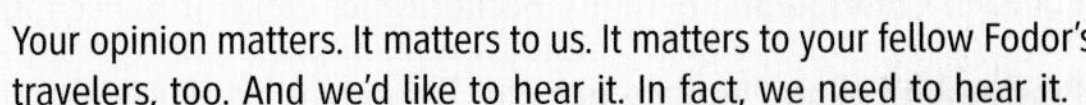

Be a Fodor's Correspondent

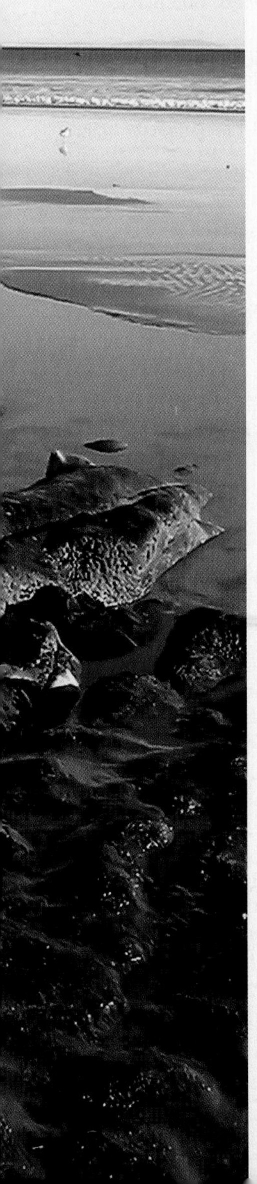

Your opinion matters. It matters to us. It matters to your fellow Fodor's travelers, too. And we'd like to hear it. In fact, we need to hear it.

When you share your experiences and opinions, you become an active member of the Fodor's community. That means we'll not only use your feedback to make our books better, but we'll publish your names and comments whenever possible. Throughout our guides, look for "Word of Mouth," excerpts of your unvarnished feedback.

Here's how you can help improve Fodor's for all of us.

Tell us when we're right. We rely on local writers to give you an insider's perspective. But our writers and staff editors—who are the best in the business—depend on you. Your positive feedback is a vote to renew our recommendations for the next edition.

Tell us when we're wrong. We're proud that we update most of our guides every year. But we're not perfect. Things change. Hotels cut services. Museums change hours. Charming cafés lose charm. If our writer didn't quite capture the essence of a place, tell us how you'd do it differently. If any of our descriptions are inaccurate or inadequate, we'll incorporate your changes in the next edition and will correct factual errors at fodors.com immediately.

Tell us what to include. You probably have had fantastic travel experiences that aren't yet in Fodor's. Why not share them with a community of like-minded travelers? Maybe you chanced upon a beach or bistro or B&B that you don't want to keep to yourself. Tell us why we should include it. And share your discoveries and experiences with everyone directly at fodors.com. Your input may lead us to add a new listing or highlight a place we cover with a "Highly Recommended" star or with our highest rating, "Fodor's Choice."

Give us your opinion instantly at our feedback center at www.fodors.com/feedback. You may also e-mail editors@fodors.com with the subject line "Northern California Editor." Or send your nominations, comments, and complaints by mail to Northern California Editor, Fodor's, 1745 Broadway, New York, NY 10019.

You and travelers like you are the heart of the Fodor's community. Make our community richer by sharing your experiences. Be a Fodor's correspondent.

Happy Traveling!

FODOR'S NORTHERN CALIFORNIA 2012

Editors: Maria Teresa Hart, Matthew Lombardi

Writers: Cindy Arora, Tanvi Chheda,Cheryl Crabtree, Alene Dawson, Maren Dougherty, Maria Hunt, Amanda Knoles, Elline Lipkin, Lea Lion, Susan MacCallum-Whitcomb, Christine Pae, Reed Parsell, Laura Randall, Natasha Sarkisian, Sharon Silva, AnnaMaria Stephens, Claire Deeks van der Lee, Christine Vovakes, Sura Wood, Bobbi Zane,
Editorial Contributors: Bethany Beckerlegge, Heidi Johansen, Claire Deeks van der Lee

Production Editors: Emily Cogburn, Evangelos Vasilakis, Carrie Parker, Anna Birinyi
Maps & Illustrations: David Lindroth and Mark Stroud, *cartographers;* Bob Blake, Rebecca Baer, *map editors;* William Wu, *information graphics*
Design: Fabrizio La Rocca, *creative director*; Guido Caroti, *art director*; Tina Malaney, Nora Rosansky, Chie Ushio, Jessica Walsh, *designers*; Melanie Marin, *associate director of photography*
Cover Photo: (Mountain Vineyard, Napa Valley) Martin Sundberg/Uppercut/Getty Images
Production Manager: Angela L. McLean

COPYRIGHT

ISBN 978-0-679-00961-0

ISSN 1543–1045

SPECIAL SALES

This book is available at special discounts for bulk purchases for sales promotions or premiums. Special editions, including personalized covers, excerpts of existing books, and corporate imprints, can be created in large quantities for special needs. For more information, write to Special Markets/Premium Sales, 1745 Broadway, MD 3-1, New York, NY 10019, or e-mail specialmarkets@randomhouse.com.

AN IMPORTANT TIP & AN INVITATION

Although all prices, opening times, and other details in this book are based on information supplied to us at press time, changes occur all the time in the travel world, and Fodor's cannot accept responsibility for facts that become outdated or for inadvertent errors or omissions. So **always confirm information when it matters,** especially if you're making a detour to visit a specific place. Your experiences—positive and negative—matter to us. If we have missed or misstated something, **please write to us.** Share your opinion instantly through our online feedback center at fodors.com/contact-us.

PRINTED IN SINGAPORE

10 9 8 7 6 5 4 3 2 1

CONTENTS

Fodor's Features

MAPS

ABOUT THIS BOOK

Our Ratings

At Fodor's, we spend considerable time choosing the best places in a destination so you don't have to. By default, anything we recommend in this book is worth visiting. But some sights, properties, and experiences are so great that we've recognized them with additional accolades. Orange **Fodor's Choice** stars indicate our top recommendations; black stars highlight places we deem **Highly Recommended;** and **Best Bets** call attention to top properties in various categories. Disagree with any of our choices? Care to nominate a new place? Visit our feedback center at www.fodors.com/feedback.

Hotels

Hotels have private bath, phone, and TV, and do not offer meals unless we specify that in the review. We always list facilities but not whether you'll be charged an extra fee to use them.

For expanded hotel reviews, visit **Fodors.com**

Restaurants

Unless we state otherwise, restaurants are open for lunch and dinner daily. We mention dress only when there's a specific requirement and reservations only when they're essential or not accepted—it's always best to book ahead.

Credit Cards

We assume that restaurants and hotels accept credit cards. If not, we'll note it in the review.

Budget Well

Hotel and restaurant price categories from ¢ to $$$$ are defined in the opening pages of the respective chapters. For attractions, we always give standard adult admission fees; reductions are usually available for children, students, and senior citizens.

Listings
- ★ Fodor's Choice
- ★ Highly recommended
- ✉ Physical address
- ✣ Directions or Map coordinates
- ☎ Telephone
- Fax
- On the Web
- E-mail
- Admission fee
- Open/closed times
- Ⓜ Metro stations
- No credit cards

Hotels & Restaurants
- Hotel
- Number of rooms
- Facilities
- Meal plans
- ✕ Restaurant
- Reservations
- Dress code
- Smoking

Outdoors
- Golf
- Camping

Other
- Family-friendly
- ⇨ See also
- Branch address
- ☞ Take note

Experience Northern California

WHAT'S NEW IN NORTHERN CALIFORNIA

Foodie's Paradise

Great dining is a staple of the California lifestyle, and a new young generation of chefs is challenging old ideas about preparing and presenting great food. Food-truck frenzy has created a moveable feast across the state. Esteemed chefs and urban foodies follow the trucks on Twitter as they move around cities 24/7 purveying delicious, cheap, fresh meals. The Spencer on the Go truck is a great example—it hangs out in SoMa in San Francisco, serving such delicacies as escargot puff lollipops.

Grape Expectations

A whole new crop of vintners and winemakers are making headlines, especially since some of them work their magic in unlikely places such as the Sierra foothills and at higher elevations in the Coast mountains. Notable is vintner Ann Kraemer, whose Shake Ridge old-vine zinfandels and tempranillo, sold under the venerable Yorba Family name, are turning heads in the Bay Area. Others include Mendocino-based Stuart Bewley, noted for the lusty Alder Springs Syrah that emerges from his 4,400-foot hillside.

All Aboard

Riding the rails can be a satisfying experience, particularly in California where the distances between destinations can run into the hundreds of miles. You can save money on gas and parking, avoid freeway traffic, and see some of the best the state has to offer.

The best trip is on the new, luxuriously appointed *Coast Starlight,* a long-distance train with sleeping cars that runs between Seattle and Los Angeles, passing some of California's most beautiful coastline as it hugs the beach. For the best surfside viewing, get a seat or a room on the left side of the train and ride south to north from San Diego to Oakland.

Head for the Hills

Things are looking up for visitors to California's alpine recreation areas, thanks to a host of enhancements. Yosemite National Park observed its 120th birthday in late 2011 with some new ways to see the park. Yosemite Guide Service offers guided day hikes, customized driving tours, and backpacking trips. You can also take Yosemite Audio Adventures CD tours with you as you explore the park.

It's Easy Being Green

The Golden State is glowing green all over. It's the only state in the nation to mandate green building codes for all new construction to reduce greenhouse emissions. California Road Trips maps 12 green itineraries including the Ultimate Eco Tour of the North Coast and Farm Fresh, drives that takes you to orchards that produce some of the best and most succulent fruit in the world.

Homegrown Hospitality

Agritourism in California isn't new, but it is on the rise, with farm tours and agricultural festivals sprouting up everywhere.

Wine country is a particularly fertile area—spurred by the success of vineyards, the area's lavender growers and olive-oil producers have started welcoming visitors. Sonoma Farm Tours include walking the land and a farm-driven dinner with paired wines.

In the Central Valley, America's number-one producer of stone fruit, you can travel themed tourist routes (like Fresno County's Blossom Trail) and tour herb gardens, fruit orchards, organic dairies, and pumpkin patches.

WHEN TO GO

Because it offers activities indoors and out, San Francisco is an all-season destination. Early spring—when the gray whale migration overlaps with the end of the elephant seal breeding season and the start of the bird migration—is the optimal time to visit Point Reyes National Seashore. Yosemite is ideal in the late spring because roads closed in winter are reopened, the summer crowds have yet to arrive, and the park's waterfalls—swollen with melting snow—run fast. Autumn is "crush time" in Napa and Sonoma valleys. Snowfall makes winter peak season for skiers in Mammoth Mountain and Lake Tahoe, where runs typically open around Thanksgiving. (They sometimes remain in operation into June.)

Climate

It's difficult to generalize much about the state's weather beyond saying that precipitation comes in winter and summers are dry in most places. As a rule, inland regions are hotter in summer and colder in winter, compared with coastal areas, which are relatively cool year-round. As you climb into the mountains, seasonal variations are more apparent: winter brings snow (at elevations above 3,000 feet), autumn is crisp, spring can go either way, and summer is sunny and warm, with only an occasional thundershower in the southern part of the state.

Microclimates

Mountains separate the California coastline from the state's interior, and the weather can sometimes vary dramatically within a 15-minute drive. On a foggy summer day in San Francisco you'll be grateful for a sweater—but head 50 mi north inland to Napa Valley, and you'll likely be content in short sleeves. Day and nighttime temperatures can also vary greatly. Temperature swings elsewhere can be even more extreme. Take Sacramento. On August afternoons the mercury hits the 90s and occasionally exceeds 100°F. Yet as darkness falls, it sometimes plummets to 40°F.

Forecasts

National Weather Service (*www.wrh.noaa.gov*).

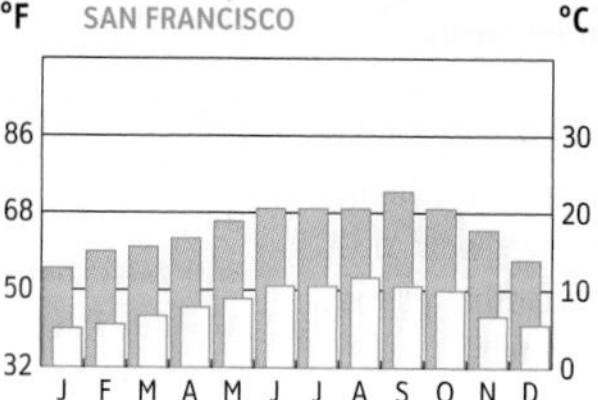

WHAT'S WHERE

The following numbers refer to chapters.

2 The Central Coast. Three of the state's top stops—swanky Santa Barbara, Hearst Castle, and Big Sur—sit along the scenic 200-mi route.

3 Monterey Bay Area. Postcard-perfect Monterey, Victorian-flavored Pacific Grove, and exclusive Carmel all share this stretch of California coast. To the north, Santa Cruz boasts a boardwalk, a UC campus, ethnic clothing shops, and plenty of surfers.

4 San Francisco. To see why so many have left their hearts here, you need to veer off the beaten path and into the city's neighborhoods—posh Pacific Heights, the Hispanic Mission, and gay-friendly Castro.

5 The Bay Area. The area that rings San Francisco is nothing like the city—but it is home to some of the nation's great universities, fabulous bay views, and Alice Waters's Chez Panisse.

6 The Wine Country. Napa and Sonoma counties retain their title as *the* California wine country, by virtue of award-winning vintages, luxe lodgings, and epicurean eats.

7 The North Coast. The star attractions here are the natural ones, from the secluded beaches and wave-battered bluffs of Point Reyes National Seashore to the towering redwood forests.

8 Redwood National Park. More than 200 mi of trails, ranging from easy to strenuous, allow visitors to see these spectacular trees in their primitive environments.

9 The Southern Sierra. In the Mammoth Lakes region, sawtooth mountains and deep powdery snowdrifts combine to create the state's premier conditions for skiing and snowboarding.

10 Yosemite National Park. The views immortalized by photographer Ansel Adams—of towering granite monoliths, verdant glacial valleys, and lofty waterfalls—are still camera-ready.

11 Sequoia and Kings Canyon National Parks. The sight of ancient redwoods towering above jagged mountains will take your breath away.

12 Sacramento and the Gold Country. The 1849 gold rush that built San Francisco and Sacramento began here, and the former mining camps strung along 185 mi of Highway 49 replay their past to the hilt.

13 Lake Tahoe. With miles of crystalline water reflecting the peaks of the High Sierra, Lake Tahoe is the perfect setting for activities like hiking and golfing in summer and skiing and snowmobiling in winter.

14 The Far North. California's far northeast corner is home to snowcapped Mount Shasta, the pristine Trinity Wilderness, and abundant backwoods character that appeals to outdoorsy types.

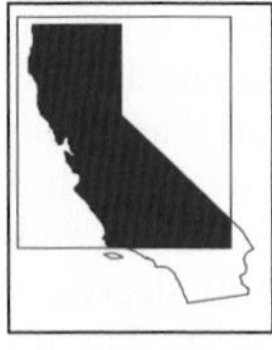

0
75 mi
0
75 km
Crescent City
Klamath
Yreka
Goose Lake
Alturas
Redwood National Park
8
Mt. Shasta
CASCADE RANGE
Burney
Shasta Lake
Arcata
Eureka
Weaverville
14
Redding
Ferndale
Lassen Volcanic National Park
Susanville
Garberville
Eel R.
Red Bluff
Sacramento Valley
Pyramid Lake
NEVADA
Leggett
Paradise
Chico
Fort Bragg
Willows
Oroville
Reno
Willits
Grass Valley
Truckee
Mendocino
Ukiah
Yuba City
49
13
CARSON CITY
Boonville
Clear Lake
Auburn
Lake Tahoe
South Lake Tahoe
Point Arena
7
Placerville
Gualala
6
Woodland
Healdsburg
SACRAMENTO
Jenner
12
Santa Rosa
Napa
Elk Grove
Yosemite National Park
Bridgeport
Fairfield
Jackson
Novato
Sonoma
Lodi
Point Reyes National Seashore
SIERRA NEVADA
Mono Lake
10
9
Stockton
Sonora
4
Berkeley
Oakland
Modesto
Yosemite Village
Mammoth Lakes
SAN FRANCISCO
5
Fremont
San Joaquin Valley
Turlock
Merced
Bishop
Palo Alto
San Jose
Big Pine
Gilroy
Chowchilla
Santa Cruz
San Luis Res.
Los Banos
Madera
Kings Canyon National Park
Castroville
PACIFIC OCEAN
Monterey
Salinas
Fresno
Pacific Grove
3
Soledad
5
11
Carmel
Visalia
Big Sur
Tulare Lake Bed
Porterville
Sequoia National Park
Coalinga
China Lake
Kernville
San Simeon
Paso Robles
Bakersfield
Ridgecrest
San Luis Obispo
McKittrick
TEHACHAPI MTS.
Tejon Pass
Santa Maria
Lancaster
Lompoc
2
Santa Barbara
Ojai
Santa Barbara Channel
Ventura
Oxnard
Pasadena

NORTHERN CALIFORNIA PLANNER

Driving Around

Driving may be a way of life in California, but it isn't cheap (gas prices here are usually among the highest in the nation). It's also not for the fainthearted; you've surely heard horror stories about California's freeways, but even the state's scenic highways and byways have their own hassles. For instance, on the dramatic coastal road between San Simeon and Carmel, twists, turns, and divinely distracting vistas frequently slow traffic; in rainy season, mudslides can close the road altogether. ⚠ **Never cross the double line when driving these roads. If you see that cars are backing up behind you on a long two-lane, no-passing stretch, do everyone (and yourself) a favor and use the first available pullout.**

On California's notorious freeways other rules apply. Nervous Nellies must resist the urge to stay in the two slow-moving ones on the far right, used primarily by trucks. To drive at least the speed limit, get yourself in the middle lane. If you're ready to bend the rules a bit, the second (lanes are numbered from 1 starting at the center) lane moves about 5 mi faster. But avoid the far-left lane (the one next to the carpool lane), where speeds range from 75 MPH to 90 MPH.

Flying In

Air travelers beginning or ending their vacation in San Francisco have two main airports to choose from: San Francisco International (SFO) or Oakland International (OAK) across the Bay. The former lands you closer to the city core (ground transportation will take about 20 minutes versus 35); but the latter is less heavily trafficked and less prone to pesky fog delays. Both airports are served by BART, the Bay Area's affordable rapid-transit system. So your decision will probably rest on which one has the best fares and connections for your particular route.

If your final destination is Monterey or Carmel, San Jose International Airport (SJC), about 40 mi south of San Francisco, is another alternative.

FAQ

I'm not particularly active. Will I still enjoy visiting a national park? Absolutely, the most popular parks really do have something for everyone. Take Yosemite. When the ultrafit embark on 12-hour trail treks, mere mortals can hike Cook's Meadow—an easy 1-mi loop that's also wheelchair accessible. If even that seems too daunting, you can hop on a free shuttle or drive yourself to sites like Glacier Point or the Mariposa Grove of Giant Sequoias.

What's the single best place to take the kids? Well, that depends on your children's ages and interests, but for its sheer smorgasbord of activities, San Francisco is hard to beat. A cable-car ride is a no-brainer—but if you have a Thomas the Tank engine fan in tow, be sure to also take a spin on the historic F-line trolleys. Other classic kid-friendly SF sights include the Exploratorium, the San Francisco Zoo, Alcatraz, the Ferry Building, and the California Academy of Sciences.

But San Francisco is filled with more offbeat activities for adventurous families. Take the kids for dim sum in Chinatown; odds are they'll enjoy picking their dishes from a rolling buffet filled with foods they've likely never seen before. Or head to Musée Mécanique to see what kids played (way) before Nintendo's Wii came out.

Need to blow off some steam? Then head to one of the city's great outdoor venues: Golden Gate Park, the Western Shoreline, the Presidio, or Aquatic Park. If you want to get out of town, take a ferry ride to Sausalito or head to Muir Woods—if you think these massive trees are tall, imagine seeing them from two or three feet lower. Up for a less wild outdoor experience? Then catch a Giants game at beautiful AT&T Park.

California sounds expensive. How can I save on sightseeing? If you're focusing on San Francisco, consider taking a pass—a Go Card Pass (☎ *800/887–9103* 🌐 *www.gocardusa.com*) that is. Sold in one-day to one-week versions, they're priced from $55 and cover dozens of tours and attractions in the city.

Many museums set aside free-admission days; call ahead to see if any of your planned stops have free days during your trip.

Prefer the great outdoors? An $80 America the Beautiful annual pass (☎ *888/275–8747* 🌐 *www.nps.gov*) admits you to every site under the National Park Service umbrella. Better yet, depending on the property, passengers in your vehicle get in free, too.

I'm not crazy about spending 14 nights in hotels. Any alternatives? If you want to pretend you're lucky enough to live in California, try a vacation or time-share rental. Aside from providing privacy (a boon for families and groups), a rental lets you set your own schedule and cook at your leisure (you'll save money, plus it's a great excuse to stock up on that fine California produce!). In terms of coverage, geographically and pricewise, HomeAway (🌐 *www.homeaway.com*) is a good place for house hunting. It lists more than 4,000 condos, cottages, beach houses, ski chalets, and villas. *For more information on California trip planning, see the Planning sections at the beginning of each chapter and at the Travel Smart Northern California chapter at the back of the book.*

NORTHERN CALIFORNIA TODAY

The People

California is as much a state of mind as a state in the union—a kind of perpetual Promised Land that has represented many things to many people. In the 18th century, Spanish missionaries came seeking converts. In the 19th, miners rushed here to search for gold. And, in the years since, a long line of Dust Bowl farmers, land speculators, Haight-Ashbury hippies, migrant workers, dot-commers, real estate speculators, and would-be actors has come chasing their own dreams.

The result is a population that leans toward idealism—without necessarily being as liberal as you might think. (Remember, this is Ronald Reagan's old stomping ground.) And despite the stereotype of the blue-eyed, blond surfer, California's population is not homogeneous either. Ten million people who live here (more than 28% of Californians) are foreign born—including former Governor Schwarzenegger. Almost half hail from neighboring Mexico; another third emigrated from Asia, following the waves of Chinese workers who arrived in the 1860s to build the railroads and subsequent waves of Indochinese refugees from the Vietnam War.

The Politics

What's blue and red and green all over? California: a predominantly Democratic state with an aggressive "go green" agenda. When he left office in 2010 (before his marital scandal broke involving "another woman"), Governor Arnold Schwarzenegger left a legacy of pushing a number of environmental initiatives including controls on gas emissions. Democratic Governor Jerry Brown, who was elected to the office for the second time in 30 years on a promise to clean up the financial mess created under Schwarzenegger, is moving his predecessor's green agenda ahead with policies that make California the greenest state in the nation supporting more green construction, wind farms, and solar panels.

The Economy

Leading all other states in terms of the income generated by agriculture, tourism, and industrial activity, California has the country's most diverse state economy. Moreover, with a gross state product of more than $2 trillion, California would be one of the top 10 economies *in the world* if it were an independent nation. But due to its wealth ($61,000 median household income) and productivity, California took a large hit in the recession that began in 2007. This affected all levels of government from local to statewide and resulted in reduction of services that Californians have long taken for granted.

But the Golden State's economic history is filled with boom and bust cycles—beginning with the mid-19th-century gold rush that started it all. Optimists already have their eyes on the next potential boom: high-tech and bio research, "green companies" focused on alternative energy, renewables, electric cars, and the like.

The Culture

Cultural organizations thrive in California. San Francisco—a city with only about 775,000 residents—has well-regarded ballet, opera, and theater companies, and is home to one of the continent's most noteworthy orchestras. Museums like San Francisco Museum of Modern Art (SFMOMA) and the de Young also represent the city's ongoing commitment to the arts. Art and culture thrive farther south in San Diego as well. Balboa Park alone holds 15 museums, opulent gardens, and three performance venues, in addition to the San Diego Zoo.

The Old Globe Theater and La Jolla Playhouse routinely originate plays that capture coveted Tony Awards in New York.

The Parks and Preserves

Cloud-spearing redwood groves, snow-tipped mountains, canyon-slashed deserts, primordial lava beds, and a seemingly endless coast: California's natural diversity is staggering—and efforts to protect it started early. The first national park here was established in 1890, and the National Park Service now oversees 30 sites in California (more than in any other state). When you factor in 278 state parks—which encompass underwater preserves, historic sites, wildlife reserves, dune systems, and other sensitive habitats—the number of acres involved is almost as impressive as the topography itself.

Due to encroaching development and pollution, keeping these natural treasures in pristine condition is an ongoing challenge. For instance, Sequoia and Kings Canyon (which is plagued by pesticides and other agricultural pollutants blown in from the San Joaquin Valley) has been named America's "smoggiest park" by the National Parks Conservation Association, and the Environmental Protection Agency has designated it as an "ozone non-attainment area with levels of ozone pollution that threaten human health."

The Cuisine

California gave us McDonald's, Denny's, Carl's Jr., Taco Bell, and, of course, In-N-Out Burger. Fortunately for those of us with fast-clogging arteries, the state also kick-started the organic food movement. Back in the 1970s, California-based chefs put American cuisine on the culinary map by focusing on freshly prepared seasonal ingredients.

Today, this focus has spawned the "locavore" or sustainable food movement—followers try to only consume food produced within a 100-mi radius of where they live, since processing and refining food and transporting goods over long distances is bad for both the body and the environment. This isn't much of a restriction in California, where a huge variety of crops grow year-round. Some 350 cities and towns have certified farmers' markets—and their stalls are bursting with a variety of goods. California has been America's top agricultural producer for the last 50 years, growing more fruits and vegetables than any other state. Dairies and ranches also thrive here, and fishing fleets harvest fish and shellfish from the rich waters offshore.

QUINTESSENTIAL NORTHERN CALIFORNIA

The Wine

If California were a country, it would rank as the world's fourth-largest wine producer, after Italy, France, and Spain. In those countries, where vino is barely considered an alcoholic beverage, wine drinking has evolved into a relaxing ritual best shared with friends and family. A modern, Americanized version of that mentality integrates wine into daily life in California, and there are many places to sample it. The Napa and Sonoma valleys come to mind first. However, there are other destinations for oenophiles who want a vintage vacation. You can find great wineries around Santa Barbara County, Monterey Bay, and Gold Country's Shenandoah Valley, too. All are respected appellations, and their winery tours and tastings will show you what all the buzz is about.

The Beach

California's beach culture is, in a word, legendary. Of course, it only makes sense that folks living in a state with a 1,264-mi coastline (a hefty portion of which sees the sun upward of 300 days a year) would perfect the art of beach-going. True aficionados begin with a reasonably fit physique, plus a stylish wardrobe consisting of flip-flops, bikinis, wet suits, and such. Mastery of at least one beach skill—surfing, boogie boarding, kayaking, Frisbee tossing, power walking, or soaking up some rays—is also essential. As a visitor, though, you need only a swimsuit and some rented equipment for most sports. You can then hit the beach almost anywhere, thanks to the California belief in coastal access as a birthright. The farther south you go, the wider, sandier, and sunnier the beaches become; moving north they are rockier and foggier, with colder and rougher surf.

Californians live in such a large and splashy state that they sometimes seem to forget about the rest of the country. They've developed a distinctive culture all their own, which you can delve into by doing as the locals do.

The Outdoors

One of California's greatest assets—the mild year-round weather enjoyed by most of the state—inspires residents to spend as much time outside as they possibly can. To be sure, they have a tremendous enthusiasm for every imaginable outdoor sport, and, up north especially, fresh-air adventures are extremely popular (which may explain why everyone there seems to own at least one pair of hiking boots). But, overall, the California-alfresco creed is more broadly interpreted. Indeed, the general rule when planning any activity is "if it can happen outside, it will!" *Plein-air* vacation opportunities include dining on patios, decks, and wharves; shopping in street markets or elaborate open-air malls; hearing almost any kind of music at moonlight concerts; touring the sculpture gardens that grace major art museums; and celebrating everything from gay pride to garlic at outdoor fairs.

The Automobile

Americans may have a love affair with the automobile, but Californians have an out-and-out obsession. Even when gas prices rev up and freeway traffic slows down, their passion burns as hot as ever. You can witness this ardor any summer weekend at huge classic- and custom-car shows held statewide. Even better, you can feel it yourself by taking the wheel. Trace an old stagecoach route through the mountains above Santa Barbara on Highway 154; race migrating whales up the coast to Big Sur; or take 17-Mile Drive along the precipitous edge of the Monterey Peninsula. Glorious for the most part, but authentically congested in some areas down south, Highway 1 runs almost the entire length of the state.

NORTHERN CALIFORNIA TOP ATTRACTIONS

Yosemite National Park

(A) Nature looms large here, both literally and figuratively. In addition to hulking Half Dome, the park is home to El Capitan (the world's largest exposed granite monolith, rising 3,593 feet above the glacier-carved valley floor) and Yosemite Falls (North America's tallest cascade). In Yosemite's signature stand of giant sequoias—the Mariposa Grove—even the trees are Bunyanesque. Needless to say, crowds can be super-size.

San Francisco

(B) Population-wise, San Francisco is smaller than Indianapolis. But when it comes to sights (and soul), this city is a giant. Start working through the standard travelers' "to do" list by strolling across the Golden Gate Bridge, taking a ferry to Alcatraz, and hopping on the Powell–Hyde cable car. Just leave enough time to explore the diverse neighborhoods where San Francisco's distinctive personality—an amalgam of gold-rush history, immigrant traditions, counterculture proclivities, and millennial materialism—is on display.

Wine Country

(C) Although the vineyard-blanketed hills of California's original Wine Country are undeniably scenic, the wine itself (preferably accompanied by the area's famed cuisine) remains the big draw here. Budding oenophiles can educate their palettes on scores of tours and tasting sessions—provided they can elbow their way through the high-season hordes.

Point Reyes National Seashore

(D) Aside from the namesake seashore, this Marin County preserve encompasses ecosystems that range from woodlands and marshlands to heathlike grasslands. The range of wildlife here is equally diverse—depending on when you visit, expect to see gray whales, rare Tule elk, and almost 500 species of birds. December through March you can also see male elephant seals compete for mates.

Lake Tahoe

(E) Deep, clear, and intensely blue, this forest-rimmed body of water straddling the California–Nevada border is one of the continent's prettiest alpine lakes. That environmental controls can keep it that way is something of a miracle, given Tahoe's popularity. Throngs of outdoor adventurers flock to the California side to ski, hike, bike, and boat. On the Nevada side, where casinos are king, gambling often wins out over fresh-air activities—but natural wonders are never far away.

Gold Country

(F) California's gold rush was one of the most significant events in U.S. history. It saved the Union and helped open the western frontier, when Argonauts flooded a 300-mi-long stretch of the Sierra foothills. Remnants of the gold rush remain to this day in the towns, diggings, trains, museums, and culture that you'll encounter along historic Highway 49; it runs north to south from Loyalton near the Nevada border to Oakhurst, just south of Yosemite. Towns along the way, mostly updated and renovated, allow you to dig into the past and discover what the excitement was all about.

NORTHERN CALIFORNIA'S TOP EXPERIENCES

Hit the Road

Kings Canyon Highway, Redwood Highway, Tioga Pass, 17-Mile Drive, the Lake Tahoe loop: California has some splendid and challenging roads. You'll drive through a tunnel formed by towering redwood trees on the Redwood Highway. If you venture over the Sierras by way of Tioga Pass (through Yosemite in summer only), you'll see emerald-green meadows, gray granite monoliths, and pristine blue lakes—and very few people.

Go for the Gold

Though California's gold rush ended more than a hundred years ago, you can still feel the '49er fever on the western face of the Sierra Nevada in Columbia, a well-preserved town populated by costumed interpreters, where you can pan for gold or tour a mine. Or visit Bodie, an eerie ghost town in the eastern Sierra that remains in a state of "arrested decay."

Think Globally, Eat Locally

Over the years California cuisine has evolved from a mere trend into a respected gastronomic tradition: one that pairs local, often organic or sustainable, ingredients with techniques inspired by European, Asian, and increasingly Indian and Middle Eastern cookery.

Embrace Your Inner Eccentric

California has always drawn creative and, well, eccentric people. And all that quirkiness has left its mark in the form of oddball architecture that makes for some fun sightseeing. Begin by touring Hearst Castle—the beautifully bizarre estate William Randolph Hearst built above San Simeon. Lake Tahoe's Vikingsholm (a re-created Viking castle) is equally odd.

Be Transported

San Franciscans take cable cars seriously—and riding on one is a tourist staple. In Sacramento the "iron horses" that opened the American West get their due at the California State Railroad Museum. When you're done looking at the exhibits, head out of town to Jamestown, where you can ride a real locomotive at the museum's Railtown 1897.

Catch the Spirit

You can learn a lot about the Golden State by visiting its places of worship. The venerable Spanish-built missions stretching from San Diego to Sonoma are obvious examples. Yet other sanctuaries—like Tin How Temple in San Francisco's Chinatown—have their own stories to tell. So does Mt. Shasta, which has both a New Age and age-old appeal. Considered sacred by Native Americans, it's also a magnet for shamans, goddess-worshippers, and the occasional alien.

Go Wild

California communities host hundreds of annual events, but some of the best are organized by Mother Nature. The most famous is the "miracle migration" that sees swallows flock back to Mission San Juan Capistrano each March. In Pacific Grove masses of monarch butterflies reliably arrive for their winter vacation every October.

People-Watch

Opportunities for world-class people-watching abound in California. Just saunter the rainbow-flagged streets of San Francisco's Castro neighborhood or the century-old boardwalk in time-warped, resiliently boho Santa Cruz.

GREAT ITINERARIES

SIERRA RICHES: YOSEMITE, GOLD COUNTRY, AND TAHOE

Day 1: Arrival/San Francisco

Straight from the airport, drop your bags at the lighthearted Hotel Monaco near Union Square and request a goldfish for your room. Chinatown, chock-full of dim sum shops, storefront temples, and open-air markets, promises unfamiliar tastes for lunch. Catch a Powell Street cable car to the end of the line and get off to see the bay views and the antique arcade games at Musée Mécanique, the hidden gem of otherwise mindless Fisherman's Wharf. No need to go any farther than cosmopolitan North Beach for cocktail hour, dinner, and live music.

Day 2: San Francisco

A Union Square stroll packs a wallop of people-watching, window-shopping, and architecture-viewing. In Golden Gate Park, linger amid the flora of the conservatory and the arboretum, soak up some art at the de Young Museum, and find serene refreshment at the Japanese Tea Garden. The Pacific surf pounds the cliffs below the Legion of Honor art museum, which has an exquisite view of the Golden Gate Bridge—when the fog stays away. Sunset cocktails at the circa-1909 Cliff House include a prospect over Seal Rock (actually occupied by sea lions). Eat dinner elsewhere: Pacific Heights, the Mission, and SoMa teem with excellent restaurants.

Day 3: Into the High Sierra

First thing in the morning, pick up your rental car and head for the hills. A five-hour drive due east brings you to Yosemite National Park, where Bridalveil Fall and El Capitan, the 350-story granite monolith, greet you on your way to Yosemite Village. Ditch the car and pick up information and refreshment before hopping on the year-round shuttle to explore. Justly famous sights cram Yosemite Valley: massive Half Dome and Sentinel Dome, thundering Yosemite Falls, and wispy Ribbon Fall and Nevada Fall. Invigorating short hikes off the shuttle route lead to numerous vantage points. Celebrate your arrival in one of the world's most sublime spots with dinner in the dramatic Ahwahnee Hotel Dining Room.

Day 4: Yosemite National Park

Ardent hikers consider John Muir Trail a must-do, tackling the rigorous 12-hour round-trip to the top of Half Dome in search of life-changing vistas. The merely mortal hike downhill from Glacier Point on Four-Mile Trail or Panorama Trail, the latter an all-day trek past waterfalls. Less demanding still is a drive to Wawona for a stroll in the Mariposa Grove of Big Trees and lunch at the 19th-century Wawona Hotel. In bad weather, take shelter in the Ansel Adams Gallery and Yosemite Museum; in fair conditions, drive up to Glacier Point for a breathtaking sunset view.

Day 5: Gold Country South

Highway 49 traces the mother lode that yielded many fortunes in gold in the 1850s and 1860s. Step into a living gold-rush town at Columbia State Historic Park, where you can ride a stagecoach and pan for riches. Sutter Creek's well-preserved downtown bursts with shopping opportunities, but the vintage goods displayed at J. Monteverde General Store are not for sale. A different sort of vintage powers the present-day bonanza of Shenandoah Valley, heart of the Sierra Foothills wine country. Taste your way through Zinfandels and Syrahs at boutique wineries such as Domaine de la Terre Rouge, Renwood, and Sobon Estate. Amador City's 1879 Imperial Hotel places you firmly in the past for the night.

Day 6: Gold Country North

In Placerville, a mineshaft invites investigation at Hangtown's Gold Bug Mine, while Marshall Gold Discovery State Historic Park encompasses most of Coloma and preserves the spot where James Marshall's 1849 find set off the California gold rush. Old Town Auburn, with its museums and courthouse, makes a good lunch stop, but if you hold out until you reach Grass Valley you can try authentic miners' pasties. A tour of Empire Mine State Historic Park takes you into a mine, and a few miles away horse-drawn carriages ply the narrow, shop-lined streets of downtown Nevada City. Backtrack to Auburn or Placerville to overnight in historic or modern lodgings.

Day 7: To the Lake

Jewel-like Lake Tahoe is a straight shot east of Placerville on Highway 50; stop for picnic provisions in commercial South Lake Tahoe. A stroll past the three magnificent estates in Pope-Baldwin Recreation area hints at the sumptuous lakefront summers once enjoyed by the elite. High above a glittering cove, Emerald Bay State Park offers one of the best lake views as well as a steep hike down to (and back up from) Vikingsholm, a replica 9th-century Scandinavian castle. Another fine, old mansion—plus a nature preserve and many hiking trails—lies in Sugar Pine Point State Park. Tahoe City offers more history and ample dining and lodging choices.

Day 8: Lake Tahoe

With advance reservations, you can tour the ultraluxe 1936 Thunderbird Lodge and its grounds. The picture-perfect beaches and bays of Lake Tahoe–Nevada State Park line the Nevada shoreline, a great place to bask in the sun or go mountain biking. For a different perspective of the lake, get out on the azure water aboard the stern-wheeler MS *Dixie II* from Zephyr Cove. In South Lake Tahoe, another view unfurls as the Heavenly Gondola travels 2½ mi up a mountain. Keep your adrenaline pumping into the evening with some action at the massive casinos clustered in Stateline, Nevada.

Day 9: Back to the City

After a morning of driving, return your rental car in San Francisco and soak up some more urban excitement. Good options include lunch at the Ferry Building, followed by a visit to the San Francisco Museum of Modern Art, or lunch in Japantown followed by shopping in Pacific Heights. People-watching excels in the late afternoon bustle of the Castro and the Haight. Say good-bye to Northern California at one of the plush lounges or trendy bars in the downtown hotels.

Day 10: Departure/San Francisco

Check the weather before you start out for the airport: Fog sometimes causes delays at SFO. On a clear day, your flight path might give you one last fabulous glimpse of the City by the Bay.

TIPS

❶ Try to time your trip for late spring or early fall to avoid the worst of the crowds and the road-closing snowfalls in Yosemite and around Lake Tahoe. Yosemite's falls peak in spring and early summer, while fall brings the grape harvest in the Sierra Nevada foothills.

❷ Parking in San Francisco is expensive and scarce. When you fly in, take a shuttle or taxi from the airport to the city, then use the excellent public transportation to get around. Car rental from downtown locations costs no more than at the airport.

❸ For a visit in any season, reserve your hotel or campground accommodations in Yosemite as far in advance as possible—up to a year ahead. Staying in the park itself will cost extra, but it will also save you precious time and miles of driving from the gateway communities.

❹ If you can stay longer, extend your Tahoe-area stay with a day in the Nevada mining boomtowns around Virginia City and a night amid the bright lights of Reno.

NORCAL'S LOCAVORE FOOD MOVEMENT

Organic, local, and *sustainable* are buzzwords in Northern California, home to hundreds of small family farmers, sustainable ranchers, and artisan producers are leading the country's back-to-the-earth food movement.

When Alice Waters opened Chez Panisse in Berkeley in 1971, she sparked a culinary revolution that continues today. Initially called California cuisine, the cooking style showcased local, seasonal ingredients in fresh preparations. It also marked a new willingness by American chefs to experiment with international influences. As the movement spread, it became known as New American cooking. This "eat local, think global" ethos has lead to a resurgence of artisanal producers across the country.

The *locavore* (focused on sustainable, local foods) movement's epicenter is still Northern California. At the Ferry Plaza Farmers Market in San Francisco alone, farmers bring over 1,200 varieties of fruits and vegetables to market every year. Chefs proudly call out their purveyors on menus and Web sites, elevating humble vegetable growers to starring culinary roles.

FARMERS MARKETS

One of the best ways to taste Northern California's bounty is by stopping by the Ferry Plaza Farmers Market, held outside of the Ferry Building on the Embarcadero, at Market Street. Held on Tuesday and Saturday mornings, the market offers produce, meats, fish, and flowers from small regional farmers and ranchers, many of whom are certified organic.

It is also a great place to pick up items for a picnic. Prepared foods like tamales and pasta are available, as are specialties like jams, breads, and cheeses from local artisan producers.

Check 🌐 *www.cuesa.org* for hours.

FRUIT

Northern California's diverse climate makes it an ideal place to grow all types of fruit, from berries to stone fruit. Farmers' markets and restaurants abound with a staggering selection of produce: Blossom Bluff Orchards, south of San Francisco, offers more than 150 varieties of stone fruits, like apricots, nectarines, and peaches. North of the city, The Apple Farm grows 80 varieties of apples, pears, persimmons, quince, and French plums. The Bay Area is also one of the best places in the country to find rare fruit varieties like aprium, cherimoya, cactus pear, jujube, and loquat; California's famous Meyer lemons—sweeter and less acidic than common lemons—are celebrated in restaurant desserts.

VEGETABLES

Some chefs give top billing to their produce purveyors, like a recently observed menu touting a salad of Star Route Farm field greens with Picholine olives, sweet herbs, and goat cheese. Along with these tantalizing items, be on the lookout for locally grown artichokes, Asian vegetables, multihued beets and carrots, and heirloom varieties of tomatoes, squash, and beans.

MEAT

Family-owned ranches and farms are prominent in the region, with many raising organic or "humane certified"

beef, pork, lamb, and poultry. Upscale Bay Area restaurants are fervent about recognizing their high-quality protein producers. From recent menus at two well-known San Francisco restaurants: Wolfe Ranch quail and foie gras crostini with Murcott mandarins, smoked bacon and bok choy, and vanilla gastrique; and Prather Ranch lamb with fava greens, cranberry beans, crispy artichokes, and salsa verde.

FISH

Diners and shoppers will find myriad seafood from local waters, from farm-raised scallops to line-caught California salmon. On menus, look for Hog Island Oysters, a local producer that raises more than three million oysters a year in Tomales Bay. Sardines netted in Monterey Bay are popular in preparations like mesquite-grilled sardines with fava beans, French radish and fennel salad, and preserved Meyer lemon.

CHEESE

Restaurant cheese plates, often served before—or in lieu of—dessert, are a great way to experience the region's excellent local cheeses. Look for selections from Cypress Grove Chevre, popular for its artisan goat cheeses, and Cowgirl Creamery, a renowned local producer of fresh and aged cow's milk cheeses. Additionally, some shops and bakeries offer fresh local butter and cheeses.

THE ULTIMATE ROAD TRIP

CALIFORNIA'S LEGENDARY HIGHWAY 1

by Cheryl Crabtree

One of the world's most scenic drives, California's State Route 1 (also known as Highway 1, the Pacific Coast Highway, the PCH) stretches along the edge of the state for nearly 660 miles, from Southern California's Dana Point to its northern terminus near Leggett, about 40 miles north of Fort Bragg. As you travel south to north, the water's edge transitions from long, sandy beaches and low-lying bluffs to towering dunes, craggy cliffs, and ancient redwood groves. The ocean changes as well; the relatively tame and surfable swells lapping the Southern California shore give way to the frigid, powerful waves crashing against weatherbeaten rocks in the north.

HIGHWAY 1 TOP 10

- Santa Monica
- Santa Barbara
- Hearst San Simeon State Historical Monument
- Big Sur
- Carmel
- 17-Mile Drive
- Monterey
- San Francisco
- Marin Headlands
- Point Reyes National Seashore

Give yourself lots of extra time to pull off the road and enjoy the scenery

STARTING YOUR JOURNEY

You may decide to drive the road's entire 660-mile route, or bite off a smaller piece. In either case, a Highway 1 road trip allows you to experience California at your own pace, stopping when and where you wish. Hike a beachside trail, dig your toes in the sand, and search for creatures in the tidepools. Buy some artichokes and strawberries from a roadside farmstand. Talk to people along the way (you'll run into everyone from soul-searching meditators, farmers, and beatniks to city-slackers and working-class folks), and take lots of pictures. Don't rush—you could easily spend a lifetime discovering secret spots along this route.

To help you plan your trip, we've broken the road into two regions (Santa Monica to Big Sur and Carmel to San Francisco); each region is then broken up into smaller segments—many of which are suitable for a day's drive. If you're pressed for time, you can always tackle a section of Highway 1, and then head inland to U.S. 101 or I-5 to reach your next destination more quickly.

For more information, please see our Highway 1 CloseUps in The Central Coast, Monterey Bay Area, and the North Coast.

WHAT'S IN A NAME?

Though it's often referred to as the Pacific Coast Highway (or PCH), sections of Highway 1 actually have different names. The southernmost section (Dana Point to Oxnard) is the Pacific Coast Highway. After that, the road becomes the Cabrillo Highway (Las Cruces to Lompoc), the Big Sur Coast Highway (San Luis Obispo County line to Monterey), the North Coast Scenic Byway (San Luis Obispo city limit to the Monterey County line), the Cabrillo Highway again (Santa Cruz County line to Half Moon Bay), and finally the Shoreline Highway (Marin City to Leggett). To make matters more confusing, smaller chunks of the road have additional honorary monikers.

Just follow the green triangular signs that say "California 1."

HIGHWAY 1 DRIVING

- Rent a convertible. (You will not regret it.)
- Begin the drive north from Santa Monica, where congestion and traffic delays pose less of a problem.
- Mind your manners on the freeway. Don't tailgate or glare at other drivers, and don't fly the finger.
- If you're prone to motion sickness, take the wheel yourself. Focusing on the landscape outside should help you feel less queasy.
- If you're afraid of heights, drive from south to north so you'll be on the mountain rather than the cliff side of the road.

2

The Central Coast

FROM VENTURA TO BIG SUR

WORD OF MOUTH

"I was blown away by the immense outdoor pool at the Hearst Castle. It is huge, and yet incredibly serene in its surroundings. The Castle is situated on top of the hills in the San Simeon area and allows for massive views of nearly 360 degrees around."

—photo by L Vantreight, Fodors.com member

WELCOME TO THE CENTRAL COAST

TOP REASONS TO GO

★ **Incredible nature:** Much of the Central Coast looks as wild and wonderful as it did centuries ago; the area is home to Channel Islands National Park, two national marine sanctuaries, state parks and beaches, and the vast and rugged Los Padres National Forest.

★ **Edible bounty:** Land and sea provide enough fresh regional foods to satisfy even the savviest of foodies—grapes, strawberries, seafood, olive oil . . . the list goes on and on. Get your fill at countless farmers' markets, wineries, and restaurants.

★ **Outdoor activities:** Kick back and revel in the casual California lifestyle. Surf, golf, kayak, hike, play tennis—or just hang out and enjoy the gorgeous scenery.

★ **Small-town charm, big-city culture:** Small, friendly, uncrowded towns offer an amazing array of cultural amenities. With all the art and history museums, theater, music, and festivals, you might start thinking you're in L.A. or San Francisco.

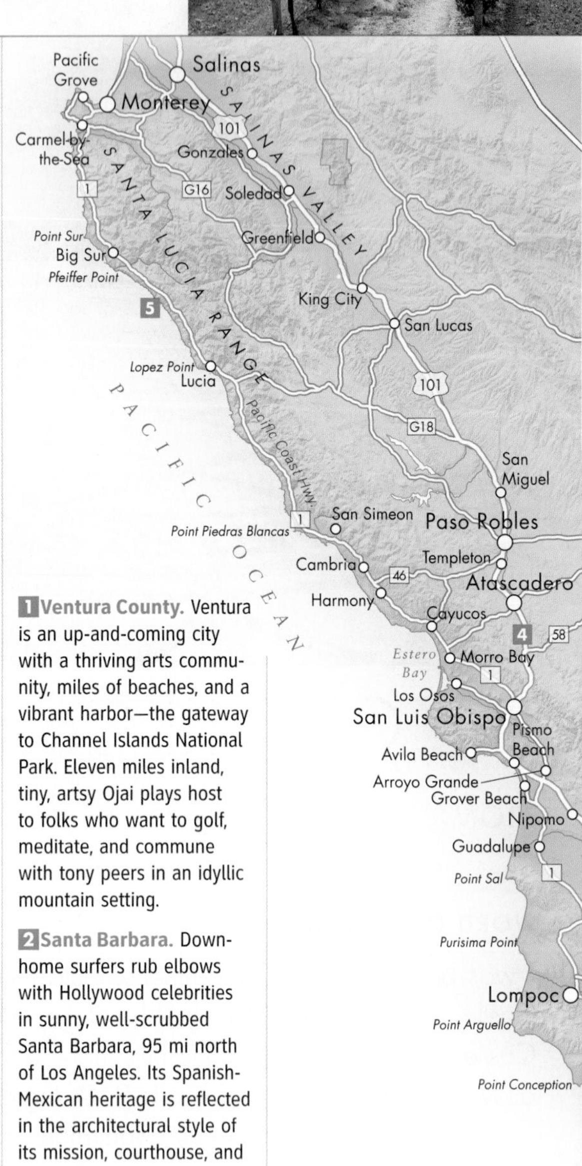

1 Ventura County. Ventura is an up-and-coming city with a thriving arts community, miles of beaches, and a vibrant harbor—the gateway to Channel Islands National Park. Eleven miles inland, tiny, artsy Ojai plays host to folks who want to golf, meditate, and commune with tony peers in an idyllic mountain setting.

2 Santa Barbara. Down-home surfers rub elbows with Hollywood celebrities in sunny, well-scrubbed Santa Barbara, 95 mi north of Los Angeles. Its Spanish-Mexican heritage is reflected in the architectural style of its mission, courthouse, and many homes and public buildings.

3 Santa Barbara County. Wineries, ranches, and small villages dominate the quintessentially Californian landscape here.

4 San Luis Obispo County. Friendly college town San Luis Obispo serves as hub of a burgeoning wine region that stretches nearly 100 mi from Pismo Beach north to Paso Robles; the 230-plus wineries here have earned reputations for high-quality vintages that rival those of northern California.

5 The Big Sur Coastline. Rugged cliffs meet the Pacific for more than 60 mi—one of the most scenic and dramatic drives in the world.

6 Channel Islands National Park. Home to 145 species of plants and animals found nowhere else on Earth, this relatively undiscovered gem of a park encompasses five islands and a mile of surrounding ocean.

GETTING ORIENTED

The Central Coast region begins about 60 mi north of Los Angeles, near the seaside city of Ventura. From there the coastline stretches north about 200 mi, winding through the small cities of Santa Barbara and San Luis Obispo, then north through the small towns of Morro Bay and Cambria to Carmel. The drive through this region, especially the section of Highway 1 from San Simeon to Big Sur, is one of the most scenic in the state.

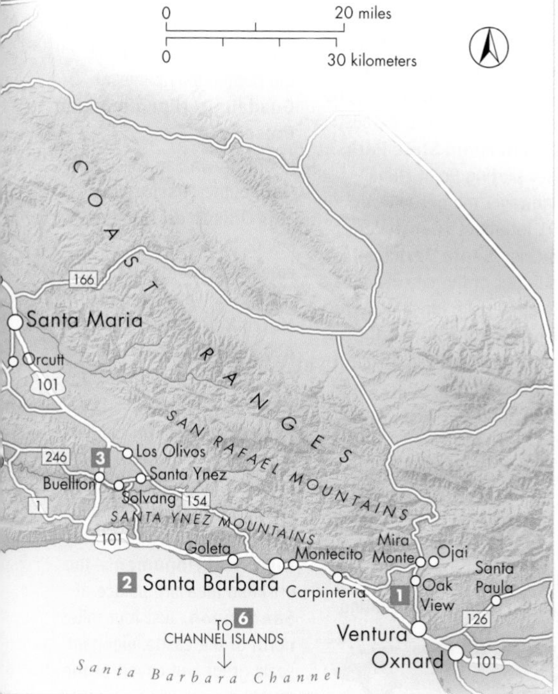

HIGHWAY 1: SANTA MONICA TO BIG SUR

Hearst Castle

THE PLAN

Distance: approx. 335 mi

Time: 3-5 days

Good Overnight Options: Malibu, Santa Barbara, Pismo Beach, San Luis Obispo, Cambria, Carmel

For more information on the sights and attractions along this portion of Highway 1, please see Los Angeles and Central Coast chapters

SANTA MONICA TO MALIBU (approx. 26 mi)

Highway 1 begins in Dana point, but it seems more appropriate to begin a PCH adventure in **Santa Monica.** Be sure to experience the beach culture, then balance the tacky pleasures of Santa Monica's amusement pier with a stylish dinner in a neighborhood restaurant.

MALIBU TO SANTA BARBARA (approx. 70 mi)

The PCH follows the curve of Santa Monica Bay all the way to **Malibu** and **Point Mugu,** near **Oxnard.** Chances are you'll experience *déjà vu* driving this 27-mile stretch: mountains on one side, ocean on the other, opulent homes perched on hillsides; you've seen this piece of coast countless times on TV and film. Be sure to walk out on the **Malibu Pier** for a great photo opp, then check out **Surfrider Beach,** with three famous points where perfect waves ignited a worldwide surfing rage in the 1960s.

Santa Monica

After Malibu you'll drive through miles of protected, largely unpopulated coastline. Ride a wave at **Zuma Beach**, scout for offshore whales at **Point Dume State Preserve,** or hike the trails at **Point Mugu State Park.** After skirting Point Mugu, Highway 1 merges with U.S. 101 for about 70 mi before reaching **Santa Barbara.** A mini-tour of the city includes a real Mexican lunch at **La Super-Rica,** a visit to the magnificent Spanish **Mission Santa Barbara,** and a walk down hopping **State Street to Stearns Wharf.**

SANTA BARBARA TO SAN SIMEON (approx. 147 mi)

North of Santa Barbara, Highway 1 morphs into the Cabrillo Highway, separating

Santa Barbara

from and then rejoining U.S. 101. The route winds through rolling vineyards and rangeland to **San Luis Obispo,** where any legit road trip includes a photo stop at the quirky **Madonna Inn.** Be sure to also climb the humungous dunes at **Guadalupe-Nipomo Dunes Preserve.**

In downtown San Luis Obispo, the **Mission San Luis Obispo de Tolosa** stands by a tree-shaded creek edged with shops and cafés. Highway 1 continues to **Morro Bay** and up the coast. About 15 mi north of Morro Bay, you'll reach the town of **Harmony** (population 18), a tiny burg with artists' studios, a wedding chapel, shops, and a winery. The road continues through **Cambria** to solitary **Hearst San Simeon State Historical Monument**—the art-filled pleasure palace at **San Simeon.** Just four miles north of the castle, elephant seals grunt and cavort at the

Big Sur

TOP 5 PLACES TO LINGER

- Point Dume State Preserve
- Santa Barbara
- Hearst San Simeon State Historical Monument
- Big Sur/Julia Pfeiffer Burns State Park
- Carmel

Piedras Blancas Elephant Seal Rookery, just off the side of the road.

SAN SIMEON TO CARMEL (approx. 92 mi)

Heading north, you'll drive through **Big Sur,** a place of ancient forests and rugged shoreline stretching 90 mi from San Simeon to **Carmel.** Much of Big Sur lies within several state parks and the 165,000-acre **Ventana Wilderness,** itself part of the **Los Padres National Forest.** This famously scenic stretch of the coastal drive, which twists up and down bluffs above the ocean, can last hours. Take your time.

At **Julia Pfeiffer Burns State Park** one easy but rewarding hike leads to an iconic waterfall off a beach-front cliff. When you reach lovely **Carmel,** stroll around the picture-perfect town's mission, galleries, and shops.

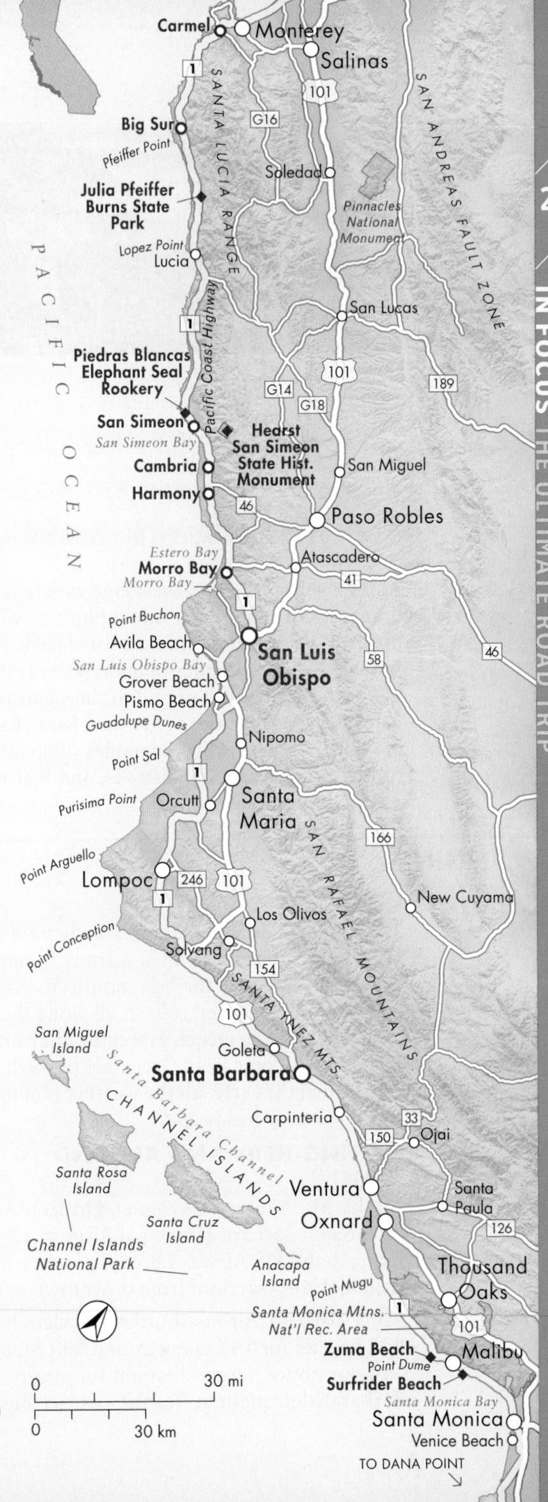

Updated by Cheryl Crabtree

Balmy weather, glorious beaches, crystal clear air, and serene landscapes have lured people to the Central Coast since prehistoric times. It's an ideal place to relax, slow down, and appreciate the good things in life.

Along the Pacific coast, the scenic variety is stunning—everything from dramatic cliffs and grass-tufted bluffs to wildlife estuaries and miles of dunes. Offshore, a pristine national park and a vast marine sanctuary protect the wild, wonderful underwater resources of this incredible corner of the planet. But not all of the Central Coast's top attractions are natural: the small cities of Ventura, Santa Barbara, and San Luis Obispo are filled with sparkling examples of Spanish-Mediterranean architecture, bustling shopping districts, and first-rate restaurants showcasing regional foods and wines.

PLANNING

WHEN TO GO

The Central Coast climate is usually mild throughout the year. If you like to sunbathe and swim in warmer (though still nippy) ocean waters, July and August are the best months to visit. Be aware that this is also high season. Fog often rolls in all along the coastal areas in early summer; you'll need a jacket, especially after sunset, close to the shore. The rains usually come from December through March. From April to early June and in the early fall the weather is almost as fine as in high season, and the pace is less hectic.

GETTING HERE AND AROUND

BY AIR

Alaska Air, American, Frontier, Horizon Air, United, and US Airways fly to Santa Barbara Municipal Airport, 12 mi from downtown. United Express and US Airways provide service to San Luis Obispo County Regional Airport, 3 mi from downtown San Luis Obispo.

Santa Barbara Airbus shuttles travelers between Santa Barbara and Los Angeles for $48 one-way and $90 round-trip (slight discount with 24-hour notice, larger discount for groups of six or more). The Santa Barbara Metropolitan Transit District Bus 11 ($1.75) runs every 30 minutes from the airport to the downtown transit center. A taxi between the airport and the hotel district runs $20 to $28.

Airport Contacts San Luis Obispo County Regional Airport ✉ *903-5 Airport Dr., San Luis Obispo* ☎ *805/781-5205* 🌐 *www.sloairport.com.* **Santa Barbara Airport** ✉ *500 Fowler Rd., Santa Barbara* ☎ *805/683-4011, 800/423-1618* 🌐 *www.flysba.com.*

Airport Transfer Contacts Santa Barbara Airbus ☎ *805/964-7759, 800/423-1618* 🌐 *www.santabarbaraairbus.com.* **Santa Barbara Metropolitan Transit District** ☎ *805/963-3366* 🌐 *www.sbmtd.gov.*

BY BUS

Greyhound provides service from San Francisco and Los Angeles to San Luis Obispo, Ventura, and Santa Barbara. From Monterey and Carmel, Monterey-Salinas Transit operates buses to Big Sur between May and mid-October. From San Luis Obispo, Central Coast Transit runs buses around Santa Maria and out to the coast. Santa Barbara Metropolitan Transit District provides local service. The Downtown/State Street and Waterfront shuttles cover their respective sections of Santa Barbara during the day. Gold Coast Transit buses serve the entire Ventura County region.

Bus Contacts Central Coast Transit ☎ *805/781-4472* 🌐 *www.slorta.org.* **Gold Coast Transit** ☎ *805/487-4222 for Oxnard and Port Hueneme, 805/643-3158 for Ojai and Ventura* 🌐 *www.goldcoasttransit.org.* **Greyhound** ☎ *800/231-2222* 🌐 *www.greyhound.com.* **Monterey-Salinas Transit** ☎ *888/678-2871* 🌐 *www.mst.org.* **San Luis Obispo Transit** ☎ *805/781-4472* 🌐 *www.slorta.org.* **Santa Barbara Metropolitan Transit District** ☎ *805/963-3366* 🌐 *www.sbmtd.gov.*

BY CAR

Driving is the easiest way to experience the Central Coast. A car gives you the flexibility to stop at scenic vista points along Highway 1, take detours through Wine Country, and drive to rural lakes and mountains. Traveling north through Ventura County to San Luis Obispo (note that from just south of Ventura up to San Luis Obispo, U.S. 101 and Highway 1 are the same road), you can take in the rolling hills, peaceful valleys, and rugged mountains that stretch for miles along the shore.

Highway 1 and U.S. 101 run north–south and more or less parallel along the Central Coast, with Highway 1 hugging the coast and U.S. 101 running inland. The most dramatic section of the Central Coast is the 70 mi between Big Sur and San Simeon. Don't expect to make good time along here: The road is narrow and twisting with a single lane in each direction, making it difficult to pass the many lumbering RVs. In fog or rain the drive can be downright nerve-racking; in wet seasons mudslides can close portions of the road. Once you start south from Carmel, there is no route east from Highway 1 until Highway 46 heads inland from Cambria to connect with U.S. 101. At Morro Bay, Highway 1 turns inland for 13 mi and connects with U.S. 101 at San Luis Obispo. From here south to Pismo Beach the two highways run concurrently. South of Pismo Beach to Las Cruces the roads separate, then run together all the way to Oxnard. Along any stretch where they are separate, U.S. 101 is the quicker route.

U.S. 101 and Highway 1 will get you to the Central Coast from Los Angeles and San Francisco. If you are coming from the east, you can take Highway 46 west from I–5 in the Central Valley (near Bakersfield) to U.S. 101 at Paso Robles, where it continues to the coast, intersecting Highway 1 a few miles south of Cambria. Highway 33 heads south from I–5 at Bakersfield to Ojai. About 60 mi north of Ojai, Highway 166 leaves Highway 33, traveling due west through the Sierra Madre to Santa Maria at U.S. 101 and continuing west to Highway 1 at Guadalupe. South of Carpinteria, Highway 150 winds from Highway 1/U.S. 101 through sparsely populated hills to Ojai. From Highway 1/U.S. 101 at Ventura, Highway 33 leads to Ojai and the Los Padres National Forest. South of Ventura, Highway 126 runs east from Highway 1/U.S. 101 to I–5.

Contacts Caltrans ☏ *800/427–7623* 🌐 *www.dot.ca.gov.*

BY TRAIN

The Amtrak *Coast Starlight,* which runs between Los Angeles and Seattle via Oakland, stops in Paso Robles, San Luis Obispo, Santa Barbara, and Oxnard. Amtrak runs several *Pacific Surfliner* trains daily between San Luis Obispo, Santa Barbara, Los Angeles, and San Diego. Metrolink Regional Rail Service trains connect Ventura and Oxnard with Los Angeles and points between.

Train Contacts Amtrak ☏ *800/872–7245, 805/963–1015 in Santa Barbara, 805/541–0505 in San Luis Obispo* 🌐 *www.amtrakcalifornia.com.* **Metrolink** ☏ *800/371–5465* 🌐 *www.metrolinktrains.com.*

TOUR OPTIONS

Cloud Climbers Jeep and Wine Tours offers four types of daily tours: wine-tasting, mountain, sunset, and a discovery tour for families. These trips to the Santa Barbara/Santa Ynez mountains and Wine Country are conducted in open-air, six-passenger jeeps. Fares range from $89 to $129 per adult. The company also offers a four-hour All Around Ojai Tour for $99 per adult and arranges biking, horseback riding, and trap-shooting tours and Paso Robles wine tours by appointment. Wine Edventures operates customized Santa Barbara County tours and narrated North County wine-country tours in 25-passenger minicoaches. Fares for the wine tours are $110 per person. The Grapeline Wine Country Shuttle leads daily wine and vineyard picnic tours with flexible itineraries in San Luis Obispo County and Santa Barbara County Wine Country; they stop at many area hotels and can provide private custom tours with advance reservations. Fares range from $88 to $115, depending on pickup location and tour choice.

Spencer's Limousine & Tours offers customized tours of the city of Santa Barbara and Wine Country via sedan, limousine, van, or minibus. A five-hour basic tour with at least four participants costs about $90 per person. Sultan's Limousine Service has a fleet of super stretches; each can take up to eight passengers on Paso Robles and Edna Valley–Arroyo Grande wine tours and tours of the San Luis Obispo County coast. Hiring a limo for a four-hour Wine Country tour typically costs $400 to $450 with tip. Sustainable Vine Wine Tours' biodiesel-powered vans can take you on a day of eco-friendly wine touring in the Santa Ynez Valley. Trips include door-to-door transportation from your location in the Santa Barbara or Santa Ynez Valley area, tastings at green-minded wineries, and a gourmet organic picnic lunch.

Tour Contacts Cloud Climbers Jeep and Wine Tours ☎ *805/646-3200* ⊕ *www.ccjeeps.com.* **The Grapeline Wine Country Shuttle** ☎ *888/894-6379* ⊕ *www.gogrape.com.* **Spencer's Limousine & Tours** ☎ *805/884-9700* ⊕ *www.spencerslimo.com.* **Sultan's Limousine Service** ☎ *805/466-3167 North SLO County, 805/544-8320 South SLO County, 805/771-0161 coastal SLO County cities* ⊕ *www.sultanslimo.com.* **Sustainable Vine Wine Tours** ☎ *805/698-3911* ⊕ *www.sustainablevine.com.* **Wine Edventures** ✉, *Santa Barbara* ☎ *805/965-9463* ⊕ *www.welovewines.com.*

VISITOR INFORMATION

Contacts San Luis Obispo County Visitors and Conference Bureau ✉ *811 El Capitan Way, #200, San Luis Obispo* ☎ *805/541-8000* ⊕ *www.sanluisobispocounty.com.* **Santa Barbara Conference and Visitors Bureau** ✉ *1601 Anacapa St., Santa Barbara* ☎ *805/966-9222* ⊕ *www.santabarbaraca.com.*

RESTAURANTS

The cuisine in Ventura and Santa Barbara is every bit as eclectic as it is in California's bigger cities; fresh seafood is a standout. The region from Solvang to Big Sur is far enough off the Interstate to ensure that nearly every restaurant or café has its own personality—from chic to down-home and funky. A foodie renaissance has overtaken the entire region from Ventura to Paso Robles, spawning dozens of new restaurants touting locavore cuisine made with fresh organic produce and meats.

Dining attire on the Central Coast is generally casual, though slightly dressy casual wear is the custom at pricier restaurants.

HOTELS

There are plenty of lodging options throughout the Central Coast—but expect to pay top dollar for any rooms along the shore, especially in summer. Moderately priced hotels and motels do exist—most just a short drive inland from their higher-price counterparts. Make your reservations as early as possible and take advantage of midweek specials to get the best rates. It's common for hotels to require minimum stays on holidays and some weekends, especially in summer, and to double their rates during festivals and other events.

WHAT IT COSTS

	¢	$	$$	$$$	$$$$
Restaurants	under $10	$10–$15	$16–$22	$23–$30	over $30
Hotels	under $90	$90–$120	$121–$175	$176–$250	over $250

Restaurant prices are for a main course at dinner, excluding sales tax of 7.25%–7.75% (depending on location). Hotel prices are for two people in a standard double room in high season, excluding service charges and 9%–10% tax.

VENTURA COUNTY

Ventura County was first settled by the Chumash Indians. Spanish missionaries were the first Europeans to arrive, followed by Americans and other Europeans, who established bustling towns, transportation networks, and highly productive farms. Since the 1920s, though, agriculture has been steadily replaced as the area's main industry—first by the oil business, and more recently, by tourism.

VENTURA

60 mi north of Los Angeles on U.S. 101.

Like Los Angeles, the city of Ventura enjoys gorgeous weather and sun-kissed beaches—but without the smog and congestion. The city is filled with classic California buildings, farmers' and fish markets, art galleries, and shops. The miles of beautiful beaches attract both athletes—bodysurfers and boogie boarders, runners and bikers—and those who'd rather doze beneath a rented umbrella all day. Ventura Harbor is home to the Channel Islands National Park Visitor Center and myriad fishing boats, restaurants, and water-activity centers where you can rent boats and take harbor cruises. Foodies can get their fix here, too; dozens of upscale cafés and wine and tapas bars have opened in recent years. Ventura is also a magnet for arts and antiques buffs who come to browse the dozens of galleries and shops in the downtown area.

GETTING HERE AND AROUND

Amtrak trains stop near the Ventura County Fairgrounds, a short walk from downtown. Metrolink trains travel from Los Angeles to southern Ventura. U.S. 101 is the main artery through town from north or south. For a scenic coastal route, drive along Highway 1 north along the coast from Santa Monica through Malibu. The road merges with U.S. 101 in Oxnard, just south of Ventura. To reach historic downtown Ventura, exit southbound U.S. 101 at Ventura Avenue or northbound U.S. 101 at California Street. Gold Coast Transit buses provide service throughout the city.

ESSENTIALS

Visitor Information Ventura Visitors and Convention Bureau ✉ *101 S. California St.* ☎ *805/648–2075, 800/483–6214* 🌐 *www.ventura-usa.com.*

EXPLORING

Visitor Center. You can pick up culinary, shopping, and other guides downtown at the visitor center run by the Ventura Visitors and Convention Bureau. ✉ *101 S. California St.* ☎ *805/648–2075, 800/483–6214* 🌐 *www.ventura-usa.com.*

Ventura Oceanfront. Four miles of gorgeous coastline stretch from the county fairgrounds at the northern border of the city of San Buenaventura, through San Buenaventura State Beach, down to Ventura Harbor in the south. The main attraction here is the San Buenaventura City Pier, a historic landmark built in 1872 and restored in 1993. Surfers rip the waves just north of the pier, and sunbathers relax on white-sand beaches on either side. The mile-long promenade and the Omer Rains Bike Trail north of the pier attract scores of joggers, surrey cyclers, and bikers throughout the year. ✉ *California St., at ocean's edge.*

TRAFFIC TIMING

The southbound freeway from Santa Barbara to Ventura and L.A. slows from 4 pm to 6 or 7 pm; the reverse is true heading from Ventura to Santa Barbara in the early morning hours. Traffic in the greater Los Angeles region can clog the roads as early as 2 pm. Traveling south, it's best to depart Santa Barbara before 1 pm, or after 6 pm. Heading north, you probably won't encounter many traffic problems until you reach the Salinas/San Jose corridor.

Lake Casitas Recreation Area. Lunker largemouth bass, rainbow trout, crappie, redears, and channel catfish live in the waters at Lake Casitas Recreation Area, an impoundment of the Ventura River. The lake is one of the country's best bass-fishing areas, and anglers come from all over the United States to test their luck. The park, nestled below the Santa Ynez Mountains' Laguna Ridge, is also a beautiful spot for pitching a tent or having a picnic. The Casitas Water Adventure, which has two water playgrounds and a lazy river for tubing and floating, is a great place to take kids in summer ($12 for an all-day pass; $6 from 5 to 7 pm). The park is 13 miles northwest of Ventura. ✉ *11311 Santa Ana Rd., off Hwy. 33* ☎ *805/649–2233, 805/649–1122 campground reservations* 🌐 *www.lakecasitas.info* *$10–$15 per vehicle, $10 per boat* ⏲ *Daily.*

Mission San Buenaventura. The ninth of the 21 California missions, Mission San Buenaventura was established in 1782 but burned to the ground in the 1790s. It was rebuilt and rededicated in 1809. A self-guided tour takes you through a small museum, a quiet courtyard, and a chapel with 250-year-old paintings. ✉ *211 E. Main St.* ☎ *805/643–4318* 🌐 *www.sanbuenaventuramission.org* *$2* ⏲ *Weekdays 10–5, Sat. 9–5, Sun. 10–4.*

WHERE TO EAT

$$$ AMERICAN **Brooks.** Innovative chef Andy Brooks and his wife Jayme—whose grandfather co-owned the famous Chi Chi supper club in Palm Springs in the 1960s—serve some of the town's finest meals in a slick, contemporary downtown dining room. The ever-changing menu centers on seasonal, mostly local, organic ingredients and features a nightly five-course tasting menu, which might include limoncello steamed mussels, cornmeal fried shrimp, or free-range chicken breast with sautéed collard greens and goat cheese-potato puree. Ask for the romaine salad dressed in the legendary Chi Chi creamy garlic dressing. Live music and hip martinis and margaritas attract a loyal following after 9 pm on weekends. ✉ *545 E. Thompson Blvd.* ☎ *805/652–7070* 🌐 *www.restaurantbrooks.com* ⏲ *Closed Mon. No lunch.*

$$ SEAFOOD **Brophy Bros.** The Ventura outpost of this wildly popular Santa Barbara restaurant provides the same fresh seafood-oriented meals in a spacious second-story setting overlooking the harbor. Feast on everything from fish and chips and crab cakes to chowder and delectable fish—often straight from the boats moored below. ✉ *1559 Spinnaker Dr., in Ventura Harbor Village* ☎ *805/639–0865* 🌐 *www.brophybros.com* *Reservations not accepted.*

¢ AMERICAN **Busy Bee Cafe.** A local favorite for decades, this classic 1950s diner has a jukebox on every table and serves hearty burgers and American comfort food (think meat loaf and mashed potatoes, pot roast, and Cobb salad). For breakfast, tuck into a huge omelet; for a snack or dessert, be sure to order a shake or hot fudge sundae from the soda fountain. *478 E. Main St. 805/643–4864 www.busybeecafe.biz.*

$ AMERICAN **Christy's.** You can get breakfast all day—don't miss the breakfast burrito—at this cozy, nautical-theme locals' hangout in the harbor, across the water from the Channel Islands. It also serves burgers, sandwiches, and soup. *1559 Spinnaker Dr. 805/642–3116.*

$$ MEDITERRANEAN **Jonathan's at Peirano's.** The main dining room here has a gazebo where you can eat surrounded by plants and local art. The menu has dishes from Spain, Portugal, France, Italy, Greece, and Morocco. Standouts are the various paellas, the *penne checca* pasta, and the ahi tuna encrusted with pepper and pistachios. The owners also run an evening tapas bar next door, which serves exotic martinis. *204 E. Main St. 805/648–4853 www.jonathansatpeiranos.com.*

WHERE TO STAY

For expanded hotel reviews, visit Fodors.com.

$$ **Crowne Plaza Ventura Beach.** An enviable SoCal location is the main draw of this full-service, 12-story hotel: on the beach, next to an historic pier, within easy walking distance of downtown restaurants and nightlife, and steps from the Amtrak train station. Pros: right on the beach, walk to downtown and main attractions, steps from waterfront activities. Cons: trains whiz by early morning, waterfront area crowded in summer, most rooms on the small side *450 E. Harbor Blvd., Ventura 800/842–0800 cpventura.com 254 rooms, 4 suites In-room: a/c, Wi-Fi. In-hotel: restaurant, bar, pool, gym, beach, water sports, laundry facilities, business center, parking, some pets allowed.*

$$ **Four Points by Sheraton Ventura Harbor.** The spacious, contemporary rooms here are still gleaming from a total renovation that was completed in 2009. **Pros:** close to island transportation; mostly quiet; short drive or bus ride to historic downtown Ventura. **Cons:** not in the heart of downtown; noisy seagulls sometimes congregate nearby. *1050 Schooner Dr. 805/658–1212 www.fourpoints.com/ventura 102 rooms, 4 suites In-room: a/c, Internet, Wi-Fi. In-hotel: restaurant, bar, pool, gym, business center, some pets allowed.*

$$ **Holiday Inn Express Ventura Harbor.** A favorite among Channel Islands visitors, this quiet, comfortable, lodge-inspired property sits right at the Ventura Harbor entrance. **Pros:** quiet at night; easy access to harbor restaurants and activities; on shuttle bus route to city attractions. **Cons:** busy area on weekends; five-minute drive to downtown sights. *1080 Navigator Dr. 805/856–9533, 800/315–2621 www.hiexpress.com 68 rooms, 23 suites In-room: no a/c, kitchen, Internet. In-hotel: pool, gym, business center, some pets allowed Breakfast.*

$$$ **Pierpont Inn.** Back in 1910, Josephine Pierpont-Ginn built the original Pierpont Inn on a hill overlooking Ventura Beach. **Pros:** near the beach; lush gardens; Tempur-Pedic mattresses and pillows. **Cons:** near the freeway and train tracks; difficult to walk downtown from here. *550*

Sanjon Rd. ☎ *805/643–6144* 🌐 *www.pierpontinn.com* *65 rooms, 9 suites, 2 cottages* *In-room: no a/c, Wi-Fi. In-hotel: restaurant, bar, pool, tennis court, gym, spa, business center* *Breakfast.*

$$$ **Ventura Beach Marriott.** Spacious, contemporary rooms, a peaceful location just steps from San Buenaventura State Beach, and easy access to historic downtown Ventura's arts and culture district make the Marriott a popular choice for travelers who want to explore Ventura. **Pros:** walk to beach and biking/jogging trails; a block from historic pier; great value for location. **Cons:** close to highway; near busy intersection. ✉ *2055 E. Harbor Blvd.* ☎ *805/643–6000, 888/236–2427* 🌐 *www.marriottventurabeach.com* *272 rooms, 12 suites* *In-room: a/c, Internet, Wi-Fi. In-hotel: restaurant, bar, pool, gym, laundry facilities, business center, parking, some pets allowed* *Breakfast.*

SPORTS AND THE OUTDOORS

The most popular outdoor activities in Ventura are beach-going and whale-watching. California gray whales migrate offshore through the Santa Barbara Channel from late December through March; giant blue and humpback whales feed here from mid-June through September. In fact, the channel is teeming with marine life year-round, so tours include more than just whale sightings.

> **HOTEL HELP**
>
> **Hot Spots.** Hot Spots provides room reservations and tourist information for destinations in Ventura, Santa Barbara, and San Luis Obispo counties. ☎ *800/793–7666* 🌐 *www.hotspotsusa.com.*

Island Packers. A cruise through the Santa Barbara Channel with Island Packers will give you the chance to spot dolphins and seals—and sometimes even whales—throughout the year. ✉ *1691 Spinnaker Dr., Ventura Harbor* ☎ *805/642–1393* 🌐 *www.islandpackers.com.*

OJAI

15 mi north of Ventura, U.S. 101 to Hwy. 33.

The Ojai Valley, which director Frank Capra used as a backdrop for his 1936 film *Lost Horizon,* sizzles in the summer when temperatures routinely reach 90°F. The acres of orange and avocado groves here evoke postcard images of agricultural Southern California from decades ago. This is a lush, slow-moving place, where many artists and celebrities have sought refuge from life in the fast lane.

GETTING HERE AND AROUND

From Ventura, reach Ojai via Highway 33, which veers east from U.S. 101 in northern Ventura and climbs inland to Ojai. From Santa Barbara, exit U.S. 101 at Highway 150 in Carpinteria, then travel inland 20 mi to Ojai (it's a twisty, two-lane country road, not recommended at night or during poor weather). You can also access Ojai from Highway 126, which runs between U.S. 101 and inland Highway 5. Exit at Santa Paula and follow Highway 150 16 mi north to Ojai. Get around Ojai Valley on the Ojai Valley Trolley.

ESSENTIALS

Visitor Information Ojai Visitors Bureau ☎ *888/652–4669* 🌐 *www.ojaivisitors.com.*

EXPLORING

Ojai Valley Trolley. The town can be easily explored on foot; you can also hop on the Ojai Valley Trolley, which follows two routes around Ojai and neighboring Miramonte between 7:15 and 5:15 on weekdays, 9 and 5 on weekends. If you tell the driver you're a visitor, you'll get an informal guided tour. 🌐 *www.ojaitrolley.com* 🎫 *50¢.*

Ojai Visitors Bureau. Maps and tourist information are available at the Ojai Visitors Bureau at the Ojai Chamber of Commerce. ✉ *201 S. Signal St.* ☎ *888/652–4669* 🌐 *www.ojaichamber.org* ⏲ *Weekdays 9–4.*

Ojai Avenue. The work of local artists is displayed in the Spanish-style shopping arcade along Ojai Avenue (Highway 150). Organic and specialty growers sell their produce on Sunday 9–1 at the farmers' market behind the arcade.

Ojai Center for the Arts. The Ojai Center for the Arts exhibits artwork and presents theater, dance, and other performances. ✉ *113 S. Montgomery St.* ☎ *805/646–0117* 🌐 *www.ojaiartcenter.org.*

Ojai Valley Museum. The Ojai Valley Museum has exhibits on the valley's history and many Native American artifacts. ✉ *130 W. Ojai Ave.* ☎ *805/640–1390* 🌐 *www.ojaivalleymuseum.org* 🎫 *$4.*

Ojai Valley Trail. The 18-mi Ojai Valley Trail is open to pedestrians, bikers, joggers, equestrians, and nonmotorized vehicles. You can access it anywhere along its route. ✉ *Parallel to Hwy. 33 from Soule Park in Ojai to ocean in Ventura* ☎ *888/652–4669* 🌐 *www.ojaivisitors.com.*

WHERE TO EAT

$$ MEDITERRANEAN

✕ **Azu.** Delectable tapas, a full bar, slick furnishings, and piped jazz music lure diners to this popular, artsy Mediterranean bistro. You can also order soups, salads, and bistro fare such as tagine, roasted chicken, and paella. Save room for the homemade gelato. ✉ *457 E. Ojai Ave.* ☎ *805/640–7987* 🌐 *www.azuojai.com* ⏱ *No lunch Sun. and Mon.*

$ ITALIAN

✕ **Boccali's.** Edging a ranch, citrus groves, and a seasonal garden that provides much of the produce for menu items, family-run Boccali's has attracted droves of loyal fans to its modest but cheery restaurant since 1986. In the warmer months, you can dine alfresco in the oak-shaded patio and lawn area and sometimes listen to live music. Best known for their hand-rolled pizzas and homestyle pastas (don't miss the eggplant lasagna), Boccali's also serves a seasonal strawberry shortcake that some patrons drive many miles to savor every year. ✉ *3277 Ojai Ave., about 2 mi east of downtown* ☎ *805/646–6116* 🌐 *www.boccalis.com* 💳 *No credit cards* ⏱ *No lunch Mon. and Tues.*

$$$ AMERICAN ★

✕ **The Ranch House.** This elegant yet laid-back eatery—said to be the best in town—has been around for decades. Main dishes such as rack of lamb in an oyster-and-mushroom cream sauce, and grilled diver scallops with curried sweet-corn sauce are not to be missed. The verdant patio is a wonderful place to have Sunday brunch. ✉ *500 S. Lomita Ave.* ☎ *805/646–2360* 🌐 *www.theranchhouse.com* ⏱ *Closed Mon. No lunch.*

$$$ CONTINENTAL

✕ **Suzanne's Cuisine.** Peppered filet mignon, linguine with steamed clams, and pan-roasted salmon with a roasted mango sauce are among the offerings at this European-style restaurant. Game, seafood, and vegetarian dishes dominate the dinner menu, and salads and soups star at lunchtime. All the breads and desserts are made on the premises. ✉ *502 W. Ojai Ave.* ☎ *805/640–1961* 🌐 *www.suzannescuisine.com* ⏱ *Closed Tues.*

WHERE TO STAY

For expanded hotel reviews, visit Fodors.com.

$

🏨 **The Blue Iguana Inn & Suites.** Artists run this Southwestern-style hotel, and their work (which is for sale) decorates the rooms. **Pros:** colorful art everywhere; secluded property; breakfast delivered to each room. **Cons:** 2 mi from the heart of Ojai; sits on the main highway to Ventura; small. ✉ *11794 N. Ventura Ave., Hwy. 33* ☎ *805/646–5277* 🌐 *www.blueiguanainn.com* 🛏 *4 rooms, 7 suites, 8 cottages* 👍 *In-room: a/c, kitchen, Wi-Fi. In-hotel: pool, some pets allowed* 🍽 *Breakfast.*

$$$ Oaks at Ojai. Rejuvenation is the name of the game at this comfortable spa resort. **Pros:** great place to get fit; peaceful retreat; healthy meals. **Cons:** rooms are basic; sits on the main highway through town. ✉ *122 E. Ojai Ave.* ☎ *805/646–5573, 800/753–6257* 🌐 *www.oaksspa.com* *44 rooms, 2 suites* *In-room: a/c, Wi-Fi. In-hotel: restaurant, pool, gym, spa, laundry facilities, business center* *All meals* ☞ *2-night minimum stay.*

$$$$ ★ **Ojai Valley Inn & Spa.** This outdoorsy, golf-oriented resort and spa is set on beautifully landscaped grounds, with hillside views in nearly all directions. **Pros:** gorgeous grounds; exceptional outdoor activities; romantic yet kid-friendly. **Cons:** expensive; staff isn't always attentive. ✉ *905 Country Club Rd.* ☎ *805/646–1111, 888/697–8780* 🌐 *www.ojairesort.com* *231 rooms, 77 suites* *In-room: a/c, Internet, Wi-Fi. In-hotel: restaurant, bar, golf course, pool, tennis court, spa, children's programs, some pets allowed.*

$$$ **Su Nido Inn.** Just a short walk from downtown Ojai sights and restaurants, this posh Mission revival–style inn is nested in a quiet neighborhood a few blocks from Libbey Park. **Pros:** walking distance from downtown; homey feel. **Cons:** no pool; can get hot during summer. ✉ *301 N. Montgomery St.* ☎ *805/646–7080, 866/646–7080* 🌐 *www.sunidoinn.com* *3 rooms, 9 suites* *In-room: a/c, kitchen, Internet, Wi-Fi. In-hotel: bar, business center.*

SANTA BARBARA

27 mi northwest of Ventura and 29 mi west of Ojai on U.S. 101.

Santa Barbara has long been an oasis for Los Angelenos seeking respite from hectic big-city life. The attractions begin at the ocean and end in the foothills of the Santa Ynez Mountains. A few miles up the coast—but still very much a part of Santa Barbara—is the exclusive residential district of Hope Ranch. Santa Barbara is on a jog in the coastline, so the ocean is actually to the south, instead of the west; for this reason, directions can be confusing. "Up" the coast toward San Francisco is west, "down" toward Los Angeles is east, and the mountains are north.

GETTING HERE AND AROUND

A car is handy but not essential if you're planning to stay in town. The beaches and downtown are easily explored by bicycle or on foot. You can also hop aboard one of the electric shuttles that cruise the downtown and waterfront every 8 to 15 minutes (25¢ each way) and connect with local buses such as Line 22, which goes to major visitor sights (🌐 *www.sbmtd.gov*).

Santa Barbara Trolley Co. A motorized San Francisco–style cable car operated by Santa Barbara Trolley Co. makes 90-minute runs from 10 to 4 past major hotels, shopping areas, and attractions. Get off whenever you like, and pick up another trolley when you're ready to move on (they come every hour). Try to get a seat on the newest vehicle in the fleet, a biodiesel trolley with all seats on the top deck. Trolleys depart from and return to Stearns Wharf. The fare is $19 for the day. ☎ *805/965–0353* 🌐 *www.sbtrolley.com.*

Santa Barbara Car Free. Visit Santa Barbara Car Free for bike route and walking-tour maps and car-free vacation packages with substantial lodging discounts. *www.santabarbaracarfree.org.*

ESSENTIALS

Visitor Information Santa Barbara Conference and Visitors Bureau *1601 Anacapa St. 805/966–9222 www.santabarbaraca.com.* **Santa Barbara Chamber of Commerce Visitor Information Center** *1 Garden St., at Cabrillo Blvd. 805/965–3021, 805/568–1811 www.sbchamber.org.*

EXPLORING

Santa Barbara's waterfront is beautiful, with palm-studded promenades and plenty of sand. In the few miles between the beaches and the hills are downtown, the old mission, and the botanic gardens.

Andree Clark Bird Refuge. This peaceful lagoon and its gardens sit north of East Beach. Bike trails and footpaths, punctuated by signs identifying native and migratory birds, skirt the lagoon. *1400 E. Cabrillo Blvd. Free.*

Carriage and Western Art Museum. The country's largest collection of old horse-drawn vehicles—painstakingly restored—is exhibited here. Everything from polished hearses to police buggies to old stagecoaches and circus vehicles is on display. In August the Old Spanish Days Fiesta borrows many of the vehicles for a jaunt about town. This is one of the city's true hidden gems, a wonderful place to help history come alive—especially for children. Docents lead tours the third Sunday of every month from 1 to 4 pm. *129 Castillo St. 805/962–2353 www.carriagemuseum.org Free Weekdays 9–3.*

★ **El Presidio State Historic Park.** Founded in 1782, El Presidio was one of four military strongholds established by the Spanish along the coast of California. The park encompasses much of the original site in the heart of downtown. El Cuartel, the adobe guardhouse, is the oldest building in Santa Barbara and the second oldest in California. *123 E. Canon Perdido St. 805/965–0093 www.sbthp.org $5 Daily 10:30–4:30.*

Karpeles Manuscript Library. Ancient political tracts and old Disney cartoons are among the holdings at this facility, which also houses one of the world's largest privately owned collections of rare manuscripts. Fifty display cases contain a sampling of the archive's million-plus documents. *21 W. Anapamu St. 805/962–5322 www.karpeles.com Free Daily 10–4.*

Fodor's Choice ★ **Mission Santa Barbara.** Widely referred to as the "Queen of Missions," this is one of the most beautiful and frequently photographed buildings in coastal California. Dating to 1786, the architecture evolved from adobe-brick buildings with thatch roofs to more permanent edifices as the mission's population burgeoned. An earthquake in 1812 destroyed the third church built on the site. Its replacement, the present structure, is still a functioning Catholic church. Mission Santa Barbara has a splendid Spanish/Mexican colonial art collection, as well as Chumash sculptures and the only Native American–made altar and tabernacle left in the California missions. Docents lead 90-minute tours ($8 adult) Thursday and Friday at 11 and Saturday at 10:30; these include

Continued on page 54

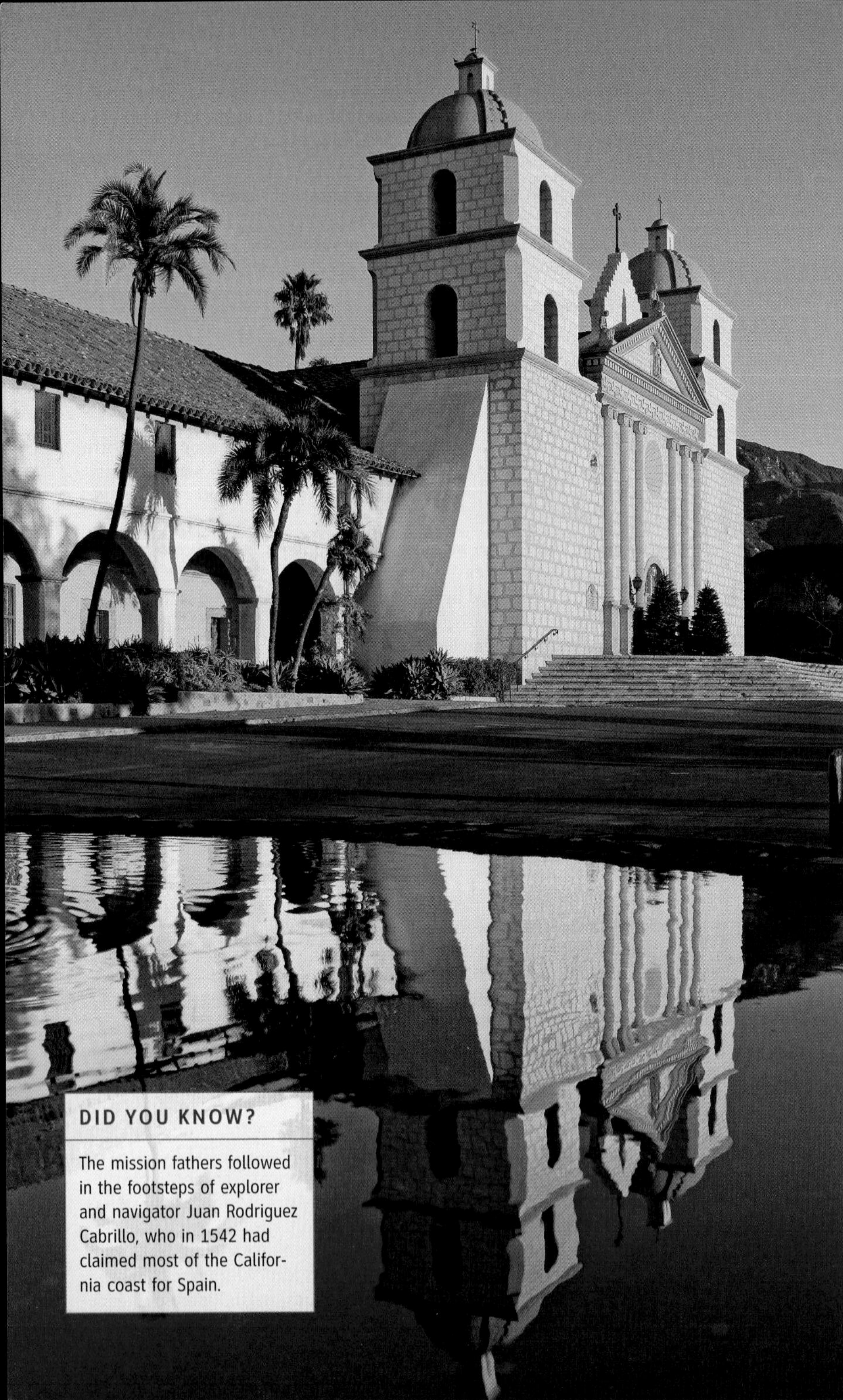
DID YOU KNOW?
The mission fathers followed in the footsteps of explorer and navigator Juan Rodriguez Cabrillo, who in 1542 had claimed most of the California coast for Spain.

ON A MISSION

Their soul may belong to Spain, their heart to the New World, but the historic missions of California, with their lovely churches, beckon the traveler on a soulful journey back to the very founding of the American West.

by Cheryl Crabtree and Robert I.C. Fisher

California history changed forever in the 18th century when Spanish explorers founded a series of missions along the Pacific coast. Believing they were following God's will, they wanted to spread the gospel and convert as many natives as possible. The process produced a collision between the Hispanic and California Indian cultures, resulting in one of the most striking legacies of Old California: the Spanish mission churches. Rising like mirages in the middle of desert plains and rolling hills, these saintly sites transport you back to the days of the Spanish colonial period.

GOD AND MAN IN CALIFORNIA

The Alta California territory came under pressure around 1750 when Spain feared foreign advances into the territory explorer Juan Rodríguez Cabrillo had claimed for the Spanish crown back in 1542. But how could Spain create a visible and viable presence halfway around the world? They decided to build on the model that had already worked well in Spain's Mexico colony. The plan involved establishing a series of missions, to be operated by the Catholic Church and protected by four of Spain's *presidios* (military outposts). The native Indians—after quick conversion to Christianity—would provide the labor force necessary to build mission towns.

FATHER OF THE MISSIONS

Father Junípero Serra is an icon of the Spanish colonial period. At the behest of the Spanish government, the diminutive padre—then well into his fifties, and despite a chronic leg infection—started out on foot from Baja California to search for suitable mission sites, with a goal of reaching Monterey. In 1769 he helped establish Alta California's first mission in San Diego and continued his travels until his death, in 1784, by which time he had founded eight more missions.

The system ended about a decade after the Mexican government took control of Alta California in the early 1820s and began to secularize the missions. The church lost horses and cattle, as well as vast tracts of land, which the Mexican government in turn granted to private individuals. They also lost laborers, as the Indians were for the most part free to find work and a life beyond the missions. In 1848, the Americans assumed control of the territory, and California became part of the United States. Today, these missions stand as extraordinary monuments to their colorful past.

Altarpiece at Mission San Gabriel Arcángel

MISSION ACCOMPLISHED

California's Mission Trail is the best way to follow in the fathers' footsteps. Here, below, are its 21 settlements, north to south.

Amazingly, all 21 Spanish missions in California are still standing—some in their pristine historic state, others with modifications made over the centuries. Many are found on or near the "King's Road"—El Camino Real—which linked these mission outposts. At the height of the mission system the trail was approximately 600 miles long, eventually extending from San Diego to Sonoma. Today the road is commemorated on portions of routes 101 and 82 in the form of roadside bell markers erected by CalTrans every one to two miles between Orange County and San Francisco.

San Francisco Solano, Sonoma (1823; this was the final California mission constructed.)

San Rafael, San Rafael (1817)

San Francisco de Asís (aka Mission Dolores), San Francisco (1776). Situated in the heart of San Francisco,

Painting from 1818, San Juan Bautista.

Mission Santa Clara de Asís

these mission grounds and nearby Arroyo de los Dolores (Creek of Sorrows) are home to the oldest intact building in the city.

Santa Clara de Asís, Santa Clara (1777). On the campus of Santa Clara University, this beautifully restored mission contains original paintings, statues, a bell, and hundreds of artifacts, as well as a spectacular rose garden.

San José, Fremont (1797)

Santa Cruz, Santa Cruz (1791)

San Juan Bautista, San Juan Bautista (1797). Immortalized in Hitchcock's *Vertigo*, this remarkably preserved pueblo contains the largest church of all the California missions, as well as 18th- and 19th-century buildings and a sprawling plaza.

San Carlos Borromeo del Río Carmelo, Carmel (1770). Carmel Mission was headquarters for the California mission system under Father Serra and the Father Presidents who succeeded him; the on-site museum includes Serra's tiny sleeping quarters (where he died in 1784).

Nuestra Señora de la Soledad, Soledad (1791)

San Antonio de Padua, Jolon (1771)

San Miguel Arcángel, San Miguel (1797). San Miguel boasts the only intact original interior work of art in any of the missions, painted in 1821 by Native American converts under the direction of Spanish artist Esteban Muras.

Mission Santa Inés

San Luis Obispo de Tolosa, San Luis Obispo (1772). Bear meat from grizzlies captured here saved the Spaniards from starving, which helped convince Father Serra to establish a mission.

La Purísima Concepción, Lompoc (1787). La Purísima is the nation's most completely restored mission complex. It is now a living-history museum with a church and nearly forty craft and residence rooms.

Santa Inés, Solvang (1804). Home to one of the most significant pieces of liturgical art created by a California mission Indian.

Santa Bárbara, Santa Barbara (1786). The "Queen of the Missions" has twin bell towers, gorgeous gardens with heirloom plant varietals, a massive collection of rare artworks and artifacts, and lovely stonework.

San Buenaventura, Ventura (1782). This was the last mission founded by Father Serra; it is still an active parish in the Archdiocese of Los Angeles.

Mission San Fernando Rey de España

San Fernando Rey de España, Mission Hills (1797)

San Gabriel Arcángel, San Gabriel (1771)

San Luis Rey de Francia, Oceanside (1798)

San Juan Capistrano, San Juan Capistrano (1776). This mission is famed for its Saint Joseph's Day (March 19) celebration of the return of swallows in the springtime. The mission's adobe walls enclose acres of lush gardens and historic buildings.

San Diego de Alcalá, San Diego (1769). This was the first California missions constructed, although the original was destroyed in 1775.

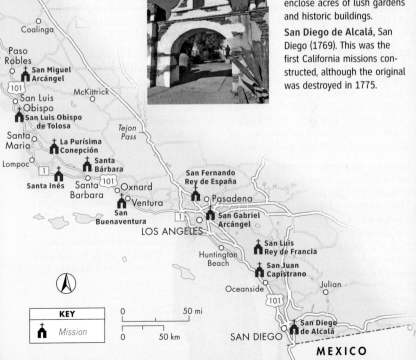

SPANISH MISSION STYLE

(left) Mission San Luis Rey de Francia; (right) Mission San Antonio de Padua

The Spanish mission churches derive much of their strength and enduring power from their extraordinary admixture of styles. They are spectacular examples of the combination of races and cultures that bloomed along Father Serra's road through Alta California.

SPIRIT OF THE PLACE

In building the missions, the Franciscan padres had to rely on available resources. Spanish churches back in Europe boasted marble floors and gilded statues. But here, whitewashed adobe walls gleamed in the sun and floors were often merely packed earth.

However simple the structures, the art within the mission confines continued to glorifiy the Church. The padres imported much finery to decorate the churches and perform the mass—silver, silk and lovely paintings to teach the life of Christ to the Indians and soldiers and settlers. Serra himself commissioned fine artists in Mexico to produce custom works using the best materials and according to exact specifications. Sculptures of angels, Mary, Joseph, Jesus and the Franciscan heroes and saints—and of course the Stations of the Cross—adorned all the missions.

AN ENDURING LEGACY

Mission architecture reflects a gorgeous blend of European and New World influences. While naves followed the simple forms of Franciscan Gothic, cloisters (with beautiful arcades) adopted aspects of the Romanesque style, and ornamental touches of the Spanish Renaissance—including red-tiled roofs and wrought-iron grilles—added even more elegance. In the 20th century, the Mission Revival Style had a huge impact on architecture and design in California, as seen in examples ranging from San Diego's Union Station to Stanford University's main quadrangle.

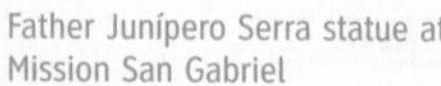

Father Junípero Serra statue at Mission San Gabriel

FOR WHOM THE BELLS TOLLED

Perhaps the most famous architectural motif of the Spanish Mission churches was the belltower. These took the form of either a campanile—a single tower called a campanario—or, more spectacularly, of an open-work espedaña, a perforated adobe wall housing a series of bells (notable examples of this form are at San Miguel Arcángel and San Diego de Alcalá). Bells were essential to maintaining the routines of daily life at the missions.

MISSION LIFE

Morning bells summoned residents to chapel for services; noontime bells introduced the main meal, while the evening bells sounded the alert to gather around 5 pm for mass and dinner. Many of the natives were happy with their new faith, and even enjoyed putting in numerous hours a week working as farmers, soapmakers, weavers, and masons.

Others, however, were less willing to abandon their traditional culture, but were coerced to abide by the new Spanish laws and mission rules. Natives were sometimes mistreated by the friars, who used a system of punishments to enforce submission to their teachings.

NATIVE TRAGEDY

In the end, mission life proved extremely destructive to the Native Californian population. European diseases and contaminated water caused the death of nearly a third, with some tribes—notably the Chumash—being virtually decimated. One friar was quoted as noting that the Indians "live well free but as soon as we reduce them to a Christian and community life . . . they fatten, sicken, and die."

Though so many native Indians died during the mission era, small numbers did survive. After the Mexican government secularized the missions in 1833, a majority of the native population was reduced to poverty. Some stayed at the missions, while others went to live in the pueblos, ranchos, and countryside—a tragic end for those whose labor was largely responsible for the magnificent mission churches we see today.

FOR MORE INFORMATION

California Missions Foundation

✉ 26555 Carmel Rancho Blvd., Ste. 7 Carmel, CA 93923

☎ 831/622-7500

🌐 www.californiamissionsfoundation.org

Top and bottom, Mission San Gabriel Arcángel.

a stroll through to the adjacent La Huerta Project—a re-creation of the Spanish-era gardens with native and heirloom plants. ✉ *2201 Laguna St.* ☎ *805/682–4149, 805/682–4713* 🌐 *www.santabarbaramission.org* 🎫 *$5* ⏲ *Daily 9–4:30.*

Montecito. Since the late 1800s the tree-studded hills and valleys of this town have attracted the rich and famous (Hollywood icons, business tycoons, dot-commers who divested before the crash, and old-money families who installed themselves here years ago). Shady roads wind through the community, which consists mostly of gated estates. Swank boutiques line Coast Village Road, where well-heeled residents such as Oprah Winfrey sometimes browse for truffle oil, picture frames, and designer sweats. Residents also hang out in the Upper Village, a chic shopping area with restaurants and cafés at the intersection of San Ysidro and East Valley roads. Montecito is about 3 mi east of Santa Barbara.

SANTA BARBARA STYLE

Why does downtown Santa Barbara look so scrubbed and uniform? After a 1925 earthquake, which demolished many buildings, the city seized a golden opportunity to create a Spanish-Mediterranean look. It established an architectural board of review, which, along with city commissions, created strict architectural codes for the downtown district: red tile roofs, earth-tone facades, arches, wrought-iron embellishments, and height restrictions (about four stories).

Lotusland. The 37-acre Montecito estate called Lotusland once belonged to Polish opera singer Ganna Walska. Many of the exotic trees and other subtropical flora were planted in 1882 by horticulturist R. Kinton Stevens. On the two-hour guided tour (the only option for visiting unless you're a member), you'll see an outdoor theater, a topiary garden, a huge collection of rare cycads (an unusual plant genus that has been around since the time of the dinosaurs), and a lotus pond. Tours are conducted mid-February through mid-November, Wednesday through Saturday at 10 and 1:30. Reservations are required. Child-friendly family tours are available for groups with children under the age of 10; contact Lotusland for scheduling. ✉ *695 Ashley Rd.* ☎ *805/969–9990* 🌐 *www.lotusland.org* 🎫 *$35*

Outdoors Santa Barbara Visitor Center. The small office provides maps and other information about Channel Islands National Park, Channel Islands National Marine Sanctuary, and the Santa Barbara Maritime Museum, which occupies the same building in the harbor. ✉ *113 Harbor Way* ☎ *805/884–1475* 🌐 *outdoorsb.noaa.gov* 🎫 *Free* ⏲ *Daily 11–5.*

Santa Barbara Botanic Garden. Scenic trails meander through the garden's 78 acres of native plants. The Mission Dam, built in 1806, stands just beyond the redwood grove and above the restored aqueduct that once carried water to Mission Santa Barbara. More than a thousand plant species thrive in various themed sections of the garden, including mountains, deserts, meadows, redwoods, and Channel Islands. ✉ *1212 Mission Canyon Rd.* ☎ *805/682–4726* 🌐 *www.sbbg.org* 🎫 *$8* ⏲ *Mar.–Oct., daily 9–6; Nov.–Feb., daily 9–5. Guided tours weekdays at 2, weekends at 11 and 2.*

Santa Barbara

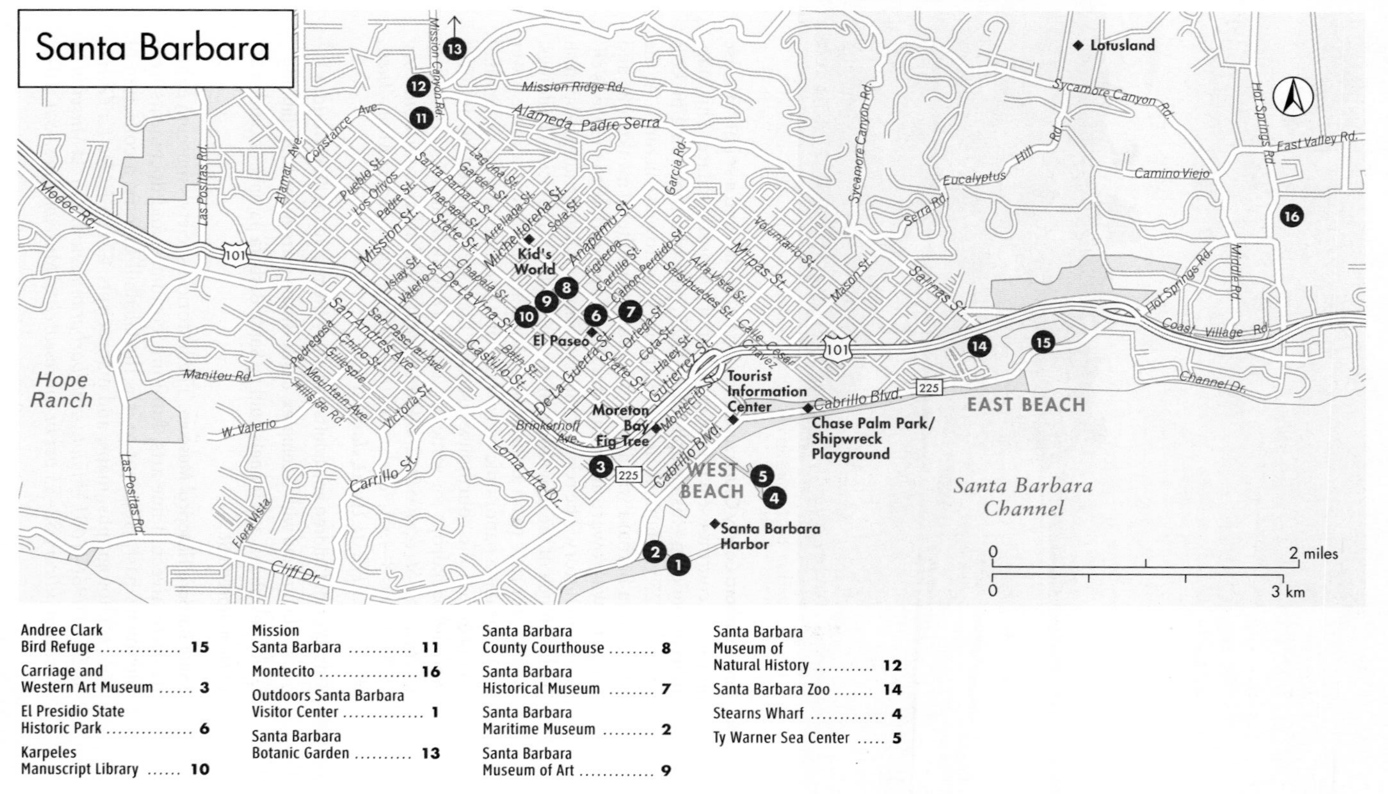

Andree Clark Bird Refuge 15
Carriage and Western Art Museum 3
El Presidio State Historic Park 6
Karpeles Manuscript Library 10
Mission Santa Barbara 11
Montecito 16
Outdoors Santa Barbara Visitor Center 1
Santa Barbara Botanic Garden 13
Santa Barbara County Courthouse 8
Santa Barbara Historical Museum 7
Santa Barbara Maritime Museum 2
Santa Barbara Museum of Art 9
Santa Barbara Museum of Natural History 12
Santa Barbara Zoo 14
Stearns Wharf 4
Ty Warner Sea Center 5

Santa Barbara's downtown is attractive, but be sure also to visit its beautiful—and uncrowded—beaches.

★ **Santa Barbara County Courthouse.** Hand-painted tiles and a spiral staircase infuse the courthouse with the grandeur of a Moorish palace. This magnificent building was completed in 1929, part of a rebuilding process after a 1925 earthquake destroyed many downtown structures. At the time, Santa Barbara was also in the midst of a cultural awakening, and the trend was toward an architectural style appropriate to the area's climate and history. The result is the harmonious Mediterranean–Spanish look of much of the downtown area, especially the municipal buildings. An elevator rises to an arched observation area in the courthouse tower that provides a panoramic view of the city. The murals in the ceremonial chambers on the courthouse's second floor were painted by an artist who did backdrops for some of Cecil B. DeMille's films. ✉ *1100 block of Anacapa St.* ☎ *805/962–6464* 🌐 *www.santabarbaracourthouse.org* ⏲ *Weekdays 8–4:45, weekends 10–4:30. Free guided tours Mon., Tues., Weds., and Fri. at 10:30, daily at 2.*

QUICK BITES

Kids' World. Children and adults can enjoy themselves at Kids' World, a public playground with a complex, castle-shape maze of fanciful climbing structures, slides, and tunnels built by Santa Barbara parents. ✉ ***Garden St. at Micheltorena St..***

Santa Barbara Historical Museum. The historical society's museum exhibits decorative and fine arts, furniture, costumes, and documents from the town's past. Adjacent to it is the Gledhill Library, a collection of books, photographs, maps, and manuscripts. ✉ *136 E. De La Guerra St.* ☎ *805/966–1601* 🌐 *www.santabarbaramuseum.com* 🎫 *Museum by donation; library $2–$5 per hr for research* ⏲ *Museum Tues.–Sat. 10–5,*

Sun. noon–5, guided tours Sat. at 2; library Tues.–Fri. 10–4, 1st Sat. of month 10–1.

Santa Barbara Maritime Museum. California's seafaring history is the focus at this museum. High-tech, hands-on exhibits, such as a sportfishing activity that lets you catch a "big one" and a local surfing history retrospective make this a fun stop for families. ✉ *113 Harbor Way* ☎ *805/962–8404* 🌐 *www.sbmm.org* 🎫 *$7* 🕒 *June–Aug., Thurs.–Tues. 10–6; Sept.–May, Thurs.–Tues. 10–5.*

Santa Barbara Museum of Art. The highlights of this museum's permanent collection include ancient sculpture, Asian art, impressionist paintings, contemporary Latin American art, and American works in several media. ✉ *1130 State St.* ☎ *805/963–4364* 🌐 *www.sbma.net* 🎫 *$9, free on Sun.* 🕒 *Tues.–Sun. 11–5. Free guided tours Tues.–Sun. at noon and 1.*

Santa Barbara Museum of Natural History. The gigantic skeleton of a blue whale greets you at the entrance of this complex. The major draws include the planetarium, space lab, and a gem and mineral display. A room of dioramas illustrates Chumash Indian history and culture. Startlingly alive-looking stuffed specimens, complete with nests and eggs, roost in the bird diversity room. Many exhibits have interactive components. Outdoors you can stroll on nature trails that wind through the serene oak-studded grounds. Admission is free on the third Sunday of each month. Ask about the Nature Pass, which includes discounted unlimited two-day admission to both the Museum of Natural History and the Ty Warner Sea Center on Stearns Wharf. ✉ *2559 Puesta del Sol Rd.* ☎ *805/682–4711* 🌐 *www.sbnature.org* 🎫 *$10* 🕒 *Daily 10–5.*

Santa Barbara Zoo. The grounds of this smallish zoo are so gorgeous people book their weddings here long in advance. The palm-studded lawns on a hilltop overlooking the beach are perfect spots for family picnics. The natural settings of the zoo shelter elephants, gorillas, exotic birds like the rare California condor, and big cats such as the rare snow leopard, a thick-furred, high-altitude dweller from Asia. For small children, there's a scenic railroad and barnyard petting zoo. ✉ *500 Niños Dr.* ☎ *805/962–5339 main line, 805/962–6310 information* 🌐 *www.santabarbarazoo.org* 🎫 *Zoo $12, parking $5* 🕒 *Daily 10–5.*

LAND SHARK!

Land and Sea Tours. Land and Sea Tours takes visitors on narrated, 90-minute land-and-sea adventures in an amphibious 49-passenger vehicle, nicknamed the Land Shark. Tours begin with a drive through the city and continue with a plunge into the harbor for a cruise along the coast. ✉ *State St. at Stearns Wharf* ☎ *805/683–7600* 🌐 *www.out2seesb.com* 🎫 *$25* 🕒 *Tours May–Oct., daily noon, 2, and 4; Nov.–Apr., daily noon and 2.*

QUICK BITES

Chase Palm Park and Shipwreck Playground. The antique carousel, large playground with a nautical theme, picnic areas, and snack bar make the scenic waterfront Chase Palm Park and Shipwreck Playground a favorite destination for kids and parents. ✉ ***Cabrillo Blvd., between Garden St. and Calle Cesar Chavez.***

Stearns Wharf. Built in 1872, historic Stearns Wharf is Santa Barbara's most visited landmark. Expansive views of the mountains, cityscape, and harbor unfold from every vantage point on the three-block-long pier. Although it's a nice walk from the Cabrillo Boulevard parking areas, you can also park on the pier and then wander through the shops or stop for a meal at one of the wharf's restaurants. ✉ *Cabrillo Blvd., at foot of State St.* ☎ *805/897–2683 info line, 805/564–5531 harbormaster* 🌐 *www.stearnswharf.org.*

Ty Warner Sea Center. A branch of the Santa Barbara Museum of Natural History, the Sea Center specializes in Santa Barbara Channel marine life and conservation. In 2005 it reopened in a new $6.5 million facility bearing the name of Ty Warner, Beanie Baby mogul and local resident, whose hefty donation helped the center complete the final stages of construction. The new Sea Center is small compared to aquariums in Monterey and Long Beach, but it's a fascinating, hands-on marine science laboratory that lets you participate in experiments, projects, and exhibits, including touch tanks. Haul up and analyze water samples, learn to identify marine mammals, and check out amazing creatures in the tide-pool lab and animal nursery. The two-story glass walls open to stunning ocean, mountain, and city views. Ask about the Nature Pass, which includes discounted unlimited two-day admission to both the Sea Center and the Museum of Natural History. ✉ *211 Stearns Wharf* ☎ *805/962–2526* 🌐 *www.sbnature.org* *$8* ⏲ *Daily 10–5.*

Urban Wine Trail. Nearly a dozen winery tasting rooms are sprinkled around the downtown area; most are within walking/biking distance of the beach and lower State Street shopping/restaurant district. ✉ *Santa Barbara* 🌐 *urbanwinetrailsb.com.*

WHERE TO EAT

$$ JAPANESE **Arigato Sushi.** You might have to wait 45 minutes for a table at this trendy, two-story restaurant and sushi bar—locals line up early for the hip, casual atmosphere and wildly creative combination rolls. Fans of authentic Japanese food sometimes disagree about the quality of the seafood, but all dishes are fresh and artfully presented. The menu includes traditional dishes as well as innovative creations such as sushi pizza on seaweed and Hawaiian sashimi salad. ✉ *1225 State St.* ☎ *805/965–6074* 🌐 *www.arigatosantabarbara.com* *Reservations not accepted* ⏲ *No lunch.*

$$ SEAFOOD **Brophy Bros.** The outdoor tables at this casual harborside restaurant have perfect views of the marina and mountains. The staff serves enormous, exceptionally fresh fish dishes—don't miss the seafood salad and chowder—and provides you with a pager if there's a long wait for a table. You can stroll along the waterfront until the beep lets you know your table's ready. This place is hugely popular, so it can be crowded and loud, especially on weekend evenings. ✉ *119 Harbor Way* ☎ *805/966–4418* 🌐 *www.brophybros.com.*

$$$ AMERICAN **Elements.** Different sections within this chic, contemporary restaurant and bar reflect nature's elements: an outdoor porch overlooking the sunken gardens at the Santa Barbara Courthouse across the street (air); the gold-tone main dining room (earth); an intimate corner with sofas for

romantic dining (fire); and an often lively, ocean-hue area where professionals unwind over specialty martinis after work at the slick granite bar. The seasonal world-fusion menu, designed around organic and sustainable foods, might include a grilled ahi tuna wrap with wasabi mayonnaise at lunch, or lemongrass and panko-crusted sea bass with curry-coconut sauce and gingered basmati rice for dinner. ✉ *129 E. Anapamu St.* ☎ *805/884–9218* 🌐 *www.elementsrestaurantandbar.com* ⏲ *Closed Mondays.*

BEST VIEWS

Drive along Alameda Padre Serra, a hillside road that begins near the mission and continues to Montecito, to feast your eyes on spectacular views of the city and the Santa Barbara Channel.

$ ✕ **Flavor of India.** Feast on authentic northern Indian dishes like tandoori chicken, saag paneer, lamb biryani, and a host of curries at this cozy local favorite in a residential Upper State neighborhood. Best bets include the combination dinners served in a traditional Indian tray and the all-you-can-eat lunch buffet ($9). ✉ *3026 State St., Santa Barbara* ☎ *805/682–6561* 🌐 *www.flavorofindiasb.com* ⏲ *Closed Sundays.*

$$$ SEAFOOD ✕ **The Hungry Cat.** The hip Santa Barbara sibling of a famed Hollywood eatery, run by chefs David Lentz and his wife Suzanne Goin, dishes up savory seafood in a small but lively nook in the downtown arts district. Feast on sea urchin, addictive peel-and-eat shrimp, and creative cocktails made from farmers' market fruits and veggies. A busy nightspot on weekends, the Cat also awakens for a popular brunch on Sunday. Night or day, come early or be prepared for a wait. ✉ *1134 Chapala St.* ☎ *805/884–4701* 🌐 *www.thehungrycat.com* ⏲ *Closed Mon. Sept.–April.*

¢ MEXICAN ★ ✕ **La Super-Rica.** Praised by Julia Child, this food stand with a patio on the east side of town serves some of the spiciest and most authentic Mexican dishes between Los Angeles and San Francisco. Fans drive for miles to fill up on the soft tacos served with yummy spicy or mild sauces and legendary beans. Three daily specials are offered each day. Portions are on the small side; order several dishes and share. ✉ *622 N. Milpas St., at Alphonse St.* ☎ *805/963–4940* 💳 *No credit cards* ⏲ *Closed Wed.*

$$$ ITALIAN ✕ **Olio e Limone.** Sophisticated Italian cuisine (with an emphasis on Sicily) is served at this restaurant near the Arlington Center for the Performing Arts. The juicy veal chop is a popular dish, but surprises abound here; be sure to try unusual dishes such as ribbon pasta with quail and sausage in a mushroom ragout, duck ravioli, or swordfish with Sicilian ratatouille. Tables are placed a bit close together, so this may not be the best spot for intimate conversations. For casual artisanal Italian fare, head next door to the Olio pizzeria/enoteca/bar. ✉ *17 W. Victoria St.* ☎ *805/899–2699* 🌐 *www.olioelimone.com* ⏲ *No lunch Sun.*

$$$ SOUTHERN ✕ **Palace Grill.** Mardi Gras energy, team-style service, lively music, and great food have made the Palace a Santa Barbara icon. Acclaimed for its Cajun and Creole dishes such as blackened redfish and jambalaya with dirty rice, the Palace also serves Caribbean fare, including a delicious coconut-shrimp dish. If you're spice-phobic, you can choose pasta, softshell crab, or filet mignon. Be prepared to wait as long as 45 minutes

for a table on Friday and Saturday night (when reservations are taken for a 5:30 seating only), though the live entertainment and free appetizers, sent out front when the line is long, will whet your appetite for the feast to come. ✉ *8 E. Cota St.* ☎ *805/963–5000* 🌐 *www.palacegrill.com.*

$$$ ✕ **Roy.** Owner-chef Leroy Gandy serves a $25 fixed-price dinner (some selections are $20, some $30)—a real bargain—that includes a small salad, fresh soup, homemade organic bread, and a selection from a rotating list of contemporary American main courses. If you're lucky, the entrée choices might include grilled local fish with a mandarin beurre blanc, or bacon-wrapped filet mignon. You can also choose from an à la carte menu of inexpensive appetizers and entrées, plus local wines. Half a block from State Street in the heart of downtown, Roy is a favorite spot for late-night dining (it's open until midnight and has a full bar). ✉ *7 W. Carrillo St.* ☎ *805/966–5636* 🌐 *www.restaurantroy.com* ⏲ *No lunch.*

$$$$ AMERICAN ★ ✕ **The Stonehouse.** Part of the San Ysidro Ranch resort, this elegantly rustic restaurant is housed in a century-old granite farmhouse. Executive chef James West harvests herbs and veggies from the on-site garden, then adds them to an array of top-quality local ingredients to create outstanding regional cuisine. The menu changes constantly but typically includes favorites such as crab cake with persimmon relish appetizer and local spiny lobster with mascarpone risotto. Dine on the radiant-heated oceanview deck with stone fireplace, next to a fountain under a canopy of loquat trees, or in the romantic, candlelit dining room overlooking a creek. The Plow & Angel pub, downstairs, offers more casual bistro fare. ✉ *900 San Ysidro La., Montecito* ☎ *805/565–1700* 🌐 *www.sanysidroranch.com* ✍ *Reservations essential* ⏲ *No lunch Mon.–Sat.*

$$$ AMERICAN ✕ **Wine Cask.** When the Wine Cask closed suddenly in February 2009, the community mourned. So did Doug Margerum, whose family had operated the venerable restaurant, tucked in a romantic courtyard in historic El Paseo, from 1982 to 2007, before selling to an out-of-towner. He teamed up with local restaurateur Mitchel Sjerven to resurrect the Wine Cask, which reopened at year's end. The "new" Wine Cask serves bistro-style meals in a casual, comfortable and classy dining room, with a gold-wood interior and a massive fireplace. The seasonal menu revolves around farmers' market ingredients (just a few blocks away twice a week) and pairs with Santa Barbara's most extensive wine list, thanks to Doug's main business as an established winemaker and the wine shop/tasting room, focused on local and specialty handcrafted vintages, just steps away (open daily, noon to 6). The more casual bar-café across the courtyard serves pizzas, salads, small plates, wines, and cocktails from lunch through late evening. ✉ *813 Anacapa St.* ☎ *805/966–9463* 🌐 *www.winecask.com* ✍ *Reservations essential* ⏲ *Closed Sundays. No lunch Sat.*

WHERE TO STAY

For expanded hotel reviews, visit Fodors.com.

$$$$ 🏨 **Canary Hotel.** The only full-service hotel in the heart of downtown, the Canary blends the feel of a casual beach getaway with tony urban sophistication. **Pros:** easy stroll to museums, shopping, dining; friendly, attentive service; adjacent fitness center. **Cons:** across from

main bus transit center; some rooms feel cramped. ✉ *31 W. Carrillo St.* ☎ *805/884–0300, 877/468–3515* 🌐 *www.canarysantabarbara.com* *77 rooms, 20 suites* *In-room: a/c, Internet, Wi-Fi. In-hotel: restaurant, bar, pool, business center, parking, some pets allowed.*

$$$$ ★ **Four Seasons Resort The Biltmore Santa Barbara.** Surrounded by lush, perfectly manicured gardens and across from the beach, Santa Barbara's grande dame has long been a favorite for quiet, California-style luxury. **Pros:** first-class resort; historic Santa Barbara character; personal service; steps from the beach. **Cons:** back rooms are close to train tracks; expensive. ✉ *1260 Channel Dr.* ☎ *805/969–2261, 800/332–3442* 🌐 *www.fourseasons.com/santabarbara* *181 rooms, 26 suites* *In-room: a/c, Internet, Wi-Fi. In-hotel: restaurant, bar, pool, tennis court, gym, spa, beach, children's programs, business center, parking, some pets allowed.*

$$$ **Hyatt Santa Barbara.** A complex of three separate buildings on three landscaped acres, plus a neighboring inn and apartment units, the Mar Monte (managed by Hyatt) provides a wide range of value-laden lodging options in a prime location—right across from East Beach and the Cabrillo Pavilion Bathhouse. **Pros:** steps from the beach; many room types and rates; walk to the zoo and waterfront shuttle. **Cons:** motelish vibe; busy area in summer. ✉ *1111 E. Cabrillo Blvd.* ☎ *805/963–0744, 800/643–1994* 🌐 *www.santabarbara.hyatt.com* *218 rooms, 5 apartments* *In-room: a/c, kitchen, Internet, Wi-Fi. In-hotel: restaurant, bar, pool, gym, spa, business center, parking, some pets allowed.*

$$$$ **Inn of the Spanish Garden.** A half block from the Presidio in the heart of downtown, this elegant Spanish-Mediterranean retreat celebrates Santa Barbara style, from tile floors, wrought-iron balconies, and exotic plants, to original art by famed local plein-air artists. **Pros:** walking distance from downtown; classic Spanish-Mediterranean style; caring staff. **Cons:** far from the beach; not much here for kids. ✉ *915 Garden St.* ☎ *805/564–4700, 866/564–4700* 🌐 *www.spanishgardeninn.com* *23 rooms* *In-room: a/c, Internet, Wi-Fi. In-hotel: bar, pool, gym, parking* *Breakfast.*

$ **Motel 6 Santa Barbara Beach.** A half block from East Beach amid fancier hotels sits this basic but comfortable motel, which was the first Motel 6 in existence. **Pros:** less than a minute's walk from the zoo and beach; friendly staff; clean and comfortable. **Cons:** no frills; motel-style rooms; no breakfast. ✉ *443 Corona Del Mar Dr.* ☎ *805/564–1392, 800/466–8356* 🌐 *www.motel6.com* *51 rooms* *In-room: a/c, Wi-Fi. In-hotel: pool, some pets allowed.*

$ **Presidio Motel.** Young globetrotting couple Chris Sewell and Kenny Osehan transformed the Presidio, a formerly funky motel, into a simple yet stylish oasis. Two artists individually decorated each room with custom vinyl stickers; all rooms include flat-panel, widescreen TVs, complimentary WiFi, and use of bicycles to tool around town. Situated in the Arts District near the Arlington Theater, this is a good choice for those who want (relatively) affordable lodging within walking distance of downtown attractions; the electric Downtown/Waterfront Shuttle stops just a few blocks away. **Pros:** great downtown location; friendly staff; hip, artsy vibe. **Cons:** smallish rooms; basic baths; thin walls. ✉ *1620 State St., Santa Barbara* ☎ *805/963–1355* 🌐 *www.thepresidiomotel.com* *16 rooms* *In-room: Wi-Fi* *Breakfast.*

$$$$ ★ **San Ysidro Ranch.** At this romantic hideaway on an historic property in the Montecito foothills—where John and Jackie Kennedy spent their honeymoon and Oprah sends her out-of-town guests—guest cottages are scattered among groves of orange trees and flower beds. All have down comforters and fireplaces, most have private outdoor spas, and one has its own pool. Seventeen miles of hiking trails crisscross 500 acres of open space surrounding the property. The Stonehouse restaurant ($$$$; see above) and Plow & Angel Bistro ($$$) are Santa Barbara institutions. **Pros:** ultimate privacy; surrounded by nature; celebrity hangout; pet-friendly. **Cons:** very expensive; too remote for some. ✉ *900 San Ysidro La., Montecito* ☎ *805/565–1700, 800/368–6788* 🌐 *www.sanysidroranch.com* *23 rooms, 4 suites, 14 cottages* *In-room: a/c, Internet, Wi-Fi. In-hotel: restaurant, bar, pool, gym, some pets allowed* ☞ *2-day minimum stay on weekends, 3 days on holiday weekends.*

$$$$ ★ **Simpson House Inn.** If you're a fan of traditional B&Bs, this property, with its beautifully appointed Victorian main house and acre of lush gardens, is for you. **Pros:** impeccable landscaping; walking distance from everything downtown; ranked among the nation's top B&Bs. **Cons:** some rooms in the main building are small; two-night minimum stay on weekends. ✉ *121 E. Arrellaga St.* ☎ *805/963–7067, 800/676–1280* 🌐 *www.simpsonhouseinn.com* *11 rooms, 4 cottages* *In-room: a/c, Wi-Fi* *Breakfast.*

NIGHTLIFE AND THE ARTS

Most major hotels present entertainment nightly during the summer season and on weekends all year. Much of the town's bar, club, and live-music scene centers on lower State Street (between the 300 and 800 blocks). The thriving arts district, with theaters, restaurants, and cafés, starts around the 900 block of State Street and continues north to the Arlington Center for the Performing Arts, in the 1300 block. Santa Barbara supports a professional symphony and a chamber orchestra. The proximity to the University of California at Santa Barbara assures an endless stream of visiting artists and performers. To see what's scheduled around town, pick up a copy of the free weekly *Santa Barbara Independent* newspaper or visit their Web site 🌐 *www.independent.com.*

NIGHTLIFE

Blue Agave. Rich leather couches, a crackling fire in chilly weather, a cigar balcony, and pool tables draw a fancy Gen-X crowd to Blue Agave for good food and designer martinis. ✉ *20 E. Cota St.* ☎ *805/899–4694.*

Dargan's. All types of people hang out at Dargan's, a lively pub with four pool tables, a great selection of draft beer and Irish whiskeys, and a full menu of traditional Irish dishes. ✉ *18 E. Ortega St.* ☎ *805/568–0702.*

James Joyce. The James Joyce, which sometimes plays host to folk and rock performers, is a good place to have a few beers and while away an evening. ✉ *513 State St.* ☎ *805/962–2688.*

Joe's Cafe. Joe's Cafe, where steins of beer accompany hearty bar food, is a fun, if occasionally rowdy, collegiate scene. ✉ *536 State St.* ☎ *805/966–4638.*

Lucky's. A slick sports bar attached to an upscale steak house owned by the maker of Lucky Brand Dungarees, Lucky's attracts a flock of hip, fashionably dressed patrons hoping to see and be seen. ✉ *1279 Coast Village Rd., Montecito* ☎ *805/565–7540.*

Milk & Honey. Swank Milk & Honey lures trendy crowds with artfully prepared tapas, coconut-mango mojitos, and exotic cocktails—despite high prices and a reputation for inattentive service. ✉ *30 W. Anapamu St.* ☎ *805/275–4232.*

SOhO. SOhO—a hip restaurant, bar, and music club—schedules an eclectic mix of live music groups, from jazz to blues to rock, every night of the week. ✉ *1221 State St.* ☎ *805/962–7776.*

THE ARTS

Arlington Center for the Performing Arts. Arlington Center for the Performing Arts, a Moorish-style auditorium, hosts major events during the two-week Santa Barbara International Film Festival every winter and presents touring performers and films throughout the year. ✉ *1317 State St.* ☎ *805/963–4408.*

Center Stage Theatre. Center Stage Theatre presents plays, music, dance, and readings. ✉ *700 block of State St., 2nd fl. of Paseo Nuevo* ☎ *805/963–0408.*

Ensemble Theatre Company. Ensemble Theatre Company stages plays by authors ranging from Tennessee Williams and Henrik Ibsen to rising contemporary dramatists. ✉ *914 Santa Barbara St.* ☎ *805/965–5400.*

Granada. Originally opened in 1924, the landmark Granada theater reopened to great fanfare in 2008 following a $50 million restoration and modernization. ✉ *1214 State St.* ☎ *805/899–3000 general info, 805/899–2222 box office.*

Lobero Theatre. The Lobero Theatre, a state landmark, hosts community theater groups and touring professionals. ✉ *33 E. Canon Perdido St.* ☎ *805/963–0761.*

Music Academy of the West. In Montecito, the Music Academy of the West showcases orchestral, chamber, and operatic works every summer. ✉ *1070 Fairway Rd.* ☎ *805/969–4726, 805/969–8787 box office.*

SPORTS AND THE OUTDOORS

BEACHES

Santa Barbara's beaches don't have the big surf of the shoreline farther south, but they also don't have the crowds. You can usually find a solitary spot to swim or sunbathe. In June and July, fog often hugs the coast until about noon.

East Beach. The wide swath of sand at the east end of Cabrillo Boulevard on the harbor front is a great spot for people-watching. East Beach has sand volleyball courts, summertime lifeguard and sports competitions, and arts-and-crafts shows on Sunday and holidays. You can use showers, a weight room, and lockers (bring your own towel) and rent umbrellas and boogie boards at the Cabrillo Bathhouse. Next door, there's an elaborate jungle-gym play area for kids. ✉ *1118 Cabrillo Blvd.* ☎ *805/897–2680.*

Arroyo Burro County Beach. The usually gentle surf at Arroyo Burro County Beach makes it ideal for families with young children. ✉ *Cliff Dr., at Las Positas Rd.*

BICYCLING **Cabrillo Bike Lane.** The level, two-lane, 3-mi Cabrillo Bike Lane passes the Santa Barbara Zoo, the Andree Clark Bird Refuge, beaches, and the harbor. There are restaurants along the way, and you can stop for a picnic along the palm-lined path looking out on the Pacific.

Wheel Fun Rentals. Wheel Fun Rentals has bikes, quadricycles, and skates; a second outlet around the block rents small electric cars and scooters. ✉ *23 E. Cabrillo Blvd.* ☎ *805/966–2282.*

BIRTHPLACE OF THE ENVIRONMENTAL MOVEMENT

In 1969, 200,000 gallons of crude oil spilled into the Santa Barbara Channel, causing an immediate outcry from residents, particularly in the UCSB community. The day after the spill, Get Oil Out (GOO) was established; the group helped lead the successful fight for legislation to limit and regulate offshore drilling in California. The Santa Barbara spill also spawned Earth Day, which is still celebrated in communities across the nation today.

BOATS AND CHARTERS **Santa Barbara Sailing Center.** Santa Barbara Sailing Center offers sailing instruction, rents and charters sailboats, and organizes dinner and sunset champagne cruises, island excursions, and whale-watching trips. ✉ *Santa Barbara Harbor launching ramp* ☎ *805/962–2826, 800/350–9090.*

Santa Barbara Water Taxi. Children beg to ride *L'il Toot*, a cheery yellow water taxi that cruises from the harbor to Stearns Wharf and back again. ✉ *Santa Barbara Harbor and Stearns Wharf, Santa Barbara* ☎ *805/896–6900* 🌐 *sbwatertaxi.com* *$4 one-way* ⏲ *Departures every half hour from 12 to 6 in summer, 12 to sunset in winter.*

SEA Landing. SEA Landing operates surface and deep-sea fishing charters year-round. ✉ *Cabrillo Blvd., at Bath St., and breakwater in Santa Barbara Harbor* ☎ *805/965–3564.*

Condor Express. From SEA Landing, the *Condor Express*, a 75-foot high-speed catamaran, whisks up to 149 passengers toward the Channel Islands on dinner cruises, whale-watching excursions, and pelagic-bird trips. ☎ *805/882–0088, 888/779–4253.*

Truth Aquatics. Truth Aquatics departs from SEA Landing in the Santa Barbara Harbor to ferry passengers on excursions to the National Marine Sanctuary and Channel Islands National Park. Their three dive boats also take scuba divers on single-day and multiday trips. ☎ *805/962–1127.*

GOLF **Sandpiper Golf Club.** Like Pebble Beach, the 18-hole, par-72 Sandpiper Golf Club sits on the ocean bluffs and combines stunning views with a challenging game. Greens fees are $139–$159; a cart (optional) is $16. ✉ *7925 Hollister Ave., 14 mi north of downtown on Hwy. 101* ☎ *805/968–1541.*

Santa Barbara Golf Club. Santa Barbara Golf Club has an 18-hole, par-70 course. The greens fees are $40–$50; a cart (optional) costs $30 per cart or $15 per person. ✉ *Las Positas Rd. and McCaw Ave.* ☎ *805/687–7087.*

TENNIS Many hotels in Santa Barbara have courts.

City of Santa Barbara Parks and Recreation Department. The City of Santa Barbara Parks and Recreation Department operates public courts with lighted play until 9 pm weekdays. You can purchase day permits ($7) at the courts, or call the department. ☎ *805/564–5473.*

Municipal Tennis Center. The 12 hard courts at the Municipal Tennis Center include an enclosed stadium court and three lighted courts open daily. ✉ *1414 Park Pl., near Salinas St. and U.S. 101.*

Pershing Park. Pershing Park has eight lighted courts available for public play after 5 pm weekdays and all day on weekends and Santa Barbara City College holidays. ✉ *100 Castillo St., near Cabrillo Blvd.*

SHOPPING

SHOPPING AREAS

State Street. State Street, roughly between Cabrillo Boulevard and Sola Street, is the commercial hub of Santa Barbara and a shopper's paradise. Chic malls, quirky storefronts, antiques emporia, elegant boutiques, and funky thrift shops abound here. You can do your shopping on foot or by a battery-powered trolley (25¢) that runs between the waterfront and the 1300 block.

Paseo Nuevo. Paseo Nuevo, an open-air mall anchored by chains such as Nordstrom and Macy's, also contains a few local institutions such as the Contemporary Arts Forum and Center Stage Theater. ✉ *700 and 800 blocks of State St.*

El Paseo. Shops, art galleries, and studios share the courtyard and gardens of El Paseo, a historic arcade. ✉ *Canon Perdido St., between State and Anacapa Sts.*

Brinkerhoff Avenue. Antiques and gift shops are clustered in restored Victorian buildings on Brinkerhoff Avenue. ✉ *2 blocks west of State St., at West Cota St.*

Summerland. Serious antiques hunters can head a few miles south of Santa Barbara to the beach town of Summerland, which is full of shops and markets.

CLOTHING

Channel Islands Surfboards. Channel Islands Surfboards stocks the latest in California beachwear, sandals, and accessories. ✉ *36 Anacapa St.* ☎ *805/966–7213.*

Diani. This upscale, European-style women's boutique across from the Arlington Theater dresses clients in designer clothing from around the world. A sibling shoe shop is just a few doors away. ✉ *1324 State St., Santa Barbara* ☎ *877/342–6474* 🌐 *www.dianiboutique.com.*

Wendy Foster. Wendy Foster is a casual-chic clothing store for women. ✉ *833 State St.* ☎ *805/966–2276.*

Santa Barbara Outfitters. Santa Barbara Outfitters carries stylish, functional clothing, shoes, and accessories for active folks: kayakers, climbers, cyclists, runners, and hikers. A connected PrAna store focuses on yoga classes, gear, and attire. ✉ *1200 State St.* ☎ *805/564–1007.*

Surf 'N Wear's Beach House. Surf 'N Wear's Beach House carries surf clothing, gear, and collectibles; it's also the home of Santa Barbara Surf

Shop and the exclusive local dealer of Surfboards by Yater. ✉ *10 State St.* ☎ *805/963–1281.*

Territory Ahead. Territory Ahead, a high-quality outdoorsy catalog company, sells fashionably rugged clothing for men and women. ✉ *Main store, 515 State St.* ☎ *805/962–5558.*

EN ROUTE

If you choose to drive north via U.S. 101 without detouring to the Solvang/Santa Ynez area, you will drive right past some good beaches. In succession from east to west, **El Capitan, Gaviota, and Refugio state beaches** all have campsites, picnic tables, and fire rings.

SANTA BARBARA COUNTY

Residents refer to the glorious 30-mi stretch of coastline from Carpinteria to Gaviota as the South Coast. The Santa Ynez Mountains divide the county geographically; U.S. 101 passes through a mountain tunnel leading inland. Northern Santa Barbara County used to be known for its sprawling ranches and strawberry and broccoli fields. Today its 100-plus wineries and 22,000 acres of vineyards dominate the landscape from the Santa Ynez Valley in the south to Santa Maria in the north.

The hit film *Sideways* was filmed almost entirely in the North County Wine Country; when the movie won Golden Globe and Oscar awards in 2005, it sparked national and international interest in visits to the region.

ESSENTIALS

Visitor Information Santa Barbara County Vintners' Association ☎ *805/688–0881* 🌐 *www.sbcountywines.com.*

The Santa Barbara Conference & Visitors Bureau. The Santa Barbara Conference & Visitors Bureau created a detailed map highlighting film location spots. Maps can be downloaded from visitor bureau Web sites: 🌐 *www.santaynezvalleyvisit.com or www.santabarbaraca.com.* ☎ *805/966–9222* 🌐 *www.santabarbaraca.com.*

SANTA YNEZ

31 mi north of Goleta via Hwy. 154.

Founded in 1882, the tiny town of Santa Ynez still has many of its original frontier buildings. You can walk through the three-block downtown area in just a few minutes, shop for antiques, and hang around the old-time saloon. At some of the eponymous valley's best restaurants, you just might bump into one of the many celebrities who own nearby ranches.

GETTING HERE AND AROUND

If you're coming from Santa Barbara, two-lane Highway 154 over San Marcos Pass is the shortest and most scenic route to Santa Ynez. You can also drive along U.S. 101 north 43 mi to Buellton, then 7 mi east through Solvang to Santa Ynez. Santa Ynez Valley Transit shuttle buses connect Santa Ynez with Solvang and other north county towns.

ESSENTIALS

Visitor Information Santa Ynez Valley Visitors Association ☎ *805/686–0053, 800/742–2843* 🌐 *www.santaynezvalleyvisit.com.*

WORD OF MOUTH

"California's Central Coast is a popular place for surfers and windsurfers. If you're not up to surfing yourself, spend some time relaxing on the beach and watching the action." —photo by Doreen Miller, Fodors.com member

EXPLORING

Chumash Casino Resort. Just south of Santa Ynez on the Chumash Indian Reservation lies the sprawling, Las Vegas–style Chumash Casino Resort. The casino has 2,000 slot machines, and the property includes three restaurants, a spa, and an upscale hotel ($$$–$$$$). ✉ *3400 E. Hwy. 246* ☎ *800/248–6274.*

WHERE TO EAT AND STAY

$$ ITALIAN ★ ✕ **Trattoria Grappolo.** Authentic Italian fare, an open kitchen, and festive, family-style seating make this trattoria equally popular with celebrities from Hollywood and ranchers from the Santa Ynez Valley. Italian favorites on the extensive menu range from thin-crust pizza to homemade ravioli, risottos, and seafood linguine to grilled lamb chops in red-wine sauce. The noise level tends to rise in the evening, so this isn't the best spot for a romantic getaway. ✉ *3687-C Sagunto St.* ☎ *805/688–6899* 🌐 *www.trattoriagrappolo.com* ⊙ *No lunch Mon.*

$$$$ **Santa Ynez Inn.** This posh two-story Victorian inn in downtown Santa Ynez was built from scratch in 2002. **Pros:** near several restaurants; unusual antiques; spacious rooms. **Cons:** high price for location; not in a historic building. ✉ *3627 Sagunto St.* ☎ *805/688–5588, 800/643–5774* 🌐 *www.santaynezinn.com* *20 rooms, 3 suites* *In-room: a/c, Internet, Wi-Fi. In-hotel: gym* *Breakfast.*

LOS OLIVOS

4 mi north of Santa Ynez on Hwy. 154.

This pretty village in the Santa Ynez Valley was once on Spanish-built El Camino Real (Royal Highway) and later a stop on major stagecoach and rail routes. It's so sleepy today, though, that the movie *Return to Mayberry* was filmed here. Tasting rooms, art galleries, antiques stores, and country markets line Grand Avenue and intersecting streets for several blocks.

GETTING HERE AND AROUND

From U.S. 101 north or south, exit at Highway 154 and drive east about 8 mi. From Santa Barbara, travel 30 mi northwest on Highway 154. Santa Ynez Valley Transit provides shuttle bus service between Los Olivos, Ballard, Solvang, and other towns.

EXPLORING

Carhartt Vineyard Tasting Room. Inside the intimate, 99-square-foot Carhartt Vineyard Tasting Room, you're likely to meet owners and winemakers Mike and Brooke Carhartt, who pour samples of their small-lot, handcrafted vintages most days. ✉ *2990-A Grand Ave.* ☎ *805/693–5100* 🌐 *www.carharttvineyard.com.*

Daniel Gehrs Tasting Room. Historic Heather Cottage, originally an early-1900s doctor's office, houses the Daniel Gehrs Tasting Room. Here you can sample Gehrs's various varietals, produced in limited small-lot quantities. ✉ *2939 Grand Ave.* ☎ *805/693–9686* 🌐 *www.danielgehrswines.com.*

Firestone Vineyard. Firestone Vineyard has been around since 1972. It has daily tours, grassy picnic areas, and hiking trails in the hills overlooking the valley; the views are fantastic. ✉ *5000 Zaca Station Rd.* ☎ *805/688–3940* 🌐 *www.firestonewine.com.*

WHERE TO EAT AND STAY

$$$$ AMERICAN Fodor's Choice ★ ✕ **Brothers Restaurant at Mattei's Tavern.** In the stagecoach days, Mattei's Tavern provided wayfarers with hearty meals and warm beds. Chef-owners and brothers Matt and Jeff Nichols renovated the 1886 building, and while retaining the original character, transformed it into one of the best restaurants in the valley. The casual, unpretentious dining rooms with their red-velvet wallpaper and historic photos reflect the rich history of the tavern. The menu changes every few weeks but often includes house favorites such as spicy fried calamari, prime rib, and salmon, and the locally famous jalapeño corn bread. There's also a full bar and an array of vintages from the custom-built cedar wine cellar. ✉ *2350 Railway Ave.* ☎ *805/688–4820* 🌐 *www.matteistavern.com* *Reservations essential* *No lunch.*

$$ AMERICAN ✕ **Los Olivos Cafe.** Site of the scene in *Sideways* where the four main characters dine together and share a few bottles of wine, this down-to-earth restaurant not only provided the setting but served the actors real food from their existing menu during filming. Part wine store and part social hub for locals, the café focuses on wine-friendly fish, pasta, and meat dishes made from local bounty, plus salads, pizzas, and burgers. Don't miss the homemade muffuletta and olive tapenade spreads. Other house favorites include an artisanal cheese plate, baked Brie with honey-roasted hazelnuts, and braised pot roast with whipped potatoes. ✉ *2879 Grand Ave.* ☎ *805/688–7265, 888/946–3748* 🌐 *www.losolivoscafe.com.*

$$$ **The Ballard Inn & Restaurant.** Set among orchards and vineyards in the tiny town of Ballard, 2 mi south of Los Olivos, this inn makes an elegant wine-country escape. **Pros:** exceptional food; attentive staff; secluded. **Cons:** some baths could use updating; several miles from Los Olivos and Santa Ynez. ✉ *2436 Baseline Ave., Ballard* ☎ *805/688–7770, 800/638–2466* 🌐 *www.ballardinn.com* *15 rooms* *In-room: a/c, no TV, Wi-Fi. In-hotel: restaurant* *Breakfast.*

$$$$ **Fess Parker's Wine Country Inn and Spa.** This luxury inn includes an elegant, tree-shaded French country–style main building and an equally attractive annex across the street with a pool, hot tub, and day spa. **Pros:** convenient wine touring base; walking distance from restaurants and galleries; well-appointed rooms. **Cons:** pricey; staff attention is inconsistent. ✉ *2860 Grand Ave.* ☎ *805/688–7788, 800/446–2455* 🌐 *www.fessparker.com* *20 rooms, 1 suite* *In-room: a/c, Internet. In-hotel: restaurant, bar, pool, gym, spa, some pets allowed* *Breakfast.*

SOLVANG

5 mi south of Los Olivos on Alamo Pintado Rd., Hwy. 246, 3 mi east of U.S. 101.

You'll know you've reached the town of Solvang when the architecture suddenly changes to half-timber buildings and windmills. This town was settled in 1911 by a group of Danish educators (the flatlands and rolling green hills reminded them of home), and even today, more than two-thirds of the residents are of Danish descent. Although it's attracted tourists for decades, in recent years it has become more sophisticated, with galleries, upscale restaurants, and wine-tasting rooms. Most shops are locally owned; the city has an ordinance prohibiting chain stores. A good way to get your bearings is to park your car in one of the many free public lots and stroll around town. Stop in at the visitor center at 2nd Street and Copenhagen Drive for maps and helpful advice on what to see and do. Don't forget to stock up on Danish pastries from the town's excellent bakeries before you leave.

GETTING HERE AND AROUND

Highway 246 West (Mission Drive) traverses the town—access the road from U.S. 101 and Buellton from the west, and Highway 154 from the east. Alamo Pintado Road connects Solvang with Ballard and Los Olivos to the north. Santa Ynez Valley Transit shuttle buses run between Solvang and other nearby towns.

ESSENTIALS

Visitor Information Solvang Conference & Visitors Bureau ✉ *1639 Copenhagen Dr.* ☎ *805/688–6144, 800/468–6765* 🌐 *www.solvangusa.com.*

EXPLORING

Alma Rosa Winery. Just outside Solvang is the Alma Rosa Winery. Owners Richard and Thekla Sanford helped put Santa Barbara County on the international wine map with a 1989 Pinot Noir. Recently the Sanfords started a new winery, Alma Rosa, with wines made from grapes grown on their 100-plus-acre certified organic vineyards in the Santa Rita Hills. You can taste the current releases at one of the most environmentally sensitive tasting rooms and picnic areas in the valley. All their vineyards are certified organic, and the Pinot Noirs and Chardonnays are exceptional. ✉ *7250 Santa Rosa Rd.* ☎ *805/688–9090* 🌐 *www.almarosawinery.com.*

Mission Santa Inés. Often called the Hidden Gem of the missions, Mission Santa Inés has an impressive collection of paintings, statuary, vestments, and Chumash and Spanish artifacts in a serene bluff-top setting. Take a self-guided tour through the museum, sanctuary, and tranquil gardens. ✉ *1760 Mission Dr.* ☎ *805/688–4815* 🌐 *www.missionsantaines.org* 🎟 *$5* ⏲ *Daily 9–4:30.*

Rideau Vineyard. Housed in an 1884 adobe, the Rideau Vineyard tasting room provides simultaneous blasts from the area's ranching past and from its hand-harvested, Rhône-varietal wine-making present. ✉ *1562 Alamo Pintado Rd.* ☎ *805/688–0717* 🌐 *www.rideauvineyard.com.*

WHERE TO EAT AND STAY

$$$ AMERICAN ✕ **The Hitching Post II.** You'll find everything from grilled artichokes to ostrich at this casual eatery just outside of Solvang, but most people come for what is said to be the best Santa Maria–style barbecue in the state. The oak used in the barbecue imparts a wonderful smoky taste. Be sure to try a glass of owner-chef-winemaker Frank Ostini's signature Highliner Pinot Noir, a star in the 2004 film *Sideways*. ✉ *406 E. Hwy. 246* ☎ *805/688–0676* 🌐 *www.hitchingpost2.com* ⏲ *No lunch.*

$$$ AMERICAN ★ ✕ **Root 246.** The name of this chic outpost at Hotel Corque is a play on the main route through the Santa Ynez Valley (Highway 246). Chef Bradley Ogden and his team tap local purveyors and shop for organic foods at farmers' markets before deciding on the day's menu. Depending

on the season, you might feast on local squid with sweet baby prawns, prime rib eye steak grilled over an oak fire and served with root vegetable gratin, or rhubarb and polenta upside-down cake. The attentive wait staff can recommend pairings from the restaurant's 1,800-bottle selection of regional wines. The gorgeous design incorporates wood, stone, tempered glass, and leather elements in several distinct areas, including a slick 47-seat dining room (but jeans and casual wine-touring attire are welcome), a more casual bar with sofas and chairs, and a hip lounge. ✉ *420 Alisal Rd.* ☎ *805/686–8681* 🌐 *www.root-246.com* 🕒 *No lunch. Closed Mondays and Tuesdays.*

$$$$ ★ **Alisal Guest Ranch and Resort.** Since 1946 this 10,000-acre ranch has been popular with celebrities and plain folk alike. **Pros:** Old West atmosphere; tons of activities; ultraprivate. **Cons:** isolated; cut off from the high-tech world; some units are aging. ✉ *1054 Alisal Rd.* ☎ *805/688–6411, 800/425–4725* 🌐 *www.alisal.com* *36 rooms, 37 suites* *In-room: no a/c, no TV, Wi-Fi. In-hotel: restaurant, bar, golf course, pool, tennis court, gym, spa, children's programs, business center* *Some meals.*

$$$ ★ **Hotel Corque.** Sleek, stunning Hotel Corque—the largest hotel in the Santa Ynez Valley—provides a full slate of upscale amenities on the edge of town. **Pros:** all front desk staff are trained concierges; short walk to shops, tasting rooms and restaurants; smoke-free property. **Cons:** no kitchenettes or laundry facilities; not low-budget. ✉ *400 Alisal Rd.* ☎ *805/688–8000, 800/624–5572* 🌐 *www.hotelcorque.com* *122 rooms, 10 suites* *In-room: a/c, Wi-Fi. In-hotel: restaurant, bar, pool, business center.*

$$ **Solvang Gardens Inn.** Lush gardens with fountains and waterfalls, friendly staff, and cheery English-country-theme rooms with antiques make for a peaceful retreat just a few blocks—but worlds away—from Solvang's main tourist area. **Pros:** homey; family-friendly; colorful gardens. **Cons:** some rooms are tiny; some need upgrades. ✉ *293 Alisal Rd.* ☎ *805/688–4404, 888/688–4404* 🌐 *www.solvanggardens.com* *16 rooms, 8 suites* *In-room: a/c, kitchen, Wi-Fi. In-hotel: spa, business center* *Breakfast.*

LOMPOC

20 mi west of Solvang on Hwy. 246.

Known as the flower-seed capital of the world, Lompoc is blanketed with vast fields of brightly colored flowers that bloom from May through August.

GETTING HERE AND AROUND

Driving is the easiest way to get to Lompoc. From Santa Barbara, follow U.S. 101 north to Highway 1 exit off Gaviota Pass, or Highway 246 west at Buellton. The City of Lompoc Transit (COLT) buses travel throughout the city and surrounding neighborhoods; COLT's Wine Country Express buses run between Lompoc, Buellton, and Solvang weekdays. COLT also provides limited service to and from downtown Santa Barbara.

EXPLORING

Lompoc Valley Flower Festival. For five days around the last weekend of June, the Lompoc Valley Flower Festival brings a parade, carnival, and crafts show to town. ☎ *805/735–8511* 🌐 *www.flowerfestival.org.*

La Purisima Mission State Historic Park. At La Purisima Mission State Historic Park you can see Mission La Purisima Concepción, the most fully restored mission in the state. Founded in 1787, it stands in a stark and still remote location and powerfully evokes the lives of California's Spanish settlers. Docents lead tours every afternoon, and displays illustrate the secular and religious activities that were part of mission life. From March through October the mission holds special events, including crafts demonstrations by costumed docents. ✉ *2295 Purisima Rd., off Hwy. 246* ☎ *805/733–3713* 🌐 *www.lapurisimamission.org* *$6 per vehicle* *Daily 9–5; tour daily at 1.*

SAN LUIS OBISPO COUNTY

San Luis Obispo County's pristine landscapes and abundant wildlife areas, especially those around Morro Bay and Montaña de Oro State Park, have long attracted nature lovers. In the south, Pismo Beach and other coastal towns have great sand and surf; inland, a booming wine region stretches from the Edna and Arroyo Grande valleys in the south to Paso Robles in the north. With historical attractions, a photogenic downtown, and busy shops and restaurants, the college town of San Luis Obispo is at the heart of the county.

ESSENTIALS

Visitor Information San Luis Obispo County Visitors and Conference Bureau ✉ *811 El Capitan Way, Suite 200, San Luis Obispo* ☎ *805/541–8000* 🌐 *www.sanluisobispocounty.com.*

PISMO BEACH

U.S. 101/Hwy. 1, about 40 mi north of Lompoc.

About 20 mi of sandy shoreline—nicknamed the Bakersfield Riviera for the throngs of vacationers who come here from the Central Valley—begins at the town of Pismo Beach. The southern end of town runs along sand dunes, some of which are open to cars and off-road vehicles; sheltered by the dunes, a grove of eucalyptus trees attracts thousands of migrating monarch butterflies November through February. A long, broad beach fronts the center of town, where a municipal pier extends into the sea at the foot of shop-lined Pomeroy Street. To the north, hotels and homes perch atop chalky oceanfront cliffs.

Fewer than 10,000 people live in this quintessential surfer haven, but Pismo Beach has a slew of hotels and restaurants with great views of the Pacific Ocean. Still, rooms can sometimes be hard to come by. Each Father's Day weekend the Pismo Beach Classic, one of the West Coast's largest classic-car and street-rod shows, overruns the town. A Dixieland jazz festival in February also draws crowds.

GETTING HERE AND AROUND

Pismo Beach straddles both sides of U.S. 101. If you're traveling from Santa Barbara and have time for a scenic drive, exit the 101 in Santa Maria and take Highway 166 8 mi west to Guadalupe and follow Highway 1 north 16 mi to Pismo Beach. South County Area Transit (SCAT) buses run throughout the city and connect with nearby towns and the city of San Luis Obispo. In summer, the free Avila Trolley extends service to Pismo Beach.

VOLCANOES?

Those funny looking, sawed-off peaks along the drive from Pismo Beach to Morro Bay are the Seven Sisters—a series of ancient volcanic plugs. Morro Rock, the northern-most sibling and a state historic monument, is the most famous and photographed of the clan.

EN ROUTE

Guadalupe-Nipomo Dunes Preserve. The spectacular Guadalupe-Nipomo Dunes Preserve stretches 18 mi along the coast south of Pismo Beach. It's the largest and most ecologically diverse dune system in the state, and a habitat for more than 200 species of birds as well as sea otters, black bears, bobcats, coyotes, and deer. The 1,500-foot Mussel Rock is the highest beach dune in the western states. As many as 20 movies have been filmed here, including Cecil B. DeMille's 1923 silent *The Ten Commandments*. The main entrances to the dunes are at Oso Flaco Lake (about 13 mi south of Pismo Beach on U.S. 101/Highway 1, then 3 mi west on Oso Flaco Road) and at the far west end of Highway 166 (Main Street) in Guadalupe. Parking at Oso Flaco Lake is $5 per vehicle.

Dunes Center. At the Dunes Center, you can get nature information and view an exhibit about *The Ten Commandments* movie set, which weather and archaeologists are slowly unearthing near Guadalupe Beach. ✉ *1055 Guadalupe St., 1 mi north of Hwy. 166* ☎ *805/343–2455* 🌐 *www.dunescenter.org* ⏲ *April-September Wed.–Sun. 10–4, Oct.-March Thurs.-Sun. 10–4.*

WHERE TO EAT

$$ SEAFOOD **✕ Cracked Crab.** This traditional New England–style crab shack imports fresh seafood daily from Australia, Alaska, and the East Coast. Fish is line-caught, much of the produce is organic, and everything is made from scratch. For a real treat, don a bib and chow through a bucket of steamed shellfish with Cajun sausage, potatoes, and corn on the cob, all dumped right onto your table. The menu changes daily. ✉ *751 Price St.* ☎ *805/773–2722* 🌐 *www.crackedcrab.com* *Reservations not accepted.*

$$ ITALIAN **✕ Giuseppe's Cucina Italiana.** The classic flavors of southern Italy are highlighted at this lively, warm downtown spot. Most recipes originate from Bari, a seaport on the Adriatic; the menu includes breads and pizzas baked in the wood-burning oven, hearty dishes such as osso buco and lamb, and homemade pastas. The wait for a table can be long at peak dinner hours, but sometimes an accordion player gets the crowd singing. Next door, their bakery sells take-out selections. ✉ *891 Price St.* ☎ *805/773–2870* 🌐 *www.giuseppesrestaurant.com* *Reservations not accepted* ⏲ *No lunch weekends.*

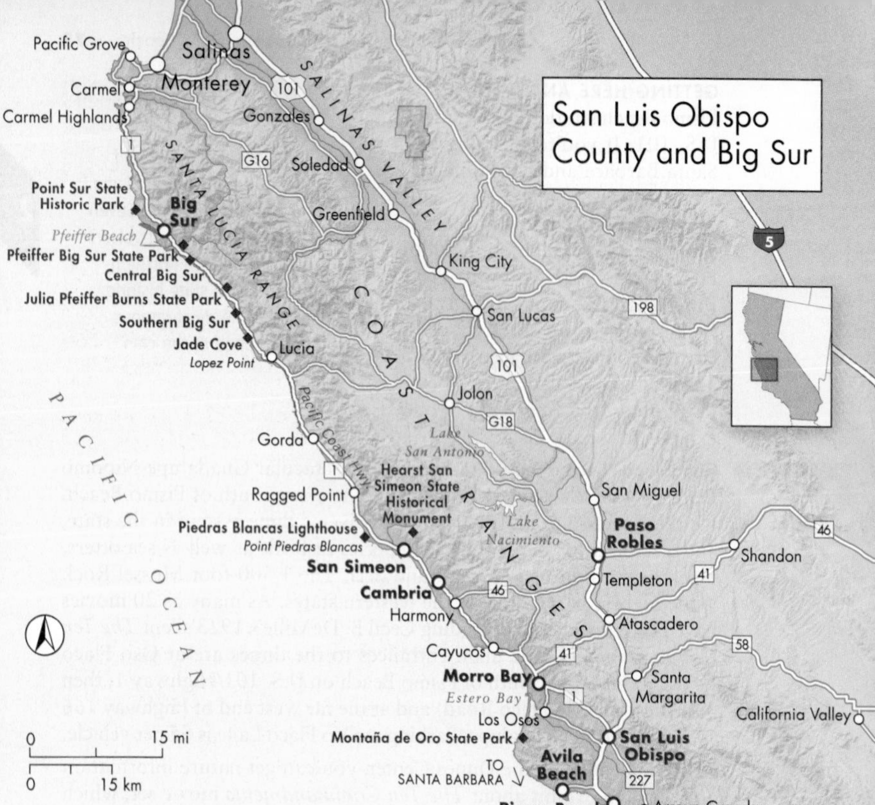

¢ SEAFOOD ✕ **Splash Café.** Folks line up all the way down the block for clam chowder served in a sourdough bread bowl at this wildly popular seafood stand. You can also order beach food such as fresh steamed clams, burgers, and fried calamari at the counter (no table service)—and many items on the menu are $8 or less. The grimy, cramped, but cheery hole-in-a-wall, a favorite with locals and savvy visitors, is open daily for lunch and dinner (plus a rock-bottom basic breakfast starting at 8 am), but closes early on weekday evenings during low season. ✉ *197 Pomeroy St.* ☎ *805/773–4653* 🌐 *www.splashcafe.com.*

WHERE TO STAY

For expanded hotel reviews, visit Fodors.com.

$$$ **The Cliffs Resort.** Perched dramatically on an oceanfront cliff, this full-service resort is surrounded by lawns and palm trees; the pool, with a cascading fountain, overlooks the sea. *2757 Shell Beach Rd., Pismo Beach* ☎ *805/773–5000, 800/342–4295* 🌐 *www.cliffsresort.com* *160 rooms* *In-room: a/c, safe, Wi-Fi. In-hotel: restaurant, bar, pool, spa, beach, parking, some pets allowed.*

$$$$ **Dolphin Bay.** Perched on grass-covered bluffs overlooking Shell Beach, this luxury resort looks and feels like an exclusive community of villas. **Pros:** lavish apartment units; as upscale as you can get; killer views; walking distance from the beach. **Cons:** hefty price tag; upper-crust vibe.

2727 Shell Beach Rd. 805/773–4300, 800/516–0112 reservations, 805/773–8900 restaurant www.thedolphinbay.com 62 suites In-room: no a/c, kitchen, Internet, Wi-Fi. In-hotel: restaurant, bar, pool, gym, spa, beach, children's programs, laundry facilities, business center, parking, some pets allowed.

$$$$ **Pismo Lighthouse Suites.** Each of the well-appointed two-room, two-bath suites at this oceanfront resort has a private balcony or patio. **Pros:** lots of space for families and groups; nice pool area. **Cons:** not easy to walk to main attractions; some units are next to busy road. *2411 Price St. 805/773–2411, 800/245–2411 www.pismolighthousesuites.com 70 suites In-room: no a/c, Internet, Wi-Fi. In-hotel: pool, gym, spa, laundry facilities Breakfast.*

$$$ **Sea Venture Resort.** The bright, homey rooms at this hotel all have fireplaces and featherbeds; most have balconies with private hot tubs, and some have beautiful ocean views. **Pros:** on the beach; excellent food; romantic rooms. **Cons:** touristy area; some rooms and facilities are beginning to age; dark hallways. *100 Ocean View Ave. 805/773–4994, 800/760–0664 www.seaventure.com 50 rooms In-room: no a/c, Internet, Wi-Fi. In-hotel: restaurant, spa, beach, business center, parking Breakfast.*

$ **Shell Beach Inn.** Just 2½ blocks from the beach, this basic but cozy motor court is a great bargain for the area. **Pros:** walking distance from the beach; clean rooms; friendly and dependable service. **Cons:** sits on a busy road; small rooms; tiny pool. *653 Shell Beach Rd. 805/773–4373, 800/549–4727 www.shellbeachinn.com 10 rooms In-room: no a/c, Wi-Fi. In-hotel: pool, some pets allowed.*

AVILA BEACH

4 mi north of Pismo Beach on U.S. 101/Hwy. 1.

Because the village of Avila Beach and the sandy, cove-front shoreline for which it's named face south into the Pacific Ocean, they get more sun and less fog than any other stretch of coast in the area. It can be bright and warm here while just beyond the surrounding hills communities shiver under the marine layer. With its fortuitous climate and protected waters, Avila's public beach draws plenty of sunbathers and families; weekends are very busy. Demolished in 1998 to clean up extensive oil seepage from a Unocal tank farm, downtown Avila Beach has sprung back to life. The seaside promenade has been fully restored and shops and hotels have quickly popped up; with mixed results the town has tried to re-create its former offbeat character. For real local color, head to the far end of the cove and watch the commercial fishing boats offload their catch on the old Port San Luis wharf. A few seafood shacks and fish markets do business on the pier while sea lions congregate below. On Fridays from mid-April through mid-September, a fish and farmers' market livens up the beach area with music, fresh local produce and seafood, and children's activities.

GETTING HERE AND AROUND

Exit U.S. 101 at Avila Beach Drive and head 3 mi west to reach the beach. The free Avila Shuttle operates weekends year-round, plus Friday afternoon/evenings from April to September. The minibuses connect Avila Beach and Port San Luis to Shell Beach, with multiple stops along the way. Service extends to Pismo Beach in summer.

WHERE TO EAT AND STAY

$$$$ 🏨 **Avila La Fonda.** Modeled after a village in early California's Mexican period, Avila La Fonda surrounds guests with rich jewel tones, fountains, and upscale comfort. **Pros:** one-of-a-kind theme and artwork; flexible room combinations; a block from the beach. **Cons:** pricey; most rooms don't have an ocean view. ✉ *101 San Miguel St.* ☎ *805/595–1700* 🌐 *www.avilalafondahotel.com* *28 rooms, 1 suite* *In-room: a/c, kitchen, Internet, Wi-Fi. In-hotel: laundry facilities, business center, some pets allowed.*

$$ 🏨 **Sycamore Mineral Springs Resort.** This wellness resort's hot mineral springs bubble up into private outdoor tubs on an oak-and-sycamore-forest hillside. **Pros:** great place to rejuvenate; nice hiking; incredible spa services. **Cons:** rooms vary in quality; 2½ mi from the beach. ✉ *1215 Avila Beach Dr., San Luis Obispo* ☎ *805/595–7302, 800/234–5831* 🌐 *www.sycamoresprings.com* *26 rooms, 50 suites* *In-room: a/c, kitchen, Internet, Wi-Fi. In-hotel: restaurant, bar, pool, spa, business center, parking.*

SAN LUIS OBISPO

8 mi north of Avila Beach on U.S. 101/Hwy. 1.

About halfway between San Francisco and Los Angeles, San Luis Obispo—nicknamed SLO—spreads out below gentle hills and rocky extinct volcanoes. Its main appeal lies in its architecturally diverse and commercially lively downtown, especially several blocks of Higuera Street. The pedestrian-friendly district bustles with shoppers, restaurant goers, and students from California Polytechnic State University, known as Cal Poly. On Thursday from 6 pm to 9 pm a farmers' market fills Higuera Street with local produce, entertainment, and food stalls. SLO is less a vacation destination than a pleasant stopover along Highway 1; it's a nice place to stay while touring the Wine Country south of town.

GETTING HERE AND AROUND

U.S. 101/Highway 1 traverses the city for several miles. From the north, Highway 1 jogs inland from the coast and merges with the interstate when it reaches the city of San Luis Obispo. SLO City Transit buses operate daily; Regional Transit Authority (SLORTA) buses connect with towns throughout the north county. The Downtown Trolley lumbers through the city's hub on Thursdays, Fridays, and Saturdays.

ESSENTIALS

Visitor Information San Luis Obispo Chamber of Commerce ✉ *1039 Chorro St.* ☎ *805/781–2777* 🌐 *www.visitslo.com.* **San Luis Obispo Vintners Association** ☎ *805/541–5868* 🌐 *www.slowine.com.* **San Luis Obispo City Visitor Information.** Visit the City of San Luis Obispo's Web site for details on nearly 40 lodging options, a current events calendar, and other visitor information. ✉ *San Luis Obispo* 🌐 *www.sanluisobispovacations.com.*

DID YOU KNOW?

You can unwind in a private tub fed by hot mineral springs at Avila Beach's Sycamore Mineral Springs Resort.

EXPLORING

★ **Mission San Luis Obispo de Tolosa.** Special events often take place on sun-dappled Mission Plaza in front of Mission San Luis Obispo de Tolosa, established in 1772. Its small museum exhibits artifacts of the Chumash Indians and early Spanish settlers, and docents sometimes lead tours of the church and grounds. ✉ *751 Palm St.* ☎ *805/543–6850* 🌐 *www.missionsanluisobispo.org* 🎟 *$3 suggested donation* ⏲ *Apr.–late-Oct., daily 9–5; late Oct.–Mar., daily 9–4.*

San Luis Obispo Children's Museum. The delightful San Luis Obispo Children's Museum has 21 indoor and outdoor activities that present a kid-friendly version of the city of San Luis Obispo. Visitors enter through an "imagination-powered" elevator, which transports them to a series of underground caverns beneath the city, while simulated lava and steam sputters from an active volcano. Kids can pick rubber fruit at a farmers' market, clamber up a clockworks tower, race to fight a fire on a fire engine, and learn about solar energy from a 15-foot sunflower. The museum attracts mostly kids under eight; older children may become bored quickly. ✉ *1010 Nipomo St.* ☎ *805/545–5874* 🌐 *www.slocm.org* 🎟 *$8* ⏲ *Apr.–Sept., Tues.–Fri. 10–4, Sat. 10–5, Sun. and select Mon. holidays 11–5; Oct.–Mar., Tues.–Fri. 10–3, Sat. 10–5, Sun. and select Mon. holidays 1–5.*

History Center of San Luis Obispo County. Across the street from the old Spanish mission, the History Center of San Luis Obispo County presents rotating exhibits on various aspects of county history—such as Native American life, California ranchos, and the impact of railroads. A separate children's room has theme activities where kids can earn prizes. Visit the center's Web site to download a self-guided historic walking tour of downtown San Luis Obispo. ✉ *696 Monterey St.* ☎ *805/543–0638* 🌐 *historycenterslo.org* 🎟 *Free* ⏲ *Wed.–Sun. 10–4.*

Edna Valley/Arroyo Grande Valley Wine Country. San Luis Obispo is the commercial center of Edna Valley/Arroyo Grande Valley Wine Country, whose appellations stretch east–west from San Luis Obispo toward the coast and toward Lake Lopez in the inland mountains. Many of the 20 or so wineries line Highway 227 and connecting roads. The region is best known for Chardonnay and Pinot Noir, although many wineries experiment with other varietals and blends. Wine-touring maps are readily available around town; note that many wineries charge a small tasting fee and most tasting rooms close at 5.

Edna Valley Vineyard. For sweeping views of the Edna Valley while you sample estate-grown Chardonnay, go to the modern tasting bar at Edna Valley Vineyard. ✉ *2585 Biddle Ranch Rd.* ☎ *805/544–5855* 🌐 *www.ednavalleyvineyard.com.*

Baileyana Winery. A refurbished 1909 schoolhouse serves as tasting room for Baileyana Winery, which produces concentrated Chardonnays, Pinot Noirs, and Syrahs. Its sister winery, Tangent, creates alternative white wines and shares the tasting room. ✉ *5828 Orcutt Rd.* ☎ *805/269–8200* 🌐 *www.baileyana.com.*

Claiborne & Churchill. An eco-friendly winery built from straw bales, Claiborne & Churchill makes small lots of exceptional Alsatian-style wines such as dry Riesling and Gewürztraminer, plus Pinot Noir and Chardonnay. ✉ *2649 Carpenter Canyon Rd.* ☎ *805/544–4066* 🌐 *www.claibornechurchill.com.*

Old Edna. While touring Edna Valley Wine Country, be sure to stop at Old Edna, a peaceful, 2-acre site that once was the town of Edna. Browse for local art, taste wines, pick up sandwiches at the gourmet deli, and stroll along Old Edna Lane. ✉ *Hwy. 227, at Price Canyon Rd.* ☎ *805/544–8062* 🌐 *www.oldedna.com.*

DEEP ROOTS

Way back in the 1700s, the Spanish padres who accompanied Father Junípero Serra planted grapevines from Mexico along California's Central Coast, and began using European wine-making techniques to turn the grapes into delectable vintages.

2

WHERE TO EAT

$$ ✕ **Big Sky Café.** A popular gathering spot three meals a day, this quintessentially Californian, family-friendly (and sometimes noisy) café turns local and organically grown ingredients into global dishes. Brazilian churasco chicken breast, Thai catfish, New Mexican *pozole* (hominy stew): just pick your continent. Vegetarians have lots to choose from. ✉ *1121 Broad St.* ☎ *805/545–5401* 🌐 *www.bigskycafe.com* *Reservations not accepted.*

$$ ITALIAN ★ ✕ **Buona Tavola.** Homemade pasta with river shrimp in a creamy tomato sauce and porcini-mushroom risotto are among the northern Italian dishes served at this casual spot. Daily fresh fish and salad specials and an impressive wine list attract a steady stream of regulars. In good weather you can dine on the flower-filled patio. The Paso Robles branch is equally enjoyable. ✉ *1037 Monterey St.* ☎ *805/545–8000* 🌐 *www.btslo.com* *No lunch weekends.*

¢ SOUTHERN ✕ **Mo's Smokehouse BBQ.** Barbecue joints abound on the Central Coast, but this one excels. A variety of Southern-style sauces seasons tender hickory-smoked ribs and shredded meat sandwiches; sides such as baked beans, coleslaw, homemade potato chips, and garlic bread extend the pleasure. ✉ *1005 Monterey St.* ☎ *805/544–6193* 🌐 *www.smokinmosbbq.com.*

$ ✕ **Novo Restaurant & Lounge.** In the colorful dining room or on the large creek-side deck, this animated downtown eatery will take you on a culinary world tour. The salads, small plates, and entrées come from nearly every continent. The wine and beer list also covers the globe (you can sample various international wines paired with tapas Sunday evenings)—and includes local favorites. Many of the decadent desserts are baked at the restaurant's sister property in Cambria, the French Corner Bakery. ✉ *726 Higuera St.* ☎ *805/543–3986* 🌐 *www.novorestaurant.com.*

WHERE TO STAY

For expanded hotel reviews, visit Fodors.com.

$$$ **Apple Farm.** Decorated to the hilt with floral bedspreads and watercolors by local artists, this Victorian country-style hotel is one of the most popular places to stay in San Luis Obispo. **Pros:** flowers everywhere; convenient to Cal Poly and Highway 101; creek-side setting. **Cons:** hordes

of tourists stop here during the day; too floral for some people's tastes. *2015 Monterey St. 800/255–2040 www.applefarm.com 104 rooms In-room: a/c, Internet, Wi-Fi. In-hotel: restaurant, pool, spa.*

$$ **Garden Street Inn.** From this fully restored 1887 Italianate Queen Anne, the only lodging in downtown SLO, you can walk to many restaurants and attractions. **Pros:** classic B&B; walking distance from everywhere downtown; nice wine-and-cheese reception. **Cons:** city noise filters through some rooms; not a great place for families. *1212 Garden St. 805/545–9802, 800/488–2045 www.gardenstreetinn.com 9 rooms, 4 suites In-room: no a/c, no TV, Wi-Fi Breakfast.*

$$$ **Madonna Inn.** From its rococo bathrooms to its pink-on-pink froufrou steak house, the Madonna Inn is fabulous or tacky, depending on your taste. **ros:** fun one-of-a-kind experience. **Cons:** rooms vary widely; must appreciate kitsch. *100 Madonna Rd. 805/543–3000, 800/543–9666 805/543–1800 www.madonnainn.com 106 rooms, 4 suites In-hotel: restaurant, bar, pool, gym, spa.*

$$ **Petit Soleil.** A cobblestone courtyard, country-French custom furnishings, and Gallic music piped through the halls evoke a Provençal mood at this cheery inn on upper Monterey Street's motel row. **Pros:** French details throughout; scrumptious breakfasts; cozy rooms. **Cons:** sits on a busy avenue; cramped parking. *1473 Monterey St. 805/549–0321, 800/676–1588 www.psslo.com 15 rooms, 1 suite In-room: no a/c, Internet, Wi-Fi Breakfast.*

NIGHTLIFE AND THE ARTS

NIGHTLIFE

The club scene in this college town is centered on Higuera Street off Monterey Street.

Frog and Peach. The Frog and Peach is a decent spot to nurse an English beer and listen to live music. *728 Higuera St. 805/595–3764.*

Koberl at Blue. A trendy urban crowd hangs out at the slick bar at Koberl at Blue, an upscale Wine Country restaurant with late-night dining, exotic martinis, and a huge list of local and imported beer and wine. *998 Monterey St. 805/783–1135.*

Linnaea's Cafe. Linnaea's Cafe, a mellow java joint, sometimes holds poetry readings, as well as blues, jazz, and folk music performances. *1110 Garden St. 805/541–5888.*

MoTav. Chicago-style MoTav draws crowds with good pub food and live entertainment in a turn-of-the-20th-century setting (complete with antique U.S. flags and a wall-mounted moose head). *725 Higuera St. 805/541–8733.*

THE ARTS

Performing Arts Center. The Performing Arts Center at Cal Poly hosts live theater, dance, and music performances by artists from around the world. *1 Grand Ave. 805/756–7222, 805/756–2787 box office, 888/233–2787 toll-free www.pacslo.org.*

Festival Mozaic. Festival Mozaic celebrates five centuries of classical music and takes place in late July and early August. *805/781–3008 www. festivalmozaic.com.*

San Luis Obispo Museum of Art. San Luis Obispo Museum of Art displays and sells a mix of traditional work and cutting-edge arts and crafts by Central Coast, national, and international artists. The museum's permanent collection conserves an artistic legacy on the Central Coast. ✉ *1010 Broad St., at Mission Plaza* ☎ *805/543–8562* 🌐 *www.sloma.org* ⏲ *Open 11–4. Closed Tues. early Sept.–late June.*

SPORTS AND THE OUTDOORS

Parks and Recreation Department. Hilly greenbelts with vast amounts of open space and extensive hiking trails surround the city of San Luis Obispo. For information on trailheads, call the city Parks and Recreation Department or visit its Web site to download a trail map. ☎ *805/781–7300* 🌐 *www.slocity.org/parksandrecreation.*

EN ROUTE

Montaña de Oro State Park. Instead of continuing north on Highway 1 from San Luis Obispo to Morro Bay, consider taking Los Osos Valley Road (off Madonna Road, south of downtown) past farms and ranches to dramatic Montaña de Oro State Park. The park has miles of nature trails along rocky shoreline, wild beaches, and hills overlooking some of California's most spectacular scenery. Check out the tide pools, watch the waves roll into the bluffs, and picnic in the eucalyptus groves. ✉ *7 mi south of Los Osos on Pecho Rd.* ☎ *805/528–0513, 805/772–7434* 🌐 *www.parks.ca.gov.*

MORRO BAY

14 mi north of San Luis Obispo on Hwy. 1.

Commercial fishermen slog around Morro Bay in galoshes, and beat-up fishing boats bob in the bay's protected waters.

GETTING HERE AND AROUND

From U.S. 101 south or north, exit at Highway 1 in San Luis Obispo and head west. Scenic Highway 1 passes through the eastern edge of town. From Atascadero, two-lane Highway 41 West treks over the mountains to east Morro Bay. RTA Route 12 buses operate year-round between Morro Bay, San Luis Obispo, Cayucos, Cambria, San Simeon, Hearst Castle. The Morro Bay Shuttle picks up riders throughout the town Friday–Monday in summer ($1.25).

ESSENTIALS

Visitor Information Morro Bay Visitors Center. Stop at the Morro Bay Visitors Center and Chamber of Commerce to pick up maps and get information from friendly staffers. ✉ *845 Embarcadero Rd., Morro Bay* ☎ *805/772–4467, 800/231–0592* 🌐 *www.morrobay.org* ⏲ *Weekdays 9-5, Sat. 10-4, Sun. 10-2.*

EXPLORING

Morro Rock. At the mouth of Morro Bay, which is both a state and national estuary, stands 576-foot-high Morro Rock, one of nine such small volcanic peaks, or morros, in the area. A short walk leads to a breakwater, with the harbor on one side and the crashing waves of the Pacific on the other. You may not climb the rock, where endangered falcons and other birds nest. Sea lions and otters often play in the water at the foot of the peak. ✉ *Northern end of Embarcadero.*

Embarcadero. The center of the action on land is the Embarcadero, where vacationers pour in and out of souvenir shops and seafood restaurants and stroll or bike along the scenic half-mile Harborwalk to Morro Rock. From here, you can get out on the bay in a kayak or tour boat. ✉ *On waterfront from Beach St. to Tidelands Park.*

★ **Morro Bay State Park Museum of Natural History.** South of downtown Morro Bay, interactive exhibits at the spiffy Morro Bay State Park Museum of Natural History teach kids and adults about the natural environment and how to preserve it—both in the Morro Bay estuary and on the rest of the planet. ✉ *State Park Rd.* ☎ *805/772–2694* 🌐 *www.ccnha.org* *$3* *Daily 10–5.*

WHERE TO EAT

$ SOUTHWESTERN ★ **Taco Temple.** The devout stand in line at this family-run diner that serves some of the freshest food around. Seafood anchors a menu of dishes—salmon burritos, superb fish tacos with mango salsa—hailing from somewhere between California and Mexico. Desserts get rave reviews, too. Make an effort to find this gem tucked away in the corner of a supermarket parking lot north of downtown—it's on the frontage road parallel to Highway 1, just north of the Highway 41 junction. ✉ *2680 Main St., at Elena* ☎ *805/772–4965* *Reservations not accepted* *No credit cards* *Closed Tues.*

$$$ SEAFOOD **Windows on the Water.** From giant picture windows at this second-floor spot, watch the sun set over the water. Fresh fish and other dishes based on local ingredients emerge from the wood-fired oven in the open kitchen; a variety of oysters on the half shell beckon from the raw bar. About 20 of the wines on the extensive, mostly California list are poured by the glass. ✉ *699 Embarcadero* ☎ *805/772–0677* 🌐 *www.windowsmb.com* *No lunch.*

WHERE TO STAY

For expanded hotel reviews, visit Fodors.com.

$$$ **Anderson Inn.** The innkeepers' friendly personal service and an oceanfront setting lure a steady stream of loyal patrons to this new inn on the Embarcadero, built from scratch in 2009. **Pros:** walk to restaurants and sights; well-appointed rooms; attentive service. **Cons:** waterfront area gets crowded on weekends and in summer; not low-budget. ✉ *897 Embarcadero, Morro Bay* ☎ *805/772–3434* 🌐 *www.andersoninnmorrobay.com* *8 rooms* *In-room: a/c, safe, Wi-Fi.*

$$$ **Cass House.** The original 1867 home of shipping pioneer Captain James Cass is now a luxurious B&B boasting colorful rose gardens in the heart of Cayucos, a tiny oceanfront enclave about 4 miles north of Morro Bay just west of Highway 1. **Pros:** historic property; some ocean views; excellent meals. **Cons:** not near Morro Bay nightlife or tourist attractions; not designed for families. ✉ *222 N. Ocean Ave., Cayucos* ☎ *805/995–3669* 🌐 *www.casshouseinn.com* *5 rooms* *In-room: no a/c, Wi-Fi. In-hotel: restaurant* *Breakfast.*

SPORTS AND THE OUTDOORS

Kayak Horizons. Kayak Horizons rents kayaks and gives lessons and guided tours. ✉ *551 Embarcadero* ☎ *805/772–6444* 🌐 *www.kayakhorizons.com.*

Lost Isle Adventures. Captain Alan Rackov's Tiki-Boat cruises into the bay and out to Morro Rock every hour starting at 11 am daily. ✉ *At Giovanni's Fish Market on the Embarcadero, 1001 Front St., Morro Bay* ☎ *805/440–8170* 🌐 *lostisleadventures.com.*

Sub-Sea Tours. Sub-Sea Tours operates glass-bottom boat and catamaran cruises, and has kayak and canoe rentals and summer whale-watching cruises. ✉ *699 Embarcadero* ☎ *805/772–9463* 🌐 *subseatours.com.*

Virg's Landing. Virg's Landing conducts deep-sea fishing and whale-watching trips. ✉ *1215 Embarcadero* ☎ *805/772–1222* 🌐 *www.virgs.com.*

PASO ROBLES

30 mi north of San Luis Obispo on U.S. 101; 25 mi northwest of Morro Bay via Hwy. 41 and U.S. 101.

In the 1860s tourists began flocking to this dusty ranching outpost to "take the cure" in a luxurious bathhouse fed by underground mineral hot springs. An Old West town, complete with opera house, emerged; grand Victorian homes went up, followed in the 20th century by Craftsman bungalows. A 2003 earthquake demolished or weakened several beloved downtown buildings, but historically faithful reconstruction has proceeded rapidly.

Today the wine industry booms and mile upon mile of vineyards envelop Paso Robles; golfers play the four local courses and spandex-clad bicyclists race along the winding back roads. A mix of down-home and upmarket restaurants, bars, antiques stores, and little shops fills the streets around oak-shaded City Park, where special events of all kinds—custom car shows, an olive festival, Friday night summer concerts—take place on many weekends. Still, Paso (as the locals call it) more or less remains cowboy country: each year in late July and early August, the city throws the two-week California Mid-State Fair, complete with livestock auctions, carnival rides, and corn dogs.

GETTING HERE AND AROUND

U.S. 101 runs through the city of Paso Robles. Highway 46 West links Paso Robles to Highway 1/Cambria on the coast. Highway 46 East connects Paso Robles with Highway 5 and the San Joaquin Valley. The Paso Express public transit system extends throughout the city.

ESSENTIALS

Visitor Information Paso Robles Wine Country Alliance ✉ *744 Oak St.* ☎ *805/239–8463* 🌐 *www.pasowine.com.* **Paso Robles Chamber of Commerce** ✉ *1225 Park St.* ☎ *888/988–7276* 🌐 *www.travelpaso.com.*

EXPLORING

Harris Stage Lines. Former pro rodeo riders and horse trainers Tom and Debby Harris offer stagecoach rides (learn to hitch the team of horses beforehand), riding/driving lessons, and an array of Old West-themed events at their Old West ranch on the north side of town. ✉ *5995 North River Rd., Paso Robles* ☎ *805/237–1860* 🌐 *www.harrisstagelines.com.*

Paso Robles Pioneer Museum. Take a look back at California's rural heritage at the Paso Robles Pioneer Museum. Displays of historical ranching paraphernalia, horse-drawn vehicles, hot springs artifacts, and photos evoke the town's old days; a one-room schoolhouse is part of the complex. ✉ *2010 Riverside Ave.* ☎ *805/239–4556* 🌐 *www.pasoroblespioneermuseum.org* 🎟 *Free* ⏲ *Thurs.–Sun. 1–4.*

River Oaks Hot Springs & Spa. The lakeside River Oaks Hot Springs & Spa, on 240 hilly acres near the intersection of U.S. 101 and Highway 46E, is a great place to relax before and after wine tasting or festival-going. Soak in a private indoor or outdoor hot tub fed by natural mineral springs, or indulge in a massage or facial. ✉ *800 Clubhouse Dr.* ☎ *805/238–4600* 🌐 *www.riveroakshotsprings.com* 🎟 *Hot tubs $13 to $24 per person per hr* ⏲ *Tues.–Sun. 9–9.*

Paso Robles Wine Country. In Paso Robles Wine Country, nearly 200 wineries and more than 26,000 vineyard acres pepper the wooded hills west of U.S. 101 and blanket the flatter, more open land on the east side. The region's brutally hot summer days and cool nights yield stellar grapes that make noteworthy wines, particularly robust reds such as Cabernet Sauvignon, Merlot, Zinfandel, and Rhône varietals such as Syrah. An abundance of exquisite whites also comes out of Paso, including Chardonnay and Rhône varietals such as Viognier. Small-town friendliness prevails at most wineries, especially smaller ones, which tend to treat visitors like neighbors. Pick up a regional wine-touring map at lodgings, wineries, and attractions around town. Most tasting rooms close at 5 pm; many charge a small fee.

Paso Robles Wine Festival. Most of the local wineries pour at the Paso Robles Wine Festival, held mid-May in City Park. The outdoor tasting—the largest such California event—includes live bands and diverse food vendors. Winery open houses and winemaker dinners round out the weekend. ✉ *Spring St., between 10th and 12th Sts., City Park* ☎ *805/239–8463, 800/549–9463* 🌐 *www.pasowine.com* 🎟 *$55 basic admission, designated driver/child $15.*

Paso Wine Centre. Choose among 48 local wines available for tasting via enomatic dispensers at Paso Wine Centre, a spacious, contemporary space with comfy sofas and handhewn oak tables just off the town square. More than 200 wines are available for purchase. ✉ *1240 Park St., Paso Robles* ☎ *805/239–9156* 🌐 *www.pasobleswinecenter.com.*

Justin Vineyards & Winery. Small but swank Justin Vineyards & Winery makes Bordeaux-style blends at the western end of Paso Robles Wine Country. This reader favorite offers winery, vineyard, and barrel-tasting tours ($15 to $100). In the tasting room there's a deli bar; a tiny high-end restaurant is also part of the complex. ✉ *11680 Chimney Rock Rd.* ☎ *805/238–6932, 800/726–0049* 🌐 *www.justinwine.com.*

Tablas Creek Vineyard. Tucked in the far-west hills of Paso Robles, Tablas Creek Vineyard makes some of the area's finest wine by blending organically grown, hand-harvested Rhône varietals such as Syrah, Grenache, Roussanne, and Viognier. Tours include a chance to graft your own grapevine; call to reserve space. ✉ *9339 Adelaida Rd.* ☎ *805/237–1231* 🌐 *www.tablascreek.com.*

★ **Pasolivo.** While touring the idyllic west side of Paso Robles, take a break from wine by stopping at Pasolivo. Find out how they make their Tuscan-style Pasolivo olive oils on a high-tech Italian press, and taste the widely acclaimed results. ✉ *8530 Vineyard Dr.* ☎ *805/227–0186* 🌐 *www.pasolivo.com.*

Wild Horse Winery & Vineyards. In southeastern Paso Robles Wine Country, Wild Horse Winery & Vineyards was a pioneer Central Coast producer. You can try delicious, well-priced Pinot Noir, Chardonnay, and Merlot in their simple tasting room. ✉ *1437 Wild Horse Winery Ct., Templeton* ☎ *805/434–2541* 🌐 *www.wildhorsewinery.com.*

Firestone Walker Fine Ales. As they say around Paso Robles, it takes a lot of beer to make good wine, and to meet that need the locals turn to Firestone Walker Fine Ales. In the brewery's taproom, sample medal-winning craft beers such as Double Barrel Ale. They close at 7 pm. ✉ *1400 Ramada Dr.* ☎ *805/238–2556* 🌐 *www.firestonebeer.com.*

LAID-BACK WINE COUNTRY

Hundreds of vineyards and wineries dot the hillsides from Paso Robles to San Luis Obispo, through the scenic Edna Valley and south to northern Santa Barbara County. The wineries offer much of the variety of northern California's Napa and Sonoma valleys—without the glitz and crowds. Since the early 1980s the region has developed an international reputation for high-quality wines, most notably Pinot Noir, Chardonnay, and Zinfandel. Wineries here tend to be small, but most have tasting rooms (some have tours), and you'll often meet the winemakers themselves.

Eberle Winery. Even if you don't drink wine, stop at Eberle Winery for a fascinating tour of the huge wine caves beneath the east-side Paso Robles vineyard. Gary Eberle, one of Paso wine's founding fathers, is obsessed with Cabernet Sauvignon. ✉ *Hwy. 46E, 3½ mi east of U.S. 101* ☎ *805/238–9607* 🌐 *www.eberlewinery.com.*

WHERE TO EAT

$$$ AMERICAN

✕ **Artisan.** Innovative renditions of traditional American comfort foods, a well-chosen list of regional wines, a stylish full bar, and a sophisticated urban vibe lure winemakers, locals, and tourists to this small, family-run American bistro in an art deco building near the town square. Chris Kobayashi (Chef Koby, recently nominated for a James Beard award) uses local, organic, wild-caught ingredients to whip up regional favorites, which might include red abalone with fried green tomatoes and pancetta, scallops with laughing bird prawns, mussels, clams, Spanish chorizo, and saffron, or flatiron steak with shallots, fries, and Cabernet butter. Try to nab a booth facing the open kitchen, and save room for the restaurant's famed homestyle desserts: brownies, peach crumbles, crème brûlée, and the like. ✉ *1401 Park St.* ☎ *805/237–8084* 🌐 *www.artisanpasorobles.com.*

$$$ FRENCH ★

✕ **Bistro Laurent.** Owner-chef Laurent Grangien has created a handsome, welcoming French bistro in an 1890s brick building across from City Park. He focuses on traditional dishes such as osso buco, cassoulet, rack of lamb, goat-cheese tart, and onion soup, but always offers a few updated dishes as daily specials. Wines, sourced from the adjacent wine shop, come from around the world. ✉ *1202 Pine St.* ☎ *805/226–8191* 🌐 *www.bistrolaurent.com* ⏲ *Closed Sun. and Mon.*

2

$$$ AMERICAN ✕ **McPhee's Grill.** The grain silos across the street and the floral oilcloths on the tables belie the sophisticated cuisine at this casual chophouse. In an 1860s building in the tiny cow town of Templeton (just south of Paso Robles), the restaurant serves creative, contemporary versions of traditional Western fare—such as oak-grilled filet mignon and cedar-planked salmon. House-label wines, made especially for McPhee's, are quite good. ✉ *416 S. Main St., Templeton* ☎ *805/434–3204* 🌐 *www.mcphees.com.*

$ FRENCH ✕ **Panolivo Family Bistro.** Scrumptious French bistro fare draws a loyal crowd of locals to this cheery downtown café, just a block north of the town square. For breakfast, try a fresh pastry or quiche, or build your own omelet. Lunch and dinner choices include traditional French dishes like snails baked in garlic-butter sauce or cassoulet as well as sandwiches, salads, and fresh pastas—including the house-made beef cannelloni. ✉ *1344 Park St.* ☎ *805/239–3366.*

$$ ✕ **Thomas Hill Organics.** In a casual bistro off a tiny alley, Joe and Debbie Thomas serve delectable locavore cuisine made from regional ingredients; much of the produce comes from their own ten-acre organic farm down the road. The menu changes weekly, depending on what's in-season and available, and includes a good selection of Central Coast wines. There's also a wine bar stocked with local vintages. A festive group of locals gathers every Monday evening for a family-style, multi-course feast ($25) with live music. Ask for a table in the outdoor courtyard on fair-weather days. ✉ *1305 Park St., Templeton* ☎ *805/226–5888* 🌐 *thomashillorganics.com* ⊗ *Closed Tuesdays.*

$$$ SOUTHWESTERN ✕ **Villa Creek.** With a firm nod to the rancho and mission cuisine of California's early Spanish settlers, chef Tom Fundero conjures distinctly modern magic with local and sustainable ingredients. The seasonal menu has included butternut-squash enchiladas and braised lamb shank with saffron risotto and classic beef bourgignon with parsnip and cauliflower purée, but you might also find duck breast with sweet-potato latkes. Central Coast wines dominate the list, with a smattering of Spanish and French selections. All brick and bare wood, the dining room can get loud when winemakers start passing their bottles from table to table, but it's always festive. For lighter appetites or wallets, the bar serves smaller plates—not to mention a killer margarita. ✉ *1144 Pine St.* ☎ *805/238–3000* 🌐 *www.villacreek.com* ⊗ *No lunch.*

WHERE TO STAY

For expanded hotel reviews, visit Fodors.com.

¢ Fodor's Choice ★ **Adelaide Inn.** Family-owned and -managed, this clean, friendly oasis with meticulous landscaping offers spacious rooms and everything you need: coffeemaker, iron, hair dryer, and peace and quiet. **Pros:** great bargain; attractive pool area; ideal for families. **Cons:** not a romantic retreat; near a busy intersection and freeway. ✉ *1215 Ysabel Ave.* ☎ *805/238–2770, 800/549–7276* 🌐 *www.adelaideinn.com* *109 rooms* *In-room: a/c, Internet, Wi-Fi. In-hotel: pool, gym, laundry facilities* *Breakfast.*

$$$$ **Hotel Cheval.** Equestrian themes surface throughout this intimate, sophisticated, European-style inn just a half-block from the main square and a short walk to some of Paso's best restaurants. **Pros:** walking distance from downtown restaurants; European-style facilities; personal

service. **Cons:** views aren't great; no pool or hot tub. ✉ *1021 Pine St.* ☎ *805/226–9995, 866/522–6999* 🌐 *www.hotelcheval.com* *16 rooms* *In-room: a/c, Internet, Wi-Fi. In-hotel: bar* *Breakfast.*

$$$ **La Bellasera Hotel & Suites.** The swankest full-service hotel for miles around, the La Bellasera, completed in 2008, caters to those looking for luxurious high-tech amenities and close proximity to major Central Coast roadways. **Pros:** new property; tons of amenities. **Cons:** far from town square; located at major intersection. ✉ *206 Alexa Court* ☎ *805/238–2834, 866/782–9669* 🌐 *www.labellasera.com* *35 rooms, 25 suites* *In-room: a/c, kitchen, Wi-Fi. In-hotel: restaurant, bar, pool, gym, spa, laundry facilities, business center, parking.*

$$ **Paso Robles Inn.** On the site of a luxurious old spa hotel by the same name, the inn is built around a lush, shady garden with a pool. **Pros:** private spring-fed hot tubs; historic property; across from park and town square. **Cons:** fronts a busy street; rooms vary in size and quality. ✉ *1103 Spring St.* ☎ *805/238–2660, 800/676–1713* 🌐 *www.pasoroblesinn.com* *92 rooms, 6 suites* *In-room: a/c, Internet, Wi-Fi. In-hotel: restaurant, bar, pool.*

CAMBRIA

28 mi west of Paso Robles on Hwy. 46; 20 mi north of Morro Bay on Hwy. 1.

Cambria, set on piney hills above the sea, was settled by Welsh miners in the 1890s. In the 1970s, the gorgeous, isolated setting attracted artists and other independent types; the town now caters to tourists, but it still bears the unmistakable imprint of its bohemian past. Both of Cambria's downtowns, the original East Village and the newer West Village, are packed with art and crafts galleries, antiques shops, cafés, restaurants, and B&Bs. Late-Victorian homes stand along side streets, and the hills are filled with redwood-and-glass residences.

GETTING HERE AND AROUND

Highway 1 leads to Cambria from north and south. From U.S. 101 at Paso Robles, Highway 246 West curves through mountains to Cambria and the coast. RTA Route 12 buses ferry passengers between San Luis Obispo and Hearst Castle, stopping in Cambria along the way.

ESSENTIALS

Visitor Information Cambria Chamber of Commerce ☎ *805/927–3624* 🌐 *www.cambriachamber.org.*

EXPLORING

Moonstone Beach Drive. Lined with low-key motels, Moonstone Beach Drive runs along a bluff above the ocean. The boardwalk that winds along the beach side of the drive makes a great walk.

Leffingwell's Landing. Leffingwell's Landing, a state picnic ground, is a good place for examining tidal pools and watching otters as they frolic in the surf. ✉ *North end of Moonstone Beach Dr.* ☎ *805/927–2070.*

Nit Wit Ridge. Arthur Beal (aka Captain Nit Wit, Der Tinkerpaw) spent 51 years building Nit Wit Ridge, a home with terraced rock gardens. For building materials, he used all kinds of collected junk: beer cans, rocks, abalone shells, car parts, TV antennas—you name it. The site, above Cambria's West Village, is a State Historic Landmark. You can drive by and peek in; better yet, call ahead for a guided tour of the house and grounds. *881 Hillcrest Dr. 805/927–2690 $10 Daily by appointment.*

WHERE TO EAT

$$$ AMERICAN **Black Cat Bistro.** Jazz wafts through the several small rooms of this intimate East Village bistro where stylish cushions line the banquettes. Start with an order of the fried olives stuffed with Gorgonzola, accompanied by a glass from the eclectic list of local and imported wines. The daily-changing menu is centered on sustainable ingredients and might include roasted rack of elk rubbed in cocoa or breast of pheasant stuffed with caramelized apples. *1602 Main St. 805/927–1600 www.blackcatbistro.com Reservations essential Closed Tues. and Wed. No lunch.*

¢ CAFÉ **French Corner Bakery.** Place your order at the counter and then sit outside to watch the passing East Village scene (if the fog has rolled in, take a seat in the tiny deli). The rich aroma of coffee and fresh breakfast pastries makes mouths water in the morning; for lunch, try a quiche with flaky crust or a sandwich on house-baked bread. *2214 Main St. 805/927–8227 Reservations not accepted No dinner.*

$$ **Robin's.** A truly multiethnic and vegetarian-friendly dining experience awaits you at this East Village cottage filled with country antiques. At dinner, choose from lobster enchiladas, pork osso buco, Thai green chicken curry, and more. Lunchtime's extensive salad and sandwich menu embraces burgers and tofu alike. Unless it's raining, ask for a table on the secluded (and heated) garden patio. *4095 Burton Dr. 805/927–5007 www.robinsrestaurant.com.*

$$$ SEAFOOD **The Sea Chest.** By far the best seafood place in town—readers give it a big thumbs-up—this Moonstone Beach restaurant fills soon after it opens at 5:30. Those in the know grab seats at the oyster bar, where they can take in spectacular sunsets while watching the chefs broil fresh halibut and steam garlicky clams. If you can't get there early, play some cribbage or checkers while you wait for a table. *6216 Moonstone Beach Dr. 805/927–4514 www.seachestrestaurant.com Reservations not accepted No credit cards Closed Tues. mid-Sept.–May. No lunch.*

WHERE TO STAY

For expanded hotel reviews, visit Fodors.com.

¢ **Bluebird Inn.** This sweet motel in Cambria's East Village sits amid beautiful gardens along Santa Rosa Creek. **Pros:** excellent value; well-kept gardens; friendly staff. **Cons:** few frills; basic rooms; on Cambria's main drag. *1880 Main St. 805/927–4634, 800/552–5434 www.bluebirdmotel.com 37 rooms In-room: a/c, Wi-Fi.*

$$ **Cambria Pines Lodge.** With lots of recreational facilities and a range of accommodations—from basic state park–style cabins to motel-style standard rooms to large fireplace suites—this 25-acre retreat up the hill from the East Village is a good choice for families. **Pros:** short walk from downtown; verdant gardens; spacious grounds. **Cons:** front desk service and housekeeping not always top-quality; some units could use an

update. ✉ *2905 Burton Dr.* ☎ *805/927–4200, 800/966–6490* 🌐 *www.cambriapineslodge.com* *72 rooms, 18 cabins, 62 suites* *In-room: a/c, Internet, Wi-Fi. In-hotel: restaurant, bar, pool, spa, business center, some pets allowed* *Breakfast.*

$$ ★ **Moonstone Landing.** Friendly staff, lots of amenities, and reasonable rates make this up-to-date motel a top pick with readers who like to stay right on Moonstone Beach. **Pros:** sleek furnishings; across from the beach; cheery lounge. **Cons:** narrow property; some rooms overlook a parking lot. ✉ *6240 Moonstone Beach Dr.* ☎ *805/927–0012, 800/830–4540* 🌐 *www.moonstonelanding.com* *29 rooms* *In-room: no a/c, Wi-Fi* *Breakfast.*

SAN SIMEON

Hwy. 1, 9 mi north of Cambria and 65 mi south of Big Sur.

Whalers founded San Simeon in the 1850s but had virtually abandoned the town by the time Senator George Hearst reestablished it 20 years later. Hearst bought up most of the surrounding ranch land, built a 1,000-foot wharf, and turned San Simeon into a bustling port. His son, William Randolph Hearst, further developed the area during the construction of Hearst Castle. Today the town, 4 mi south of the entrance to Hearst San Simeon State Historical Monument, is basically a strip of gift shops and mediocre motels along Highway 1.

GETTING HERE AND AROUND

Highway 1 is the only way to reach San Simeon. From northern California, follow Highway 1 from Big Sur south to San Simeon. From U.S. 101 north or south, exit at Highway 1 in San Luis Obispo and follow it northwest 42 mi to San Simeon. Alternative rural routes to reach Highway 1 from the 101 include Highway 41 West (Atascadero to Morro Bay) and Highway 46 West (Paso Robles to Cambria).

EXPLORING

★ **Hearst Castle.** Hearst Castle, officially known as "Hearst San Simeon State Historical Monument," sits in solitary splendor atop La Cuesta Encantada (the Enchanted Hill). Its buildings and gardens spread over 127 acres that were the heart of newspaper magnate William Randolph Hearst's 250,000-acre ranch. Hearst devoted nearly 30 years and about $10 million to building this elaborate estate. He commissioned renowned architect Julia Morgan—who also designed buildings at the University of California at Berkeley—but he was very much involved with the final product, a hodgepodge of Italian, Spanish, Moorish, and French styles. The 115-room main building and three huge "cottages" are connected by terraces and staircases and surrounded by pools, gardens, and statuary. In its heyday the castle was a playground for Hearst and his guests, many of them Hollywood celebrities. Construction began in 1919 and was never officially completed. Work was halted in 1947 when Hearst had to leave San Simeon because of failing health. The Hearst family presented the property to the State of California in 1958.

Access to the castle is through the large visitor center at the foot of the hill, which contains a collection of Hearst memorabilia and a giant-screen theater that shows a 40-minute film giving a sanitized version of Hearst's life and of the castle's construction. Buses from the visitor center zigzag up the hillside to the neoclassical extravaganza, where guides conduct three different daytime tours of various parts of the main house and grounds. All three tours include movie tickets and take you to the indoor and outdoor pools. Tours last about two hours, including the bus ride up the hill, about 40 minutes with a guide, and time to stroll the grounds on your own.

The Grand Rooms Tour provides a good overview of the highlights; the others focus on the upstairs suites, cottages, and kitchens. In spring and fall, docents in period costume portray Hearst's guests and staff for an evening tour, which begins at sunset.(The Web site has specific dates.) All tours include a ½-mi walk and between 150 and 400 stairs. Reservations for the tours, which can be made up to eight weeks in advance, are necessary. ✉ *San Simeon State Park, 750 Hearst Castle Rd.* ☎ *800/444–4445* 🌐 *www.hearstcastle.com* 🎫 *Daytime tours $25,* ⏲ *Tours daily 8:20–3:20, later in summer; additional tours take place most Fri. and Sat. evenings Mar.–May and Sept.–Dec.*

Old San Simeon. Turn west from Highway 1 across from the Hearst Castle entrance to see Old San Simeon, an 1850s whaling village that morphed into an outpost for Hearst employees. There's a historic one-room schoolhouse and Spanish-style buildings; don't miss Sebastian's General Store in an 1852 building. Now a state historic landmark, Sebastian's houses a café with excellent sandwiches and salads, a store, and a wine tasting room. ✉ *West of Highway 1, across from Hearst Castle entrance, San Simeon.*

Piedras Blancas Elephant Seal Rookery. A large and growing colony (at last count 15,000 members) of elephant seals gathers every year at Piedras Blancas Elephant Seal Rookery, on the beaches near Piedras Blancas Lighthouse. The huge males with their pendulous, trunklike noses typically start appearing on shore in late November, and the females begin to arrive in December to give birth—most babies are born in the last two weeks of January. The newborn pups spend about four weeks nursing before their mothers head out to sea, leaving them on their own; the "weaners" leave the rookery when they are about 3½ months old. The seals return in the spring and summer months to molt or rest, but not en masse as in winter. You can watch them from a boardwalk along the bluffs just a few feet above the beach; do not attempt to approach them, as they are wild animals. Docents are often on hand to give background information and statistics. The rookery is just south of Piedras Blancas Lighthouse (4½ mi north of Hearst San Simeon State Historical Monument); the nonprofit Friends of the Elephant Seal runs a small visitor center and gift shop at their San Simeon office. ✉ *Friends of the Elephant Seal, 250 San Simeon Ave., Suite 3* ☎ *805/924–1628* 🌐 *www.elephantseal.org.*

WHERE TO STAY

For expanded hotel reviews, visit Fodors.com.

$$ **Best Western Cavalier Oceanfront Resort.** Reasonable rates, an oceanfront location, evening bonfires, and well-equipped rooms—some with wood-burning fireplaces and private patios—make this motel one of the best choices in San Simeon. **Pros:** on the bluffs; fantastic views; close to Hearst Castle; bluff bonfires. **Cons:** room amenities and sizes vary; pools are small and sometimes crowded. *9415 Hearst Dr. 805/927–4688, 800/826–8168 www.cavalierresort.com 90 rooms In-room: a/c, Internet, Wi-Fi. In-hotel: restaurant, pool, gym, laundry facilities, business center, some pets allowed.*

$$ **The Morgan San Simeon.** On the ocean side of Highway 1, near San Simeon restaurants and shops, the Morgan offers a range of motel-style rooming options while paying tribute to famed Hearst Castle architect Julia Morgan. **Pros:** fascinating artwork; easy access to Hearst Castle and Highway 1; some ocean views. **Cons:** not right on beach; no fitness room or laundry facilities. *9135 Hearst Dr. 805/927–3878, 800/451–9900 www.hotel-morgan.com 54 rooms, 1 suite In-room: Wi-Fi. In-hotel: bar, pool, spa Breakfast.*

BIG SUR COASTLINE

Long a retreat of artists and writers, Big Sur is a place of ancient forests and rugged shoreline, stretching 90 mi from San Simeon to Carmel. Residents have protected it from overdevelopment, and much of the region lies within several state parks and the more than 165,000-acre Ventana Wilderness, itself part of the Los Padres National Forest.

ESSENTIALS

Visitor Information Big Sur Chamber of Commerce *831/667–2100 www.bigsurcalifornia.org.*

SOUTHERN BIG SUR

Hwy. 1 from San Simeon to Julia Pfeiffer Burns State Park.

This especially rugged stretch of oceanfront is a rocky world of mountains, cliffs, and beaches.

GETTING HERE AND AROUND

Highway 1 is the only major access route from north or south. From the south, access Highway 1 from U.S. 101 in San Luis Obispo. From the north, take rural routes Highway 46 West (Paso Robles to Cambria) or Highway 41 West (Atascadero to Morro Bay). Nacimiento-Fergusson Road snakes through mountains and forest from U.S. 101 at Jolon about 25 mi to Highway 1 at Kirk Creek, about 4 mi south of Lucia; this curvy, at times precipitous road is a motorcyclist favorite, not recommended for the faint of heart or during inclement weather.

EXPLORING

Fodor's Choice ★ **Highway 1.** One of California's most spectacular drives, Highway 1 snakes up the coast north of San Simeon. Numerous pullouts along the way offer tremendous views and photo ops. On some of the beaches,

WORD OF MOUTH

"The Central Coast in all its glory: I proposed to my fiancé 10 minutes after I took this photo in Julia Pfeiffer Burns State Park." —photo by Valhalla, Fodors.com member

huge elephant seals lounge nonchalantly, seemingly oblivious to the attention of rubberneckers—but keep your distance.

CalTrans. In rainy seasons, portions of Highway 1 north and south of Big Sur are sometimes shut down by mudslides. Contact CalTrans for road conditions. ☎ *800/427–7623* 🌐 *www.dot.ca.gov*

Jade Cove. In Los Padres National Forest just north of the town of Gorda is Jade Cove, a well-known jade-hunting spot. Rock hunting is allowed on the beach, but you may not remove anything from the walls of the cliffs. ✉ *Hwy. 1, 34 mi north of San Simeon.*

Julia Pfeiffer Burns State Park. Julia Pfeiffer Burns State Park provides some fine hiking, from an easy ½-mi stroll with marvelous coastal views to a strenuous 6-mi trek through the redwoods. The big attraction here, an 80-foot waterfall that drops into the ocean, gets crowded in summer; still, it's an astounding place to sit and contemplate nature. Migrating whales, as well as harbor seals and sea lions, can sometimes be spotted not far from shore. ✉ *Hwy. 1, 53 mi north of San Simeon, 15 mi north of Lucia* ☎ *831/667–2315* 🌐 *www.parks.ca.gov* *$10* ⏲ *Daily sunrise–sunset.*

WHERE TO STAY

For expanded hotel reviews, visit Fodors.com.

$$ **Ragged Point Inn.** At this cliff-top resort—the only inn and restaurant for miles around—glass walls in most rooms open to awesome, unobstructed ocean views. **Pros:** on the cliffs; great food; idyllic views. **Cons:** busy road stop during the day; often booked for weekend weddings. ✉ *19019 Hwy. 1, 20 mi north of San Simeon, Ragged Point* ☎ *805/927–4502, 805/927–5708 restaurant* 🌐 *raggedpointinn.com* *30 rooms* *In-room: no a/c, kitchen. In-hotel: restaurant, laundry facilities.*

$$ **Treebones Resort.** Perched on a hilltop, surrounded by national forest and stunning, unobstructed ocean views, this yurt resort opened in 2004. **Pros:** 360-degree views; spacious pool area; comfortable beds. **Cons:** steep paths; no private bathrooms; more than a mile from the nearest store; not a good place for families with children under six. ✉ *71895 Hwy. 1, Willow Creek Rd., 32 mi north of San Simeon, 1 mi north of Gorda* ☎ *805/927–2390, 877/424–4787* 🌐 *www.treebonesresort.com* *16 yurts, 5 campsites, 1 human nest w/campsite* *In-room: no a/c. In-hotel: restaurant, pool, spa, laundry facilities, business center, some pets allowed* *Breakfast.*

CENTRAL BIG SUR

Hwy. 1, from Partington Cove to Bixby Bridge.

The countercultural spirit of Big Sur—which instead of a conventional town is a loose string of coast-hugging properties along Highway 1—is alive and well today. Its few residents include the very wealthy, the enthusiastically outdoorsy, and the thoroughly evolved: since the 1960s the Esalen Institute, a center for alternative education and East–West philosophical study, has attracted seekers of higher consciousness and devotees of the property's hot springs. Today, posh and rustic resorts hidden among the redwoods cater to visitors drawn from near and far by the extraordinary scenery and serene isolation.

2

GETTING HERE AND AROUND

From the north, follow Highway 1 south from Carmel. From the south, access scenic Highway 1 from U.S. 101 at San Luis Obispo. Alternate connections from U.S. 101 north or south are rural roads Highway 46 West (Paso Robles to Cambria) and Highway 41 West (Atascadero to Morro Bay). MST Line 22 Big Sur travels between Monterey, Carmel, and Big Sur on weekends (daily in summer).

EXPLORING

Pfeiffer Beach. Through a hole in one of the gigantic boulders at secluded Pfeiffer Beach, you can watch the waves break first on the sea side and then on the beach side. Keep a sharp eye out for the unsigned, ungated road to the beach: it branches west of Highway 1 between the post office and Pfeiffer Big Sur State Park. The 2-mile, one-lane road descends sharply. ✉ *Off Hwy. 1, 1 mi south of Pfeiffer Big Sur State Park* 🎟 *$10 per vehicle per day.*

Pfeiffer Big Sur State Park. Among the many hiking trails at Pfeiffer Big Sur State Park ($10 per vehicle for day use) a short route through a redwood-filled valley leads to a waterfall. You can double back or continue on the more difficult trail along the valley wall for views over miles of treetops to the sea. Stop in at the Big Sur Station visitor center, off Highway 1, less than ½ mi south of the park entrance, for information about the entire area; it's open 8–4:30. ✉ *47225 Hwy. 1* ☎ *831/667–2315* 🌐 *www.parks.ca.gov* 🎟 *$10 per vehicle* 🕙 *Daily dawn–dusk.*

★ **Point Sur State Historic Park.** Point Sur State Historic Park is the site of an 1889 lighthouse that still stands watch from atop a large volcanic rock. Four lighthouse keepers lived here with their families until 1974, when the light station became automated. Their homes and working spaces are open to the public only on 2½- to 3-hour ranger-led tours. Considerable walking, including up two stairways, is involved. Strollers are not allowed. ✉ *Hwy. 1, 7 mi north of Pfeiffer Big Sur State Park* ☎ *831/625–4419* 🌐 *www.pointsur.org* 🎟 *$10* 🕙 *Tours generally Nov.–Mar., weekends at 10, Wed. at 1; Apr.–Oct., Sat. and Wed. at 10 and 2, Sun. at 10; call to confirm.*

Bixby Creek Bridge. The graceful arc of Bixby Creek Bridge is a photographer's dream. Built in 1932, it spans a deep canyon, more than 100 feet wide at the bottom. From the parking area on the north side you can admire the view or walk across the 550-foot span. ✉ *Hwy. 1, 6 mi north of Point Sur State Historic Park, 13 mi south of Carmel.*

WHERE TO EAT

$$ ✕ **Big Sur Roadhouse.** At this colorful, casual bistro, feast on innovative, well-executed California Latin–fusion fare. Crispy striped bass atop a pillow of carrot-coconut puree, tangy-smoky barbecue chicken breast beneath a julienne of jicama and cilantro: the zesty, balanced flavors wake up your mouth. Emphasizing new-world vintages, the wine list is gently priced. The chocolate-caramel layer cake may bring tears to your eyes. ✉ *Hwy. 1, 1 mi north of Pfeiffer Big Sur State Park* ☎ *831/667–2264* 🌐 *www.bigsurroadhouse.com* 🕙 *Closed Tues. No lunch.*

$$$ AMERICAN ✕ **Deetjen's Big Sur Inn.** The candlelighted, creaky-floor restaurant in the main house at the historic inn of the same name is a Big Sur institution. It serves spicy seafood paella, steak, and rack of lamb for dinner and wonderfully flavorful eggs Benedict for breakfast. The chef procures much of the fish, meats, and produce from purveyors who practice sustainable farming and fishing practices. ✉ *Hwy. 1, 3½ mi south of Pfeiffer Big Sur State Park* ☎ *831/667–2377* ⊕ *www.deetjens.com* ⊗ *No lunch.*

$$$ AMERICAN ✕ **Nepenthe.** It may be that no other restaurant between San Francisco and Los Angeles has a better coastal view; no wonder Orson Welles and Rita Hayworth once owned the place. The food and drink are overpriced but good; there are burgers, sandwiches, and salads for lunch, and fresh fish and hormone-free steaks for dinner. For the real show, settle on the terraced deck in the late afternoon, order a glass from the extensive wine list, and watch the sun slip into the Pacific Ocean. The less expensive, outdoor Café Kevah serves brunch and lunch. ✉ *Hwy. 1, 2½ mi south of Big Sur Station* ☎ *831/667–2345* ⊕ *www.nepenthebigsur.com.*

$$$$ AMERICAN ✕ **The Restaurant at Ventana.** Closed for remodeling for more than a year after a kitchen fire, the Restaurant at Ventana (formerly Cielo) rose from the ashes in stunning fashion in fall 2009. Redwood, copper, and cedar elements pay tribute to the historic natural setting, while gleaming new fixtures and dining accoutrements place the restaurant firmly in the 21st century. Chef Trueman Jones' seasonal menu showcases fine California cuisine, from rabbit loin and California white sea bass to artichokes and abalone, and a full slate of regional and international wines. Much of the produce comes from the restaurant's organic vegetable garden. The restaurant is also open for lunch—ask for a table on the outdoor terrace, where ocean views unfold on clear, sunny days. ✉ *Hwy. 1, 1½ mi south of Pfeiffer Big Sur State Park* ☎ *831/667–2242* ⊕ *www.ventanainn.com* ⚠ *Reservations essential.*

$$$$ AMERICAN ✕ **Sierra Mar.** Ocean-view dining doesn't get much better than this. Perched at cliff's edge 1,200 feet above the Pacific at the ultra-chic Post Ranch Inn, Sierra Mar serves cutting-edge American food made from mostly organic, seasonal ingredients, including a stellar four-course prix-fixe menu. The restaurant's wine list is one of the most extensive in the nation. ✉ *Hwy. 1, 1½ mi south of Pfeiffer Big Sur State Park* ☎ *831/667–2800* ⚠ *Reservations essential.*

WHERE TO STAY

$$$ **Big Sur Lodge.** The modern motel-style cottages in Pfeiffer Big Sur State Park sit in a meadow surrounded by trees and flowering shrubbery. Renovated in 2005, with Mission-style furnishings and vaulted ceilings, some rooms have fireplaces and some have kitchens; all have a deck or patio. The larger, multi-bedded rooms and suites are a good choice for families. **Pros:** near trailheads; good camping alternative. **Cons:** basic rooms; walk to main lodge. ✉ *47225 Hwy. 1(Pfeiffer Big Sur State Park)* ☎ *831/667–3100, 800/424–4787* ⊕ *www.bigsurlodge.com* *61 rooms* *In-room: kitchen, no TV. In-hotel: restaurant, bar, pool.*

¢ **Deetjen's Big Sur Inn.** This historic 1930s Norwegian-style property is endearingly rustic and charming, especially if you're willing to go with a camplike flow. **Pros:** surrounded by Big Sur history; tons of character; wooded grounds. **Cons:** rustic; thin walls; some rooms don't have private baths. ✉ *Hwy. 1, 3½ mi south of Pfeiffer Big Sur State Park* ☎ *831/667–2377* 🌐 *www.deetjens.com* *20 rooms, 15 with bath* *In-room: no a/c, no TV. In-hotel: restaurant.*

$$$$ **Post Ranch Inn.** This luxurious retreat, designed exclusively for adult getaways, has remarkably environmentally conscious architecture. **Pros:** world-class resort; spectacular views; gorgeous property with hiking trails. **Cons:** expensive; austere design; not a good choice if you're scared of heights. ✉ *Hwy. 1, 1½ mi south of Pfeiffer Big Sur State Park* ✉ *Hwy. 1, Box 219* ☎ *831/667–2200, 888/524–4787* 🌐 *www.postranchinn.com* *39 units* *In-room: a/c, Internet, Wi-Fi. In-hotel: restaurant, bar, pool, gym, spa, business center* *Breakfast.*

Fodor's Choice ★

$$$$ **Ventana Inn & Spa.** Hundreds of celebrities, from Oprah Winfrey to Sir Anthony Hopkins, have escaped to Ventana, a romantic resort on 243 tranquil acres 1,200 feet above the Pacific. **Pros:** nature trails everywhere; great food; secluded. **Cons:** simple breakfast; no ocean view from rooms. ✉ *Hwy. 1, almost 1 mi south of Pfeiffer Big Sur State Park* ☎ *831/667–2331, 800/628–6500* 🌐 *www.ventanainn.com* *25 rooms, 31 suites* *In-room: a/c, Internet, Wi-Fi. In-hotel: restaurant, bar, pool, gym, spa* *Breakfast.*

Fodor's Choice ★

2

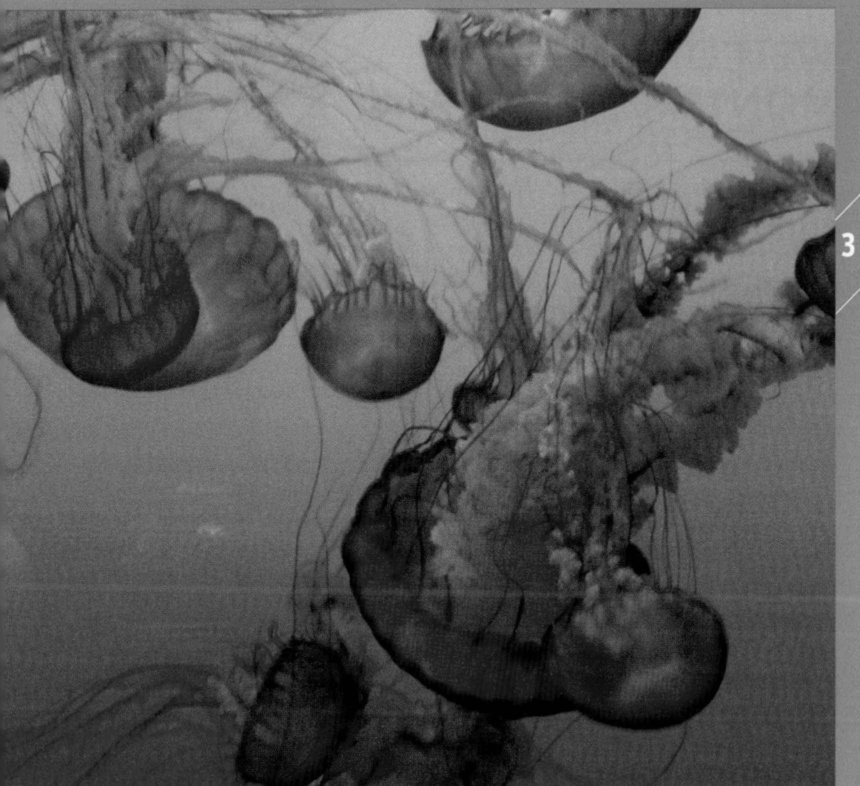

3

The Monterey Bay Area

FROM CARMEL TO SANTA CRUZ

WORD OF MOUTH

"To be able to see, up close, the wonders of the ocean, is an amazing experience at the wonderful Monterey Bay Aquarium."
—photo by mellifluous, Fodors.com member

WELCOME TO THE MONTEREY BAY AREA

TOP REASONS TO GO

★ **Marine life:** Monterey Bay is home to the world's third-largest marine sanctuary, home to whales, otters, and other underwater creatures.

★ **Getaway central:** For more than a century, urbanites have come to the Monterey Bay area to unwind, relax, and have fun. It's a great place to browse unique shops and galleries, ride a giant roller coaster, or play a round of golf on a world-class course.

★ **Nature preserves:** More than the sea is protected here—the region boasts nearly 30 state parks, beaches, and preserves, fantastic places for walking, jogging, hiking, and biking.

★ **Wine and dine:** The area's rich agricultural bounty translates to abundant fresh produce, great wines, and fabulous dining. It's no wonder more than 300 culinary events take place here every year.

★ **Small-town vibes:** Even the cities here are friendly, walkable places where you'll feel like a local.

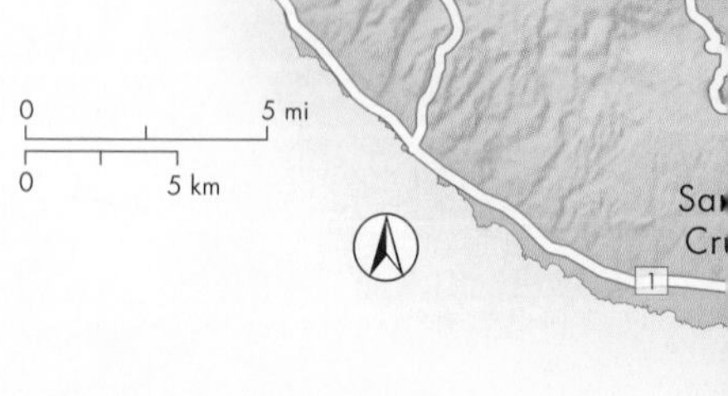

1 Carmel and Pacific Grove. Exclusive Carmel-by-the-Sea and Carmel Valley Village burst with historic charm, fine dining, and unusual boutiques that cater to celebrity residents and well-heeled visitors. Nearby 17-Mile Drive—quite possibly the prettiest stretch of road you'll ever travel—runs between Carmel-by-the-Sea and Victorian-studded Pacific Grove, home to thousands of migrating monarch butterflies between October and February.

2 Monterey. A former Spanish military outpost, Monterey's well-preserved historic district is a hands-on history lesson. Cannery Row, the former center of Monterey's once-thriving sardine industry, has been reborn as a tourist attraction with shops, restaurants, hotels, and the Monterey Bay Aquarium.

3 Around the Bay. Much of California's lettuce, berries, artichokes, and Brussels sprouts come from Salinas and Watsonville. Salinas is also home of the National Steinbeck Center, and Moss Landing and Watsonville encompass pristine wildlife wetlands. Aptos, Capitola, and Soquel are former lumber towns that became popular seaside resorts more than a century ago. Today they're filled with antiques shops, restaurants, and wine-tasting rooms; you'll also find some of the bay's best beaches along the shore here.

4 Santa Cruz. Santa Cruz shows its colors along an old-time beach boardwalk and municipal wharf. A University of California campus imbues the town with arts and culture and a liberal mind-set.

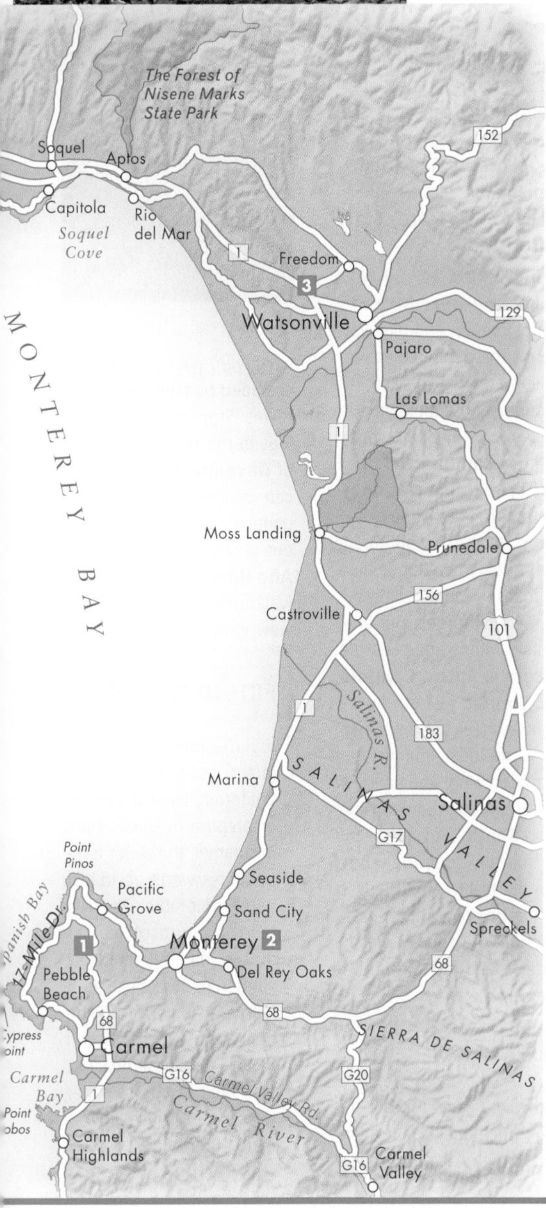

The Forest of Nisene Marks State Park
Soquel
Aptos
Capitola
Rio del Mar
Soquel Cove
Freedom
Watsonville
Pajaro
Las Lomas
MONTEREY BAY
Moss Landing
Prunedale
Castroville
Salinas R.
Marina
SALINAS VALLEY
Salinas
Point Pinos
Pacific Grove
Seaside
Sand City
Spanish Bay
17-Mile Dr.
Monterey
Spreckels
Pebble Beach
Del Rey Oaks
Cypress Point
Carmel
SIERRA DE SALINAS
Carmel Bay
Carmel Valley Rd.
Carmel River
Point Lobos
Carmel Highlands
Carmel Valley
152
1
129
156
101
183
G17
68
G16
G20

GETTING ORIENTED

North of Big Sur the coastline softens into lower bluffs, windswept dunes, pristine estuaries, and long, sandy beaches, bordering one of the world's most amazing marine environments—the Monterey Bay. On the Monterey Peninsula, at the southern end of the bay, are Carmel-by-the-Sea, Pacific Grove, and Monterey; Santa Cruz sits at the northern tip of the crescent. In between, Highway 1 cruises along the coastline, passing windswept beaches piled high with sand dunes. Along the route are wetlands, artichoke and strawberry fields, and workaday towns such as Castroville and Watsonville.

HIGHWAY 1: CARMEL TO SAN FRANCISCO

San Francisco

THE PLAN

Distance: approx. 123 mi

Time: 2-4 days

Good Overnight Options: Carmel, Monterey, Santa Cruz, Half Moon Bay, San Francisco

For more information on the sights and attractions along this portion of Highway 1, please see chapters Montery Bay, San Francisco, and Bay Area.

CARMEL TO MONTEREY (approx. 4 mi)

Between **Carmel** and **Monterey,** the Highway 1 cuts across the base of the Monterey Peninsula. Pony up the toll and take a brief detour to follow famous **17-Mile Drive,** which traverses a surf-pounded landscape of cypress trees, sea lions, gargantuan estates, and the world famous **Pebble Beach Golf Links.** Take your time here as well, and be sure to allow lots of time for pulling off to enjoy the gorgeous views.

Monterey

If you have the time, spend a day checking out the sights in **Monterey,** especially the kelp forests and bat rays of the **Monterey Bay Aquarium** and the adobes and artifacts of **Monterey State Historic Park.**

MONTEREY TO SANTA CRUZ (approx. 42 mi)

From Monterey the highway rounds the gentle curve of Monterey Bay, passing through sand dunes and artichoke fields on its way to **Moss Landing** and the **Elkhorn Slough National Estuarine Marine Preserve.** Kayak or walk through the protected wetlands here, or board a pontoon safari boat—don't forget your binoculars. The historic seaside villages of **Aptos, Capitola,** and **Soquel,** just off the highway near the bay's midpoint, are ideal stopovers for beachcombing, antiquing, and hiking through redwoods. In boho **Santa Cruz,** just 7 mi north, walk along the **wharf,** ride the historic roller coaster on the **boardwalk,** and perch on the cliffs to watch surfers peel through tubes at **Steamer Lane.**

SANTA CRUZ TO SAN FRANCISCO (approx. 77 mi)

Highway 1 hugs the ocean's edge once again as it departs Santa Cruz and runs northward past a string of secluded beaches and small towns. Stop and stretch your legs in the tiny, artsy town of **Davenport,** where you can wander through several galleries and enjoy sumptuous views from the bluffs. At **Año Nuevo State Reserve,** walk down to the dunes to view gargantuan elephant

Davenport cliffs, Devenport

FRIGID WATERS

If you're planning to jump in the ocean in Northern California, wear a wetsuit or prepare to shiver. Even in summer, the water temperatures warm up to just barely tolerable. The fog tends to burn off earlier in the day at relatively sheltered beaches near Monterey Bay's midpoint, near Aptos, Capitola and Santa Cruz. These beaches also tend to attract softer waves than those on the bay's outer edges.

Half Moon Bay

TOP 5 PLACES TO LINGER

- 17 Mile Drive
- Monterey
- Santa Cruz
- Año Nuevo State Reserve
- Half Moon Bay

seals lounging on shore, then break for a meal or snack in **Pescadero** or **Half Moon Bay.**

From Half Moon Bay to **Daly City,** the road includes a number of shoulderless twists and turns that demand slower speeds and nerves of steel. Signs of urban development soon appear: mansions holding fast to Pacific cliffs and then, as the road veers slightly inland to merge with Skyline Boulevard, boxlike houses sprawling across **Daly City** and **South San Francisco.**

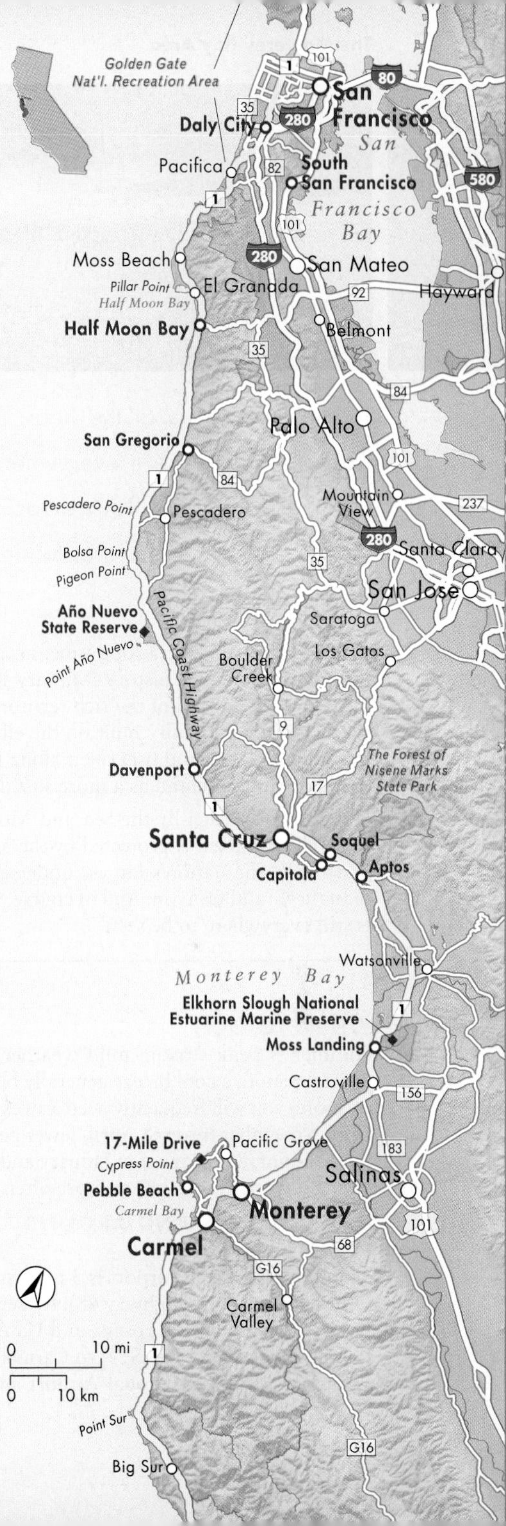

Golden Gate Nat'l. Recreation Area
San Francisco
Daly City
Pacifica
South San Francisco
San Francisco Bay
Moss Beach
San Mateo
Pillar Point
El Granada
Half Moon Bay
Hayward
Half Moon Bay
Belmont
Palo Alto
San Gregorio
Mountain View
Pescadero Point
Pescadero
Santa Clara
Bolsa Point
Pigeon Point
San Jose
Año Nuevo State Reserve
Saratoga
Pacific Coast Highway
Point Año Nuevo
Los Gatos
Boulder Creek
The Forest of Nisene Marks State Park
Davenport
Santa Cruz
Soquel
Capitola
Aptos
Watsonville
Monterey Bay
Elkhorn Slough National Estuarine Marine Preserve
Moss Landing
Castroville
17-Mile Drive
Pacific Grove
Cypress Point
Pebble Beach
Salinas
Carmel Bay
Monterey
Carmel
Carmel Valley
0 10 mi
0 10 km
Point Sur
Big Sur
1 101 80 35 280 82 580 92 84 237 9 17 156 183 68 G16

Updated by Cheryl Crabtree

Natural beauty is at the heart of this region's enormous appeal—you sense it everywhere, whether you're exploring one of Monterey Bay's attractive coast-side towns, relaxing at a luxurious resort, or touring the coast on the lookout for marine life.

It's been this way for a long time: an abiding current of plenty runs through the region's history. Military buffs see it in centuries' worth of battles for control of the rich territory. John Steinbeck saw it in the success of a community built on the elbow grease of farm laborers in the Salinas Valley and fishermen along Cannery Row. Biologists see it in the ocean's potential as a more sustainable source of food.

Downtown Carmel-by-the-Sea and Monterey are walks through history. The bay itself is protected by the Monterey Bay National Marine Sanctuary, the nation's largest undersea canyon—bigger and deeper than the Grand Canyon. And of course, the backdrop of natural beauty is still everywhere to be seen.

PLANNING

WHEN TO GO

Summer is peak season; mild weather brings in big crowds. In this coastal region, a cool breeze generally blows and fog often rolls in from offshore; you will frequently need a sweater or windbreaker. Off-season, from November through April, fewer people visit and the mood is mellower. Rainfall is heaviest in January and February, but autumn through spring days are crystal clear more often than in summer.

GETTING HERE AND AROUND

BY AIR

Monterey Peninsula Airport is 3 mi east of downtown Monterey (take Olmstead Road off Highway 68). It's served by Allegiant Air, American Eagle, United/United Express, and US Airways. Taxi service to downtown runs about $15 to $17; to Carmel the fare is $23 to $32. To and from San Jose International Airport and San Francisco International

Airport, Monterey Airbus starts at $35 and the Early Bird Airport Shuttle runs $75 to $190.

Airport Contacts **Monterey Peninsula Airport** ✉ *200 Fred Kane Dr., Monterey* ☎ *831/648–7000* 🌐 *www.montereyairport.com.*

Taxi Contacts **Central Coast Cab Company** ☎ *831/626–3333.* **Monterey Airbus** ☎ *831/373–7777* 🌐 *www.montereyairbus.com.* **Early Bird Airport Shuttle** ☎ *831/462–3933* 🌐 *www.earlybirdairportshuttle.com.* **Yellow Checker Cabs** ☎ *831/646–1234.*

3

BY BUS

Greyhound serves Santa Cruz and Salinas from San Francisco and San Jose three or four times daily. The trips take about 3 and 4½ hours, respectively. Monterey-Salinas Transit provides frequent service between the peninsula's towns and many major sightseeing spots and shopping areas. Fares are $1, $2, or $3, depending on the line. Commuter lines, e.g., between Monterey and San Jose, cost $10. A day pass costs $6 to $12, depending on how many zones you'll be traveling through. Monterey-Salinas Transit also runs the MST Trolley, which links major attractions on the Monterey waterfront. The free shuttle operates late May through early September, daily from 10 to 7; from July 5 through early September service is extended weekends and holidays from 10 to 8.

Bus Contacts **Greyhound** ☎ *800/231–2222* 🌐 *www.greyhound.com.* **Monterey-Salinas Transit** ☎ *888/678–2871* 🌐 *www.mst.org.*

BY CAR

Highway 1 runs south–north along the coast, linking the towns of Carmel-by-the-Sea, Monterey, and Santa Cruz; some sections have only two lanes. The freeway, U.S. 101, lies to the east, roughly parallel to Highway 1. The two roads are connected by Highway 68 from Pacific Grove to Salinas; Highway 156 from Castroville to Prunedale; Highway 152 from Watsonville to Gilroy; and Highway 17 from Santa Cruz to San Jose. Highway 17 crosses the redwood-filled Santa Cruz Mountains. ■ **TIP→ Traffic near Santa Cruz can crawl to a standstill during commuter hours.**

The drive south from San Francisco to Monterey can be made comfortably in three hours or less. The most scenic way is to follow Highway 1 down the coast past flower, pumpkin, and artichoke fields and small seaside communities. Unless you drive on sunny weekends when locals are heading for the beach, the two-lane coast highway may take no longer than the freeway. A sometimes-faster route is I–280 south from San Francisco to Highway 17, north of San Jose. A third option is to follow U.S. 101 south through San Jose to Prunedale and then take Highway 156 west to Highway 1 south into Monterey.

From Los Angeles the drive to Monterey can be made in five to six hours by heading north on U.S. 101 to Salinas and then west on Highway 68. The spectacular but slow alternative is to take U.S. 101 to San Luis Obispo and then follow the hairpin turns of Highway 1 up the coast. Allow about three extra hours if you take this route.

BY TRAIN

Amtrak's *Coast Starlight* runs between Los Angeles, Oakland, and Seattle. From the train station in Salinas, connecting Amtrak Thruway buses serve Monterey and Carmel-by-the-Sea; from San Jose, connecting buses serve Santa Cruz.

Train Contacts Amtrak ☎ *800/872–7245* 🌐 *www.amtrakcalifornia.com.* **Salinas Amtrak Station** ✉ *30 Railroad Ave., Salinas* ☎ *800/872–7245.*

TOUR OPTIONS

California Parlor Car Tours operates motor-coach tours from San Francisco that include one or two days in Monterey and Carmel. Ag Venture Tours runs wine-tasting, sightseeing, and agricultural tours in the Monterey, Salinas, Carmel Valley, and Santa Cruz areas.

Tour Contacts Ag Venture Tours ☎ *831/761–8463* 🌐 *www.agventuretours.com.* **California Parlor Car Tours** ☎ *415/474–7500, 800/227–4250* 🌐 *www.calpartours.com.*

VISITOR INFORMATION

Contacts Monterey County Convention & Visitors Bureau ☎ *877/666–8373* 🌐 *www.seemonterey.com.* **Monterey County Vintners and Growers Association** ☎ *831/375–9400* 🌐 *www.montereywines.org.* **Pajaro Valley Chamber of Commerce & Agriculture** ✉ *449 Union St., Watsonville* ☎ *831/724–3900* 🌐 *www.pajarovalleychamber.com.* **Salinas Valley Chamber of Commerce** ✉ *119 E. Alisal St., Salinas* ☎ *831/751–7725* 🌐 *www.salinaschamber.com.* **San Lorenzo Valley Chamber of Commerce** ✉ *Box 1510, Felton* ☎ *831/222–2120* 🌐 *www.slvchamber.org.* **Santa Cruz County Conference and Visitors Council** ✉ *303 Water St., Santa Cruz* ☎ *831/425–1234, 800/833–3494* 🌐 *www.santacruz.org.* **Santa Cruz Mountain Winegrowers Association** ✉ *7605-A Old Dominion Ct., Aptos* ☎ *831/685–8463* 🌐 *www.scmwa.com.*

RESTAURANTS

Between San Francisco and Los Angeles, some of the finest dining to be found is around Monterey Bay. The surrounding waters are full of fish, wild game roams the foothills, and the inland valleys are some of the most fertile in the country—local chefs draw on this bounty for their fresh, truly California cuisine. Except at beachside stands and inexpensive eateries, where anything goes, casual but neat dress is the norm. Only a few places require formal attire.

HOTELS

Monterey-area accommodations range from no-frills motels to luxurious hotels. Pacific Grove, amply endowed with ornate Victorian houses, has quietly turned itself into the region's B&B capital; Carmel also has charming inns in residential areas. Truly lavish resorts, with everything from featherbeds to heated floors, cluster in exclusive Pebble Beach and pastoral Carmel Valley.

High season runs April through October. Rates in winter, especially at the larger hotels, may drop by 50% or more, and B&Bs often offer midweek specials in the off-season. However, special events throughout the year can fill lodgings far in advance. Whatever the month, even the simplest of the area's lodgings are expensive, and many properties require a two-night stay on weekends. ⚠ **Many of the fancier accommodations are not suitable for children, so if you're traveling with kids, be sure to ask before you book.**

Bed and Breakfast Inns of Santa Cruz County. Bed and Breakfast Inns of Santa Cruz County, an association of innkeepers, can help you find a bed-and-breakfast. *www.santacruzbnb.com.*

WHAT IT COSTS

	¢	$	$$	$$$	$$$$
Restaurants	under $10	$10–$15	$16–$22	$23–$30	over $30
Hotels	under $90	$90–$120	$121–$175	$176–$250	over $250

Restaurant prices are for a main course at dinner, excluding sales tax of 8.25%–9.5% (depending on location). Hotel prices are for two people in a standard double room in high season, excluding service charges and 10%–10.5% tax.

3

CARMEL AND PACIFIC GROVE

CARMEL-BY-THE-SEA

26 mi north of Big Sur on Hwy. 1.

Although the community has grown quickly through the years and its population quadruples with tourists on weekends and in summer, Carmel-by-the-Sea, commonly referred to as Carmel, retains its identity as a quaint village. Self-consciously charming, the town is populated by many celebrities, major and minor, and has more than its share of quirky ordinances. For instance, women wearing high heels do not have the right to pursue legal action if they trip and fall on the cobblestone streets, and drivers who hit a tree and leave the scene are charged with hit-and-run.

Buildings still have no street numbers (street names are written on discreet white posts) and consequently no mail delivery (if you really want to see the locals, go to the post office). Artists started this community, and their legacy is evident in the numerous galleries. Wandering the side streets off Ocean Avenue, where you can poke into hidden courtyards and stop at cafés for tea and crumpets, is a pleasure.

GETTING HERE AND AROUND

From north or south follow Highway 1 to Carmel. To access Highway 1 from U.S. 101 take Highway 156 West from Prunedale, about 10 mi north of Salinas, or Highway 68 from Salinas. Head west at Ocean Avenue to reach the main village hub. In summer the MST Carmel-by-the-Sea Trolley loops around town to the beach and mission every 30 minutes or so.

ESSENTIALS

Visitor Information **Carmel Chamber of Commerce** *San Carlos, between 5th and 6th 831/624–2522, 800/550–4333 www.carmelcalifornia.org.*

Carmel Walks. For insight into Carmel's colorful history and culture, join a guided two-hour Carmel Walks tour through hidden courtyards, gardens, and pathways around town. Tours ($25) depart from the Pine Inn courtyard on Lincoln near Ocean Avenue Tues.–Fri. at 10 and Sat. at 10 and 2; call to reserve a spot. *Lincoln St. at 6th Ave. 831/642–2700 www.carmelwalks.com.*

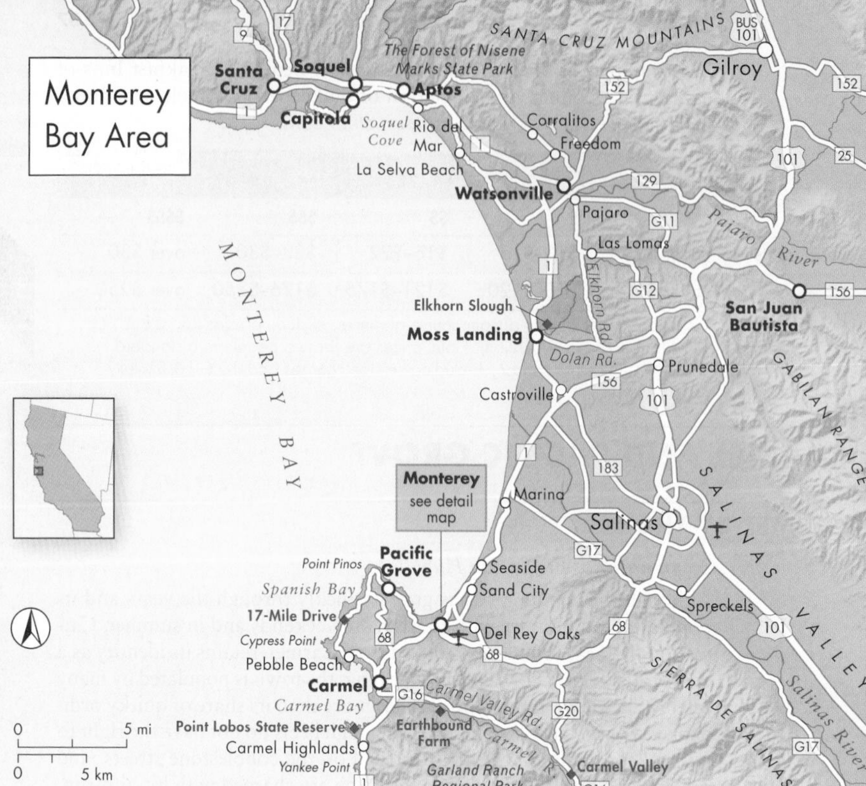

EXPLORING

Ocean Avenue. Downtown Carmel's chief lure is shopping, especially along its main street, Ocean Avenue, between Junipero Avenue and Camino Real; the architecture here is a mishmash of ersatz Tudor, Mediterranean, and other styles.

Carmel Plaza. Carmel Plaza, in the east end of the village proper, holds more than 50 shops and restaurants. ✉ *Ocean and Junipero Aves.* ☎ *831/624–1385* 🌐 *www.carmelplaza.com.*

★ **Carmel Mission.** Long before it became a shopping and browsing destination, Carmel was an important religious center during the establishment of Spanish California. That heritage is preserved in the Mission San Carlos Borroméo del Rio Carmelo, more commonly known as the Carmel Mission. Founded in 1771, it served as headquarters for the mission system in California under Father Junípero Serra. Adjoining the stone church is a tranquil garden planted with California poppies. Museum rooms at the mission include an early kitchen, Serra's spartan sleeping quarters, and the first college library in California. ✉ *3080 Rio Rd., at Lasuen Dr.* ☎ *831/624–3600* 🌐 *www.carmelmission.org* 🎟 *$6.50* ⏲ *Mon.–Sat. 9:30–5, Sun. 10:30–5.*

WORD OF MOUTH

"The beauty of Point Lobos State Reserve was so stunning, I could not believe it. Here you have a mix of tall cliffs, crashing waves, gorgeous wild flowers, abundant wild life (seals, sea otters, deer), and sheltered emerald-green coves with white sandy beaches."
—Birder

Tor House. Scattered throughout the pines in Carmel-by-the-Sea are houses and cottages originally built for the writers, artists, and photographers who discovered the area decades ago. Among the most impressive dwellings is Tor House, a stone cottage built in 1919 by poet Robinson Jeffers on a craggy knoll overlooking the sea. Portraits, books, and unusual art objects fill the low-ceiling rooms. The highlight of the small estate is Hawk Tower, a detached edifice set with stones from the Carmel coastline—as well as one from the Great Wall of China. The docents who lead tours (six people maximum) are well informed about the poet's work and life. Advance reservations for tours via e-mail at *thf@torhouse.org* are recommended. *26304 Ocean View Ave.* *831/624–1813* *www.torhouse.org* *$10* *Tours on hr Fri. and Sat. 10–3* *No children under 12.*

Carmel Beach. Carmel-by-the-Sea's greatest attraction is its rugged coastline, with pine and cypress forests and countless inlets. Carmel Beach, an easy walk from downtown shops, has sparkling white sands and magnificent sunsets. **■TIP→ Dogs are allowed to romp off-leash here.** *End of Ocean Ave.*

Carmel River State Beach. This sugar-white beach, stretching 106 acres along Carmel Bay, is adjacent to a bird sanctuary, where you might spot pelicans, kingfishers, hawks, and sandpipers. *Off Scenic Rd. south of Carmel Beach* *831/624–4909, 831/649–2836* *www.parks.ca.gov* *Free* *Daily 8 am–½ hr after sunset.*

★ **Point Lobos State Reserve.** A 350-acre headland harboring a wealth of marine life, this reserve lies a few miles south of Carmel. The best way to explore here is to walk along one of the many trails. The Cypress Grove Trail leads through a forest of Monterey cypress (one of only two natural groves remaining), which clings to the rocks above an emerald-green cove. Sea Lion Point Trail is a good place to view sea lions. From those and other trails you may also spot otters, harbor seals, and (in winter and spring) migrating whales. An additional 750 acres of the reserve is an undersea marine park open to qualified scuba divers. **■TIP→ Arrive early (or in late afternoon) to avoid crowds; the parking lots fill up.** No pets are allowed. *Hwy. 1* *831/624–4909, 831/624–8413 for scuba-diving reservations* *www.pointlobos.org* *$10 per vehicle* *Daily 8 am–½ hr after sunset.*

WHERE TO EAT

$$$ FRENCH BISTRO ★ **André's Bouchée.** The food here presents an innovative bistro-style take on local ingredients. A Monterey Bay sea scallop reduction adorns pan-seared veal tenderloin; grilled rib-eye steaks are topped with a shallot–Cabernet Sauvignon sauce. With its copper wine bar, the dining room feels more urban than most of Carmel; perhaps that's why this is the "cool" place in town to dine. The stellar wine list sources the selection

at adjoining Andre's Wine Merchant. ✉ *Mission St., between Ocean and 7th Aves.* ☎ *831/626–7880* 🌐 *www.andresbouchee.com* ✍ *Reservations essential* ⏲ *No lunch Mon. and Tues.*

$$$ CONTINENTAL ✕ **Anton and Michel.** Carefully prepared European cuisine is the draw at this airy restaurant. The rack of lamb is carved at the table, the grilled Halloumi cheese and tomatoes are meticulously stacked and served with basil and kalamata olive tapenade, and the desserts are set aflame before your eyes. In summer, you (and your dog!) can have lunch served in the courtyard; inside, the dining room looks onto a lighted fountain. ✉ *Mission St. and 7th Ave.* ☎ *831/624–2406* 🌐 *www.antonandmichel.com* ✍ *Reservations essential.*

$$$$ ★ ✕ **Casanova.** Built in a former home, this cozy restaurant inspires European-style celebration and romance—chairs are painted in all colors, accordions hang from the walls, and tiny party lights dance along the low ceilings. All entrées include antipasti and your choice of appetizers, which all but insist that you sit back and enjoy a long meal. The food consists of delectable seasonal dishes from southern France and northern Italy. Private dining and a special menu are offered at Van Gogh's Table, a special table imported from France's Auberge Ravoux, the artist's final residence. ✉ *5th Ave., between San Carlos and Mission Sts.* ☎ *831/625–0501* 🌐 *www.casanovarestaurant.com* ✍ *Reservations essential.*

$ AMERICAN ✕ **The Cottage Restaurant.** For the best breakfast in Carmel, look no further: The menu here offers six different preparations of eggs Benedict, and all kinds of sweet and savory crepes. This family-friendly spot serves sandwiches, pizzas, and homemade soups at lunch and simple entreés at dinner, but the best meals appear on the breakfast menu (good thing it's served all day). ✉ *Lincoln St., between Ocean and 7th Aves.* ☎ *831/625–6260* 🌐 *www.cottagerestaurant.com* ⏲ *No dinner Sun.–Wed.*

$$$ SEAFOOD ✕ **Flying Fish Grill.** Simple in appearance yet bold with its flavors, this Japanese–California seafood restaurant is one of Carmel's most inventive eateries. Among the best entrées is the almond-crusted sea bass served with Chinese cabbage and rock shrimp stir-fry. The warm, wood-lined dining room is broken up into very private booths. For the entrance, go down the steps near the gates to Carmel Plaza. ✉ *Mission St., between Ocean and 7th Aves.* ☎ *831/625–1962* ⏲ *No lunch.*

$ AMERICAN ✕ **Jack London's.** If anyone's awake after dinner in Carmel, he's at Jack London's. This publike local hangout is the only Carmel restaurant to serve food until midnight (Sunday through Thursday until 11). The menu includes everything from nachos to steaks. ✉ *Su Vecino Court on Dolores St., between 5th and 6th Aves.* ☎ *831/624–2336* 🌐 *jacklondons.com.*

$ AMERICAN ✕ **Katy's Place.** Locals flock to Katy's cozy, country-style eatery to fill up on hearty eggs Benedict dishes. (There are 16 types to choose from, each made with three fresh eggs.) The huge breakfast menu also includes omelets, pancakes, and eight types of Belgian waffles. An assortment of salads, sandwiches, and burgers is available at lunch—try the grilled calamari burger with melted Monterey Jack cheese. ✉ *Mission St., between 5th and 6th Aves.* ☎ *831/624–0199* 🌐 *www.katysplacecarmel.com* ▭ *No credit cards* ⏲ *No dinner.*

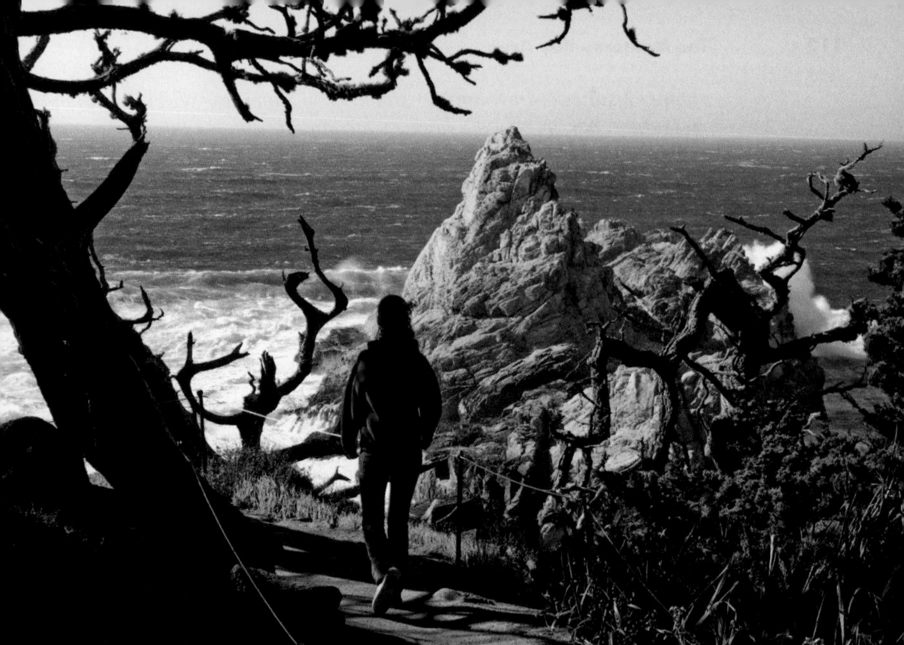

Point Lobos Reserve State Park is home to one of the only two natural stands of Monterey Cypress in the world.

$$$ FRENCH ✕ **L'Escargot.** Chef-owner Kericos Loutas personally sees to each plate of food served at this romantic and mercifully unpretentious French restaurant (which also has a full bar). Take his recommendation and order the duck confit in puff pastry or the bone-in steak in truffle butter; or, if you can't decide, choose the three-course prix-fixe dinner. Service is warm and attentive. ✉ *Mission St., between 4th and 5th Aves.* ☎ *831/620–1942* 🌐 *www.escargot-carmel.com* ✍ *Reservations essential* ⏲ *No lunch.*

$ AMERICAN ✕ **Tuck Box.** This bright little restaurant is in a cottage right out of a fairy tale, complete with a stone fireplace that's lighted on rainy days. Handmade scones are the house specialty, and are good for breakfast or afternoon tea. ✉ *Dolores St., between Ocean and 7th Aves.* ☎ *831/624–6365* 🌐 *www.tuckbox.com* ✍ *Reservations not accepted* ▭ *No credit cards* ⏲ *No dinner.*

WHERE TO STAY

For expanded reviews, visit Fodors.com.

$$$$ 🏨 **Cypress Inn.** The decorating style here is luxurious but refreshingly simple. **Pros:** luxury without snobbery; popular lounge; traditional British-style afternoon tea. **Cons:** not for the pet-phobic. ✉ *Lincoln St. and 7th Ave., Box Y* ☎ *831/624–3871, 800/443–7443* 🌐 *www.cypress-inn.com* 🛏 *39 rooms, 5 suites* ♨ *In-room: a/c, Wi-Fi. In-hotel: restaurant, bar, some pets allowed* 🍽 *Breakfast.*

$$$$ ★ 🏨 **Highlands Inn, A Hyatt Hotel.** High on a hill overlooking the Pacific, this place has superb views. **Pros:** killer views; romantic getaway; great food. **Cons:** thin walls; must drive to Carmel. ✉ *120 Highlands Dr.* ☎ *831/620–1234, 800/233–1234* 🌐 *highlandsinn.hyatt.com* 🛏 *46*

rooms, 2 suites ♿ *In-room: no a/c, kitchen, Internet, Wi-Fi. In-hotel: restaurant, bar, pool, gym, laundry facilities, business center.*

$$$$ Fodor's Choice ★ **L'Auberge Carmel.** Stepping through the doors of this elegant inn is like being transported to a little European village. **Pros:** in town but off the main drag; four blocks from the beach; full-service luxury. **Cons:** touristy area; not a good choice for families. ✉ *Monte Verde, at 7th Ave.* ☎ *831/624–8578* 🌐 *www.laubergecarmel.com* *20 rooms* ♿ *In-room: a/c, Wi-Fi. In-hotel: restaurant, bar* 🍴 *Breakfast.*

$$ **Mission Ranch.** The property at Mission Ranch is gorgeous and includes a sprawling sheep pasture, bird-filled wetlands, and a sweeping view of the ocean. **Pros:** farm setting; pastoral views; great for tennis buffs. **Cons:** busy parking lot; must drive to the heart of town. ✉ *26270 Dolores St.* ☎ *831/624–6436, 800/538–8221, 831/625-9040 restaurant* 🌐 *www.missionranchcarmel.com* *31 rooms* ♿ *In-room: no a/c. In-hotel: restaurant, bar, tennis court, gym, business center* 🍴 *Breakfast.*

$$ **Sea View Inn.** In a residential area a few hundred feet from the beach, this restored 1905 home has a double parlor with two fireplaces, Oriental rugs, canopy beds, and a spacious front porch. **Pros:** quiet; private; close to the beach. **Cons:** small building; uphill trek to the heart of town. ✉ *Camino Real, between 11th and 12th Aves.* ☎ *831/624–8778* 🌐 *www.seaviewinncarmel.com* *8 rooms, 6 with private bath* ♿ *In-room: no a/c, no TV, Wi-Fi* 🍴 *Breakfast.*

$$$$ **Tickle Pink Inn.** Atop a towering cliff, this inn has views of the Big Sur coastline, which you can contemplate from your private balcony. **Pros:** close to great hiking; intimate; dramatic views. **Cons:** close to a big hotel; lots of traffic during the day. ✉ *155 Highland Dr.* ☎ *831/624–1244, 800/635–4774* 🌐 *www.ticklepink.com* *23 rooms, 10 suites, 1 cottage* ♿ *In-room: no a/c, Wi-Fi. In-hotel: business center* 🍴 *Breakfast.*

$$$$ ★ **Tradewinds Carmel.** Its sleek decor inspired by the South Seas, this converted motel encircles a courtyard with waterfalls, a meditation garden, and a fire pit. **Pros:** serene; within walking distance of restaurants; friendly service. **Cons:** no pool; long walk to the beach. ✉ *Mission St., at 3rd Ave.* ☎ *831/624–2776* 🌐 *www.tradewindscarmel.com* *26 rooms, 2 suites* ♿ *In-room: no a/c, safe, Wi-Fi. In-hotel: spa, some pets allowed* 🍴 *Breakfast.*

SHOPPING

ART GALLERIES

Carmel Art Association. Carmel Art Association exhibits the original paintings and sculptures of local artists. ✉ *Dolores St., between 5th and 6th Aves.* ☎ *831/624–6176* 🌐 *www.carmelart.org.*

Galerie Plein Aire. Galerie Plein Aire showcases oil paintings by a group of local artists. ✉ *Dolores St., between 5th and 6th Aves.* ☎ *831/625–5686* 🌐 *www.galeriepleinaire.com.*

Weston Gallery. Run by the family of the late Edward Weston, Weston Gallery is hands down the best photography gallery around, with contemporary color photography complemented by classic black-and-whites. ✉ *6th Ave., between Dolores and Lincoln Sts.* ☎ *831/624–4453* 🌐 *www.westongallery.com.*

SPECIALTY SHOPS

Bittner. Bittner has a fine selection of collectible and vintage pens from around the world. ✉ *Ocean Ave., between Mission and San Carlos Sts.* ☎ *831/626–8828, 888/248–8637 toll free* 🌐 *www.bittner.com.*

Intima. Intima is the place to find European lingerie that ranges from lacy to racy. ✉ *Mission St., between Ocean and 7th Aves.* ☎ *831/625–0599.*

Jan de Luz. Jan de Luz monograms and embroiders fine linens (including bathrobes) while you wait. ✉ *Dolores St., between Ocean and 7th Aves.* ☎ *831/622–7621* 🌐 *www.jandeluz.com.*

Madrigal. Madrigal carries sportswear, sweaters, and accessories for women. ✉ *Carmel Plaza and Mission St.* ☎ *831/624–3477.*

3

CARMEL VALLEY

10 mi east of Carmel, Hwy. 1 to Carmel Valley Rd.

Carmel Valley Road, which heads inland from Highway 1 south of Carmel-by-the-Sea, is the main thoroughfare through this valley, a secluded enclave of horse ranchers and other well-heeled residents who prefer the area's sunny climate to the fog and wind on the coast. Once thick with dairy farms, the valley has recently proved itself as a venerable wine appellation. Tiny Carmel Valley Village, about 13 mi southeast of Carmel-by-the-Sea via Carmel Valley Road, has several crafts shops and art galleries, as well as tasting rooms for numerous local wineries.

GETTING HERE AND AROUND

From U.S. 101 north or south, exit at Highway 68 and head west toward the coast. Scenic, two-lane Laureles Grade winds over the mountains to Carmel Valley Road, just a few miles north of Carmel Valley Village. You can also continue on Highway 68 to Monterey, then head south on Highway 1 to Carmel and turn east on Carmel Valley Road.

EXPLORING

Bernardus Tasting Room. At Bernardus Tasting Room, you can sample many of the wines—including older vintages and reserves—from the nearby Bernardus Winery and Vineyard. ✉ *5 W. Carmel Valley Rd.* ☎ *831/298–8021, 800/223–2533* 🌐 *www.bernardus.com* ⏲ *Daily 11–5.*

Earthbound Farm. Pick up fresh veggies, ready-to-eat meals, gourmet groceries, flowers, and gifts at 32-acre Earthbound Farm, the world's largest grower of organic produce. You can also take a romp in the kid's garden, cut your own herbs, and stroll through the chamomile aromatherapy labyrinth. On Saturday from April through December the farm offers special events, from bug walks to garlic-braiding workshops. ✉ *7250 Carmel Valley Rd.* ☎ *831/625–6219* 🌐 *www.ebfarm.com* 🎫 *Free* ⏲ *Mon.–Sat. 8–6:30, Sun. 9–6.*

Garland Ranch Regional Park. Garland Ranch Regional Park has hiking trails across nearly 4,500 acres of property that includes meadows, forested hillsides, and creeks. ✉ *Carmel Valley Rd., 9 mi east of Carmel-by-the-Sea* ☎ *831/659–4488.*

Château Julien. The extensive Château Julien winery, recognized internationally for its Chardonnays and Merlots, gives weekday tours at 10:30 and 2:30 and weekends at 12:30 and 2:30, all by appointment. The tasting room is open daily. ✉ *8940 Carmel Valley Rd.* ☎ *831/624–2600* 🌐 *www.chateaujulien.com* ⏱ *Weekdays 8–5, weekends 11–5.*

WINE TOURING WITH THE MST

Why risk driving while wine tasting when you can hop aboard the Carmel Valley Grapevine Express? This Monterey-Salinas Transit bus travels between downtown Monterey and Carmel Valley Village, with stops near wineries, restaurants, and shopping centers. Buses depart daily every hour from 11 to 6. At $6 for a ride-all-day pass, it's an incredible bargain. For more information, call ☎ *888/678–2871* or visit 🌐 *www.mst.org.*

WHERE TO EAT

$$ STEAKHOUSE **Café Rustica.** Italian-inspired country cooking is the focus at this lively roadhouse. Specialties include roasted meats, pastas, and thin-crust pizzas from the wood-fired oven. Because of the tile floors, it can get quite noisy inside; opt for a table outside if you want a quieter meal. ✉ *10 Delfino Pl.* ☎ *831/659–4444* 🌐 *www.caferusticacarmel.com* *Reservations essential* ⏱ *Closed Mon.*

$ AMERICAN **Wagon Wheel Coffee Shop.** This local hangout decorated with wagon wheels, cowboy hats, and lassos serves up terrific hearty breakfasts, including oatmeal and banana pancakes, eggs Benedict, and biscuits and gravy. The lunch menu includes a dozen different burgers and other sandwiches. ✉ *Valley Hill Center, Carmel Valley Rd., next to Quail Lodge* ☎ *831/624–8878* *No credit cards* ⏱ *No dinner.*

$$$ AMERICAN **Will's Fargo.** On the main street of Carmel Valley Village since the 1920s, this restaurant calls itself a "dressed-up saloon." Steer horns and gilt-frame paintings adorn the walls of the Victorian-style dining room; you can also eat on the patios. The menu is mainly seafood and steaks, including a 20-ounce porterhouse. ✉ *16 E. Carmel Valley Rd.* ☎ *831/659–2774* 🌐 *www.bernardus.com* ⏱ *No lunch. Closed Tues. and Wed.*

WHERE TO STAY

For expanded hotel reviews, visit Fodors.com.

$$$$ Fodor's Choice ★ **Bernardus Lodge.** Even before you check in at this luxury spa resort, the valet hands you a glass of Sauvignon Blanc. **Pros:** exceptional personal service; outstanding food and wine. **Cons:** some guests can seem snooty; pricey. ✉ *415 Carmel Valley Rd.* ☎ *831/658–3400, 888/648–9463* 🌐 *www.bernardus.com* *56 rooms, 1 suite* *In-room: a/c, Internet, Wi-Fi. In-hotel: restaurant, bar, pool, tennis court, gym, spa, business center.*

$$$$ **Carmel Valley Ranch Resort & Spa.** Hotel scion John Pritzker bought this 500-acre all-suites resort in 2009 and committed more than $30 million to transform the property into an upscale experiential getaway nonpareil. **Pros:** stunning natural setting; tons of activities; state-of-the-art amenities. **Cons:** must drive several miles to shops and nightlife; pricey. ✉ *1 Old Ranch Rd.* ☎ *831/626–2510* ☎ *855/687–7262* 🌐 *www.carmelvalleyranch.com* *139 suites* *In-room: a/c, Wi-Fi. In-hotel: restaurant, bar, golf course, pool, tennis court, gym, spa, children's programs, some pets allowed.*

$$$$ Fodor's Choice ★ **Stonepine Estate Resort.** Set on 330 pastoral acres, this former estate of the Crocker banking family has been converted to a luxurious inn. **Pros:** supremely exclusive. **Cons:** difficult to get a reservation; far from the coast. ✉ *150 E. Carmel Valley Rd.* ☎ *831/659–2245* 🌐 *www.stonepineestate.com* *3 rooms, 9 suites, 3 cottages* *In-room: no a/c, safe, kitchen, Wi-Fi. In-hotel: restaurant, golf course, pool, tennis court, gym, some pets allowed.*

GOLF

Rancho Cañada Golf Club. Rancho Cañada Golf Club is a public course with 36 holes, some of them overlooking the Carmel River. Fees range from $40 to $70, plus $19 per rider for cart rental, depending on course and tee time. ✉ *4860 Carmel Valley Rd., 1 mi east of Hwy. 1* ☎ *831/624–0111.*

3

17-MILE DRIVE

Fodor's Choice ★ *Off North San Antonio Rd. in Carmel-by-the-Sea or off Sunset Dr. in Pacific Grove.*

Primordial nature resides in quiet harmony with palatial late-20th-century estates along 17-Mile Drive, which winds through an 8,400-acre microcosm of the Monterey coastal landscape. Dotting the drive are rare Monterey cypress, trees so gnarled and twisted that Robert Louis Stevenson described them as "ghosts fleeing before the wind." Some sightseers balk at the $9.50-per-car fee collected at the gates—this is one of only two private toll roads west of the Mississippi—but most find the drive well worth the price. An alternative is to grab a bike. **■ TIP→ Cyclists tour for free. Visitors who dine at a Pebble Beach restaurant receive a fee refund if they show a receipt at the exit gate.**

GETTING HERE AND AROUND

If you drive south from Monterey on Highway 1, exit at 17-Mile-Drive/Sunset Drive in Pacific Grove to find the northern entrance gate. Coming from Carmel, exit at Ocean Avenue and follow the road almost to the beach; turn right on N. San Antonio Road to the Carmel Gate. You can also enter through the Highway 1 Gate at Scenic Drive/Sunridge Road. MST buses provide regular service in and around Pebble Beach.

EXPLORING

Pebble Beach Golf Links. You can take in views of the impeccable greens at Pebble Beach Golf Links over a drink or lunch at the Lodge at Pebble Beach. The ocean plays a major role in the 18th hole of the famed links. Each February the course is the main site of the AT&T Pebble Beach Pro-Am (formerly the Bing Crosby Pro-Am), where show business celebrities and golf pros team up for one of the nation's most glamorous tournaments. ✉ *17-Mile Dr., near Lodge at Pebble Beach* ☎ *800/654–9300* 🌐 *www.pebblebeach.com.*

Crocker Marble Palace. Many of the stately homes along 17-Mile Drive reflect the classic Monterey or Spanish Mission style typical of the region. A standout is the Crocker Marble Palace, about a mile south of the Lone Cypress (⇨ *below*). It's a private waterfront estate inspired by a Byzantine castle, easily identifiable by its dozens of marble arches.

Lone Cypress. The most-photographed tree along 17-Mile Drive is the weather-sculpted Lone Cypress, which grows out of a precipitous outcropping above the waves about 1½ mi up the road from Pebble Beach Golf Links. You can stop for a view of the Lone Cypress at a parking area, but you can't walk out to the tree.

Seal Rock. Sea creatures and birds—as well as some very friendly ground squirrels—make use of Seal Rock, the largest of a group of islands about 2 mi north of Lone Cypress.

Bird Rock. Bird Rock, the largest of several islands at the southern end of the Monterey Peninsula Country Club's golf course, teems with harbor seals, sea lions, cormorants, and pelicans.

WHERE TO STAY

For expanded hotel reviews, visit Fodors.com.

$$$$ ★ **Casa Palmero.** This exclusive spa resort evokes a stately Mediterranean villa. **Pros:** ultimate in pampering; more private than sister resorts; right on the golf course. **Cons:** pricey; may be *too* posh for some. ✉ *1518 Cypress Dr.* ☎ *831/622–6650, 800/654–9300* 🌐 *www.pebblebeach.com* *21 rooms, 3 suites* *In-room: a/c, Wi-Fi. In-hotel: bar, golf course, pool, spa.*

$$$$ **Inn at Spanish Bay.** This resort sprawls across a breathtaking stretch of shoreline, and has lush, 600-square-foot rooms. **Pros:** attentive service; tons of amenities; spectacular views. **Cons:** huge hotel; four miles from other Pebble Beach Resort facilities. ✉ *2700 17-Mile Dr.* ☎ *831/647–7500, 800/654–9300* 🌐 *www.pebblebeach.com* *252 rooms, 17 suites* *In-room: no a/c, Internet, Wi-Fi. In-hotel: restaurant, bar, golf course, pool, tennis court, gym, beach, business center.*

$$$$ ★ **Lodge at Pebble Beach.** All rooms have fireplaces and many have wonderful ocean views at this circa 1919 resort. **Pros:** world-class golf; borders the ocean and fairways; fabulous facilities. **Cons:** some rooms are on the small side; very pricey. ✉ *1700 17-Mile Dr.* ☎ *831/624–3811, 800/654–9300* 🌐 *www.pebblebeach.com* *142 rooms, 19 suites* *In-room: no a/c, Internet, Wi-Fi. In-hotel: restaurant, bar, golf course, pool, tennis court, gym, spa, beach, business center, some pets allowed.*

GOLF

Links at Spanish Bay. The Links at Spanish Bay, which hugs a choice stretch of shoreline, is designed in the rugged manner of a traditional Scottish course, with sand dunes and coastal marshes interspersed among the greens. The greens fee is $260, plus $35 per person for cart rental (cart is included for resort guests); nonguests can reserve tee times up to two months in advance. ✉ *17-Mile Dr., north end* ☎ *831/624–3811, 831/624–6611, 800/654–9300.*

Pebble Beach Golf Links. Pebble Beach Golf Links attracts golfers from around the world, despite a greens fee of $495, plus $35 per person for an optional cart (complimentary cart for guests of the Pebble Beach and Spanish Bay resorts). Tee times are available to guests who book a minimum two-night stay. Nonguests can reserve a tee time only one day in advance on a space-available basis (up to a year for groups); resort guests can reserve up to 18 months in advance. ✉ *17-Mile Dr., near Lodge at Pebble Beach* ☎ *831/624–3811, 831/624–6611, 800/654–9300.*

DID YOU KNOW?

The Lone Cypress has stood on this rock for more than 250 years. The tree is the official symbol of Pebble Beach.

Peter Hay. Peter Hay, a 9-hole, par-3 course, charges $30 per person, no reservations necessary. ✉ *17-Mile Dr.* ☎ *831/622–8723.*

Poppy Hills. Poppy Hills, a splendid 18-hole course designed in 1986 by Robert Trent Jones Jr., has a greens fee of $200; an optional cart costs $36. Individuals may reserve up to one month in advance, groups up to a year. ✉ *3200 Lopez Rd., at 17-Mile Dr.* ☎ *831/625–2035* 🌐 *www.poppyhillsgolf.com.*

Spyglass Hill. Spyglass Hill is among the most challenging Pebble Beach courses. With the first five holes bordering on the Pacific and the other 13 reaching deep into the Del Monte Forest, the views offer some consolation. The greens fee is $360, and an optional cart costs $35 (the cart is complimentary for resort guests). Reservations are essential and may be made up to one month in advance (18 months for guests). ✉ *Stevenson Dr. and Spyglass Hill Rd.* ☎ *831/624–3811, 831/624–6611, 800/654–9300.*

PACIFIC GROVE

3 mi north of Carmel-by-the-Sea on Hwy. 68.

This picturesque town, which began as a summer retreat for church groups more than a century ago, recalls its prim and proper Victorian heritage in its host of tiny board-and-batten cottages and stately mansions. However, long before the church groups flocked here the area received thousands of annual pilgrims—in the form of bright orange-and-black monarch butterflies. They still come, migrating south from Canada and the Pacific Northwest to take residence in pine and eucalyptus groves from October through March. In Butterfly Town USA, as Pacific Grove is known, the sight of a mass of butterflies hanging from the branches like a long, fluttering veil is unforgettable.

A prime way to enjoy Pacific Grove is to walk or bicycle the 3 mi of city-owned shoreline along Ocean View Boulevard, a cliff-top area landscaped with native plants and dotted with benches meant for sitting and gazing at the sea. You can spot many types of birds here, including colonies of web-foot cormorants crowding the massive rocks rising out of the surf.

GETTING HERE AND AROUND

Reach Pacific Grove via Highway 68 off Highway 1, just south of Monterey. From Cannery Row in Monterey, head north until the road merges with Ocean Boulevard and follow it along the coast. MST buses travel within Pacific Grove and surrounding towns.

EXPLORING

Monarch Grove Sanctuary. The Monarch Grove Sanctuary is a fairly reliable spot for viewing the butterflies between October and February. ✉ *1073 Lighthouse Ave., at Ridge Rd.* 🌐 *www.pgmuseum.org.*

Pacific Grove Museum of Natural History. Contact the Pacific Grove Museum of Natural History for the latest information about the butterfly population. If you're in Pacific Grove when the monarch butterflies aren't, you can view the well-crafted butterfly tree exhibit at the museum. ✉ *165 Forest Ave.* ☎ *831/648–5716* 🌐 *www.pgmuseum.org* *$3 suggested donation* ⏲ *Tues.–Sun. 10–5.*

Pryor House. Among the Victorians of note is the Pryor House, a massive, shingled, private residence with a leaded- and beveled-glass doorway. ✉ *429 Ocean View Blvd.*.

Green Gables. Green Gables, a romantic Swiss Gothic–style mansion with peaked gables and stained-glass windows, is a B&B. ✉ *5th St. and Ocean View Blvd.* ☎ *800/722–1774* 🌐 *www.greengablesinnpg.com.*

Lovers Point Park. The view of the coast is gorgeous from Lovers Point Park, on Ocean View Boulevard midway along the waterfront. The park's sheltered beach has a children's pool and picnic area, and the main lawn has a sandy volleyball court and snack bar. ☎ *831/648–5730.*

Point Pinos Lighthouse. At the 1855-vintage Point Pinos Lighthouse, the oldest continuously operating lighthouse on the West Coast, you can learn about the lighting and foghorn operations and wander through a small museum containing U.S. Coast Guard memorabilia. ✉ *Lighthouse Ave., off Asilomar Blvd.* ☎ *831/648–3176* 🌐 *www.pgmuseum.org* *$2* ⏲ *Thurs.–Mon. 1–4.*

Asilomar State Beach. Asilomar State Beach, a beautiful coastal area, is on Sunset Drive between Point Pinos and the Del Monte Forest in Pacific Grove. The 100 acres of dunes, tidal pools, and pocket-size beaches form one of the region's richest areas for marine life—including surfers, who migrate here most winter mornings. ☎ *831/646–6440* 🌐 *www.parks.ca.gov.*

WHERE TO EAT

$$$ MEDITERRANEAN ✕ **Fandango.** The menu here is mostly Mediterranean and southern French, with such dishes as calves' liver and onions and paella served in a skillet. The decor follows suit: stone walls and country furniture give the restaurant the earthy feel of a European farmhouse. This is where locals come when they want to have a big dinner with friends, drink wine, have fun, and generally feel at home. ✉ *223 17th St.* ☎ *831/372–3456* 🌐 *www.fandangorestaurant.com.*

$$ SEAFOOD ✕ **Fishwife.** Fresh fish with a Latin accent makes this a favorite of locals for lunch or a casual dinner. Standards are the sea garden salads topped with your choice of fish and the fried seafood plates with fresh veggies. Large appetites appreciate the fisherman's bowls, which feature fresh fish served with rice, black beans, spicy cabbage, salsa, vegetables, and crispy tortilla strips. ✉ *1996½ Sunset Dr., at Asilomar Blvd.* ☎ *831/375–7107* 🌐 *www.fishwife.com.*

$$ ITALIAN ✕ **Joe Rombi's.** Pastas, fish, steaks, and chops are the specialties at this modern trattoria, which is the best in town for Italian food. The look is spare and clean, with colorful antique wine posters decorating the white walls. Next door, Joe Rombi's La Piccola Casa serves lunch and early dinner Wednesday through Sunday. ✉ *208 17th St.* ☎ *831/373–2416* 🌐 *www.joerombi.com* ⏲ *Closed Mon. and Tues. No lunch.*

$$$ NEW AMERICAN ★ ✕ **Passionfish.** South American artwork and artifacts decorate the room, and Latin and Asian flavors infuse the dishes at Passionfish. Chef Ted Walter—lauded for his commitment to using eco-friendly, sustainable ingredients—shops at local farmers' markets several times a week to find the best produce, fish, and meat available, then pairs it with creative sauces. The ever-changing menu might include crispy squid with spicy

orange-cilantro vinaigrette. ✉ *701 Lighthouse Ave.* ☎ *831/655–3311* 🌐 *www.passionfish.net* ⏲ *No lunch.*

$ MEXICAN ✕ **Peppers Mexicali Cafe.** A local favorite, this cheerful white-walled storefront serves traditional dishes from Mexico and Latin America, with an emphasis on fresh seafood. Excellent red and green salsas are made throughout the day, and there's a large selection of beers, along with fresh lime margaritas. ✉ *170 Forest Ave.* ☎ *831/373–6892* 🌐 *www.peppersmexicalicafe.com* ⏲ *Closed Tues. No lunch Sun.*

$$ AMERICAN ✕ **Red House Café.** When it's nice out, sun pours through the big windows of this cozy restaurant and across tables on the porch; when fog rolls in, the fireplace is lit. The American menu changes with the seasons, but typically includes grilled lamb fillets atop mashed potatoes for dinner and a huge Dungeness crab cake over salad for lunch. Breakfast on weekends is a local favorite. ✉ *662 Lighthouse Ave.* ☎ *831/643–1060* 🌐 *www.redhousecafe.com* ⏲ *Closed Mon.*

$$ AMERICAN ✕ **Taste Café and Bistro.** A favorite of locals, Taste serves hearty European-inspired food in a casual, airy room with high ceilings and an open kitchen. Meats, such as grilled marinated rabbit, roasted half chicken, and filet mignon, are the focus. ✉ *1199 Forest Ave.* ☎ *831/655–0324* 🌐 *www.tastecafebistro.com* ⏲ *Closed Mon.*

WHERE TO STAY

For expanded reviews, go to Fodors.com.

$$$ ★ **Green Gables Inn.** Stained-glass windows and ornate interior details compete with spectacular ocean views at this Queen Anne–style mansion, built by a businessman for his mistress in 1888. **Pros:** exceptional views; impeccable attention to historic detail. **Cons:** some rooms are small; thin walls. ✉ *301 Ocean View Blvd.* ☎ *831/375–2095, 800/722–1774* 🌐 *www.greengablesinnpg.com* *10 rooms, 3 with bath; 1 suite* *In-room: no a/c, Wi-Fi. In-hotel: business center* *Breakfast.*

$$ **The Inn at 213 Seventeen Mile Drive.** Set in a residential area just past town, this carefully restored 1920s Craftsman-style home and cottage are surrounded by gardens and redwood, cypress, and eucalyptus trees. **Pros:** killer gourmet breakfast; historic charm; verdant gardens. **Cons:** far from restaurants and shops; few extra amenities. ✉ *213 17-Mile Dr., at Lighthouse Dr.* ☎ *831/642–9514, 800/526–5666* 🌐 *www.innat17.com* *14 rooms* *In-room: no a/c, Wi-Fi. In-hotel: some pets allowed* *Breakfast.*

$$ **Lighthouse Lodge and Resort.** Near the tip of the peninsula, this complex straddles Lighthouse Avenue—the lodge is on one side, the all-suites Lighthouse Resort facility on the other. **Pros:** near lighthouse and 17-Mile Drive; friendly reception; many room options. **Cons:** next to a cemetery; lodge rooms are basic. ✉ *1150 and 1249 Lighthouse Ave.* ☎ *831/655–2111, 800/858–1249* 🌐 *www.lhls.com* *64 rooms, 31 suites* *In-room: no a/c, Wi-Fi. In-hotel: pool, spa, some pets allowed* *Breakfast.*

$$$ **Martine Inn.** The glassed-in parlor and many guest rooms at this 1899 Mediterranean-style villa have stunning ocean views. **Pros:** romantic; fancy breakfast; ocean views. **Cons:** not child-friendly; sits on a busy thoroughfare. ✉ *255 Ocean View Blvd.* ☎ *831/373–3388, 800/852–5588* 🌐 *www.martineinn.com* *24 rooms* *In-room: no a/c, Internet, Wi-Fi. In-hotel: business center* *Breakfast.*

MONTEREY

2 mi southeast of Pacific Grove via Lighthouse Ave.; 2 mi north of Carmel-by-the-Sea via Hwy. 1.

Early in the 20th century Carmel Martin, the first mayor of the city of Monterey, saw a bright future for his town: "Monterey Bay is the one place where people can live without being disturbed by manufacturing and big factories. I am certain that the day is coming when this will be the most desirable place in the whole state of California." It seems that Mayor Martin was not far off the mark.

3

GETTING HERE AND AROUND

From San Jose or San Francisco, take U.S. 101 south to Highway 156 West at Prunedale. Head west about 8 mi to Highway 1 and follow it about 15 mi south. From San Luis Obispo, take U.S. 101 north to Salinas and drive west on Highway 68 about 20 mi to reach Monterey. In summer the MST Monterey Trolley travels from downtown Monterey along Cannery Row to the Aquarium and back.

ESSENTIALS

Visitor Information Monterey County Convention & Visitors Bureau ☎ *877/666–8373* 🌐 *www.seemonterey.com.*

EXPLORING

A Taste of Monterey. Without driving the back roads, you can taste the wines of more than 90 area vintners while taking in fantastic bay views. Purchase a few bottles and pick up a map and guide to the county's wineries and vineyards. ✉ *700 Cannery Row, Suite KK* ☎ *831/646–5446, 888/646–5446* 🌐 *www.tastemonterey.com* 🎟 *Wine tastings $10–$20* ⏲ *Daily 11–6.*

California's First Theatre. This adobe began its life in 1846 as a saloon and lodging house for sailors. Four years later stage curtains were fashioned from army blankets, and some U.S. officers staged plays to the light of whale oil lamps. As of this writing, the building is not open but you can stroll in the garden. ✉ *Monterey State Historic Park, Scott and Pacific Sts.* ☎ *831/649–7118* 🌐 *www.parks.ca.gov/mshp* 🎟 *Free* ⏲ *Call for hrs.*

Cannery Row. When John Steinbeck published the novel *Cannery Row* in 1945, he immortalized a place of rough-edged working people. The waterfront street, edging a mile of gorgeous coastline, once was crowded with sardine canneries processing, at their peak, nearly 200,000 tons of the smelly silver fish a year. During the mid-1940s, however, the sardines disappeared from the bay, causing the canneries to close. Through the years the old tin-roof canneries have been converted into restaurants, art galleries, and malls with shops selling T-shirts, fudge, and plastic sea otters. Recent tourist development along the row has been more tasteful, however, and includes several stylish inns and hotels, wine tasting rooms, and upscale specialty shops. ✉ *Cannery Row, between Reeside and David Aves.* 🌐 *www.canneryrow.com.*

Casa Soberanes. A classic low-ceiling adobe structure built in 1842, this was once a Custom House guard's residence. Exhibits at the house survey life

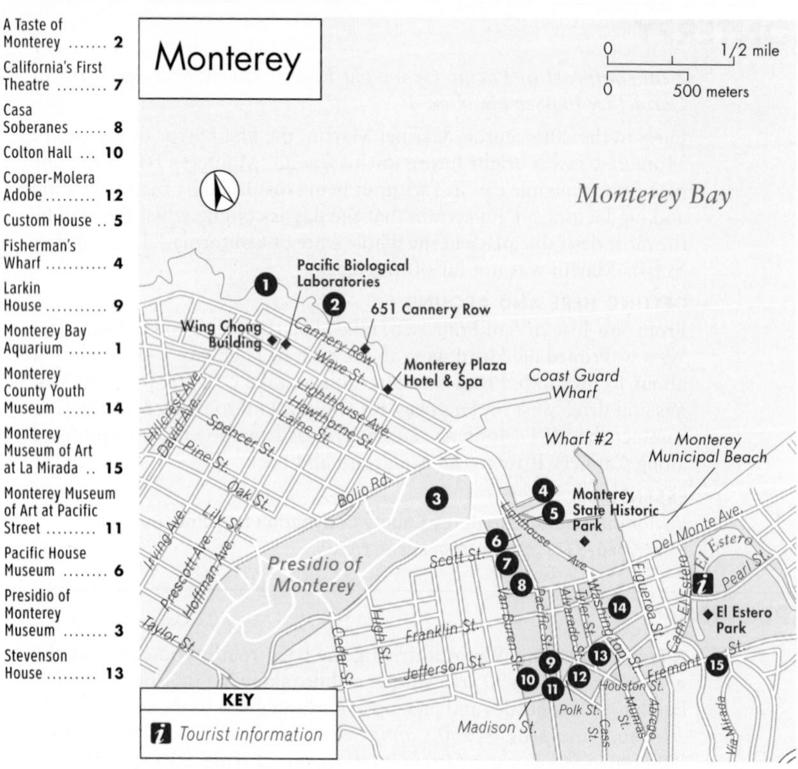

in Monterey from the era of Mexican rule to the present. The building is currently closed, but feel free to stop at the peaceful rear garden, which has a lovely rose-covered arbor and sitting benches. ✉ *Monterey State Historic Park, 336 Pacific St.* ☎ *831/649–7118* 🌐 *www.parks.ca.gov/mshp* 🎫 *Free.*

Colton Hall. A convention of delegates met in 1849 to draft the first state constitution at California's equivalent of Independence Hall. The stone building, which has served as a school, a courthouse, and the county seat, is a city-run museum furnished as it was during the constitutional convention. The extensive grounds outside the hall surround the Old Monterey Jail. ✉ *500 block of Pacific St., between Madison and Jefferson Sts.* ☎ *831/646–5648* 🌐 *www.monterey.org/museum/coltonhall.html* 🎫 *Free* 🕒 *Daily 10–4.*

Cooper-Molera Adobe. The restored 2-acre complex includes a house dating from the 1820s, a visitor center, a bookstore, and a large garden enclosed by a high adobe wall. The mostly Victorian-era antiques and memorabilia that fill the house provide a glimpse into the life of a prosperous early sea merchant's family. If the house is closed, you can still visit the Cooper Museum visitor center and pick up walking tour maps and walk around the grounds. ✉ *Monterey State Historic Park, Polk and Munras Sts.* ☎ *831/649–7118, 831/649–7111* 🌐 *www.parks.ca.gov/mshp* 🎫 *$5* 🕒 *Weekends. Call for hrs.*

Custom House. This adobe structure, built by the Mexican government in 1827—now California's oldest standing public building—was the first stop for sea traders whose goods were subject to duties. At the beginning of the Mexican-American War, in 1846, Commodore John Sloat raised the American flag over the building and claimed California for the United States. The house's lower floor displays cargo from a 19th-century trading ship. While the house is currently closed, you can still visit the cactus gardens and stroll around the plaza. ✉ *Monterey State Historic Park, 1 Custom House Plaza, across from Fisherman's Wharf* ☎ *831/649–7118* 🌐 *www.parks.ca.gov/mshp* 🎟 *Free* 🕒 *Weekends 10–4.*

JOHN STEINBECK'S CANNERY ROW

"Cannery Row in Monterey in California is a poem, a stink, a grating noise, a quality of light, a tone, a habit, a nostalgia, a dream. Cannery Row is the gathered and scattered, tin and iron and rust and splintered wood, chipped pavement and weedy lots and junk heaps, sardine canneries of corrugated iron, honky tonks, restaurants and whore houses, and little crowded groceries, and laboratories and flophouses."
—John Steinbeck, *Cannery Row*

Fisherman's Wharf. The mournful barking of sea lions provides a steady soundtrack all along Monterey's waterfront, but the best way to actually view the whiskered marine mammals is to walk along one of the two piers across from Custom House Plaza. Fisherman's Wharf is lined with souvenir shops, seafood restaurants, and whale-watching tour boats. It's undeniably touristy, but still a lively and entertaining place. Up the harbor to the right is Wharf No. 2, a working municipal pier where you can see fishing boats unloading their catches to one side, and fishermen casting their lines into the water on the other. The pier has a couple of low-key restaurants, from whose seats lucky customers may spot otters and harbor seals. ✉ *At end of Calle Principal* ☎ *831/649–6544* 🌐 *www.montereywharf.com.*

Larkin House. A veranda encircles the second floor of this architecturally significant two-story adobe built in 1835, whose design bears witness to the Mexican and New England influences on the Monterey style. The rooms are furnished with period antiques, many of them brought from New Hampshire by the building's namesake, Thomas O. Larkin, an early California statesman. The building is closed weekdays, but you can stroll the historic gardens and peek in the windows. ✉ *Monterey State Historic Park, 464 Calle Principal, between Jefferson and Pacific Sts.* ☎ *831/649–7118* 🌐 *www.parks.ca.gov/mshp* 🎟 *$5* 🕒 *Weekends; call for hrs.*

Fodor's Choice ★

Monterey Bay Aquarium. The minute you hand over your ticket at this extraordinary aquarium you're surrounded by sea creatures; right at the entrance, you can see dozens of them swimming in a three-story-tall, sunlit kelp forest tank. The beauty of the exhibits here is that they are all designed to give a sense of what it's like to be in the water with the animals—sardines swim around your head in a circular tank, and jellyfish drift in and out of view in dramatically lighted spaces that suggest the ocean depths. A petting pool gives you a hands-on experience with bat rays, and the million-gallon Open Seas tank shows the vast variety of creatures (from sharks to placid-looking turtles) that live in the eastern Pacific. A Splash Zone with 45 interactive bilingual exhibits opened in 2008: here, kids (and kids-at-heart) can commune with sea dragons, potbellied seahorses, and other fascinating creatures. The only drawback to the experience is that it must be shared with the throngs of people that crowd the place daily; most think it's worth it. To avoid the crowds, arrive as soon as the aquarium opens or visit after 2 pm, when field trip groups depart and youngsters head home for their naps. Weekend evenings in summer, the aquarium stays open later and is usually less crowded during the extended hours. **■TIP→ Reserve a lunch table at the aquarium's restaurant, perched on ocean's edge. Otters and other sea creatures often frolic just outside the floor-to-ceiling windows.** ✉ *886 Cannery Row* ☎ *800/555–3656 info, 800/756–3737 for advance tickets* 🌐 *www.montereybayaquarium.org* 🎫 *$30* ⏲ *Late May–June and early Sept., daily 9:30–6; July and Aug., weekdays 9:30–6, weekends 9:30–8; early Sept.–late May, daily 10–5.*

MONTEREY: FORMER CAPITAL OF CALIFORNIA

In 1602 Spanish explorer Sebastián Vizcaíno stepped ashore on a remote California peninsula. He named it after the viceroy of New Spain—Count de Monte Rey. Soon the Spanish built a military outpost, and the site was the capital of California until the state came under American rule.

Monterey County Youth Museum (MY Museum). Monterey Bay comes to life from a child's perspective in this fun-filled, interactive indoor exploration center that opened in the heart of the historic district in late 2008. The seven exhibit galleries showcase the science and nature of the Big Sur coast, theater arts, Pebble Beach golf, and beaches. There's also a live performance theater, a creation station, a hospital emergency room, and an agriculture corner where kids follow artichokes, strawberries, and other fruits and veggies on their evolution from sprout to harvest to farmers' markets. ✉ *425 Washington St.* ☎ *831/649–6444* 🌐 *www.mymuseum.org* 🎫 *$7* ⏲ *Mon., Tues., and Thurs.–Sat. 10–5, Sun. noon–5.*

Monterey Museum of Art at La Mirada. Asian and European antiques fill this 19th-century adobe house. A newer 10,000-square-foot gallery space, designed by Charles Moore, houses Asian and California regional art. Outdoors are magnificent rose and rhododendron gardens. A single fee covers admission to the La Mirada and Pacific Street facilities of the Monterey Museum of Art. ✉ *720 Via Mirada, at Fremont St.* ☎ *831/372–3689* 🌐 *www.montereyart.org* 🎫 *$5* ⏲ *Wed.–Sat. 11–5, Sun. 1–4.*

Dennis the Menace Playground. El Estero Park's Dennis the Menace Playground is an imaginative play area designed by the late Hank Ketcham, the well-known cartoonist. The equipment is on a grand scale and made for daredevils; there's a roller slide, a clanking suspension bridge, and a real Southern Pacific steam locomotive. You can rent a rowboat or a paddleboat for cruising around U-shaped Lake El Estero, populated with an assortment of ducks, mud hens, and geese. The park is open 10 to dusk and closed Tuesday September–May. ✉ *Pearl St. and Camino El Estero* ☎ *831/646–3866.*

Trained "seals" that perform in circuses are actually California sea lions, intelligent, social animals that live (and sleep) close together in groups.

Monterey Museum of Art at Pacific Street. Photographs by Ansel Adams and Edward Weston, as well as works by other artists who have spent time on the peninsula, are on display here. There's also a colorful collection of international folk art; the pieces range from Kentucky hearth brooms to Tibetan prayer wheels. A single fee covers admission to the Pacific Street and La Mirada facilities of the Monterey Museum of Art. ✉ *559 Pacific St., across from Colton Hall* ☎ *831/372–5477* 🌐 *www.montereyart.org* 🎫 *$5* 🕓 *Wed.–Sat. 11–5, Sun. 1–4.*

Monterey State Historic Park. You can glimpse Monterey's early history in the well-preserved adobe buildings scattered along several city blocks. Far from being a hermetic period museum, the park facilities are an integral part of the day-to-day business life of the town—within some of the buildings are a store, a theater, and government offices. At some of the historic houses, the gardens (open daily 10 to 5 in summer, 10 to 4 rest of the year) are worthy sights themselves. ■ **TIP→ At this writing, many buildings are closed and tours on hiatus due to state park budget cuts. Visit the Web site for up-to-date information.** ✉ *20 Custom House Plaza* ☎ *831/649–7118* 🌐 *www.parks.ca.gov/mshp* 🎫 *Free* 🕓 *Call for hrs.*

Pacific House Museum. Once a hotel and saloon, this visitor center and museum now commemorates early-California life with gold-rush relics and photographs of old Monterey. The upper floor displays Native American artifacts, including gorgeous baskets and pottery. ✉ *Monterey State Historic Park, 10 Custom House Plaza* ☎ *831/649–7118* 🌐 *www.parks.ca.gov/mshp* 🎫 *Free* 🕓 *Open weekends 10–4.*

Presidio of Monterey Museum. This spot has been significant for centuries as a town, a fort, and the site of several battles, including the skirmish

CLOSE UP

The Underwater Kingdom

Although Monterey's coastal landscapes are stunning, their beauty is more than equaled by the wonders that lie offshore. The huge Monterey Bay National Marine Sanctuary—which stretches 276 mi, from north of San Francisco almost all the way down to Santa Barbara—teems with abundant life, and has topography as diverse as that aboveground.

The preserve's 5,322 square mi include vast submarine canyons, which reach down 10,663 feet at their deepest point. They also encompass dense forests of giant kelp—a kind of seaweed that can grow more than a hundred feet from its roots on the ocean floor. These kelp forests are especially robust off Monterey.

The sanctuary was established in 1992 to protect the habitat of the many species that thrive in the bay. Some animals can be seen quite easily from land. In summer and winter you might glimpse the offshore spray of gray whales as they migrate between their summer feeding grounds in Alaska and their breeding grounds in Baja. Clouds of marine birds—including white-faced ibis, three types of albatross, and more than 15 types of gull—skim above the waves, or roost in the rock islands along 17-Mile Drive. Sea otters dart and gambol in the calmer waters of the bay; and of course, you can watch the sea lions—and hear their round-the-clock barking—on the wharves in Santa Cruz and Monterey.

The sanctuary supports many other creatures, however, that remain unseen by most on-land visitors. Some of these are enormous, such as the giant blue whales that arrive to feed on plankton in summer; others, like the more than 22 species of red algae in these waters, are microscopic. So whether you choose to visit the Monterey Bay Aquarium, take a whale-watch trip, or look out to sea with your binoculars, remember you're seeing just a small part of a vibrant underwater kingdom.

in which the pirate Hipoleto Bruchard conquered the Spanish garrison that stood here. Its first incarnation was as a Native American village for the Rumsien tribe; then it became known as the landing site for explorer Sebastián Vizcaíno in 1602, and father of the California missions, Father Serra, in 1770. The indoor museum tells the stories; the outdoor sites are marked with plaques. ✉ *Corporal Ewing Rd., Presidio of Monterey* ☎ *831/646–3456* 🌐 *www.monterey.org/museum/pom/* 🎫 *Free* 🕒 *Mon. 10–1, Thurs.–Sat. 10–4, Sun. 1–4.*

Stevenson House. This house was named in honor of author Robert Louis Stevenson, who boarded here briefly in a tiny upstairs room. Items from his family's estate furnish Stevenson's room; period-decorated chambers elsewhere in the house include a gallery of the author's memorabilia and a children's nursery stocked with Victorian toys and games. ✉ *Monterey State Historic Park, 530 Houston St.* ☎ *831/649–7118* 🌐 *www.parks.ca.gov/mshp* 🎫 *Free* 🕒 *Open Sat. 1–4.*

WHERE TO EAT

¢ AMERICAN — ✕ **Café Lumiere.** Attached to the lobby of Monterey's art-house cinema, this café shows work by local artists. Eat a light breakfast or lunch, drink coffee, or choose a pot of tea from the extensive selection. The menu includes baked goods, cakes, sandwiches, granola, and other breakfast items. Most patrons bring their laptops for the free Wi-Fi, and most tables are shared. Close to downtown bars, it's open until 10 pm. ✉ *365 Calle Principal* ☎ *831/920–2451* 🌐 *www.montereylumiere.com.*

$$ SEAFOOD — ✕ **Monterey's Fish House.** Casual yet stylish, and removed from the hubbub of the wharf, this always-packed seafood restaurant attracts locals and frequent visitors to the city. If the dining room is full, you can wait at the bar and savor deliciously plump oysters on the half shell. The bartenders and waitstaff will gladly advise you on the perfect wine to go with your poached, blackened, or oak-grilled seafood. ✉ *2114 Del Monte Ave.* ☎ *831/373–4647* ⊙ *No lunch weekends.*

$$$ AMERICAN Fodor's Choice ★ — ✕ **Montrio Bistro.** This quirky, converted firehouse, with its rawhide walls and iron indoor trellises, has a wonderfully sophisticated menu. Chef Tony Baker uses organic produce and meats and sustainably sourced seafood to create imaginative dishes that reflect local agriculture, such as artichokes stuffed with fire-roasted Brie, and grilled lamb tenderloin with rosemary, garlic sauce, and broccolini. Likewise, the wine list draws primarily on California, and many come from the Monterey area. ✉ *414 Calle Principal* ☎ *831/648–8880* 🌐 *www.montrio.com* ✍ *Reservations essential* ⊙ *No lunch.*

$ AMERICAN — ✕ **Old Monterey Café.** Breakfast here gets constant local raves. Its fame rests on familiar favorites in many incarnations: a dozen kinds of omelets, and pancakes from blueberry to cinnamon-raisin-pecan. The lunch and dinner menus have good soups, salads, and sandwiches, and this is a great place to relax with an afternoon cappuccino. ✉ *489 Alvarado St.* ☎ *831/646–1021* 🌐 *www.cafemonterey.com* ✍ *Reservations not accepted.*

$$ AMERICAN — ✕ **Tarpy's Roadhouse.** Fun, dressed-up American favorites—a little something for everyone—are served in this renovated early-1900s stone farmhouse several miles outside town. The kitchen cranks out everything from Cajun-spiced prawns to meat loaf with Marsala-mushroom gravy to grilled ribs and steaks. Eat indoors by a fireplace or outdoors in the courtyard. ✉ *2999 Monterey–Salinas Hwy., Hwy. 68* ☎ *831/647–1444* 🌐 *www.tarpys.com.*

WHERE TO STAY

For expanded reviews, go to Fodors.com.

$ — **Best Western Beach Resort Monterey.** With a great waterfront location about 2 mi north of town—with views of the bay and the city skyline—and a surprising array of amenities, this hotel is one of the best values in town. **Pros:** on the beach; great value; family-friendly. **Cons:** several miles from major attractions; big-box mall neighborhood. ✉ *2600 Sand Dunes Dr.* ☎ *831/394–3321, 800/242–8627* 🌐 *www.montereybeachresort.com* *196 rooms* *In-room: a/c, Wi-Fi. In-hotel: restaurant, bar, pool, gym, beach, business center, parking, some pets allowed.*

$$$$ — **InterContinental The Clement Monterey.** Spectacular bay views, assiduous service, a slew of upscale amenities, and a superb waterfront location

next to the aquarium propelled this full-service luxury hotel to immediate stardom when it opened in 2008. **Pros:** a block from the aquarium; fantastic views from some rooms; great for families. **Cons:** a tad formal; not budget-friendly. ✉ *750 Cannery Row* ☎ *831/375–4500, 866/781-2406 toll free* 🌐 *www.ictheclementmonterey.com* *192 rooms, 16 suites* *In-room: a/c, Internet, Wi-Fi. In-hotel: restaurant, bar, pool, gym, spa, children's programs, business center, some pets allowed.*

THE FIRST ARTICHOKE QUEEN

Castroville, a tiny town off Highway 1 between Monterey and Watsonville, produces about 95% of U.S. artichokes. Back in 1948, the town chose its first queen to preside during its Artichoke Festival—a beautiful young woman named Norma Jean Mortenson, who later changed her name to Marilyn Monroe.

$$ ★ **Monterey Bay Lodge.** Location (on the edge of Monterey's El Estero Park) and superior amenities give this cheerful facility an edge over other motels in town. **Pros:** within walking distance of beach and playground; quiet at night; good family choice. **Cons:** near busy boulevard. ✉ *55 Camino Aguajito* ☎ *831/372–8057, 800/558–1900* 🌐 *www.montereybaylodge.com* *43 rooms, 3 suites* *In-room: a/c, Internet, Wi-Fi. In-hotel: restaurant, pool, some pets allowed.*

$$$ **Monterey Plaza Hotel and Spa.** This hotel commands a waterfront location on Cannery Row, where you can see frolicking sea otters from the wide outdoor patio and many room balconies. **Pros:** on the ocean; lots of amenities; attentive service. **Cons:** touristy area; heavy traffic. ✉ *400 Cannery Row* ☎ *831/646–1700, 800/334–3999* 🌐 *www.montereyplazahotel.com* *280 rooms, 10 suites* *In-room: a/c, Internet, Wi-Fi. In-hotel: restaurant, bar, gym, spa, business center.*

$$$$ Fodor's Choice ★ **Old Monterey Inn.** This three-story manor house was the home of Monterey's first mayor, and today it remains a private enclave within walking distance of downtown. **Pros:** gorgeous gardens; refined luxury; serene. **Cons:** must drive to attractions and sights; fills quickly. ✉ *500 Martin St.* ☎ *831/375–8284, 800/350–2344* 🌐 *www.oldmontereyinn.com* *6 rooms, 3 suites, 1 cottage* *In-room: a/c, Internet, Wi-Fi. In-hotel: spa, business center, some pets allowed* *Breakfast.*

$ **Quality Inn Monterey.** This attractive motel has a friendly, country-inn feeling. **Pros:** indoor pool; bargain rates; cheerful innkeepers. **Cons:** street is busy during the day; some rooms are dark. ✉ *1058 Munras Ave.* ☎ *831/372–3381* 🌐 *www.qualityinnmonterey.com* *55 rooms* *In-room: a/c, Internet, Wi-Fi. In-hotel: pool* *Breakfast.*

$$$ **Spindrift Inn.** This boutique hotel on Cannery Row has beach access and a rooftop garden that overlooks the water. **Pros:** close to aquarium; steps from the beach; friendly staff. **Cons:** throngs of visitors outside; can be noisy; not good for families. ✉ *652 Cannery Row* ☎ *831/646–8900, 800/841–1879* 🌐 *www.spindriftinn.com* *45 rooms* *In-room: no a/c, Wi-Fi. In-hotel: business center* *Breakfast.*

THE ARTS

★ **Dixieland Monterey.** Dixieland Monterey, held on the first full weekend of March, presents traditional jazz bands at waterfront venues on the harbor. ☎ *831/675–0298, 888/349–6879* 🌐 *www.dixieland-monterey.com.*

Monterey Bay Blues Festival. The Monterey Bay Blues Festival draws blues fans to the Monterey Fairgrounds the last weekend in June. ☎ *831/394–2652* 🌐 *www.montereyblues.com.*

Monterey Jazz Festival. The Monterey Jazz Festival, the world's oldest, attracts jazz and blues greats from around the world to the Monterey Fairgrounds on the third full weekend of September. ☎ *925/275–9255 ticket office, 831/373–3366* 🌐 *www.montereyjazzfestival.org.*

Bruce Ariss Wharf Theater. The Bruce Ariss Wharf Theater focuses on American musicals past and present. ✉ *One Fisherman's Wharf* ☎ *831/372–1373.*

3

SPORTS AND THE OUTDOORS

Throughout most of the year, the Monterey Bay area is a haven for those who love tennis, golf, surfing, fishing, biking, hiking, scuba diving, and kayaking. In the rainy winter months, when the waves grow larger, adventurous surfers flock to the water.

Monterey Bay National Marine Sanctuary. The Monterey Bay National Marine Sanctuary, home to mammals, seabirds, fishes, invertebrates, and plants, encompasses a 276-mi shoreline and 5,322 square mi of ocean. Ringed by beaches and campgrounds, it's a place for kayaking, whale-watching, scuba diving, and other water sports. ☎ *831/647–4201* 🌐 *montereybay.noaa.gov.*

BICYCLING

Bay Bikes. For bicycle and surrey rentals and tours, visit Bay Bikes. ✉ *585 Cannery Row* ☎ *831/655–2453* 🌐 *www.baybikes.com.*

Adventures by the Sea, Inc. Adventures by the Sea, Inc. offers bike tours and rents surreys and tandem and standard bicycles. ✉ *299 Cannery Row and 210 Alvarado Mall next to the Portola Plaza Hotel* ☎ *831/372–1807, 831/648–7236* 🌐 *www.adventuresbythesea.com.*

FISHING

Randy's Fishing and Whale Watching Trips. Randy's Fishing and Whale Watching Trips, a small family-run business, has been operating since 1949. ✉ *66 Fisherman's Wharf* ☎ *831/372–7440, 800/251–7440* 🌐 *www.randysfishingtrips.com.*

SCUBA DIVING

Monterey Bay waters never warm to the temperatures of their Southern California counterparts (the warmest they get is low 60s), but that's one reason why the marine life here is among the world's most diverse.

Aquarius Dive Shop. The staff at Aquarius Dive Shop gives diving lessons and tours, and rents equipment. Their scuba-conditions information line is updated daily. ✉ *2040 Del Monte Ave.* ☎ *831/375–1933, 831/657–1020 diving conditions* 🌐 *www.aquariusdivers.com.*

WALKING

Monterey Bay Coastal Trail. From Custom House Plaza, you can walk along the coast in either direction on the 29-mi-long Monterey Bay Coastal Trail for spectacular views of the sea. It runs all the way from north of Monterey to Pacific Grove, with sections continuing around Pebble Beach. ☎ *831/372–3196* 🌐 *www.mtycounty.com/pgs-parks/bike-path.html.*

WHALE-WATCHING

Thousands of gray whales pass close by the Monterey Coast on their annual migration between the Bering Sea and Baja California. The gigantic creatures are sometimes visible through binoculars from shore, but a whale-watching cruise is the best way to get a close look at these magnificent mammals. The migration south takes place from December through March; January is prime viewing time. The whales migrate north from March through June. In addition, some 2,000 blue whales and 600 humpbacks pass the coast and are easily spotted in late summer and early fall.

★ **Monterey Bay Whale Watch.** Monterey Bay Whale Watch, which operates out of the Monterey Bay Whale Watch Center at Fisherman's Wharf, gives three- to five-hour tours led by marine biologists. ✉ *84 Fisherman's Wharf* ☎ *831/375–4658* 🌐 *www.montereybaywhalewatch.com.*

Monterey Whale Watching. Monterey Whale Watching provides three tours a day on a 150-passenger high-speed cruiser and a large 75-foot boat. ✉ *96 Fisherman's Wharf #1* ☎ *831/372–2203, 800/979–3370* 🌐 *www.montereywhalewatching.com.*

AROUND THE BAY

As Highway 1 follows the curve of the bay between Monterey and Santa Cruz, it passes through a rich agricultural zone. Opening right onto the bay, where the Salinas and Pajaro rivers drain into the Pacific, a broad valley brings together fertile soil, an ideal climate, and a good water supply to create optimum growing conditions for crops such as strawberries, artichokes, Brussels sprouts, and broccoli. Several beautiful beaches line this part of the coast.

MOSS LANDING

17 mi north of Monterey on Hwy. 1.

Moss Landing is not much more than a couple of blocks of cafés and restaurants, art galleries, and studios plus a busy fishing port, but therein lies its charm. It's a fine place to overnight or stop for a meal and get a dose of nature.

GETTING HERE AND AROUND

From Highway 1 north or south, exit at Moss Landing Road on the ocean side. From U.S. 101, take Highway 156 West from Prunedale 8 mi to Castroville and follow Highway 1 about 3 mi to Moss Landing Road. Public transit via MST connects Moss Landing with all Monterey County destinations and the Watsonville Transit Center in southern Santa Cruz County.

SALINAS AND JOHN STEINBECK'S LEGACY

National Steinbeck Center. Salinas (17 mi east of Monterey), a hardworking city surrounded by vegetable fields, honors the memory and literary legacy of John Steinbeck, its most well-known native, at the modern National Steinbeck Center. Exhibits document the life of the Pulitzer- and Nobel-prize winner and the history of the local communities that inspired Steinbeck novels such as *The Grapes of Wrath.* Highlights include reproductions of the green pickup-camper from *Travels with Charley* and of the bunkroom from *Of Mice and Men*; you can watch actors read from Steinbeck's books on video screens throughout the museum. The museum is the centerpiece of the revival of Old Town Salinas, where handsome turn-of-the-20th-century stone buildings have been renovated and filled with shops and restaurants.

Steinbeck House. Two blocks from the National Steinbeck Center is the author's Victorian birthplace, Steinbeck House. It operates as a lunch spot Tuesday through Saturday and displays some Steinbeck memorabilia. ✉ *132 Central Ave., Salinas* ☎ *831/424–2735* ✉ *1 Main St., 17 mi east of Monterey via Hwy. 68, Salinas* ☎ *831/796–3833 administration, 831/775–4721 admission* 🌐 *www.steinbeck.org* *$11* ⏲ *Daily 10–5.*

ESSENTIALS

Visitor Information **Monterey County Convention & Visitors Bureau** ✉ *Box 1770, Monterey* ☎ *877/666–8373* 🌐 *www.seemonterey.com.* **Moss Landing Chamber of Commerce** ✉ *8071 Moss Landing Rd., Monterey* ☎ *831/633-4501*

EXPLORING

★ **Elkhorn Slough National Estuarine Research Reserve.** In the Elkhorn Slough National Estuarine Research Reserve, 1,400 acres of tidal flats and salt marshes form a complex environment that supports some 300 species of birds. A walk or a kayak trip along the meandering waterways and wetlands can reveal hawks, white-tailed kites, owls, herons, and egrets. Sea otters, sharks, rays, and many other animals also live or visit here. On weekends guided walks from the visitor center to the heron rookery begin at 10 and 1. Although the reserve lies across the town line in Watsonville, you reach its entrance through Moss Landing. ✉ *1700 Elkhorn Rd., Watsonville* ☎ *831/728–2822* 🌐 *www.elkhornslough.org* *$2.50* ⏲ *Wed.–Sun. 9–5.*

Elkhorn Slough Safari. Aboard a 27-foot pontoon boat operated by Elkhorn Slough Safari, a naturalist leads an up-close look at wetlands denizens. Advance reservations are required for the two-hour tours ($35). ✉ *Moss Landing Harbor* ☎ *831/633–5555* 🌐 *www.elkhornslough.com.*

WHERE TO EAT AND STAY

$ SEAFOOD ✕ **Phil's Fish Market & Eatery.** Exquisitely fresh, simply prepared seafood (try the cioppino) is on the menu at this warehouselike restaurant on the harbor; all kinds of glistening fish are on offer at the market in the front. ■ **TIP→ Phil's Snack Shack, a tiny sandwich-and-smoothie joint, serves quicker meals at the north end of town.** ✉ *7600 Sandholdt Rd.* ☎ *831/633–2152* 🌐 *www.philsfishmarket.com.*

$$ **Captain's Inn.** Commune with nature and pamper yourself with upscale creature comforts at this green-certified getaway in the heart of town. **Pros:** walk to restaurants and shops; tranquil natural setting; homey atmosphere **Cons:** rooms in historic building don't have water views; far from urban amenities; not appropriate for young children. *8122 Moss Landing Rd., Moss Landing 831/633–5550 www.captainsinn.com 10 In-room: no a/c, Internet, Wi-Fi. In-hotel: spa, parking Breakfast.*

WATSONVILLE

7 mi north of Moss Landing on Hwy. 1.

If ever a city was built on strawberries, Watsonville is it. Produce has long driven the economy here, and this is where the county fair takes place each September.

GETTING HERE AND AROUND

From Santa Cruz or Monterey, follow Highway 1 to Watsonville. Santa Cruz Metropolitan Transit District buses operate throughout the county; buses run regularly from the Santa Cruz Transit Center to the Watsonville Transit Center. From U.S. 101, take Highway 152 West from Gilroy (a curvy but scenic road over the mountains) or Highway 129 West from just north of San Juan Bautista.

EXPLORING

Agricultural History Project. One feature of the Santa Cruz County Fairgrounds is the Agricultural History Project, which preserves the history of farming in the Pajaro Valley. In the Codiga Center and Museum you can examine antique tractors and milking machines, peruse an exhibit on the era when Watsonville was the "frozen food capitol of the West," and watch experts restore farm implements and vehicles. *2601 E. Lake Ave. 831/724–5898 www.aghistoryproject.org $2 suggested donation Thurs.–Sun. noon–4.*

Watsonville Fly-in & Air Show. Every Labor Day weekend, aerial performers execute elaborate aerobatics at the Watsonville Fly-in & Air Show. More than 300 classic, experimental, and military aircraft are on display; concerts and other events fill three days. *Watsonville Municipal Airport, 100 Aviation Way 831/763–5600 www.watsonvilleflyin.org $15.*

APTOS

7 mi north of Watsonville on Hwy. 1.

Backed by a redwood forest and facing the sea, downtown Aptos—known as Aptos Village—is a place of wooden walkways and false-fronted shops. Antiques dealers cluster along Trout Gulch Road, off Soquel Drive east of Highway 1.

GETTING HERE AND AROUND

Use Highway 1 to reach Aptos from Santa Cruz or Monterey. Exit at State Park Drive to reach the main shopping hub and Aptos Village. You can also exit at Freedom Boulevard or Rio del Mar. Soquel Drive is the main artery through town.

SAN JUAN BAUTISTA

About as close to early-19th-century California as you can get, San Juan Bautista (15 mi east of Watsonville on Highway 156) has been protected from development since 1933, when much of it became a state park. Small antiques shops and restaurants occupy the Old West and art deco buildings that line 3rd Street.

The wide green plaza of San Juan Bautista State Historic Park is ringed by 18th- and 19th-century buildings, many of them open to the public. The cemetery of the long, low, colonnaded mission church contains the unmarked graves of more than 4,300 Native American converts. Nearby is an adobe home furnished with Spanish-colonial antiques, a hotel frozen in the 1860s, a blacksmith shop, a stable, a pioneer cabin, and a jailhouse.

The first Saturday of each month, costumed volunteers engage in quilting bees, tortilla making, and other frontier activities. *www.san-juan-bautista.ca.us.*

3

ESSENTIALS

Visitor Information **Aptos Chamber of Commerce** *7605-A Old Dominion Ct. 831/688–1467 www.aptoschamber.com.*

EXPLORING

Seacliff State Beach. Sandstone bluffs tower above Seacliff State Beach, a favorite of locals. You can fish off the pier, which leads out to a sunken World War I tanker ship built of concrete. *201 State Park Dr. 831/685–6442 www.parks.ca.gov $10 per vehicle.*

WHERE TO EAT AND STAY

$$$ MEDITERRANEAN ★ **Bittersweet Bistro.** A large old tavern with cathedral ceilings houses this popular bistro, where chef-owner Thomas Vinolus draws culinary inspiration from the Mediterranean. The menu changes seasonally, but regular highlights include pan-seared Monterey Bay petrale sole, seafood *puttanesca* (pasta with a spicy sauce of garlic, tomatoes, anchovies, and olives), and fire-roasted pork tenderloin. The decadent chocolate desserts are not to be missed. You can order many of the entrées in small or regular portions. Lunch is available to go from the express counter. *787 Rio Del Mar Blvd. 831/662–9799 www.bittersweetbistro.com.*

$$$ **Best Western Seacliff Inn.** A favorite lair of families and business travelers, this 6-acre Best Western near Seacliff State Beach is more resort than hotel. **Pros:** walking distance from the beach; family-friendly; includes hot breakfast buffet. **Cons:** close to the freeway; occasional nighttime bar noise. *7500 Old Dominion Ct. 831/688–7300, 800/367–2003 www.seacliffinn.com 139 rooms, 10 suites In-room: a/c, Internet, Wi-Fi. In-hotel: restaurant, bar, pool, gym, laundry facilities Breakfast.*

$$$ **Flora Vista.** Multicolor fields of flowers, strawberries, and veggies unfold in every direction at this luxury neo-Georgian inn set on two serene acres in a rural community just south of Aptos; Sand Dollar Beach is just a short walk away. **Pros:** super-private; near the beach; flowers everywhere. **Cons:** no restaurants or nightlife within walking distance; not a good place for kids. *1258 San Andreas Rd., La Selva*

Beach ☎ *831/724–8663, 877/753–5672* 🌐 *www.floravistainn.com* ⇆ *5 rooms* 🛈 *In-room: no a/c, Wi-Fi. In-hotel: tennis court* 🍽 *Breakfast.*

$$$$ **Seascape Beach Resort.** On a bluff overlooking Monterey Bay, Seascape is a full-fledged resort that makes it easy to unwind. **Pros:** time-share-style apartments; access to miles of beachfront; superb views. **Cons:** far from city life; most bathrooms are small. ✉ *1 Seascape Resort Dr.* ☎ *831/688–6800, 800/929–7727* 🌐 *www.seascaperesort.com* ⇆ *285 suites* 🛈 *In-room: no a/c, kitchen, Wi-Fi. In-hotel: restaurant, bar, pool, gym, spa, beach, children's programs, laundry facilities, business center.*

CAPITOLA AND SOQUEL

4 mi northwest of Aptos on Hwy. 1.

On the National Register of Historic places as California's first seaside resort town, the village of Capitola has been in a holiday mood since the late 1800s. Its walkable downtown is jam-packed with casual eateries, surf shops, and ice-cream parlors. Inland, across Highway 1, antiques shops line Soquel Drive in the town of Soquel. Wineries dot the Santa Cruz Mountains beyond.

GETTING HERE AND AROUND

From Santa Cruz or Monterey, follow Highway 1 to the Capitola/Soquel (Bay Avenue) exit about 7 mi south of Santa Cruz and head toward the ocean to reach Capitola. Turn east and you'll find the heart of Soquel Village. On summer weekends, park for free in the lot behind the Crossroads Center just a block west of the freeway and hop aboard the free Capitola Shuttle to the village.

ESSENTIALS

Visitor Information Capitola-Soquel Chamber of Commerce ✉ *716-G Capitola Ave.* ☎ *831/475–6522, 800/474-6522* 🌐 *www.capitolachamber.com.*

EXPLORING

New Brighton State Beach. New Brighton State Beach, once the site of a Chinese fishing village, is now a popular surfing and camping spot. Its Pacific Migrations Visitor Center traces the history of the Chinese and other peoples who settled around Monterey Bay, as well as the migratory patterns of the area's wildlife, such as monarch butterflies and gray whales. **TIP→ New Brighton Beach connects with Seacliff Beach, and at low tide you can walk or run along this scenic stretch of sand for nearly 16 mi south (you might have to wade through a few creeks). The 1½-mi stroll from New Brighton to Seacliff's cement ship is a local favorite.** ✉ *1500 State Park Dr.* ☎ *831/464–6330* 🌐 *www.parks.ca.gov* 🎫 *$10 per vehicle.*

WHERE TO EAT AND STAY

¢ SEAFOOD **Carpo's.** Locals line up in droves at Carpo's counter, hankering for mouthwatering, casual family meals. The menu leans heavily toward seafood, but also includes burgers, salads, and steaks. Favorites include the fishermen's baskets of fresh battered snapper, calamari and prawns, seafood kabobs, and homemade olallieberry pie. Nearly everything here costs less than $10. Go early to beat the crowds, or be prepared to wait for a table. ✉ *2400 Porter St.* ☎ *831/476–6260* 🌐 *www.carposrestaurant.com.*

¢ CAFÉ **Gayle's Bakery & Rosticceria.** Whether you're in the mood for an orange-olallieberry muffin, a wild rice and chicken salad, or tri-tip on garlic toast, this bakery-cum-deli's varied menu is likely to satisfy. Munch your chocolate macaroon on the shady patio or dig into the daily blue-plate dinner—there's a junior blue plate for the kids—amid the whirl inside. *504 Bay Ave. 831/462–1200 www.gaylesbakery.com.*

$$ AMERICAN **Michael's on Main.** Classic comfort food with a creative gourmet twist, reasonable prices, and attentive service draw a lively crowd of locals to this upscale-but-casual creek-side eatery. Chef Michael Clark's commitment to locally sustainable fisheries and farmers has earned him community accolades and infuses dishes with the inimitable taste that comes from using fresh local ingredients. The menu changes seasonally, but you can always count on finding such home-style dishes as pork osso bucco in red wine tomato citrus sauce as well as unusual entrées like pistachio-crusted salmon with mint vinaigrette. For a quiet conversation spot, ask for a table on the romantic patio overlooking the creek. The busy bar area hosts live music Wednesday through Saturday. *2591 Main St. 831/479–9777 www.michaelsonmain.net Closed Mon.*

$$$ CONTINENTAL **Shadowbrook.** To get to this romantic spot overlooking Soquel Creek, you can take a cable car or walk the stairs down a steep, fern-lined bank beside a running waterfall. Dining room options include the rooftop Redwood Room, the wood-paneled Wine Cellar, and the airy, glass-enclosed Garden Room. Prime rib and grilled seafood are the stars of the simple menu. A cheaper menu of light entrées is available in the lounge. *1750 Wharf Rd. 831/475–1511, 800/975–1511 www.shadowbrook-capitola.com No lunch.*

$$$$ **Inn at Depot Hill.** This inventively designed B&B in a former rail depot sees itself as a link to the era of luxury train travel. **Pros:** short walk to beach and village; historic charm; excellent service. **Cons:** fills quickly; hot tub conversation on the patio may irk second-floor guests. *250 Monterey Ave. 831/462–3376, 800/572–2632 www.innatdepothill.com 12 rooms In-room: no a/c, Wi-Fi Breakfast.*

CALIFORNIA'S OLDEST RESORT TOWN

As far as anyone knows for certain, Capitola is the oldest seaside resort town on the Pacific Coast. In 1856 a pioneer acquired Soquel Landing, the picturesque lagoon and beach where Soquel Creek empties into the bay, and built a wharf. Another man opened a campground along the shore, and his daughter named it Capitola after a heroine in a novel series. After the train came to town in the 1870s, thousands of vacationers began arriving to bask in the sun on the glorious beach.

3

SANTA CRUZ

5 mi west of Capitola on Hwy. 1; 48 mi north of Monterey on Hwy. 1.

The big city on this stretch of the California coast, Santa Cruz (pop. 57,500) is less manicured than Carmel or Monterey. Long known for its surfing and its amusement-filled beach boardwalk, the town is a mix of grand Victorian-era homes and rinky-dink motels. The opening of the University of California campus in the 1960s swung the town sharply to the left, and the counterculture more or less lives on here. At the same time, the revitalized downtown and an insane real-estate market reflect the city's proximity to Silicon Valley and to a growing wine country in the surrounding mountains.

GETTING HERE AND AROUND

From San Francisco Bay Area, take Highway 17 South over the mountains to Santa Cruz, where it merges with Highway 1. Use Highway 1 to get around the area and to access all Monterey Bay coastal destinations. The main Santa Cruz Transit Center is in the heart of downtown, a short walk from the Wharf and Boardwalk; from here, connect with public transit throughout the Monterey Bay and San Francisco Bay areas.

ESSENTIALS

Visitor Information Santa Cruz County Conference and Visitors Council ✉ *303 Water St.* ☎ *831/425-1234, 800/833-3494* 🌐 *www.santacruzcounty.travel.*

EXPLORING

Santa Cruz Beach Boardwalk. Santa Cruz has been a seaside resort since the mid-19th century. Along one end of the broad, south-facing beach, the Santa Cruz Beach Boardwalk has entertained holidaymakers for almost as long—it celebrated its 100th anniversary in 2007. Its Looff carousel and classic wooden Giant Dipper roller coaster, both dating from the early 1900s, are surrounded by high-tech thrill rides and easy-going kiddie rides with ocean views. Video and arcade games, a mini-golf course, and a laser-tag arena pack one gigantic building, which is open daily even if the rides aren't running. You have to pay to play, but you can wander the entire boardwalk for free while sampling delicacies such as corn dogs and garlic fries. ✉ *Along Beach St.* ☎ *831/423–5590, 831/426–7433* 🌐 *www.beachboardwalk.com* *$30 day pass for unlimited rides, or pay per ride* ⏲ *Apr.–early Sept., daily; early Sept.–late May, weekends, weather permitting; call for hrs.*

Santa Cruz Municipal Wharf. Jutting half a mile into the ocean near one end of the Santa Cruz Beach Boardwalk, the Santa Cruz Municipal Wharf is topped with seafood restaurants; souvenir shops; and outfitters offering bay cruises, fishing trips, and boat rentals. A salty sound track drifts up from under the wharf, where barking sea lions lounge in heaps on crossbeams. ✉ *Beach St., at Pacific Ave.* ☎ *831/420–6025* 🌐 *www.santacruzwharf.com.*

West Cliff Drive. West Cliff Drive winds along the top of an oceanfront bluff from the municipal wharf to Natural Bridges State Beach. It's a spectacular drive, but it's much more fun to walk, blade, or bike the paved path that parallels the road. Groups of surfers bob and swoosh in Monterey Bay at several points near the foot of the bluff, especially at a break known as Steamer Lane. Named for a surfer who died here in 1965, nearby Mark Abbott Memorial Lighthouse stands at Point Santa Cruz, the cliff's major promontory. From here you can watch pinnipeds hang out, sunbathe, and frolic on Seal Rock.

★ **Santa Cruz Surfing Museum.** The Santa Cruz Surfing Museum, inside the Mark Abbott Memorial Lighthouse, traces local surfing history back to the early 20th century. Historical photographs show old-time surfers, and a display of boards includes rarities such as a heavy redwood plank predating the fiberglass era and the remains of a modern board chomped by a great white shark. Surfer-docents are on-site to talk about the old days. ✉ *701 W. Cliff Dr.* ☎ *831/420–6289* 🌐 *www.santacruzsurfingmuseum.org* 🎫 *$2 suggested donation* ⏲ *Sept.–June, Thurs.–Mon. noon–4; July and Aug., Weds.–Mon. 10–5.*

Natural Bridges State Beach. At the end of West Cliff Drive lies Natural Bridges State Beach, a stretch of soft sand edged with tide pools and sea-sculpted rock bridges. **■ TIP→ From October to early March a colony of monarch butterflies roosts in a eucalyptus grove.** ✉ *2531 W. Cliff Dr.* ☎ *831/423–4609* 🌐 *www.parks.ca.gov* 🎫 *Beach free, parking $10* ⏲ *Daily 8 am–sunset. Visitor center Oct.–Feb., daily 10–4; Mar.–Sept., weekends 10–4.*

Seymour Marine Discovery Center. Seymour Marine Discovery Center, part of Long Marine Laboratory at UCSC's Institute of Marine Sciences, looks more like a research facility than a slick aquarium. Interactive exhibits demonstrate how scientists study the ocean, and the aquarium displays creatures of particular interest to marine biologists. The 87-foot blue whale skeleton is one of the world's largest. Tours (sign up when you arrive) take place at 11, 1, 2, and 3. ✉ *100 Shaffer Rd., off Delaware St. west of Natural Bridges State Beach* ☎ *831/459–3800* 🌐 *seymourcenter.ucsc.edu* 🎫 *$6* ⏲ *Tues.–Sat. 10–5, Sun. noon–5.*

Wilder Ranch State Park. In the Cultural Preserve of Wilder Ranch State Park you can visit the homes, barns, workshops, and bunkhouse of a 19th-century dairy farm. Nature has reclaimed most of the ranch land, and native plants and wildlife have returned to the 7,000 acres of forest, grassland, canyons, estuaries, and beaches. Hike, bike, or ride horseback on miles of ocean-view trails. ✉ *Hwy. 1, 1 mi north of Santa Cruz* ☎ *831/426–0505 Interpretive Center, 831/423–9703 trail information* 🌐 *www.parks.ca.gov* 🎫 *Parking $10* ⏲ *Daily 8 am–sunset.*

Pacific Avenue. When you've had your fill of the city's beaches and waters, take a stroll in downtown Santa Cruz, especially on Pacific Avenue between Laurel and Water streets. Vintage boutiques and mountain sports stores, sushi bars and Mexican restaurants, day spas, and nightclubs keep the main drag and the surrounding streets hopping mid-morning until late evening.

Santa Cruz Mission State Historic Park. On the northern fringes of downtown, Santa Cruz Mission State Historic Park preserves the site of California's 12th Spanish mission, built in the 1790s and destroyed by an earthquake in 1857. A museum in a restored 1791 adobe and a half-scale replica of the mission church are part of the complex. ✉ *144 School St.* ☎ *831/425–5849* 🌐 *www.parks.ca.gov* 🎫 *Free* ⏲ *Thurs.–Sat. 10–4.*

HAWAIIAN ROYALTY SURFS THE BAY

In 1885 relatives of Hawaiian Queen Kapiolani reputedly visited Santa Cruz and surfed near the mouth of the San Lorenzo River. Nearly 20 years later, legendary Hawaiian surfer Duke Kahanamoku also surfed the Santa Cruz swells.

Mystery Spot. Hokey tourist trap or genuine scientific enigma? Since 1940, curious throngs baffled by the Mystery Spot have made it one of the most visited attractions in Santa Cruz. The laws of gravity and physics don't appear to apply in this tiny patch of redwood forest, where balls roll uphill and people stand on a slant. Advance online tickets ($6) are recommended for weekend and holiday visits. ✉ *465 Mystery Spot Rd.* ☎ *831/423–8897* 🌐 *www.mysteryspot.com* 🎫 *$5 on site, $6 in advance, parking $5* ⏲ *Late May–early Sept., daily 10–7; early Sept.–late May, weekdays 10–4, weekends 10–5.*

University of California at Santa Cruz. The modern 2,000-acre campus of the University of California at Santa Cruz nestles in the forested hills above town. Its sylvan setting, sweeping ocean vistas, and redwood architecture make the university worth a visit. Campus tours, offered several times daily (reserve in advance), offer a glimpse of college life and campus highlights. They run about an hour and 45 minutes and combine moderate walking with shuttle transport.

UCSC Arboretum. Half a mile beyond the main campus entrance, the UCSC Arboretum is a stellar collection of gardens arranged by geography. A walking path leads through areas dedicated to the plants of California, Australia, New Zealand, and South Africa. ✉ *1156 High St.* ☎ *831/427–2998* 🌐 *arboretum.ucsc.edu* 🎫 *$5* ⏲ *Daily 9–5, guided tours by appointment* ✉ *Main entrance at Bay and High Sts.* ☎ *831/459–0111* 🌐 *www.ucsc.edu.*

OFF THE BEATEN PATH

Santa Cruz Mountains. Highway 9 heads northeast from Santa Cruz into hills densely timbered with massive coastal redwoods. The road winds through the lush San Lorenzo Valley, past hamlets consisting of a few cafés, antiques shops, and old-style tourist cabins. Here, residents of the hunting-and-fishing persuasion coexist with hardcore flower-power survivors and wannabes. Along Highway 9 and its side roads are about a dozen **wineries,** most notably Bonny Doon Vineyard, Organic Wineworks, and David Bruce Winery. ■ **TIP→ The Santa Cruz Mountains Winegrowers** Association (🌐 www.scmwa.com) distributes a wine-touring map at many lodgings and attractions around Santa Cruz.

Felton. On your way into Felton, stop at the tiny, brick-red Bigfoot Discovery Museum, then take a walk in Henry Cowell Redwoods State Park. Off Graham Hill Road in town are a covered bridge and Roaring Camp Railroads, where you can take a vintage train to Bear Mountain year-round or down the San Lorenzo Gorge to Santa Cruz Main Beach in summer. ✉ *Hwy. 9, 7 mi north of Santa Cruz* ☎ *831/222–2120* 🌐 *www.slvchamber.org.*

Ben Lomond. Ben Lomond has the rough-hewn Henfling's Tavern, which presents a broad spectrum of live American and international music, and the kitschy chalet-style Tyrolean Inn, a Bavarian restaurant (no lunch) offering German beer and music. ✉ *Hwy. 9, 3 mi north of Felton* ☎ *831/222–2120* 🌐 *www.slvchamber.org.*

Boulder Creek. In Boulder Creek, buildings from the 1880s–1920s line the main street; pick up the walking-tour pamphlet, available at many local businesses, to learn more. ✉ *Hwy. 9, 2 mi north of Brookdale* ☎ *831/222–2120* 🌐 *www.slvchamber.org.*

Big Basin Redwoods State Park. Boulder Creek is the gateway to Big Basin Redwoods State Park. In California's oldest state park (established in 1902), more than 80 mi of hiking trails thread through redwood groves and past waterfalls. ✉ *Hwy. 236, Big Basin Way, 9 mi northwest of Boulder Creek, Boulder Creek* ☎ *831/338–8860* 🌐 *www.parks.ca.gov*

WHERE TO EAT

$ SEAFOOD ★ ✕ **Crow's Nest.** A local favorite since 1969, this classic California beachside eatery sits right on the water in Santa Cruz Harbor. Vintage surfboards and local surf photography line the walls in the main dining room; nearly every table overlooks the sand and surf. Seafood and steaks, served with local veggies, dominate the menu; favorite appetizers include the chilled shrimp-stuffed artichoke and crispy tempura prawns, served with rice pilaf. No need to pile high on your first trip to the endless salad bar—you can return as often as you like. For sweeping ocean views and more casual fare (think fish tacos and burgers), head upstairs to the Breakwater Bar & Grill. Live entertainment several days a week makes for a dynamic atmosphere year-round. ✉ *2218 E. Cliff Dr.* ☎ *831/476–4560* 🌐 *www.crowsnest-santacruz.com.*

$$ ITALIAN ✕ **Gabriella Café.** The work of local artists hangs on the walls of this petite, romantic café in a tile-roof cottage. Featuring organic produce from area farms, the seasonal Italian menu has offered wild mushroom risotto, grilled quail with quince mostarda, and roasted beet salad with arugula, goat cheese and pistachios. ✉ *910 Cedar St.* ☎ *831/457–1677* 🌐 *www.gabriellacafe.com.*

$$$ ITALIAN ✕ **La Posta.** Locals and tourists alike cram into La Posta's cozy, modern-rustic dining room, lured by authentic Italian fare made with fresh local produce. Near everything is house-made, from pizzas and breads baked in the brick oven to pasta and vanilla bean gelato (eggs come from a chicken coop out back). The seasonal menu changes often, but always includes flavorful dishes with a Santa Cruz flair, like fried artichokes, ravioli filled with crab, chicken with Brussels sprouts, or sautéed fish, caught sustainably from local waters. Come Sunday for a lively, family-style, fixed-price dinner—four courses for just $30. ✉ *538 Seabright Ave.* ☎ *831/457–2782* 🌐 *www.lapostarestaurant.com* ⏲ *Closed Mon. No lunch.*

$$$ CONTINENTAL ★ ✕ **Oswald.** Sophisticated yet unpretentious European-inspired California cooking is the order of the day at this intimate and stylish bistro. The menu changes seasonally, but might include such items as perfectly prepared sherry-steamed mussels or sautéed duck breast. Sit at the slick marble bar and order a creative concoction like bourbon mixed with

local apple and lemon juices or gin with cucumber and ginger beer, or choose from a range of wines and spirits. ✉ *121 Soquel Ave., at Front St.* ☎ *831/423–7427* 🌐 *www.oswaldrestaurant.com* ⏲ *Closed Mon. No lunch weekends.*

$ AMERICAN ✕ **Seabright Brewery.** Great burgers, big salads, and stellar microbrews make this a favorite hangout in the youthful Seabright neighborhood east of downtown. Sit outside on the large patio or inside at a comfortable, spacious booth; both are popular with families. ✉ *519 Seabright Ave.* ☎ *831/426–2739* 🌐 *www.seabrightbrewery.com.*

$$ MEDITERRANEAN ✕ **Soif.** Wine reigns at this sleek bistro and wine shop that takes its name from the French word for thirst. The lengthy list includes selections from near and far, dozens of which you can order by the taste or glass. Infused with the tastes of the Mediterranean, small plates and mains are served at the copper-top bar, the big communal table, and private tables. A jazz combo or solo pianist plays some evenings. ✉ *105 Walnut Ave.* ☎ *831/423–2020* 🌐 *www.soifwine.com* ⏲ *No lunch.*

¢ AMERICAN ✕ **Zachary's.** This noisy café filled with students and families defines the funky essence of Santa Cruz. It also dishes up great breakfasts: stay simple with sourdough pancakes, or go for Mike's Mess—eggs scrambled with bacon, mushrooms, and home fries, then topped with sour cream, melted cheese, and fresh tomatoes. ■ **TIP→ If you arrive after 9 am, expect a long wait for a table; lunch is a shade calmer, but closing time is 2:30 pm.** ✉ *819 Pacific Ave.* ☎ *831/427–0646* *Reservations not accepted* ⏲ *Closed Mon. No dinner.*

WHERE TO STAY

For expanded reviews, go to Fodors.com.

$$$ **Babbling Brook Inn.** Though it's smack in the middle of Santa Cruz, this B&B has lush gardens, a running stream, and tall trees that make you feel as if you're in a secluded wood. **Pros:** close to UCSC; walking distance from downtown shops; woodsy feel. **Cons:** near a high school; some rooms are close to a busy street. ✉ *1025 Laurel St.* ☎ *831/427–2437, 800/866–1131* 🌐 *www.babblingbrookinn.com* *13 rooms* *In-room: no a/c, Wi-Fi* *Breakfast.*

$$$ **Chaminade Resort & Spa.** A full-on renovation of the entire property, completed in 2009, sharpened this hilltop resort's look, enhanced its amenities, and qualified it for regional green certification. **Pros:** far from city life; spectacular property; ideal spot for romance and rejuvenation. **Cons:** must drive to attractions and sights; near major hospital. ✉ *1 Chaminade La.* ☎ *800/283–6569 reservations, 831/475–5600* 🌐 *www.chaminade.com* *112 rooms, 44 suites* *In-room: a/c, Internet, Wi-Fi. In-hotel: restaurant, bar, pool, tennis court, gym, spa, business center, some pets allowed.*

¢ **Harbor Inn.** Family-run, friendly, and funky, this basic but sparkling-clean lodge offers exceptional value just a few blocks from Santa Cruz Harbor and Twin Lakes Beach. **Pros:** affordable; free Wi-Fi; park your car and walk to the beach. **Cons:** not fancy; not near downtown. ✉ *645 7th Ave.* ☎ *831/479–9731* 🌐 *www.harborinn.info* *17 rooms, 2 suites* *In-room: no a/c, Wi-Fi. In-hotel: some pets allowed.*

$$$ **Pacific Blue Inn.** Green themes reign in this three-story, eco-friendly B&B, built from scratch in 2009 on a sliver of prime property on the outer edge of Pacific Avenue, downtown Santa Cruz's main drag. **Pros:** free bicycles; five-minute walk to boardwalk and wharf; right in downtown. **Cons:** tiny property; not suitable for children. *636 Pacific Ave. 831/600–8880 www.pacificblueinn.com 9 rooms In-room: Wi-Fi. In-hotel: some pets allowed Breakfast.*

$$$ **Pleasure Point Inn.** Tucked in a residential neighborhood at the east end of town, this modern Mediterranean-style B&B sits right across the street from the ocean and a popular surfing beach (where surfing lessons are available). **Pros:** fantastic views; ideal for checking the swells; quirky neighborhood. **Cons:** few rooms; several miles from major attractions. *2–3665 E. Cliff Dr. 831/475–4657 www.pleasurepointinn.com 4 rooms In-room: no a/c, Wi-Fi. In-hotel: beach Breakfast.*

3

$$$$ ★ **Santa Cruz Dream Inn.** Just a short stroll from the boardwalk and wharf, this full-service luxury hotel is the only lodging in Santa Cruz directly on the beach. **Pros:** directly on the beach; easy parking; walk to boardwalk and downtown. **Cons:** expensive; area gets congested on busy weekends. *175 W. Cliff Dr. 831/426–4330, 866/774–7735 reservations 831/427–2025 www.dreaminnsantacruz.com 149 rooms, 16 suites In-room: a/c, Wi-Fi. In-hotel: restaurant, bar, pool, beach, business center, parking.*

$$$ ★ **West Cliff Inn.** Perched on the bluffs across from Cowell Beach, this posh nautical-theme inn commands sweeping views of the boardwalk and Monterey Bay. **Pros:** killer views; walking distance from the beach; close to downtown. **Cons:** boardwalk noise; street traffic. *174 West Cliff Dr. 800/979–0910 toll free, 831/457-2200 www.westcliffinn.com 7 rooms, 2 suites, 1 cottage In-room: a/c, Wi-Fi. In-hotel: business center, some pets allowed Breakfast.*

NIGHTLIFE AND THE ARTS

NIGHTLIFE

★ **Catalyst.** Dance with the crowds at the Catalyst, a huge, grimy downtown club that has regularly featured big names, from Neil Young to the Red Hot Chili Peppers. *1011 Pacific Ave. 831/423–1338 www.catalystclub.com.*

Kuumbwa Jazz Center. Renowned in the international jazz community, and drawing performers such as Herbie Hancock, Pat Metheny, and Charlie Hunter, the nonprofit Kuumbwa Jazz Center bops with live music most nights; the café serves meals an hour before most shows. *320–2 Cedar St. 831/427–2227 www.kuumbwajazz.org.*

Moe's Alley. Blues, salsa, reggae, funk: you name it, Moe's Alley has it all, six nights a week. *1535 Commercial Way 831/479–1854 www.moesalley.com.*

THE ARTS

Cabrillo Festival of Contemporary Music. Each August, the Cabrillo Festival of Contemporary Music brings some of the world's finest artists to the Santa Cruz Civic Auditorium to play groundbreaking symphonic music, including major world premieres. ☎ *831/426–6966, 831/420–5260 box office* 🌐 *www.cabrillomusic.org.*

Santa Cruz Baroque Festival. Using period and reproduction instruments, the Santa Cruz Baroque Festival presents a wide range of classical music at various venues throughout the year. As the name suggests, the focus is on 17th- and 18th-century composers such as Bach and Handel. ☎ *831/457–9693* 🌐 *www.scbaroque.org.*

Shakespeare Santa Cruz. Shakespeare Santa Cruz stages a six-week Shakespeare festival in July and August that may also include the occasional modern dramatic performance. Most performances are outdoors under the redwoods. A holiday program takes place in December. ✉ *SSC/UCSC Theater Arts Center, 1156 High St.* ☎ *831/459–2121, 831/459–2159 tickets* 🌐 *www.shakespearesantacruz.org.*

SPORTS AND THE OUTDOORS

BICYCLING

Another Bike Shop. Mountain bikers should head to Another Bike Shop for tips on the best trails around and a look at cutting-edge gear made and tested locally. ✉ *2361 Mission St.* ☎ *831/427–2232* 🌐 *www.anotherbikeshop.com.*

Bicycle Shop Santa Cruz. Park the car and rent a beach cruiser at Bicycle Shop Santa Cruz. ✉ *1325 Mission St.* ☎ *831/454–0909* 🌐 *www.thebicycleshopsantacruz.com.*

BOATS AND CHARTERS

Chardonnay Sailing Charters. Chardonnay Sailing Charters cruises Monterey Bay year-round on a variety of trips, such as whale-watching, astronomy, and winemaker sails. The 70-foot *Chardonnay II* leaves from the yacht harbor in Santa Cruz. Food and drink are served on many of their cruises. Reservations are essential. ☎ *831/423–1213* 🌐 *www.chardonnay.com.*

Stagnaro Sport Fishing. Stagnaro Sport Fishing operates salmon, albacore, and rock-cod fishing expeditions; the fees ($50 to $75) include bait. The company also runs whale-watching, dolphin, and sealife cruises ($45) year-round. ✉ *June–Aug., Santa Cruz Municipal Wharf; Sept.–May, Santa Cruz West Harbor* ☎ *831/427–2334* 🌐 *www.stagnaros.com.*

GOLF

Pasatiempo Golf Club. Designed by famed golf architect Dr. Alister MacKenzie in 1929, semiprivate Pasatiempo Golf Club, set amid undulating hills just above the city, often ranks among the nation's top championship courses in annual polls. Golfers rave about the spectacular views and challenging terrain. The greens fee is $220; an electric cart is $30 per player. ✉ *20 Clubhouse Rd.* ☎ *831/459–9155* 🌐 *www.pasatiempo.com.*

CLOSE UP

O'Neill: A Santa Cruz Icon

O'Neill wet suits and beachwear weren't exactly born in Santa Cruz, but as far as most of the world is concerned, the O'Neill brand is synonymous with Santa Cruz and surfing legend.

The O'Neill wet suit story began in 1952, when Jack O'Neill and his brother Robert opened their first Surf Shop in a garage across from San Francisco's Ocean Beach. While shaping balsa surfboards and selling accessories, the O'Neills experimented with solutions to a common surfer problem: frigid waters. Tired of being forced back to shore, blue-lipped and shivering, after just 20 or 30 minutes riding the waves, they played with various materials and eventually designed a neoprene vest.

In 1959 Jack moved his Surf Shop 90 mi south to Cowell Beach in Santa Cruz. It quickly became a popular surf hangout, and O'Neill's new wet suits began to sell like hotcakes. In the early 1960s the company opened a warehouse for manufacturing on a larger scale. Santa Cruz soon became a major surf city, attracting wave-riders to prime breaks at Steamer Lane, Pleasure Point, and The Hook. In 1965 O'Neill pioneered the first wet-suit boots, and in 1971 Jack's son invented the surf leash. By 1980, O'Neill stood at the top of the world wet-suit market.

O'Neill operates two flagship stores, one downtown and one close to Jack O'Neill's home on Pleasure Point. Check out the latest versions, along with casual beachwear and surfing gear. You can also pop into a smaller outlet on the Santa Cruz Wharf.

O'Neill Surf Shop ✉ *110 Cooper St.* ☎ *831/469–4377* 🌐 *www.oneill.com..*

3

KAYAKING

Kayak Connection. In March, April, and May paddle out in the bay to mingle with gray whales and their calves on their northward journey to Alaska with Kayak Connection. Kayak Connection also guides other tours around Monterey Bay, including Natural Bridges State Beach, Capitola, and Elkhorn Slough. ✉ *413 Lake Ave. #3, Santa Cruz Harbor* ☎ *831/479–1121* 🌐 *www.kayakconnection.com.*

Venture Quest Kayaking. Explore hidden coves and kelp forests with Venture Quest Kayaking. The company's guided nature tours depart from Santa Cruz Wharf or Harbor, depending on the season. A two-hour kayak nature tour and introductory lesson costs $55. A three-hour kayak rental is $30 and includes wet suit and gear. Venture Quest also arranges tours at other Monterey Bay destinations, including Capitola and Elkhorn Slough. ✉ *#2 Santa Cruz Wharf* ☎ *831/427–2267, 831/425–8445* 🌐 *www.kayaksantacruz.com.*

SURFING

Pleasure Point. Surfers gather for spectacular waves and sunsets at Pleasure Point. ✉ *E. Cliff and Pleasure Point Drs.*

Steamer Lane. Steamer Lane, near the lighthouse on West Cliff Drive, has a decent break. The area plays host to several competitions in summer.

Club-Ed Surf School and Camps. Find out what all the fun is about at Club-Ed Surf School and Camps. Your first private or group lesson ($85 and up) includes all equipment. ✉ *Cowell Beach, at Santa Cruz Dream Inn* ☎ *831/464–0177* 🌐 *www.club-ed.com.*

Paradise Surf Shop. The most welcoming place in town to buy or rent surf gear is Paradise Surf Shop. The shop is owned and run by women who aim to help everyone feel comfortable on the water. ✉ *3961 Portola Dr.* ☎ *831/462–3880* 🌐 *www.paradisesurf.com.*

Cowell's Beach Surf Shop. Cowell's Beach Surf Shop sells bikinis, rents surfboards and wet suits, and offers lessons. ✉ *30 Front St.* ☎ *831/427–2355* 🌐 *www.cowellssurfshop.com.*

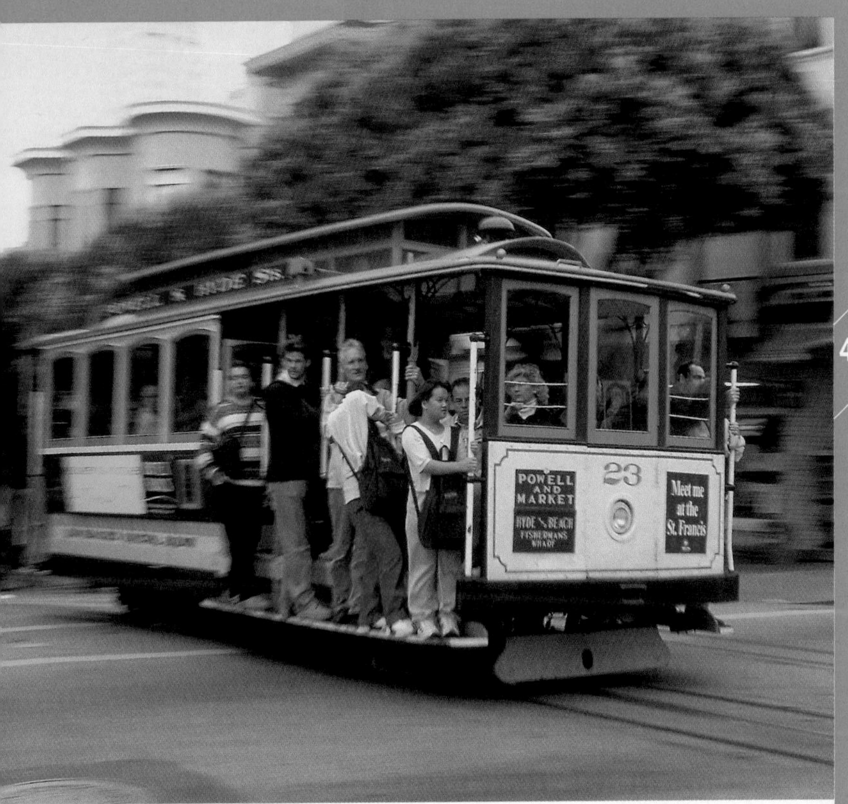

San Francisco

WORD OF MOUTH

"The part I was really looking forward to was walking down [Telegraph Hill] and looking for parrots. I'd seen the movie *The Wild Parrots of Telegraph Hill,* and the neighborhood was one of the things that meant 'San Francisco' to me. The neighborhood itself was beautiful, and we did indeed see parrots."

—sunny16

WELCOME TO SAN FRANCISCO

TOP REASONS TO GO

★ **The bay:** It's hard not to gasp as you catch sight of sunlight dancing on the water when you crest a hill, or watch the Golden Gate Bridge vanish and reemerge in the summer fog.

★ **The food:** San Franciscans are serious about what they eat, and with good reason. Home to some of the nation's best chefs, top restaurants, and finest local produce, it's hard not to eat well here.

★ **The shopping:** Shopaholics visiting the city will not be disappointed: San Francisco is packed with browsing destinations, everything from quirky boutiques to massive malls.

★ **The good life:** A laid-back atmosphere, beautiful surroundings, and oodles of cultural, culinary, and aesthetic pleasures . . . if you spend too much time here, you might not leave!

★ **The great outdoors:** From Golden Gate Park to sidewalk cafés in North Beach, San Franciscans relish their outdoor spaces.

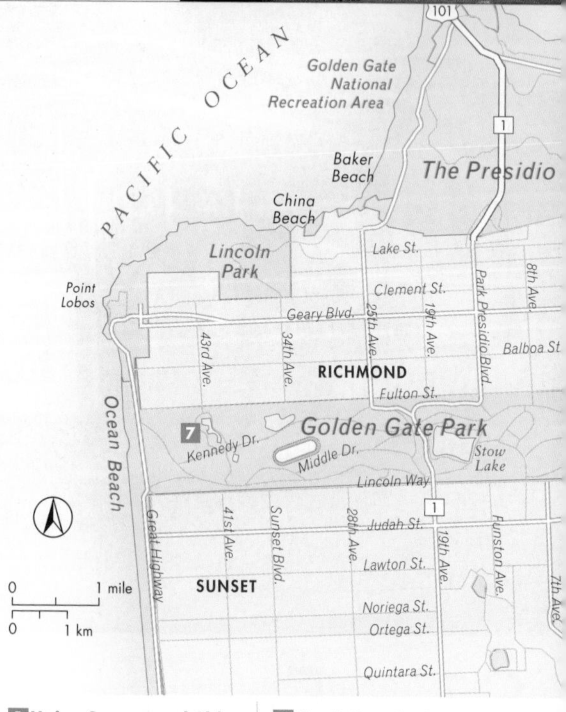

1 Union Square and Chinatown. Union Square has hotels, public transportation, and shopping; walking through Chinatown is like visiting another country.

2 SoMa and Civic Center. SoMa is anchored by SFMOMA and Yerba Buena Gardens; the city's performing arts venues are in Civic Center.

3 Nob Hill and Russian Hill. Nob Hill is old money San Francisco; Russian Hill's steep streets have excellent eateries and shopping.

4 North Beach. This small Italian neighborhood is a great place to enjoy an espresso.

5 On the Waterfront. Head here to visit the exquisitely restored Ferry Building, Fisherman's Wharf, Pier 39, and Ghirardelli Square.

6 The Marina and the Presidio. The Marina has trendy boutiques, restaurants, and cafés; the wooded Presidio offers great views of the Golden Gate Bridge.

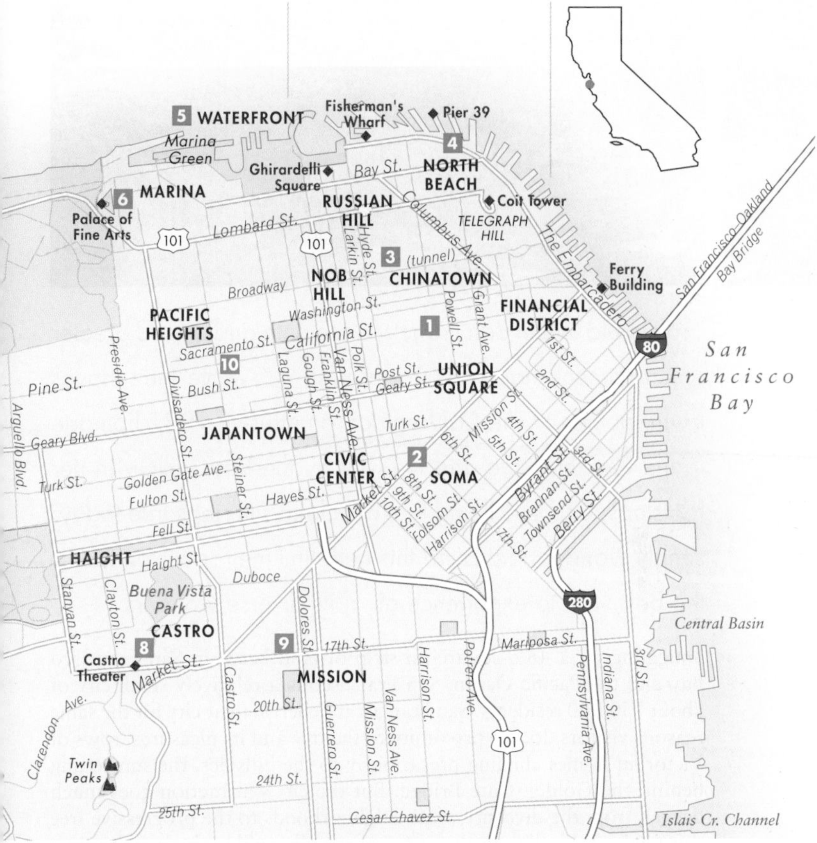

5 WATERFRONT
Fisherman's Wharf
Pier 39
Marina Green
4
Ghirardelli Square
Bay St.
NORTH BEACH
6
MARINA
RUSSIAN HILL
Columbus Ave.
Coit Tower
Palace of Fine Arts
101
Lombard St.
101
Hyde St.
Larkin St.
TELEGRAPH HILL
The Embarcadero
San Francisco-Oakland Bay Bridge
3 (tunnel)
Ferry Building
Broadway
NOB HILL
CHINATOWN
Washington St.
FINANCIAL DISTRICT
PACIFIC HEIGHTS
California St.
1
Powell St.
Grant Ave.
Sacramento St.
10
80
San Francisco Bay
1st St.
2nd St.
Presidio Ave.
Laguna St.
Gough St.
Franklin St.
Van Ness Ave.
Polk St.
Post St.
Geary St.
UNION SQUARE
Pine St.
Bush St.
Divisadero St.
Arguello Blvd.
Geary Blvd.
JAPANTOWN
Turk St.
Mission St.
4th St.
5th St.
6th St.
Turk St.
Golden Gate Ave.
Steiner St.
CIVIC CENTER
2
SOMA
3rd St.
Fulton St.
Hayes St.
Market St.
8th St.
9th St.
10th St.
Folsom St.
Harrison St.
Bryant St.
Brannan St.
Townsend St.
Berry St.
7th St.
Fell St.
HAIGHT
Haight St.
Duboce
Buena Vista Park
Stanyan St.
Clayton St.
CASTRO
280
Central Basin
9
Dolores St.
17th St.
Mariposa St.
8
Castro Theater
Market St.
MISSION
Harrison St.
Potrero Ave.
Pennsylvania Ave.
Indiana St.
3rd St.
Castro St.
20th St.
Guerrero St.
Mission St.
Van Ness Ave.
101
Clarendon Ave.
Twin Peaks
24th St.
25th St.
Cesar Chavez St.
Islais Cr. Channel

4

7 Golden Gate Park and the Western Shoreline. San Francisco's 1,000-acre backyard has sports fields, windmills, museums, and gardens; the windswept Western Shoreline stretches for miles.

8 The Haight, the Castro, and Noe Valley. After you've seen the blockbuster sights, come to these neighborhoods to see where the city's heart beats.

9 The Mission. This Latino neighborhood has destination restaurants, bargain ethnic eateries, and a hip bar scene.

10 Pacific Heights and Japantown. Pacific Heights has some of the city's most opulent real estate; Japantown is packed with authentic Japanese shops and restaurants.

GETTING ORIENTED

San Francisco is a compact city; just 46½ square mi. Essentially a tightly packed cluster of extremely diverse neighborhoods, the city dearly rewards walking. The areas that most visitors cover are easy (and safe) to reach on foot, but many have steep—make that *steep*—hills.

Updated by Denise M. Leto, Michele Bigley, Marcia Gagliardi, Fiona G. Parrott, Sura Wood

"You could live in San Francisco a month and ask no greater entertainment than walking through it," wrote Inez Hayes Irwin, author of *The Californiacs*, an effusive 1921 homage to the Golden State and the City by the Bay. Follow in her footsteps, and you'll find that her claim still rings true today: simply wandering around this beautiful metropolis on foot is the best way to experience all of its diverse wonders.

Snuggling on a 46½-square-mi strip of land between San Francisco Bay and the Pacific Ocean, San Francisco is a relatively small city of about 750,000 residents. San Franciscans cherish their city for the same reasons visitors do: the proximity to the bay and its pleasures, rows of Victorian homes clinging precariously to the hillsides, the sun setting behind the Golden Gate Bridge. But the city's attraction goes much deeper, from the diversity of its neighborhoods to the progressive free spirit here. Take all these things together, and you'll begin to understand why many San Franciscans can't imagine calling anyplace else home—despite the dizzying cost of living.

San Francisco's charms are great and small. You won't want to miss Golden Gate Park, the Palace of Fine Arts, The Golden Gate Bridge, or a cable car ride over Nob Hill. But a walk down the Filbert Street Steps or through Macondray Lane or an hour gazing at murals in the Mission or the thundering Pacific from the cliffs of Lincoln Park can be equally inspiring.

PLANNING

WHEN TO GO

You can visit San Francisco comfortably any time of year. Possibly the best time to visit San Francisco is September and October, when the city's summerlike weather brings outdoor concerts and festivals. The climate here always feels Mediterranean and moderate—with a foggy, sometimes chilly bite. The temperature rarely drops below 40°F, and anything warmer than 80°F is considered a heat wave. Be prepared for rain in winter, especially December and January. Winds off the ocean can add to the chill factor. That old joke about summer in SF feeling like winter is true at heart, but once you move inland, it gets warmer. (And some locals swear the thermostat has inched up in recent years.)

GETTING HERE AND AROUND

AIR TRAVEL

The major gateway to San Francisco is San Francisco International Airport (SFO), 15 mi south of the city. It's off U.S. 101 near Millbrae and San Bruno. Oakland International Airport (OAK) is across the bay, not much farther away from downtown San Francisco (via I–80 east and I–880 south), but rush-hour traffic on the Bay Bridge may lengthen travel times considerably. San Jose International Airport (SJC) is about 40 mi south of San Francisco; travel time depends largely on traffic flow, but plan on an hour and a half with moderate traffic.

4

Airports **San Francisco International Airport** (*SFO ☎ 800/435–9736* or *650/821–8211 🌐 www.flysfo.com*). **Oakland International Airport** (*OAK ☎ 510/563–3300 🌐 www.flyoakland.com*). **San Jose International Airport** (*SJC ☎ 408/392–3600 🌐 www.sjc.org*).

Airport Transfers **American Airporter** (*☎ 415/202–0733 🌐 www.americanairporter.com*). **BayPorter Express** (*☎ 415/467–1800 🌐 www.bayporter.com*). **Caltrain** (*☎ 800/660–4287 🌐 www.caltrain.com*). **East Bay Express Airporter** (*☎ 877/526–0304 🌐 www.eastbaytransportation.com*). **Lorrie's Airport Service** (*☎ 415/334–9000 🌐 www.gosfovan.com*). **Marin Airporter** (*☎ 415/461–4222 🌐 www.marinairporter.com*). **Marin Door to Door** (*☎ 415/457–2717 🌐 www.marindoortodoor.com*). **SamTrans** (*☎ 800/660–4287 🌐 www.samtrans.com*). **South & East Bay Airport Shuttle** (*☎ 800/548–4664 🌐 www.southandeastbayairportshuttle.com*). **SuperShuttle** (*☎ 800/258–3826 🌐 www.supershuttle.com*). **VIP Airport Shuttle** (*☎ 408/986–6000 or 800/235–8847 🌐 www.viptransportgroup.com*).

BART TRAVEL

Bay Area Rapid Transit (BART) trains, which run until midnight, travel under the bay via tunnel to connect San Francisco with Oakland, Berkeley, Pittsburgh/Bay Point, Richmond, Fremont, Dublin/Pleasanton, and other small cities and towns in between. Within San Francisco, stations are limited to downtown, the Mission, and a couple of outlying neighborhoods.

Trains travel frequently from early morning until evening on weekdays. After 8 pm weekdays and on weekends there's often a 20-minute wait between trains on the same line. Trains also travel south from San Francisco as far as Millbrae. BART trains connect downtown San Francisco to San Francisco International Airport; a ride is $8.10.

Intracity San Francisco fares are $1.75; intercity fares are $3.10 to $5.95. BART bases its ticket prices on miles traveled, and does not offer price breaks by zone. The easy-to-read maps posted in BART stations list fares based on destination, radiating out from your starting point of the current station.

Contact **Bay Area Rapid Transit** (*BART ☎ 415/989–2278 or 650/992–2278 🌐 www.bart.gov*).

BOAT AND FERRY TRAVEL

Several ferry lines run out of San Francisco. Blue & Gold Fleet operates a number of routes, including service to Sausalito ($10 one-way) and Tiburon ($10 one-way). Tickets are sold at Pier 41 (between Fisherman's Wharf and Pier 39), where the boats depart. Alcatraz Cruises, owned by Hornblower Yachts, operates the ferries to Alcatraz Island ($22 including audio tour and National Park Service ranger-led programs) from Pier 33, about a half-mile east of Fisherman's Wharf ($3 shuttle buses serve several area hotels and other locations). Boats leave 10 times a day (14 times a day in summer), and the journey itself is 30 minutes. Allow roughly 2½ hours for a round-trip jaunt. Golden Gate Ferry runs daily to and from Sausalito and Larkspur (each costs $8.25 one-way), leaving from Pier 1, behind the San Francisco Ferry Building. The Alameda/Oakland Ferry operates daily between Alameda's Main Street Ferry Building, Oakland's Jack London Square, and San Francisco's Pier 41 and the Ferry Building ($6.25 one-way); some ferries go only to Pier 41 or the Ferry Building, so ask when you board. Purchase tickets onboard.

Ferry Lines Alameda/Oakland Ferry (☎ *510/522–3300* ⊕ *www.eastbayferry.com*). **Alcatraz Cruises** (☎ *415/981–7625* ⊕ *www.alcatrazcruises.com*). **Blue & Gold Fleet** (☎ *415/705–8200* ⊕ *www.blueandgoldfleet.com*). **Golden Gate Ferry** (☎ *415/923–2000* ⊕ *www.goldengateferry.org*). **San Francisco Ferry Building** (✉ *1 Ferry Bldg., at foot of Market St. on Embarcadero* ☎ *415/983–8030* ⊕ *www.ferrybuildingmarketplace.com*).

CABLE CAR TRAVEL

The fare (for one direction) is $6 (Muni Passport holders only pay a $1 supplement). You can buy tickets on board (exact change isn't necessary) or at the kiosks at the cable car turnarounds at Hyde and Beach streets and at Powell and Market streets.

The heavily traveled Powell–Mason and Powell–Hyde lines begin at Powell and Market streets near Union Square and terminate at Fisherman's Wharf; lines for these routes can be long, especially in summer. The California Street line runs east and west from Market and California streets to Van Ness Avenue; there is often no wait to board this route.

CAR TRAVEL

Driving in San Francisco can be a challenge because of the one-way streets, snarly traffic, and steep hills. The first two elements can be frustrating enough, but those hills are tough for unfamiliar drivers. **■ TIP→ Remember to curb your wheels when parking on hills—turn wheels away from the curb when facing uphill, toward the curb when facing downhill. You can get a ticket if you don't do this.**

MUNI TRAVEL

The San Francisco Municipal Railway, or Muni, operates light-rail vehicles, the historic F-line streetcars along Fisherman's Wharf and Market Street, trolley buses, and the world-famous cable cars. Light rail travels along Market Street to the Mission District and Noe Valley (J line), the Ingleside District (K line), and the Sunset District (L, M, and N lines); during peak hours (Mon.–Fri., 6 am–9 am and 3 pm–7 pm) the J line continues around the Embarcadero to the Caltrain station at 4th and King streets. The T line light rail runs from the Castro, down Market

Street, around the Embarcadero, and south past Hunters Point and Monster Park to Sunnydale Avenue and Bayshore Boulevard. Muni provides 24-hour service on select lines to all areas of the city.

On buses and streetcars the fare is $2. Exact change is required, and dollar bills are accepted in the fare boxes. For all Muni vehicles other than cable cars, 90-minute transfers are issued free upon request at the time the fare is paid. These are valid for two additional transfers in any direction. Cable cars cost $6 and include no transfers *(see Cable Car Travel, above)*.

One-day ($13), three-day ($20), and seven-day ($26) Passports valid on the entire Muni system can be purchased at several outlets, including the cable car ticket booth at Powell and Market streets and the visitor information center downstairs in Hallidie Plaza. A monthly ticket, called a Fast Pass, is available for $70, and can be used on all Muni lines (including cable cars) and on BART within city limits. The San Francisco CityPass, a discount ticket booklet to several major city attractions, also covers all Muni travel for seven consecutive days.

The San Francisco Municipal Transit and Street Map ($3) is a useful guide to the extensive transportation system. You can buy the map at most bookstores and at the San Francisco Visitor Information Center, on the lower level of Hallidie Plaza at Powell and Market streets.

Outside the city, AC Transit serves the East Bay, and Golden Gate Transit serves Marin and Sonoma counties.

Bus Lines AC Transit (☎ *510/839–2882* 🌐 *www.actransit.org*). **Golden Gate Transit** (☎ *511 or 415/455–2000* 🌐 *www.goldengate.org*). **San Francisco Municipal Railway System** (*Muni* ☎ *311 or 415/701–3000* 🌐 *www.sfmta.com*).

TAXI TRAVEL

Taxi service is notoriously bad in San Francisco, and hailing a cab can be frustratingly difficult in some parts of the city, especially on weekends. Popular nightspots such as the Mission, SoMa, North Beach, the Haight, and the Castro have a lot of cabs but a lot of people looking for taxis, too. Midweek, and during the day, you shouldn't have much of a problem—unless it's raining. In a pinch, hotel taxi stands are an option, as is calling for a pick-up. But be forewarned: taxi companies frequently don't answer the phone in peak periods. The absolute worst time to find a taxi is Friday afternoon and evening; plan well ahead, and if you're going to the airport, make a reservation or book a shuttle instead. Most taxi companies take advance reservations for airport and out-of-town runs but not in-town transfers.

Taxis in San Francisco charge $3.10 for the first 1/5 mi (one of the highest base rates in the United States), 45¢ for each additional 1/5 mi, and 45¢ per minute in stalled traffic. There is no charge for additional passengers; there is no surcharge for luggage. For trips outside city limits, multiply the metered rate by 1.5.

Taxi Companies DeSoto Cab (☎ *415/970–1300*). **Luxor Cab** (☎ *415/282–4141*). **Veteran's Taxicab** (☎ *415/648–1313*). **Yellow Cab** (☎ *415/626–2345*).

Complaints San Francisco Police Department Taxi Complaints (☎ *415/553–1447*).

TRAIN TRAVEL

Amtrak trains travel to the Bay Area from some cities in California and the United States. The *Coast Starlight* travels north from Los Angeles to Seattle, passing the Bay Area along the way, but contrary to its name, the train runs inland through the Central Valley for much of its route through Northern California; the most scenic stretch is in Southern California, between San Luis Obispo and Los Angeles. Amtrak also has several routes between San Jose, Oakland, and Sacramento. The *California Zephyr* travels from Chicago to the Bay Area, and has spectacular alpine vistas as it crosses the Sierra Nevada mountains. San Francisco doesn't have an Amtrak train station but does have an Amtrak bus station, at the Ferry Building, which provides service to trains in Emeryville, just over the Bay Bridge. Shuttle buses also connect the Emeryville train station with downtown Oakland, the Caltrain station, and other points in downtown San Francisco.

Caltrain connects San Francisco to Palo Alto, San Jose, Santa Clara, and many smaller cities en route. In San Francisco, trains leave from the main depot, at 4th and Townsend streets, and a rail-side stop at 22nd and Pennsylvania streets. One-way fares are $2.75 to $11.50, depending on the number of zones through which your travel tickets are valid for four hours after purchase time. A ticket is $6 from San Francisco to Palo Alto, at least $8 to San Jose. You can also buy a day pass ($5.25–$22.75) for unlimited travel in a 24-hour period. It's worth waiting for an express train for trips that last 1 to 1¾ hours. On weekdays, trains depart three or four times per hour during the morning and evening, twice per hour during daytime non-commute hours, and as little as once per hour in the evening. Weekend trains run once per hour. The system shuts down at midnight. There are no onboard ticket sales. You must buy tickets before boarding the train or risk paying a $250 fine for fare evasion.

INFORMATION

Amtrak (☎ *800/872–7245* 🌐 *www.amtrak.com*). **Caltrain** (☎ *800/660–4287* 🌐 *www.caltrain.com*). **San Francisco Caltrain station** (✉ *700 4th St., at King St.*, ☎ *800/660–4287*).

VISITOR INFORMATION

The San Francisco Convention and Visitors Bureau can mail you brochures, maps, and festivals and events listings. Once you're in town, you can stop by their info center near Union Square. Information about the Wine Country, redwood groves, and northwestern California is available at the California Welcome Center on Pier 39.

Contacts San Francisco Visitor Information Center (✉ *Hallidie Plaza, lower level, 900 Market St., Union Sq.* ☎ *415/391–2000 TDD* 🌐 *www.onlyinsanfrancisco.com*).

EXPLORING SAN FRANCISCO

UNION SQUARE AND CHINATOWN

The Union Square area bristles with big-city bravado, while just a stone's throw away is a place that feels like a city unto itself, Chinatown. The two areas share a strong commercial streak, although manifested very differently. In Union Square the crowds zigzag among international brands, trailing glossy shopping bags. A few blocks north, people dash between small neighborhood stores, their arms draped with plastic totes filled with groceries or souvenirs.

EXPLORING IN UNION SQUARE

Maiden Lane. Known as Morton Street in the raffish Barbary Coast era, this former red-light district reported at least one murder a week during the late 19th century. Things cooled down after the 1906 fire destroyed the brothels, and these days Maiden Lane is a chic, boutique-lined pedestrian mall stretching two blocks, between Stockton and Kearny streets. Wrought-iron gates close the street to traffic most days between 11 and 5, when the lane becomes a patchwork of umbrella-shaded tables.

At **140 Maiden Lane** you can see the only Frank Lloyd Wright building in San Francisco. Walking through the brick archway and recessed entry feels a bit like entering a glowing cave. The interior's graceful, curving ramp and skylights are said to have been his model for the Guggenheim Museum in New York. Xanadu Gallery, which showcases Baltic, Latin American, and African folk art, now occupies the space. ✉ *Between Stockton and Kearny Sts., Union Square.*

San Francisco Visitor Information Center. A multilingual staff operates this facility below the cable car terminus. Staffers answer questions and provide maps and pamphlets. You can also pick up discount coupons—the savings can be significant, especially for families—and hotel brochures here. If you're planning to hit the big-ticket stops like the California Academy of Sciences, the Exploratorium, and SFMOMA, and ride the cable cars, consider picking up a CityPass here (or at any of the attractions it covers). **■ TIP→ The CityPass ($64, $39 ages 5–12), good for nine days including seven days of transit, will save you about 50%.** Also buy your Muni Passport here. ✉ *Hallidie Plaza, lower level, Powell and Market Sts., Union Square* ☎ *415/391–2000 or 415/283–0177* 🌐 *www.onlyinsanfrancisco.com* ⏲ *Weekdays 9–5, Sat. 9–3; also Sun. 9–3 in May–Oct.*

Union Square. The heart of San Francisco's downtown since 1850, the landscaped, 2½-acre square is about the only place you can sit for free in this part of town. Back in 2002, the public responded to Union Square's redesign with a resounding shrug. With its pretty landscaping, easier street access, and the addition of a café (welcome, but nothing special), it certainly was an improvement over the previous concrete wasteland. Four globular lamp sculptures by the artist R.M. Fischer preside over the space; there's also a café, an open-air stage, a visitor information booth, and a front-row seat to the cable car tracks. And there's a familiar kaleidoscope of characters: office workers sunning and brown-bagging, street musicians, shoppers taking a rest, kids chasing pigeons, and a fair number of homeless people.

The square takes its name from the violent pro-Union demonstrations staged here before the Civil War. At center stage, Robert Ingersoll Aitken's *Victory Monument* commemorates Commodore George Dewey's victory over the Spanish fleet at Manila in 1898. The 97-foot Corinthian column, topped by a bronze figure symbolizing naval conquest, was dedicated by Theodore Roosevelt in 1903 and withstood the 1906 earthquake. After the earthquake and fire of 1906, the square was dubbed Little St. Francis because of the temporary shelter erected for residents of the St. Francis Hotel. Actor John Barrymore (grandfather of actress Drew Barrymore and a notorious carouser) was among the guests pressed into volunteering to stack bricks in the square. His uncle, thespian John Drew, remarked, "It took an act of God to get John out of bed and the United States Army to get him to work."

CABLE CAR TERMINUS

Two of the three cable car lines begin and end their runs at Powell and Market streets, a couple of blocks south of Union Square. These two lines are the most scenic, and both pass near Fisherman's Wharf, so they're usually clogged with first-time sightseers. The wait to board a cable car at this intersection is longer than at any other stop in the system. If you'd rather avoid the mob, board the less-touristy California line at the bottom of Market Street, at Drumm Street.

On the eastern edge of Union Square, **TIX Bay Area** (☎ *415/433–7827 info only* 🌐 *www.theatrebayarea.org*) provides half-price day-of-performance tickets to all types of performing-arts events, as well as regular full-price box-office services. Union Square covers a convenient four-level garage, allegedly the first underground garage in the world. ✉ *Bordered by Powell, Stockton, Post, and Geary Sts., Union Square.*

Westin St. Francis Hotel. The second-oldest hotel in the city, established in 1904, was conceived by railroad baron and financier Charles Crocker and his associates as a hostelry for their millionaire friends. Swift service and sumptuous surroundings have always been hallmarks of the property. After the hotel was ravaged by the 1906 fire, a larger, more luxurious Italian Renaissance–style residence was opened in 1907 to attract loyal clients from among the world's rich and powerful. The hotel's checkered past includes the ill-fated 1921 bash in the suite of the silent-film comedian Fatty Arbuckle, at which a woman became ill and later died. Arbuckle endured three sensational trials for rape and murder before being acquitted, by which time his career was kaput. In 1975 Sara Jane Moore, standing among a crowd outside the hotel, attempted to shoot then-president Gerald Ford. As might be imagined, no plaques in the lobby commemorate these events. ■ **TIP→ One of the best views in the city is from the glass elevators here—and best of all, a ride is free. Zip up to the 32nd floor for a bird's-eye view; the lights of the nighttime cityscape are particularly lovely.** Don't be shy if you're not a guest: some visitors make this a stop every time they're in town. Every November the hotel's pastry chef creates a spectacular, rotating 12-foot gingerbread castle, on display in the

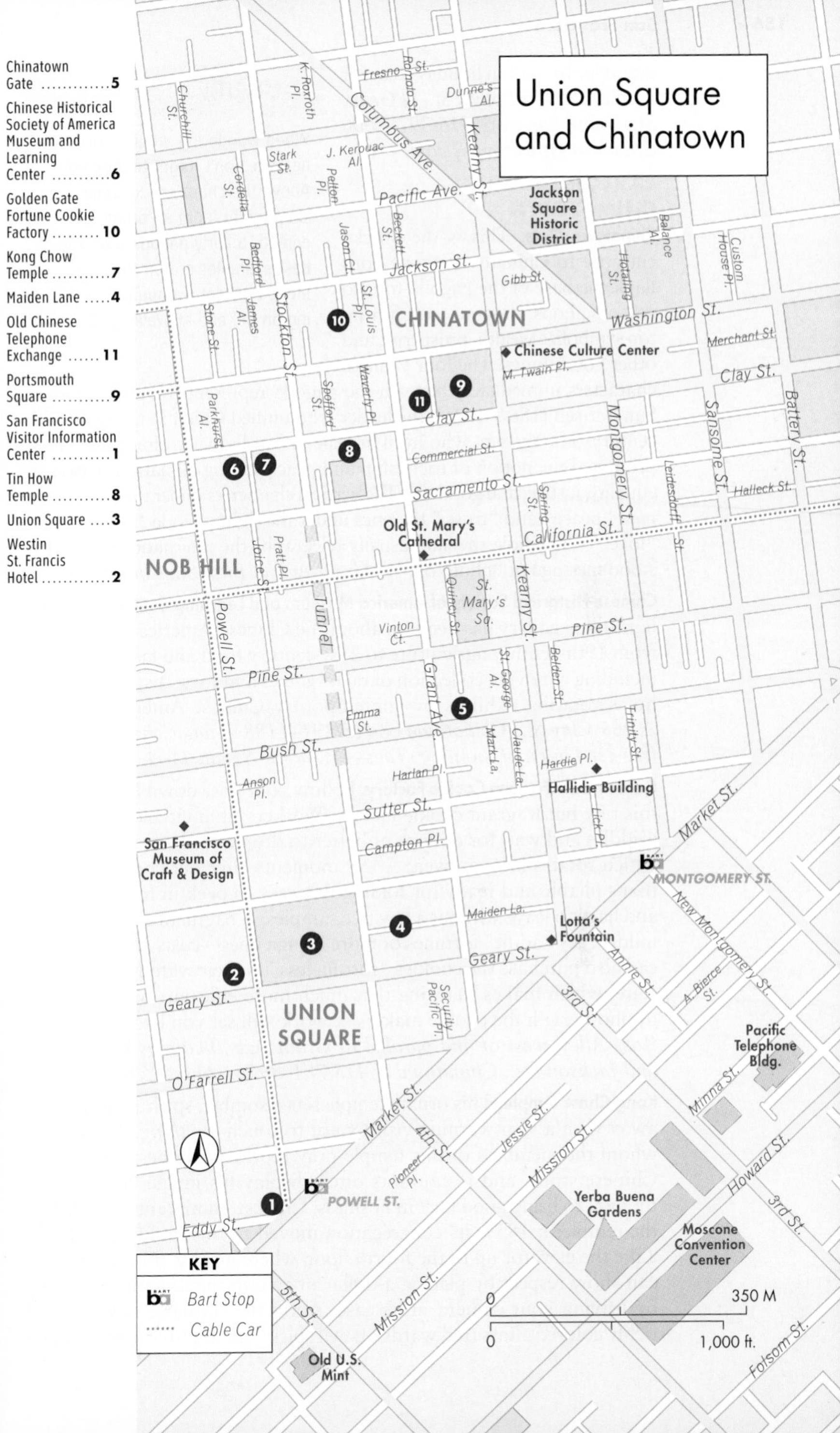
Union Square and Chinatown
Chinatown Gate 5
Chinese Historical Society of America Museum and Learning Center 6
Golden Gate Fortune Cookie Factory 10
Kong Chow Temple 7
Maiden Lane 4
Old Chinese Telephone Exchange 11
Portsmouth Square 9
San Francisco Visitor Information Center 1
Tin How Temple 8
Union Square 3
Westin St. Francis Hotel 2
Jackson Square Historic District
CHINATOWN
Chinese Culture Center
Old St. Mary's Cathedral
NOB HILL
St. Mary's Sq.
Hallidie Building
San Francisco Museum of Craft & Design
MONTGOMERY ST.
Lotta's Fountain
UNION SQUARE
Pacific Telephone Bldg.
POWELL ST.
Yerba Buena Gardens
Moscone Convention Center
Old U.S. Mint
Fresno St.
Romolo St.
Dunne's Al.
K. Rexroth Pl.
Churchill St.
Columbus Ave.
Kearny St.
Stark St.
J. Kerouac Al.
Cordelia St.
Pelton Pl.
Pacific Ave.
Jason Ct.
Beckett St.
Bedford Pl.
Jackson St.
Gibb St.
Balance Al.
Hotaling St.
Custom House Pl.
James Al.
Stockton St.
St. Louis Pl.
Stone St.
Washington St.
Merchant St.
M. Twain Pl.
Clay St.
Spofford St.
Waverly Pl.
Parkhurst Al.
Montgomery St.
Sansome St.
Battery St.
Commercial St.
Leidesdorff St.
Sacramento St.
Halleck St.
Spring St.
California St.
Pratt Pl.
Joice St.
Tunnel
Quincy St.
Powell St.
Vinton Ct.
Pine St.
Grant Ave.
St. George Al.
Belden St.
Emma St.
Mark La.
Claude La.
Trinity St.
Bush St.
Hardie Pl.
Harlan Pl.
Anson Pl.
Sutter St.
Lick Pl.
Market St.
Campton Pl.
New Montgomery St.
Maiden La.
Geary St.
Annie St.
A. Bierce St.
3rd St.
Security Pacific Pl.
O'Farrell St.
Minna St.
4th St.
Jessie St.
Mission St.
Howard St.
Pioneer Pl.
Eddy St.
5th St.
Folsom St.
KEY
Bart Stop
Cable Car
0
350 M
0
1,000 ft.

grand lobby—a fun holiday treat for families. ✉ *335 Powell St., at Geary St., Union Square* ☎ *415/397–7000* 🌐 *www.westinstfrancis.com.*

LOOK UP!

When wandering around Chinatown, don't forget to look up! Above the chintziest souvenir shop might loom an ornate balcony or a curly pagoda roof. The best examples are on the 900 block of Grant Avenue (at Washington St.) and at Waverly Place.

EXPLORING IN CHINATOWN

Chinatown Gate. This is the official entrance to Chinatown. Stone lions flank the base of the pagoda-topped gate; the lions, dragons, and fish up top symbolize wealth, prosperity, and other good things. The four Chinese characters immediately beneath the pagoda represent the philosophy of Sun Yat-sen (1866–1925), the leader who unified China in the early 20th century. Sun Yat-sen, who lived in exile in San Francisco for a few years, promoted the notion of friendship and peace among all nations based on equality, justice, and goodwill. The vertical characters under the left pagoda read "peace" and "trust," the ones under the right pagoda "respect" and "love." The whole shebang usually telegraphs the internationally understood message of "photo op." ✉ *Grant Ave. at Bush St., Chinatown.*

Chinese Historical Society of America Museum and Learning Center. This airy, light-filled gallery has displays about the Chinese-American experience from 19th-century agriculture to 21st-century food and fashion trends, including a moving collection of racist games and toys. A separate room hosts rotating exhibits by contemporary Chinese-American artists. ✉ *965 Clay St., Chinatown* ☎ *415/391–1188* 🌐 *www.chsa.org* 🎫 *$3, free 1st Thurs. of month* ⏲ *Tues.–Fri. noon–5, Sat. 11–4.*

Golden Gate Fortune Cookie Factory. Follow your nose down Ross Alley to this tiny but fragrant cookie factory. Workers sit at circular motorized griddles and wait for dollops of batter to drop onto a tiny metal plate, which rotates into an oven. A few moments later out comes a cookie that's pliable and ready for folding. It's easy to peek in for a moment, and hard to leave without a few free samples. A bagful of cookies—with mildly racy "adult" fortunes or more benign ones—costs about $4. You can also purchase the cookies "fortuneless" in their waferlike unfolded state, which makes snacking that much more efficient. Being allowed to photograph the cookie makers at work will set you back 50¢. ✉ *56 Ross Alley, west of and parallel to Grant Ave., between Washington and Jackson Sts., Chinatown* ☎ *415/781–3956* 🎫 *Free* ⏲ *Daily 9–8.*

Kong Chow Temple. This ornate temple sets a somber, spiritual tone right away with a sign warning visitors not to touch *anything*. The god to whom the members of this temple pray represents honesty and trust. Chinese stores and restaurants often display his image because he's thought to bring good luck in business. Chinese immigrants established the temple in 1851; its congregation moved to this building in 1977. Take the elevator up to the fourth floor, where incense fills the air. You can show respect by placing a dollar or two in the donation box and by leaving your camera in its case. Amid the statuary, flowers, and richly colored altars (red wards off evil spirits and signifies virility, green

Continued on page 163

CHINATOWN

Chinatown's streets flood the senses. Incense and cigarette smoke mingle with the scents of briny fish and sweet vanilla. Rooflines flare outward, pagoda-style. Loud Cantonese bargaining and honking car horns rise above the sharp clack of mah-jongg tiles and the eternally humming cables beneath the street.

Most Chinatown visitors march down Grant Avenue, buy a few trinkets, and call it a day. Do yourself a favor and dig deeper. This is one of the largest Chinese communities outside Asia, and there is far more to it than buying a back-scratcher near Chinatown Gate. To get a real feel for the neighborhood, wander off the main drag. Step into a temple or an herb shop and wander down a flag-draped alley. And don't be shy: residents welcome guests warmly, though rarely in English.

Whatever you do, don't leave without eating something. Noodle houses, bakeries, tea houses, and dim sum shops seem to occupy every other storefront. There's a feast for your eyes as well: in the market windows on Stockton and Grant, you'll see hanging whole roast ducks, fish, and shellfish swimming in tanks, and strips of shiny, pink-glazed Chinese-style barbecued pork.

CHINATOWN'S HISTORY

Sam Brannan's 1848 cry of "Gold!" didn't take long to reach across the world to China. Struggling with famine, drought, and political upheaval at home, thousands of Chinese jumped at the chance to try their luck in California. Most came from the Pearl River Delta region, in the Guangdong province, and spoke Cantonese dialects. From the start, Chinese businesses circled around Portsmouth Square, which was conveniently central. Bachelor rooming houses sprang up, since the vast majority of new arrivals were men. By 1853, the area was called Chinatown.

The Street of Gamblers (Ross Alley), 1898 (top). The first Chinese telephone operator in Chinatown (bottom).

COLD WELCOME

The Chinese faced discrimination from the get-go. Harrassment became outright hostility as first the gold rush, then the work on the Transcontinental Railroad petered out. Special taxes were imposed to shoulder aside competing "coolie labor." Laws forbidding the Chinese from moving outside Chinatown kept the residents packed in like sardines, with nowhere to go but up and down—thus the many basement establishments in the neighborhood. State and federal laws passed in the 1870s deterred Chinese women from immigrating, deeming them prostitutes. In the late 1870s, looting and arson attacks on Chinatown businesses soared.

The coup de grace, though, was the Chinese Exclusion Act, passed by the U.S.

Chinatown's Grant Avenue.

Women and children flooded into the neighborhood after the Great Quake.

Congress in 1882, which slammed the doors to America for "Asiatics." This was the country's first significant restriction on immigration. The law also prevented the existing Chinese residents, including American-born children, from becoming naturalized citizens. With a society of mostly men (forbidden, of course, from marrying white women), San Francisco hoped that Chinatown would simply die out.

OUT OF THE ASHES

When the devastating 1906 earthquake and fire hit, city fathers thought they'd seize the opportunity to kick the Chinese out of Chinatown and get their hands on that desirable piece of downtown real estate. Then Chinatown businessman Look Tin Eli had a brainstorm of Disneyesque proportions.

He proposed that Chinatown be rebuilt, but in a tourist-friendly, stylized, "Oriental" way. Anglo-American architects would design new buildings with pagoda roofs and dragon-covered columns. Chinatown would attract more tourists—the curious had been visiting on the sly for decades—and add more tax money to the city's coffers. Ka-ching: the sales pitch worked.

PAPER SONS

For the Chinese, the 1906 earthquake turned the virtual "no entry" sign into a flashing neon "welcome!" All the city's immigration records went up in smoke, and the Chinese quickly began to apply for passports as U.S. citizens, claiming their old ones were lost in the fire. Not only did thousands of Chinese become legal overnight, but so did their sons in China, or "sons," if they weren't really related. Whole families in Chinatown had passports in names that weren't their own; these "paper sons" were not only a windfall but also an uncomfortable neighborhood conspiracy. The city caught on eventually and set up an immigration center on Angel Island in 1910. Immigrants spent weeks or months being inspected and interrogated while their papers were checked. Roughly 250,000 people made it through. With this influx, including women and children, Chinatown finally became a more complete community.

A GREAT WALK THROUGH CHINATOWN

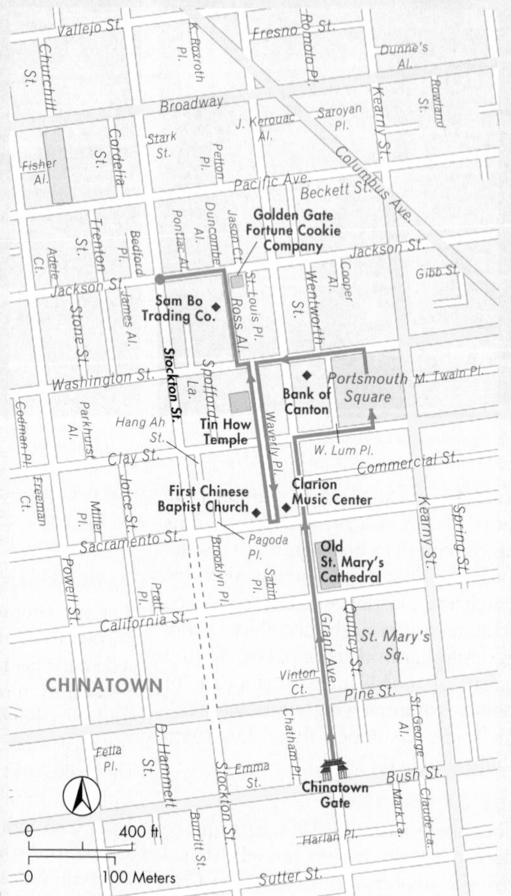

■ Start at the Chinatown Gate and walk ahead on Grant Avenue, entering the souvenir gauntlet. (You'll also pass Old St. Mary's Cathedral.)

■ Make a right on Clay Street and walk to Portsmouth Square. Sometimes it feels like the whole neighborhood's here, playing chess and exercising.

■ Head up Washington Street to the elaborately pagodaed Old Chinese Telephone Exchange building, now the Bank of Canton. Across Grant, look left for Waverly Place. Here Republic of China flags flap over some of the neighborhood's most striking buildings, including Tin How Temple.

■ At the Sacramento Street end of Waverly Place stands the oddly beautiful brick First Chinese Baptist Church of 1908. Just across the way, the Clarion Music Center is chock-full of unusual instruments, as well as exquisite lion-dance sets.

■ Head back to Washington Street and check out the herb shops, like the Superior Trading Company (No. 839) and the Great China Herb Co. (No. 857).

■ Follow the scent of vanilla from Washington Street down Ross Alley (entrance across from Superior Trading Company) to the Golden Gate Fortune Cookie Factory. Then head across the alley to Sam Bo Trading Co., where religious items are stacked chockablock in the narrow space. Tell the friendly owners your troubles and they'll prepare a package of joss papers, joss sticks, and candles, and tell you how and when to offer them up.

■ Turn left on Jackson Street; ahead is the real Chinatown's main artery, Stockton Street. This is where most residents do their grocery shopping; if it's Saturday, get ready for throngs (and their elbows). Look toward the back of stores for Buddhist altars with offerings of oranges and grapefruit. From here you can loop one block east back to Grant.

ALL THE TEA IN CHINATOWN

Preparing a perfect brew at Red Blossom Tea.

San Francisco's close ties to Asia have always made it more tea-conscious than other American burgs, but these days the city is in the throes of a tea renaissance, with new tasting rooms popping up in every neighborhood. Below are our favorite spots for every tea under the sun.

Red Blossom Tea. A light and modern shop—the staff really know their stuff. It's a favorite among younger tea enthusiasts, who swear by its excellent bang-for-the-buck value. While Red Blossom doesn't do formal tastings or sell tea by the cup, they'll gladly brew up perfect samples of the teas you're interested in. ✉ *831 Grant Ave.* ☎ *415/395–0868.*

Vital Tea Leaf. Tastings here work like those for wine—one of the gregarious, knowledgeable servers chooses the teas and describes them as you sample. It's a great spot for tea newbies to get their feet wet without a hard sell, but local connoisseurs grumble about the high prices and the self-promotion. ✉ *1044 Grant Ave.* ☎ *415/981–2388.*

Imperial Tea Court. If you want to visit the most respected of traditional tea purveyors, you'll need to venture outside of Chinatown. Imperial Tea Court's serene Powell Street oasis closed unexpectedly in 2007, but you'll find the same great selection and expertise at their fancy new digs in the Ferry Building. ☎ *415/544–9830.*

WAITING FOR CUSTARD

As you're strolling down Grant Avenue, past the plastic Buddhas and yin/yang balls, be sure to stop at the Golden Gate Bakery (No. 1029) for some delicious eggy *dan tat* (custard tarts). These flaky-crusted treats are heaven for just a buck. There's often a line, but it's worth the wait.

DON'T-MISS SHOPS

Locals snap up flowers from an outdoor vendor.

If you're in the market for a pair of chirping metal crickets (oh you'll hear them, trust us), you can duck into any of the obvious souvenir-stuffed storefronts. But if you're looking for something special, head for these tempting sources. **■TIP→ Fierce neighborhood competition keeps prices within reason, but for popular wares like jade, it pays to shop around before making a serious investment. Many stores accept cash only.**

Chinatown Kite Shop. Family-run shop selling bright, fun-shaped kites—dragons, butterflies, sharks—since the 1960s. ⊠ *717 Grant Ave.* ☎ *415/989–5182.*

Dragon House. A veritable museum: the store sells authentic, centuries-old antiques like ivory carvings. ⊠ *455 Grant Ave.* ☎ *415/421–3693.*

Old Shanghai. One of the largest selections of hand-painted robes, formal dresses, and jackets in Chinatown, plus chic Asian-inspired pieces. ⊠ *645 Grant Ave.* ☎ *415/986–1222.*

CHINATOWN WITH KIDS

It can be tough for the little ones to keep their hands to themselves, especially when all sorts of curios spill out onto the sidewalk at just the right height. To burn off some steam (in them) and relieve some stress (in you), take them to the small but spruce playground in St. Mary's Square, across California from Old St. Mary's. If that setting's too tranquil, head to the more boisterous Willie Wong Playground, on Sacramento Street at Waverly Place.

symbolizes longevity, and gold connotes majesty), a couple of plaques announce that "mrs. harry s. truman came to this temple in june 1948 for a prediction on the outcome of the election . . . this fortune came true." The temple's balcony has a good view of Chinatown. ✉ *855 Stockton St., Chinatown* ☎ *No phone* 🎟 *Free* ⏲ *Mon.–Sat. 9–4.*

Old Chinese Telephone Exchange. After the 1906 earthquake, many Chinatown buildings were rebuilt in Western style with pagoda roof and fancy balconies slapped on. This building—today the Bank of Canton—is the exception, an example of top-to-bottom Chinese architecture. The intricate three-tier pagoda was built in 1909. The exchange's operators were renowned for their prodigious memories, about which the San Francisco Chamber of Commerce boasted in 1914: "These girls respond all day with hardly a mistake to calls that are given (in English or one of five Chinese dialects) by the name of the subscriber instead of by his number—a mental feat that would be practically impossible to most high-schooled American misses." ✉ *Bank of Canton, 743 Washington St., Chinatown.*

Portsmouth Square. Chinatown's living room buzzes with activity. The square, with its pagoda-shape structures, is a favorite spot for morning tai chi; by noon dozens of men huddle around Chinese chess tables, engaged in not-always-legal competition. Kids scamper about the square's two grungy playgrounds (warning: the bathrooms are sketchy). Back in the late 19th century this land was near the waterfront, and Robert Louis Stevenson, the author of *Treasure Island,* often dropped by, chatting up the sailors who hung out here. Some of the information he gleaned about life at sea found its way into his fiction. A bronze galleon sculpture, a tribute to Stevenson, is anchored in a corner of the square. ✉ *Bordered by Walter Lum Pl. and Kearny, Washington, and Clay Sts., Chinatown.*

Tin How Temple. Duck into the inconspicuous doorway, climb three flights of stairs—on the second floor is a mah-jongg parlor whose patrons hope the spirits above will favor them—and be assaulted by the aroma of incense in this tiny, altar-filled room. Day Ju, one of the first three Chinese to arrive in San Francisco, dedicated this temple to the Queen of the Heavens and the Goddess of the Seven Seas in 1852. In the temple's entryway, elderly ladies can often be seen preparing "money" to be burned as offerings to various Buddhist gods or as funds for ancestors to use in the afterlife. Hundreds of red-and-gold lanterns cover the ceiling; the larger the lamp, the larger its donor's contribution to the temple. Gifts of oranges, dim sum, and money left by the faithful, who kneel mumbling prayers, rest on altars to various gods. Tin How presides over the middle back of the temple, flanked by one red and one green lesser god. Take a good look around, since taking photographs is not allowed. ✉ *125 Waverly Pl., Chinatown* ☎ *No phone* 🎟 *Free, donations accepted* ⏲ *Daily 9–4.*

SOMA AND CIVIC CENTER

To a newcomer, SoMa (short for "south of Market") and Civic Center may look like cheek-by-jowl neighbors—they're divided by Market Street. To locals, though, these areas are firmly separate entities, especially since Market Street itself is considered such a strong demarcation line. SoMa is less a neighborhood than it is a sprawling area of wide, traffic-heavy boulevards lined with office high-rises and pricey live-work lofts. Across Market Street from the western edge of SoMa is Civic Center, with San Francisco's eye-catching, gold-domed City Hall. Tickets to a show at one of the neighborhood's grand performance halls are the main reason to venture here.

EXPLORING SOMA

California Historical Society. If you're not a history buff, the CHS might seem like an obvious skip—who wants to look at fading old photographs and musty artifacts? If the answer is an indignant "I do!" or if you're just curious, these airy galleries are well worth a stop. A rotating selection draws from the society's vast repository of Californiana—hundreds of thousands of photographs, publications, paintings, and gold-rush paraphernalia. ■ **TIP→ From out front, take a look across the street: this is the best view of the three-story photo mosaic at the Museum of African Diaspora.** ✉ *678 Mission St., SoMa* ☎ *415/357–1848* 🌐 *www.californiahistoricalsociety.org* 🎫 *$3* 🕑 *Wed.–Sat. noon–4:30; galleries close between exhibitions.*

Cartoon Art Museum. Krazy Kat, Zippy the Pinhead, Batman, and other colorful cartoon icons greet you at the Cartoon Art Museum, established with an endowment from cartoonist-icon Charles M. Schulz. The museum's strength is its changing exhibits, which explore such topics as America from the perspective of international political cartoons, and the output of women and African-American cartoonists. Serious fans of cartoons—especially those on the quirky underground side—will likely enjoy the exhibits; those with a casual interest may be disappointed. The museum store carries loads of cool titles to add to your collection. ✉ *655 Mission St., SoMa* ☎ *415/227–8666* 🌐 *www.cartoonart.org* 🎫 *$7, pay what you wish 1st Tues. of month* 🕑 *Tues.–Sun. 11–5.*

Contemporary Jewish Museum. Fascinating museum buildings are sprouting up all over the city, and this Daniel Liebeskind–designed CJM is a real coup for SoMa. It's impossible to ignore that diagonal blue cube. The all-new addition jutting into a painstakingly restored power substation is a physical manifestation of the Hebrew phrase *l'chaim* (to life). And even if the architectural philosophy behind the design seems a bit esoteric, the blue, steel-clad cube—one of the most striking structures in town—creates a unique, light-filled space that merits a stroll through the lobby even if current exhibits don't entice you into the galleries. Be sure to check out the seam where old building meets new. ✉ *736 Mission St., between 3rd and 4th Sts., SoMa* ☎ *415/655–7800* 🌐 *www.thejcm.org* 🎫 *$10, $5 Thurs. after 5 pm* 🕑 *Thurs. 1–8, Fri.–Tues. 11–5.*

Rincon Center. The only reason to visit what is basically a modern office building is the striking Works Project Administration mural by Anton Refregier in the lobby of the Streamline Moderne–style former post

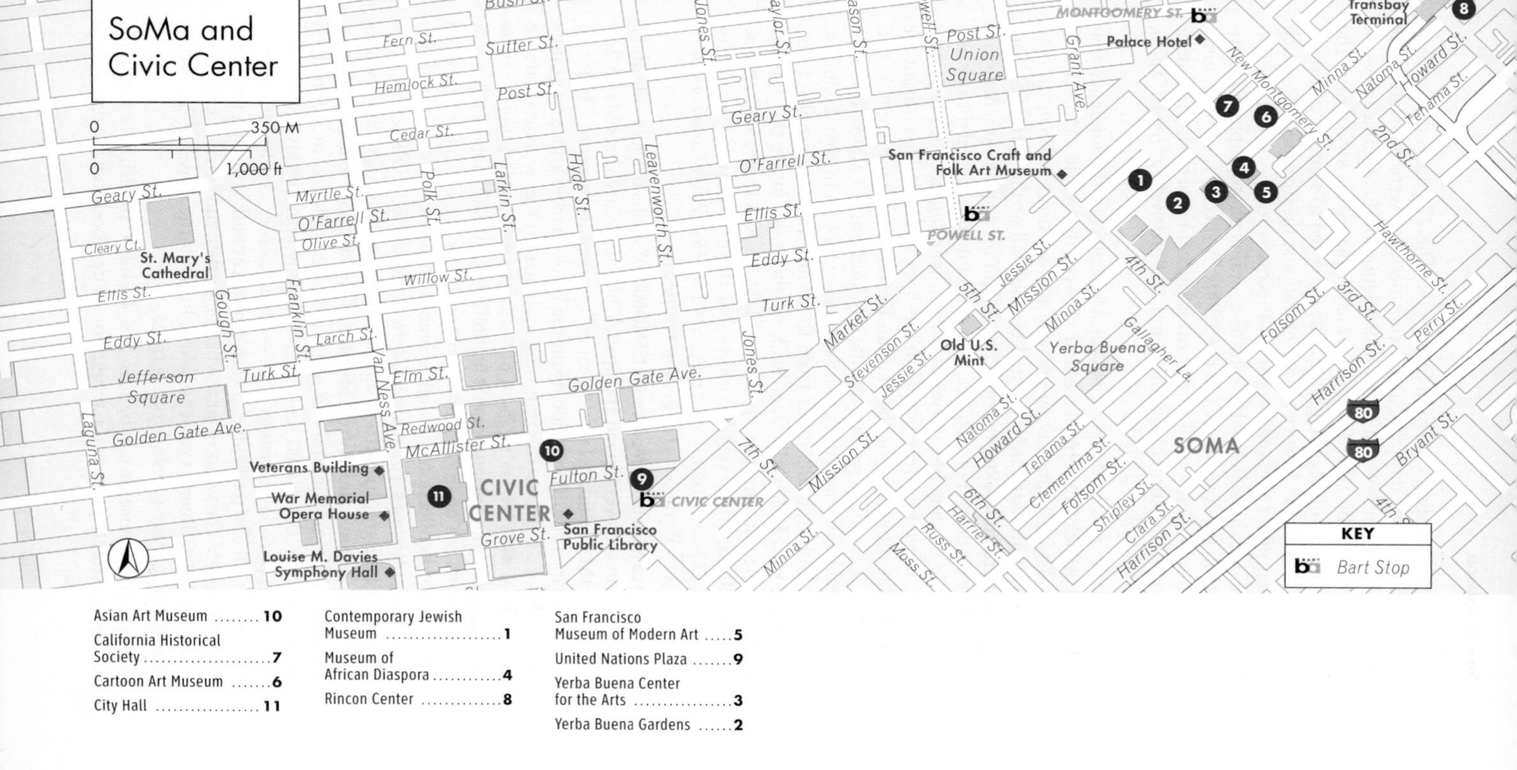

Asian Art Museum 10
California Historical Society 7
Cartoon Art Museum 6
City Hall 11
Contemporary Jewish Museum 1
Museum of African Diaspora 4
Rincon Center 8
San Francisco Museum of Modern Art 5
United Nations Plaza 9
Yerba Buena Center for the Arts 3
Yerba Buena Gardens 2

office on the building's Mission Street side. The 27 panels depict California life from the days when Native Americans were the state's sole inhabitants through World War I. Completion of this significant work was interrupted by World War II (which explains the swastika in the final panel) and political infighting. The latter led to some alteration in Refregier's "radical" historical interpretations; they exuded too much populist sentiment for some of the politicians who opposed the artist. A permanent exhibit below the murals contains photographs and artifacts of life in the Rincon area in the 1800s. A sheer five-story column of water resembling a mini-rainstorm is the centerpiece of the indoor arcade around the corner from the mural. ✉ *Bordered by Steuart, Spear, Mission, and Howard Sts., SoMa.*

Museum of the African Diaspora (MoAD). Dedicated to the influence that people of African descent have had all over the world, MoAD provokes discussion from the get-go with the question, "When did you discover you are African?" painted on the wall at the entrance. With no permanent collection, the museum is light on displays and heavy on interactive exhibits. For instance, you can sit in a darkened theater and listen to the moving life stories of slaves; hear snippets of music that helped create genres from gospel to hip-hop; and see videos about the Civil Rights movement or the Haitian Revolution. Some grumble that sweeping generalities replace specific information, but almost everyone can appreciate the museum's most striking exhibit in the front window. The three-story mosaic, made from thousands of photographs, forms the image of a little girl's face. Walk up the stairs inside the museum and view the photographs up close—Malcolm X is there, Muhammad Ali, too, along with everyday folks—but the best view is from across the street. ✉ *685 Mission St., SoMa* ☎ *415/358–7200* 🌐 *www.moadsf.org* 🎟 *$10* 🕒 *Wed.–Sat. 11–6, Sun. noon–5.*

Fodor's Choice ★ **San Francisco Museum of Modern Art (SFMOMA).** With its brick facade and a striped central tower lopped at a lipstick-like angle, architect Mario Botta's SFMOMA building fairly screams "modern-art museum." Indeed it is. The stripes continue inside, from the black marble and gray granite of the floors right up the imposing staircase to the wooden slats on the ceiling. ■ **TIP→ Taking in all of SFMOMA's four exhibit floors can be overwhelming, so having a plan is helpful. Keep in mind that the museum's heavy hitters are on floors 2 and 3.** Floor 2 gets the big-name traveling exhibits and collection highlights such as Matisse's *Woman with the Hat,* Diego Rivera's *The Flower Carrier,* and Georgia O'Keeffe's *Black Place 1.* Photography buffs should hustle up to floor 3, with its works by Ansel Adams and Alfred Stieglitz. The large-scale contemporary exhibits on floors 4 and 5 can usually be seen quickly (or skipped). If it's on display, don't miss sculptor Jeff Koons' memorably creepy, life-size gilded porcelain *Michael Jackson and Bubbles,* on the fifth floor at the end of the Turret Bridge, a vertiginous catwalk dangling under the central tower. The window at the bridge's other end offers a great view over the Yerba Buena Gardens below. In 2009 the museum opened its fifth-floor, garage-top sculpture garden.

Seating in the museum can be scarce, so luckily Caffè Museo, accessible from the street, provides a refuge for quite good, reasonably priced

Light streams in through the skylight atop the bold striped cylinder of the San Francisco Museum of Modern Art (SFMOMA).

drinks and light meals. It's easy to drop a fortune at the museum's large store, chockablock with fun gadgets, artsy doodads of all kinds, very modern furniture, and possibly the best selection of kids' books in town. **TIP→ No ticket is required to visit the lobby, so if it's the architecture you're interested in, save yourself the admission and have a gander for free.** *151 3rd St., SoMa 415/357–4000 www.sfmoma.org $18, free 1st Tues. of month, ½ price Thurs. 6–9 Labor Day–Memorial Day, Fri.–Tues. 11–5:45, Thurs. 11–8:45; Memorial Day–Labor Day, Fri.–Tues. 10–5:45, Thurs. 10–8:45.*

Yerba Buena Center for the Arts. If SFMOMA's for your parents, this Center is for you. You never know what's going to be on at this facility in the Yerba Buena Gardens, but whether it's an exhibit of Mexican street art (graffiti to laypeople), innovative modern dance, or baffling video installations, it's likely to be memorable. The productions here tend to draw a young, energetic crowd, and lean hard toward the cutting edge. *701 Mission St., SoMa 415/978–2787 www.ybca.org Galleries $7, free 1st Tues. of month Thurs.–Sat. noon–8, Sun. noon–6, 1st Tues. of the month noon–8.*

★ **Yerba Buena Gardens.** There's not much south of Market that encourages lingering outdoors, or indeed walking at all, with this notable exception. These two blocks encompass the **Center for the Arts, Metreon, Moscone Convention Center,** and the convention center's rooftop **Children's Creativity Museum,** but the gardens themselves are the everyday draw. Office workers escape to the green swath of the East Garden. The memorial to Martin Luther King Jr. is the focal point here. Powerful streams of water surge over large, jagged stone columns, mirroring the enduring force of King's words that are carved on the stone walls and on glass blocks behind the waterfall. Moscone North is behind the memorial, and an overhead walkway leads to Moscone South and its rooftop attractions. **■TIP→ The gardens are liveliest during the week and especially during the Yerba Buena Gardens Festival (May–October, www.ybgf.org), when free performances run from Latin music to Balinese dance.**

Atop the Moscone Convention Center perch a few lures for kids. The historic Looff carousel ($3 for two rides) twirls daily 11 to 6. South of the carousel is the Children's Creativity Museum (☎ *415/820–3320* 🌐 *www.zeum.org*), a high-tech, interactive arts-and-technology center (adults, $10; kids 3–18, $8) geared to children ages eight and over. Kids can walk through a model of San Francisco complete with hologram landmarks, make Claymation videos, work in a computer lab, and view exhibits and performances. The museum is open 1 to 5 Wednesday through Friday and 11 to 5 weekends during the school year and Tuesday through Sunday 11 to 5 when school's out. Also part of the rooftop complex are gardens, an ice-skating rink, and a bowling alley. ✉ *Bordered by 3rd, 4th, Mission, and Folsom Sts., SoMa* ☎ *No phone* 🌐 *www.yerbabuenagardens.org* 🎟 *Free* 🕒 *Daily sunrise–10 pm.*

HAYES VALLEY

Hayes Valley, right next door to the Civic Center, is an offbeat neighborhood with terrific eateries, cool watering holes, and great browsing in its funky clothing and home-decor boutiques. Swing down main drag Hayes Street, between Franklin and Laguna, and you can hit the highlights, including two very popular restaurants, Absinthe and Suppenküche. Comfy Place Pigalle (at Hayes and Octavia streets) is also a favorite for its living-room atmosphere, wines, and microbrews. Locals love this quarter, but without any big-name draws it remains off the radar for most visitors.

EXPLORING CIVIC CENTER

★ **Asian Art Museum.** Expecting a building full of Buddhas and jade? Well, yeah, you can find plenty of that here. Happily, though, you don't have to be a connoisseur of Asian art to appreciate a visit to this splendidly renovated museum, whose monumental exterior conceals a light, open, and welcoming space. The fraction of the museum's items on display (about 2,500 pieces from a 15,000-plus-piece collection) is laid out thematically and by region, making it easy to follow developments.

Begin on the third floor, where highlights of Buddhist art in Southeast Asia and early China include a large, jewel-encrusted, exquisitely painted 19th-century Burmese Buddha and clothed rod puppets from Java. On the second floor you can find later Chinese works, as well as pieces from Korea and Japan. Look for a cobalt tiger jauntily smoking a pipe on a whimsical Korean jar and delicate Japanese tea implements. The ground floor displays rotating exhibits, including contemporary and traveling shows. **■TIP→ If you'd like to attend one of the occasional tea ceremonies and tastings at the Japanese Teahouse, call ahead, since preregistration is required.** ✉ *200 Larkin St., between McAllister and Fulton Sts., Civic Center* ☎ *415/581–3500* 🌐 *www.asianart.org*

$12, free 1st Sun. of month; $10 some Thurs. 5–9; tea ceremony $27, includes museum ⏲ *Tues.–Sun. 10–5; Feb.–Sept., Thurs. until 9.*

City Hall. This imposing 1915 structure with its massive gold-leaf dome—higher than the U.S. Capitol's—is about as close to a palace as you're going to get in San Francisco. (Alas, the metal detectors take something away from the grandeur.) The classic granite-and-marble behemoth was modeled after St. Peter's Cathedral in Rome. Architect Arthur Brown Jr., who also designed Coit Tower and the War Memorial Opera House, designed an interior with grand columns and a sweeping central staircase. San Franciscans were thrilled, and probably a bit surprised, when his firm built City Hall in just a few years. The building it replaced, dubbed "the new City Hall ruin," had lined the pockets of corrupt builders and politicians during its 27 years of construction. That 1899 structure collapsed in about 27 seconds in the 1906 earthquake, revealing trash and newspapers mixed into the building materials.

4

City Hall was spruced up and seismically retrofitted in the late 1990s, but the sense of history remains palpable. Some noteworthy events that have taken place here include the marriage of Marilyn Monroe and Joe DiMaggio (1954); the hosing—down the central staircase—of civil-rights and freedom-of-speech protesters (1960); the murders of Mayor George Moscone and openly gay supervisor Harvey Milk (1978); the torching of the lobby by angry members of the gay community in response to the light sentence given to the former supervisor who killed both men (1979); and the registrations of scores of gay couples in celebration of the passage of San Francisco's Domestic Partners Act (1991). February 2004 has come to be known as the Winter of Love: thousands of gay and lesbian couples responded to Mayor Gavin Newsom's decision to issue marriage licenses to same-sex partners, turning City Hall into the site of raucous celebration and joyful nuptials for a month before the state Supreme Court ordered the practice stopped. That celebratory scene replayed during 2008, when scores of couples were wed between the court's June ruling that everyone enjoys the civil right to marry and the November passage of California's ballot proposition banning same-sex marriage. (Stay tuned . . .) Free tours are offered weekdays at 10, noon, and 2.

The South Light Court houses a modest, rotating display from the collection of the **Museum of the City of San Francisco** (*www.sfmuseum.org*), including historical items, maps, and photographs. That enormous, 700-pound iron head once crowned the *Goddess of Progress* statue, which topped the old City Hall building when it crumbled during the 1906 earthquake. Unlike the building, the statue survived the earthquake in one piece, but the subsequent removal proved too much for it.

Across Polk Street is **Civic Center Plaza,** with lawns, walkways, seasonal flower beds, a playground, and an underground parking garage. This sprawling space is generally clean but somewhat grim. A large part of the city's homeless population hangs out here, despite frequently being shunted away, so the plaza can feel dodgy. ✉ *Bordered by Van Ness Ave. and Polk, Grove, and McAllister Sts., Civic Center* ☎ *415/554–6023* *www.sfgov.org/site/cityhall* *Free* ⏲ *Weekdays 8–8.*

United Nations Plaza. Locals know this plaza for two things: its Wednesday and Sunday farmers' market—cheap and earthy to the Ferry Building's pricey and beautiful—and its homeless population, which seems to return no matter how many times the city tries to shunt them aside. Brick pillars listing various nations and the dates of their admittance into the United Nations line the plaza, and its floor is inscribed with the goals and philosophy of the United Nations charter, which was signed at the War Memorial Opera House in 1945. ✉ *Fulton St. between Hyde and Market Sts., Civic Center.*

NOB HILL AND RUSSIAN HILL

In place of the quirky charm and cultural diversity that mark other San Francisco neighborhoods, Nob Hill exudes history and good breeding. Topped with some of the city's most elegant hotels, Gothic Grace Cathedral, and private blue-blood clubs, it's the pinnacle of privilege. One hill over, across Pacific Avenue, is another old-family bastion, Russian Hill. It may not be quite as wealthy as Nob Hill, but it's no slouch—and it's known for its jaw-dropping views.

Nob Hill was officially dubbed during the 1870s when "the Big Four"—Charles Crocker, Leland Stanford, Mark Hopkins, and Collis Huntington, who were involved in the construction of the transcontinental railroad—built their hilltop estates. The lingo is thick from this era: those on the hilltop were referred to as "nabobs" (originally meaning a provincial governor from India) and "swells," and the hill itself was called Snob Hill, a term that survives to this day. By 1882 so many estates had sprung up on Nob Hill that Robert Louis Stevenson called it "the hill of palaces." But the 1906 earthquake and fire destroyed all the palatial mansions except for portions of the Flood brownstone. History buffs may choose to linger here, but for most visitors, a casual glimpse from a cable car will be enough.

Essentially a tony residential neighborhood of spiffy pieds-à-terre, Victorian flats, Edwardian cottages, and boxlike condos, Russian Hill also has some of the city's loveliest stairway walks, hidden garden ways, and steepest streets—brave drivers can really have some fun here—not to mention those bay views. Several stories explain the origin of Russian Hill's name. One legend has it that Russian farmers raised vegetables here for Farallon Islands seal hunters; another attributes the name to a Russian sailor of prodigious drinking habits who drowned when he fell into a well on the hill. A plaque at the top of the Vallejo Steps gives credence to the version that says sailors of the Russian-American company were buried here in the 1840s. Be sure to visit the sign for yourself—its location offers perhaps the finest vantage point on the hill.

EXPLORING NOB HILL

Cable Car Museum. The Cable Car Museum is one of the city's best free offerings and an absolute must for kids. (You can even ride a cable car there, since all three lines stop between Russian Hill and Nob Hill.) The museum, which is inside the city's last cable car barn, takes the top off the system to let you see how it all works. Eternally humming and squealing, the massive powerhouse cable wheels steal the show. You

Cable Car Museum 3
Feusier House 5
Grace Cathedral 2
Ina Coolbrith Park 4
Lombard Street 7
Macondray Lane 6
Pacific Union Club 1
San Francisco Art Institute 8

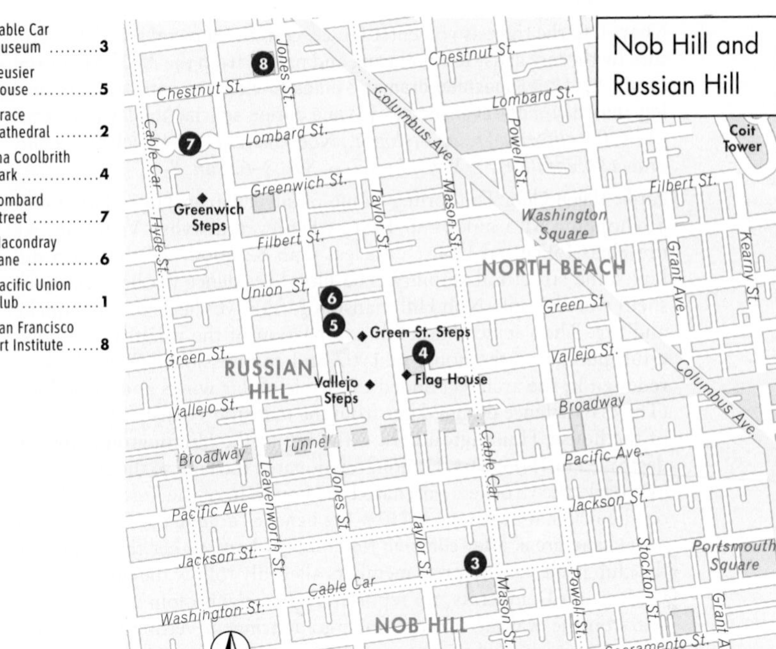

can also climb aboard a vintage car and take the grip, let the kids ring a cable car bell (briefly), and check out vintage gear dating from 1873.

The gift shop sells cable car paraphernalia, including an authentic gripman's bell for $600 (it'll sound like Powell Street in your house every day). For significantly less, you can pick up a key chain made from a piece of worn-out cable. ✉ *1201 Mason St., at Washington St. Nob Hill* ☎ *415/474–1887* 🌐 *www.cablecarmuseum.com* 🎫 *Free* 🕒 *Oct.–Mar., daily 10–5; Apr.–Sept., daily 10–6.*

Grace Cathedral. Not many churches can boast a Keith Haring sculpture and not one but two labyrinths. The seat of the Episcopal Church in San Francisco, this soaring Gothic-style structure, erected on the site of Charles Crocker's mansion, took 53 years to build, wrapping up in 1964. The gilded bronze doors at the east entrance were taken from casts of Lorenzo Ghiberti's incredible Gates of Paradise, which are on the Baptistery in Florence, Italy. A black-and-bronze stone sculpture of St. Francis by Beniamino Bufano greets you as you enter.

The 35-foot-wide labyrinth, a large, purplish rug with a looping pattern, is a replica of the 13th-century stone maze on the floor of Chartres Cathedral. All are encouraged to walk the ¼-mi-long labyrinth, a ritual based on the tradition of meditative walking. There's also a terrazzo outdoor labyrinth on the church's north side. The AIDS Interfaith

Chapel, to the right as you enter Grace, contains a metal tryptich sculpture by the late artist Keith Haring and panels from the AIDS Memorial Quilt. ■ **TIP→ Especially dramatic times to view the cathedral are during Thursday-night evensong (5:15) and during special holiday programs.** ✉ *1100 California St., at Taylor St., Nob Hill* ☎ *415/749–6300* 🌐 *www.gracecathedral.org* ⏲ *Weekdays 7–6, Sat. 8–6, Sun. 8–7.*

Pacific Union Club. The former home of silver baron James Flood cost a whopping $1.5 million in 1886, when even a stylish Victorian like the Haas-Lilienthal House cost less than $20,000. All that cash did buy some structural stability. The Flood residence (to be precise, its shell) was the only Nob Hill mansion to survive the 1906 earthquake and fire. The Pacific Union Club, a bastion of the wealthy and powerful, purchased the house in 1907 and commissioned Willis Polk to redesign it; the architect added the semicircular wings and third floor. (The ornate fence design dates from the mansion's construction.) West of the house, Huntington Park is the site of the Huntington mansion, destroyed in 1906. Mrs. Huntington donated the land to the city for use as a park; the Crockers purchased the Fountain of the Tortoises, based on the original in Rome. ■ **TIP→ The benches around the fountain offer a welcome break after climbing Nob Hill.** It's hard to get the skinny on the club itself; its 700 or so members allegedly follow the directive "no women, no Democrats, no reporters." Those who join usually spend years on the waiting list and undergo a stringent vetting process, the rigors of which might embarrass the NSA. Needless to say, the club is closed to the public. ✉ *1000 California St., Nob Hill.*

EXPLORING RUSSIAN HILL

Feusier House. Octagonal houses were once thought to make the best use of space and enhance the physical and mental well-being of their occupants. A brief mid-19th-century craze inspired the construction of several in San Francisco. Only the Feusier House, built in 1857, and the Octagon House in Pacific Heights remain standing. A private residence, the Feusier House is easy to overlook unless you look closely—it's dwarfed by the large-scale apartments around it. Across from the Feusier House is the **1907 Firehouse** (✉ *1088 Green St., Russian Hill*). Louise M. Davies, the local art patron for whom Symphony Hall is named, bought it from the city in 1957. The firehouse is closed to the public, but it's worth taking in the exterior. ✉ *1067 Green St., Russian Hill.*

★ **Ina Coolbrith Park.** If you make it all the way up here, you may have the place all to yourself, or at least feel that you do. The park's terraces are carved from a hill so steep that it's difficult to see if anyone else is there or not. Locals love this park because it feels like a secret no one else knows about—one of the city's magic hidden gardens, with a meditative setting and spectacular views of the bay peeking out from among the trees. A poet, Oakland librarian, and niece of Mormon prophet Joseph Smith, Ina Coolbrith (1842–1928) introduced Jack London and Isadora Duncan to the world of books. For years she entertained literary greats in her Macondray Lane home near the park. In 1915 she was named poet laureate of California. ✉ *Vallejo St. between Mason and Taylor Sts., Russian Hill.*

Continued on page 177

CABLE CARS

The moment it dawns on you that you severely underestimated the steepness of the San Francisco hills will likely be the same moment you look down and realize those tracks aren't just for show—or just for tourists.

Sure, locals rarely use the cable cars for commuting these days. (That's partially due to the $6 fare—hear that, Muni?) So you'll likely be packed in with plenty of fellow sightseers. You may even be approaching cable-car fatigue after seeing its image on so many souvenirs. But if you fear the magic is gone, simply climb on board, and those jaded thoughts will dissolve. Grab the pole and gawk at the view as the car clanks down an insanely steep grade toward the bay. Listen to the humming cable, the clang of the bell, and the occasional quip from the gripman. It's an experience you shouldn't pass up, whether on your first trip or your fiftieth.

HOW CABLE CARS WORK

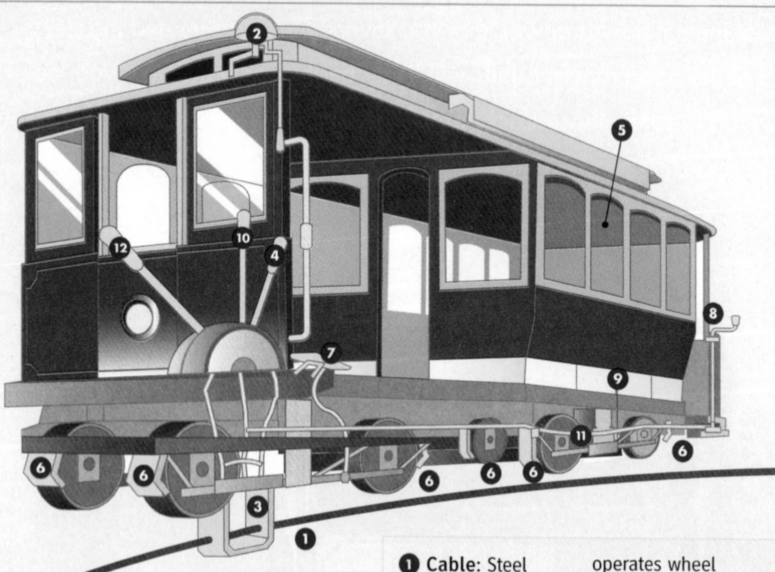

The mechanics are pretty simple: cable cars grab a moving subterranean cable with a "grip" to go. To stop, they release the grip and apply one or more types of brakes. Four cables, totaling 9 miles, power the city's three lines. If the gripman doesn't adjust the grip just right when going up a steep hill, the cable will start to slip and the car will have to back down the hill and try again. This is an extremely rare occurrence—imagine the ribbing the gripman gets back at the cable car barn!

Gripman: Stands in front and operates the grip, brakes, and bell. Favorite joke, especially at the peak of a steep hill: "This is my first day on the job folks . . ."

Conductor: Moves around the car, deals with tickets, alerts the grip about what's coming up, and operates the rear wheel brakes.

❶ **Cable:** Steel wrapped around flexible sisal core; 2 inches thick; runs at a constant 9½ mph.

❷ **Bells:** Used for crew communication; alerts other drivers and pedestrians.

❸ **Grip:** Vice-like lever extends through the center slot in the track to grab or release the cable.

❹ **Grip Lever:** Left-hand lever; operates grip.

❺ **Car:** Entire car weighs 8 tons.

❻ **Wheel Brake:** Steel brake pads on each wheel.

❼ **Wheel Brake Lever:** Foot pedal; operates wheel brakes.

❽ **Rear Wheel Brake Lever:** Applied for extra traction on hills.

❾ **Track Brake:** 2-foot long sections of Monterey pine push down against the track to help stop the car.

❿ **Track Brake Lever:** Middle lever; operates track brakes.

⓫ **Emergency Brake:** 18-inch steel wedge, jams into street slot to bring car to an immediate stop.

⓬ **Emergency Brake Lever:** Right-hand lever, red; operates emergency brake.

ROUTES

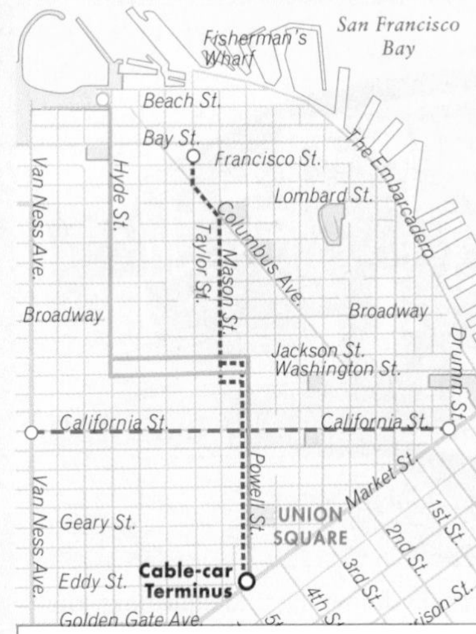

Cars run at least every 15 minutes, from around 6 AM to about 1 AM.

Powell–Hyde line: Most scenic, with classic Bay views. Begins at Powell and Market streets, then crosses Nob Hill and Russian Hill before a white-knuckle descent down Hyde Street, ending near the Hyde Street Pier.

Powell–Mason line: Also begins at Powell and Market streets, but winds through North Beach to Bay and Taylor streets, a few blocks from Fisherman's Wharf.

California line: Runs from the foot of Market Street, at Drumm Street, up Nob Hill and back. Great views (and aromas and sounds) of Chinatown on the way up. Sit in back to catch glimpses of the Bay. ■ TIP→ **Take the California line if it's just the cable-car experience you're after—the lines are shorter, and the grips and conductors say it's friendlier and has a slower pace.**

RULES OF THE RIDE

Tickets. A whopping $6 each way. There are ticket booths at all three turnarounds, or you can pay the conductor after you board (they can make change). Try not to grumble about the price—they're embarrassed enough as it is.

■ TIP→ **If you're planning to use public transit a few times, or if you'd like to ride back and forth on the cable car without worrying about the price, consider a one-day Muni passport ($14). You can get passports online, at the Powell Street turnaround, the TIX booth on Union Square, or the Fisherman's Wharf cable-car ticket booth at Beach and Hyde streets.**

All Aboard. You can board on either side of the cable car. It's legal to stand on the running boards and hang on to the pole, but keep your ears open for the gripman's warnings. ■ TIP→ **Grab a seat on the outside bench for the best views.**

Most people wait (and wait) in line at one of the cable car turnarounds, but you can also hop on along the route. Board wherever you see a white sign showing a figure climbing aboard a brown cable car; wave to the approaching driver, and wait until the car stops.

Riding on the running boards can be part of the thrill.

CABLE CAR HISTORY

HALLIDIE FREES THE HORSES

In the 1850s and '60s, San Francisco's streetcars were drawn by horses. Legend has it that the horrible sight of a car dragging a team of horses downhill to their deaths roused Andrew Smith Hallidie to action. The English immigrant had invented the "Hallidie Ropeway," essentially a cable car for mined ore, and he was convinced that his invention could also move people. In 1873, Hallidie and his intrepid crew prepared to test the first cable car high on Russian Hill. The anxious engineer peered down into the foggy darkness, failed to see the bottom of the hill, and promptly turned the controls over to Hallidie. Needless to say, the thing worked . . . but rides were free for the first two days because people were afraid to get on.

SEE IT FOR YOURSELF

The **Cable Car Museum** is one of the city's best free offerings and an absolute must for kids. (You can even ride a cable car there, since all three lines stop between Russian Hill and Nob Hill.) The museum, which is inside the city's last cable-car barn, takes the top off the system to let you see how it all works. Eternally humming and squealing, the massive powerhouse cable wheels steal the show. You can also climb aboard a vintage car and take the grip, let the kids ring a cable-car bell (briefly, please!), and check out vintage gear dating from 1873.

✉ *1201 Mason St., at Washington St., Nob Hill* ☎ *415/474–1887* 🌐 *www.cablecarmuseum.com* *Free* *Oct.–Mar., daily 10–5; Apr.–Sept., daily 10–6*

■ TIP→ The gift shop sells cable car paraphernalia, including an authentic gripman's bell for $600 (it'll sound like Powell Street in your house every day). For significantly less, you can pick up a key chain made from a piece of worn-out cable.

CHAMPION OF THE CABLE CAR BELL

Each June the city's best and brightest come together to crown a bell-ringing champion at Union Square. The crowd cheers gripmen and conductors as they stomp, shake, and riff with the rope. But it's not a popularity contest; the ringers are judged by former bell-ringing champions who take each ping and gong very seriously.

Lombard Street. The block-long "Crookedest Street in the World" makes eight switchbacks down the east face of Russian Hill between Hyde and Leavenworth streets. Residents bemoan the traffic jam outside their front doors, and occasionally the city attempts to discourage drivers by posting a traffic cop near the top of the hill, but the determined can find a way around. If no one is standing guard, join the line of cars waiting to drive down the steep hill, or avoid the whole mess and walk down the steps on either side of Lombard. You take in super views of North Beach and Coit Tower whether you walk or drive—though if you're the one behind the wheel, you'd better keep your eye on the road lest you become yet another of the many folks who ram the garden barriers. ■ **TIP→ Can't stand the throngs? Thrill seekers of a different stripe may want to head two blocks south of Lombard to Filbert Street. At a gradient of 31.5%, the hair-raising descent between Hyde and Leavenworth streets is the city's steepest. Go slowly!** ✉ *Lombard St. between Hyde and Leavenworth Sts., Russian Hill.*

4

Fodor's Choice ★ **Macondray Lane.** San Francisco has no shortage of impressive, grand homes, but it's the tiny fairy-tale lanes that make most folks want to move here, and Macondray Lane is the quintessential hidden garden. Enter under a lovely wooden trellis and proceed down a quiet, cobbled pedestrian lane lined with Edwardian cottages and flowering plants and trees. ■ **TIP→ Watch your step—the cobblestones are quite uneven in spots.** A flight of steep wooden stairs at the end of the lane leads to Taylor Street—on the way down you can't miss the bay views. If you've read any of Armistead Maupin's *Tales of the City* books, you may find the lane vaguely familiar. It's the thinly disguised setting for part of the series' action. ✉ *Between Jones and Taylor Sts., and Union and Green Sts., Russian Hill.*

★ **San Francisco Art Institute.** A Moorish-tile fountain in a tree-shaded courtyard draws the eye as soon as you enter the institute. The number-one reason for a visit is Mexican master Diego Rivera's *Making of a Fresco Showing the Building of a City* (1931), in the student gallery to your immediate left inside the entrance. Rivera himself is in the fresco—his broad behind is to the viewer—and he's surrounded by his assistants. They in turn are surrounded by a construction scene, laborers, and city notables such as sculptor Robert Stackpole and architect Timothy Pfleuger. *The Making of a Fresco* is one of three San Francisco murals painted by Rivera. The number-two reason to come here is the café, or more precisely the eye-popping, panoramic view from the café, which serves surprisingly decent food for a song.

The older portions of the Art Institute, including the lovely Mission-style bell tower, were erected in 1926. To this day, otherwise pragmatic people claim that ghostly footsteps can be heard in the tower at night. Ansel Adams created the school's fine-arts photography department in 1946, and school directors established the country's first fine-arts film program. Notable faculty and alumni have included painter Richard Diebenkorn and photographers Dorothea Lange, Edward Weston, and Annie Leibovitz. The **Walter & McBean Galleries** (☎ *415/749–4563* ⏲ *Tues.–Sat. 11–6*) exhibit the often provocative works of established artists. ✉ *800 Chestnut St., North Beach* ☎ *415/771–7020* 🌐 *www.sfai.edu* 🎫 *Galleries free* ⏲ *Student gallery daily 8:30–8:30.*

NORTH BEACH

San Francisco novelist Herbert Gold calls North Beach "the longest-running, most glorious American bohemian operetta outside Greenwich Village." Indeed, to anyone who's spent some time in its eccentric old bars and cafés, North Beach evokes everything from the Barbary Coast days to the no-less-rowdy Beatnik era. Italian bakeries appear frozen in time, homages to Jack Kerouac and Allen Ginsberg pop up everywhere, and the modern equivalent of the Barbary Coast's "houses of ill repute," strip joints, do business on Broadway. With its outdoor café tables, throngs of tourists, and holiday vibe, this is probably the part of town Europeans are thinking of when they say San Francisco is the most European city in America.

EXPLORING NORTH BEACH

★ **City Lights Bookstore.** Take a look at the exterior of the store: the replica of a revolutionary mural destroyed in Chiapas, Mexico, by military forces; the poetry in the windows; and the sign that says "Turn your sell [sic] phone off. Be here now." This place isn't just doling out best sellers. Designated a city landmark, the hangout of Beat-era writers—Allen Ginsberg and store founder Lawrence Ferlinghetti among them—remains a vital part of San Francisco's literary scene. Browse the three levels of sometimes haphazardly arranged poetry, philosophy, politics, fiction, history, and local 'zines, to the tune of creaking wood floors. **■ TIP→ Be sure to check their calendar of literary events.**

Back in the day, the basement was a kind of literary living room, where writers like Ginsberg and Kerouac would read and even receive mail. Ferlinghetti cemented City Lights' place in history by publishing Ginsberg's *Howl and Other Poems* in 1956. The small volume was ignored in the mainstream . . . until Ferlinghetti and the bookstore manager were arrested for corruption of youth and obscenity. In the landmark First Amendment trial that followed, the judge exonerated both, saying a work that has "redeeming social significance" can't be obscene. *Howl* went on to become a classic.

Kerouac Alley, branching off Columbus Avenue next to City Lights, was rehabbed in 2007. Embedded in the pavement are quotes from Lawrence Ferlinghetti, Maya Angelou, Confucius, John Steinbeck, and of course, the namesake himself. ✉ *261 Columbus Ave., North Beach* ☎ *415/362–8193* 🌐 *www.citylights.com* ⏲ *Daily 10 am–midnight.*

★ **Coit Tower.** Whether you think it resembles a fire-hose nozzle or something more, ahem, adult, this 210-foot tower is among San Francisco's most distinctive skyline sights. Although the monument wasn't intended as a tribute to firemen, it's often considered as such because of the donor's special attachment to the local fire company. As the story goes, a young gold rush–era girl, Lillie Hitchcock Coit (known as Miss Lil), was a fervent admirer of her local fire company—so much so that she once deserted a wedding party and chased down the street after her favorite engine, Knickerbocker No. 5, while clad in her bridesmaid finery. She became the Knickerbocker Company's mascot and always signed her name "Lillie Coit 5." When Lillie died in 1929 she left the city $125,000 to "expend in an appropriate manner . . . to the beauty of San Francisco."

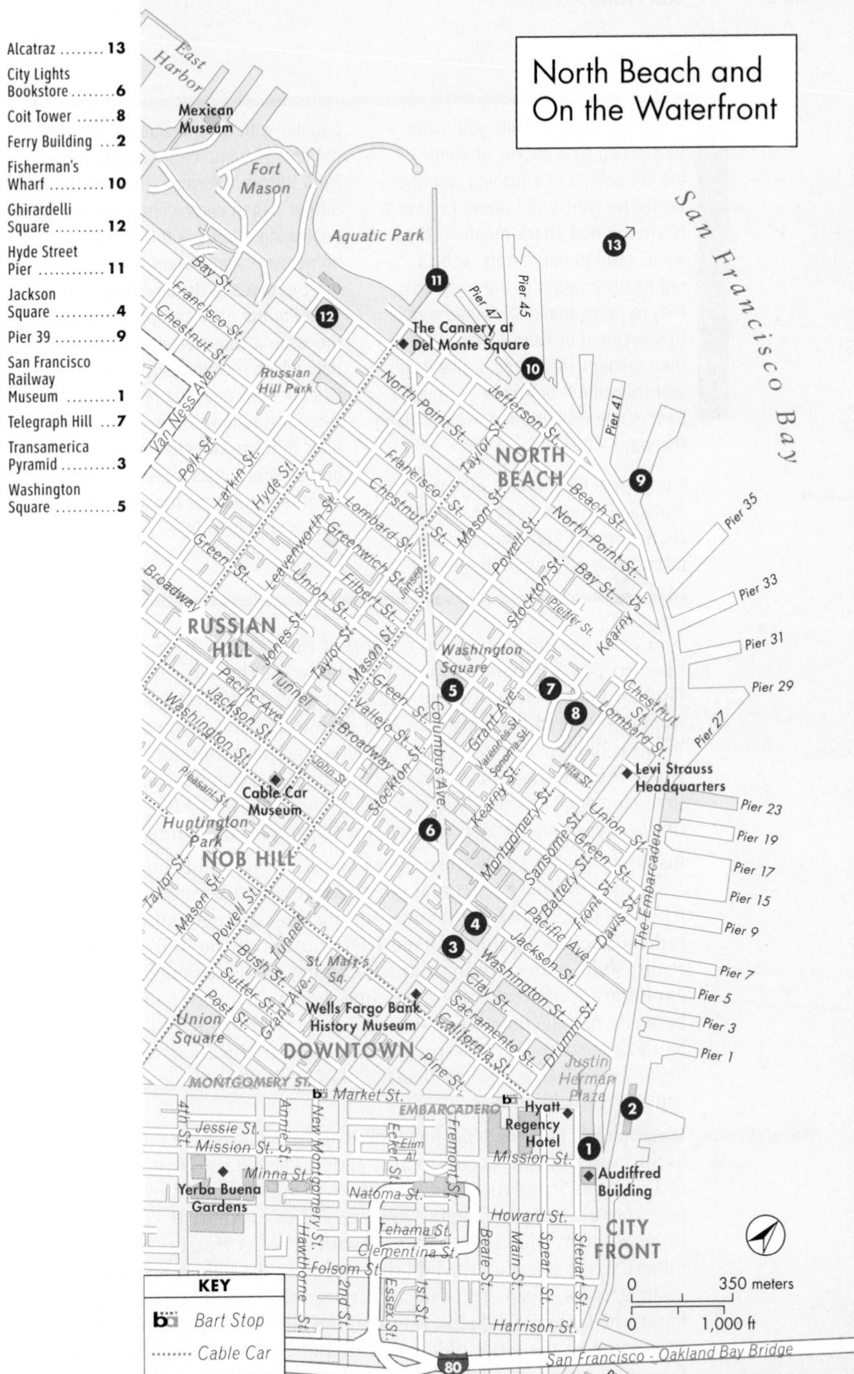

North Beach and On the Waterfront
Alcatraz 13
City Lights Bookstore 6
Coit Tower 8
Ferry Building 2
Fisherman's Wharf 10
Ghirardelli Square 12
Hyde Street Pier 11
Jackson Square 4
Pier 39 9
San Francisco Railway Museum 1
Telegraph Hill 7
Transamerica Pyramid 3
Washington Square 5
East Harbor
Mexican Museum
Fort Mason
Aquatic Park
San Francisco Bay
The Cannery at Del Monte Square
Russian Hill Park
NORTH BEACH
RUSSIAN HILL
Washington Square
Levi Strauss Headquarters
Cable Car Museum
Huntington Park
NOB HILL
St. Mary's Sq.
Wells Fargo Bank History Museum
Union Square
DOWNTOWN
Justin Herman Plaza
Hyatt Regency Hotel
Audiffred Building
Yerba Buena Gardens
CITY FRONT
EMBARCADERO
MONTGOMERY ST.
Pier 47
Pier 45
Pier 41
Pier 35
Pier 33
Pier 31
Pier 29
Pier 27
Pier 23
Pier 19
Pier 17
Pier 15
Pier 9
Pier 7
Pier 5
Pier 3
Pier 1
Pier 26
Bay St.
Francisco St.
Chestnut St.
Van Ness Ave.
Polk St.
Larkin St.
Hyde St.
Leavenworth St.
Jones St.
Taylor St.
Mason St.
North Point St.
Jefferson St.
Beach St.
Lombard St.
Greenwich St.
Filbert St.
Union St.
Green St.
Broadway
Jansen St.
Powell St.
Stockton St.
Pfeiffer St.
Kearny St.
Grant Ave.
Varennes St.
Sonoma St.
Alta St.
Columbus Ave.
Vallejo St.
Pacific Ave.
Jackson St.
Washington St.
Tunnel
John St.
Pleasant St.
Montgomery St.
Sansome St.
Battery St.
Front St.
Davis St.
The Embarcadero
Clay St.
Sacramento St.
California St.
Pine St.
Bush St.
Sutter St.
Post St.
Drumm St.
Market St.
Jessie St.
Mission St.
Minna St.
Natoma St.
Tehama St.
Clementina St.
Folsom St.
Howard St.
Harrison St.
Bryant St.
Taber Pl.
4th St.
Annie St.
New Montgomery St.
Hawthorne St.
2nd St.
Ecker St.
Elim Al.
Essex St.
1st St.
Fremont St.
Beale St.
Main St.
Spear St.
Steuart St.
San Francisco - Oakland Bay Bridge
80
0
350 meters
1,000 ft
KEY
Bart Stop
Cable Car

CLOSE UP

The Birds

While on Telegraph Hill, you might be startled by a chorus of piercing squawks and a rushing sound of wings. No, you're not about to have a Hitchcock bird-attack moment. These small, vivid green parrots with cherry-red heads number in the hundreds; they're descendants of former pets that escaped or were released by their owners. (The birds dislike cages and they bite if bothered . . . must've been some disillusioned owners along the way.)

The parrots like to roost high in the aging cypress trees on the hill, chattering and fluttering, sometimes taking wing en masse. They're not popular with most residents, but they did find a champion in local bohemian Mark Bittner, a former street musician. Bittner began chronicling their habits, publishing a book and battling the homeowners who wanted to cut down the cypresses. A documentary, *The Wild Parrots of Telegraph Hill*, made the issue a cause célèbre. In 2007 City Hall, which recognizes a golden goose when it sees one, stepped in and brokered a solution to keep the celebrity birds in town. The city will cover the homeowners' insurance worries and plant new trees for the next generation of wild parrots.

—Denise M. Leto

You can ride the elevator to the top of the tower—the only thing you have to pay for here—to enjoy the view of the Bay Bridge and the Golden Gate Bridge; due north is Alcatraz Island. ■ **TIP→ The views from the base of the tower are also expansive—and free. Parking at Coit Tower is limited; in fact, you may have to wait (and wait) for a space. Save yourself some frustration and take the 39 bus, which goes all the way up to the tower's base, or, if you're in good shape, hike up.** ⇨ *For more details on the lovely stairway walk, see the Telegraph Hill listing.*

Inside the tower, 19 Depression-era murals depict California's economic and political life. The federal government commissioned the paintings from 25 local artists, and ended up funding quite a controversy. The radical Mexican painter Diego Rivera inspired the murals' socialist-realist style, with its biting cultural commentary, particularly about the exploitation of workers. At the time the murals were painted, clashes between management and labor along the waterfront and elsewhere in San Francisco were widespread. ✉ *Telegraph Hill Blvd. at Greenwich St. or Lombard St., North Beach* ☎ *415/362–0808* 🎫 *Free; elevator to top $5* ⏲ *Daily 10–6.*

Fodor's Choice ★ **Telegraph Hill.** Hill residents have some of the best views in the city, as well as the most difficult ascents to their aeries. The hill rises from the east end of Lombard Street to a height of 284 feet and is capped by Coit Tower *(see above)*. Imagine lugging your groceries up that! If you brave the slope, though, you can be rewarded with a "secret treasure" SF moment. Filbert Street starts up the hill, then becomes the Filbert Steps when the going gets too steep. You can cut between the Filbert Steps and another flight, the Greenwich Steps, on up to the hilltop. As you climb, you can pass some of the city's oldest houses and be surrounded by beautiful, flowering private gardens. In some places the trees grow over the stairs so they feel like a green tunnel; elsewhere, you'll have wide-open views of the bay. And the telegraphic name? It comes from the hill's status as the first Morse code signal station back in 1853. ✉ *Bordered by Lombard, Filbert, Kearny, and Sansome Sts., North Beach.*

Washington Square. Once the daytime social heart of Little Italy, this grassy patch has changed character numerous times over the years. The Beats hung out in the 1950s, hippies camped out in the 1960s and early '70s, and nowadays you're just as likely to see kids of Southeast Asian descent tossing a Frisbee as Italian men or women chatting about their children and the old country. In the morning elderly Asians perform the motions of tai chi, but by mid-morning groups of conservatively dressed Italian men in their 70s and 80s begin to arrive. Any time of day, the park may attract a number of homeless people, who stretch out to rest on the benches and grass, and young locals sunbathing or running their dogs. Lillie Hitchcock Coit, in yet another show of affection for San Francisco's firefighters, donated the statue of two firemen with a child they rescued. **■TIP→ The North Beach Festival, the city's oldest street fair, celebrates the area's Italian culture here each June.** ✉ *Bordered by Columbus Ave. and Stockton, Filbert, and Union Sts., North Beach.*

4

ON THE WATERFRONT

San Francisco's waterfront neighborhoods have fabulous views and utterly different personalities. Kitschy, overpriced Fisherman's Wharf struggles to maintain the last shreds of its existence as a working wharf, while Pier 39 is a full-fledged consumer circus. The Ferry Building draws well-heeled locals with its culinary pleasures, firmly reconnecting the Embarcadero to downtown. Between the Ferry Building and Pier 39 a former maritime no-man's-land is filling in with Alcatraz Landing's fashionable waterfront restaurants, restored pedestrian-friendly piers, and in 2013, the new Exploratorium.

Today's shoreline was once Yerba Buena Cove, filled in during the latter half of the 19th century, when San Francisco was a brawling, extravagant gold-rush town. Jackson Square, now a genteel and upscale corner of the inland Financial District, was the heart of the Barbary Coast, bordering some of the roughest wharves in the world. Below Montgomery Street (in today's Financial District), between California Street and Broadway, lies a remnant of these wild days: more than 100 ships abandoned by frantic crews and passengers caught up in gold fever lie under the foundations of buildings here.

EXPLORING THE WATERFRONT

Fodor's Choice ★ **Alcatraz.** Thousands of visitors a day take the 15-minute ferry ride to "the Rock" to walk in the footsteps of Alcatraz's notorious criminals. Definitely take the splendid audio tour; gravelly voiced former inmates and hardened guards bring one of America's most notorious penal colonies to life. Plan your schedule to allow at least three hours for the visit and boat rides combined, and buy tickets in advance, even in the off-season. ✉ *Pier 33, Embarcadero* ☎ *415/981–7625* 🌐 *www.nps.gov/alca* 🎟 *$26, including audio tour; $33 evening tour, including audio* ⏲ *Ferry departs every 30–45 mins Sept.–late May, daily 9:30–2:15, 4:20* *for evening tour Thurs.–Mon. only; late May–Aug., daily 9:30–4:15, 6:30 and 7:30 for evening tour.*

Fodor's Choice ★ **Ferry Building.** Renovated in 2003, the Ferry Building is the jewel of the Embarcadero. The beacon of the port area, erected in 1896, has a 230-foot clock tower modeled after the campanile of the cathedral in Seville, Spain. On the morning of April 18, 1906, the tower's four clock faces, powered by the swinging of a 14-foot pendulum, stopped at 5:17—the moment the great earthquake struck—and stayed still for 12 months.

Today San Franciscans flock to the street-level Market Hall, stocking up on supplies from local favorites such as Acme Bread, Scharffen Berger Chocolate, Cowgirl Creamery, and Blue Bottle Coffee. Lucky diners claim a coveted table at Slanted Door, the city's beloved high-end Vietnamese restaurant. The seafood bars at Hog Island Oyster Company and Ferry Plaza Seafood have fantastic city panoramas—or you can take your purchases around to the building's bay side, where benches face views of the Bay Bridge. Saturday mornings the plaza in front of the building buzzes with an upscale, celebrity-chef-studded farmers' market. Extending from the piers on the north side of the building south to the Bay Bridge, the waterfront promenade is a favorite among joggers and picnickers, with a front-row view of the sailboats slipping by. The Ferry Building also serves actual ferries: from behind the building they sail to Sausalito, Larkspur, Tiburon, and the East Bay. ✉ *Embarcadero at foot of Market St., Embarcadero* 🌐 *www.ferrybuildingmarketplace.com.*

QUICK BITES

Even locals love the cheery Buena Vista Café (✉ *2765 Hyde St., Fisherman's Wharf* ☎ *415/474–5044*), which claims to be the first place in the United States to have served Irish coffee. The café opens at 9 am weekdays (8 am weekends) and dishes up a great breakfast. They serve about 2,000 Irish coffees a day, so it's always crowded; try for a table overlooking nostalgic Victorian Park and its cable car turntable.

Fisherman's Wharf. It may be one of the city's best-known attractions, but the wharf is a no-go zone for most locals, who shy away from the difficult parking, overpriced food, and cheesy shops at third-rate shopping centers like the Cannery at Del Monte Square. If you just can't resist a visit here, come early to avoid the crowds and get a sense of the wharf's functional role—it's not just an amusement park replica.

Most of the entertainment at the wharf is schlocky and overpriced, with one notable exception: the splendid **Musée Mécanique** (☎ *415/346–2000* ⏲ *Weekdays 10–7, weekends 10–8*), a time-warped arcade with antique mechanical contrivances, including peep shows and nickelodeons. Some favorites are the giant and rather creepy "Laffing Sal" (you enter the museum through his gaping mouth), an arm-wrestling machine, the world's only steam-powered motorcycle, and mechanical fortune-telling figures that speak from their curtained boxes. Note the depictions of race that betray the prejudices of the time: stoned Chinese figures in the "Opium-Den" and clown-faced African-Americans eating watermelon in the "Mechanical Farm." Admission is free, but you'll need quarters to bring the machines to life.

Thousands of visitors take ferries to Alcatraz each day to walk in the footsteps of the notorious criminals who were held on "The Rock."

Among the two floors of exhibits at **Ripley's Believe It or Not! Museum** (✉ *175 Jefferson St., Fisherman's Wharf* ☎ *415/771–6188* 🌐 *www.ripleysf.com* 🎫 *$16.99* ⏲ *Late June–Labor Day, Sun.–Thurs. 9 am–11 pm, Fri. and Sat. 9 am–midnight; Labor Day–early June, Sun.–Thurs. 10–10, Fri. and Sat., 10 am–midnight*)is a tribute to San Francisco—an 8-foot-long scale model of a cable car, made entirely of matchsticks.

Notables from local boy Robin Williams to King Tut await at the **Wax Museum** (✉ *145 Jefferson St.,Fisherman's Wharf* ☎ *415/202–0400 or 800/439–4305* 🌐 *www.waxmuseum.com*), open daily 10–9. Admission is $14.

The **USS Pampanito** (✉ *Pier 45, Fisherman's Wharf* ☎ *415/775–1943* 🌐 *www.maritime.org/pamphome.htm* ⏲ *Oct.–Memorial Day, Sun.–Thurs. 9–6, Fri. and Sat. 9–8; Memorial Day–Sept., Thurs.–Tues. 9–8, Wed. 9–6*) provides an intriguing if mildly claustrophobic glimpse into life on a submarine during World War II. The sub sank six Japanese warships and damaged four others. Admission is $10; the family pass is a great deal at $20 for two adults and up to four kids.

✉ *Jefferson St. between Leavenworth St. and Pier 39, Fisherman's Wharf*

Ghirardelli Square. Most of the redbrick buildings in this early-20th-century complex were once part of the Ghirardelli factory. Now tourists come here to pick up the famous chocolate, though you can purchase it all over town and save yourself a trip to what is essentially a mall. But this is the only place to watch the cool chocolate manufactory in action. (If you're a chocoholic, this definitely beats the Cannery.) There are no fewer than three Ghirardelli stores here, as well as gift shops and a couple of restaurants—including Ana Mandara—that even locals love. Fairmont recently opened an upscale urban time-share directly on the square. Placards throughout the square describe the factory's history. ✉ *900 North Point St., Fisherman's Wharf* ☎ *415/775–5500* 🌐 *www.ghirardellisq.com.*

F-LINE TROLLEYS

The **F-line**, the city's system of vintage electric trolleys gives the cable cars a run for their money as San Francisco's best-loved mode of transportation. These beautifully restored streetcars—some dating from the 19th century—run from the Castro all the way down Market Street to the Embarcadero, then north to Fisherman's Wharf. Each car is unique, restored to the colors of its city of origin, from New Orleans and Philadelphia to Moscow and Milan. Purchase tickets on board; exact change is required. 🌐 *www.streetcar.org* 🎟 *$2.*

★ **Hyde Street Pier.** Cotton candy and souvenirs are all well and good, but if you want to get to the heart of the Wharf—boats—there's no better place to do it than at this pier, by far one of the Wharf area's best bargains. Depending on the time of day, you might see boatbuilders at work or children pretending to man an early-1900s ship.

Don't pass up the centerpiece collection of historic vessels, part of the **San Francisco Maritime National Historic Park,** almost all of which can be boarded. The newly restored *Balclutha,* an 1886 full-rigged three-masted sailing vessel that's more than 250 feet long, sailed around Cape Horn 17 times; kids especially love the *Eureka,* a side-wheel passenger and car ferry, for her onboard collection of vintage cars; the *Hercules* is a steam-powered tugboat. The *C.A. Thayer,* a three-masted schooner, recently underwent a painstaking restoration and is back on display. Across the street from the pier and almost a museum in itself is the San Francisco Maritime National Historic Park's **Visitor Center** (✉ *499 Jefferson St., at Hyde St., Fisherman's Wharf* ☎ *415/447–5000* ⏲ *Jun.–Aug., daily 9:30–5:30; Sept.–May, daily 9:30–5*), happily free of mind-numbing, text-heavy displays. Instead, fun large-scale exhibits, such as a huge First Order Fresnel lighthouse lens and a shipwrecked boat, make this an engaging and relatively quick stop. Though it's still undergoing long-term restoration, the **Maritime Museum** (✉ *900 Beach St., at Polk St., Fisherman's Wharf* ⏲ *lobby open daily 10–4*) is worth a peek now to see its lobby mural, a gorgeous underwater dreamscape. ✉ *Hyde and Jefferson Sts., Fisherman's Wharf* ☎ *415/561–7100* 🌐 *www.nps.gov/safr* 🎟 *Ships $5* ⏲ *Jun.–Aug., daily 9:30–5:30; Sept.–May, daily 9:30–5.*

Jackson Square. This was the heart of the Barbary Coast of the Gay '90s (the 1890s, that is). Although most of the red-light district was destroyed in the fire that followed the 1906 earthquake, old redbrick buildings and narrow alleys recall the romance and rowdiness of San Francisco's early days. The days of brothels and bar fights are long gone—now Jackson Square is a genteel, quiet corner of the Financial District. It's of interest to the historically inclined and antiques-shop browsers, but otherwise safely skipped.

Some of the city's first business buildings, survivors of the 1906 quake, still stand between Montgomery and Sansome streets. After a few decades of neglect, these old-timers were adopted by preservation-minded interior designers and wholesale furniture dealers for use as showrooms. In 1972 the city officially designated the area—bordered by Columbus Avenue on the west, Broadway and Pacific Avenue on the north, Washington Street on the south, and Sansome Street on the east—San Francisco's first historic district. When property values soared, many of the fabric and furniture outlets fled to Potrero Hill. Advertising agencies, attorneys, and antiques dealers now occupy the Jackson Square–area structures.

Restored 19th-century brick buildings line Hotaling Place, which connects Washington and Jackson streets. The lane is named for the head of the **A.P. Hotaling Company whiskey distillery** (✉ *451 Jackson St., at Hotaling Pl.*), which was the largest liquor repository on the West Coast in its day. (Hotaling whiskey is still made in the city, by the way; look for their single malts for a sip of truly local flavor.) It takes a bit of conjuring to evoke the wild Barbary Coast days when checking out the now-gentrified gold rush–era buildings in the 700 block of **Montgomery Street.** But this was an especially colorful block. Author Mark Twain was a reporter for the spunky *Golden Era* newspaper, which occupied No. 732 (now part of the building at No. 744). From 1959 to 1996 the late ambulance-chaser extraordinaire, lawyer Melvin Belli, had his headquarters there. There was never a dull moment in Belli's world; he represented clients from Mae West to Gloria Sykes (who in 1964 claimed that a cable car accident turned her into a nymphomaniac) to Jim and Tammy Faye Bakker. Whenever he won a case, he fired a cannon and raised the Jolly Roger. Belli was also known for receiving a letter from the never-caught Zodiac killer. It seems fitting that the building sat for years, deteriorating and moldering, while the late attorney's sons fought wife number five (joined with Belli in holy matrimony just three months before his death). She eventually won, but today the dilapidated building is for sale. ✉ *Jackson Sq. district, bordered by Broadway and Washington, Kearny, and Sansome Sts., Financial District.*

Pier 39. The city's most popular waterfront attraction draws millions of visitors each year who come to browse through its vertiginous array of shops and concessions hawking every conceivable form of souvenir. The pier can be quite crowded, and the numerous street performers may leave you feeling more harassed than entertained. Arriving early in the morning ensures you a front-row view of the sea lions, but if you're here to shop—and make no mistake about it, Pier 39 wants your money—be aware that most stores don't open until 9:30 or 10 (later in winter).

Pick up a buckwheat hull–filled otter neck wrap or a plush sea lion to snuggle at the **Marine Mammal Center Store** (☎ *415/289–7373*), whose proceeds benefit Sausalito's respected wild-animal hospital, the Marine Mammal Center.

Sales of the excellent books, maps, and collectibles—including a series of gorgeous, distinctive art deco posters for Alcatraz, the Presidio, Fort Point, and the other members of the Golden Gate National Recreation Area—at the **National Park Store** (☎ *415/433–7221*) help to support the National Park Service.

Brilliant colors enliven the double-decker **San Francisco Carousel** (*$3 per ride*), decorated with images of such city landmarks as the Golden Gate Bridge and Lombard Street.

Follow the sound of barking to the northwest side of the pier to view the sea lions that flop about the floating docks.

At **Aquarium of the Bay** (*415/623–5300 or 888/732–3483 www.aquariumofthebay.org $16.95 Jun.–Sept., 9–8 daily; Mar.–May and Oct., Mon.–Thurs. 10–7, Fri.–Sun. 10–8; Nov.–Feb., Mon.–Thurs. 10–7, Fri.–Sun. 10–7*) moving walkways transport you through a space surrounded on three sides by water filled with indigenous San Francisco Bay marine life, from fish and plankton to sharks. Many find the aquarium overpriced; if you can, take advantage of the family rate ($39.95 for two adults and two kids under 12).

WHISKEY RHYME

The Italianate Hotaling building survived the disastrous 1906 quake and fire—a miracle considering the thousands of barrels of inflammable liquid inside. A plaque on the side of the structure repeats a famous query: "if, as they say, God spanked the town for being over frisky, why did he burn the churches down and save hotaling's whiskey?"

The **California Welcome Center** (*415/981–1280 www.visitcwc.com Daily 10–6*), on Pier 39's second level, offers Internet use for $5 per half hour.

Parking (free with validation from a Pier 39 restaurant) is at the Pier 39 Garage, off Powell Street at the Embarcadero. *Beach St. at Embarcadero, Fisherman's Wharf www.pier39.com.*

San Francisco Railway Museum. A labor of love brought to you by the same vintage-transit enthusiasts responsible for the F-line's revival, this one-room museum and store celebrates the city's storied streetcars and cable cars with photographs, models, and artifacts. The permanent exhibit includes the replicated end of a streetcar with a working cab—complete with controls and a bell—for kids to explore; the cool, antique Wiley birdcage traffic signal; and models and display cases to view. Right on the F-line track, just across from the Ferry Building, this is a great quick stop. *77 Steuart St., Embarcadero 415/974–1948 www.streetcar.org Free Tues.–Sun. 10–6.*

Transamerica Pyramid. It's neither owned by Transamerica nor is it a pyramid, but this 853-foot-tall obelisk *is* the most photographed of the city's high-rises. Excoriated in the design stages as "the world's largest architectural folly," the icon was quickly hailed as a masterpiece when it opened in 1972. Today it's probably the city's most recognized structure after the Golden Gate Bridge. A fragrant redwood grove along the east side of the building, replete with benches and a cheerful fountain, is a placid patch in which to unwind. *600 Montgomery St., Financial District www.transamerica.com.*

THE MARINA AND THE PRESIDIO

Yachts bob at their moorings, satisfied-looking folks jog along the Marina Green, and multimillion-dollar homes overlook the bay in this picturesque, if somewhat sterile, neighborhood. Does it all seem a bit too perfect? Well, it got this way after the hard knock of Loma Prieta—the current pretty face was put on after hundreds of homes collapsed in the 1989 earthquake. Just west of this waterfront area is a more natural beauty: the Presidio. Once a military base, this beautiful, sprawling park is mostly green space, with hills, woods, and the marshlands of Crissy Field.

EXPLORING THE MARINA

★ **Exploratorium.** Walking into this fascinating "museum of science, art, and human perception" is like visiting a mad scientist's laboratory. Most of the exhibits are supersize, and you can play with everything. Get an Alice in Wonderland feeling in the distortion room, where you seem to shrink and grow as you walk across the slanted, checkered floor. In the shadow room, a powerful flash freezes an image of your shadow on the wall; jumping is a favorite pose. "Pushover" demonstrates cow-tipping, but for people: stand on one foot and try to keep your balance while a friend swings a striped panel in front of you (trust us, you're going to fall).

More than 650 other exhibits focus on sea and insect life, computers, electricity, patterns and light, language, the weather, and much more. "Explainers"—usually high-school students on their days off—demonstrate cool scientific tools and procedures, like DNA sample-collection and cow-eye dissection. One surefire hit is the pitch-black, touchy-feely Tactile Dome. In this geodesic dome strewn with textured objects, you crawl through a course of ladders, slides, and tunnels, relying solely on your sense of touch. Not surprisingly, lovey-dovey couples sometimes linger in the "grope dome," but be forewarned: the staff will turn on the lights if they have to. ■ **TIP→ Reservations are required for the Tactile Dome, and will get you 75 minutes of access. You have to be at least seven years old to go through the dome, and the space is not for the claustrophobic.** The Exploratorium is preparing to move into its new home at Pier 15 in 2013. ✉ *3601 Lyon St., at Marina Blvd., Marina* ☎ *415/561–0360 general information; 415/561–0362 Tactile Dome reservations* 🌐 *www.exploratorium.edu* 🎟 *$15, free 1st Wed. of month; Tactile Dome $5 extra* 🕙 *Tues.–Sun. 10–5.*

Fort Mason Center. Originally a depot for the shipment of supplies to the Pacific during World War II, the fort was converted into a cultural center in 1977. Here you can find the vegetarian restaurant Greens and shops, galleries, and performance spaces, most of which are closed Monday. There's also plentiful free parking—a rarity in the city.

You have to be seriously into Italian-American culture to appreciate the text- and photograph-heavy exhibits at the **Museo Italo-Americano** (✉ *Bldg. C* ☎ *415/673–2200* 🌐 *museoitaloamericano.org* 🕙 *Tues.–Sun. noon–4*), but depending on the exhibit, it might be worth a glance if you're already at Fort Mason. Plus, it's free. The temporary exhibits downstairs at the free **SFMOMA Artists Gallery** (✉ *Bldg. A* ☎ *415/441–4777*) can be great, but head upstairs and check out the paintings, sculptures, prints, and photographs for sale and for rent. It's a fun scene, with folks flipping through the works like posters. You won't find a Picasso or a Rembrandt here, but you can find works of high quality by emerging Northern California artists—and where else can you get a $50,000 work of art to hang on your wall for $400 (a month)? It's open Tuesday through Saturday 11:30–5:30. ✉ *Buchanan St. and Marina Blvd., Marina* ☎ *415/345–7500 event information* 🌐 *www.fortmason.org*.

Fodor's Choice ★ **Palace of Fine Arts.** At first glance this stunning, rosy rococo palace seems to be from another world, and indeed, it's the sole survivor of the many tinted-plaster structures (a temporary classical city of sorts) built for the 1915 Panama-Pacific International Exposition, the world's fair that celebrated San Francisco's recovery from the 1906 earthquake and fire. The expo buildings originally extended about a mile along the shore. Bernard Maybeck designed this faux–Roman classic beauty, which was reconstructed in concrete and reopened in 1967.

A victim of the elements, the Palace completed a piece-by-piece renovation in 2008, though the pseudo-Latin language adorning the exterior urns continues to stump scholars. The massive columns (each topped with four "weeping maidens"), great rotunda, and swan-filled lagoon have been used in countless fashion layouts, films, and wedding photo shoots. After admiring the lagoon, look across the street to the house at 3460 Baker Street. If the maidens out front look familiar, they should—they're original casts of the lovely "garland ladies" you can see in the Palace's colonnade. The house was on the market in 2007; if you'd had a cool $8 million, it could've been yours. ✉ *Baker and Beach Sts., Marina* ☎ *415/561–0364 Palace history tours* 🌐 *www.exploratorium.edu/palace* 🎫 *Free* ⏲ *Daily 24 hrs.*

EXPLORING THE PRESIDIO

Fort Point. Dwarfed today by the Golden Gate Bridge, this brick fortress constructed between 1853 and 1861 was designed to protect San Francisco from a Civil War sea attack that never materialized. It was also used as a coastal-defense fortification post during World War II, when soldiers stood watch here. This National Historic Site is now a sprawling museum filled with military memorabilia, surrounding a lonely, windswept courtyard. The building has a gloomy air and is suitably atmospheric. (It's usually chilly and windy, too, so bring a jacket.) On days when Fort Point is staffed, guided group tours and cannon drills take place. The top floor affords a unique angle on the bay. ■ **TIP→ Take care when walking along the front side of the building, as it's slippery, and the waves have a dizzying effect.** Note that the fort is open only Friday through Sunday. The fort's popular guided candlelight tours, available only in winter, sell out in advance, so be sure to book ahead. Southeast of this structure is the **Fort Point Mine Depot,** an army facility that functioned as the headquarters for underwater mining operations throughout World War II. Today it's the Warming Hut, a National Park Service café and bookstore. ✉ *Marine Dr. off Lincoln Blvd., Presidio* ☎ *415/556–1693* 🌐 *www.nps.gov/fopo* 🎫 *Free* ⏲ *Fri.–Sun. 10–5.*

Fodor's Choice ★ **Golden Gate Bridge.** The suspension bridge that connects San Francisco with Marin County has long wowed sightseers with its simple but powerful art deco design. Completed in 1937 after four years of

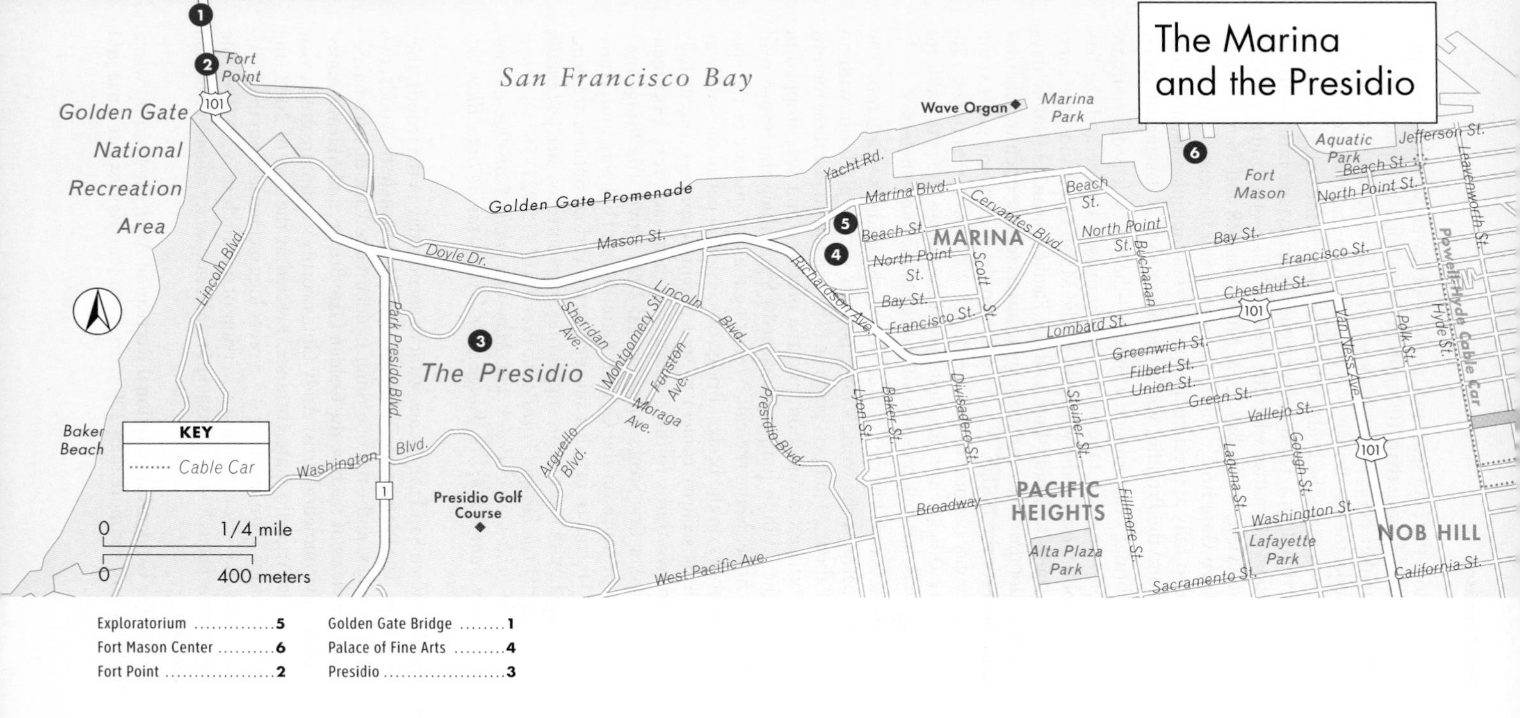
The Marina and the Presidio
San Francisco Bay
Golden Gate National Recreation Area
Fort Point
Wave Organ
Marina Park
Aquatic Park
Fort Mason
Golden Gate Promenade
MARINA
The Presidio
PACIFIC HEIGHTS
NOB HILL
Presidio Golf Course
Alta Plaza Park
Lafayette Park
Baker Beach
Powell-Hyde Cable Car
Yacht Rd.
Marina Blvd.
Cervantes Blvd.
Beach St.
North Point St.
Bay St.
Francisco St.
Chestnut St.
Lombard St.
Greenwich St.
Filbert St.
Union St.
Green St.
Vallejo St.
Broadway
Washington St.
Sacramento St.
California St.
Jefferson St.
Leavenworth St.
Hyde St.
Polk St.
Van Ness Ave.
Gough St.
Laguna St.
Fillmore St.
Steiner St.
Buchanan St.
Scott St.
Divisadero St.
Baker St.
Lyon St.
Richardson Ave.
Mason St.
Doyle Dr.
Lincoln Blvd.
Sheridan Ave.
Montgomery St.
Funston Ave.
Moraga Ave.
Arguello Blvd.
Presidio Blvd.
Park Presido Blvd.
Washington Blvd.
West Pacific Ave.
KEY
Cable Car
0 1/4 mile
0 400 meters
Exploratorium 5
Fort Mason Center 6
Fort Point 2
Golden Gate Bridge 1
Palace of Fine Arts 4
Presidio 3

construction, the 2-mi span and its 750-foot towers were built to withstand winds of more than 100 mph. It's also not a bad place to be in an earthquake: designed to sway up to 27.7 feet, the Golden Gate Bridge, unlike the Bay Bridge, was undamaged by the 1989 Loma Prieta quake. (If you're on the bridge when it's windy, stand still and you can feel it swaying a bit.) Though it's frequently gusty and misty—always bring a jacket, no matter what the weather's like—the bridge provides unparalleled views of the Bay Area. Muni buses 28 and 76 make stops at the Golden Gate Bridge toll plaza, on the San Francisco side. However, drive to fully appreciate the bridge from multiple vantage points in and around the Presidio; you'll be able to park at designated areas.

From the bridge's eastern-side walkway—the only side pedestrians are allowed on—you can take in the San Francisco skyline and the bay islands; look west for the wild hills of the Marin Headlands, the curving coast south to Land's End, and the Pacific Ocean. On sunny days sailboats dot the water, and brave windsurfers test the often-treacherous tides beneath the bridge. A vista point on the Marin side gives you a spectacular city panorama. ■ **TIP→ May 27, 2012 marks the bridge's 75th anniversary. Officials have decided against closing the bridge to traffic for a bridge walk, but look for some official celebration nonetheless.**

But there's a well-known, darker side to the bridge's story, too. The bridge is perhaps the world's most popular suicide platform, with an average of about 20 jumpers per year. (The first leaped just three months after the bridge's completion, and the official count was stopped in 1995 as the 1,000th jump approached.) Signs along the bridge read "There is hope. Make the call," referring the disconsolate to the special telephones on the bridge. Bridge officers, who patrol the walkway and watch by security camera to spot potential jumpers, successfully talk down two-thirds to three-quarters of them each year. Documentary filmmaker Eric Steel's controversial 2006 movie *The Bridge* once again put pressure on the Golden Gate Bridge Highway and Transportation District to install a suicide barrier; various options are being considered, with most locals supporting an unobtrusive net. ✉ *Lincoln Blvd. near Doyle Dr. and Fort Point, Presidio* ☎ *415/921–5858* 🌐 *www.goldengatebridge.org* ⏲ *Pedestrians Mar.–Oct., daily 5 am–9 pm; Nov.–Feb., daily 5 am–6 pm; hrs change with daylight saving time. Bicyclists daily 24 hrs.*

★ **Presidio.** When San Franciscans want to spend a day in the woods, they head here. The Presidio has 1,400 acres of hills and majestic woods, two small beaches, and—the one thing Golden Gate Park doesn't have—stunning views of the bay, the Golden Gate Bridge, and Marin County. Famed environmental artist Andy Goldsworthy's sculpture greets visitors at the Arguello Gate entrance. Erected at the end of 2008, the 100-plus-foot *Spire*, made of 37 cypress logs reclaimed from the Presidio, looks like a rough, natural version of a church spire. ■ **TIP→ The best lookout points lie along Washington Boulevard, which meanders through the park.**

Part of the **Golden Gate National Recreation Area,** the Presidio was a military post for more than 200 years. Don Juan Bautista de Anza and

Armed with only helmets, safety harnesses, and painting equipment, a full-time crew of 38 painters keeps the Golden Gate Bridge clad in International Orange.

a band of Spanish settlers first claimed the area in 1776. It became a Mexican garrison in 1822, when Mexico gained its independence from Spain; U.S. troops forcibly occupied the Presidio in 1846. The U.S. Sixth Army was stationed here until October 1994, when the coveted space was transferred into civilian hands.

Today the area is being transformed into a self-sustaining national park with a combination of public, commercial, and residential projects. In 2005 Bay Area filmmaker George Lucas opened the **Letterman Digital Arts Center,** his 23-acre digital studio "campus," along the eastern edge of the land. Seventeen of those acres are exquisitely landscaped and open to the public, but not even landscaping this perfect can compete with the wilds of the Presidio.

The battle over the fate of the rest of the Presidio is ongoing. Many older buildings have been reconstructed; the issue now is how to fill them. The original plan described a nexus for arts, education, and environmental groups. Since the Presidio's overseeing trust must make the park financially self-sufficient by 2013, which means generating enough revenue to keep afloat without the federal government's monthly $20 million checks, many fear that money will trump culture. The Asian-theme SenSpa and a new Walt Disney museum have opened, and a lodge at the Main Post is in the planning stages. With old military housing now repurposed as apartments and homes with rents up to $10,000 a month, there's some concern that the Presidio will become an incoherent mix of pricey real estate. Still, the $6 million that Lucas shells out annually for rent does plant a lot of saplings.

The Presidio also has two beaches, a golf course, a visitor center, and picnic sites; the views from the many overlooks are sublime.

★ Especially popular is **Crissy Field,** a stretch of restored marshland along the sand of the bay. Kids on bikes, folks walking dogs, and joggers share the paved path along the shore, often winding up at the Warming Hut, a combination café and fun gift store at the end of the path, for a hot chocolate in the shadow of the Golden Gate Bridge. Midway along the Golden Gate Promenade that winds along the shore is the Gulf of the Farallones National Marine Sanctuary Visitor Center, where kids can get a close-up view of small sea creatures and learn about the rich ecosystem offshore. Temporarily relocated to East Beach, just across from the Exploratorium, Crissy Field Center offers great children's programs and has cool science displays; grab lunch at the Beach Hut Café next door. West of the Golden Gate Bridge is sandy **Baker Beach,** beloved for its spectacular views and laid-back vibe (read: you'll see naked people here). This is one of those places that inspires local pride. ✉ *Between Marina and Lincoln Park, Presidio* 🌐 *www.nps.gov/prsf and www.presidio.gov.*

GOLDEN GATE PARK AND THE WESTERN SHORELINE

More than 1,000 acres, stretching from the Haight all the way to the windy Pacific coast, Golden Gate Park is a vast patchwork of woods, trails, lakes, lush gardens, sports facilities, museums—even a herd of buffalo. There's more natural beauty beyond the park's borders, along San Francisco's wild Western Shoreline.

EXPLORING GOLDEN GATE PARK

Fodor's Choice ★ **California Academy of Sciences.** With its native plant–covered living roof, retractable ceiling, three-story rain forest, gigantic planetarium, living coral reef, and frolicking penguins, the Cal Academy is one of the city's most spectacular treasures. Dramatically designed by Renzo Piano, it's an eco-friendly, energy-efficient adventure in biodiversity and green architecture. The roof's large mounds and hills mirror the local topography, and Piano's audacious design completes the dramatic transformation of the park's Music Concourse. Moving away from a restrictive role as a backward-looking museum that catalogued natural history, the new academy is all about sustainability and the future, but you'll still find those beloved dioramas in African Hall.

By the time you arrive, hopefully you've decided which shows and programs to attend, looked at the academy's floor plan, and designed a plan to cover it all in the time you have. And if not, here's the quick version: Head left from the entrance to the wooden walkway over otherworldly leopard rays in the Philippine Coral Reef, then continue to the Swamp to see the famous albino alligator. Swing through African Hall and gander at the penguins, take the elevator up to the living roof, then return to the main floor and get in line to explore the Rainforests of the World, ducking free-flying butterflies and watching for other live surprises. You'll end up below ground in the Amazonian Flooded Rainforest, where you can explore the academy's other aquarium exhibits.

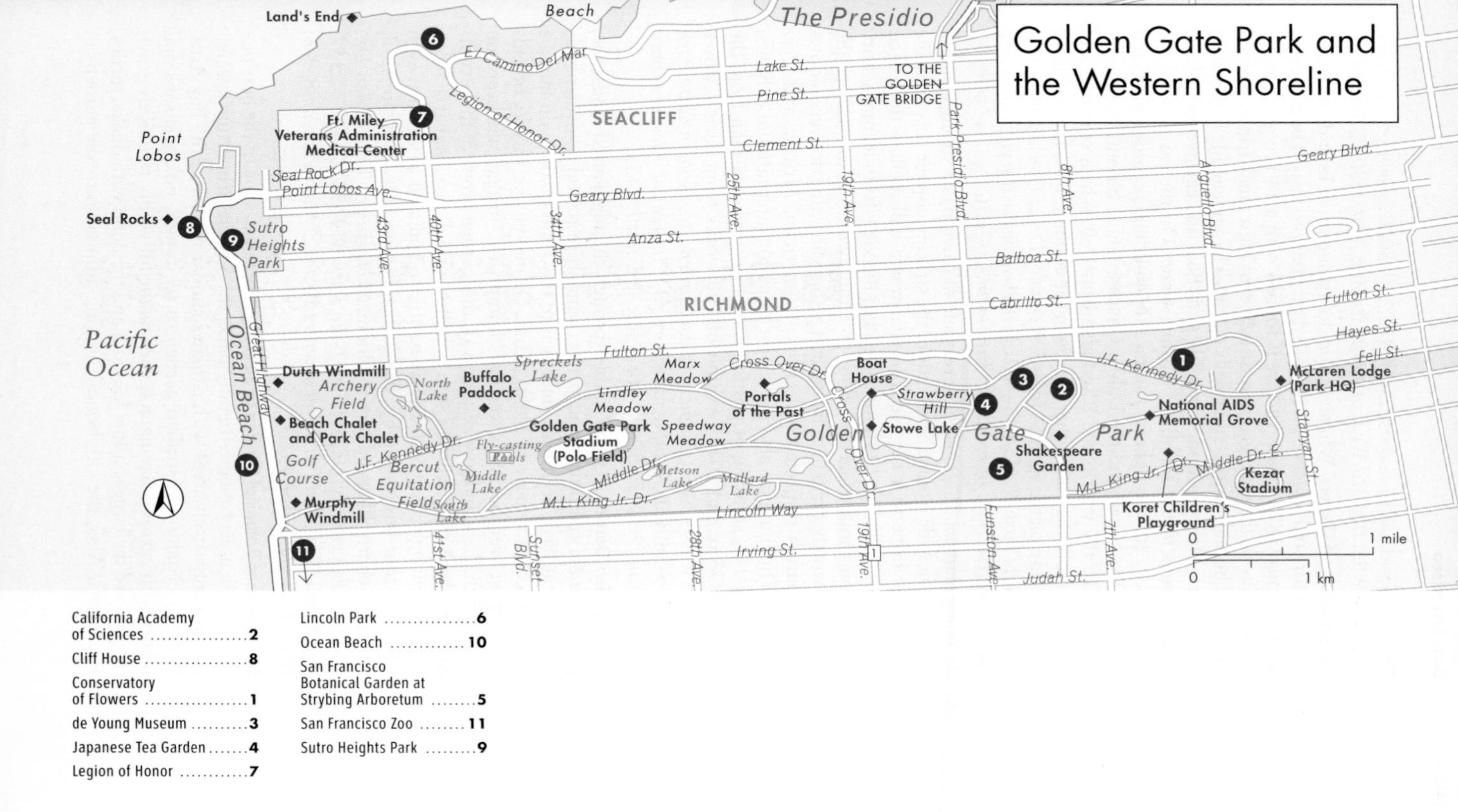

California Academy of Sciences	2
Cliff House	8
Conservatory of Flowers	1
de Young Museum	3
Japanese Tea Garden	4
Legion of Honor	7
Lincoln Park	6
Ocean Beach	10
San Francisco Botanical Garden at Strybing Arboretum	5
San Francisco Zoo	11
Sutro Heights Park	9

Phew. ✉ *55 Music Concourse Dr.* ☎ *415/379–8000* 🌐 *www.calacademy.org* 🎫 *$29.95, free 3rd Wed. of month* ⏲ *Mon.–Sat. 9:30–5, Sun. 11–5.*

Conservatory of Flowers. Whatever you do, be sure to at least drive by the Conservatory of Flowers—it's just too darn pretty to miss. The gorgeous, white-framed 1878 glass structure is topped with a 14-ton glass dome. Stepping inside the giant greenhouse is like taking a quick trip to the rain forest; it's humid, warm, and smells earthy. The undeniable highlight is the Aquatic Plants section, where lily pads float and carnivorous plants dine on bugs to the sounds of rushing water. On the east side of the conservatory (to the right as you face the building), cypress, pine, and redwood trees surround the Dahlia Garden, which blooms in summer and fall. To the west is the Rhododendron Dell, which contains 850 varieties, more than any other garden in the country. It's a favorite local Mother's Day picnic spot. ✉ *John F. Kennedy Dr. at Conservatory Dr., Golden Gate Park* ☎ *415/666–7001* 🌐 *www.conservatoryofflowers.org* 🎫 *$7, free 1st Tues. of month* ⏲ *Tues.–Sun. 10–4:30.*

★ **de Young Museum.** It seems that everyone in town has a strong opinion about the new de Young. Some adore the striking copper façade, while others just hope that the green patina of age will mellow the effect. Most maligned is the 144-foot tower, but the view from its ninth-story observation room, ringed by floor-to-ceiling windows and free to the public, is worth a trip here by itself. The building almost overshadows the de Young's respected collection of American, African, and Oceanic art. The museum also plays host to major international exhibits, such as 2010's showing of postimpressionist works on loan from the Musée d'Orsay and 2011's exhibit of 100 works from Paris's Musée National Picasso. ✉ *50 Hagiwara Tea Garden Dr., Golden Gate Park* ☎ *415/750–3600* 🌐 *deyoung.famsf.org* 🎫 *$10, free 1st Tues. of month* ⏲ *Tues.–Sun. 9:30–5:15; mid-Jan.–Nov., Fri. until 8:45.*

Japanese Tea Garden. As you amble through the manicured landscape, past Japanese sculptures and perfect miniature pagodas, over ponds of carp that have been here since before the 1906 quake, you may be transported to a more peaceful plane. Or maybe the shrieks of kids clambering over the almost vertical "humpback" bridges will keep you firmly in the here and now. Either way, this garden is one of those tourist spots that's truly worth a stop (a half-hour will do). And at 5 acres, it's large enough that you'll always be able to find a bit of serenity, even when the tour buses drop by. The garden is especially lovely in April, when the cherry blossoms are in bloom. ✉ *Hagiwara Tea Garden Dr., off John F. Kennedy Dr., Golden Gate Park* ☎ *415/752–4227* 🎫 *$7, free Mon., Wed., and Fri. if you enter by 10 am* ⏲ *Mar.–Oct., daily 9–6; Nov.–Feb., daily 9–4:45.*

San Francisco Botanical Garden at Strybing Arboretum. One of the best picnic spots in a very picnic-friendly park, the 55-acre arboretum specializes in plants from areas with climates similar to that of the Bay Area. Walk the Eastern Australian garden to see tough, pokey shrubs and plants with cartoon-like names, such as the hilly-pilly tree. Kids gravitate toward the large shallow fountain and the pond with ducks, turtles, and egrets. Alas, the city began charging admission to the gardens in

2010, so it's a slightly less alluring picnic spot compared to the free stretches in front of the Conservatory of Flowers and on the Music Concourse between the de Young and the Cal Academy. ✉ *Enter the park at 9th Ave. at Lincoln Way, Golden Gate Park* ☎ *415/661–1316* 🌐 *www.sfbotanicalgarden.org* 🎫 *$7, free 2nd Tues. of month* ⏲ *Apr.–Oct., daily 9–6; Nov.–Mar., daily 10–5.*

EXPLORING THE WESTERN SHORELINE

Cliff House. A meal at the Cliff House isn't about the food—the spectacular ocean view is what brings folks here. The vistas, which include offshore Seal Rock (the barking marine mammals who reside there are actually sea lions), can be 30 mi or more on a clear day—or less than a mile on foggy days. ■ **TIP→ Come for drinks just before sunset; then head back into town for dinner.**

4

Three buildings have occupied this site since 1863. The current building dates from 1909; a 2004 renovation has left a strikingly attractive restaurant and a squat concrete viewing platform out back. The complex, owned by the National Park Service, includes a gift shop.

Sitting on the observation deck is the **Giant Camera,** a camera obscura with its lens pointing skyward housed in a cute yellow-painted wooden shack. Built in the 1940s and threatened many times with demolition, it's now on the National Register of Historic Places. Step into the dark, tiny room inside (for a $3 fee); a fascinating 360-degree image of the surrounding area—which rotates as the "lens" on the roof rotates—is projected on a large, circular table. ■ **TIP→ In winter and spring you may also glimpse migrating gray whales from the observation deck.**

To the north of the Cliff House are the ruins of the once-grand glass-roof **Sutro Baths,** which you can explore on your own (they look a bit like water-storage receptacles). Adolf Sutro, eccentric onetime San Francisco mayor and Cliff House owner, built the bath complex, including a train out to the site, in 1896, so that everyday folks could enjoy the benefits of swimming. Six enormous baths (some freshwater and some seawater), more than 500 dressing rooms, and several restaurants covered 3 acres north of the Cliff House and accommodated 25,000 bathers. Likened to Roman baths in a European glass palace, the baths were for decades the favorite destination of San Franciscans in search of entertainment. The complex fell into disuse after World War II, was closed in 1952, and burned down (under officially questionable circumstances, wink wink) during demolition in 1966. ✉ *1090 Point Lobos Ave., Outer Richmond* ☎ *415/386–3330* 🌐 *www.cliffhouse.com* 🎫 *Free* ⏲ *Weekdays 9 am–9:30 pm, weekends 9 am–10 pm.*

Fodor's Choice ★ **Legion of Honor.** The old adage of real estate—location, location, location—is at full force here. You can't beat the site of this museum of European art atop cliffs overlooking the ocean, the Golden Gate Bridge, and the Marin Headlands. A pyramidal glass skylight in the entrance court illuminates the lower-level galleries, which exhibit prints and drawings, English and European porcelain, and ancient Assyrian, Greek, Roman, and Egyptian art. The 20-plus galleries on the upper level display the permanent collection of European art (paintings, sculpture, decorative arts, and tapestries) from the 14th century to the present day.

The noteworthy Auguste Rodin collection includes two galleries devoted to the master and a third with works by Rodin and other 19th-century sculptors. An original cast of Rodin's *The Thinker* welcomes you as you walk through the courtyard. As fine as the museum is, the setting and view outshine the collection and make a trip here worthwhile.

The **Legion Café,** on the lower level, serves tasty light meals (soup, sandwiches, grilled chicken) inside and on a garden terrace. (Unfortunately, there's no view.) Just north of the museum's parking lot is George Segal's *The Holocaust,* a stark white installation that evokes life in concentration camps during World War II. It's haunting at night, when backlighted by lights in the Legion's parking lot. **■ TIP→ Admission to the Legion also counts as same-day admission to the de Young Museum.** ✉ *34th Ave. at Clement St., Outer Richmond* ☎ *415/750–3600* 🌐 *legionofhonor.famsf.org* 🎟 *$10, $2 off with Muni transfer, free 1st Tues. of month* ⏲ *Tues.–Sun. 9:30–5:15.*

★ **Lincoln Park.** Although many of the city's green spaces are gentle and welcoming, Lincoln Park is a wild 275-acre park with windswept cliffs and panoramic views. The newly renovated Coastal Trail, the park's most dramatic one, leads out to **Lands End;** pick it up west of the Legion of Honor (at the end of El Camino del Mar) or from the parking lot at Point Lobos and El Camino del Mar. Time your hike to hit Mile Rock at low tide, and you might catch a glimpse of two wrecked ships peeking up from their watery graves. ⚠ **Do be careful if you hike here; landslides are frequent, and many people have fallen into the sea by standing too close to the edge of a crumbling bluff top.**

On the tamer side, large Monterey cypresses line the fairways at Lincoln Park's 18-hole golf course, near the Legion of Honor. At one time this land was the Golden Gate Cemetery, where the dead were segregated by nationality; most were indigent and interred without ceremony in the potter's field. In 1900 the Board of Supervisors voted to ban burials within city limits, and all but two city cemeteries (at Mission Dolores and the Presidio) were moved to Colma, a small town just south of San Francisco. When digging has to be done in the park, bones occasionally surface again. ✉ *Entrance at 34th Ave. at Clement St., Outer Richmond.*

Ocean Beach. Stretching 3 mi along the western side of the city from the Richmond to the Sunset, this sandy swath of the Pacific coast is good for jogging or walking the dog—but not for swimming. The water is so cold that surfers wear wet suits year-round, and riptides are strong. As for sunbathing, it's rarely warm enough here; think meditative walking instead of sun worshipping.

Paths on both sides of the Great Highway lead from Lincoln Way to Sloat Boulevard (near the zoo); the beachside path winds through landscaped sand dunes, and the paved path across the highway is good for biking and in-line skating. (Though you have to rent bikes elsewhere.) The **Beach Chalet** restaurant and brewpub is across the Great Highway from Ocean Beach, about five blocks south of the Cliff House. ✉ *Along Great Hwy. from Cliff House to Sloat Blvd. and beyond.*

San Francisco Zoo. Awash in bad press since one of its tigers escaped its enclosure and killed a visitor on Christmas Day 2007, the zoo is touting its metamorphosis into the "New Zoo," a wildlife-focused recreation center that inspires visitors to become conservationists. Integrated exhibits group different species of animals from the same geographic areas together in enclosures that don't look like cages. The zoo's superstar exhibit is **Grizzly Gulch,** where orphaned sisters Kachina and Kiona enchant visitors with their frolicking and swimming. The **Lemur Forest** has five varieties of the bug-eyed, long-tailed primates from Madagascar, and **Gorilla Preserve is** one of the largest and most natural gorilla habitats of any zoo in the world. The **Children's Zoo** includes an insect zoo, a meerkat and prairie-dog exhibit, a restored 1921 Dentzel carousel, and a mini–steam train. ✉ *Sloat Blvd. and 47th Ave., Sunset* ✥ *Muni L–Taraval streetcar from downtown* ☎ *415/753–7080* 🌐 *www.sfzoo.org* *$15, $1 off with Muni transfer* ⏲ *Mid-Mar.–Oct., daily 10–5; Nov.–mid-Mar., daily 10–4.*

4

Sutro Heights Park. Crows and other large birds battle the heady breezes at this cliff-top park on what were once the grounds of the home of Adolph Sutro, an eccentric mining engineer and former San Francisco mayor. An extremely wealthy man, Sutro may have owned about 10% of San Francisco at one point, but he couldn't buy good taste: a few remnants of his gaudy, faux-classical statue collection still stand (including the lions at what was the main gate). Monterey cypresses and Canary Island palms dot the park, and photos on placards depict what things looked like before the house burned down in 1896, from the greenhouse to the ornate carpet-bed designs.

All that remains of the main house is its foundation. Climb up for a sweeping view of the Pacific Ocean and the Cliff House below (which Sutro owned), and try to imagine what the perspective might have been like from one of the upper floors. San Francisco City Guides (☎ *415/557–4266*) runs a free Saturday tour of the park that starts at 2 (meet at the lion statue at 48th and Point Lobos avenues). ✉ *Point Lobos and 48th Aves., Outer Richmond.*

THE HAIGHT, THE CASTRO, AND NOE VALLEY

Once you've seen the blockbuster sights and you're getting curious about the neighborhoods where the city's soul resides, come out to these three areas. They wear their personalities large and proud, and all are perfect for just strolling around. You can move from the Haight's residue of 1960s counterculture to the Castro's connection to 1970s and '80s gay life to 1990s gentrification in Noe Valley. Although history thrust the Haight and the Castro onto the international stage, both are anything but stagnant—they're still dynamic areas well worth exploring. Noe Valley may lack the headlines, but a mellow morning walk here will make you feel like a local.

EXPLORING THE HAIGHT

Haight-Ashbury Intersection. On October 6, 1967, hippies took over the intersection of Haight and Ashbury streets to proclaim the "Death of Hip." If they thought hip was dead then, they'd find absolute

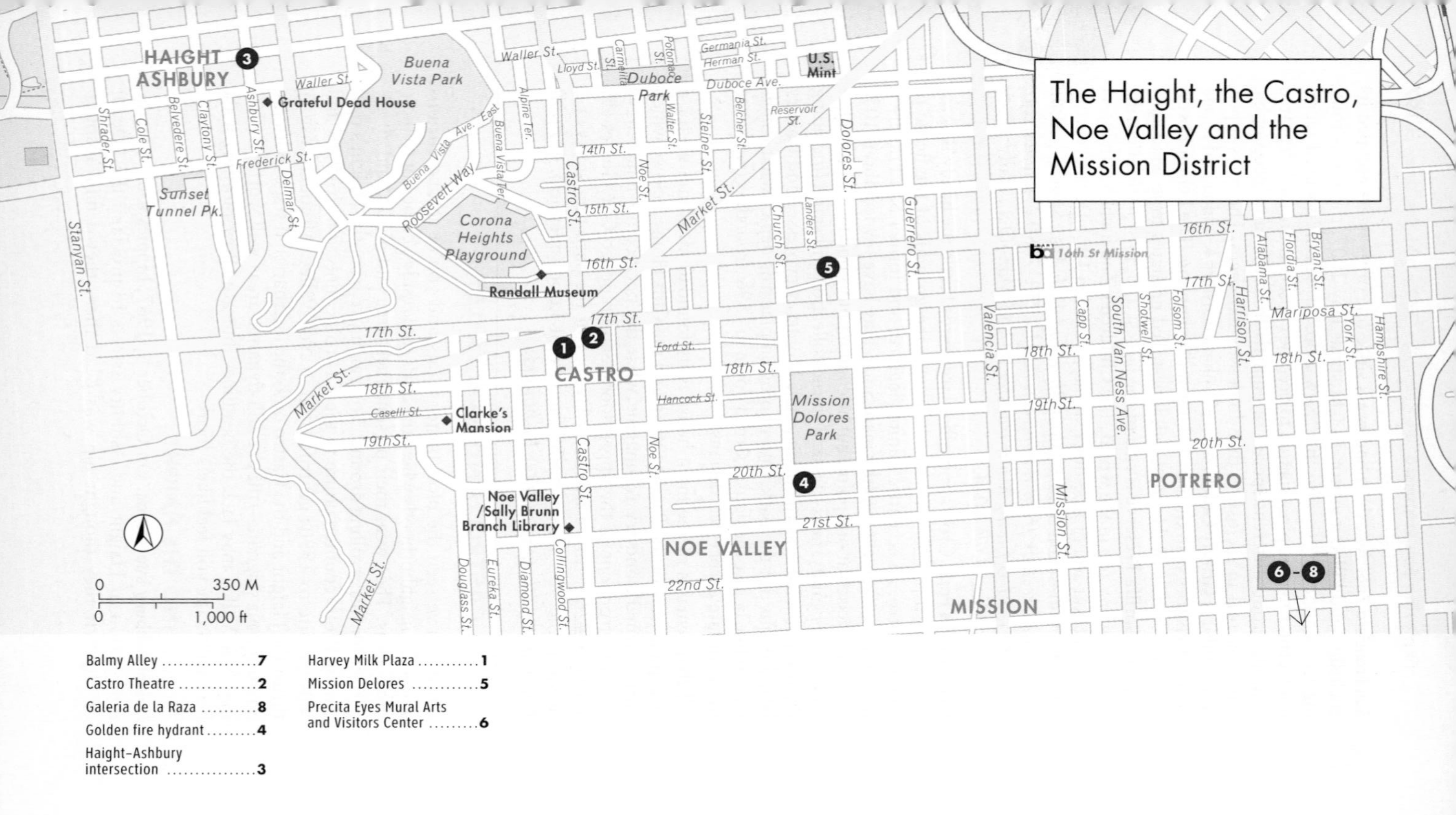

The Haight, the Castro, Noe Valley and the Mission District
HAIGHT ASHBURY
Grateful Dead House
Buena Vista Park
Waller St.
Lloyd St.
Carmelita St.
Potomac St.
Duboce Park
Germania St.
Herman St.
Duboce Ave.
U.S. Mint
Reservoir St.
Shrader St.
Cole St.
Belvedere St.
Claytony St.
Ashbury St.
Frederick St.
Buena Vista Ave. East
Buena Vista Ter.
Alpine Ter.
14th St.
Noe St.
Walter St.
Steiner St.
Belcher St.
Dolores St.
Sunset Tunnel Pk.
Delmar St.
Roosevelt Way
Corona Heights Playground
Castro St.
15th St.
Market St.
Church St.
Landers St.
Guerrero St.
Stanyan St.
16th St.
Randall Museum
16th St Mission
Alabama St.
Flordia St.
Bryant St.
17th St.
Harrison St.
Mariposa St.
Capp St.
South Van Ness Ave.
Shotwell St.
Folsom St.
York St.
Hampshire St.
Valencia St.
18th St.
Ford St.
CASTRO
Hancock St.
Mission Dolores Park
Caselli St.
Clarke's Mansion
19thSt.
20th St.
POTRERO
Noe Valley /Sally Brunn Branch Library
21st St.
Mission St.
NOE VALLEY
22nd St.
MISSION
Douglass St.
Eureka St.
Diamond St.
Collingwood St.
0 350 M
0 1,000 ft
Balmy Alley 7
Castro Theatre 2
Galeria de la Raza 8
Golden fire hydrant 4
Haight–Ashbury intersection 3
Harvey Milk Plaza 1
Mission Delores 5
Precita Eyes Mural Arts and Visitors Center 6

confirmation of it today, what with the only tie-dye in sight on the famed corner being Ben & Jerry's storefront.

Everyone knows the Summer of Love had something to do with free love and LSD, but the drugs and other excesses of that period have tended to obscure the residents' serious attempts to create an America that was more spiritually oriented, more environmentally aware, and less caught up in commercialism. The Diggers, a radical group of actors and populist agitators, for example, operated a free shop a few blocks off Haight Street. Everything really was free at the free shop; people brought in things they didn't need and took things they did. (The group also coined immortal phrases like "Do your own thing.")

Among the folks who hung out in or near the Haight during the late 1960s were writers Richard Brautigan, Allen Ginsberg, Ken Kesey, and Gary Snyder; anarchist Abbie Hoffman; rock performers Marty Balin, Jerry Garcia, Janis Joplin, and Grace Slick; LSD champion Timothy Leary; and filmmaker Kenneth Anger. If you're keen to feel something resembling the hippie spirit these days, there's always Hippie Hill, just inside the Haight Street entrance of Golden Gate Park. Think drum circles, guitar players, and whiffs of pot smoke.

EXPLORING THE CASTRO

★ **Castro Theatre.** Here's a classic way to join in the Castro community: grab some popcorn and catch a flick at this gorgeous, 1,500-seat art deco theater; opened in 1922, it's the grandest of San Francisco's few remaining movie palaces. The neon marquee, which stands at the top of the Castro strip, is the neighborhood's great landmark. The Castro was the fitting host of 2008's red-carpet preview of Gus Van Sant's film *Milk*, starring Sean Penn as openly gay San Francisco supervisor Harvey Milk. The theater's elaborate Spanish baroque interior is fairly well preserved. Before many shows the theater's pipe organ rises from the orchestra pit and an organist plays pop and movie tunes, usually ending with the Jeanette McDonald standard "San Francisco" (go ahead, sing along). The crowd can be enthusiastic and vocal, talking back to the screen as loudly as it talks to them. Classics such as *Who's Afraid of Virginia Woolf?* take on a whole new life, with the assembled beating the actors to the punch and fashioning even snappier comebacks for Elizabeth Taylor. Head here to catch classics, a Fellini film retrospective, or the latest take on same-sex love. ✉ *429 Castro St., Castro* ☎ *415/621–6120*.

Harvey Milk Plaza. An 18-foot-long rainbow flag, the symbol of gay pride, flies above this plaza named for the man who electrified the city in 1977 by being elected to its Board of Supervisors as an openly gay candidate. In the early 1970s Milk had opened a camera store on the block of Castro Street between 18th and 19th streets. The store became the center for his campaign to open San Francisco's social and political life to gays and lesbians.

The liberal Milk hadn't served a full year of his term before he and Mayor George Moscone, also a liberal, were shot in November 1978 at City Hall. The murderer was a conservative ex-supervisor named Dan White, who had recently resigned his post and then became enraged when Moscone wouldn't reinstate him. Milk and White had often

A colorful mosaic mural in the Castro.

been at odds on the board, and White thought Milk had been part of a cabal to keep him from returning to his post. Milk's assassination shocked the gay community, which became infuriated when the infamous "Twinkie defense"—that junk food had led to diminished mental capacity—resulted in a manslaughter verdict for White. During the so-called White Night Riot of May 21, 1979, gays and their allies stormed City Hall, torching its lobby and several police cars.

Milk, who had feared assassination, left behind a tape recording in which he urged the community to continue the work he had begun. His legacy is the high visibility of gay people throughout city government; a bust of him was unveiled at City Hall on his birthday in 2008, and the 2008 film *Milk* gives insight into his life. A plaque at the base of the flagpole lists the names of past and present openly gay and lesbian state and local officials. ✉ *Southwest corner of Castro and Market Sts., Castro.*

EXPLORING NOE VALLEY

Golden Fire Hydrant. When all the other fire hydrants went dry during the fire that followed the 1906 earthquake, this one kept pumping. Noe Valley and the Mission District were thus spared the devastation wrought elsewhere in the city, which explains the large number of pre-quake homes here. Every year on April 18 (the anniversary of the quake) folks gather here to share stories about the earthquake, and the famous hydrant gets a fresh coat of gold paint. ✉ *Church and 20th Sts., southeast corner, across from Dolores Park, Noe Valley.*

CASTRO AND NOE WALK

The Castro and Noe Valley are both neighborhoods that beg to be walked—or ambled through, really, without time pressure or an absolute destination. Hit the Castro first, beginning at Harvey Milk Plaza under the gigantic rainbow flag. If you're going on to Noe Valley, first head east down Market Street for the cafés, bistros, and shops, then go back to Castro Street and head south, past the glorious art deco Castro Theatre, checking out boutiques and cafés along the way (Cliff's Variety, at 479 Castro St., is a must). To tour Noe Valley, go east down 18th Street to Church (at Dolores Park), and then either strap on your hiking boots and head south over the hill or hop the J-Church to 24th Street, the center of this rambling neighborhood.

MISSION DISTRICT

The Mission has a number of distinct personalities: it's the Latino neighborhood, where working-class folks raise their families and where gangs occasionally clash; it's the hipster hood, where tattooed and pierced twenty- and thirtysomethings hold court in the coolest cafés and bars in town; it's a culinary epicenter, with the strongest concentration of destination restaurants and affordable ethnic cuisine; and it's the artists' quarter, where murals adorn literally blocks of walls. It's also the city's equivalent of the Sunshine State—this neighborhood's always the last to succumb to fog.

EXPLORING THE MISSION DISTRICT

Balmy Alley. Mission District artists have transformed the walls of their neighborhood with paintings, and Balmy Alley is one of the best-executed examples. Murals fill the one-block alley, with newer ones continually filling in the blank spaces. Local children working with adults started the project in 1971. Since then dozens of artists have steadily added to it, with the aim of promoting peace in Central America, as well as community spirit and AIDS awareness. ■ **TIP→ Be alert here: the 25th Street end of the alley adjoins a somewhat dangerous area.** ✉ *24th St. between and parallel to Harrison and Treat Sts., alley runs south to 25th St., Mission.*

Galería de la Raza. San Francisco's premier showcase for contemporary Latino art, the gallery exhibits the works of mostly local artists. Events include readings and spoken word by local poets and writers, screenings of Latin American and Spanish films, and theater works by local minority theater troupes. Just across the street, amazing art festoons the 24th Street/York Street Minipark, a tiny urban playground. A mosaic-covered Quetzalcoatl serpent plunges into the ground and rises, creating hills for little ones to clamber over, and mural-covered walls surround the space. ✉ *2857 24th St., at Bryant St., Mission* ☎ *415/826–8009* 🌐 *www.galeriadelaraza.org* ⏲ *Gallery Tues. 1–7, Wed.–Sat. noon–6.*

★ **Mission Dolores.** Two churches stand side by side at this mission, including the small adobe **Mission San Francisco de Asís,** the oldest standing structure in San Francisco. Completed in 1791, it's the sixth of the 21 California missions founded by Father Junípero Serra in the 18th and early 19th centuries. Its ceiling depicts original Ohlone Indian basket designs, executed in vegetable dyes. The tiny chapel includes frescoes and a hand-painted wooden altar. There's a hidden treasure here, too. In 2004 an archaeologist and an artist crawling along the ceiling's rafters opened a trap door behind the altar and rediscovered the mission's original mural, painted with natural dyes by Native Americans in 1791. The centuries have taken their toll, so the team photographed the 20-by-22-foot mural and began digitally restoring the photographic version. Among the images is a dagger-pierced Sacred Heart of Jesus. There's a small museum covering the mission's founding and history, and the pretty little mission cemetery (made famous by a scene in Alfred Hitchcock's *Vertigo*) maintains the graves of mid-19th-century European immigrants. (The remains of an estimated 5,000 Native Americans lie in unmarked graves.) Services are held in both the Mission San Francisco de Asís and next door in the handsome multi-dome basilica. ✉ *Dolores and 16th Sts., Mission* ☎ *415/621–8203* 🌐 *www.missiondolores.org* 🎫 *$5 donation, audio tour $7* ⏲ *Nov.–Apr., daily 9–4; May–Oct., daily 9–4:30.*

Precita Eyes Mural Arts and Visitors Center. Founded by muralists, this nonprofit arts organization designs and creates murals. The artists themselves lead informative guided walks of murals in the area. Most tours start with a 45-minute slide presentation. The bike and walking trips, which take between one and three hours, pass several dozen murals. May is Mural Awareness Month, with visits to murals-in-progress and presentations by artists. You can pick up a map of 24th Street's murals at the center and buy art supplies, T-shirts, postcards, and other mural-related items. Bike tours are available by appointment; Saturday's 11 am walking tour meets at Cafe Venice, at 24th and Mission streets. (All other tours meet at the center.) ✉ *2981 24th St., Mission* ☎ *415/285–2287* 🌐 *www.precitaeyes.org* 🎫 *Center free, tours $12–$15* ⏲ *Center weekdays 10–5, Sat. 10–4, Sun. noon–4; walks weekends at 11 and 1:30 or by appointment.*

PACIFIC HEIGHTS AND JAPANTOWN

Pacific Heights and Japantown are something of an odd couple: privileged, old-school San Francisco and the workaday commercial center of Japanese-American life in the city, stacked virtually on top of each other. The sprawling, extravagant mansions of Pacific Heights gradually give way to the more modest Victorians and unassuming housing tracts of Japantown. The most interesting spots in Japantown huddle in the Japan Center, the neighborhood's two-block centerpiece, and along Post Street. You can find plenty of authentic Japanese treats in the shops and restaurants, if you have a special interest in these.

■ TIP→ Japantown is a relatively safe area, but the Western Addition, south of Geary Boulevard, can be dangerous even during the daytime. Avoid going too far west of Fillmore Street on either side of Geary.

EXPLORING PACIFIC HEIGHTS

Alta Plaza Park. Golden Gate Park's fierce longtime superintendent, John McLaren, designed Alta Plaza in 1910, modeling its terracing on that of the Grand Casino in Monte Carlo, Monaco. From the top you can see

Marin to the north, downtown to the east, Twin Peaks to the south, and Golden Gate Park to the west. Kids love the many play structures at the large, enclosed playground at the top; everywhere else is dog territory. ✉ *Bordered by Clay, Steiner, Jackson, and Scott Sts., Pacific Heights.*

Franklin Street buildings. What at first looks like a stone facade on the **Golden Gate Church** (✉ *1901 Franklin St., Pacific Heights*) is actually redwood painted white. A Georgian-style residence built in the early 1900s for a coffee merchant sits at 1735 Franklin. On the northeast corner of Franklin and California streets is a **Christian Science church**; built in the Tuscan revival style, it's noteworthy for its terra-cotta detailing. The **Coleman House** (✉ *1701 Franklin St., Pacific Heights*) is an impressive twin-turret Queen Anne mansion that was built for a gold-rush mining and lumber baron. Don't miss the large, brilliant-purple stained-glass window on the house's north side. ✉ *Franklin St. between Washington and California Sts., Pacific Heights.*

Haas-Lilienthal House. A small display of photographs on the bottom floor of this elaborate, gray 1886 Queen Anne house makes clear that despite its lofty stature and striking, round third-story tower, the house was modest compared with some of the giants that fell victim to the 1906 earthquake and fire. The Foundation for San Francisco's Architectural Heritage operates the home, whose carefully kept rooms provide an intriguing glimpse into late-19th-century life through period furniture, authentic details (antique dishes in the kitchen built-in), and photos of the family who occupied the house until 1972. Volunteers conduct one-hour house tours three days a week and informative two-hour walking tours ($8) of the Civic Center, Broadway, and Union Street areas on Saturday afternoon, and of the eastern portion of Pacific Heights on Sunday afternoon (call or check Web site for schedule). ✉ *2007 Franklin St., between Washington and Jackson Sts., Pacific Heights* ☎ *415/441–3004* 🌐 *www.sfheritage.org* 💵 *Entry $8* ⏲ *1-hr tour Wed. and Sat. noon–3, Sun. 11–4; 2-hr tour Sun. at 12:30.*

Noteworthy Victorians. Two **Italianate Victorians** (✉ *1818 and 1834 California St., Pacific Heights*) stand out on the 1800 block of California. A block west is the Victorian-era **Atherton House** (✉ *1990 California St., Pacific Heights*), whose mildly daffy design incorporates Queen Anne, Stick-Eastlake, and other architectural elements. Many claim the house—now apartments—is haunted by the ghosts of its 19th-century residents, who regularly whisper, glow, and generally cause a mild fuss. The oft-photographed **Laguna Street Victorians,** on the west side of the 1800 block of Laguna Street, cost between $2,000 and $2,600 when they were built in the 1870s. No bright colors here though—most of the paint jobs are in soft beiges or pastels. ✉ *California St. between Franklin and Octavia Sts., and Laguna St. between Pine and Bush Sts., Pacific Heights.*

Octagon House. This eight-sided home sits across the street from its original site on Gough Street; it's one of two remaining octagonal houses in the city (the other is on Russian Hill), and the only one open to the public. White quoins accent each of the eight corners of the pretty blue-gray exterior, and a colonial-style garden completes the picture. Inside, it's full of antique American furniture, decorative arts (paintings, silver, rugs), and documents from the 18th and 19th centuries. A deck of Revolutionary-era hand-painted playing cards takes an antimonarchist position: in place of kings, queens, and jacks, the American upstarts substituted American statesmen, Roman goddesses, and Indian chiefs. ✉ *2645 Gough St., Pacific Heights* ☎ *415/441–7512* *Free, donations encouraged* ⏲ *Feb.–Dec., 2nd Sun. and 2nd and 4th Thurs. of month noon–3; group tours weekdays by appointment.*

Spreckels Mansion. Shrouded behind tall juniper hedges at the corner of lovely winding, brick Octavia Street, overlooking Lafayette Park, the estate was built for sugar heir Adolph Spreckels and his wife Alma. Mrs. Spreckels was so pleased with her house that she commissioned George Applegarth to design another building in a similar vein: the Legion of Honor. One of the city's great iconoclasts, Alma Spreckels was the model for the bronze figure atop the Victory Monument in Union Square. Today this house belongs to prolific romance novelist Danielle Steel. ✉ *2080 Washington St., at Octavia St., Pacific Heights.*

Whittier Mansion. With a Spanish-tile roof and scrolled bay windows on all four sides, this is one of the most elegant 19th-century houses in the state. Unlike other grand mansions lost in the 1906 quake, the Whittier Mansion was built so solidly that only a chimney toppled over during the disaster. ✉ *2090 Jackson St., Pacific Heights.*

EXPLORING JAPANTOWN

★ **Japan Center.** Cool and curious trinkets, noodle houses and sushi joints, a destination bookstore, and a peek at Japanese culture high and low await at this 5-acre complex designed in 1968 by noted American architect Minoru Yamasaki. Architecturally, the development hasn't aged well, and its Peace Plaza, where seasonal festivals are held, is an unwelcoming sea of cement. The Japan Center includes the shop- and restaurant-filled Kintetsu and Kinokuniya buildings; the excellent Kabuki Springs & Spa; the Hotel Kabuki; and the Sundance Kabuki, Robert Redford's fancy, reserved-seating cinema/restaurant complex.

The Kinokuniya Bookstores, in the Kinokuniya Building, have an extensive selection of Japanese-language books, *manga* (graphic novels), books on design, and English-language translations and books on Japanese topics. Just outside, follow the Japanese teenagers to Pika Pika, where you and your friends can step into a photo booth and then use special effects and stickers to decorate your creation. On the bridge connecting the center's two buildings, check out Shige Antiques for *yukata* (lightweight cotton kimonos) for kids and lovely silk kimonos, and Asakichi and its tiny incense shop for tinkling wind chimes and display-worthy teakettles. Continue into the Kintetsu Building for a selection of Japanese restaurants.

Between the Miyako Mall and Kintetsu Building are the five-tier, 100-foot-tall **Peace Pagoda** and the Peace Plaza. The pagoda, which draws on the 1,200-year-old tradition of miniature round pagodas dedicated to eternal peace, was designed in the late 1960s by Yoshiro Taniguchi to convey the "friendship and goodwill" of the Japanese people to the people of the United States. The plaza itself is a shadeless,

DID YOU KNOW?

These soft-colored Victorian homes in Pacific Heights are closer to the original hues sported back in the 1900s. It wasn't until the 1960s that the bold, electric colors now seen around SF gained popularity. Before that, the most typical house paint color was a standard gray.

- Alta Plaza Park 10
- Franklin Street buildings 5
- Haas-Lilienthal House 4
- Japan Center 7
- Japan Center Mall 8
- Kabuki Springs & Spa 9
- Noteworthy Victorians 6
- Octagon House .. 1
- Spreckels Mansion 3
- Whittier Mansion 2

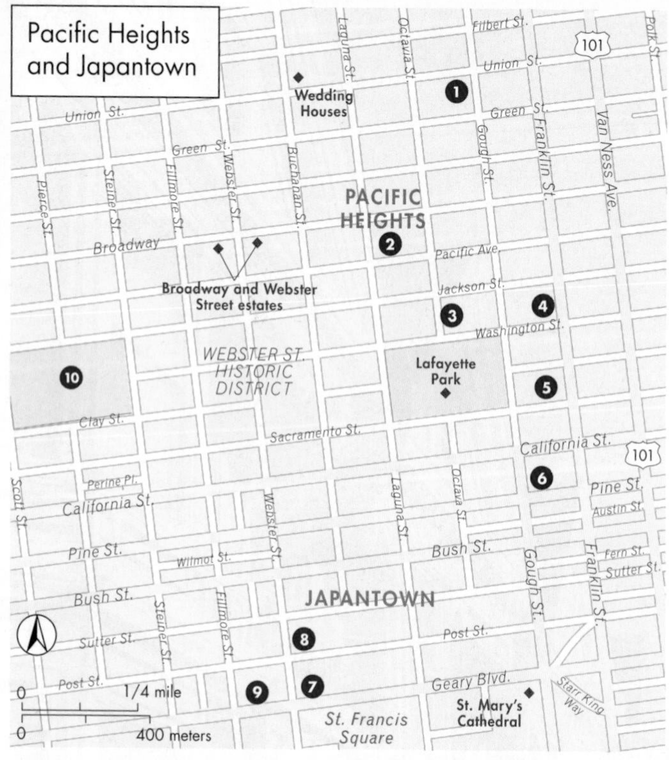

unwelcoming stretch of cement with little seating. Continue into the Miyako Mall to Ichiban Kan, a Japanese dollar store where you can pick up fun Japanese kitchenware, tote bags decorated with hedgehogs, and erasers shaped like food. ✉ *Bordered by Geary Blvd. and Fillmore, Post, and Laguna Sts., Japantown* ☎ *No phone.*

Japan Center Mall. The buildings lining this open-air mall are of the shoji school of architecture. The mall's many good restaurants draw a lively crowd of nearby workers for lunch, but the atmosphere remains weirdly hushed. The shops are geared more toward locals—travel agencies, electronics shops—but there are some fun Japanese-goods stores. Arrive early in the day and you may score some fabulous mochi (a soft, sweet Japanese rice treat) at **Benkyodo** (✉ *1747 Buchanan St., Japantown* ☎ *415/922–1244*). It's easy to spend hours among the fabulous origami and craft papers at **Paper Tree** (✉ *1743 Buchanan St., Japantown* ☎ *415/921–7100*), open since the 1960s. You can have a seat on local artist Ruth Asawa's twin origami-style fountains, which sit in the middle of the mall; they're squat circular structures made of fieldstone, with three levels for sitting and a brick floor. ✉ *Buchanan St. between Post and Sutter Sts., Japantown* ☎ *No phone.*

★ **Kabuki Springs & Spa.** This serene spa is one Japantown destination that draws locals from all over town, from hipster to grandma,

Japanese-American or not. Balinese urns decorate the communal bath area of this house of tranquillity, and you're just as likely to hear soothing flute or classical music as you are Kitaro.

The massage menu has also expanded well beyond traditional Shiatsu technique. The experience is no less relaxing, however, and the treatment regimen includes facials, salt scrubs, and mud and seaweed wraps. You can take your massage in a private room with a bath or in a curtained-off area. The communal baths ($22 weekdays, $25 weekends) contain hot and cold tubs, a large Japanese-style bath, a sauna, a steam room, and showers. Bang the gong for quiet if your fellow bathers are speaking too loudly.

The clothing-optional baths are open for men only on Monday, Thursday, and Saturday; women bathe on Wednesday, Friday, and Sunday. Bathing suits are required on Tuesday, when the baths are coed. Men and women can reserve private rooms daily. An 80-minute massage-and-bath package with a private room costs $110; a package that includes a 50-minute massage and the use of the communal baths costs $100. ✉ *1750 Geary Blvd., Japantown* ☎ *415/922–6000* 🌐 *www.kabukisprings.com* ⏲ *Daily 10–10.*

4

WHERE TO EAT

San Francisco is a vital culinary crossroads, with nearly every ethnic cuisine represented. Although locals have long headed to the Mission District for Latin food, Chinatown for Asian food, and North Beach for Italian food, they also know that every part of the city offers dining experiences beyond the neighborhood tradition.

Some renowned restaurants are booked weeks or even months in advance. But you can get lucky at the last minute if you're flexible—and friendly. Most restaurants keep a few tables open for walk-ins and VIPs. Show up for dinner early (5:30 pm) or late (after 9 pm) and politely inquire about any last-minute vacancies or cancellations.

Use the coordinate (⊕ A1) at the end of each listing to locate a site on the corresponding map.

WHAT IT COSTS

	¢	$	$$	$$$	$$$$
Restaurants	under $10	$10–$17	$18–$24	$25–$35	over $35

Prices are for a main course at dinner, excluding tax.

UNION SQUARE

$$$ AMERICAN ✕ **Canteen.** Blink, and you'll miss this place. Chef-owner Dennis Leary has transformed this narrow coffee shop into one of the most sought-after dinner reservations in town. The homey place has just 20 counter seats and a quartet of wooden booths. But that's all Leary, with a modest open kitchen and a single assistant, can handle. The dinner menu,

which changes often, offers only four first courses, four mains, and three or four desserts. A typical meal might start with veal meatballs with fennel-artichoke puree, followed by a gratin of chanterelles and tomatoes, or pork tenderloin with braised cranberry beans and fig-olive jus, and then a dreamy vanilla soufflé or almond torte. On Tuesday night a three-course prix-fixe menu is in force (no choices within each course) for $35 (seatings are at 6 pm and 8 pm). Because this is a one-man band, there are set times to dine other nights in the week: 6 pm, 7:30 pm, and 9:15 pm. ✉ *817 Sutter St., Union Square* ☎ *415/928–8870* 🌐 *www.sfcanteen.com* ✍ *Reservations essential* ⏲ *Closed Mon. No lunch Tues.–Thu. or weekends* ✧ *D4.*

FINANCIAL DISTRICT

$$$
SPANISH

✕ **Bocadillos.** The name means "sandwiches," but that's only half the story here. You'll find 13 bocadillos at lunchtime: plump rolls filled with everything from serrano ham to Catalan sausage with arugula to a memorable lamb burger. But at night chef-owner Gerald Hirigoyen, who also owns the high-profile Piperade, focuses on tapas, offering some two-dozen choices, including a savory octopus carpaccio, an equally superb pig's trotters with herbs, and patatas bravas (potatoes) with *romesco* sauce (a thick combination of red pepper, tomato, almonds, and garlic). His wine list is well matched to the food. A youngish crowd typically piles into the modern, red-brick-wall dining space, so be prepared to wait for a seat. A large communal table is a good perch for singles. If you're in the neighborhood at breakfast time, there is plenty here to keep you happy, including a scrambled eggs and cheese bocadillo or house-made chorizo and eggs. ✉ *710 Montgomery St., Financial District* ☎ *415/982–2622* 🌐 *www.bocasf.com* ✍ *Reservations not accepted* ⏲ *Closed Sun. No lunch Sat.* ✧ *F3.*

BEST BETS FOR SAN FRANCISCO DINING

With thousands of restaurants to choose from, how will you decide where to eat? Fodor's writers and editors have selected their favorite restaurants by price, cuisine, and experience in the Best Bets lists below. In the first column, Fodor's Choice designations represent the "best of the best" in every price category. You can also search by neighborhood for excellent eats—just peruse the following pages.

Fodor's Choice ★

A16, $$$, p. 218
Acquerello, $$$$, p. 216
Aziza, $$$, p. 221
Boulevard, $$$$, p. 211
Coi, $$$$, p. 215
Delfina, $$$, p. 220
Gary Danko, $$$$, p. 218
L'Osteria del Forno, $, p. 215
Quince, $$$, p. 210
Swan Oyster Depot, $$, p. 216
Zuni Café, $$$, p. 217

By Price

¢

Pho Hoa Clement, p. 221

$

L'Osteria del Forno, p. 215
SanJalisco, p. 220

$$

Swan Oyster Depot, p. 216

$$$

A16, p. 218
Aziza, p. 221
Canteen, p. 207
Delfina, p. 220
Quince, p. 210
Zuni Café, p. 217

$$$$

Acquerello, p. 216
Boulevard, p. 211
Coi, p. 215
Gary Danko, p. 218

By Cuisine

AMERICAN

Canteen, $$$, p. 207
Nopa, $$$, p. 221

CHINESE

R&G Lounge, $$, p. 214
Yank Sing, $, p. 210

FRENCH

Masa's, $$$$, p. 215

INDIAN

Indian Oven, $$, p. 220

ITALIAN

A16, $$$, p. 218
Delfina, $$$, p. 220

JAPANESE

Mifune, $, p. 217

LATIN AMERICAN

La Mar Cebicheria Peruana, $$$, p. 214

MEDITERRANEAN

Zuni Café, $$$, p. 217

MEXICAN

SanJalisco, $, p. 220

SEAFOOD

Hog Island Oyster Company, $$, p. 211
Plouf, $$, p. 210
Swan Oyster Depot, $$, p. 216

VIETNAMESE

Slanted Door, $$$, p. 214

By Experience

BAY VIEWS

Slanted Door, $$$, p. 214

BRUNCH

Rose's Café, $$, p. 218

BUSINESS DINING

Boulevard, $$$$, p. 211

CHILD-FRIENDLY

Yank Sing, $, p. 210

COMMUNAL TABLE

Bocadillos, $$$, p. 208
Nopa, $$$, p. 221

HISTORIC INTEREST

Boulevard, $$$$, p. 211
Swan Oyster Depot, $$, p. 216

HOT SPOTS

A16, $$$, p. 218
Nopa, $$$, p. 221
Spruce, $$$$, p. 216

SMALL PLATES

Bocadillos, $$$, p. 208

4

$$ SEAFOOD

Plouf. This French-friendly spot is a gold mine for mussel lovers, with six preparations to choose from, plus a mussels and clams combo, all at a modest price. Among the best are *marinière* (white wine, garlic, and parsley) and one combining coconut milk, lime juice, and chili. Add a side of the skinny fries and that's all most appetites need. The menu changes seasonally, and includes lamb shank and filet mignon to satisfy any unrepentant carnivores. Many of the appetizers—oysters on the half shell, clam croquettes, ceviche—stick to seafood, as well. The tables are squeezed together in the bright, lively dining room, so you might overhear neighboring conversations. On temperate days and nights, try for one of the outdoor tables. *40 Belden Pl., Financial District 415/986–6491 www.ploufsf.com Closed Sun. No lunch Sat. F3.*

$$$ ITALIAN Fodor's Choice ★

Quince. Previously housed in a small, almost quaint, former apothecary in Pacific Heights, this smart, wildly praised restaurant has taken up residence in a much bigger, high-design, and elegant space in Jackson Square. Michael Tusk, who has cooked at the legendary Chez Panisse and Oliveto, oversees the kitchen, where he uses only the finest local ingredients to turn out his Italian-inspired cuisine. The menu changes regularly, featuring a delicious selection of their famed pastas and seasonal dishes, such as chestnut tagliatelle with squab sugo, rabbit with flageolet beans, and fig crostata with burnt-honey ice cream. Don't pass up the cheese course—it's one of the city's finer selections. The 800-bottle-strong wine list is top-notch, but can get pricey (the $35 corkage means you won't save much by bringing your own bottle), and the service is both refined and friendly. (You can also slink next door to Quince's new casual offshoot, Cotogna, for an affordable and rustic meal, both for lunch and dinner.) *470 Pacific St., Financial District 415/775–8500 www.quincerestaurant.com Reservations essential No lunch F3.*

$ CHINESE

Yank Sing. This is the granddaddy of the city's dim sum teahouses. It opened in a plain-Jane storefront in Chinatown in 1959, but left its Cantonese neighbors behind for the high-rises of downtown by the 1970s. This brightly decorated location on quiet Stevenson Street (there's also a big, brassy branch in the Rincon Center) serves some of San Francisco's best dim sum to office workers on weekdays and to big, boisterous families on weekends. The kitchen cooks up some 100 varieties of dim sum on a rotating basis, offering 60 different types daily. These include both the classic (steamed pork buns, shrimp dumplings, egg custard tartlets) and the creative (scallion-skewered prawns tied with bacon, lobster and tobiko roe dumplings, basil seafood dumplings). The Shanghai soup dumplings are a classic—and some of the best in the city. A take-out counter makes a meal on the run a satisfying and penny-wise compromise when office duties—or touring—won't wait. *49 Stevenson St., Financial District 415/541–4949 www.yanksing.com No dinner F4.*

POTRERO HILL

$$ FRENCH

✕ **Chez Papa.** France arrived on Potrero Hill with Chez Papa, which delivers food, waiters, and charm that would be right at home in Provence. The modest corner restaurant, with a Mediterranean blue awning, big windows overlooking the street, and a small heated patio, caters to a lively crowd that makes conversation difficult. Small plates include mussels in wine, *brandade de morue* (salt-cod gratin), and caramelized onion tart with anchovies. Big plates range from rack of lamb and salmon with braised endives to homey lamb daube. Leave space for a typically Gallic crème brûlée or wedge of lemon tart. The $31.95 prix fixe is also a good deal for the penny wise. To accommodate the overflow of Hill residents who have packed this place since Day One, the owners opened the tiny (and more casual) Chez Maman (crepes, burgers with blue cheese, salads) halfway down the block. ✉ *1401 18th St., Potrero Hill* ☎ *415/824–8205* ⏲ *No lunch Sun.* ✥ *G5.*

4

EMBARCADERO

$$$$ AMERICAN Fodor's Choice ★

✕ **Boulevard.** Two of San Francisco's top restaurant celebrities—chef Nancy Oakes and designer Pat Kuleto—are responsible for this high-profile, high-priced eatery in the magnificent 1889 Audiffred Building, a Parisian look-alike and one of the few downtown structures to survive the 1906 earthquake. Kuleto's Belle Époque interior and Oakes's sophisticated American food with a French accent attract well-dressed locals and flush out-of-towners. The menu changes seasonally, but count on standout appetizers and generous portions of dishes like gnocchi and Maine lobster, pan-roasted halibut with three side dishes (grains, squash blossoms, and spinach), and wood-grilled extra-thick pork chop with roasted heirloom apples. Save room (and calories) for one of the dynamite desserts, such as caramelized apple brioche pudding. There's counter seating for folks too hungry to wait for a table, and an American Kobe and Chianina beef burger at lunchtime that lets you eat with the swells without raiding your piggybank. The well-chosen wine list and excellent service are also hallmarks here. ✉ *1 Mission St., Embarcadero* ☎ *415/543–6084* 🌐 *www.boulevardrestaurant.com* ✍ *Reservations essential* ⏲ *No lunch weekends* ✥ *G4.*

$$ SEAFOOD

✕ **Hog Island Oyster Company.** Hog Island, a thriving oyster farm in Tomales Bay, north of San Francisco, serves up its harvest at this attractive raw bar and retail shop in the busy Ferry Building. The U-shape counter and a handful of tables seat no more than three-dozen diners, who come here for impeccably fresh oysters (from Hog Island and elsewhere) or clams (from Hog Island) on the half shell. Other mollusk-centered options include a first-rate oyster stew, clam chowder, and steamer clams with Israeli couscous. The bar also turns out what is arguably the best grilled-cheese sandwich (with three artisanal cheeses on artisanal bread) this side of Wisconsin. You need to eat early, however, as the bar closes at 8 on weekdays and 6 on weekends. Happy hour, 5 to 7 on Monday and Thursday, is an oyster lover's dream and jam-packed: chef's choice of oysters for a buck apiece and beer for $3.50. ✉ *Ferry Bldg., Embarcadero at Market St., Embarcadero* ☎ *415/391–7117* 🌐 *www.hogislandoysters.com* ✥ *H3.*

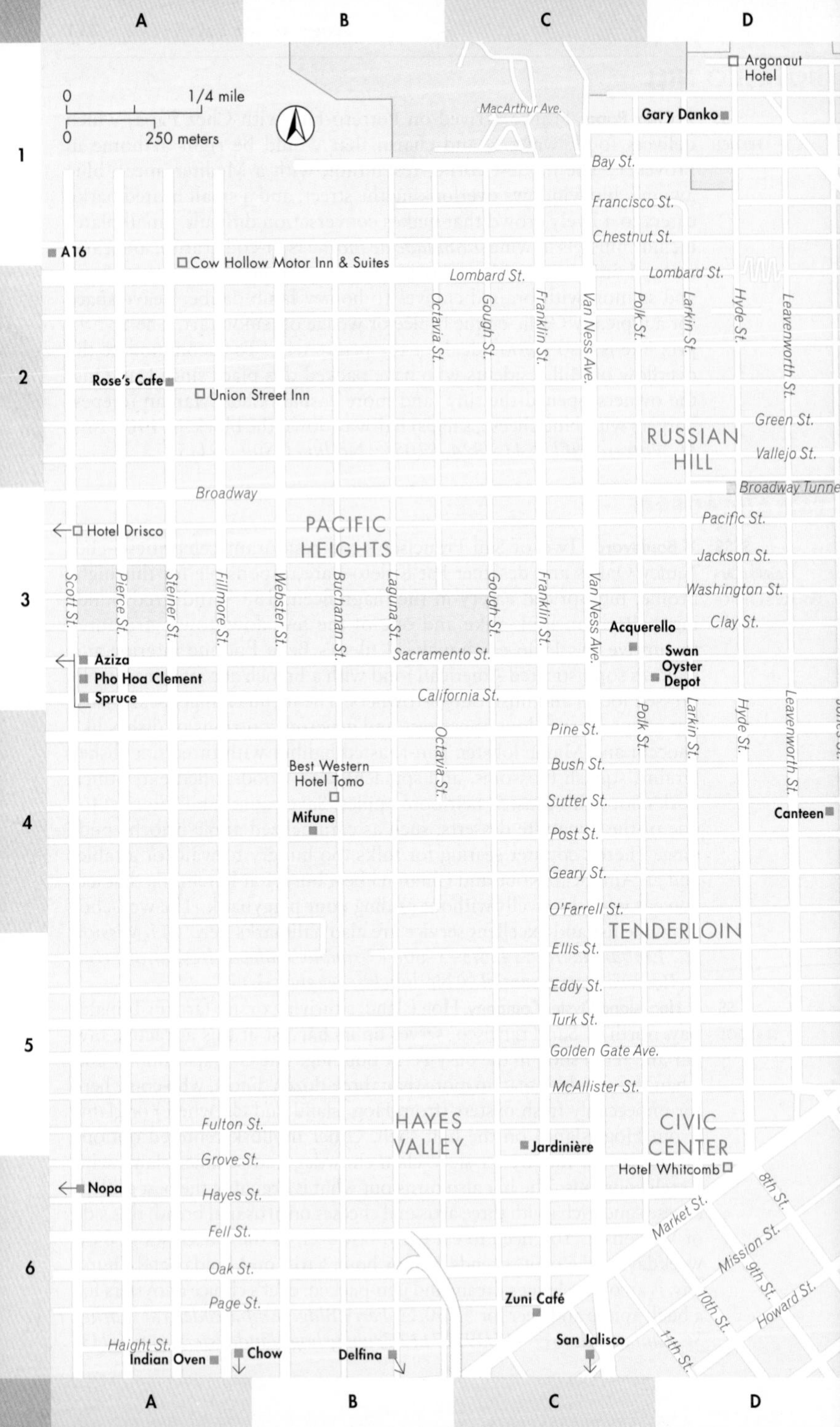

A
B
C
D
1
2
3
4
5
6
0
1/4 mile
0
250 meters
Argonaut Hotel
MacArthur Ave.
Gary Danko
Bay St.
Francisco St.
Chestnut St.
A16
Cow Hollow Motor Inn & Suites
Lombard St.
Lombard St.
Octavia St.
Gough St.
Franklin St.
Van Ness Ave.
Polk St.
Larkin St.
Hyde St.
Leavenworth St.
Rose's Cafe
Union Street Inn
Green St.
RUSSIAN HILL
Vallejo St.
Broadway
Broadway Tunnel
Pacific St.
Hotel Drisco
PACIFIC HEIGHTS
Jackson St.
Washington St.
Scott St.
Pierce St.
Steiner St.
Fillmore St.
Webster St.
Buchanan St.
Laguna St.
Gough St.
Franklin St.
Van Ness Ave.
Acquerello
Clay St.
Aziza
Pho Hoa Clement
Spruce
Sacramento St.
Swan Oyster Depot
California St.
Polk St.
Larkin St.
Hyde St.
Leavenworth St.
Jones St.
Pine St.
Octavia St.
Bush St.
Best Western Hotel Tomo
Sutter St.
Mifune
Canteen
Post St.
Geary St.
O'Farrell St.
TENDERLOIN
Ellis St.
Eddy St.
Turk St.
Golden Gate Ave.
McAllister St.
Fulton St.
HAYES VALLEY
CIVIC CENTER
Grove St.
Jardinière
Hotel Whitcomb
Nopa
Hayes St.
8th St.
Market St.
Fell St.
Mission St.
Oak St.
9th St.
10th St.
Howard St.
Page St.
Zuni Café
11th St.
Haight St.
San Jalisco
Indian Oven
Chow
Delfina

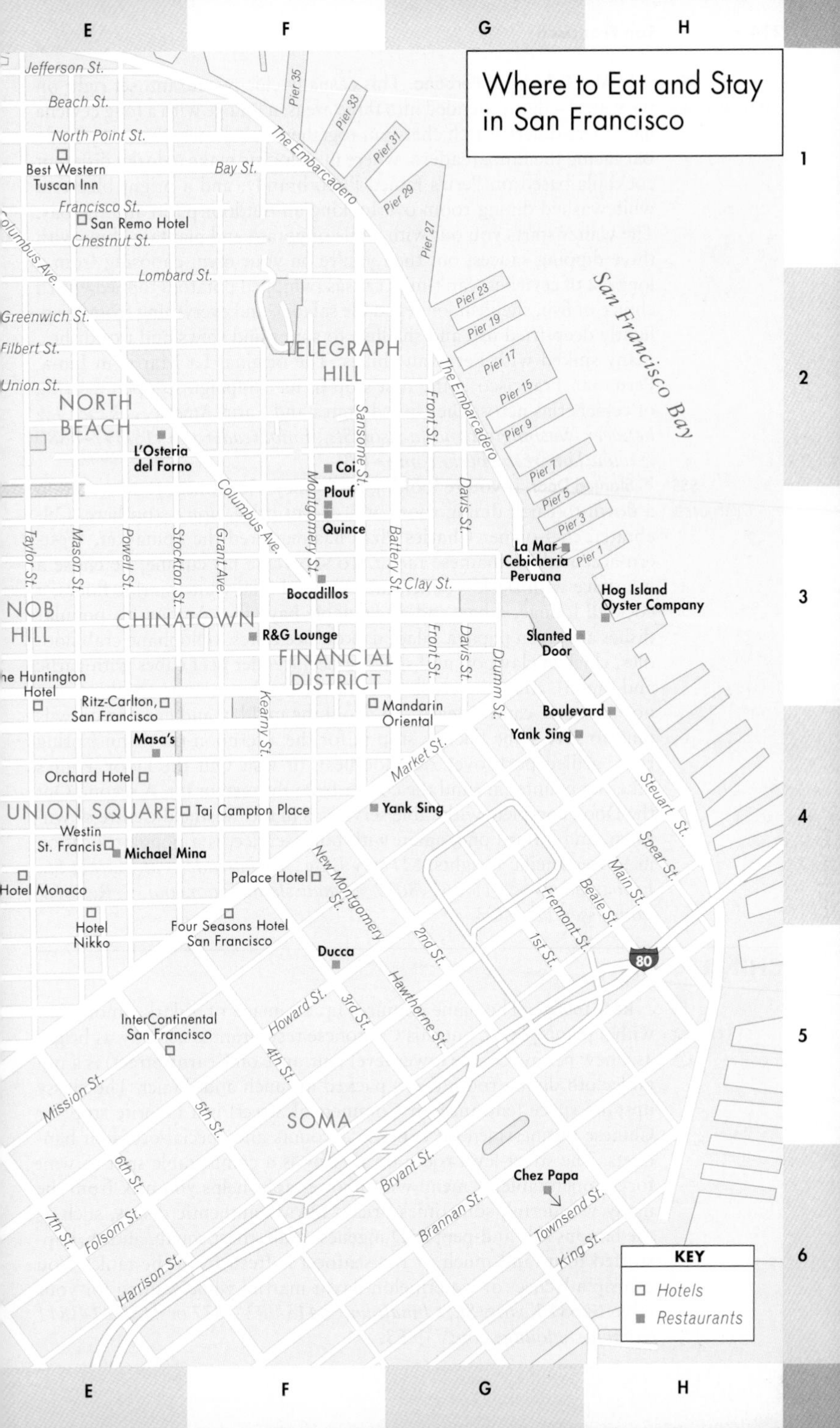

Where to Eat and Stay in San Francisco
E
F
G
H
1
2
3
4
5
6
Jefferson St.
Beach St.
North Point St.
Best Western Tuscan Inn
Bay St.
Francisco St.
San Remo Hotel
Chestnut St.
Columbus Ave.
Lombard St.
Greenwich St.
Filbert St.
Union St.
NORTH BEACH
L'Osteria del Forno
TELEGRAPH HILL
Pier 35
Pier 33
Pier 31
Pier 29
Pier 27
Pier 23
Pier 19
Pier 17
Pier 15
Pier 9
Pier 7
Pier 5
Pier 3
Pier 1
The Embarcadero
San Francisco Bay
Coi
Plouf
Quince
Sansome St.
Montgomery St.
Front St.
Davis St.
Battery St.
Clay St.
La Mar Cebicheria Peruana
Hog Island Oyster Company
Taylor St.
Mason St.
Powell St.
Stockton St.
Grant Ave.
Bocadillos
NOB HILL
CHINATOWN
R&G Lounge
FINANCIAL DISTRICT
Slanted Door
Drumm St.
The Huntington Hotel
Ritz-Carlton, San Francisco
Kearny St.
Mandarin Oriental
Boulevard
Yank Sing
Masa's
Market St.
Orchard Hotel
UNION SQUARE
Taj Campton Place
Yank Sing
Steuart St.
Spear St.
Westin St. Francis
Michael Mina
Main St.
Beale St.
Fremont St.
Hotel Monaco
Palace Hotel
New Montgomery St.
Hotel Nikko
Four Seasons Hotel San Francisco
2nd St.
1st St.
Ducca
80
Hawthorne St.
InterContinental San Francisco
Howard St.
3rd St.
4th St.
Mission St.
5th St.
SOMA
6th St.
Bryant St.
Chez Papa
Brannan St.
Townsend St.
7th St.
Folsom St.
Harrison St.
King St.
KEY
Hotels
Restaurants

$$$ LATIN AMERICAN ✕ **La Mar Cebicheria Peruana.** This casually chic restaurant, set right on the water's edge, is divided into three areas: a lounge with a long ceviche bar where diners watch chefs put together their plates; the savvy Pisco Bar facing the Embarcadero, where mixologists make a dozen different cocktails based on Peru's famed Pisco brandy; and a bright blue and whitewashed dining room overlooking an outdoor patio and the bay. The waiter starts you out with a pile of potato and plantain chips with three dipping sauces, but then you're on your own, choosing from a long list of ceviches, can't-miss causas (whipped potatoes topped with a choice of fish, shellfish, or vegetable salads), and everything from crisp, lightly deep-fried fish and shellfish to soups and stews and rice dishes, many spiked with Peruvian chilies. The original La Mar is in Lima, Peru. San Francisco is the first stop in its campaign to open a string of cebicherias across the United States and Latin America. ☒ *Pier 1½ between Washington and Jackson Sts., Embarcadero* ☎ *415/397–8880* 🌐 *www.lamarcebicheria.com* ✣ *H3.*

$$$ VIETNAMESE ✕ **Slanted Door.** If you're looking for homey Vietnamese food served in a down-to-earth dining room at a decent price, *don't* stop here. Celebrated chef-owner Charles Phan has mastered the upmarket, Western-accented Vietnamese menu. To showcase his cuisine, he chose a big space with sleek wooden tables and chairs, white marble floors, a cocktail lounge, a bar, and an enviable bay view. Among his popular dishes are green papaya salad, daikon rice cakes, cellophane crab noodles, chicken clay pot, and shaking beef (tender beef cubes with garlic and onion). Alas, the crush of fame means that no one speaking in a normal voice can be heard. To avoid the midday and evening crowds (and to save some bucks), stop in for the afternoon-tea menu (spring rolls, grilled pork over rice noodles), or visit Out the Door, Phan's take-out counter around the corner from the restaurant. A second Out the Door, complete with table service, is in the Westfield Centre downtown, and a third one, again with table service, is a popular location in Lower Pacific Heights. ☒ *Ferry Bldg., Embarcadero at Market St., Embarcadero* ☎ *415/861–8032* 🌐 *www.slanteddoor.com* ✍ *Reservations essential* ✣ *G3.*

CHINATOWN

$$ CHINESE ✕ **R&G Lounge.** The name conjures up an image of a dark, smoky bar with a piano player, but this Cantonese restaurant is actually as bright as a new penny. On the lower level (entrance on Kearny Street) is a no-tablecloth dining room that's packed at lunch and dinner. The classy upstairs space (entrance on Commercial Street) is a favorite stop for Chinese businessmen on expense accounts and special-occasion banquets. The street-level room on Kearny is a comfortable spot to wait for an open table. A menu with photographs helps you pick from the many wonderful, sometimes pricey, always authentic dishes, such as the famous salt-and-pepper Dungeness crab, roast squab, and shrimp-stuffed tofu (and much of the seafood is fresh from the tank). You can sip a lychee- or watermelon-flavor martini while waiting for your table. ☒ *631 Kearny St., Chinatown* ☎ *415/982–7877 or 415/982–3811* 🌐 *www.rnglounge.comV* ✣ *F3.*

NORTH BEACH

$$$$ NEW AMERICAN Fodor's Choice ★ **Coi.** Daniel Patterson, who has made a name for himself both as a chef and as a pundit on contemporary restaurant trends, has created a destination restaurant, an intriguing 50-seat spot on the gritty end of Broadway. Coi (pronounced *kwa*) is really two restaurants. One is an intimate 30-seat formal dining room—ascetic gold-taupe banquettes on two walls—that offers an 11-course tasting menu ($135). The highly seasonal and obsessively sourced food matches the space in sophistication, with such inspired dishes as chilled fennel consommé with sea urchin and purslane, Prather Ranch beef with black garlic, and Monterey Bay abalone with nettle-dandelion salsa verde. The menu in the more casual—and more casually priced—lounge is à la carte, with fewer than a dozen items, including a crisp-skinned roast chicken, a bowl of udon noodles, and a grilled Gruyère cheese sandwich (and you don't need reservations to nab a seat). ✉ *373 Broadway, North Beach* ☎ *415/393–9000* 🌐 *www.coirestaurant.com* *Reservations not accepted for lounge* ⏲ *Closed Sun. and Mon. No lunch* ✣ *F2.*

$ ITALIAN Fodor's Choice ★ **L'Osteria del Forno.** A staff chattering in Italian and seductive aromas drifting from the open kitchen make customers who pass through the door of this modest storefront, with its sunny yellow walls and friendly waitstaff, feel as if they've stumbled into a homey trattoria in Italy. Each day the kitchen produces small plates of simply cooked vegetables (grilled radicchio wrapped in prosciutto, roasted carrots and fennel), a few pastas, a daily special or two, milk-braised pork, a roast of the day, creamy polenta, and thin-crust pizzas—including a memorable "white" pie topped with porcini mushrooms and mozzarella. (All the hot dishes come out of an oven—no stove here, so don't come expecting a large selection of pastas.) Wine drinkers will find a good match for any dish they order on the all-Italian list, which showcases gems from limited-production vineyards. At lunch try one of North Beach's best focaccia sandwiches. ✉ *519 Columbus Ave., North Beach* ☎ *415/982–1124* 🌐 *www.losteriadelforno.com* *No credit cards* ⏲ *Closed Tues.* ✣ *E2.*

NOB HILL

$$$$ FRENCH **Masa's.** Although the toque has been passed to several chefs since the death of founding chef Masataka Kobayashi, this 25-year-old restaurant, with its chocolate-brown walls, white fabric ceiling, and red-silk-shaded lanterns, is still one of the country's most celebrated food temples. Chef Gregory Short, who worked alongside Thomas Keller at the famed French Laundry for seven years, is at the helm these days, and his tasting menus of three, four, and seven courses, including a vegetarian option, are pleasing both diners and critics. The fare is dubbed New French, and all the dishes are laced with fancy ingredients, leaving diners struggling to choose between foie gras, langoustines, and squab. In fall, when northern Italy's exquisite white truffles are in season, Short typically puts together a tasting menu that tucks them into every course, including dessert, which in a past season featured a white-truffle ice-cream float. Wine drinkers are bound to find something that suits them, with an award-winning list that includes many small-production wines

from around the globe. Be prepared for a decidedly stuffy, though not suffocating, atmosphere (a jacket is preferred for gentlemen). ✉ *Hotel Vintage Court, 648 Bush St., Nob Hill* ☎ *415/989–7154* 🌐 *www.masasrestaurant.com* *Reservations essential* *Closed Sun. and Mon. No lunch* ✥ *E4.*

VAN NESS/POLK

$$$$ ITALIAN Fodor's Choice ★ **Acquerello.** For years, devotees of chef-owner Suzette Gresham-Tognetti's high-end but soulful Italian cooking have been swooning over her incomparable Parmesan budino, ridged pasta with foie gras and truffles, and veal loin involtini stuffed with seasonal vegetables. Dishes are complex, refined, and also feature some cutting-edge touches and techniques. Dinners are prix-fixe, with three ($64), four ($78), or five ($90) courses and at least six choices within each course. Tognetti also tempts with a chef's eight-course tasting menu ($180, with wine pairings). The cheese course is definitely worth saving room for. Co-owner Giancarlo Paterlini (and his son) oversee the service and the list of Italian wines, both of which are superb. The room, with its vaulted ceiling and terra-cotta and pale-ocher palette, suits the refined food. This is a true San Francisco dining gem that is worth every penny. ✉ *1722 Sacramento St., Van Ness/Polk* ☎ *415/567–5432* 🌐 *www.acquerello.com* *Closed Sun. and Mon. No lunch* ✥ *C3.*

$$ SEAFOOD Fodor's Choice ★ **Swan Oyster Depot.** Half fish market and half diner, this small, slim, family-run seafood operation, open since 1912, has no tables, only a narrow marble counter with about a dozen-and-a-half stools. Most people come in to buy perfectly fresh salmon, halibut, crabs, and other seafood to take home. Everyone else hops onto one of the rickety stools to enjoy a bowl of clam chowder—the only hot food served—a dozen oysters, half a cracked crab, a slice of crusty sourdough, a big shrimp salad, or a smaller shrimp cocktail. Come early or late to avoid a long wait. ✉ *1517 Polk St., Van Ness/Polk* ☎ *415/673–1101* *Reservations not accepted* *No credit cards* *Closed Sun. No dinner* ✥ *D3.*

PACIFIC HEIGHTS

$$$$ NEW AMERICAN **Spruce.** One of the hottest reservations in town from the day it opened, Spruce caters to the city's social set, with the older crowd sliding into the mohair banquettes in the early hours and the younger set taking their places after eight. The large space, a former 1930s auto barn, shelters a high-style dining room and a more casual bar-cum-library lounge. Charcuterie, bavette steak with bordelaise sauce and duck-fat fries, and sweetbreads reflect the French slant of the modern American menu. If you can't wrangle a table, stop in at the take-out café next door, which carries not only sandwiches, salads, and pastries (like the exquisite palmiers) but also anything from the dining room menu to go. And if you are watching your pocketbook, you can graze off the bar menu and watch the swells come and go. ✉ *3640 Sacramento St., Pacific Heights* ☎ *415/931–5100* 🌐 *www.sprucesf.com* *Reservations essential* *No lunch weekends* ✥ *A3.*

JAPANTOWN

$ JAPANESE ✕ **Mifune.** Thin brown soba and thick white udon are the stars at this long-popular North American outpost of an Osaka-based noodle empire. A line regularly snakes out the door, but the house-made noodles, served both hot and cold and with a score of toppings, are worth the wait. Seating is at wooden tables, where diners of every age can be heard slurping down big bowls of such traditional Japanese combinations as *nabeyaki udon,* wheat noodles topped with tempura, chicken, and fish cake; and *tenzaru,* cold noodles and hot tempura with gingery dipping sauce served on lacquered trays. The noodle-phobic can choose from a few rice dishes and sushi. ✉ *Japan Center, Kintetsu Bldg., 1737 Post St., Japantown* ☎ *415/922–0337* 🌐 *www.mifune.com* ✥ *B4.*

4

HAYES VALLEY

$$$$ NEW AMERICAN ✕ **Jardinière.** A special anniversary? An important business dinner? A fat tax refund? These are the reasons you book a table at Jardinière. The restaurant takes its name from its chef-owner, Traci Des Jardins, and the sophisticated interior, with its eye-catching oval atrium and curving staircase, fills nightly with locals and out-of-towners alike. The equally sophisticated French-cum-Californian dining-room menu, served upstairs in the atrium, changes daily, but regularly includes such high-priced adornments as caviar, foie gras, and truffles. Downstairs, the lounge menu, with smaller plates and smaller prices ($8 to $18), is ideal for when you want to eat light while visiting with friends or tame your hunger before or after the nearby opera or symphony. Cheese lovers will appreciate the wide variety of choices—both Old World and New—housed in the glassed-in cheese-aging chamber in the rear of the restaurant. ✉ *300 Grove St., Hayes Valley* ☎ *415/861–5555* 🌐 *www.jardiniere.com* *Reservations essential* ⏲ *No lunch* ✥ *C5.*

$$$ MEDITERRANEAN Fodor's Choice ★ ✕ **Zuni Café.** After one bite of chef Judy Rodgers' succulent brick-oven-roasted whole chicken with Tuscan bread salad, you'll understand why she's a national star. Food is served here on two floors; the rabbit warren of rooms on the second level includes a balcony overlooking the main dining room. The crowd is a disparate mix that reflects the makeup of the city: casual and dressy, young and old, hip and staid. At the long copper bar, trays of briny-fresh oysters on the half shell are dispensed along with cocktails and wine. The southern French–Italian menu changes daily (though the signature chicken, prepared for two, is a fixture—sadly its already-dear cost is what keeps rising). Rotating dishes include house-cured anchovies with Parmigiano-Reggiano, deep-fried squid and lemons, ricotta gnocchi with seasonal vegetables, and brick-oven squab with polenta. Desserts are simple and satisfying, and include crumbly crusted tarts and an addictive cream-laced coffee granita. The lunchtime (and late-night) burger on rosemary focaccia with a side of shoestring potatoes is a favorite with locals. ✉ *1658 Market St., Hayes Valley* ☎ *415/552–2522* 🌐 *www.zunicafe.com* ⏲ *Closed Mon.* ✥ *C6.*

FISHERMAN'S WHARF

$$$$ NEW AMERICAN Fodor's Choice ★ ✕ **Gary Danko.** Be prepared to wait your turn for a table behind chef Gary Danko's legion of loyal fans, who typically keep the reservation book chock-full here (plan on reserving two months in advance). The cost of a meal ($68–$102) is pegged to the number of courses, from three to five. The decadent menu, which changes seasonally, may include risotto with lobster and rock shrimp, seared foie gras with Fuji apples, braised veal breast with sweetbreads, and quail stuffed with mushrooms and quinoa. A diet-destroying chocolate soufflé with two sauces is usually among the desserts. So, too, is a "no-cholesterol" Grand Marnier soufflé with raspberry sorbet, perfect for diners with a conscience or a heart problem. The wine list is the size of a small-town phone book, and the banquette-lined room, with beautiful wood floors and stunning (but restrained) floral arrangements, is as memorable as the food. ✉ *800 N. Point St., Fisherman's Wharf* ☎ *415/749–2060* 🌐 *www.garydanko.com* ✍ *Reservations essential* ⊗ *No lunch* ✥ *D1.*

COW HOLLOW

$$ ITALIAN ✕ **Rose's Café.** Sleepy-headed locals turn up at Rose's for the breakfast pizza of smoked ham, eggs, and Fontina; house-baked pastries and breads; poached eggs with Yukon Gold potato and mushroom hash; or soft polenta with mascarpone and jam. Midday is time for a roasted chicken and Fontina sandwich; pizza with eggplant, roasted peppers, and smoked mozzarella; or linguine with clams. Evening hours find customers eating their way through more pizza and pasta if they are on a budget, and skirt steak and roasted chicken if they aren't. The ingredients are top-notch, the service is friendly, and the seating is in comfortable booths, at tables, and at a counter. At the outside tables, overhead heaters keep you toasty when the temperature dips. Expect long lines for Sunday brunch. ✉ *2298 Union St., Cow Hollow* ☎ *415/775–2200* 🌐 *www.rosescafesf.com* ✥ *A2.*

MARINA

$$$ ITALIAN Fodor's Choice ★ ✕ **A16.** Marina residents—and, judging from the crowds, everybody else—gravitate to this lively trattoria, named for the autostrada that winds through Italy's sunny south. The kitchen serves the food of Naples and surrounding Campania, such as *burrata* (cream-filled mozzarella) with olive oil and crostini and crisp-crust pizzas, including a classic Neapolitan Margherita (mozzarella, tomato, and basil). Among the regularly changing mains are rustic pastas like maccaronara with ragu napoletana and house-made ricotta salata, and grilled yellowtail with cherry tomato and fennel agrodolce (sweet and sour sauce). A big wine list of primarily southern Italian with some California wines suits the fare perfectly. The long space includes an animated bar scene near the door; ask for a table in the quieter alcove at the far end. Reservations are easier to snag mid-week. ✉ *2355 Chestnut St., Marina* ☎ *415/771–2216* 🌐 *www.a16sf.com* ⊗ *No lunch Sat.–Tues.* ✥ *A1.*

CLOSE UP

Eating with Kids

Kids can be fussy eaters, but parents can be, too, so picking places that will satisfy both is important. Fortunately, there are plenty of excellent possibilities all over town.

If you're downtown for breakfast, stop at the touristy but venerable **Sears Fine Food** (✉ *439 Powell St., near Post St.* ☎ *415/986–0700* ✥ *4:F3*), home of "the world-famous Swedish pancakes." Eighteen of the silver-dollar-size beauties cost less than a movie ticket. Nearby in Chinatown, **City View Restaurant** (✉ *662 Commercial St., near Kearny St.* ☎ *415/398–2838* ✥ *1:E4*) serves a varied selection of dim sum, with tasty pork buns for kids and more exotic fare for adults.

If you found yourself dragging the kids through SFMOMA, you can win them back with lunch at the nearby **Crêpe O Chocolate** (✉ *75 O'Farrell St., between Stockton St. and Grant Ave.* ☎ *415/362–0255* ✥ *4:G4*), where they can fill up on a turkey and cheese sandwich and a crepe filled with peanut butter and chocolate—and you can, too. Try **Pluto's** (✉ *627 Irving St., between 7th and 8th Sts.* ☎ *415/753–8867* ✥ *2:A6*) after a visit to Golden Gate Park. Small kids love the chicken nuggets, which arrive with good-for-you carrot and celery sticks, whereas bigger kids will likely opt for one of the two-fisted sandwiches or make-your-own salads. Everyone will want a double fudge brownie for dessert. **Barney's Gourmet Burgers** (✉ *3344 Steiner St., near Union St.* ☎ *415/563–0307* ✥ *3:C6*), not far from Fort Mason and the Exploratorium, caters to older kids and their parents with mile-high burgers and giant salads. But Barney's doesn't forget "kids under 8," who have their own menu featuring a burger, an all-beef frank, chicken strips with ranch dressing, and more. The Ferry Building (✥ 1:G4) on the Embarcadero has plenty of kid-friendly options, from **Mijita Cocina Mexicana**, which has its own kids' menu, to **Gott's Roadside Tray Gourmet**, for burgers, shakes, and more. (And the outdoor access can help keep the little ones entertained.) The Mission has dozens of no-frills taco-and-burrito parlors; especially worthy is the bustling **La Corneta** (✉ *2731 Mission St., between 23rd and 24th Sts.* ☎ *415/252–9560* ✥ *2:F6*), which has a baby burrito. Banana splits and hot-fudge sundaes are what **St. Francis Fountain** (✉ *2801 24th St., at York St.* ☎ *415/826–4200* ✥ *3:H6*) is known for, along with its vintage decor (and popularity with hipsters for weekend brunch). Opened in 1918, it recalls the early 1950s, and the menu, with its burgers, BLTs, grilled-cheese sandwiches, and chili with corn bread, is timeless. In Lower Haight, the small **Rosamunde Sausage Grill** (✉ *545 Haight St., between Steiner and Fillmore Sts.* ☎ *415/437–6851* ✥ *3:D3*) serves just that—a slew of different sausages, from Polish to duck to Weisswurst (Bavarian veal). You get your choice of two toppings, like grilled onions, sauerkraut, and chili, and since there are only six stools, plan on takeout. Hint: head to nearby Duboce Park, with its cute playground.

Finally, both kids and adults love to be by the ocean, and the **Park Chalet** (✉ *1000 Great Hwy., at Fulton St.* ☎ *415/386–8439* ✥ *3:A3*), hidden behind the two-story Beach Chalet, offers pizza, mac and cheese, sticky ribs, a big banana split.

THE MISSION

$$$ ITALIAN Fodor's Choice ★ ✕ **Delfina.** "Irresistible." That's how countless die-hard fans describe Craig and Anne Stoll's Delfina. Such wild enthusiasm has made patience the critical virtue for anyone wanting a reservation here (although walk-ins can find some success at a counter and in the bar area). The interior is comfortable, with hardwood floors, aluminum-top tables, a tile bar, and a casual, friendly atmosphere. The menu changes daily, and among the usual offerings are grilled squid with warm white-bean salad and excellent tripe (they're also known for their spaghetti). If Piemontese fresh white truffles have made their way to San Francisco, you are likely to find hand-cut tagliarini dressed with butter, cream, and the pricey aromatic fungus on the menu alongside dishes built on more prosaic ingredients. The panna cotta is best in class. The storefront next door is home to pint-size Pizzeria Delfina. And for folks who can't get to the Mission, the Stolls have opened a second pizzeria on California Street in lively Lower Pacific Heights. ✉ *3621 18th St., Mission* ☎ *415/552–4055* 🌐 *www.delfinasf.com* ✍ *Reservations essential* ⏲ *No lunch* ✣ *B6.*

$ MEXICAN ✕ **SanJalisco.** This old-time, sun-filled, colorful, family-run restaurant is a neighborhood gem (and it's not just because it serves breakfast all day). At brunch, try the hearty *chilaquiles,* made from day-old tortillas cut into strips and cooked with cheese, eggs, chilies, and sauce. Or order eggs scrambled with cactus or with *chicharrones* (crisp pork skins) and served with freshly made tortillas. Soup offerings change daily, with Tuesday's *albondigás* (meatballs) comfort food at its best. On weekends, adventurous eaters may opt for *birria,* a spicy goat stew, or *menudo,* a tongue-searing soup made from tripe, calf's foot, and hominy. The latter is a time-honored hangover cure. Bring plenty of change for the jukebox loaded with Latin hits. ✉ *901 S. Van Ness Ave., Mission* ☎ *415/648–8383* 🌐 *www.sanjalisco.com* ✣ *C6.*

THE CASTRO

$ AMERICAN ✕ **Chow.** Wildly popular and consciously unpretentious, Chow is a funky yet savvy diner where soporific standards like hamburgers, pizzas, and spaghetti with meatballs are treated with culinary respect. A magnet for penny-pinchers, the restaurant has built its top-notch reputation on honest fare made with fresh local ingredients priced to sell. Salads, pastas, and mains come in two sizes to accommodate big and small appetites, there's a daily sandwich special, and kids can peruse their mini-menu. Because reservations are restricted to large parties, folks hoping to snag seats usually surround the doorway. Come early (before 6:30) or late (after 10) to reduce the wait, and don't even think about leaving without trying the ginger cake with caramel sauce. ✉ *215 Church St., Castro* ☎ *415/552–2469* 🌐 *www.chowfoodbar.com* ✣ *A6.*

THE HAIGHT

$$ INDIAN ✕ **Indian Oven.** This white tablecloth northern Indian restaurant draws diners from all over the city who come for the tandoori specialties—chicken, lamb, breads. Classics like *saag paneer* (spinach with Indian

cheese), aloo gobhi (potato, cauliflower, and spices), and *bengan bartha* (roasted eggplant with onions and spices) are also excellent. The chef wants to keep his clientele around for the long haul, too, and puts a little "heart healthy" icon next to some of the menu items. On Friday and Saturday nights famished patrons overflow onto the sidewalk as they wait for open tables. If you try to linger over a mango *lassi* or an order of the excellent kheer (rice pudding) on one of these nights, you'll probably be hurried along by a waiter. For better service, come on a slower weeknight. ✉ *233 Fillmore St., Lower Haight* ☎ *415/626–1628* 🌐 *www.indianovensf.com* ⊙ *No lunch* ✥ *A6.*

$$$ AMERICAN ✕ **Nopa.** In the mid-2000s North of the Panhandle became the city's newest talked-about neighborhood in part because of the big, bustling Nopa, which is cleverly named after it. This casual space, with its high ceilings, concrete floor, long bar, and sea of tables, suits the high-energy crowd of young suits mixed with stylish neighborhood residents that fill it every night. They come primarily for the rustic fare, like an irresistible flatbread topped with fennel sausage and chanterelles; the vegetable tagine with lemon yogurt; smoky, crisp-skinned rotisserie chicken; a juicy grass-fed hamburger with thick-cut fries; one of the city's best pork chops; and for dessert, the donut-like sopapillas. But they also love the lively spirit of the place. Unfortunately, that buzz sometimes means that raised voices are the only way to communicate with fellow diners. A big communal table and the friendly bar ease the way for anyone dining out on his or her own. ✉ *560 Divisadero St., Haight* ☎ *415/864–8643* 🌐 *www.nopasf.com* ⊙ *No lunch* ✥ *A6.*

4

RICHMOND

$$$ MOROCCAN Fodor's Choice ★ ✕ **Aziza.** Chef-owner Mourad Lahlou's California-Moroccan food boasts a healthy dose of modernity that keeps locals coming back for his unique flavors. Diners enjoy inspired and gorgeously plated first courses like sardines with green charmoula and black garlic, or duck liver with chestnut, persimmon, and ras el hanout. The main courses are equally elegant, ranging from squab with smoked farro to lamb shank with apricot, turnips, and barley. Desserts here are a can't-miss. The attractive three-room dining area, done in blue, saffron, and white, is a warm, inviting sea of tiles, arches, and candlelight. The wine list is very food-friendly, with some organic and biodynamic options, while cocktail enthusiasts can pick from more than two-dozen inspired potions. ✉ *5800 Geary Blvd., Richmond* ☎ *415/752–2222* 🌐 *www.aziza-sf.com* ⊙ *Closed Tues. No lunch* ✥ *A4.*

¢ VIETNAMESE ✕ **Pho Hoa Clement.** The menu at this homey Formica-and-linoleum spot is big and remarkably cheap. You can order everything from sandwiches and salads to rice dishes and noodle plates. But the soups are what shine, from the two-dozen varieties of *pho,* rice noodles in beef broth, to a dozen types of *hu tieu,* seafood and pork noodle soups. All of them are served in three sizes—small, medium, and large—usually separated by just 75¢, and no bowl is skimpy. Regulars, many of whom hail from Southeast Asia, favor the shrimp, fish ball, and pork slices soup with clear noodles and the special combo *pho* with rare steak, well-done brisket, tendon, and tripe. ✉ *239 Clement St., Inner Richmond* ☎ *415/379–9008* ✥ *A4.*

WHERE TO STAY

San Francisco is one of the country's best hotel towns, offering a rich selection of properties that satisfy most tastes and budgets. Whether you're seeking a cozy inn, a kitschy motel, a chic boutique, or a grande dame hotel, this city has got the perfect room for you.

Use the coordinate (⊕ A1) at the end of each listing to locate a site on the corresponding map.

WHAT IT COSTS					
	¢	$	$$	$$$	$$$$
Hotels	under $100	$100–$200	$201–$300	$301–$400	over $400

Prices are for a standard double room in high season, excluding 14% tax.

CIVIC CENTER/VAN NESS

For expanded hotel reviews, visit Fodors.com.

$ **Hotel Whitcomb.** Built in 1910, this historic hotel (formerly the Ramada Plaza) was the temporary seat of city government from 1912 to 1915 before becoming a hotel in 1916. **Pros:** good location; rich architectural and historic legacy; opulent lobby; airport shuttle; free Wi-Fi. **Cons:** difficult to find street parking; area can be dodgy at night; rooms are not as flashy as the lobby. ✉ *1231 Market St., Civic Center* ☎ *415/626–8000 or 800/227–4747* 🌐 *www.hotelwhitcomb.com* *447 rooms, 13 suites* *In-room: Wi-Fi. In-hotel: restaurant, room service, bar, gym, parking* *No meals* ⊕ *D6.*

FINANCIAL DISTRICT

$$$$ Fodor's Choice ★ **Mandarin Oriental, San Francisco.** Two towers connected by glass-enclosed sky bridges compose the top 11 floors of San Francisco's third tallest building, offering spectacular panoramas from every room; the windows open so you can hear that trademark San Francisco sound: the "ding ding" of the cable cars some 40 floors below (and some rooms even include binoculars). **Pros:** spectacular "bridge-to-bridge" views; attentive service; in the running for the most comfy beds in the city. **Cons:** located in a business area that's quiet on weekends; restaurant is excellent but expensive (as is the hotel). ✉ *222 Sansome St., Financial District* ☎ *415/276–9600 or 800/622–0404* 🌐 *www.mandarinoriental.com/sanfrancisco* *151 rooms, 7 suites* *In-room: Wi-Fi. In-hotel: restaurant, room service, bar, gym, business center, parking, some pets allowed* *No meals* ⊕ *F4.*

FISHERMAN'S WHARF/NORTH BEACH

$$ Fodor's Choice ★ **Argonaut Hotel.** When the four-story Haslett Warehouse was a fruit-and-vegetable canning complex in 1907, boats docked right up against the building; today it's a hotel with a nautical decor—think anchors, ropes, compasses, and a row of cruise-ship deck chairs in the lobby—that reflects its unique partnership with the San Francisco Maritime

National Historical Park. **Pros:** bay views; clean rooms; near Hyde Street cable car; sofa beds; toys for the kids. **Cons:** nautical theme isn't for everyone; cramped public areas; service can be hit or miss; location is a bit of a trek from other parts of town. ✉ *495 Jefferson St., at Hyde St., Fisherman's Wharf* ☎ *415/563–0800 or 866/415–0704* 🌐 *www.argonauthotel.com* *239 rooms, 13 suites* *In-room: Internet, Wi-Fi. In-hotel: restaurant, room service, bar, gym, parking, some pets allowed* *No meals* ✥ *D1.*

$$ **Best Western Tuscan Inn.** Described by some Fodors.com users as a "hidden treasure," this hotel's redbrick facade barely hints at the Tuscan country villa that lies within. **Pros:** wine and beer hour; downhome feeling; great location near Fisherman's Wharf. **Cons:** congested touristy area; small rooms. ✉ *425 N. Point St., at Mason St., Fisherman's Wharf* ☎ *415/561–1100 or 800/648–4626* 🌐 *www.tuscaninn.com* *212 rooms, 12 suites* *In-room: Wi-Fi. In-hotel: restaurant, room service, bar, business center, parking, some pets allowed* *No meals* ✥ *E1.*

¢ Fodor's Choice ★ **San Remo Hotel.** A few blocks from Fisherman's Wharf, this three-story 1906 Italianate Victorian—once home to longshoremen and Beat poets—has a narrow stairway from the street leading to the front desk and labyrinthine hallways; rooms are small but charming, with lace curtains, forest-green-painted wood floors, brass beds, and other antique furnishings. **Pros:** inexpensive; historic; cozy. **Cons:** some rooms are dark; no private bath; spartan amenities. ✉ *2237 Mason St., North Beach* ☎ *415/776–8688 or 800/352–7366* 🌐 *www.sanremohotel.com* *64 rooms with shared baths, 1 suite* *In-room: no a/c, no phone, no TV, Wi-Fi. In-hotel: laundry facilities, parking* *No meals* ✥ *E1.*

JAPANTOWN

$ Fodor's Choice ★ **Best Western Hotel Tomo.** Japanese Pop, or J-Pop as it is known across the pond, comes alive in this newly reinvented Japantown boutique hotel, located just a couple of blocks from the chic Fillmore district, Yoshi's, and the Fillmore Theatre. **Pros:** J-Pop style; anime playing on the lobby TV and manga in your room; great price in a fun neighborhood. **Cons:** small rooms; far from downtown. ✉ *1800 Sutter St., Japantown* ☎ *415/921–4000* 🌐 *www.hoteltomo.com* *125 rooms, 1 suite* *In-room: a/c, Internet. In-hotel: restaurant, bar, gym.* *No meals* ✥ *B4*

NOB HILL

$$$$ Fodor's Choice ★ **The Huntington Hotel.** The venerable ivy-covered hotel, a family-owned property for three generations, has provided gracious personal service to everyone from Bogart and Bacall to Picasso and Pavarotti. **Pros:** personal service; an aura of old San Francisco; guests have access to the primo spa with city views; cable car passes by right out front. **Cons:** up a steep hill from downtown. ✉ *1075 California St., Nob Hill* ☎ *415/474–5400 or 800/227–4683* 🌐 *www.huntingtonhotel.com* *96 rooms, 40 suites* *In-room: kitchen (some), Wi-Fi. In-hotel: restaurant, room service, bar, pool, gym, spa, parking* *No meals* ✥ *E3.*

BEST BETS FOR SAN FRANCISCO LODGING

Fodor's offers a selective listing of quality lodging experiences at every price range, from the city's best budget motel to its most sophisticated luxury hotel. Here we've compiled our top recommendations by price and experience. The very best properties—in other words, those that provide a particularly remarkable experience in their price range—are designated in the listings with the Fodor's Choice logo.

Fodor's Choice ★

Argonaut Hotel, $$, p. 222

Best Western Hotel Tomo, $, p. 223

Cow Hollow Motor Inn and Suites, $, p. 225

Four Seasons Hotel San Francisco, $$$$, p. 225

Hotel Drisco, $$$, p. 225

Hotel Monaco, San Francisco, $$$$, p. 226

Hotel Nikko, San Francisco, $$$, p. 226

Huntington Hotel, $$$$, p. 223

InterContinental San Francisco, $$$$, p. 225

Mandarin Oriental, San Francisco, $$$$, p. 222

Orchard Hotel, $$$$, p. 226

Palace Hotel, San Francisco, $$$$, p. 226

Ritz-Carlton, San Francisco, $$$$, p. 225

San Remo Hotel, ¢, p. 223

Union Street Inn, $$, p. 225

By Price

¢

San Remo Hotel, p. 223

$

Cow Hollow Motor Inn, p. 225

$$

Union Street Inn, p. 225

$$$

Hotel Drisco, p. 225

Hotel Nikko, p. 226

$$$$

Mandarin Oriental, p. 222

Orchard Hotel, p. 226

Ritz-Carlton, p. 225

By Experience

BUSINESS TRAVELERS

Four Seasons, $$$$, p. 225

Hotel Nikko, $$$, p. 226

GREAT CONCIERGE

Ritz-Carlton, $$$$, p. 225

HISTORICAL FLAVOR

Hotel Whitcomb, $, p. 222

Palace Hotel, $$$$, p. 226

Westin St. Francis, $, p. 227

MOST KID-FRIENDLY

Argonaut Hotel, $$$, p. 222

Best Western Hotel Tomo, $, p. 223

Four Seasons, $$$$, p. 225

MOST ROMANTIC

Hotel Drisco, $$$, p. 225

Palace Hotel, $$$$, p. 226

TOP B&BS

Hotel Drisco, $$$, p. 225

TOP SPAS

Mandarin Oriental, $$$$, p. 222

$$$$ Fodor'sChoice ★ **Ritz-Carlton, San Francisco.** A preferred destination for travel-industry honchos, movie stars, and visitors alike, this hotel—a stunning tribute to beauty and attentive, professional service—completed a $12.5-million renovation of its guest rooms and meeting spaces in 2006. **Pros:** terrific service; all-day food service on Club Level; beautiful surroundings. **Cons:** expensive; hilly location. ✉ *600 Stockton St., at California St., Nob Hill* ☎ *415/296–7465* 🌐 *www.ritzcarlton.com* *276 rooms, 60 suites* *In-room: Wi-Fi. In-hotel: restaurants, room service, bars, pool, gym, business center, parking, some pets allowed* *No meals* ✣ *E3.*

PACIFIC HEIGHTS/COW HOLLOW

4

$ Fodor'sChoice ★ **Cow Hollow Motor Inn and Suites.** Suites at this large, family-owned modern motel are more spacious than average, with sitting and dining areas, dark-wood furniture, and wallpaper with muted yellow, brown, and green patterns. **Pros:** suites are the size of apartments; good for families; covered parking in building. **Cons:** congested neighborhood has a fratty feeling; rooms are on a loud street. ✉ *2190 Lombard St., Marina* ☎ *415/921–5800* 🌐 *www.cowhollowmotorinn.com* *117 rooms, 12 suites* *In-room: a/c, kitchen (some), Wi-Fi. In-hotel: parking* *No meals* ✣ *A2.*

$$$ Fodor'sChoice ★ **Hotel Drisco.** Pretend you're a resident of one of the wealthiest and most beautiful residential neighborhoods in San Francisco at this understated, elegant 1903 Edwardian hotel. **Pros:** great service; comfortable rooms; quiet residential retreat. **Cons:** small rooms; far from downtown. ✉ *2901 Pacific Ave., Pacific Heights* ☎ *415/346–2880 or 800/634–7277* 🌐 *www.hoteldrisco.com* *29 rooms, 19 suites* *In-room: no a/c. In-hotel: business center* *Breakfast* ✣ *A3.*

$$ Fodor'sChoice ★ **Union Street Inn.** Precious family antiques and unique artwork helped British innkeepers Jane Bertorelli and David Coyle (former chef for the Duke and Duchess of Bedford) transform this green-and-cream 1902 Edwardian into a delightful B&B. **Pros:** personal service; Jane's excellent full breakfast; romantic setting. **Cons:** on a congested street; no a/c; no elevator. ✉ *2229 Union St., Cow Hollow* ☎ *415/346–0424* 🌐 *www.unionstreetinn.com* *6 rooms* *In-room: no a/c, Wi-Fi. In-hotel: parking* *Breakfast* ✣ *A2.*

SOMA

$$$$ Fodor'sChoice ★ **Four Seasons Hotel San Francisco.** Occupying floors 5 through 17 of a skyscraper, this luxurious (and award-winning) hotel, designated as the "heart of the city," is sandwiched between multimillion-dollar condos, elite shops, and a premier sports-and-fitness complex. **Pros:** near museums, galleries, restaurants, and clubs; terrific fitness facilities; luxurious rooms and amenities. **Cons:** pricey. ✉ *757 Market St., SoMa* ☎ *415/633–3000, 800/332–3442, or 800/819–5053* 🌐 *www.fourseasons.com/sanfrancisco* *231 rooms, 46 suites* *In-room: Internet, Wi-Fi. In-hotel: restaurant, room service, bar, pool, gym, spa, business center, parking, some pets allowed* *No Meals* ✣ *F4.*

$$$$ Fodor'sChoice ★ **InterContinental San Francisco.** The arctic-blue glass exterior and subdued, Zen-like lobby of this sparkling new hotel may be as bland as an airport concourse, but it's merely a prelude to the spectacularly

light, expansive, thoughtfully laid-out guest rooms, which have all the ultramodern conveniences. **Pros:** a stone's throw from the Moscone Center; well-equipped gym; near hip clubs and edgy eateries; perfect for a weekend getaway. **Cons:** conservative decor is a bit short on character; borders a rough neighborhood; a bit far from many major points of interest for tourists. ✉ *888 Howard St., SoMa* ☎ *415/616–6500 or 888/811–4273* 🌐 *www.intercontinentalsanfrancisco.com* *536 rooms, 14 suites* *In-room: Wi-Fi. In-hotel: restaurant, room service, bar, pool, gym, spa, parking, some pets allowed* *No meals* ✥ *F5.*

$$$$ Fodor's Choice ★ **Palace Hotel, San Francisco.** "Majestic" is the word that best sums up this landmark hotel, which was the world's largest and most luxurious when it opened in 1875. It was completely rebuilt after the 1906 earthquake and fire, and the carriage entrance reemerged as the grand Garden Court restaurant. **Pros:** gracious service; close to Union Square; near BART. **Cons:** design from another era; smallish rooms with even smaller baths; many nearby establishments closed on weekends; west-facing rooms can be warm and stuffy. ✉ *2 New Montgomery St., SoMa* ☎ *415/512–1111 or 888/627–7196* 🌐 *www.sfpalace.com* *518 rooms, 34 suites* *In-room: Internet. In-hotel: restaurants, room service, bar, pool, gym, parking* *No meals* ✥ *F4.*

UNION SQUARE/DOWNTOWN

$$$$ Fodor's Choice ★ **Hotel Monaco, San Francisco.** A cheery 1910 Beaux-Arts facade and snappily dressed doormen welcome you into a plush lobby dominated by a French inglenook fireplace, vaulted ceilings painted with whimsical murals of hot-air balloons, a marble staircase, and a large metal baobab tree dedicated to hotelier Bill Kimpton. **Pros:** amazing service; stylish; full of character; near theater district; staff offers guests a goldfish to keep them company. **Cons:** close to the Tenderloin; some discount-rate rooms are small. ✉ *501 Geary St., Union Square* ☎ *415/292–0100 or 866/622–5284* 🌐 *www.monaco-sf.com* *181 rooms, 20 suites* *In-room: Wi-Fi. In-hotel: restaurant, room service, bar, gym, spa, business center, parking, some pets allowed* *No meals* ✥ *E4.*

$$$ Fodor's Choice ★ **Hotel Nikko, San Francisco.** The vast surfaces of gray-flecked white marble and gurgling fountains in the neoclassical lobby of this business traveler hotel have the sterility of an airport; however the crisply designed rooms in muted tones, with flat-screen TVs, modern bathrooms with sinks that sit on top of black vanities, plus separate showers and tubs, please jet-setters. **ros:** friendly multilingual staff; ultramodern baths; very clean. **Cons:** rooms and antiseptic lobby lack color; some may find the atmosphere cold; expensive parking. ✉ *222 Mason St., Union Square* ☎ *415/394–1111 or 800/248–3308* 🌐 *www.hotelnikkosf.com* *510 rooms, 22 suites* *In-room: Wi-Fi. In-hotel: restaurant, room service, bar, pool, gym, business center, parking, some pets allowed* *No meals* ✥ *E4.*

$$$$ Fodor's Choice ★ **Orchard Hotel.** The 104-room hotel embraces state-of-the-art technology—from CD and DVD players in each room to Wi-Fi access throughout the building—mixing cutting-edge Silicon Valley chic with classic European touches. **Pros:** cutting-edge technology; sizable boutique-style rooms; tech savvy quarters. **Cons:** can be a bit pricey. ✉ *665*

Bush St., Union Square ☎ *415/362–8878 or 888/717–2881* 🌐 *www.theorchardhotel.com* *104 rooms, 9 suites* *In-room: Wi-Fi. In-hotel: restaurant, room service, parking, some pets allowed* *No meals* ✥ *E4.*

$$$$ **Taj Campton Place San Francisco.** Beauty and highly attentive service remain the hallmarks of this exquisite jewel-like, top-tier hotel. **Pros:** attentive service; first-class restaurant; abundant natural light. **Cons:** smallish rooms; pricey (but worth it). ✉ *340 Stockton St., Union Square* ☎ *415/781–5555 or 866/332–1670* 🌐 *www.camptonplace.com* *101 rooms, 9 suites* *In-room: Wi-Fi. In-hotel: restaurant, room service, bar, gym, parking, some pets allowed* *No meals* ✥ *E4.*

$ **Westin St. Francis.** The site of sensational, headline scandals, this hotel's past is shrouded in as much infamy as stardust: this is the place where Sara Jane Moore tried to assassinate Gerald Ford, where Al Jolson died playing poker; Suite 1219–1221 was the scene of a massive scandal, which erupted when a 30-year-old aspiring actress died after a night of heavy boozing in the close company of silent film comedian Fatty Arbuckle. **Pros:** fantastic beds; prime location; spacious rooms, some with great views. **Cons:** some guests comment on the long wait at check-in; rooms in original building can be small; glass elevators are not for the faint of heart. ✉ *335 Powell St., Union Square* ☎ *415/397–7000 or 800/917–7458* 🌐 *www.westinstfrancis.com* *1,157 rooms, 38 suites* *In-room: Internet, Wi-Fi. In-hotel: restaurants, room service, bars, spa, business center, parking, some pets allowed* *No Meals* ✥ *E4.*

4

NIGHTLIFE

This small city packs the punch of a much larger metropolis after dark. Downtown cool, trendy, relaxed, quirky, and downright outrageous could all be used to describe San Francisco's diverse and vibrant collection of bars, clubs, and performance venues.

THE 4-1-1

Entertainment information is printed in the pink Sunday "Datebook" section (🌐 *www.sfgate.com/datebook*) and the more calendar-based Thursday "96 Hours" section (🌐 *www.sfgate.com/96hours*) in the *San Francisco Chronicle*. Also consult any of the free alternative weeklies, notably the *SF Weekly* (🌐 *www.sfweekly.com*), which blurbs nightclubs and music, and the *San Francisco Bay Guardian* (🌐 *www.sfbg.com*), which lists neighborhood, avant-garde, and budget events. SF Station (🌐 *www.sfstation.com*; online only) has an up-to-date calendar of entertainment goings-on.

BARS AND LOUNGES

★ **Cliff House.** A bit classier than the Beach Chalet, with a more impressive, sweeping view of Ocean Beach, the Cliff House is our pick if you must choose just one oceanfront restaurant/bar. Sure, it's the site of many high-school prom dates, and you could argue that the food and drinks are overpriced, and some say the sleek facade looks like a mausoleum—but the views are terrific. The best window seats are reserved for diners, but there's a small upstairs lounge where you can watch gulls sail high

Fodor's Choice ★

Mandarin Oriental

Argonaut Hotel

Hotel Drisco

Palace Hotel

Union Street Inn

Fodor's Choice ★

Four Seasons Hotel

Orchard Hotel

Hotel Nikko

The Ritz-Carlton

4

above the vast blue Pacific. Come before sunset. ✉ *1090 Point Lobos, at Great Hwy., Lincoln Park* ☎ *415/386–3330* 🌐 *www.cliffhouse.com.*

WINE BARS

★ **Eos Restaurant and Wine Bar.** Though it's just a few blocks away, Cole Valley is a world apart from funky, grungy Haight Street. Eos, along with the handful of restaurants and bars that line this part of Cole Street, manages to be both sophisticated and unpretentious—and truly fantastic. This narrow and romantically lighted space, with more than 400 wines by the bottle and 40-plus by the glass, offers two different wine flights—one red and one white—every month. The adjoining restaurant's excellent East-meets-West cuisine is available at the bar. ✉ *901 Cole St., at Carl St., Haight* ☎ *415/566–3063* 🌐 *www.eossf.com.*

★ **Hôtel Biron.** Sharing an alleylike block with the backs of Market Street restaurants, this tiny, cavelike (in a good way) spot displays rotating artwork of the Mission School aesthetic on its brick walls. The clientele is well-behaved twenty- to thirtysomethings who enjoy the cramped quarters, good range of wines and prices, off-the-beaten path location, soft lighting, and hip music. ✉ *45 Rose St., off Market St., Hayes Valley* ☎ *415/703–0403* 🌐 *www.hotelbiron.com.*

★ **MatrixFillmore.** Don a pair of Diesel jeans and a Michael Kors sweater and sip cosmos or Cabernet with the Marina's bon vivants. This is the premier spot in the "Triangle" (short for Bermuda Triangle, named for all of the singles who disappear in the bars clustered at Greenwich and Fillmore streets). Although there's a small dance floor where some folks bump and grind to high-energy DJ-spun dance tracks, the majority of the clientele usually vies for the plush seats near the central open fireplace, flirts at the bar, or huddles for romantic tête-à-têtes in the back. The singles scene can be overwhelming on weekends. ✉ *3138 Fillmore St., between Greenwich and Filbert Sts., Marina* ☎ *415/563–4180* 🌐 *www.matrixfillmore.com.*

Tonga Room. Since 1947 the Tonga Room has given San Francisco a taste of high Polynesian kitsch. Fake palm trees, grass huts, a lagoon (three-piece combos play pop standards on a floating barge), and faux monsoons—courtesy of sprinkler-system rain and simulated thunder and lightning—grow more surreal as you quaff fruity cocktails. ✉ *Fairmont San Francisco, 950 Mason St., at California St., Nob Hill* ☎ *415/772–5278.*

★ **Vesuvio Café.** If you're only hitting one bar in North Beach, it should be this one. The low-ceiling second floor of this raucous boho hangout, little altered since its 1960s heyday (when Jack Kerouac frequented the place), is a fine vantage point for watching the colorful Broadway and Columbus Avenue intersection. Another part of Vesuvio's appeal is its diverse, always-mixed clientele (20s to 60s), from neighborhood regulars and young couples to Bacchanalian posses of friends. ✉ *255 Columbus Ave., at Broadway, North Beach* ☎ *415/362–3370* 🌐 *www.vesuvio.com.*

GAY AND LESBIAN NIGHTLIFE

The *Bay Area Reporter* (☎ *415/861–5019* 🌐 *www.ebar.com*), a biweekly newspaper, lists gay and lesbian events in its calendar. The biweekly *San Francisco Bay Times* (☎ *415/626–0260* 🌐 *www.sfbaytimes.com*) is aimed at gay and lesbian readers.

GAY MALE BARS

★ **Eagle Tavern.** Bikers are courted with endless drink specials and, increasingly, live rock music at this humongous indoor-outdoor leather bar, one of the few SoMa bars remaining from the days before AIDS and gentrification. The Sunday-afternoon "Beer Busts" (3–6 pm) are a social high point and benefit charitable organizations. It's a surprisingly welcoming place for people from all walks of life. ✉ *398 12th St., at Harrison St., SoMa* ☎ *415/626–0880* 🌐 *www.sfeagle.com.*

★ **Martuni's.** A mixed crowd enjoys cocktails in the semi-refined environment of this elegant bar at the intersection of the Castro, the Mission, and Hayes Valley; variations on the martini are a specialty. In the intimate back room a pianist plays nightly, and patrons take turns boisterously singing show tunes. It's a favorite post-theater spot—especially after the symphony or opera, which are within walking distance. ✉ *4 Valencia St., at Market St., Mission* ☎ *415/241–0205.*

★ **The Stud.** Mingle with glam trannies, tight-teed pretty boys, ladies and their ladies, and a handful of straight onlookers who dance to the live DJ and watch world-class drag performers on the small stage. The entertainment is often campy, pee-your-pants funny, and downright talented. Each night's music is different—from funk, soul, and hip-hop to '80s tunes and disco favorites. The club is sometimes closed Sunday. ✉ *1284 Harrison St., at Ninth St., SoMa* ☎ *415/863–6623* 🌐 *www.studsf.com.*

LESBIAN BARS

★ **Lexington Club.** According to its slogan, "every night is ladies' night" at this all-girl club geared to urban alterna-dykes in their 20s and 30s (think piercings and tattoos, not lipstick). **■ TIP→ The women's room has awesome graffiti.** ✉ *3464 19th St., at Lexington St., Mission* ☎ *415/863–2052* 🌐 *www.lexingtonclub.com.*

JAZZ CLUBS

★ **Yoshi's.** The legendary Oakland club that has pulled in some of the world's best jazz musicians—Pat Martino, Branford Marsalis, Betty Carter, and Dizzy Gillespie, to name just a few—opened a San Francisco location in late 2007. The new club has terrific acoustics, a 9-foot Steinway grand piano (broken in by Chick Corea), and seating for 411; it's been hailed as "simply the best jazz club in the city." Yoshi's also serves Japanese food in an adjoining restaurant set in a soaring two-story space, decorated with blond wood and hanging paper lanterns (you can also order food at café tables in the club). Sightlines are good from just about any vantage point, including the back balcony. Be advised, the club is located on a tough block in an even tougher neighborhood; so, take advantage of the valet parking. ✉ *1330 Fillmore St., at Eddy St., Japantown* ☎ *415/655–5600* 🌐 *www.yoshis.com.*

ROCK, POP, HIP-HOP, FOLK, AND BLUES CLUBS

★ **Bimbo's 365 Club.** The plush main room and adjacent lounge of this club, here since 1951, retain a retro vibe perfect for the "Cocktail Nation" programming that keeps the crowds entertained. For a taste of the old-school San Francisco nightclub scene, you can't beat this place. Indie low-fi and pop bands like Stephen Malkmus and the Jicks and Camera Obscura fill the bill. ✉ *1025 Columbus Ave., at Chestnut St., North Beach* ☎ *415/474–0365* 🌐 *www.bimbos365club.com.*

Fodor's Choice ★ **BooM BooM RooM.** John Lee Hooker's old haunt has been an old-school blues haven for years, attracting top-notch acts from all around the country. Luck out with legendary masters like James "Super Chikan" Johnson, or discover new blues and funk artists. ✉ *1601 Fillmore St., at Geary Blvd., Japantown* ☎ *415/673–8000* 🌐 *www.boomboomblues.com.*

★ **Bottom of the Hill.** This is a great live-music dive—in the best sense of the word—and truly the epicenter for independent rock in the Bay Area. The club has hosted some great acts over the years, including the Strokes and the Throwing Muses. Rap and hip-hop acts occasionally make it to the stage. ✉ *1233 17th St., at Texas St., Potrero Hill* ☎ *415/621–4455* 🌐 *www.bottomofthehill.com.*

The Fillmore. This is *the* club that all the big names, from Coldplay to Clapton, want to play. San Francisco's most famous rock-music hall serves up a varied menu of national and local acts: rock, reggae, grunge, jazz, folk, acid house, and more. Most tickets cost $20–$30, and some shows are open to all ages. **■ TIP→ Avoid steep service charges by buying tickets at the Fillmore box office on Sunday (10–4).** ✉ *1805 Geary Blvd., at Fillmore St., Western Addition* ☎ *415/346–6000* 🌐 *www.thefillmore.com.*

Fodor's Choice ★ **Great American Music Hall.** You can find top-drawer entertainment at this great, eclectic nightclub. Acts range from the best in blues, folk, and jazz to up-and-coming college-radio and American-roots artists to of-the-moment indie rock stars (OK Go, Mates of State) and the establishment (Cowboy Junkies). The colorful marble-pillared emporium (built in 1907 as a bordello) also accommodates dancing at some shows. Pub grub is available most nights. ✉ *859 O'Farrell St., between Polk and Larkin Sts., Tenderloin* ☎ *415/885–0750* 🌐 *www.gamh.com.*

THE ARTS

San Francisco's symphony, opera, and ballet all perform in the Civic Center area, also home to the 928-seat Herbst Theatre, which hosts many fine soloists and ensembles.

TICKETS

City Box Office (✉ *180 Redwood St., Suite 100, off Van Ness Ave. between Golden Gate Ave. and McAllister St., Civic Center* ☎ *415/392–4400* 🌐 *www.cityboxoffice.com*), a charge-by-phone service, offers tickets for many performances and lectures. You can buy tickets in person at its downtown location weekdays 9:30 to 5:30. **San Francisco Performances** (✉ *500 Sutter St., Suite 710* ☎ *415/398–6449* 🌐 *www.performances.org*) brings an eclectic array of top-flight global music and dance talents to various venues—mostly the Yerba Buena Center for the Arts, Davies Symphony Hall, and Herbst Theatre. Artists have included the Los Angeles Guitar Quartet, Edgar Meyer, the Paul Taylor Dance Company, and Midori. Tickets can be purchased in person, online, or by phone.

You can charge tickets for everything from jazz concerts to Giants games by phone or online through **Tickets.com** (☎ *800/955–5566* 🌐 *www.tickets.com*). Half-price, same-day tickets for many local and touring stage shows go on sale (cash only) at 11 am Tuesday through Saturday at the **TIX Bay Area** (✉ *Powell St. between Geary and Post Sts., Union Square* ☎ *415/433–7827* 🌐 *www.tixbayarea.com*) booth on Union Square. TIX is also a full-service ticket agency for theater and music events around the Bay Area, open Tuesday through Friday 11 to 6, Saturday 10 to 6, and Sunday 10 to 3.

4

THE 4-1-1

The best guide to the arts is the Sunday "Datebook" section (🌐 *www.sfgate.com/datebook*), printed on pink paper, in the *San Francisco Chronicle*. The four-day entertainment supplement "96 Hours" (🌐 *www.sfgate.com/96hours*) is in the Thursday *Chronicle*. Also be sure to check out the city's free alternative weeklies, including *SF Weekly* (🌐 *www.sfweekly.com*) and the more avant-garde *San Francisco Bay Guardian* (🌐 *www.sfbg.com*).

DANCE

Fodor's Choice ★ **San Francisco Ballet.** For ballet-lovers, this company is reason alone to come to the Bay Area. Under artistic director Helgi Tomasson, the San Francisco Ballet's works—both classical and contemporary—have won critical raves. The primary season runs from February through May. Its repertoire includes full-length ballets such as *Don Quixote* and *Sleeping Beauty*; the December presentation of the *Nutcracker* is one of the most spectacular in the nation. The company also performs bold new dances from star choreographers such as William Forsythe and Mark Morris, alongside modern classics by George Balanchine and Jerome Robbins. Tickets and information are available at the **War Memorial Opera House.** ✉ *War Memorial Opera House, 301 Van Ness Ave., Civic Center* ☎ *415/865–2000* 🌐 *www.sfballet.org* ⏲ *Weekdays 10–4.*

MUSIC

Fodor's Choice ★ **San Francisco Symphony.** One of America's top orchestras, the San Francisco Symphony performs from September through May, with additional summer performances of light classical music and show tunes; visiting artists perform here the rest of the year. The orchestra and its charismatic music director, Michael Tilson Thomas, who is known for his daring programming of 20th-century American works (most notably his Grammy Award–winning Mahler cycle), often perform with soloists of the caliber of Andre Watts, Gil Shaham, and Renée Fleming. The adventuresome side of the organization is amply illustrated by this symphony's collaboration with the heavy-metal group Metallica. David Byrne has performed here, as well. Tickets run about $15–$100.

Built as a bordello in 1907, the Great American Music Hall now pulls in top-tier performers.

Many members of the San Francisco Symphony perform in the **Summer in the City** (☎ *415/864–6000* 🌐 *www.sfsymphony.org*) concert series, held in the 2,400-seat Davies Symphony Hall. The schedule includes light classics and Broadway, country, and movie music. ✉ *Davies Symphony Hall, 201 Van Ness Ave., at Grove St., Civic Center* ☎ *415/864–6000* 🌐 *www.sfsymphony.org*.

MUSIC FESTIVALS

Fodor's Choice ★ **Stern Grove Festival.** The nation's oldest continual free summer music festival hosts Sunday-afternoon performances of symphony, opera, jazz, pop music, and dance. The amphitheater is in a beautiful eucalyptus grove below street level, perfect for picnicking before the show. (Dress for cool weather.) ✉ *Sloat Blvd. at 19th Ave., Sunset* ☎ *415/252–6252* 🌐 *www.sterngrove.org*.

OPERA

Fodor's Choice ★ **San Francisco Opera.** Founded in 1923, this world-renowned company has resided in the Civic Center's War Memorial Opera House since the building's completion in 1932. Over its split season—September through January and June through July—the opera presents about 70 performances of 10 to 12 operas. Translations are projected above the stage during almost all non-English operas. Long considered a major international company and the most important operatic organization in the United States outside New York, the opera frequently embarks on productions with European opera companies and unconventional projects, some with a popular cultural edge designed attract younger audiences. Ticket prices can range from $25 to $195. The full-time box office (Monday 10–5, Tuesday–Friday 10–6) is at 199 Grove Street, at Van Ness Avenue. ✉ *War Memorial Opera House, 301 Van Ness Ave., at Grove St., Civic Center* ☎ *415/864–3330 tickets* 🌐 *www.sfopera.com.*

THEATER

★ **American Conservatory Theater.** Not long after its founding in the mid-1960s, the city's major nonprofit theater company became one of the nation's leading regional theaters. During its season, which runs from early fall to late spring, ACT presents approximately eight plays, from classics to contemporary works, often in rotating repertory. In December ACT stages a much-loved version of Charles Dickens's *A Christmas Carol.* The **ACT ticket office** (✉ *405 Geary St., Union Square* ☎ *415/749–2228*) is next door to **Geary Theater,** the company's home. ✉ *Geary Theater, 415 Geary St., Union Square* 🌐 *www.act-sf.org.*

Fodor's Choice ★ **Teatro ZinZanni.** Contortionists, chanteuses, jugglers, illusionists, and circus performers ply the audience as you're served a surprisingly good five-course dinner in a fabulous antique Belgian traveling-dance-hall tent (the location of which is moving to a new permanent home in 2011). Be ready to laugh, and arrive early for a front-and-center table. Reservations are essential; tickets are $125 to $150, call or check the Web site for prices and location. And dress fancy. ☎ *415/438–2668* 🌐 *www.zinzanni.org.*

SPORTS AND THE OUTDOORS

BASEBALL

Fodor's Choice ★ The 2010 World Champion **San Francisco Giants** (✉ *AT&T Park, 24 Willie Mays Plaza, between 2nd and 3rd Sts., SoMa* ☎ *415/972–2000 or 800/734–4268* 🌐 *sanfrancisco.giants.mlb.com*) play in beautiful, classic AT&T Park. **Tickets.com** (☎ *877/473–4849* 🌐 *www.tickets.com*) sells game tickets over the phone and charges a per-ticket fee of $5–$24, plus a per-call processing fee of up to $3.50. The **Giants Dugout** (✉ *AT&T Park, 24 Willie Mays Plaza, SoMa* ☎ *415/972–2000 or 800/734–4268* ✉ *4 Embarcadero Center, Embarcadero* ☎ *415/951–8888*) sells tickets in any of its stores (check the Web site, 🌐 *sanfrancisco.giants.mlb.com/sf/ballpark/dugout_stores.jsp*, for all locations); a surcharge is added at all but the ballpark store.

BICYCLING

The **San Francisco Bicycle Coalition** (☎ *415/431–2453* 🌐 *www.sfbike.org*) has extensive information about the policies and politics of riding a bicycle in the city and lists local events for cyclists on its Web site. You can also download (but not print) a PDF version of the *San Francisco Bike Map and Walking Guide.*

WHERE TO RENT

Bike and Roll. You can rent bikes here for $8 per hour or $32 per day; discounted weekly rates are available. They have three locations and also have complimentary maps. ✉ *899 Columbus Ave., North Beach*

✉ 353 Jefferson St. between Jones and Leavenworth Sts., Fisherman's Wharf ✉ 2800 Leavenworth St., Fisherman's Wharf ☎ 415/229–2000 or 888/245–3929 ⊕ www.bicyclerental.com.

Blazing Saddles. This outfitter rents bikes for $8 to $9 an hour, depending on the type of bike, or $32 to $88 a day, and shares tips on sights to see along the paths. *✉ 2715 Hyde St., Fisherman's Wharf ✉ 433 Mason St., Union Sq. ✉ Pier 41, Fisherman's Wharf ✉ 465 Jefferson St., at Hyde St., Fisherman's Wharf ✉ 2555 Powell St., Fisherman's Wharf ✉ 1095 Columbus, North Beach ✉ 721 Beach St.,, North Beach ☎ 415/202–8888 ⊕ www.blazingsaddles.com.*

NO UPHILL BATTLE

Don't want to get stuck slogging up 30-degree inclines? Then be sure to pick up a copy of the foldout *San Francisco Bike Map and Walking Guide* ($3), which indicates street grades by color and delineates bike routes that avoid major hills and heavy traffic. You can pick up a copy in bicycle shops, select bookstores, or at the San Francisco Bicycle Coalition's Web site (⊕ *www.bikesf.org*).

SHOPPING

MAJOR SHOPPING DISTRICTS

THE CASTRO AND NOE VALLEY

The Castro, often called the gay capital of the world, is also a major shopping destination for all travelers. It's filled with men's clothing boutiques and home-accessories stores geared to the neighborhood's fairly wealthy demographic. Of course, there are plenty of places hawking kitsch, too, and if you're looking for something to shock your Aunt Martha back home, you've come to the right place. Just south of the Castro on 24th Street, largely residential Noe Valley is an enclave of fancy-food stores, bookshops, women's clothing boutiques, and specialty gift stores.

CHINATOWN

The intersection of Grant Avenue and Bush Street marks the gateway to Chinatown. The area's 24 blocks of shops, restaurants, and markets are a nonstop tide of activity. Dominating the exotic cityscape are the sights and smells of food: crates of bok choy, tanks of live crabs, cages of live partridges, and hanging whole chickens. Racks of Chinese silks, colorful pottery, baskets, and carved figurines are displayed chockablock on the sidewalks, alongside fragrant herb shops where your bill might be tallied on an abacus. And if you need to knock off souvenir shopping for the kids and coworkers in your life, the dense and multiple selections of toys, T-shirts, mugs, magnets, decorative boxes, and countless other trinkets make it a quick, easy, and inexpensive proposition.

FISHERMAN'S WHARF

A constant throng of sightseers crowds Fisherman's Wharf, and with good reason: Pier 39, the Anchorage, Ghirardelli Square, and the Cannery are all here, each with shops and restaurants, as well as outdoor entertainment—musicians, mimes, and magicians. Best of all are the

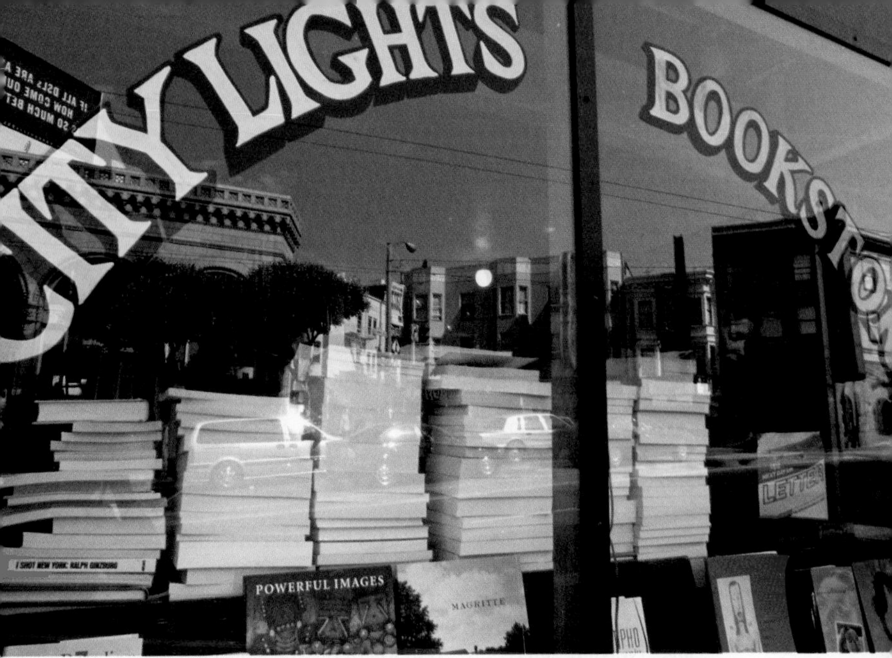

The beat movement of the 1950s was born in San Francisco's most famous bookstore, City Lights.

Wharf's view of the bay and its proximity to cable car lines, which can shuttle shoppers directly to Union Square. Many of the tourist-oriented shops border on tacky, peddling the requisite Golden Gate tees, taffy, and baskets of shells, but tucked into the mix are a few fine galleries, clothing shops, and groceries that even locals will deign to visit.

THE HAIGHT

Haight Street is a perennial attraction for visitors, if only to see the sign at Haight and Ashbury streets—the geographic center of the Flower Power movement during the 1960s, so it can be a bummer to find this famous intersection is now the turf for Gap and Ben & Jerry's. Don't be discouraged; it's still possible to find high-quality vintage clothing, funky shoes, folk art from around the world, and used records and CDs galore in this always-busy neighborhood.

HAYES VALLEY

A community park called Hayes Green breaks up a crowd of cool shops just west of the Civic Center. Here you can find everything from hip housewares to art galleries to handcrafted jewelry. The density of unique stores—as well as the absence of chains anywhere in sight—makes it a favorite destination for many San Francisco shoppers.

JAPANTOWN

Unlike the ethnic enclaves of Chinatown, North Beach, and the Mission, the 5-acre Japan Center (✉ *Bordered by Laguna, Fillmore, and Post Sts. and Geary Blvd.* ☎ *No phone*) is under one roof. The three-block complex includes a reasonably priced public garage and three shop-filled buildings. Especially worthwhile are the Kintetsu and Kinokuniya buildings, where shops sell things like bonsai trees, tapes and records, jewelry, antique kimonos, *tansu* (Japanese chests), electronics, and colorful glazed dinnerware and teapots.

THE MARINA DISTRICT

With the city's highest density of (mostly) non-chain stores, the Marina is an outstanding shopping nexus. But it's nobody's secret—those with plenty of cash and style to burn flood the boutiques to snap up luxe accessories and housewares. Union Street and Chestnut Street in particular cater to the shopping whims of the grown-up sorority sisters and frat boys who live in the surrounding pastel Victorians.

THE MISSION

The aesthetic of the resident Pabst Blue Ribbon–downing hipsters and starving-artist types contributes to the affordability and individuality of shopping here. These night owls keep the city's best thrift stores, vintage-furniture shops, alternative bookstores, and, increasingly, small clothing boutiques afloat. As the Mission gentrifies, though, bargain hunters find themselves trekking the long blocks in search of truly local flavor. Thankfully, many of the city's best bakeries and cafés are sprinkled throughout the area.

NORTH BEACH

Although it's sometimes compared to New York City's Greenwich Village, North Beach is only a fraction of the size, clustered tightly around Washington Square and Columbus Avenue. Most of its businesses are small eateries, cafés, and shops selling clothing, antiques, and vintage wares. Once the center of the Beat movement, North Beach still has a bohemian spirit that's especially apparent at the rambling City Lights Bookstore, where Beat poetry lives on.

PACIFIC HEIGHTS

The rest of the city likes to deprecate its wealthiest neighborhood, but no one has any qualms about weaving through the mansions to come to Fillmore and Sacramento streets to shop. With grocery and hardware stores sitting alongside local clothing ateliers and international designer outposts, these streets manage to mix small-town America with big-city glitz. After you've splurged on a cashmere sweater or a handblown glass vase, snag an outdoor seat at Peet's or Coffee Bean; it's the perfect way to pass an afternoon watching the parade of Old Money, dogs, and strollers.

UNION SQUARE

Serious shoppers head straight to Union Square, San Francisco's main shopping area and the site of most of its department stores, including Macy's, Neiman Marcus, Barneys, and Saks Fifth Avenue along with Borders Books, Music & Cafe. Nearby are such platinum-card international boutiques as Yves Saint Laurent, Cartier, Emporio Armani, Gucci, Hermès, Louis Vuitton, and Gianni Versace.

The **Westfield San Francisco Shopping Centre,** anchored by Bloomingdale's and Nordstrom, is a mammoth mall; it's notable for its gorgeous atriums and its top-notch dining options (no typical food courts here—instead, you'll find branches of a few top local restaurants). The area is also home to the new Barneys CO-OP; the New York institution's SF outpost has high, urban fashion on seven exquisitely appointed floors.

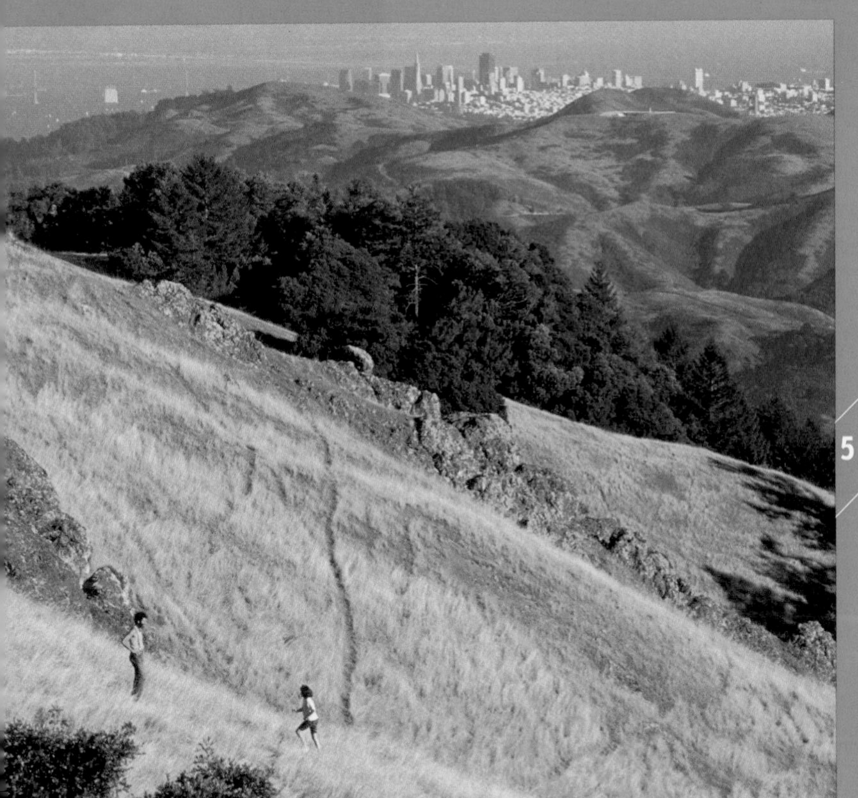

5

The Bay Area

WITH MARIN COUNTY, BERKELEY, OAKLAND, AND THE COASTAL PENINSULA

WORD OF MOUTH

"We . . . caught the ferry over to Sausalito. A stroll along the sheltered waterfront and a close-quarters view of Alcatraz on the way back rounded out a perfect stay in the City by the Bay."

—kiwi_rob

WELCOME TO THE BAY AREA

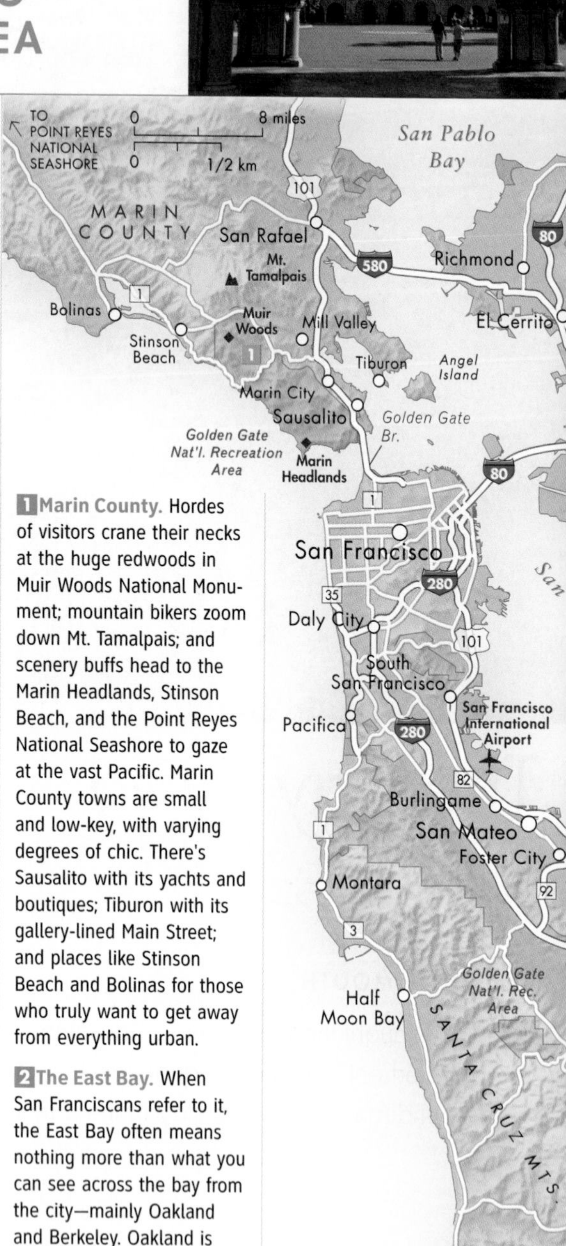

TOP REASONS TO GO

★ **Walk among giants:** Walking into Muir Woods, a mere 12 mi north of the Golden Gate Bridge, is like entering a cathedral built by God.

★ **Attend a reading:** Chances are, an author you admire will be reading somewhere in the Bay Area during your trip. Berkeley draws an especially erudite crowd; Q&A sessions can feel like a grad-school discussion.

★ **Bite into the "Gourmet Ghetto":** Eat your way through this area of Berkeley, starting with a slice of pizza from the Cheeseboard.

★ **Sit on a dock by the bay:** Admire the beauty and tranquility of the Bay Area from the rocky, picturesque shores of Sausalito.

★ **Find solitude at Point Reyes National Seashore:** Head here to hike beautifully rugged—and deserted—beaches.

1 Marin County. Hordes of visitors crane their necks at the huge redwoods in Muir Woods National Monument; mountain bikers zoom down Mt. Tamalpais; and scenery buffs head to the Marin Headlands, Stinson Beach, and the Point Reyes National Seashore to gaze at the vast Pacific. Marin County towns are small and low-key, with varying degrees of chic. There's Sausalito with its yachts and boutiques; Tiburon with its gallery-lined Main Street; and places like Stinson Beach and Bolinas for those who truly want to get away from everything urban.

2 The East Bay. When San Franciscans refer to it, the East Bay often means nothing more than what you can see across the bay from the city—mainly Oakland and Berkeley. Oakland is gritty and diverse, home to a buzzing arts scene, Jack London Square, and famous jazz joint Yoshi's. Berkeley, defined by its University of California campus and liberal-to-radical politics, is a place of renegade spirits, bursting bookstores, and creature comforts like Alice Waters' Chez Panisse.

3 The Coastal Peninsula. The coastal towns between Santa Cruz and San Francisco have long been agricultural outposts, supplying food for the missions and the towns that succeeded them. Today artichokes and other cool-weather crops still grow in coastal fields, but the big attraction here is the beaches. The shoreline is nearly all public and varies widely from long, sandy stretches to tide pool–covered flats.

GETTING ORIENTED

Cross the Golden Gate Bridge and head north to reach Marin County's rolling hills and green expanses, where residents enjoy an haute-suburban lifestyle. East of the city, across the San Francisco Bay, are Berkeley and Oakland, which most Bay Area residents refer to as the East Bay. Life here feels more relaxed than in the city—but every bit as vibrant. To the south of San Francisco lies the peninsula; which part you see depends on your route: Highway 1 passes through a sparsely populated landscape along the coast, while inland a tangle of freeways leads to bustling Silicon Valley.

5

Updated by Fiona G. Parrott and Cheryl Crabtree

It's rare for a metropolis to compete with its suburbs for visitors, but the view from any of San Francisco's hilltops shows that the Bay Area's temptations extend far beyond the city limits.

To the north is Marin County, the beauty queen: small but chic villages like Tiburon and Mill Valley plus dramatic coastal scenery. East of town are two energetic urban centers, Berkeley and Oakland. Formerly radical Berkeley is getting more glam, while Oakland is slowly shaking off its image as San Francisco's ugly stepsister. Along the peninsula south of San Francisco you'll find a largely undeveloped coastline dotted with small towns and wild beaches—a place so peaceful it's hard to believe that behind the rolling green hills lies Silicon Valley.

PLANNING

WHEN TO GO

For such a small place, the Bay Area has a surprisingly varied climate. The rainy season runs from about November through March, and temperatures in the 50s and 60s are generally constant across the region. But on any given day between April and November, 10 different local cities can have 10 different forecasts. Some things hold constant: protected from the fog, inland areas stay warm and dry, while coastal areas seesaw between sun and fog (and rarely get truly hot). The East Bay is usually warmer and sunnier than points west, though when the fog rolls in hard it can hit here, too.

Berkeley is a university town, and the rhythm of the school year might affect your visit. It's easier to navigate the streets and find parking near the university between semesters, but there's also less buzz around town. Surprisingly, summer is chock-full of students attending the many summer sessions on campus. Moving-in weeks before the fall semester bring a massive influx of students *and* parents and other family members—definitely not the best time to take a campus tour.

GETTING HERE AND AROUND

BART TRAVEL

If you don't want to worry about finding a parking space, using public transportation to reach Berkeley or Oakland is ideal. BART (Bay Area Rapid Transit) has several central stops in both towns. The under- and above-ground trains make stops in downtown Berkeley and in several parts of Oakland, including Rockridge. Use the Lake Merritt Station for the Oakland Museum and southern Lake Merritt; the Oakland City Center–12th Street Station for downtown, Chinatown, and Old Oakland; and the 19th Street Station for the Paramount Theatre and the north side of Lake Merritt. From the Berkeley (not North Berkeley) Station, walk a block up Center Street to get to the western edge of campus. Both trips take 30 to 45 minutes one way from the center of San Francisco.

Contacts BART (☎ *510/465–2278* 🌐 *www.bart.gov*).

BOAT AND FERRY TRAVEL

For sheer romance, nothing beats the ferry; there's service from San Francisco to Sausalito and Tiburon in Marin County, and to Alameda and Oakland in the East Bay.

The Golden Gate Ferry crosses the bay to Sausalito from the south wing of San Francisco's Ferry Building (at Market Street and the Embarcadero). Blue & Gold Fleet ferries depart daily for Sausalito and Tiburon from Pier 41 at Fisherman's Wharf; weekday commuter ferries leave from the Ferry Building for Tiburon. The trip to Sausalito takes 30 minutes; to Tiburon, it takes 20 minutes. Expect more crowds on weekends and during peak commute times.

The Angel Island–Tiburon Ferry sails across the strait to the island daily April through September and weekends the rest of the year.

The Alameda/Oakland Ferry runs several times daily between San Francisco's Ferry Building or Pier 39, Alameda, and the Clay Street dock near Oakland's Jack London Square; one-way tickets are $6.25. The trip lasts 30 to 45 minutes, depending on your departure point, and leads to the heart of Oakland's gentrified shopping and restaurant district. Arriving in Oakland by boat conveys a historic sense of the city's heyday as a World War II–era shipbuilding center. Purchase tickets on board.

Boat and Ferry Lines Angel Island–Tiburon Ferry (☎ *415/435–2131* 🌐 *www.angelislandferry.com*). **Blue & Gold Fleet** (☎ *415/705–8200* 🌐 *www.blueandgoldfleet.com*). **Golden Gate Ferry** (☎ *415/923–2000* 🌐 *www.goldengateferry.org*). **Alameda/Oakland Ferry** (☎ *510/522–3300* 🌐 *www.eastbayferry.com*).

BUS TRAVEL

Golden Gate Transit buses travel to Sausalito, Tiburon, and Mill Valley from 1st and Mission streets as well as from other points in San Francisco. For Mt. Tamalpais State Park and West Marin (e.g., Stinson Beach, Bolinas and Point Reyes Station), take Bus 10, 70, or 80 to Marin City; in Marin City transfer to the West Marin Stagecoach; call or check online for routes and schedules. San Francisco MuniBus 76 runs hourly from 4th and Townsend streets to the Marin Headlands Visitor Center on Sunday and major holidays only. The trip takes roughly 45 minutes.

AC Transit buses run frequently between San Francisco's TransBay Terminal (at 1st and Mission streets) and the East Bay. AC Transit's F and FS lines stop near the university and 4th Street shopping in Berkeley. Lines C and P travel to Piedmont in Oakland. The O bus stops at the edge of Chinatown near downtown Oakland.

Bus Lines **Golden Gate Transit** (☎ *415/455-2000* 🌐 *www.goldengate.org*). **San Francisco Muni** (☎ *415/701-2311* 🌐 *www.sfmuni.com*). **West Marin Stagecoach** (☎ *415/526-3239* 🌐 *www.marintransit.org/stage.html*). **AC Transit** (☎ *511* 🌐 *www.actransit.org*).

CAR TRAVEL

To visit the outer reaches of Marin, a car is essential (unless you want to spend all day on the bus). Head north on U.S.101 and cross the Golden Gate Bridge. For Sausalito, take the first exit, Alexander Avenue, just past Vista Point; after winding all the way down the hill to the water, the road becomes Bridgeway. Continue north on Bridgeway to the municipal parking lot near the center of town—but expect the lot to be full on weekends, in which case you should continue north and hunt for street spots. For Tiburon, exit at Tiburon Boulevard. For Mill Valley, exit at East Blithedale, continue west on East Blithedale to Throckmorton Avenue, and turn left to reach Lytton Square. All three trips take 20 to 45 minutes one way, depending on traffic.

The Marin Headlands are a logical stop en route to Sausalito, but reaching them can be tricky. After exiting on Alexander Avenue, take the first left (signs read San Francisco/U.S. 101 South), pass through a tunnel under the freeway, and make a hard right up the steep hill just before the road merges back on to the bridge toward San Francisco. You should see a small sign that says Forts Barry and Cronkhite. Conzelman Road follows the cliffs that face the ocean and becomes one-way before a spectacular drop toward Point Bonita; Bunker Road is a less spectacular inland route through Rodeo to the forts.

For Muir Woods and Mt. Tamalpais, take the Route 1–Stinson Beach exit off U.S. 101 and follow Route 1 west and then north. Both trips may take from 30 minutes to more than an hour, depending on traffic. Allow plenty of extra time on summer weekends.

To reach the East Bay from San Francisco, take I–80 East across the Bay Bridge. For most of Berkeley, take the University Avenue exit through downtown Berkeley to the campus or take the Ashby Avenue exit and turn left on Telegraph Avenue to the traditional campus entrance; there's a parking garage on Channing Way. For Oakland, take I–580 off the Bay Bridge to the Grand Avenue exit for Lake Merritt. To reach downtown and the waterfront, take I–980 from I–580 and exit at 12th Street. Both trips take about 30 minutes unless it's rush hour or a weekend afternoon, when you should count on an hour.

SIGHTSEEING GUIDES

Blue & Gold Fleet has a one-hour narrated tour of the San Francisco Bay, for $22, with frequent daily departures from Pier 39 in San Francisco. Super Sightseeing offers a four-hour bus tour of Muir Woods. The tour, which stops in Sausalito en route, leaves at 9 am and 2 pm daily from North Point and Taylor Street at Fisherman's Wharf and costs

$50 ($47 senior citizens, $26 ages 5–11); 24-hour advance reservations are recommended. Great Pacific Tour Co. runs four-hour morning and afternoon tours of Muir Woods and Sausalito for $55 ($53 senior citizens, $43 ages 5–11), with hotel pickup in 14-passenger vans with excellent interpretation.

By Bus and Van Blue & Gold Fleet (☎ *415/705–8200* 🌐 *www.blueandgoldfleet.com*). **Great Pacific Tour Co.** (☎ *415/626–4499* 🌐 *www.greatpacifictour.com*). **Super Sightseeing** (☎ *415/353–5310* 🌐 *www.supersightseeing.com*).

RESTAURANTS

The Bay Area is home to some of the most popular and innovative restaurants in the country, including Chez Panisse Café & Restaurant, in Berkeley, and Lark Creek Inn, in Larkspur—for which reservations must be made well in advance. Expect an emphasis on locally grown produce, hormone-free meats, and California wine. The coast provides a spectacular waterfront setting for dining as well as lodging; in many instances the views are the most important part of the experience. Keep in mind that many Marin cafés don't serve dinner, and that dinner service ends on the early side. (No 10 pm reservations in this neck of the woods.)

5

HOTELS

There aren't many hotels in Berkeley or Oakland, but Marin is a destination where hotels package themselves as cozy retreats. Summer is often booked well in advance, despite weather that is often mercurial and sometimes downright chilly. Along the coastal peninsula, accommodations tend to have homegrown character and cater to San Franciscans and weekend visitors here for a romantic getaway. Because of the weekend demand on the coast you'd be wise to make reservations as far in advance as possible. Inland Peninsula and South Bay lodgings generally attract business travelers—most are chain motels and hotels, though a handful of B&Bs have popped up in recent years. During the week, when business conventions are in full swing, many of these hotels are fully booked up two weeks in advance. However, some are nearly empty on weekends—this is when rates plummet and package deals abound.

WHAT IT COSTS

	¢	$	$$	$$$	$$$$
Restaurants	under $10	$10–$14	$15–$22	$23–$30	over $30
Hotels	under $90	$90–$149	$150–$199	$200–$250	over $250

Restaurant prices are per person for a main course at dinner, or the equivalent. Hotel prices are for two people in a standard double room in high season.

VISITOR INFORMATION

Contact Marin Convention & Visitors Bureau (*1 Mitchell Blvd., Suite B, San Rafael* ☎ *415/925–2060* 🌐 *www.visitmarin.org*).

MARIN COUNTY

Marin is quite simply a knockout—some go so far as to call it spectacular and wild. This isn't an extravagant claim, since more than 40% of the county (180,000 acres), including the majority of the coastline, is parkland. The territory ranges from chaparral, grassland, and coastal scrub to broadleaf and evergreen forest, redwood, salt marsh, and rocky shoreline.

WORD OF MOUTH

"Be sure to get out onto the water. A ferry ride to Sausalito, Tiburon, or Larkspur will reward you with wonderful views and there are things to be seen in each of those places."
—Grasshopper

Regardless of its natural beauty, what gave the county its reputation was Cyra McFadden's 1977 book *The Serial,* a literary soap opera that depicted the county as a bastion of hot-tubbing and "open" marriages. Indeed old-time bohemian, but also increasingly jet-set, Marinites still spend a lot of time outdoors, and surfing, cycling, and hiking are common after-work and weekend activities. Adrenaline junkies mountain bike down Mt. Tamalpais, and those who want solitude take a walk on one of Point Reyes's many empty beaches. The hot tub remains a popular destination after hours, but things have changed since the boho days. Artists and musicians who arrived in the 1960s have set the tone for mellow country towns, but Marin is now undeniably chic, with BMWs supplanting VW buses as the cars of choice.

Most cosmopolitan is Sausalito, the town just over the Golden Gate Bridge from San Francisco. Across the inlet from Sausalito, Tiburon and Belvedere are lined with grand homes that regularly appear on fund-raising circuits, and to the north, landlocked Mill Valley is a hub of wining and dining and tony boutiques.

In general, the farther you get from the Golden Gate Bridge the more country things become, and West Marin is about as far as you can get from the big city, both physically and ideologically. Separated from the inland county by the slopes and ridges of giant Mt. Tamalpais, this territory beckons to mavericks, artists, ocean lovers, and other free spirits. Stinson Beach has tempered its isolationist attitude to accommodate out-of-towners, as have Inverness and Point Reyes Station. Bolinas, on the other hand, would prefer you not know its location.

SAUSALITO

2 mi north of Golden Gate Bridge.

Bougainvillea-covered hillsides and an expansive yacht harbor give Sausalito the feel of an Adriatic resort. The town sits on the northwestern edge of San Francisco Bay, where it's sheltered from the ocean by the Marin Headlands; the mostly mild weather here is perfect for strolling and outdoor dining. Nevertheless, morning fog and afternoon winds can roll over the hills without warning, funneling through the central part of Sausalito once known as Hurricane Gulch.

South on Bridgeway (toward San Francisco), which snakes between the bay and the hills, a waterside esplanade is lined with restaurants on piers that lure diners with good seafood and even better views. Stairs along the west side of Bridgeway climb the hill to wooded neighborhoods filled with both rustic and opulent homes. As you amble along Bridgeway past boutiques, gift shops, and galleries, you'll notice the absence of basic services. If you need an aspirin or some groceries (or if you want to see the locals), you'll have to head to Caledonia Street, which runs parallel to Bridgeway, north of the ferry terminus and inland a couple of blocks. The streets closest to the ferry landing flaunt their fair share of shops selling T-shirts and kitschy souvenirs. Venture into some of the side streets or narrow alleyways to catch a bit more of the town's taste for eccentric jewelry and handmade crafts.

■ TIP→ The ferry is the best way to get to Sausalito from San Francisco; you get more romance (and less traffic) and disembark in the heart of downtown.

Like much of San Francisco, Sausalito had a raffish reputation before it went upscale. Discovered in 1775 by Spanish explorers and named Sausalito (Little Willow) for the trees growing around its springs, the town served as a port for whaling ships during the 19th century. By the mid-1800s wealthy San Franciscans were making Sausalito their getaway across the bay. They built lavish Victorian summer homes in

The crowded piers and rolling hillside of the Sausalito waterfront.

the hills, many of which still stand. In 1875 the railroad from the north connected with ferryboats to San Francisco, bringing the merchant and working classes with it. This influx of hardworking, fun-loving folk polarized the town into "wharf rats" and "hill snobs," and the waterfront area grew thick with saloons, gambling dens, and bordellos. Bootleggers flourished during Prohibition, and shipyard workers swelled the town's population in the 1940s.

Sausalito developed its bohemian flair in the 1950s and '60s, when a group of artists, led by a charismatic Greek portraitist named Varda, established an artists' colony and a houseboat community here. Today more than 450 houseboats are docked in Sausalito, which has since also become a major yachting center. Some of the houseboats are ragged, others deluxe, but all are quirky (one, a miniature replica of a Persian castle, even has an elevator inside). For a close-up view of the community, head north on Bridgeway—Sausalito's main thoroughfare—from downtown, turn right on Gate Six Road, and park where it dead-ends at the public shore. Keep a respectful distance; these are homes, after all, and the residents become a bit prickly from too much ogling.

ESSENTIALS

Visitor Information Sausalito Chamber of Commerce (✉ *780 Bridgeway* ☎ *415/332–0505 or 415/331–7262* 🌐 *www.sausalito.org*).

GETTING HERE AND AROUND

From San Francisco by car or bike, follow US 101 north across the Golden Gate Bridge and take the first exit, Alexander Avenue, just past Vista Point; continue down the winding hill to the water to where the road becomes Bridgeway. Buses 10 and 22 will drop you off in downtown Sausalito, and the ferries dock downtown as well. The center of town is flat, with plenty of sidewalks and bay views. It's a pleasure and a must to explore on foot.

EXPLORING

Bay Area Discovery Museum. Sitting at the base of the Golden Gate Bridge, this indoor-outdoor museum offers entertaining and enlightening hands-on exhibits for children under 8. Kids and their families can fish from a boat at the indoor wharf, imagine themselves as marine biologists in the Wave Workshop, and play outdoors at Lookout Cove (made up of scaled-down sea caves, tidal pools, and even a re-created shipwreck). At Tot Zone, toddlers and preschoolers can dress up in animal costumes and crawl through miniature tunnels. From San Francisco, take the Alexander Avenue exit from U.S. 101 and follow signs to East Fort Baker. ✉ *557 McReynolds Rd., at East Fort Baker* ☎ *415/339–3900* 🌐 *www.baykidsmuseum.org* 🎫 *$10; children under 1 free* ⏲ *Tues.–Fri. 9–4, weekends 10–5.*

Bay Model. An anonymous-looking World War II shipyard building holds one of Sausalito's great treasures: the sprawling (more than 1½ acres) Bay Model of the entire San Francisco Bay and the San Joaquin–Sacramento River delta, complete with flowing water. The U.S. Army Corps of Engineers uses the model to reproduce the rise and fall of tides, the flow of currents, and the other physical forces at work on the bay. *2100 Bridgeway, at Marinship Way* ☎ *415/332–3870 recorded information, 415/332–3871 operator assistance* 🌐 *www.spn.usace.army.mil/bmvc* 🎫 *Free* ⏲ *Memorial Day–Labor Day, Tues.–Fri. 9–4, weekends 10–5; Labor Day–Memorial Day, Tues.–Sat. 9–4.*

Drinking Fountain. On the waterfront between the Hotel Sausalito and the Sausalito Yacht Club is an unusual historic landmark—a drinking fountain. It's inscribed with "Have a drink on Sally" in remembrance of Sally Stanford, the former San Francisco madam who later became the town's mayor in the 1970s. Sassy Sally, as they called her, would have appreciated the fountain's eccentric custom attachment: a knee-level basin that reads "Have a drink on Leland" in memory of her beloved dog.

NEED A BREAK?

Judging by the crowds gathered outside Hamburgers (✉ *737 Bridgeway* ☎ *415/332–9471*), you'd think someone was juggling flaming torches out front. They're really gaping at the juicy hand-formed beef patties sizzling on a rotating grill. Brave the line (it moves fast), get your food to go, and head for the esplanade to enjoy the sweeping views. Hours are 11 am to 5 pm.

5

Plaza Viña del Mar. The landmark Plaza Viña del Mar, named for Sausalito's sister city in Chile, marks the center of town. Flanked by two 14-foot-tall elephant statues (created in 1915 for the Panama-Pacific International Exposition), the fountain is a great setting for snapshots and people-watching. ✉ *Bridgeway and Park St.*

Sausalito Visitors Center and Historical Exhibit. Get your bearings and find out what's happening in town at the Sausalito Visitors Center and Historical Exhibit, operated by the town's historical society. It's closed Monday. ✉ *780 Bridgeway* ☎ *415/332–0505.*

WHERE TO EAT

$$$ SEAFOOD Fodor's Choice ★

✕ **Fish.** If you're wondering where the locals go, this is the place. For fresh seafood, you can't beat this gleaming dockside fish house a mile north of downtown. Order at the counter and then grab a seat by the floor-to-ceiling windows or at a picnic table on the pier, overlooking the yachts and fishing boats. Most of the sustainably caught fish is hauled in from the owner's boats, right at the dock outside. Try the ceviche, crab Louis, cioppino, barbecue oysters, or anything fresh that day that's being grilled over the oak-wood fire. Outside, kids can doodle with sidewalk chalk on the pier. ✉ *350 Harbor Dr.* ☎ *415/331–3474* *Reservations not accepted* *No credit cards.*

$$ FRENCH BISTRO

✕ **Le Garage.** When Sausalito executives and entrepreneurs want a stylish lunch with a bayside setting, they head to Chef Olivier Souvestre's local lunch hot spot. Brittany born Souvestre serves traditional French bistro fare in a relaxed, sidewalk café–style setting. The menu is small, but the dishes are substantial in flavor and presentation. Standouts include frisée salad with poached egg, bacon, croutons, and pancetta vinaigrette; steak frites with a shallot confit and crispy fries; and a chef's selection of cheese or charcuterie with soup and mixed greens. The restaurant only seats 35 inside and 15 outside, so to avoid a long wait for lunch, arrive before 11:30 or after 1:30. ✉ *85 Liberty Ship Way, Suite #109, Sausalito* ☎ *415/332–5625* *No dinner Sun.*

$ SCANDINAVIAN

✕ **Lighthouse Cafe.** A cozy spot with a long coffee bar and dose of Scandinavian flair, this local establishment has been a favorite brunch destination for nearly two decades. The hearty Norwegian salmon omelet with spinach and cream cheese or fruit pancakes, as well as a wide selection of grilled burgers, sandwiches, and Danish specials like meatballs with potato salad always hit the spot, especially on chilly days. They don't take reservations, which means you might need to join the crowd (there normally is one) and wait in line for a table. ✉ *1311 BridgewaySausalito* ☎ *415/331–3034* *www.lighthouse-restaurants.com* *No reservations* *No dinner.*

$$ AMERICAN

✕ **Paradise Bay.** The views from this gem of a restaurant—which is a five-minute walk north of the tourist hub—will make you feel like you're in a secluded paradise; boats, sea kayaks, and the beautiful bay stretch before you. Outdoor seating in the Bay Area doesn't get much better than this, and the inventive, well-balanced, local- and organic-based menu won't disappoint either. Try the Paradise Bay cioppino in a rich tomato-fennel broth or the grilled organic lamb sirloin with goat cheese and garlic flan. The trio crème brûlée—espresso, mango, and coconut—is divine, as is the extensive cocktail list. This is also the perfect place for weekend brunch—the buttermilk ginger pancakes topped with banana and mango are out of this world. ✉ *1200 Bridgeway* ☎ *415/331–3226.*

$$ ITALIAN ★ ✕ **Poggio.** One of the few restaurants in Sausalito to attract both food-savvy locals and tourists, Poggio serves modern Tuscan cuisine in a handsome, open-wall space that spills onto the street. Expect dishes such as grilled lamb chops with roasted eggplant, braised artichokes with polenta, featherlight gnocchi, and pizzas from the open kitchen's wood-fired oven. ✉ *777 Bridgeway* ☎ *415/332–7771* ✍ *Reservations essential.*

$$ JAPANESE ★ ✕ **Sushi Ran.** Sushi aficionados swear that this is the Bay Area's best for raw fish, but don't overlook the excellent Pacific Rim fusions, a result of Japanese ingredients and French cooking techniques, served up in unusual presentations. Because Sushi Ran is so highly ranked among area foodies, book two to seven days in advance for dinner. Otherwise, expect a long wait, which you can soften by sipping one of the 45 by-the-glass sakes from the outstanding wine-and-sake bar. ■ **TIP→ If you wander in after a day of sightseeing and can't get a table, you can dine in the noisy bar.** ✉ *107 Caledonia St.* ☎ *415/332–3620* ⏲ *No lunch weekends.*

5

WHERE TO STAY

For expanded hotel reviews, visit Fodors.com.

$$$ **Casa Madrona.** What began as a small inn in a 19th-century landmark house has expanded over the decades to incorporate a variety of lodgings and a full-service spa, all tiered down the hill in the center of town. **Pros:** elegant new furniture, spacious rooms, central location. **Cons:** rooms in older section don't have a/c or full elevator access, parking is pricey. ✉ *801 Bridgeway* ☎ *415/332–0502 or 800/567–9524* 🌐 *www.casamadrona.com* *60 rooms, 6 suites* *In-room: Wi-Fi. In-hotel: restaurant, spa, fitness center, concierge.*

$$$$ **Cavallo Point.** Set in Golden Gate National Park, this luxury hotel and resort's location is truly one of a kind, featuring turn-of-the-century buildings converted into well-appointed yet eco-friendly rooms. **Pros:** stunning views and numerous activities: a cooking school, yoga classes, and nature walks; spa with a tea bar; art gallery. **Cons:** landscaping feels incomplete, isolated from urban amenities. ✉ *601 Murray Circle, Fort Baker, Sausalito* ☎ *415/339–4700* 🌐 *www.cavallopoint.com* *68 historic and 74 contemporary guest rooms* *In-room: no a/c (some), Internet, Wi-Fi. In hotel: restaurant, room service, bar, meditation pool, gym, spa, water sports, parking, some pets allowed (fee), no-smoking rooms.*

$$ **Hotel Sausalito.** Handmade furniture and tasteful original art and reproductions give this well-run inn the feel of a small European hotel. **Pros:** great staff, excellent central location, feels like home away from home. **Cons:** no room service, some rooms feel cramped. ✉ *16 El Portal* ☎ *415/332–0700 or 888/442–0700* 🌐 *www.hotelsausalito.com* *14 rooms, 2 suites* *In-room: Wi-Fi. In-hotel: concierge* *Breakfast.*

$$$$ **The Inn Above Tide.** This is the only hotel in the Bay Area with balconies literally hanging over the water, and each of its rooms has a perfect-10 view that takes in wild Angel Island as well as the city lights across the bay. **Pros:** great complimentary breakfast, minutes from restaurants/attractions, free in-room binoculars let you indulge in the incredible views. **Cons:** costly parking, some rooms are on the

small side. ⊠ *30 El Portal* ☎ *415/332–9535 or 800/893–8433* ⊕ *www.innabovetide.com* *29 rooms, 3 suites* *In-room: a/c, Wi-Fi. In-hotel: concierge* *Breakfast.*

SPORTS AND THE OUTDOORS

Specializing in sea kayaking, **Sea Trek Ocean Kayaking Center** (⊠ *Schoonmaker Point Marina, off Libertyship Way* ☎ *415/488–1000* ⊕ *www.seatrekkayak.com*) offers guided half-day trips underneath the Golden Gate Bridge and full- and half-day trips to Angel Island, both for beginners. Starlight and full-moon paddles are particularly popular. Trips for experienced kayakers, classes, and rentals are also available. Prices start at $20 per hour for rentals; $65 for a three-hour guided trip.

SF Bay Adventures (⊠ *60 Liberty Ship Way, Suite 4,* ☎ *415/331–0444* ⊕ *www.sfbayadventures.com*) lead specialized nautical tours out and around the bay. Their expert skippers give sunset and full-moon sails as well as fascinating eco and great white shark tours. If you're interested, they can arrange for you to spend the night in a lighthouse or even barbecue on Angel Island.

THE ARTS

The annual **Sausalito Art Festival** (☎ *415/332–3555 or 415/331–3757* ⊕ *www.sausalitoartfestival.org*), held over Labor Day weekend, attracts more than 50,000 people to the northern waterfront area; Blue & Gold Fleet ferries from San Francisco dock at the pier adjacent to the festival. Tickets are $20.

SHOPPING

Something/Anything Gallery. Right where Broadway ends and curves toward the dock, this gallery has a huge array of jewelry and gifts, from unique watches to humorous pendants. With friendly service and carefully crafted mementos of Sausalito, it's easy to find an inexpensive souvenir. ⊠ *20 Princess St., Sausalito* ☎ *415/339–8831.*

Sausalito Ferry Co. This somewhat eccentric but fun local shop is a great place to buy trendy T-shirts, wallets, and clocks. There are plenty of solar-powered bobbleheads, outrageous cocktail napkins, even one-of-a kind key chains. There's often a crowd huddled in front of the store admiring the window display. ⊠ *688 Bridgeway* ☎ *415/332–9590* ⊕ *www.sausalitoferry.com.*

TIBURON

2 mi north of Sausalito, 7 mi north of Golden Gate Bridge.

On a peninsula that was called Punta de Tiburon (Shark Point) by the Spanish explorers, this beautiful Marin County community retains the feel of a village, despite the encroachment of commercial establishments from the downtown area. The harbor faces Angel Island across Raccoon Strait, and San Francisco is directly south across the bay—which makes the views from the decks of harbor restaurants a major attraction. Tiburon is slightly more low-key than Sausalito, and the community favors Sunday brunch and cocktail hour. Since its incarnation, in 1884, when ferries from San Francisco connected the point with a railroad to San Rafael, the town has centered on the waterfront. ■ **TIP→ The ferry is the most relaxing (and fastest) way to get here whenever the weather is pleasant, particularly in summer, allowing you to skip traffic and parking problems. Think about avoiding a midweek visit to Tiburon. Although there will be fewer strollers on the street, most shops close either Tuesday or Wednesday, or both.**

ESSENTIALS

Visitor Information **Tiburon Peninsula Chamber of Commerce** (✉ *96-B Main St.* ☎ *415/435–5633* 🌐 *www.tiburonchamber.org*).

GETTING HERE AND AROUND

By car, head north from San Francisco on US-101 and take the CA 131 exit toward Tiburon Boulevard/E. Blithedale Avenue. Tiburon Boulevard goes briefly inland, then hugs the bay with remarkable views; it's just over four miles from the freeway to downtown. Golden Gate Transit buses 8 and 19 will also take you from San Francisco to downtown Tiburon, as will the Blue & Gold Fleet Ferry service. Tiburon's Main Street is made for wandering down, as are the footpaths that frame the water's edge.

EXPLORING

Ark Row. Past the pink-brick bank building, Main Street is known as Ark Row, and has a tree-shaded walk lined with antiques and specialty stores. Look closely, and you can see that some of the buildings are actually old houseboats. They floated in Belvedere Cove before being beached and transformed into stores. If you're curious about architectural history, the Tiburon Heritage & Arts Commission prints a self-guided walking-tour map, which you can pick up at local businesses. *Ark Row, parallel to Main St.* 🌐 *www.landmarks-society.org*

Main Street. Tiburon's narrow Main Street is on the bay side; you can browse the shops and galleries or relax on a restaurant's deck jutting out over the harbor.

Old St. Hilary's Landmark and Wildflower Preserve. The stark-white Old St. Hilary's Landmark and Wildflower Preserve, an 1886 Carpenter Gothic church barged over from Strawberry Point in 1957, overlooks the town and the bay from its hillside perch. ■ **TIP→ The church is surrounded by a wildflower preserve that's spectacular in May and June, when the rare black jewel flower blooms.** Expect a steep walk uphill to reach the preserve. ✉ *201 Esperanza St., off Mar West St.* ☎ *415/435–1853* 🌐 *www.*

landmarks-society.org *$2 suggested donation* *Apr.–Oct., Wed. and Sun. 1–4 and by appointment.*

Windsor Vineyards. This vineyard gives free tastings of its Sonoma County wines (head for the chardonnay) in a converted 19th-century rooming house on Ark Row. *72 Main St.* *415/435–3113* *www.windsorvineyards.com* *Fri. and Sat. 10–7, Sun.–Thurs. 10–6.*

WORD OF MOUTH

"San Francisco's Marin Headlands is part of the National Park Service, and is a wonderful place for hiking, biking, and walking on the beach. It is also home to the most breath-taking view of the Golden Gate Bridge and the city skyline." —DoreenD

WHERE TO EAT

$$$ AMERICAN **The Caprice.** For more than fifty years this Tiburon landmark has been the place to come to mark special occasions. Perched on a cliff overlooking the bay, it boasts views that are truly spectacular. Looking out from your table it almost feels as if you're eating on water. The soft-yellow walls and starched white tablecloths help to make the space bright and light. Elegant comfort food is their premise, with choices like seared day boat scallops or pan-roasted filet mignon. Polishing off the warm chocolate cake with almond ice cream while gazing out at the sunset and porpoises bobbing in the waves below is a near perfect end to the evening. *2000 Paradise Dr.* *415/435–3400* *www.thecaprice.com* *Closed Mon.*

$$ MEXICAN **Guaymas.** The festive Guaymas restaurant at the ferry terminal claims a knockout view of the bay, handsome whitewashed adobe walls, tile floors, and a heated terrace bar—and it serves a top-notch margarita. A large open kitchen churns out fairly authentic Mexican dishes such as ceviche, *carnitas uruapan* (slow-roasted pork with salsa and black beans), mesquite-grilled fish, tamales, and a long list of others. **TIP→ Sunday lunch is very popular, so make a reservation.** *5 Main St.* *415/435–6300* *Reservations essential.*

$ AMERICAN **New Morning Cafe.** If you ran straight for the morning ferry and didn't have time to eat, nab breakfast at this homey café with cozy booths and bright tablecloths. Omelets and scrambles are served all day long alongside more innovative egg dishes such as the "Scrumptious," which mixes in vegetables. If you're past morning treats, choose from the many soups, salads, and sandwiches. It's open 6:30 am to 2:30 pm weekdays and 6:30 am to 4 pm weekends. *1696 Tiburon Blvd.* *415/435–4315* *No dinner.*

$$ AMERICAN **Sam's Anchor Cafe.** Open since 1921, this casual dockside restaurant with mahogany wainscoting is the town's most famous eatery. Today most people flock here for the deck, where out-of-towners and old salts sit shoulder to shoulder for bay views, beer, seafood, and Ramos fizzes. The lunch menu has the usual suspects—burgers, sandwiches, salads, fried fish with tartar sauce—and you'll sit on plastic chairs at tables covered with blue-and-white-checked oilcloths. At night you can find standard seafood dishes with vegetarian and meat options. Expect a wait for outside tables on weekends (there are no reservations for deck seating or weekend lunch). Mind the seagulls; they know no restraint. *27 Main St.* *415/435–4527.*

$ PIZZA ✕ **Waypoint Pizza.** A nautical decor theme and a tasty "between the sheets" pizza-style sandwich are signatures of this creative pizzeria that also serves slices and whole gourmet pies. Booths are brightened with blue-checked tablecloths, and a playful air is added by indoor deck chairs, a picnic table complete with umbrella, and lighthouse salt-and-pepper shakers. If you're dining alone, peruse the aluminum rack for an excellent selection of magazines and newspapers. ✉ *15 Main St.* ☎ *415/435–3440.*

WHERE TO STAY

For expanded hotel reviews, visit Fodors.com.

$$ ★ **Waters Edge Hotel.** Checking into this elegant hotel feels like tucking away into a inviting retreat by the water—the views are stunning and the lighting is perfect. **Pros:** complimentary wine and cheese for guests every evening, restaurants/sights are minutes away. **Cons:** no room service, fitness center is offsite, not a great place to bring small children. ✉ *25 Main St.* ☎ *415/789–5999 or 877/789–5999* 🌐 *www.marinhotels.com* *23 rooms* *In-room: Wi-Fi. In-hotel: concierge* *Breakfast.*

5

SHOPPING

The Candy Store on Main Street. If you long for sheets of candy dots or chewy wax bottles, come here to score the retro candy of your childhood. There's also ice cream, freshly made fudge, and a space-age-looking dispenser for pucker powder. ✉ *7 Main St., Tiburon* ☎ *415/435–0434.*

Schoenberg Guitars. Small, narrow, and chockablock with handmade guitars, this shop is a treat even for those who don't play music. Dozens, if not hundreds, of guitars varying in size, shape, and color hang from the walls and stand against the polished wood floor. There is an organized beauty to the layout of this place and a comforting sense of musical harmony. ✉ *106 Main St.* ☎ *415/789–0846.*

MILL VALLEY

2 mi north of Sausalito, 4 mi north of Golden Gate Bridge.

One of just a few towns that are simultaneously woodsy and chic, Mill Valley has a dual personality. Here, as elsewhere in the county, the foundation is a superb natural setting. Virtually surrounded by parkland, the town lies at the base of Mt. Tamalpais, the Bay Area's tallest mountain, and includes dense redwood groves traversed by countless creeks. But this is no lumber camp. Smart restaurants and chichi boutiques line the streets, and more rock stars than one might suspect make their homes here.

The rustic village flavor is not a modern conceit but a holdover from the town's early days as a logging camp. In 1896 the Mill Valley and Mt. Tamalpais Scenic Railroad—called "the crookedest railroad in the world" because of its curvy tracks—began transporting visitors from Mill Valley to the top of Mt. Tam and down to Muir Woods, and the town soon became a vacation retreat for joyriding city slickers. The trains stopped running in the 1940s, but you can see the old railway depot: the 1924 building has been transformed into the popular Depot Bookstore & Cafe, at 87 Throckmorton Avenue.

The small downtown area, no more than five blocks square, has the constant bustle of a leisure community; even at noon on a Tuesday, people are out shopping for fancy cookware and lacy pajamas.

ESSENTIALS

Visitor Information Mill Valley Chamber of Commerce (✉ *85 Throckmorton Ave.* ☎ *415/388–9700* 🌐 *www.millvalley.org*).

GETTING HERE AND AROUND

By car, from San Francisco head north on U.S. 101 then exit at East Blithedale, continue west on East Blithedale to Throckmorton Avenue; turn left to reach Lytton Square, then park. The Golden Gate Transit Route 4 bus leaves for Mill Valley from 8th and Folsom (downtown San Francisco) every thirty minutes during commute hours. Check their schedule for details. Once here, explore the streets on foot; the town is great for strolling.

EXPLORING

Lytton Square. In the center of it all is this square, at the corner of Miller and Throckmorton avenues, where locals and visitors congregate on weekends to socialize in the many coffeehouses.

Old Mill Park. To see one of the numerous outdoor oases that make Mill Valley so appealing, follow Throckmorton Avenue ¼ mi south from Lytton Square to Old Mill Park, a shady patch of redwoods that shelters a playground and reconstructed sawmill. From the park, Cascade Drive winds its way past creek-side homes to the trailheads of several forest paths.

OFF THE BEATEN PATH

Marin County Civic Center. This wonder of arches, circles, and skylights was Frank Lloyd Wright's last major architectural undertaking. You can wander about on your own or take a docent-led tour of the complex. Tours ($5) leave from the gift shop, on the second floor, on Wednesday mornings at 10:30. If you can't make it on a Wednesday, pick up the self-guided tour map for 50 cents at the gift shop. Don't miss the photographs on the first floor, which show Marin County homes designed by Wright. There's also an excellent California library here for bibliophiles and oral-history buffs. ✉ *3501 Civic Center Dr., on San Pedro Rd., San Rafael* ☎ *415/499–7009* *Free* *Weekdays 8–5.*

WHERE TO EAT

$$$ AMERICAN

✕ **The Balboa Café.** With intimate lighting, rich wood accents, and fresh-pressed white linens, this cafe offers an upscale dining experience. Hanging on the walls are old black-and-white photos depicting Mill Valley in its lumber years. The bar is so busy that you'll be lucky if your elbow gets anywhere near it. Although the cocktails are not as stiff as their price tags, the food is creative, local, and beautifully presented. Try the Black Angus rib eye, wild mushroom risotto, or seared sea scallops—and be sure to save room for the blueberry brioche bread pudding. The wine list is extensive, and even offers wines from Marin County. If you prefer something on the lighter side, they purify and carbonate their own water. ✉ *38 Miller Ave.* ☎ *415/381–7321* *Reservations essential.*

$$$ AMERICAN ✕ **Buckeye Roadhouse.** This is Mill Valley's secret den of decadence, where house-smoked meats and fish, grilled steaks, and old-fashioned dishes such as brisket bring the locals coming back for more. They also serve beautiful organic, locally grown salads and desserts so heavenly—like their rich but light crème brûlée—you'll just about melt into the floor. The look of the 1937 roadhouse is decidedly hunting-lodge chic, with trophy heads and a river-rock fireplace dominating one wall. Marin County's Jaguar-driving bon vivants pack the place every night. The busy but cozy bar with elegant mahogany paneling and soft lighting is a good place to quench your thirst for a Marin martini or Californian Merlot. ✉ *15 Shoreline Hwy.* ☎ *415/331–2600* *Reservations essential.*

$ FRENCH/AMERICAN ✕ **Champagne.** This adorable little bakery/café on Mill Valley's main shopping street is a nice place to pop into for breakfast, a light lunch, dinner, or afternoon pick-me-up. Filled with light, authentic French decor and only a dozen tables, Champagne serves amazing crêpes with roasted chicken, creamed spinach, and Swiss cheese, as well as an assortment of savory flatbreads—try the pesto and tomato version. It's a popular place for breakfast, too, with a wide selection of omelets, as well as the perennial favorite: brioche French toast with bacon. The afternoon crowd keeps the tables busy as they chat over cappuccinos, raspberry-almond croissants, and meringue cookies. There's also a tempting assortment of baked goods to take home with you. ✉ *41 Throckmorton Ave.* ☎ *415/380–0410.*

$$ AMERICAN ✕ **The Dipsea Cafe.** There is no better place for breakfast than the Dipsea, which is named after the gorgeous trail that stretches from Mill Valley to Stinson Beach. Locals crowd its cozy interior most mornings, but weekends are especially popular. Choose from huge plates of French toast, eggs Benedict, and huevos rancheros; the homemade fries and jam that accompany the breakfast entrées are to die for. The café also serves hearty lunches, like Chinese salad with seared salmon and enormous BLTs. This is a great spot to fuel up on your way to Muir Woods or Stinson Beach. ✉ *200 Shoreline Hwy.* ☎ *415/381–0298* *No dinner Sun.–Thurs.*

$ MEXICAN ✕ **Joe's Taco Lounge.** A funky, bright lounge (and it really does feel like someone's lounge), this is a fun place to go for a casual, cheap, and delicious Mexican meal. There are all sorts of colorful relics on the walls, and chili-pepper lights adorn the windows. The signature dishes are fish tacos and snapper burritos—which are generous in both size and flavor. The organic burger with spicy fries and the fire-grilled corn on the cob are also yummy. Choose from a wide selection of Mexican beers or go for a wine-based margarita, which is refreshingly tasty. This is a popular place for families between 5 and 7 pm. ✉ *382 Miller Ave.* ☎ *415/383–8164.*

$$$ NEW AMERICAN ★ ✕ **Lark Creek Inn.** Occupying a refurbished 100-year-old house surrounded by lush, mature gardens and towering redwoods, this is one of Marin's prettiest—and best—restaurants, especially for Sunday brunch. The menu, which changes daily, highlights top-notch meats and organic produce from local farmers. Try the Caesar salad, which boasts a secret ingredient and is succulently presented with whole leaf spears. Butterscotch pudding, their signature dessert, sounds humble, but has deep flavor. Sit outside

on the patio or inside the country-elegant dining room beneath a dramatic greenhouse ceiling. Be mindful that all this beauty of place and its plates comes at a price. ✉ *234 Magnolia Ave., Larkspur* ☎ *415/924–7766* ✍ *Reservations essential* ⊗ *No lunch Mon.–Sat.*

$$ ITALIAN ✕ **Piazza D'Angelo.** In the heart of downtown, busy D'Angelo's is known for its osso buco and veal saltimbocca, as well as pastas and delicious crème brûlée. The food is authentic and fresh; another draw is the scene, especially in the lounge area, which hosts a lively cocktail hour packed with beautiful people and serves food until 10 or 11 pm—late for Mill Valley. The sprawling space encompasses a bright front room, romantic booths, and a warm patio. ✉ *22 Miller Ave.* ☎ *415/388–2000.*

WORD OF MOUTH

"Mountain Home Inn is perfect [since] it is just above Muir Woods, in fact there is a trail down to Muir Woods just across the street from Mountain Home. It's 1,000 feet down, over a mile, steep but the trail is good, with wooden steps. . . ."
—sequoia370

WHERE TO STAY

For expanded hotel reviews, visit Fodors.com.

$$$ **Mill Valley Inn.** The only hotel in downtown Mill Valley has smart-looking rooms done up in Tuscan colors of ocher and olive, with handcrafted beds, armoires, and lamps by local artisans. **Pros:** minutes from local shops and restaurants, great complimentary Continental breakfast. **Cons:** dark in winter months because of surrounding trees, some rooms are not accessible via elevator. ✉ *165 Throckmorton Ave.* ☎ *415/389–6608 or 800/595–2100* 🌐 *www.marinhotels.com* *25 rooms, 1 suite, 2 cottages* *In-room: a/c, Wi-Fi. In-hotel: no elevator (some)* *Breakfast.*

$$$ ★ **Mountain Home Inn.** Abutting 40,000 acres of state and national parks, the inn sits on the skirt of Mt. Tamalpais, where you can follow hiking trails all the way to Stinson Beach. **Pros:** amazing deck and views, peaceful, remote setting. **Cons:** nearest town is a 20-minute drive away, restaurant can get very crowded on sunny weekend days. ✉ *810 Panoramic Hwy.* ☎ *415/381–9000* 🌐 *www.mtnhomeinn.com* *10 rooms* *In-room: no a/c, no TV, Wi-Fi. In-hotel: restaurant, bar* *Breakfast.*

NIGHTLIFE AND THE ARTS

The well-regarded **Mill Valley Film Festival** (☎ *415/383–5256* 🌐 *www.mvff.com*), held annually in early October, shows everything from features and documentaries to experimental works.

The **Mill Valley Fall Arts Festival** (☎ *415/383–5256* 🌐 *www.mvfaf.org*) takes place in mid-September in Old Mill Park, with live music, a kids' stage, and artisans selling crafts, jewelry, and art.

Beerworks. Serving over one hundred local, national, and international beers, from ale to port to lager, Beerworks truly has a beer for everyone at its long polished bar. They also serve tapas-style foods: cheese plates, olives, homemade pretzels, and sandwiches. It's the perfect place to rest your feet after wandering the town or hiking Mt. Tamalpais. ✉ *173 Throckmorton Ave.* ☎ *415/336–3596.*

SHOPPING

The area around Throckmorton Avenue in downtown Mill Valley brims with stylish and quirky stores—indies as well as chains. One of the chains, Banana Republic, actually began life here as a small safari-focused retailer.

Book Passage. This sprawling independent bookstore in nearby Corte Madera is a magnet for book lovers. The calendar of author events is packed with readings by such big names as Alice Walker, Calvin Trillin, Michael Connelly, and Peter Mayle. Pick-me-up snacks are available at the in-store café. ✉ *The Marketplace, 51 Tamal Vista Blvd., Corte Madera* ☎ *415/927–0960 or 800/999–7909.*

Jay Lina's. Budget fashionistas are lured into this chic consignment store, where Prada dresses, Seven jeans, even Chanel bags are offered at reasonable prices. The items are carefully selected and easy to find; no need to rummage crowded racks. ✉ *19 E. Blithedale Ave.* ☎ *415/388–4682.* 5

Maison Rêve. French farmhouse meets contemporary style here. Clusters of interesting objects, such as vintage glass bottles, gather gracefully in vignettes. The price range is admirable, with unique finds possible at a reasonable cost. They also have charming children's gifts. ✉ *108 Throckmorton Ave., Mill Valley* ☎ *415/383–9700.*

The Tyler Florence Shop. Stock up here on everything you need for cooking—even kitchen gadgets you didn't know existed. This celebrity chef shop has the works, from chicken-shaped hardboiled egg holders to charms for crystal flutes, even copper frying pans. And if you want to escape into one of Florence's many cookbooks, there's a little library in the back with leather sofas and animal heads hanging from the wall. ✉ *59 Throckmorton Ave.* ☎ *415/380–9200* 🌐 *www.tylerflorence.com.*

THE MARIN HEADLANDS

★ The term "Golden Gate" may now be synonymous with the world-famous bridge, but it originally referred to the grassy, poppy-strewn hills flanking the passageway into San Francisco Bay. To the north of the gate lie the Marin Headlands, part of the Golden Gate National Recreation Area (GGNRA) and the most dramatic scenery in these parts. The raw beauty of the headlands, which consist of several small but steep bluffs, is particularly striking if you've just come from the enclosed silence of the nearby redwood groves. Windswept hills plunge down to the ocean, and creek-fed thickets shelter swaying wildflowers.

The headlands stretch from the Golden Gate Bridge to Muir Beach. Photographers flock to the southern headlands for shots of the city, with the Golden Gate Bridge in the foreground and the skyline on the horizon. Equally remarkable are the views north along the coast and out to sea, where the Farallon Islands are visible on clear days. ■ **TIP→ Almost any of the roads, all very windy, offer great coast views, especially as you drive at higher elevations. You'll see copious markers for scenic spots.**

The headlands' strategic position at the mouth of San Francisco Bay made them a logical site for World War II military installations. Today you can explore the crumbling concrete batteries where naval guns protected the approaches from the sea; kids especially love climbing on these structures. The headlands' main attractions are centered on Forts Barry and Cronkhite, which lie just across Rodeo Lagoon from each other. Fronting the lagoon is Rodeo Beach, a dark stretch of sand that attracts sand-castle builders and dog owners.

⚠ **Note: The beaches at the Marin Headlands are not safe for swimming. The giant cliffs are steep and unstable, so hiking down them can be dangerous. Stay on trails. Head farther north, to Muir Beach and beyond, for better ocean access.**

GETTING HERE AND AROUND

Driving from San Francisco, head north on U.S. 101, then exit on Alexander Avenue. From there take the first left (signs read "San Francisco/ U.S. 101 South"), go through the tunnel under the freeway, and turn right up the hill where the sign reads "Forts Barry and Cronkhite." The MuniBus 76 runs hourly from 4th and Townsend streets to the Marin Headlands Visitor Center on Sunday and major holidays only. Once here, it's important to get out of your car or bus and explore this beautiful countryside.

EXPLORING

Green Gulch Zen Center. Giant eucalyptus trees frame the long winding road that leads to this tranquil retreat. There are mediation programs on Sundays, workshops, and events, as well as an extensive organic garden. Visitors are welcome to roam freely through the acres of gardens that reach down toward Muir Beach. If you follow the main dirt road it will take you to a walking path that brings you to the beach. It's a peaceful walk surrounded by trees, birds, and the ocean breeze. ✉ *1601 Shoreline Hwy., Muir Beach* ☎ *415/383–3134* 🌐 *www.sfzc.org* 🎟 *Free* 🕑 *Tues.–Sat. 9–noon and 2–4, Sun. 9–10 am.*

Headlands Center for the Arts. If you're an art lover, stop by the Headlands Center for the Arts, where you can see contemporary art in a rustic natural setting. All but one of the center's nine converted military buildings are usually closed to the public, but you can visit the main building (the former barracks) to see several changing installations. The downstairs "archive room" features an odd assortment of objects found and created by residents, such as natural rocks, interesting glass bottles filled with collected items, and unusual masks. Stop by the industrial gallery space, two flights up, to see what the resident visual artists are up to—most of the work is quite contemporary. The center also hosts biweekly public programs, from artist talks to open studios. Call for current schedules. ✉ *944 Fort Barry* ☎ *415/331–2787* 🌐 *www.headlands.org* 🕑 *Weekdays 10–5, Sun. noon–5.*

Marin Headlands Visitor Center. The Marin Headlands Visitor Center, open daily 9:30 to 4:30, sells a useful guide to historic sites and wildlife, and has exhibits on the area's history and ecology. Pick up the park newspaper, which has a calendar of events, including a schedule of guided walks. Kids will enjoy the "please touch" educational sites and small play area inside. ✉ *Fort Barry, Field and Bunker Rds., Bldg. 948* ☎ *415/331–1540* 🌐 *www.nps.gov/goga/marin-headlands.htm.*

Shutterbugs rejoice in catching a scenic Muir Beach sunset.

Marine Mammal Center. If you're curious about the rehabilitation of sea life in the Pacific, stop by this hospital for rescued seals, sea lions, dolphins, and otters. You can glimpse the mammals convalescing in the pool out front, then visit the small gift shop. You can still look in on the preserved military base mess hall, pet a sealskin inside the gift shop, or watch the seal cam. ✉ *2000 Bunker Rd., Fort Cronkhite* ☎ *415/289–7325* 🌐 *www.tmmc.org.*

Muir Beach. Small but scenic, this beach—a rocky patch of shoreline off Route 1 in the northern headlands—is a good place to stretch your legs and gaze out at the Pacific. Locals often walk their dogs here; families and cuddling couples come for picnicking and sunbathing. At one end of the sand is a cluster of waterfront homes, and at the other are the bluffs of Golden Gate National Recreation Area. The beach also has an interesting history—Janis Joplin's ashes are scattered here among the sands and this is where Ken Kesey hosted his second Acid Test.

★ **Point Bonita Lighthouse.** At the end of Conzelman Road, in the southern headlands, is the Point Bonita Lighthouse, a restored beauty that still guides ships to safety with its original 1855 refractory lens. Half the fun of a visit is the steep ½-mi walk from the parking area down to the lighthouse, which takes you through a rock tunnel and across a suspension bridge. Signposts along the way detail the bravado of surfmen, as the early lifeguards were called, and the tenacity of the "wickies," the first keepers of the light. ✉ *End of Conzelman Rd.* 🎟 *Free* ⏲ *Sat.–Mon. 12:30–3:30.*

WHERE TO STAY

For expanded hotel reviews, visit Fodors.com.

¢ **Marin Headlands Hostel.** As hostels go, it's hard to beat this beautifully situated, well-maintained property in a valley on the north side of the headlands, the only lodging in the GGNRA that isn't a campsite. **Pros:** plenty of peace and quiet, great prices, rural setting. **Cons:** no Wi-Fi, difficult to get to without a car or bike, far from restaurants and shops. ✉ *941 Fort Barry* ☎ *415/331–2777* 🌐 *www.norcalhostels.org/marin* *7 private rooms, 8 dormitory rooms; all with shared bath* *In-room: no a/c, no phone, no TV. In-hotel: no elevator, laundry facilities.*

$$$ ★ **Pelican Inn.** From its slate roof to its whitewashed plaster walls, this inn looks so Tudor that it's hard to believe it was built in the 1970s. **Pros:** 5-minute walk to beach, great bar and restaurant, peaceful setting. **Cons:** 20-minute drive to nearby attractions, no Wi-Fi or wheelchair access to bedrooms. ✉ *10 Pacific Way, off Rte. 1, Muir Beach* ☎ *415/383–6000* 🌐 *www.pelicaninn.com* *7 rooms* *In-room: no a/c, no phone, no TV. In-hotel: restaurant, bar, no elevator* *Breakfast.*

MUIR WOODS NATIONAL MONUMENT

Fodor's Choice ★

12 mi northwest of the Golden Gate Bridge.

GETTING HERE AND AROUND

To get here from San Francisco by car, take U.S. 101 north across the Golden Gate Bridge to the Mill Valley/Stinson Beach exit, then follow signs to Highway 1 north. On weekends and holidays, Memorial Day through Labor Day, Golden Gate Transit operates a shuttle ($3 roundtrip) from Mill Valley every half hour. Park in Marin City at the Gateway Shopping Center (look for lighted signs directing you from U.S. 101) or at the Manzanita Park-and-Ride, at the Highway 1 exit off U.S. 101 (look for the lot under the elevated freeway), or take connecting bus service from San Francisco with Golden Gate Transit. Once here, you need to explore the wilderness. Get out of your machine and wander through this pristine patch of nature.

EXPLORING

Muir Woods National Monument. One hundred fifty million years ago, ancestors of redwood and sequoia trees grew throughout the United States. Today the *Sequoia sempervirens* can be found only in a narrow, cool coastal belt from Monterey to Oregon. The 550 acres of Muir Woods National Monument contain some of the most majestic redwoods in the world—some nearly 250 feet tall and 1,000 years old. The stand was saved from destruction in 1905, when it was purchased by a couple who donated it to the federal government. Three years later it was named after naturalist John Muir, whose environmental campaigns helped to establish the national park system. His response: "This is the best tree lover's monument that could be found in all of the forests of the world. Saving these woods from the ax and saw is in many ways the most notable service to God and man I have heard of since my forest wandering began."

Muir Woods, part of the Golden Gate National Recreation Area, is a pedestrian's park. The trails vary in difficulty and length. Beginning

DID YOU KNOW?

The gorgeous old-growth redwood trees in Muir Woods are often enveloped in fog, a useful dampness for the trees, especially to counteract the dry summers.

from the park headquarters, a 2-mi, wheelchair-accessible **loop trail** crosses streams and passes ferns and azaleas, as well as magnificent redwood groves. Among the most famous are **Bohemian Grove** and the circular formation called **Cathedral Grove.** On summer weekends visitors oohing and aahing in a dozen languages line the trail. If you prefer a little more serenity, consider the challenging **Dipsea Trail,** which climbs west from the forest floor to soothing views of the ocean and the Golden Gate Bridge. For a complete list of trails, check with rangers, who can also help you pick the best one for your ability level.

WORD OF MOUTH

"We spent one day hiking in Muir Woods. Beautiful was an understatement. It was peaceful and we saw lots of deer. You can really feel one with nature here."

—SAO

■ **TIP→ The weather in Muir Woods is usually cool and often wet, so wear warm clothes and shoes appropriate for damp trails.** Picnicking and camping aren't allowed, and pets aren't permitted. Parking can be difficult here—the lots are small and the crowds are large—so try to come early in the morning or late in the afternoon. The **Muir Woods Visitor Center** has a wide selection of books and exhibits on redwood trees and the history of Muir Woods. ✉ *Panoramic Hwy. off Hwy. 1, approximately 12 mi north of Golden Gate Bridge* ☎ *415/388–2595 park information, 415/925–4501 shuttle information* 🌐 *www.nps.gov/muwo* 🎫 *$5* 🕑 *Daily 8 am–sunset.*

MT. TAMALPAIS STATE PARK

16 mi northwest of Golden Gate Bridge.

GETTING HERE AND AROUND

By car, take the Route 1–Stinson Beach exit off U.S. 101 and follow Route 1 west and then north. From San Francisco the trip can take from 30 minutes up to an hour, depending on traffic. By bus, take the 10, 70 or 80 to Marin City; in Marin City transfer to the West Marin Stagecoach. Call or check online for routes and schedules (☎ *415/226-0855* 🌐 *www.marintransit.org/stage.html*). Once here, the only way to explore is on foot or by bike.

EXPLORING

Mt. Tamalpais State Park. Although the summit of Mt. Tamalpais is only 2,571 feet high, the mountain rises practically from sea level, dominating the topography of Marin County. Adjacent to Muir Woods National Monument, Mt. Tamalpais State Park affords views of the entire Bay Area and the Pacific Ocean to the west. The mountain was sacred to Native Americans, who saw in its profile—as you can see today—the silhouette of a sleeping Indian maiden. Locals fondly refer to it as the "Sleeping Lady." For years the 6,300-acre park has been a favorite destination for hikers. There are more than 200 mi of trails, some rugged but many developed for easy walking through meadows, grasslands, and forests and along creeks. Mt. Tam, as it's called by locals, is also the birthplace (in the 1970s) of mountain biking, and today many spandex-clad bikers whiz down the park's winding roads.

The park's major thoroughfare, the Panoramic Highway, snakes its way up from U.S. 101 to the **Pantoll Ranger Station** (✉ *3801 Panoramic Hwy., at Pantoll Rd.* ☎ *415/388–2070* 🌐 *www.parks.ca.gov*). The office is staffed sporadically, depending on funding, but if you leave a phone message, a ranger will call you back (within several days) during business hours. From the ranger station, the Panoramic Highway drops down to the town of Stinson Beach. Pantoll Road branches off the highway at the station, connecting up with Ridgecrest Boulevard. Along these roads are numerous parking areas, picnic spots, scenic overlooks, and trailheads. Parking is free along the roadside, but there's a fee at the ranger station and at some of the other parking lots.

WORD OF MOUTH

"The Redwoods at Muir Woods National Monument may be smaller than some you can find at Redwood or Sequoia National Park, but they are still gigantic... and are impressive even on a rainy February day!"

—dansnktwom

The **Mountain Theater,** also known as the Cushing Memorial Theater, is a natural amphitheater just off Ridgecrest Boulevard. Constructed in the 1930s, the theater has terraced stone seats for 3,750 people. Every May and June hundreds of locals tote overstuffed picnic baskets up the short trail to the Mountain Theater to see the **Mountain Play** (☎ *415/383–1100* 🌐 *www.mountainplay.org*), a presentation of popular musicals such as *The Music Man* and *My Fair Lady.* Depending on the play, this can be a great family activity. The **Rock Spring Trail** starts at the Mountain Theater and gently climbs about 1¾ mi to the **West Point Inn,** once a stop on the Mt. Tam railroad route. Relax at a picnic table and stock up on water before forging ahead, via Old Railroad Grade Fire Road and the Miller Trail, to Mt. Tam's Middle Peak, about 2 mi uphill.

Starting from the Pan Toll Ranger Station, the precipitous **Steep Ravine Trail** brings you past stands of coastal redwoods and, in the springtime, numerous small waterfalls. Take the connecting **Dipsea Trail** to reach the town of Stinson Beach and its swath of golden sand. If you're too weary to make the 3½-mi trek back up, Golden Gate Transit Bus 63 (Saturday, Sunday, and holidays from mid-March through early December) takes you from Stinson Beach back to the ranger station.

STINSON BEACH

20 mi northwest of Golden Gate Bridge.

GETTING HERE AND AROUND

If you're driving, take the Route 1–Stinson Beach exit off U.S. 101 and follow Route 1 west and then north. The journey from San Francisco can take from 30 minutes to more than an hour, depending on traffic. By bus, take the 10, 70, or 80 to Marin City; in Marin City transfer to the West Marin Stagecoach. Call or check online for routes and schedules. The town is intimate and perfect for casual walking.

EXPLORING

Stinson Beach. The most expansive stretch of sand in Marin County is as close (when the fog hasn't rolled in) as you can get in the region to the feel of a Southern California beach. ⚠ **Swimming here is recommended only from early May through September, when lifeguards are on duty, because the undertow can be strong and shark sightings, although infrequent, aren't unusual.** There are several clothing-optional areas (such as Red Rock Beach). On any hot summer weekend every road to Stinson Beach is jam-packed, so factor this into your plans. The town itself is very down to earth—like tonier Mill Valley, but more relaxed.

WHERE TO EAT AND STAY

$$$ AMERICAN **Parkside Cafe.** Most people know the Parkside for its beachfront snack bar (cash only), but inside is the best restaurant in Stinson Beach. The food is classic Cal cuisine, with appetizers such as day-boat scallops, ceviche, and mains such as lamb with goat-cheese-stuffed red peppers. Breakfast, a favorite among locals, is served until 2 pm. Eat on the sunny patio, which is sheltered from the wind by creeping vines, or by the fire in the contemporary dining room. *43 Arenal Ave. 415/868–1272.*

$$ AMERICAN **Sand Dollar.** The town's oldest restaurant still attracts all the old salts from Muir Beach to Bolinas, but these days they sip whiskey over an up-to-date bar or beneath market umbrellas on the spiffy deck. The food is good—try the panfried sand dabs (small flatfish) and pear salad with blue cheese—but the big draw is the lively atmosphere. Musicians play on weekends in summer, and on sunny afternoons the deck gets so packed that people sit on the fence rails sipping beer. *3458 Rte. 1 415/868–0434 No lunch Tues. Nov.–Mar.*

$ **Stinson Beach Motel.** Built in the 1930s, this motel surrounds three courtyards that burst with flowering greenery, and rooms are immaculate, simple, and summery, with freshly painted walls, good mattresses, and some kitchenettes. **Pros:** minutes from the beach, cozy, unpretentious rooms. **Cons:** smaller rooms feel a little cramped, not much to do once the sun sets. *3416 Hwy. 1 415/868–1712 www.stinsonbeachmotel.com 7 rooms In-room: no a/c, no phone, kitchen (some), Wi-Fi (some). In-hotel: no elevator.*

BOLINAS

7 mi north of Stinson Beach.

The tiny town of Bolinas wears its 1960s idealism on its sleeve, attracting potters, poets, and peace lovers to its quiet streets. With a funky gallery, a general store selling organic produce, a café, and an offbeat saloon, the main thoroughfare, Wharf Road, looks like a hippie-fied version of Main Street USA.

GETTING HERE AND AROUND

Although privacy-seeking locals openly dislike tourism and have torn down signs to the town, Bolinas isn't difficult to find: heading north from Stinson Beach follow Route 1 west and then north. Make a left at the first road just past the Bolinas Lagoon (Bolinas-Olema Road), and then turn left at the stop sign. The road dead-ends smack-dab in the middle of the tiny town, so drive slowly lest you find yourself in a confrontation with an angry local. By bus, take the 10, 70, or 80 to Marin City; in Marin City transfer to the West Marin Stagecoach. Call or check online for routes and schedules. The town is small; walking is the only way to see it.

WHERE TO EAT

$$ AMERICAN **Coast Cafe.** Decked out in a nautical theme with surfboards and buoys, the dining room at the Coast serves dependably good American fare, including specials such as shepherd's pie, pot roast, local fresh fish, grass-fed steaks, and gorgeous salads. It's also open for breakfast on weekends. ✉ *46 Wharf Rd.* ☎ *415/868–2298.*

POINT REYES NATIONAL SEASHORE

Fodor's Choice ★ *Bear Valley Visitor Center is 12 mi north of Bolinas.*

GETTING HERE AND AROUND

Take the Route 1–Stinson Beach exit off U.S. 101 if you're driving, and follow Route 1 west and then north toward McKennas Gulch Fire Road. Turn left at Sir Francis Drake Boulevard. If you're going by bus, take the 10, 70, or 80 to Marin City; in Marin City transfer to the West Marin Stagecoach. Call or check online for routes and schedules. Once you arrive, the best way to get around is on foot.

EXPLORING

Point Reyes National Seashore. One of the Bay Area's most spectacular treasures and the only national seashore on the West Coast, the 66,500-acre Point Reyes National Seashore (🌐 *www.nps.gov/pore*) encompasses hiking trails, secluded beaches, and rugged grasslands as well as **Point Reyes** itself, a triangular peninsula that juts into the Pacific. The town is a quaint, one-main-drag affair, with a charming bakery, some good gift shops with imported goods, and a few places to eat. It's nothing fancy, but that's part of its relaxed charm.

The infamous San Andreas Fault runs along the eastern edge of the park and up the center of Tomales Bay; take the short **Earthquake Trail** from the visitor center to see the impact near the epicenter of the 1906 earthquake that devastated San Francisco. A ½-mi path from the visitor center leads to **Kule Loklo,** a brilliantly reconstructed Miwok village that sheds light on the daily lives of the region's first inhabitants. From here trails also lead to the park's free campgrounds (camping permits are required). ■ **TIP→ In late winter and spring, wildlife enthusiasts should make a stop at Chimney Rock, just before the lighthouse, and take the short walk to the Elephant Seal Overlook.** Even from up on the cliff, the males look enormous as they spar for the resident females.

Bear Valley Visitor Center. The Bear Valley Visitor Center, open weekdays 9 to 5 and weekends 8 to 5, has informative exhibits about the park wildlife. Rangers here dispense information about beaches, whale-watching, hiking trails, and camping. ✉ *Bear Valley Rd. west of Rte. 1* ☎ *415/464–5100* 🌐 *www.nps.gov/pore/planyourvisit/visitorcenters.htm.*

Duxbury Reef. Mile-long Duxbury Reef is the largest shale intertidal reef in North America. Look for starfish, barnacles, sea anemones, purple urchins, limpets, sea mussels, and the occasional abalone. But check a

5

tide table (www.wrh.noaa.gov/mtr/marine.php) or the local papers if you plan to explore the reef—it's accessible only at low tide. To get here, take Mesa Road and turn left onto Overlook Drive and then right on Elm Avenue.

Point Reyes Bird Observatory. In the southernmost part of Point Reyes National Seashore, accessed through Bolinas, is the free Point Reyes Bird Observatory. Those not interested in birds might find it ho-hum, but birders adore it. The compact visitor center, open daily 9 to 5, is small yet has excellent interpretive exhibits, including a comparative display of real birds' talons. What really warrants a visit, though, are the surrounding woods, which harbor nearly 225 bird species. As you hike the quiet trails through forest and along ocean cliffs, you're likely to see biologists banding birds to aid in the study of their life cycles. *Mesa Rd. 415/868–0655 www.prbo.org.*

★ **Point Reyes Lighthouse.** In operation since December 1, 1870, this lighthouse is one of the premier attractions of the Point Reyes National Seashore. It occupies the tip of Point Reyes, 22 mi from the Bear Valley Visitor Center, a scenic 45-minute drive over hills scattered with old cattle ranches. The lighthouse originally cast a rotating beam lighted by four wicks that burned lard oil. Keeping the wicks lighted and the lens soot-free in Point Reyes's perpetually foggy climate was a constant struggle that reputedly drove the early attendants to alcoholism and insanity. On busy whale-watching weekends (late December through mid-April), parking at the forged-iron-plate lighthouse may be restricted by park staff; on these days buses shuttle visitors from the Drakes Beach lot to the top of the stairs leading down to the lighthouse (bus $5, admission free). Once there, consider whether you have it in you to walk down—and up—the 308 steps to the lighthouse. The view from the bottom is worth the effort, but the whales are visible from the cliffs above the lighthouse. *Western end of Sir Francis Drake Blvd. 415/669–1534 Thurs.–Mon. 10–4:30; weather lens room 2:30–4, except during very windy weather.*

WHERE TO EAT

$ AMERICAN **Pine Cone Diner.** For California country-kitchen cooking, the Pine Cone is where it's at. A block off the main drag, this oh-so-cute diner serves great traditional breakfasts as well as Mexican specialties such as huevos rancheros. At lunch expect hearty homemade soups, fresh salads, and thick sandwiches, all made with local, organic ingredients. The dinner menu has a good selection of comfort food. **TIP→ Kids love the outdoor picnic tables.** *60 4th St., Point Reyes Station 415/663–1536 No credit cards No dinner.*

$$ AMERICAN **Station House Cafe.** In good weather hikers fresh from the park fill the garden to enjoy alfresco dining, and on weekends there's not a spare seat on the banquettes in the wide-open dining room. The focus is on traditional American food—fresh popovers hit the table as soon as you arrive—and there's a little of everything on the menu. Grilled salmon, barbecued oysters, and burgers are all predictable hits. The place is also open for breakfast, and there's a full bar, too. *11180 Rte. 1, Point Reyes Station 415/663–1515 Closed Wed.*

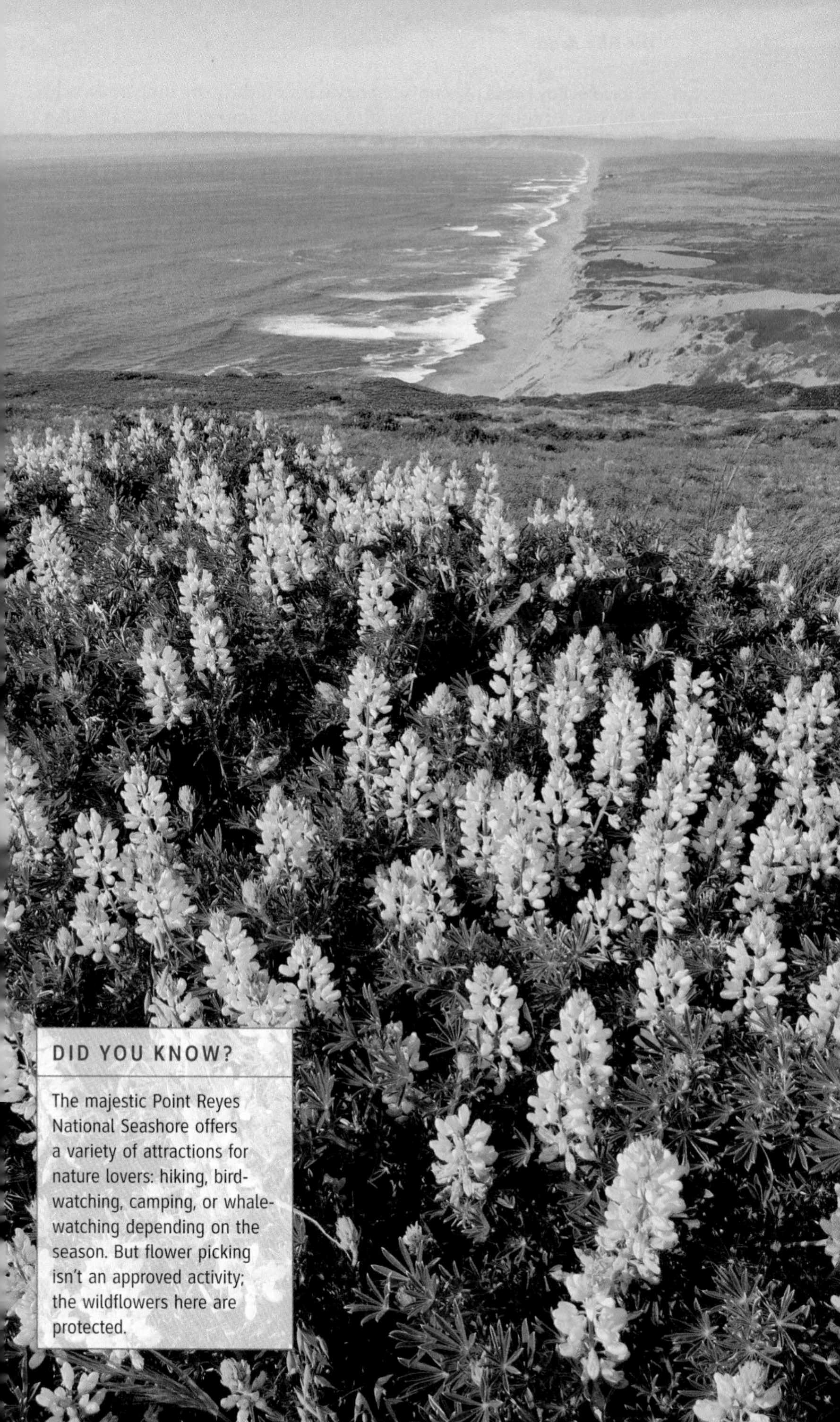

DID YOU KNOW?

The majestic Point Reyes National Seashore offers a variety of attractions for nature lovers: hiking, bird-watching, camping, or whale-watching depending on the season. But flower picking isn't an approved activity; the wildflowers here are protected.

$ AMERICAN ★ **Tomales Bay Foods.** A renovated hay barn off the main drag houses this collection of food shops, a favorite stopover among Bay Area foodies. Watch workers making Cowgirl Creamery cheese; then buy some at a counter that sells exquisite artisanal cheeses from around the world. Tomales Bay Foods showcases local organic fruits and vegetables and premium packaged foods, and the kitchen turns the best ingredients into creative sandwiches, salads, and soups. You can eat at a small café table or on the lawn or take it away for a picnic. The shops are open until 6 pm. *80 4th St., Point Reyes Station 415/663–9335 cheese shop, 415/663–8478 deli Closed Mon. and Tues.*

WHERE TO STAY

For expanded hotel reviews, visit Fodors.com.

$$ **Inverness Valley Inn.** Nestled within a 15-acre valley on the north end of town, this secluded getaway offers private cabins with plenty of room and peace and quiet. **Pros:** spacious accommodations, great place to bring kids. **Cons:** over 3 mi from downtown Inverness, don't expect to swim laps in the pool. *13275 Sir Francis Drake Blvd., Inverness 415/669–7250 www.invernessvalleyinn.com 20 cabins In-room: no a/c, kitchen, Wi-Fi. In-hotel: tennis courts, pool, spa, no elevator, some pets allowed.*

$$ **Olema Inn & Restaurant.** Built in 1876, this inn retains all its 19th-century architectural charm but has been decorated in a sophisticated, uncluttered style. **Pros:** great restaurant, magnificent scenery. **Cons:** no elevator means carrying your luggage up the stairs, the carpets need to be replaced. *10000 Sir Francis Drake Blvd., Olema 415/663–9559 www.theolemainn.com 6 rooms In-room: no a/c, no phone, Wi-Fi. In-hotel: no elevator, Wi-Fi, some pets allowed Closed Tues. No lunch weekdays.*

$$ **Ten Inverness Way.** This is the kind of down-to-earth place where you sit around after breakfast and share tips for hiking Point Reyes or linger around the living room with its stone fireplace and library. **Pros:** great base for exploring nearby wilderness, peaceful garden and friendly staff. **Cons:** overly folksy decor, some rooms are on the small side, poor cell-phone reception. *10 Inverness Way, Inverness 415/669–1648 www.teninvernessway.com 4 rooms, 1 suite In-room: no a/c, no phone, no TV. In-hotel: restaurant, Wi-Fi, no elevator, some age restrictions Breakfast.*

SPORTS AND THE OUTDOORS

Blue Waters Kayaking (*12938 Sir Francis Drake Blvd., Inverness 415/669–2600 www.bwkayak.com*) rents kayaks and offers tours and lessons. **Five Brooks Stable** (*8001 Hwy. 1, Olema 415/663–1570 www.fivebrooks.com*) rents horses and equipment. Trails from the stables wind through Point Reyes National Seashore and along the beaches. Rides run from one to six hours and cost $40 to $240.

THE EAST BAY

When San Franciscans refer to it, the East Bay often means nothing more than what you can see across the bay from the city—mainly Oakland and Berkeley, both of which are in Alameda County. In fact, the East Bay stretches north and east of Alameda to Contra Costa County, which itself has emerged as a powerful business nexus. East Bay towns south of Alameda and Contra Costa counties have become bedroom communities for workers in the high-tech industry. These begin to run into one another, reaching critical mass on the edge of Silicon Valley.

OAKLAND

Directly east of Bay Bridge.

Often overshadowed by San Francisco's beauty and Berkeley's storied counterculture, Oakland's allure lies in its amazing diversity. Here you can find a Nigerian clothing store, a beautifully renovated Victorian home, a Buddhist meditation center, and a lively salsa club, all within the same block. Oakland's multifaceted nature reflects its colorful and often tumultuous history. Once a cluster of Mediterranean-style homes and gardens that served as a bedroom community for San Francisco, the city became a hub of shipbuilding and industry almost overnight when the United States entered World War II. New jobs in the city's shipyards and factories attracted thousands of workers, including some of the first female welders, and the city's neighborhoods were imbued with a proud but gritty spirit. In the 1960s and '70s this intense community pride gave rise to such militant groups as the Black Panther Party and the Symbionese Liberation Army, but they were little match for the economic hardships and racial tensions that plagued Oakland. In many neighborhoods the reality was widespread poverty and gang violence—subjects that dominated the songs of such Oakland-bred rappers as the late Tupac Shakur.

Today Oakland is a mosaic of its past. The affluent have once again flocked to the city's hillside homes as a warmer, more spacious, and more affordable alternative to San Francisco, and a constant flow of newcomers—many from Central America and Asia—ensures continued diversity, vitality, and growing pains. Many neighborhoods to the west and south of downtown remain run-down and unsafe, but a renovated downtown area—including one of the most vibrant arts scenes in the Bay Area—and the thriving though sterile Jack London Square have injected new energy into the city.

Everyday life here revolves around the neighborhood, with a main business strip attracting both shoppers and strollers. In some areas, such as high-end Piedmont and Rockridge, you'd swear you were in Berkeley or San Francisco's Noe Valley or Cow Hollow. These are perfect places for browsing, eating, or just relaxing between sightseeing trips to Oakland's architectural gems, rejuvenated waterfront, and numerous green spaces. Between Rockridge and Piedmont and to the west, you can find the Temescal District, along Telegraph Avenue just south of 51st Street, which is beginning to attract a small collection of eateries and shops.

ESSENTIALS

Visitor Information Oakland Convention and Visitors Bureau (✉ *463 11th St.* ☎ *510/839–9000* 🌐 *www.oaklandcvb.com*).

GETTING HERE AND AROUND

Driving from San Francisco, take I–80 East across the Bay Bridge, then take I–580 to the Grand Avenue exit for Lake Merritt. To reach downtown and the waterfront, take I–980 from I–580 and exit at 12th Street. By BART, use the Lake Merritt Station for the Oakland Museum and southern Lake Merritt; the Oakland City Center–12th Street Station for downtown, Chinatown, and Old Oakland; and the 19th Street Station for the Paramount Theatre and the north side of Lake Merritt. By bus, take the AC Transit's C and P lines to get to Piedmont in Oakland. The O bus stops at the edge of Chinatown near downtown Oakland. Once you arrive, be aware of how quickly neighborhoods can change. Walking is safe and advised downtown as well as in the Piedmont and Rockridge areas, but avoid walking west and south of downtown.

WORD OF MOUTH

"I believe the downtown/historic area of Oakland is undergoing/has undergone a bit of a renaissance—galleries, restaurants, etc.... I'm not referring to Jack London Square, which does have the dubious honor of being home to the oldest bar in California. Anyone know if that's true? That tiny old place that slants?"

—Leely

EXPLORING

Chinatown. Across Broadway from Old Oakland but worlds apart, Chinatown is a densely packed, bustling neighborhood. Unlike its San Francisco counterpart, Oakland's Chinatown makes no concessions to tourists; you won't find baskets of trinkets lining the sidewalk and souvenir displays in the shop windows. But supermarkets such as **Yuen Hop Noodle Company and Asian Food Products** (✉ *824 Webster St.*), open since 1931, overflows with goodies. And the line for sweets, breads, and towering cakes snakes out the door of **Napoleon Super Bakery** (✉ *810 Franklin St.*).

College Avenue. The main shopping drag in Rockridge, College Avenue is a busy thoroughfare. By day it's crowded with shoppers buying fresh flowers, used books, and clothing; by night the same folks are back for dinner and locally brewed ales in the numerous restaurants and pubs. The hub of College Avenue life in Rockridge is **Market Hall** (✉ *5655 College Ave.* ☎ *510/250–6000* 🌐 *www.rockridgemarkethall.com*), an airy European-style marketplace with pricey specialty-food shops. The avenue ends at the California College of the Arts campus.

Jack London Square. Shops, restaurants, small museums, and historic sites line Jack London Square, which is named after one of California's best-known authors; London wrote *The Call of the Wild and The Sea Wolf*, among many other books. When he lived in Oakland, he spent many a day boozing and brawling in the waterfront area. The tiny, wonderful **Heinold's First and Last Chance Saloon** (✉ *48 Webster St.* ☎ *510/839–6761*) was one of London's old haunts. It has been serving since 1883, although it's a little worse for the wear since the 1906

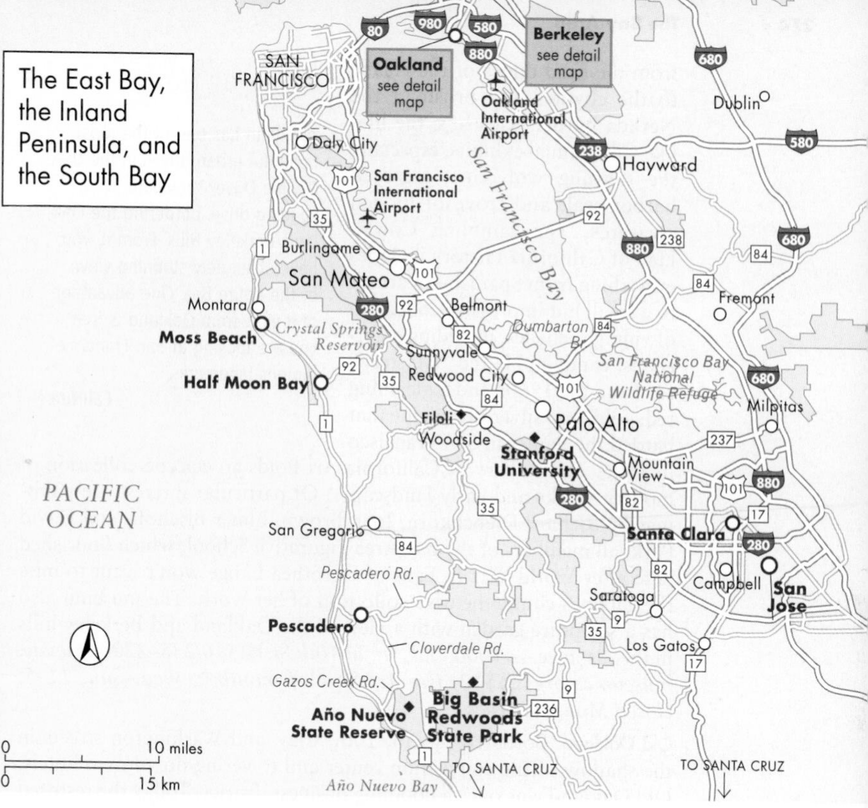

earthquake. The Klondike cabin in which London spent a summer in the late 1890s was moved from Alaska and reassembled here, next door to Heinold's saloon, in 1970. The square also contains a bronze bust of London. **TIP→ Since it's on the waterfront, the square is an obvious spot for tourists to visit and it's worth a peek if you take a ferry that docks here; to really get a feel for Oakland, though, you're better off browsing downtown, or at least in Rockridge.** ✉ *Embarcadero at Broadway* ☎ *866/295–9853* 🌐 *www.jacklondonsquare.com.*

Lake Merritt. Centering the middle of downtown Oakland is this 155-acre natural saltwater lake. Joggers and power-walkers charge along the 3-mi path that encircles the lake, crew teams often glide across the water, and boatmen guide snuggling couples in authentic Venetian gondolas. **Gondola Servizio** (✉ *1520 Lakeside Drive., Lake Merritt* ☎ *510/663–6603* 🌐 *www.gondolaservizio.com*) is by the sign that says "Sailboat House, Gondola Servizio." Fares start at $40 per couple for 30 minutes. ✉ *1520 Lakeside Dr.*

★ **Oakland Museum of California.** One of Oakland's top attractions, the Oakland Museum of California is an excellent introduction to a tour of California, and its detailed exhibits on the state's art, history, and natural wonders can help fill the gaps on a brief visit. You can travel through the state's myriad ecosystems in the Natural Sciences Gallery, from the sand dunes of the Pacific to the coyotes and brush of the Nevada border. Kids love the life-like wild-animal exhibits, especially the snarling wolverine, big-eyed harbor seal, and trove of hidden creatures. The rambling Cowell Hall of California History includes everything from Spanish-era armor to a small but impressive collection of vintage vehicles, including a gorgeous, candy-apple-red "Mystery" car from the 1960s and a gleaming red, gold, and silver fire engine that battled the flames in San Francisco in 1906. The Gallery of California Art holds an eclectic collection of modern works and early landscapes. Of particular interest are paintings by Richard Diebenkorn, Joan Brown, Elmer Bischoff, and David Park, all members of the Bay Area Figurative School, which flourished here after World War II. Fans of Dorothea Lange won't want to miss the gallery's comprehensive collection of her work. The museum also has a sculpture garden with a view of the Oakland and Berkeley hills in the distance. ✉ *1000 Oak St., at 10th St.* ☎ *510/238–2200* 🌐 *www.museumca.org* 🎟 *$12, free 1st Sun. of month* ⏱ *Wed.–Sun. 11–5, closed Mon. and Tues.*

WORD OF MOUTH

"Oakland has one of the most beautiful urban drives in the USA: Skyline Drive/Boulevard. It's a winding drive, bordering the Oakland/Berkeley Hills. From it, you have absolutely stunning views of the entire Bay. One advantage of a view from Oakland is that you are looking at San Francisco's famous landmarks."

—CaliNurse

Old Oakland. Bordered by 7th, 10th, Clay, and Washington streets in the shadow of the convention center and towering downtown hotels, Old Oakland was once a booming business district. Today the restored Victorian storefronts lining these four blocks house restaurants, cafés, shops, galleries, and a lively three-block farmers' market, which takes place Friday morning. Architectural consistency distinguishes the area from surrounding streets and lends it a distinct neighborhood feel. **Ratto's International Market** (✉ *827 Washington St.* ☎ *510/832–6503*), the Italian grocer that's been dishing up meat, cheese, imported sweets, and liquor to the neighborhood since 1897, has fresh deli sandwiches. **Pacific Coast Brewing Company** (✉ *906 Washington St.* ☎ *510/836–2739*) is a homey place for some pub grub or a microbrew on the outside patio.

★ **Paramount Theatre.** Given Oakland's reputation for Victorian and Craftsman homes, newcomers are generally surprised by the profusion of art-deco architecture in the downtown neighborhood around the 19th Street BART station. Some of these buildings have fallen into disrepair, but the Paramount Theatre, perhaps the most glorious example of art-deco architecture in the city, if not the entire Bay Area, still operates as a venue for concerts and performances of all kinds, from the Oakland Ballet to Tom Waits and Elvis Costello. You can take a two-hour tour of the building, which starts near the box office on 21st Street at 10 am on the first and third Saturday of each month. Just behind the Paramount on Telegraph Avenue, the Fox Theater, another art-deco landmark, was saved from the wrecking ball and is being lovingly restored. ✉ *2025 Broadway* ☎ *510/465–6400* 🌐 *www.paramounttheatre.com* 🎟 *Tour $5.*

A fun place to wet your whistle: Heinold's First and Last Chance Saloon.

Rockridge. The upscale neighborhood of Rockridge is one of Oakland's most desirable places to live. Explore the tree-lined streets that radiate out from College Avenue just north and south of the Rockridge BART station for a look at California bungalow architecture at its finest.

Rotary Nature Center and Waterfowl Refuge. Lakeside Park, which surrounds the north side of Lake Merritt, has several outdoor attractions, including a children's park. The Rotary Nature Center and Waterfowl Refuge is the nesting site of herons, egrets, geese, and ducks in spring and summer. Migrating birds pass through from September through February, and you can watch the birds being fed daily at 3:30 (year-round). ✉ *600 Bellevue Ave.* ☎ *510/238–3739* 🌐 *www.oaklandnet.com/parks/facilities/rnc.asp* 🎫 *Free* 🕒 *Daily 10–5.*

WHERE TO EAT

$ MEDITERRANEAN ✕ **À Côté.** This is the place for Mediterranean food in the East Bay. It's all about small plates, cozy tables, and family-style eating here—and truly excellent food. The butternut-squash ravioli, Alsatian goose sausage, and pear-and-walnut flatbread are all lovely choices. And you won't find a better plate of pommes frites anywhere. The restaurant offers over 40 wines by the glass from an extensive, ever-changing wine list. Desserts here are tempting: try the warm crème-fraîche pound cake with apple confit, vanilla ice cream, and huckleberry sauce or a tangy pomegranate sorbet. The heavy wooden tables, cool tiles, and natural light make this a coveted destination for students, families, couples, and after-work crowds. ✉ *5478 College Ave., Rockridge* ☎ *510/655–6469* ✍ *Reservations not accepted* 🕒 *No lunch.*

Jack London Square 5
Lake Merritt 3
Oakland Museum of California 4
Paramount Theatre 1
Rotary Nature Center and Waterfowl Refuge 2

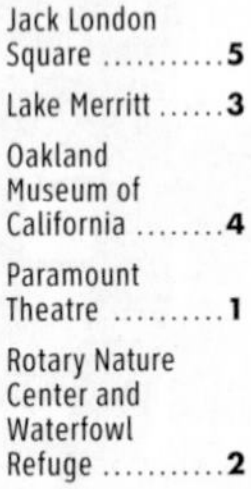

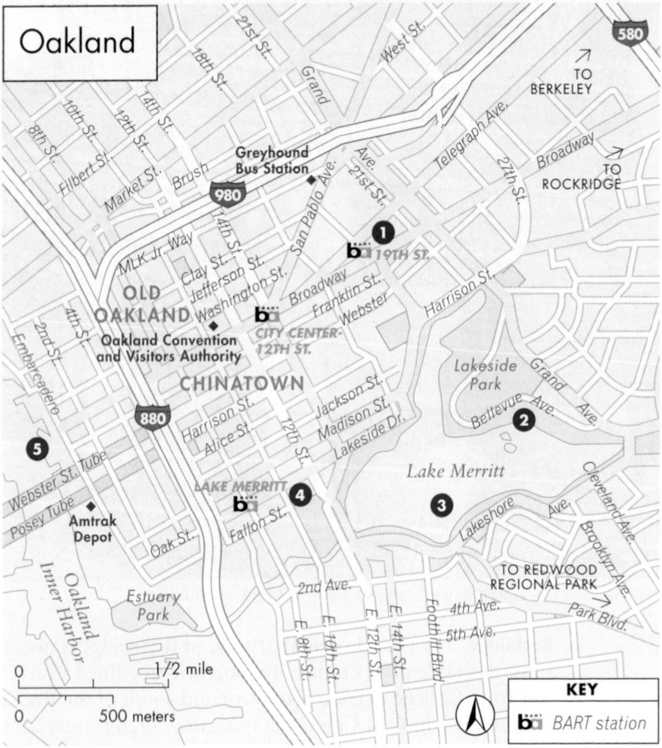

$ AMERICAN

✕ **Brown Sugar Kitchen.** Chef and owner Tanya Holland uses local, organic, and seasonal products in the menu that incorporates her African-American heritage together with her culinary education in France. She blends sweet and savory flavors like no one else, and offers up a wine list that is both unique and wide-ranging. The dining room is fresh and bright, with a long sleek counter, red leather stools, and spacious booths and tables. This is *the* place to come for chicken and waffles. ✉ *2534 Mandela Pkwy., Oakland* ☎ *510/839–7685* 🌐 *www.brownsugarkitchen.com* ⊙ *Closed Mon. No dinner.*

$$$ AMERICAN

✕ **Camino.** This first solo venture from chef-owner Russell Moore (a Chez Panisse alum of 21 years) and co-owner Allison Hopelain was quite the labor of love. Many of the menu's simple, seasonal, and straightforward dishes emerge from the enormous crackling camino (Italian for "fireplace"). Everything is made with top-notch ingredients, including local sardines; grilled lamb and sausage with shell beans; and grilled white sea bass with green beans and new potatoes. The menu of approximately eight dishes rotates nightly, with vegetarian options such as eggplant gratin available as well. The restaurant is decorated in a craftsman-meets-refectory style, with brick walls and two long redwood communal tables filled with East Bay couples and friends. Seasonally inspired cocktails from the small bar are not to be missed; the gin-based drink with house-made cherry and hibiscus bitters is notably delicious.

⌧ *3917 Grand Ave., Oakland* ☎ *510/547–5035* ⊙ *Closed Tues. No lunch (weekend brunch 10–2).*

$$ MEXICAN ✕ **Doña Tomás.** A neighborhood favorite, this spot in Oakland's up-and-coming Temescal District serves seasonal Mexican fare to a hip but low-key crowd. Mexican textiles and art adorn walls in two long rooms; there's also a vine-covered patio. Banish all images of taquería grub and tuck into starters such as quesadillas filled with butternut squash and goat cheese and entrées such as *albondigas en sopa de zanahoria* (pork-and-beef meatballs in carrot puree). A fine selection of tequilas rounds out the offerings. ⌧ *5004 Telegraph Ave.* ☎ *510/450–0522* ⊙ *Closed Sun. and Mon. No lunch.*

$ CAFÉ ✕ **L'Amyx Tea Bar.** Light through the large windows bathes the blond-wood tables, comfy chairs, and long bar, all filled with absorbed students, chatting friends, and tired shoppers in need of a boost. A small area in the back sells first-rate tea accoutrements, but sink into a couch or private nook to bask in much more than the usual cuppa. Try a tea smoothie or an herbal remedy such as Tealaxation. ⌧ *4179 Piedmont Ave.* ☎ *510/594–8322.*

$$ FRENCH ✕ **Luka's Taproom & Lounge.** Luka's is a real taste of downtown Oakland: hip and urban, with an unpretentious vibe. Diners nibble on *frites* any Belgian would embrace and entrées like *choucroute garni* (sauerkraut with duck confit, ham hock, and pork shoulder). The brews draw 'em in, too—you'd be hard pressed to find a larger selection of Belgian beer this side of the pond—and the DJs in the adjacent lounge keep the scene going late. ⌧ *2221 Broadway, at West Grand Ave.* ☎ *510/451–4677* ⊙ *No lunch Sat.*

$$ MEDITERRANEAN ✕ **Oliveto Cafe & Restaurant.** Respected chef Jonah Rhodehamel is at the helm of this locally renowned eatery that anchors Market Hall in the Rockridge neighborhood. The first-class dining room upstairs serves straightforward Italian cuisine; the menu changes daily, but might include house-made duck prosciutto, pan-seared swordfish, or spit-roasted leg of lamb. Downstairs, in the terra-cotta-wall café, everything from a morning espresso to pizza to a full-blown Italian meal (at half the upstairs price) can be enjoyed at one of the small tables or at the bar. ⌧ *5655 College Ave.* ☎ *510/547–5356* ⊙ *No lunch weekends in restaurant.*

WHERE TO STAY

For expanded hotel reviews, visit Fodors.com.

$ **Executive Inn & Suites.** This two-building hotel is convenient to both the Oakland airport and downtown Oakland, and to make up for its removed location, the property offers free shuttle service to the Oakland airport, BART stations, and Jack London Square. **Pros:** free parking, west-facing rooms overlook the peaceful waters of the Oakland Estuary, all rooms have microwaves and fridges. **Cons:** east-facing rooms look out onto the freeway and can be noisy, the decor is overly bright and busy. ⌧ *1755 Embarcadero, off I–880 at 16th St. exit* ☎ *510/536–6633 or 800/346–6331* 🌐 *www.executiveinnoakland.com* *143 rooms, 81 suites* *In-room: a/c, microwave, Internet, Wi-Fi (some). In-hotel: restaurant, bar, pool, gym, laundry facilities, concierge, airport shuttle, parking* *Breakfast.*

$ **Washington Inn Hotel.** This stylish four-story brick hotel sits across the street from the convention center in the heart of Old Oakland. **Pros:** central location, old fashion charm. **Cons:** some rooms feel cramped and need to be freshened up. ✉ *495 10th St., at Washington St.* ☎ *510/452–1776* 🌐 *www.thewashingtoninn.com* *47 rooms, 6 suites* *In-room: Wi-Fi. In-hotel: restaurant, bar, gym, parking* *Breakfast.*

$$ **Waterfront Hotel.** One of Oakland's more appealing neighborhoods is home to this thoroughly modern waterfront hotel. **Pros:** great location, dog-friendly. **Cons:** passing trains can be noisy, some rooms have yet to be renovated. ✉ *10 Washington St., Jack London Sq.* ☎ *510/836–3800 or 800/729–3638* 🌐 *www.waterfrontplaza.com* *143 rooms* *In-room: a/c, Wi-Fi. In-hotel: restaurant, room service, bar, pool, gym, concierge, parking.*

NIGHTLIFE AND THE ARTS

Oakland is where practicing artists have found cheaper rent and loft spaces. Oakland's underground arts scene—visual arts, indie music, spoken word, film—is definitely buzzing.

Fodor's Choice ★ **Café van Kleef.** When Dutch artist Peter van Kleef first opened his gallery in this downtown space, the booze flowed freely—and free, for lack of a liquor license. That gallery has morphed into this candle-strewn, funky café-bar that crackles with creative energy. Van Kleef has a lot to do with the convivial atmosphere; the garrulous owner loves sharing tales about his quirky, floor-to-ceiling collection of mementos, including what he claims are Cassius Clay's boxing gloves and Dorothy's ruby slippers. The café also has a consistently solid calendar of live music, heavy on the jazz side. And the drinks may not be free anymore, but they're quite possibly the stiffest in town. ✉ *1621 Telegraph Ave., between 16th and 17th Sts.* ☎ *510/763–7711* 🌐 *www.cafevankleef.com.*

Mama Buzz Café. At this well-worn café-gallery, a kind of living room for the indie arts crowd, you can get the lowdown on one of the most diverse arts communities around. In addition to coffee and light fare, the calendar includes poetry readings, live-music events, art exhibits, and hard-to-categorize events such as Punk Rock Haircut Night (get a new 'do, cheap), the Knitty Gritty knitting circle, and the Left-Wing Letter Bee. The owners publish the 'zine *Kitchen Sink.* ✉ *2318 Telegraph Ave.* ☎ *510/465–4073*

Fodor's Choice ★ **Yoshi's.** Oma Sosa and Charlie Hunter are among the musicians who play at Yoshi's, one of the area's best jazz venues. Monday through Saturday shows start at 8 pm and 10 pm; Sunday shows usually start at 2 pm and 8 pm. The cover runs from $16 to $30. ✉ *510 Embarcadero St., between Washington and Clay Sts.* ☎ *510/238–9200* 🌐 *www.yoshis.com.*

SPORTS AND THE OUTDOORS

BASEBALL The American League's **Oakland A's** (✉ *McAfee Coliseum, 7000 Coliseum Way, off I–880, north of Hegenberger Rd.* ☎ *510/638–4900* 🌐 *oakland.athletics.mlb.com*), formally the Oakland Athletics, play at the **McAfee Coliseum.** Same-day tickets can usually be purchased at the stadium box office (Gate D), but advance purchase is recommended. On Wednesday, entry is a bargain at $2, and you can buy a hot dog for a dollar. To get to the game, take a BART train to the Coliseum/Oakland Airport Station.

BASKETBALL The National Basketball Association's **Golden State Warriors** (✉ *Oakland Arena, 7000 Coliseum Way, off I–880, north of Hegenberger Rd.* ☎ *510/986–2200 or 888/479–4667* 🌐 *www.nba.com/warriors*) play at the **Oakland Arena** from November through April. Basketball tickets are available through **Ticketmaster** (☎ *415/421–8497* 🌐 *www.ticketmaster.com*). You can take a BART train to the game. Get off at the Coliseum/Oakland Airport Station.

WORD OF MOUTH

"The weather is nicer [in Oakland] than San Francisco, because we have the same breeze without so much fog."

—oaklander

FOOTBALL The National Football League's **Oakland Raiders** (✉ *McAfee Coliseum, 7000 Coliseum Way, off I–880, north of Hegenberger Rd., Oakland* ☎ *510/864–5000* 🌐 *www.raiders.com*) play at **McAfee Coliseum.** Tickets, sold through **Tickets.com** (☎ *510/762–2277* 🌐 *www.tickets.com*), are usually available, except for high-profile games.

SHOPPING

College Avenue is great for upscale strolling, shopping, and people-watching. The streets around Lake Merritt and Grand Lake have more casual fare and smaller boutiques.

Diesel. Wandering bibliophiles collect armfuls of the latest fiction and nonfiction here. The loftlike space, with its high ceilings and spare design, encourages airy contemplation, and on chilly days (a rarity) there's a fire going in the hearth. Keep an eye out for their excellent reading series. ✉ *5433 College Ave., Oakland* ☎ *510/653–9965.*

Maison d'Etre. Close to the Rockridge BART station, this store crystallizes the funky-chic shopping scene of Rockridge. Look for impulse buys like whimsical watches, imported fruit tea blends, and a basket of funky slippers near the back. ✉ *5640 College Ave., Oakland* ☎ *510/658–2801.*

BERKELEY

2 mi northeast of Bay Bridge.

The birthplace of the Free Speech Movement, the radical hub of the 1960s, the home of arguably the nation's top public university, and the city whose government condemned the bombing of Afghanistan—Berkeley is all of those things. The city of 100,000 facing San Francisco across the bay is also culturally diverse, a breeding ground for social trends, a bastion of the counterculture, and an important center for Bay Area writers, artists, and musicians. Berkeley residents, students, and faculty spend hours nursing various coffee concoctions while they read, discuss, and debate at any of the dozens of cafés that surround the campus. Oakland may have Berkeley beat when it comes to cutting-edge arts, and the city may have forfeited some of its renegade 1960s spirit, as some residents say, but unless a guy in a hot-pink satin body suit, skull cap, and cape rides a unicycle around *your* town, you'll likely find that Berkeley remains plenty offbeat.

It's the quintessential university town, and many who graduated years ago still bask in daily intellectual conversation, great weather, and good food. Residents will walk out of their way to go to the perfect bread shop or consult with their favorite wine merchant. And every September, residents gently lampoon themselves during the annual "How Berkeley Can You Be?" parade and festival where they celebrate their tie-dyed past and consider its new incarnations.

ESSENTIALS

Visitor Information Berkeley Convention and Visitors Bureau (✉ *2030 Addison St. #102* ☎ *510/549–7040* 🌐 *www.visitberkeley.com*).

GETTING HERE AND AROUND

BART is the easiest way to get to Berkeley from San Francisco. Alight at the Berkeley (not North Berkeley) Station, walk a block up Center Street to get to the western edge of campus. AC Transit buses F and FS lines stop near the university and 4th Street shopping in Berkeley. By car, take I–80 east across the Bay Bridge then take the University Avenue exit through downtown Berkeley to the campus or take the Ashby Avenue exit and turn left on Telegraph Avenue to the traditional campus entrance. Once you arrive, explore on foot. There's a lot to see, and the city is very pedestrian friendly.

EXPLORING

4th Street. An industrial area on 4th Street north of University Avenue has been converted into a pleasant shopping stretch, with popular eateries and shops selling handcrafted and eco-conscious goods. About six blocks long, this compact area is busiest on bright weekend afternoons. Popular destinations are the Stained Glass Garden, Hear Music, and the Crate and Barrel Outlet, along with a mini-slew of upscale boutiques and wonderful paper stores.

NEED A BREAK?

With a jazz combo playing in the storefront and a long line snaking down the block, Cheeseboard Pizza (✉ *151 Shattuck Ave.* ☎ *510/549–3055* ⏲ *Tues.–Fri. 11:30–2 and 4:30–7, Sat. 11:30–3*) taps into the pulse of the Gourmet Ghetto. This cooperatively owned take-out spot draws devoted customers with the smell of just-baked garlic, fresh vegetables, and perfect sauces. Next door at the bakery–cheese shop, customers take a playing card instead of a number and are served in suites.

Elmwood. South of campus, along College Avenue between Ashby Avenue and Claremont, shops and cafés pack the area known as Elmwood, a local favorite for browsing. **Nabolom Bakery** (✉ *2708 Russell St.* ☎ *510/845–2253*), which has been around since 1976, is a workers' collective where politics and delicious pastries collide. Shingled houses line tree-shaded streets nearby.

Telegraph Avenue. Berkeley's student-oriented thoroughfare, Telegraph Avenue is also the best place to get a dose of the city's famed counterculture. On any given day you might encounter a troop of chanting Hare Krishnas or a drumming band of Rastafarians. First and foremost, however, Telegraph is a place for socializing and shopping, the only uniquely Berkeley shopping experience in town and a definite

Berkeley Visitor Information Center **1**
Lawrence Hall of Science **6**
Phoebe A. Hearst Museum of Anthropology **4**
Sather Tower **2**
Sproul Plaza **3**
University of California, Berkeley Art Museum & Pacific Film Archive...... **5**

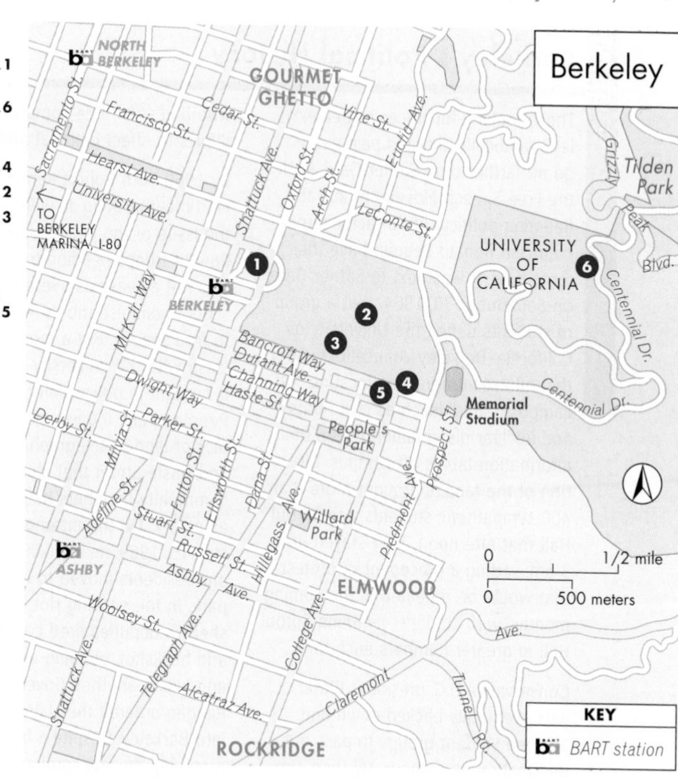

don't-miss. ■ **TIP→ Take care when wandering the street at night, as things can feel a bit edgy. The nearby People's Park, mostly harmless by day, is best avoided at night.** Cafés, bookstores, poster shops, and street vendors line the avenue. T-shirt vendors and tarot-card readers come and go on a whim, but a few establishments—**Rasputin Music** (No. 2401), **Amoeba Music** (No. 2455), and **Moe's Books** (No. 2476)—are neighborhood landmarks. Allen Ginsberg wrote his acclaimed poem "Howl" at **Caffe Mediterraneum** (No. 2475), a relic of 1960s-era café culture.

University of California. The state legislature chartered the University of California in 1868 as the founding campus of the state university system, and established it five years later on a rising plain of oak trees split by Strawberry Creek. Frederick Law Olmsted, who designed New York City's Central Park, proposed the first campus plan. University architects over the years have included Bernard Maybeck as well as Julia Morgan, who designed Hearst Castle at San Simeon. The central campus occupies 178 acres, bounded by Bancroft Way to the south, Hearst Avenue to the north, Oxford Street to the west, and Gayley Road to the east. With more than 30,000 students and a full-time faculty of 1,400, the university, known simply as "Cal," is one of the leading intellectual centers in the United States and a major site for scientific research. (🌐 *www.berkeley.edu*)

CLOSE UP

Berkeley's Political History

Those looking for traces of Berkeley's politically charged past need go no farther than Sather Gate. Both the Free Speech Movement and the fledgling political life of actor-turned-politician Ronald Reagan have their roots here. It was next to Sather Gate, on September 30, 1964, that a group of students defied the University of California–Berkeley chancellor's order that all organizations advocating "off-campus issues" (such as civil rights and nuclear disarmament) keep their information tables off campus. Citation of the tablers brought more than 400 sympathetic students into Sproul Hall that afternoon. They stayed until 3 am, setting a precedent of protest that would be repeated in the coming months, with students jamming Sproul Hall in greater numbers each time.

Conservative U.C. president Clark Kerr eventually backed down and allowed student groups to pass out information on campus. By then, the Free Speech Movement had gathered momentum, and the conflict had made a national hero of student leader Mario Savio. Political newcomer Ronald Reagan played on Californians' unease about the unruly Berkeley students in his successful 1966 bid for governor, promising to rein in the "unwashed kooks."

By the end of the 1960s, the cohesion of the groups making up the Free Speech Movement had begun to fray. Some members began questioning the efficacy of sit-ins and other nonviolent tactics that had, until then, been the hallmark of Berkeley student protests. The Black Panthers, headquartered just over the border in Oakland, were ascending into the national spotlight, and their "take no prisoners" approach appealed to some Berkeley activists who had seen little come of their efforts to affect national policy.

By 1969 both Robert Kennedy and Martin Luther King Jr. were dead, and the issue of the day—stopping the flow of troops heading to Vietnam—was not as easy as overpowering a school administration's resistance to free speech. But a more dramatic clash with the university came when it brought in police units to repossess People's Park, a university-owned plot of land at Telegraph Avenue and Haste Street that students and community members had adopted as a park. On the afternoon of May 15, 1969, nearly 6,000 students and residents moved to reclaim the park. In the ensuing riot, police and sheriff's deputies fired both tear gas and buckshot, blinding one observer and killing another. Governor Ronald Reagan ordered the National Guard into Berkeley. Despite a ban on public assembly, crowds continued to gather and march in the days after the first riot. The park changed hands several times in the following tear-gas-filled months, with the fence coming down for the last time in 1972.

A colorful mural on the side of Amoeba Records (Haste Street at Telegraph Avenue) offers the protestors' version of park history. Although the area around People's Park and Sather Gate may seem quiet now, issues such as affirmative action and tuition increases still bring protests to the steps of Sproul. Protests over civil rights, war, and other inequities march through the center of the campus, though students also gather to rally for sports events, social gatherings, and shows of school spirit.

–Chris Baty

The **Berkeley Visitor Information Center** (✉ *University Hall, Room 101, 2200 University Ave., at Oxford St.* ☎ *510/642–5215* ⏲ *Weekdays 8:30–4:30*) is the starting point for the free, student-guided tours of the campus, which last 1½ hours and start at 10 on weekdays. (Weekend tours depart from Sather Tower, *see below.*)

Student-guided campus tours leave from **Sather Tower,** the campus landmark popularly known as the Campanile, at 10 on Saturday and 1 on Sunday. The 307-foot structure, modeled on St. Mark's Tower in Venice and completed in 1914, can be seen for miles. The carillon is played daily at 7:50 am, noon, and 6 pm and for an extended 45-minute concert Sunday at 2. Take the elevator up 175 feet; then walk another 38 steps to the observation deck for a view of the campus and a close-up look at the iron bells, each of which weighs up to 10,500 pounds. ✉ *South of University Dr.* 🎫 *$2* ⏲ *Weekdays 10–4, Sat. 10–5, Sun. 10–1:30 and 3–5.*

Sproul Plaza (✉ *Telegraph Ave. and Bancroft Way*), just inside the U.C. Berkeley campus border on Bancroft Way, was the site of several free-speech and civil-rights protests in the 1960s. Today a lively panorama of political and social activists, musicians, and students show off Berkeley's flair for the bizarre. Preachers orate atop milk crates, amateur entertainers bang on makeshift drum sets, and protesters distribute leaflets about everything from marijuana to the Middle East. No matter what the combination, on weekdays when school is in swing, it always feels like a carnival. **■ TIP→ Walk through at noon for the liveliest show of student spirit.**

The collection of the **Phoebe A. Hearst Museum of Anthropology** counts almost 4 million artifacts, of which fewer than 1% are on display at any time. The Native Californian Cultures gallery showcases items related to the native peoples of California. Changing exhibits may cover the archaeology of ancient America or spotlight the museum's especially strong ancient Egyptian holdings. Mood music enhances the experience. ✉ *Kroeber Hall, Bancroft Way, at end of College Ave.* ☎ *510/642–3682* 🌐 *hearstmuseum.berkeley.edu* 🎫 *Free; guided tour $5* ⏲ *Wed.–Sat. 10–4:30, Sun. noon–4.*

The **University of California, Berkeley Art Museum & Pacific Film Archive** has an interesting collection of works that spans five centuries. Changing exhibits line the spiral ramps and balcony galleries. Look for the museum's enormous orange-red statue of a man hammering, which can be seen from the outside when strolling by its floor-to-ceiling windows. Don't miss the museum's series of vibrant paintings by abstract expressionist Hans Hofmann. On the ground floor, the Pacific Film Archive has a library and hosts programs about historic and contemporary films, but the exhibition theater is across the street at 2575 Bancroft Way, near Bowditch Street. The downstairs galleries, which house rotating exhibits, are always free. The museum's raw foods café is famous, and you can also find some cooked options, too. ✉ *2626 Bancroft Way, entrance to theater at 2575 Bancroft Way, between College and Telegraph* ☎ *510/642–0808, 510/642–1124 film-program infor-*

mation *www.bampfa.berkeley.edu* *$10, free 1st Thurs. of month* *Wed.–Sun. 11–5, Fri. 11–9.*

Thanks to Berkeley's temperate climate, about 13,500 species of plants from all over the world flourish in the 34-acre **University of California Botanical Garden.** Free garden tours are given Thursday, Saturday, and Sunday at 1:30. Benches and shady picnic tables make this a relaxing place to take in breathtaking views. *200 Centennial Dr.* *510/643–2755* *botanicalgarden.berkeley.edu* *$9, free 1st Thurs. of month* *Daily 9–5. Closed 1st Tues. of month.*

At the fortresslike **Lawrence Hall of Science,** a dazzling hands-on science center, kids can look at insects under microscopes, solve crimes using chemical forensics, and explore the physics of baseball. On weekends there are special lectures, demonstrations, and planetarium shows. The museum runs a popular (and free) stargazing program, which is held on the first and third Saturday of each month, weather permitting. (Call for times.) *Centennial Dr. near Grizzly Peak Blvd.* *510/642–5132* *www.lawrencehallofscience.org* *$12* *Daily 10–5.*

Vine Street. Another top culinary destination is this street, an offshoot of the "Gourmet Ghetto." In a historic building, **Vintage Berkeley** (*2113 Vine St.* *510/665–8600*) gathers locals in its large front garden for nightly wine-tastings of California wines from smaller vineyards. Take the stairs up to the top floor of Walnut Square to find **Love at First Bite** (*1510 Walnut St., Suite G* *510/848–5727*) a cupcakery showcasing scrumptious confections. **Twig & Fig** (*210 Vine St., Suite B* *510/848–5599*) invites you in for a peek at its three rhythmically clacking letterpresses. Stop in for one-of-a-kind papery gifts and publications such as *Inside the Brambles,* a local's guide to Tilden Park. Of all the coffeehouses in caffeine-crazed Berkeley, the one that deserves a pilgrimage is **Peet's** (*2124 Vine St.* *510/841–0564*). When this spot, the original, opened at Vine and Walnut streets in 1966, the unparalleled coffee was roasted in the store and brewed by the cup. Named after the Dutch last name of the founder, Peet's has since expanded, but this isn't a café where you can sit on sofas or order quiche. It's strictly coffee, tea, and sweets to go.

Walnut Square. Northwest of the U.C. Berkeley campus, Walnut Square, at Walnut and Vine streets, has coffee shops and an eclectic assortment of boutiques proffering such goodies as holistic products for your pet, African masks, and French children's clothing. Around the corner on Shattuck Avenue is Chez Panisse Café & Restaurant, at the heart of what is locally known as the **Gourmet Ghetto,** a three-block stretch of specialty shops and eateries. Your senses will immediately perk up as you enter the upscale market **Epicurious Garden** (*1509–1513 Shattuck Ave.*), which has everything from impeccable sushi to gelato. Outside, you can find a terraced garden—the only place to sit—that winds up four levels and ends at the Imperial Tea Court. The restaurant Taste anchors this zone; it offers a rechargeable wine-tasting card that guests use to help themselves to one-ounce automated pours from new wine selections.

WHERE TO EAT

Dining in Berkeley is a low-key affair; even in the finest restaurants—and some are quite fine—most folks dress casually. Late diners be forewarned: Berkeley is an "early to bed" kind of town.

¢ AMERICAN **Bette's Oceanview Diner.** Buttermilk pancakes are just one of the specialties at this 1930s-inspired diner complete with checkered floors and burgundy booths. Huevos rancheros and lox and eggs are other breakfast options; kosher franks, generous slices of pizza, and a slew of sandwiches are available for lunch. The wait for a seat can be quite long; thankfully, 4th Street was made for strolling. ■ TIP→ **If you're starving, head to Bette's to Go, next door, for takeout.** *1807 4th St. 510/644–3230 Reservations not accepted No dinner.*

$$$ AMERICAN **Café Rouge.** You can recover from 4th Street shopping in this spacious two-story bistro complete with zinc bar, skylights, and festive lanterns. The short, seasonal menu ranges from the sophisticated, such as rack of lamb and juniper-berry-cured pork chops, to the homey, like spit-roasted chicken or pork loin, or cheddar-topped burgers. If you visit by day, be certain to peek at the meat market in the back. *1782 4th St. 510/525–1440 No dinner Mon.*

$$ SPANISH **César.** Suitably keeping near-Spanish hours for the Spanish cuisine here, dinners are served late at César, whose kitchen closes at 11:30 pm on Friday and Saturday and at 11 pm the rest of the week. Couples spill out from its street-level windows on warm nights, or rub shoulders at the polished bar or center communal table. Founded by a trio of former Chez Panisse chefs, César is like a first cousin to Chez Panisse, each restaurant recommending the other if there's a long wait ahead. For tapas and perfectly grilled bocadillos (small sandwiches), there's no better choice. The bar also makes a mean martini and has an impressive wine list. ■ TIP→ **Come early to get seated quickly and also to hear your tablemates; the room gets loud when the bar is in full swing.** *1515 Shattuck Ave. 510/883–0222 Reservations not accepted.*

$$$$ AMERICAN Fodor's Choice ★ **Chez Panisse Café & Restaurant.** At Chez Panisse even humble pizza is reincarnated, with innovative toppings of the freshest local ingredients. The downstairs portion of Alice Waters' legendary eatery is noted for its formality and personal service. The daily-changing multicourse dinners are prix-fixe ($$$$), with the cost slightly lower on weekdays. Upstairs, in the informal café, the crowd is livelier, the prices are lower ($$$), and the ever-changing menu is à la carte. The food is simpler, too: penne with new potatoes, arugula, and sheep's-milk cheese; fresh figs with Parmigiano-Reggiano cheese and arugula; and grilled tuna with Savoy cabbage, for example. Legions of loyal fans insist that Chez Panisse lives up to its reputation and delivers a dining experience well worth the price. Visiting foodies won't want to miss a meal

A TASTING TOUR

For an unforgettable foodie experience, take Lisa Rogovin's **Culinary Walking Tour** (*510/540-6444 www.gourmetghetto.org*). You'll taste your way through the Gourmet Ghetto, learn some culinary history, and meet the chefs behind the food. Tours run Thursdays from 11 am to 2:15 pm and cost $75 per person.

5

here; be sure to make reservations a few weeks ahead of time. ✉ *1517 Shattuck Ave., north of University Ave.* ☎ *510/548–5525 restaurant, 510/548–5049 café* ✍ *Reservations essential* ⊗ *Closed Sun. No lunch in the restaurant.*

> **WORD OF MOUTH**
>
> "I am a BIG fan of the Cafe at Chez Panisse and still go there even after having started eating there in the '70s.... While in that area you might also check out The Cheeseboard Pizza.... This is unlike any pizza you have ever had. Pastries can (and should be) taken at Masse's just up Shattuck from The Cheeseboard."
>
> —PamSF

$$ MEDITERRANEAN ★ ✕ **Lalime's.** Inside a charming, flower-covered house, this restaurant serves dishes that reflect the entire Mediterranean region. The menu, constantly changing and unfailingly great, depends on the availability of fresh seasonal ingredients. Choices might include grilled *ahi* tuna or creamy Italian risotto. Light colors used in the dining room, which has two levels, help to create a cheerful mood. A star in its own right, Lalime's is a good second choice if Chez Panisse is booked. ✉ *1329 Gilman St.* ☎ *510/527–9838* ✍ *Reservations essential* ⊗ *No lunch.*

$ MEXICAN ✕ **Picante.** A barnlike space full of cheerful Mexican tiles and folk-art masks, Picante is a find for anyone seeking good Mexican food for a song. The *masa* (flour) is freshly ground for the tortillas and tamales, the salsas are complex, and the flavor combinations are inventive. Try tamales filled with butternut squash and chilies or a simple taco of roasted poblanos and sautéed onions; we challenge you to finish a plate of super nachos. ✉ *1328 6th St.* ☎ *510/525–3121* ✍ *Reservations not accepted.*

$$ AMERICAN ✕ **Rick & Ann's.** Haute comfort food is the focus here. The brunches are legendary for quality and value, and customers line up outside the door before the restaurant opens on the weekend. If you come during prime brunch hours, expect a long wait, but their soft-style eggs are worth it. Pancakes, waffles, and French toast are more flavorful than usual, with variations such as potato-cheese and orange-rice pancakes. Lunch and dinner offer burgers, favorites such as Mom's macaroni and cheese, and chicken potpie, but always with a festive twist. Reservations are accepted 48 hours in advance for dinner and for lunch parties of six or more, but, alas, you can't reserve a table for brunch. ✉ *2922 Domingo Ave.* ☎ *510/649–8538* ⊗ *No dinner Mon.*

$ AMERICAN ✕ **Saul's.** Well known for its homemade sodas and enormous sandwiches, the Saul's of today also uses sustainably sourced seafood, grass-fed beef, and organic eggs. The restaurant is a Berkeley institution and has a loyal clientele that swears by their pastrami sandwiches, stuffed cabbage rolls, and tuna melts. For breakfast, the challah French toast is so thick it's almost too big to bite and the deli omelets are served pancake style. The high ceilings and red-leather booths add to the friendly atmosphere. Don't overlook the glass deli case where you can order food to go. ✉ *1475 Shattuck Ave.* ☎ *510/848–3354* 🌐 *www.saulsdeli.com* ✍ *Reservations not accepted.*

The pioneer restaurant Chez Panisse focuses on seasonal local ingredients.

WHERE TO STAY

For inexpensive lodging, investigate University Avenue, west of campus. The area is noisy, congested, and somewhat dilapidated, but does include a few decent motels and chain properties. All Berkeley lodgings, except for the swanky Claremont, are strictly mid-range.

For expanded hotel reviews, visit Fodors.com.

$$$$ Fodor's Choice ★ **Claremont Resort and Spa.** Straddling the Oakland–Berkeley border, the hotel beckons like a gleaming white castle in the hills, luring traveling executives that come for the business amenities, including T-1 Internet connections, guest email addresses, and oversize desks. **Pros:** amazing spa, supervised childcare, some rooms have great views of the bay. **Cons:** parking is pricey; additional facilities charge for use of spa, tennis courts, pool, gym etc.; no Wi-Fi in rooms; breakfast is an additional fee. ✉ *41 Tunnel Rd., at Ashby and Domingo Aves.* ☎ *510/843–3000 or 800/551–7266* 🌐 *www.claremontresort.com* *249 rooms, 30 suites* *In-room: a/c, Internet. In-hotel: restaurants, bars, tennis courts, pools, gym, spa, children's programs, concierge, parking.*

$ **French Hotel.** The only hotel in north Berkeley, one of the best walking neighborhoods in town, this three-level brick structure has a certain *pensione* feel—guests check in at a counter at the back of the café, and the only public space in the hotel is the hallway to the elevator. **Pros:** great location, reasonable price. **Cons:** nearby trains and delivery trucks can be noisy, rear rooms are small and dark. ✉ *1538 Shattuck Ave.* ☎ *510/548–9930* *18 rooms* *In-room: no a/c, Wi-Fi. In-hotel: restaurant, concierge, parking.*

$ **Holiday Inn Express.** Convenient to the freeway and 4th Street shopping, this inviting, peach-and-beige hotel offers lots of bang for the buck. **Pros:** newly decorated rooms, good breakfast. **Cons:** area can get noisy and congested with traffic during commute hours, a fifteen minute drive to UC campus. ⊠ *1175 University Ave.* ☎ *510/548–1700 or 866/548–1700* 🌐 *www.hiexberkeley.com* *69 rooms, 3 suites with spas* *In-room: a/c, Wi-Fi. In-hotel: gym, laundry facilities, parking* *Breakfast.*

$$ **Hotel Durant.** Long a mainstay of parents visiting their children at U.C. Berkeley, this boutique hotel is also a good option for those who want to be a short walk from Telegraph Avenue. **Pros:** blackout shades, organic bathrobes. **Cons:** downstairs bar can get a little noisy during Cal games, pricey parking. ⊠ *2600 Durant Ave.* ☎ *510/845–8981* 🌐 *www.hoteldurant.com* *139 rooms, 5 suites* *In-room: a/c (some), Wi-Fi. In-hotel: restaurant, room service, bar, concierge, parking.*

$ ★ **Hotel Shattuck Plaza.** This elegant boutique hotel in the heart of Berkeley combines turn-of-the-century glamour (the hotel was built in 1910) with all the contemporary amenities. **Pros:** central location; modern facilities; great views; great restaurant. **Cons:** pricey parking; limited fitness center. ⊠ *2086 Allston Way,* ☎ *510/845–7300* 🌐 *www.hotelshattuckplaza.com* *199 rooms, 17 suites* *In-room: a/c, Wi-Fi. In-hotel: restaurant, room service, bar, gym, parking.*

NIGHTLIFE AND THE ARTS

Berkeley Repertory Theatre. One of the region's highly respected resident professional companies and a Tony Award winner for Outstanding Regional Theatre (in 1997), the theater performs classic and contemporary plays from autumn to spring. Well-known pieces such as *Mother Courage* and *Oliver Twist* mix with edgier fare. The theater's complex is near BART's Downtown Berkeley Station. ⊠ *2025 Addison St.* ☎ *510/647–2949* 🌐 *www.berkeleyrep.org.*

Berkeley Symphony Orchestra. Under artistic director Kent Nagano, this ensemble has risen to considerable prominence. The works of 20th-century composers are a focus, but traditional pieces are also performed. The orchestra plays a handful of concerts each year, in Zellerbach Hall and other locations. ⊠ *1942 University Ave., Suite 207* ☎ *510/841–2800* 🌐 *www.berkeleysymphony.org.*

★ **Cal Performances.** The series, running from September through May at various U.C. Berkeley venues, offers the Bay Area's most varied bill of internationally acclaimed artists in all disciplines, from classical soloists to the latest jazz, world-music, theater, and dance ensembles. Look for frequent campus colloquia or preshow talks featuring Berkeley's professors. ⊠ *University of California, 101 Zellerbach Hall, Suite 4800, Telegraph Ave. and Bancroft Way* ☎ *510/642–9988* 🌐 *www.calperfs.berkeley.edu.*

Fodor's Choice ★ **Freight & Salvage Coffee House.** Some of the most talented practitioners of folk, blues, Cajun, and bluegrass perform in this alcohol-free space, one of the finest folk houses in the country. Most tickets are less than $20. ✉ *2020 Addison St.* ☎ *510/644–2020* 🌐 *www.thefreight.org.*

WORD OF MOUTH

"Berkeley has always taken pride in being one of the most car-UNfriendly cities in the U.S. And this is in a metropolitan area for which a car is completely unnecessary."

—PaulRabe

SHOPPING

Fodor's Choice ★ **Amoeba Music.** Heaven for audiophiles, this legendary Berkeley favorite is *the* place to go to for new and used CDs, records, cassettes, and DVDs. The dazzling stock includes thousands of titles for all music tastes—no matter what you're looking for, you can probably find it here. The store even has its own record label. There are now branches in San Francisco and Hollywood, but this is the original. ✉ *2455 Telegraph Ave., at Haste St.* ☎ *510/549–1125.*

5

Body Time. Founded in Berkeley in 1970, this local chain emphasizes the premium-quality ingredients it uses in its natural perfumes and skin-care and aromatherapy products. Sustainably harvested essential oils that you can combine and dilute to create your own personal fragrances are the specialty. Its distinct Citrus, Lavender-Mint, and China Rain scents are all popular. ✉ *1942 Shattuck Ave.* ☎ *510/841–5818.*

Kermit Lynch Wine Merchant. Lynch's newsletters describing his finds are legendary, as is his friendship with Alice Waters of Chez Panisse. Credited for taking American appreciation of French wine to another level, this shop is a great place to peruse as you educate your palate. The friendly salespeople can direct you to the latest French bargains. ✉ *1605 San Pablo Ave., at Dwight Way* ☎ *510/524–1524.*

Moe's Books. The spirit of Moe—the cantankerous, cigar-smoking late proprietor—lives on in this four-story house of books. Students and professors come here for used books, including large sections of literary and cultural criticism, art books, and literature in foreign languages. ■ **TIP→ Wear good shoes and eat lunch first; you won't want to come out for hours.** ✉ *2476 Telegraph Ave., near Haste St.* ☎ *510/849–2087.*

Rasputin Music. A huge selection of new music for every taste draws crowds. In any other town its stock of used CDs and vinyl would certainly be unsurpassed. ✉ *2403 Telegraph Ave., at Channing Way* ☎ *510/848–9004.*

THE COASTAL PENINSULA

Bookended by San Francisco and Silicon Valley are some surprisingly low-key and unspoiled natural treasures. The vistas here are the Pacific and rolling hills, making it easy to forget the hustle and bustle that's just out of sight.

MOSS BEACH

20 mi south of San Francisco on Hwy. 1.

Moss Beach was a busy outpost during Prohibition, when regular shipments of liquid contraband from Canada were unloaded at the secluded beach and hauled off to San Francisco. The town stayed under the radar out of necessity, with only one local hotel and bar (now the Distillery) where Bay Area politicians and gangsters could go for a drink while waiting for their shipments. Today, although it has grown into a cheerful surfing town with charming inns and restaurants, it is still all but invisible from the highway—a good hideaway for those allergic to crowds.

GETTING HERE AND AROUND

To get to Moss Beach from San Francisco, take Highway 1, also known as the Coast Highway, south along the San Mateo coast. SamTrans buses (☎ *800/660–4287 or 510/817-1717* 🌐 *www.samtrans.org*) travel to Moss Beach from the Daly City BART (Bay Area Rapid Transit) station.

EXPLORING

The biggest Moss Beach attraction is the **Fitzgerald Marine Reserve** (✉ *California and North Lake Sts.* ☎ *650/728–3584*), a 3-mi stretch of bluffs and tide pools. Since the reserve was protected in 1969, scientists have discovered 25 new aquatic species here; depending on the tide, you'll most likely find shells, anemones, or starfish.

Just off the coast at Moss Beach is **Mavericks**. When there's a big swell, it's one of the biggest surfing breaks in the world. Waves here have reportedly reached 60 feet in height, and surfers get towed out to them by Jet Skis. The break is a mile offshore, so seeing it from the coast can be tough and requires a challenging hike.

The intrepid can get photocopied directions at the Distillery restaurant, then drive 3 mi south for the trail out of **Pillar Point Harbor**. Even if you're not hunting for waves, the harbor is a nice place to wander, with its laid-back restaurants and waters full of fishing boats and sea lions.

Brought here in 1928 after two horrible shipwrecks on the point, the **Point Montara Lighthouse,** which originally stood in Mayo Beach on Cape Cod from 1881 to 1922, still has its original light keeper's quarters from the late 1800s. Gray whales pass this point during their migration from November through April, so bring your binoculars. Visiting hours coincide with morning and afternoon check-in and check-out times at the adjoining youth hostel ($24 to $29 dorm beds, $68 to $78 private room). ✉ *16th St., at Hwy. 1, Montara* ☎ *650/728–7177* 🌐 *www.norcalhostels.org* ⏲ *Visitor access daily 9:30 am–sunset.*

WHERE TO EAT

$$$ MEDITERRANEAN ★ **Cafe Gibraltar.** While the cuisine here is broadly called Mediterranean, in the kitchen of chef-owner Jose Luiz Ugalde that term can mean lamb shoulder braised with artichoke hearts and house-cured olives in a tomato sauce, or pot au feu with fresh local Dungeness crab and other seafood simmered in a tomato-saffron broth. The imaginative dishes are served in a warm, pretty dining room; peach walls are lighted by flickering candles, and the booths are adorned with curtains and pillows. Two miles south of Moss Beach on the east side of the highway, the restaurant is a bit hard to find—but definitely worth the hunt. At signs for Pillar Point Harbor, turn inland onto Capistrano, then right onto Alhambra. *425 Ave. Alhambra, at Palma Ave., El Granada 650/560–9039 www.cafegibraltar.com Closed Mon. No lunch.*

$$ SEAFOOD **Sam's Chowder House.** An East Coast–style seafood joint in the Bay Area? This waterfront restaurant isn't textbook Cape Cod, but that's OK—dine here, and you'll get the best of both coasts: true New England–style clam chowder and lump crab cakes and ahi tuna poke with sesame oil and scallions or local halibut with mango salsa. Indoor seats are in one of several long dining rooms; outdoor seats are warmed by gas fire pits and heaters on chilly days; and every seat in the house looks out to the water. The attached market sells fresh fish and picnic food. *4210 N. Hwy. 1 650/712–0245 www.samschowderhouse.com.*

HALF MOON BAY

7 mi south of Moss Beach on Hwy. 1.

It may be the largest and most visited of the coastal communities, but Half Moon Bay is still by all measures a small town. Looking from the highway you'd hardly even know it was there. Turn onto Main Street, though, and you'll find five blocks of galleries, shops, and cafés, many of which occupy renovated 19th-century buildings. While traditionally this was an agricultural center for local growers of artichokes and other coastal crops, in recent years it has also come to be a haven for Bay Area retirees.

GETTING HERE AND AROUND

To get to Half Moon Bay from San Francisco, take Highway 1, also known as the Coast Highway, south along the length of the San Mateo coast. SamTrans buses (*800/660–4287 or 510/817-1717 www.samtrans.org*) travel to Half Moon Bay from the Daly City BART (Bay Area Rapid Transit) station.

ESSENTIALS

Visitor Information Half Moon Bay Chamber of Commerce (*235 Main St., Half Moon Bay 650/726–8380 www.halfmoonbaychamber.org*).

EXPLORING

The town comes to life on the third weekend in October, when 250,000 people gather for the **Half Moon Bay Art and Pumpkin Festival** (*650/726–9652*). Highlights include a parade, pie-eating contests, street performers and a "weigh-off" of giant pumpkins, some as big as 1,200 pounds.

5

The 4-mi stretch of **Half Moon Bay State Beach** (✉ *Hwy. 1, west of Main St.* ☎ *650/726–8819*) is perfect for long walks, kite flying, and picnic lunches, though the 50°F water and dangerous currents make swimming inadvisable. There are three access points, one in Half Moon Bay and two south of town off the highway. To find them, look for road signs that have a picture of footsteps.

WHERE TO EAT

$$$ MEDITERRANEAN ★ ✕ **Cetrella**. This is the coast at its most dressed up. The restaurant is all polished wood and pressed tablecloths, and hits every gourmet mark—adventurous wine list, sumptuous cheese course, and live jazz on Friday and Saturday nights. The creative menu (which changes daily) pairs regional produce and fish with choice imported ingredients, like tangy Italian *Burrata di Bufala* cheese. What results is sophisticated but not stuffy, for instance the Catalonian shellfish stew, which has a tomato, almond, and saffron broth and comes with a lobster cracker and extra napkins. The café has a smaller and cheaper but no less delectable menu. ✉ *845 Main St.* ☎ *650/726–4090* 🌐 *www.cetrella.com* ⏲ *No lunch. Closed Mon.*

$$ ITALIAN ★ ✕ **Pasta Moon**. As one of the best restaurants on the coast between San Francisco and Monterey, Pasta Moon boasts a friendly, laid-back staff and fun, jovial crowd. Local produce flavors the seasonal menu, which includes such highlights as wood-fired pizzas and braised lamb shank. Beware: the dining room can get slightly noisy on weekend nights, when live music plays in the bar and lounge. ✉ *315 Main St.* ☎ *650/726–5125* 🌐 *www.pastamoon.com.*

WHERE TO STAY

For expanded hotel reviews, visit Fodors.com.

$$ 🏨 **Old Thyme Inn**. The owners of this 1898 Princess Anne Victorian love herbs and flowers; if you have a green thumb of your own, this is the place for you. **Pros:** pretty; laid-back; comfortable. **Cons:** close quarters when the inn is full. ✉ *779 Main St.* ☎ *650/726–1616 or 800/720–4277* 🌐 *www.oldthymeinn.com* *7 rooms* *In-room: no a/c, Wi-Fi* 🍽 *Breakfast.*

$$$$ ★ 🏨 **The Ritz-Carlton**. With its enormous and elegantly decorated rooms, secluded oceanfront property, and a staff that waits on guests hand and foot, this golf and spa resort defines opulence. **Pros:** four-star service; total luxury; ocean views. **Cons:** formal; not within walking distance of anything. ✉ *1 Miramontes Point Rd.* ☎ *650/712–7000 or 800/241–3333* 🌐 *www.ritzcarlton.com* *239 rooms, 22 suites* *In-room: a/c, Internet, Wi-Fi. In-hotel: restaurants, bars, golf courses, tennis courts, gym, spa, children's programs, business center, some pets allowed.*

SPORTS

The **Bike Works** (✉ *520 Kelly St.* ☎ *650/726–6708*) rents bikes and can provide information on organized rides up and down the coast. If you prefer to go it alone, try the 3-mi bike trail that leads from Kelly Avenue in Half Moon Bay to Mirada Road in Miramar.

PESCADERO

17 mi south of Half Moon Bay on Hwy. 1.

As you walk down Stage Road, Pescadero's main street, it's hard to believe you're only 30 minutes from Silicon Valley. If you could block out the throngs of weekend cyclists, the downtown area could almost serve as the backdrop for a western movie. (In fact, with few changes, Duarte's Tavern could fill in as the requisite saloon.) This is a good place to stop for a bite or to browse for antiques. The real attractions, though, are the spectacular beaches and hiking in the area.

GETTING HERE AND AROUND

Pescadero is two miles inland from Highway 1 on Pescadero Creek Road.

EXPLORING

Stop for a spell at **Harley Farms**, a restored 1910 farm with 200 alpine goats on 12 acres of pasture. It's a fully operational dairy, renowned for its delicious cheeses: chevre, fromage blanc, ricotta, and feta. A two-hour tour follows the milk trail as it moves from goat to dairy, then from curd to cheese. During the week you can walk around the yard and read detailed signage describing the buildings and operations. The Harley Farms Shop sells cheese (samples available), lotions, soaps, and gift items. Monthly dinners in the old hay loft showcase local, in-season produce. ✉ *205 North St.,* ☎ *650/879–0480* 🌐 *www.harleyfarms.com* 🎫 *Tours $20* ⏲ *Shop daily 11 to 5; tours weekends at 11 and 1.*

If a quarantine is not in effect (watch for signs), from November through April you can look for mussels amid tidal pools and rocky outcroppings at **Pescadero State Beach**, then roast them at the barbecue pits. Any time of year is good for exploring the beach, the north side of which has several secluded spots along sandstone cliffs. Across U.S. 101, the **Pescadero Marsh Natural Preserve** has hiking trails that cover 600 acres of marshland. Early spring and fall are the best times to come, when there are lots of migrating birds and other wildlife to see. ✉ *14½ mi south of Half Moon Bay on Hwy. 1* ☎ *650/879–2170* 🎫 *Free, parking $8* ⏲ *Daily 8 am–sunset.*

WHERE TO EAT

$$ AMERICAN ✕ **Duarte's Tavern**. Though it has been noted by national press, this 19th-century roadhouse continues to serve simple American fare with a modest, hometown attitude. The restaurant's bar, for instance, is a great place to sip a whiskey; but it's also the town's liquor store, which means some locals take their orders to go. The no-frills dining room offers a solid menu based on locally grown vegetables and fresh fish. House specialties include abalone ($40), artichoke soup, and old-fashioned olallieberry pie à la mode (which *Life* magazine once named best in the United States). ✉ *202 Stage Rd.* ☎ *650/879–0464* 🌐 *www.duartestavern.com.*

WHERE TO STAY

$$ 🏨 **Costanoa.** This eco-adventure resort, a popular getaway for Silicon Valley techies and other urbanites, connects guests with outdoor experiences in an incredibly pristine location. **Pros:** stunning natural setting; many accommodation options **Cons:** can get noisy during high

season; not super-luxe, no private baths in cabins and tent bungalows. ✉ *2001 Rossi Rd.*, ☎ *650/879-1100, 877/262-7848* 🌐 *www.costanoa.com* *39 rooms, 1 suite, 12 cabins, 76 tent cabins, 65 RV sites, 13 tent sites* *In-room: a/c (some), no safe, no TV, Wi-Fi. In-hotel: restaurant, bar, spa, laundry facilities, children's programs, parking* *No meals.*

AÑO NUEVO STATE RESERVE

13 mi south of Pescadero on Hwy. 1.

GETTING HERE AND AROUND

You need your own vehicle to get here. The reserve is on Highway 1, 13 miles south of Pescadero and 21 miles north of Santa Cruz.

EXPLORING

★ **Año Nuevo State Reserve.** At the height of mating season, upward of 4,000 elephant seals congregate at Año Nuevo, one of the world's only approachable mainland rookeries. The seals are both vocal and spectacularly big (especially the males, which can weigh up to 2½ tons), and some are in residence year-round. An easy, 1½-hour round-trip walk takes you to the dunes, from which you can look down onto the animals lounging on the shoreline. Note that during mating season (mid-December through March), visitors may do the hike only as part of a 2½-hour guided tour, for which reservations must be made well in advance. The area's visitor center has a fascinating film about the seals and some natural-history exhibits (including a sea otter's pelt that you can touch). Dogs are not allowed, even in cars in the parking lot. ✉ *Hwy. 1, 13 mi south of Pescadero* ☎ *650/879–2025; 800/444–4445 for tour reservations* *Tour $7, parking $10* *Guided tours leave every 15 min, mid-Dec.–Mar., daily 8:45–3.*

BIG BASIN REDWOODS STATE PARK

17 mi north of Santa Cruz on Hwy. 1.

GETTING HERE AND AROUND

You need your own vehicle to get here. Coming from the coast, access the park at Waddell Creek (off Highway 1, 17 mi north of Santa Cruz), where a confluence of waterways pours out of the redwoods and into the ocean.

EXPLORING

Big Basin Redwoods State Park. California's oldest state park is the best place to see old-growth redwoods without going north of San Francisco (and it's far less crowded than Muir Woods and other famous spots). The parkland ranges from sea level up to 2,000 feet in elevation, which means the landscape changes often, from dark redwood groves to oak pastures that are deep green in winter and bleached nearly white in summer. The mountain setting also makes for countless waterfalls, most visible during the winter rains. The visitor center is inland, at park headquarters in Boulder Creek. Staffing at the park's coastal entrance is spotty, but there are always park information and camping check-in available at a self-service kiosk.

CLOSE UP

The Inland Peninsula

Driving south of San Francisco along the San Mateo coast, it's hard to believe that inland, behind the rolling hills, is Silicon Valley. And while the high-tech hub is known more for its semiconductors and Fortune 500 companies than its sightseeing, it does have a few highlights worth stopping for—especially if you're already driving through on I–280.

Adorable Palo Alto and its intellectual neighbor, **Stanford University** (✉ *450 Serra Mall, Stanford* ☎ *650/723–2300* 🌐 *www.stanford.edu*), are about 35 mi south of San Francisco. Stanford's gorgeous grounds are home to a primordial-looking cactus garden, a stone sculpture by Scottish artist Andy Goldsworthy, aboriginal artworks from Papua New Guinea, and an excellent art museum—The Iris and B. Gerald Cantor Center for Visual Arts—whose lawn is planted with bronzes works by Rodin. Free one-hour walking tours of the campus leave daily at 11 and 3:15 from the visitor center in the front hall of Memorial Auditorium.

In the center of Santa Clara University's campus is the **Mission Santa Clara de Asis**. Roof tiles of the current building, a reproduction of the original, were salvaged from earlier structures, which dated from the 1790s and 1820s. Early adobe walls and a spectacular garden with 4,500 roses remain intact as well. ✉ *500 El Camino Real* ☎ *408/554–4023* 🌐 *www.scu.edu/visitors/mission* 🎫 *Free* ⏲ *Self-guided tours daily 1–sundown.*

At the southern end of Silicon Valley, San Jose is home to several good museums.

The permanent collection at the **San Jose Museum of Art** (✉ *110 S. Market St., San Jose* ☎ *408/294–2787* 🌐 *www.sjmusart.org* 🎫 *$8* ⏲ *Tues.–Sun. 11–5*) focuses on cutting-edge California and Latino artists.

The **Tech Museum of Innovation** (✉ *201 S. Market St., San Jose* ☎ *408/294–8324* 🌐 *www.thetech.org* 🎫 *$8* ⏲ *Daily 10–5*) is a hands-on, high-tech children's museum.

The **Rosicrucian Egyptian Museum** (✉ *1342 Naglee Ave., San Jose* ☎ *408/947–3635* 🌐 *www.egyptianmuseum.org* 🎫 *$9* ⏲ *Mon., Wed., and Fri. 10–5, Thurs. 10–8, weekends 11–6*) showcases an exquisite collection of Egyptian and Babalonian antiquities.

5

A short walk on the Marsh Trail leads to the **Rancho Del Oso Nature Center** (☎ *831/427–2288* ⏲ *Weekends noon–4*), which has natural-history exhibits and is the starting point for several self-guided nature walks.

Mountain bikers, horseback riders, and hikers can take the nearly level Canyon Road (a dirt fire road) back up the creek and into the woods. Hikers looking for solitude might consider a more strenuous, uphill climb on Clark Connection to Westridge Trail, which rewards hard work with spectacular views of the ocean. Those who don't want to go anywhere can just stay on the windswept beach, where the main attraction is watching kite surfers get huge air on the windy shoreline waves. ✉ *21600 Big Basin Way, Boulder Creek* ☎ *831/338–8860* 🎫 *$10 parking fee.*

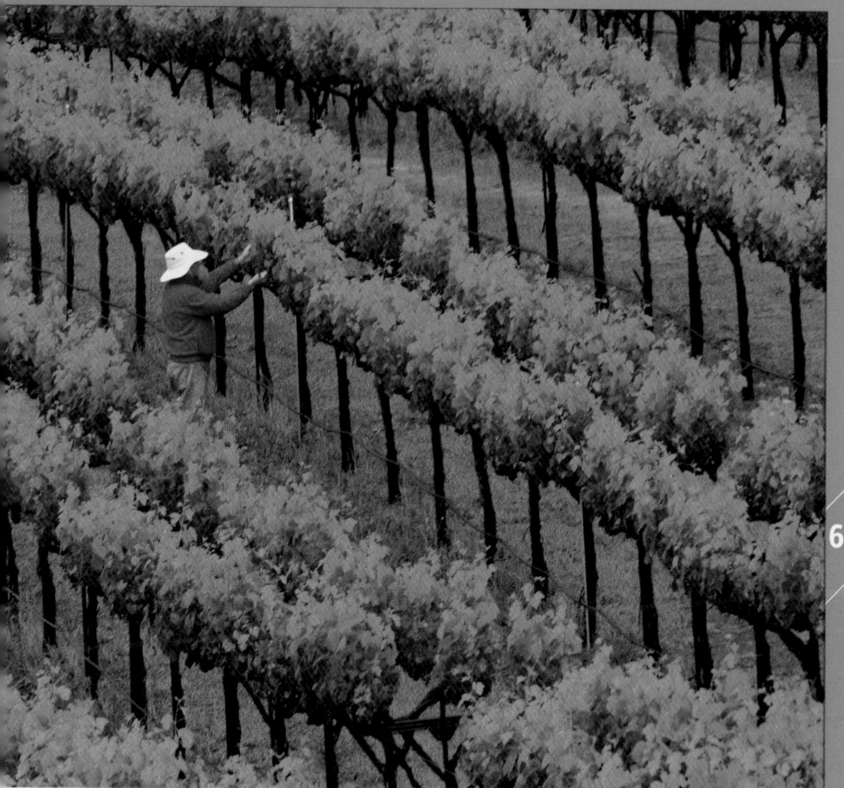

6

The Wine Country

WORD OF MOUTH

"Both Napa and Sonoma are great. Napa is almost wall-to-wall wineries, Sonoma is more rural. The further north you go in either valley, the less busy it gets."

—zootsi

WELCOME TO WINE COUNTRY

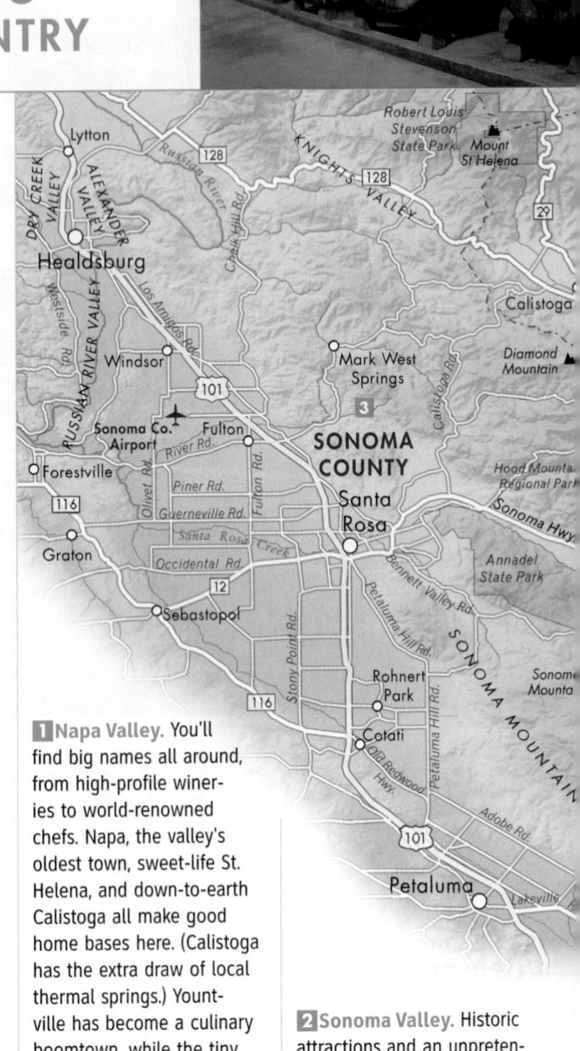

TOP REASONS TO GO

★ **Biking:** Cycling is one of the best ways to see the Wine Country—the Russian River and Dry Creek valleys are particularly beautiful.

★ **Browsing the farmers' markets:** Almost every town in Napa and Sonoma has a seasonal farmers' market, each rounding up an amazing variety of local produce.

★ **Wandering di Rosa:** Though this art and nature preserve is just off the busy Carneros Highway, it's a relatively unknown treasure. The galleries and gardens are filled with hundreds of artworks.

★ **Canoeing on the Russian River:** Trade in your car keys for a paddle and glide down the Russian River. May through October is the best time to be on the water.

★ **Touring Wineries:** Let's face it: this is the reason you're here, and the range of excellent sips to sample would make any oenophile giddy.

1 Napa Valley. You'll find big names all around, from high-profile wineries to world-renowned chefs. Napa, the valley's oldest town, sweet-life St. Helena, and down-to-earth Calistoga all make good home bases here. (Calistoga has the extra draw of local thermal springs.) Yountville has become a culinary boomtown, while the tiny communities of Oakville and Rutherford are surrounded by major vintners like Robert Mondavi and Francis Ford Coppola. Rutherford in particular is the source for outstanding Cabernet Sauvignon.

2 Sonoma Valley. Historic attractions and an unpretentious attitude prevail here. The town of Sonoma, with its atmospheric central plaza, is rich with 19th-century buildings. Glen Ellen, meanwhile, has a special connection with author Jack London.

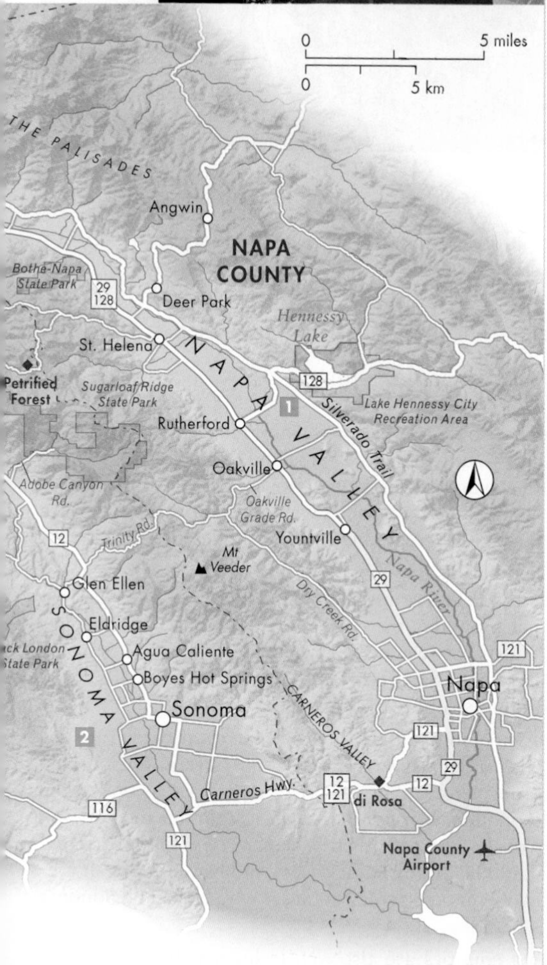

GETTING ORIENTED

The Napa and Sonoma valleys run roughly parallel, northwest to southeast, and are separated by the Mayacamas Mountains. Northwest of the Sonoma Valley are several more important viticultural areas in Sonoma County, including the Dry Creek, Alexander, and Russian River valleys. The Carneros region, which spans southern Sonoma and Napa counties, is just north of San Pablo Bay, and the closest of all these wine regions to San Francisco.

0 5 miles
0 5 km
THE PALISADES
Angwin
NAPA COUNTY
Bothe-Napa State Park
29
128
Deer Park
Hennessy Lake
St. Helena
NAPA VALLEY
Petrified Forest
Sugarloaf Ridge State Park
128
Lake Hennessy City Recreation Area
1
Silverado Trail
Rutherford
Oakville
Adobe Canyon Rd.
Oakville Grade Rd.
Yountville
12
Trinity Rd.
Mt Veeder
Napa River
29
Glen Ellen
Dry Creek Rd.
Eldridge
SONOMA VALLEY
ck London State Park
Agua Caliente
121
Boyes Hot Springs
CARNEROS VALLEY
Napa
Sonoma
2
121
29
12
121
12
Carneros Hwy.
di Rosa
116
121
Napa County Airport

3 Elsewhere in Sonoma. The winding, rural roads here feel a world away from Napa's main drag. The lovely Russian River, Dry Creek, and Alexander valleys are all excellent places to seek out Pinot Noir, Zinfandel, and Chardonnay. The small town of Healdsburg gets lots of attention, thanks to its terrific restaurants, bed-and-breakfasts, and chic boutiques.

Updated by Sharron Wood

Life is lived well in the California Wine Country. Eating and, above all, drinking are cultivated as high arts. If you've been daydreaming about driving through vineyards, stopping here and there for a wine tasting or a picnic, well, that fantasy is just everyday life here.

It's little wonder that so many visitors to San Francisco take a day or two—or five or six—to unwind in the Napa and Sonoma valleys. They join the locals in the tasting rooms, from serious wine collectors making their annual pilgrimages to wine newbies who don't know the difference between a Merlot and Mourvèdre but are eager to learn.

The state's wine industry is booming, and the Napa and Sonoma valleys have long led the field. For instance, in 1975 Napa Valley had no more than 20 wineries; today there are more than 275. A recent up-and-comer is the Carneros region, which overlaps Napa and Sonoma counties at the head of the San Francisco Bay. (Chardonnay and Pinot Noir grapes thrive on its cool, windy hillsides.)

Great dining and wine go hand in hand, and the local viticulture has naturally encouraged a robust passion for food. Several outstanding chefs have taken root here, sealing the area's reputation as one of the best restaurant destinations in the country. The lust for fine food doesn't stop at the doors of the bistros, either. Whether you visit an artisanal olive-oil producer, nibble locally made cheese, or browse the fresh vegetables in the farmers' markets, you'll soon see why Napa and Sonoma are a food-lover's paradise.

Napa and Sonoma counties are also rich in history. In the town of Sonoma, for example, you can explore buildings from California's Spanish and Mexican past. Some wineries, such as Napa Valley's Beringer, have cellars or tasting rooms dating to the late 1800s. The town of Calistoga is a flurry of Steamboat Gothic architecture, gussied up with the fretwork favored by late-19th-century spa goers. Modern architecture is the exception rather than the rule, but one standout example is the postmodern extravaganza of Clos Pegase winery in Calistoga.

Binding all these temptations together is the sheer scenic beauty of the place. Much of Napa Valley's landscape unspools in orderly, densely planted rows of vines. Sonoma's vistas are broken by rolling hills or stands of ancient oak and madrone trees. Even the climate cooperates, as the warm summer days and refreshingly cool evenings that make the area one of the world's best grape-growing regions make perfect weather for traveling, too. If you're inspired to dig further into the Wine Country, grab a copy of *Fodor's InFocus Napa & Sonoma* or the in-depth *Compass American Guide: California Wine Country.*

PLANNING

WHEN TO GO

"Crush," the term used to indicate the season when grapes are picked and crushed, usually takes place in September or October, depending on the weather. From September until November the entire Wine Country celebrates its bounty with street fairs and festivals. The Sonoma County Harvest Fair, with its famous grape stomp, is held the first weekend in October. Golf tournaments, wine auctions, and art and food fairs occur throughout the fall.

In season (April through November), Napa Valley draws crowds of tourists, and traffic along Route 29 from St. Helena to Calistoga is often backed up on weekends. The Sonoma Valley, Santa Rosa, and Healdsburg are less crowded. In season and over holiday weekends it's best to book lodging, restaurant, and winery reservations at least a month in advance. Many wineries give tours at specified times and require appointments.

To avoid crowds, visit the Wine Country during the week and get an early start (most wineries open around 10). Because many wineries close as early as 4 or 4:30—and almost none are open past 5—you'll need to get a reasonably early start if you want to fit in more than one or two, especially if you're going to enjoy the leisurely lunch customary in the Wine Country. Summer is usually hot and dry, and autumn can be even hotter, so dress appropriately if you go during these times.

GETTING HERE AND AROUND

AIR TRAVEL

If you'd like to bypass San Francisco or Oakland, you can fly directly to the small Charles M. Schulz Sonoma County Airport (STS) in Santa Rosa on Horizon Air, which has direct flights from Los Angeles, Portland, Las Vegas, and Seattle. Rental cars are available from Avis, Budget, Enterprise, and Hertz at the airport.

BUS TRAVEL

Bus travel is an inconvenient way to explore the Wine Country. Service is infrequent and buses from San Francisco can only get you to Santa Rosa or the town of Vallejo, south of Napa—neither of which is close to the vineyards. Sonoma County Transit offers daily bus service to points all over the county. VINE (Valley Intracity Neighborhood Express) provides bus service within the city of Napa and between other Napa Valley towns.

Bus Lines **Greyhound** (☎ *800/231–2222*). **Sonoma County Transit** (☎ *707/576–7433 or 800/345–7433*). **VINE** (☎ *707/251–2800*).

CAR TRAVEL

Driving your own car is by far the best way to explore the Wine Country. Well-maintained roads zip through the centers of the Napa and Sonoma valleys, while scenic routes thread through the backcountry. Distances between towns are fairly short, and you can often drive from one end of the Napa or Sonoma valley to the other in less than an hour—if there's no significant traffic. This may be a relatively rural area, but the usual rush hours still apply, and high-season weekend traffic can be excruciatingly slow, especially on Route 29.

Five major roads cut through the Napa and Sonoma valleys. U.S. 101 and Routes 12 and 121 travel through Sonoma County. Route 29 heads north from Napa. The 25-mi Silverado Trail, which runs parallel to Route 29 north from Napa to Calistoga, is Napa Valley's more scenic, less-crowded alternative to Route 29.

■ **TIP→ Remember, if you're wine tasting, either select a designated driver or be careful of your wine intake. (When you're taking just a sip or two of any given wine, it can be hard to keep track of how much you're drinking.)** Also, keep in mind that you'll likely be sharing the road with cyclists; keep a close eye on the shoulder.

When calculating the time it will take you to drive between the Napa and Sonoma valleys, remember that the Mayacamas Mountains are between the two. If it's not too far out of your way, you might want to travel between the two valleys along Highway 12/121 to the south, or along Highway 128 to the north, to avoid the slow, winding drive on the Oakville Grade, which connects Oakville, in Napa, and Glen Ellen, in Sonoma.

From San Francisco to Napa: Cross the Golden Gate Bridge, then go north on U.S. 101. Next go east on Route 37 toward Vallejo, then north on Route 121, also called the Carneros Highway. Turn left (north) when Route 121 runs into Route 29. This should take about 1½ hours when traffic is light.

From San Francisco to Sonoma: Cross the Golden Gate Bridge, then go north on U.S. 101, east on Route 37 toward Vallejo, and north on Route 121, aka the Carneros Highway. When you reach Route 12, take it north. If you're going to any of the Sonoma County destinations north of the valley, take U.S. 101 all the way north through Santa Rosa to Healdsburg. This should take about an hour, not counting substantial traffic.

From Berkeley and other East Bay towns: Take Interstate 80 north to Route 37 west, then on to Route 29 north. To head up the Napa Valley, continue on Route 29; to reach Sonoma County, turn off Route 29 onto Route 121 heading north. Getting from Berkeley to Napa will take at least 45 minutes, from Berkeley to Sonoma at least an hour.

RESTAURANTS

Star chefs from around the world have come into the Wine Country's orbit, drawn by the area's phenomenal produce, artisanal foods, and wines. These days, many visitors come to Napa and Sonoma as much for the restaurants' tasting menus as for the wineries' tasting rooms.

Although excellent meals can be found virtually everywhere in the region, the small town of Yountville has become a culinary crossroads under the influence of chef Thomas Keller. If a table at Keller's famed French Laundry is out of reach, keep in mind that he's also behind a number of more modest restaurants in town. In St. Helena the elegant Restaurant at Meadowood has just as much critical acclaim as the French Laundry, yet is considerably easier to get into. And the buzzed-about restaurants in Sonoma County, including Cyrus and Farmhouse Inn, offer plenty of mouthwatering options.

Inexpensive eateries include high-end delis that serve superb picnic fare, and brunch is a cost-effective strategy at pricey restaurants, as is sitting at the bar and ordering a few appetizers instead of sitting down to a full-blown meal.

With few exceptions (which are noted in individual restaurant listings), dress is informal. Where reservations are indicated as essential, you may need to make them a week or more ahead. In summer and early fall you may need to book several weeks ahead.

HOTELS

Napa and Sonoma know the tourism ropes well; their inns and hotels range from low-key to utterly luxurious, and generally maintain high standards. Most of the bed-and-breakfasts are in historic Victorian and Spanish buildings, and the breakfast part of the equation often involves fresh local produce. The newer hotels tend to have a more modern, streamlined aesthetic and elaborate, spalike bathrooms. Many hotels and B&Bs have excellent restaurants on their grounds, and those that don't are still just a short drive away from gastronomic bliss.

However, all of this comes with a hefty price tag. As the cost of vineyards and grapes has risen, so have lodging rates. Santa Rosa, the largest population center in the area, has the widest selection of moderately priced rooms. Try there if you've failed to reserve in advance or have a limited budget. In general, all accommodations in the area often have lower rates on weeknights, and prices are about 20% lower in winter.

On weekends, two- or even three-night minimum stays are commonly required, especially at smaller inns and B&Bs. If you'd prefer to stay a single night, though, innkeepers are usually more flexible in winter. Many B&Bs book up long in advance of the summer and fall seasons. Many B&Bs and small inns also discourage the presence of children though fall short of actually prohibiting them. If you're traveling with children, be sure to ask about them when booking to make sure they will receive a warm welcome.

BED-AND-BREAKFAST ASSOCIATIONS

Bed & Breakfast Association of Sonoma Valley (☎ *800/969–4667* 🌐 *www.sonomabb.com*). **The Wine Country Inns of Sonoma County** (☎ *800/946–3268* 🌐 *www.winecountryinns.com*).

WHAT IT COSTS	¢	$	$$	$$$	$$$$
Restaurants	under $10	$10–$17	$18–$24	$25–$35	over $35
Hotels	under $100	$100–$199	$200–$299	$300–$399	over $400

Restaurant prices are per person for a main course at dinner, or a prix fixe meal if that is the only option, excluding tax. Hotel prices are for two people in a standard double room in high season, excluding tax.

TOURS

Full-day guided tours of the Wine Country generally include lunch, and cost about $60–$100 per person. Reservations are usually required.

Beau Wine Tours (✉ *21707 8th St. E, Sonoma* ☎ *707/938–8001 or 800/387–2328* 🌐 *www.beauwinetours.com*) organizes personalized tours of Napa and Sonoma in their limos, vans, and shuttle buses. **Gray Line** (✉ *Pier 43½, Embarcadero, San Francisco* ☎ *415/434–8687 or 888/428–6937* 🌐 *www.grayline.com*) has a tour that covers both the southern Napa and Sonoma valleys in a single day, with a stop for lunch in Yountville. **Great Pacific Tour Co.** (✉ *518 Octavia St., Hayes Valley, San Francisco* ☎ *415/626–4499* 🌐 *www.greatpacifictour.com*) operates full-day tours of Napa and Sonoma, including a restaurant lunch, in passenger vans that seat 14. In addition to renting bikes by the day, **Wine Country Bikes** (✉ *61 Front St., Healdsburg* ☎ *707/473–0610* 🌐 *www.winecountrybikes.com*) organizes both one-day and multiday trips throughout Sonoma County.

THE NAPA VALLEY

When it comes to wine production in the United States, Napa Valley rules the roost, with more than 275 wineries and many of the biggest brands in the business. Vastly diverse soils and microclimates give Napa winemakers the chance to make a tremendous variety of wines. But what's the area like beyond the glossy advertising and boldface names?

The handful of small towns strung along Highway 29 are where wine-industry workers live, and they're also where most of the area lodging is. Napa—the valley's largest town—lures with its few cultural attractions and accommodations that are (relatively) reasonably priced. A few miles farther north, compact Yountville is a culinary boomtown, densely packed with top-notch restaurants and hotels, including a few luxury properties. Continuing north, St. Helena teems with elegant boutiques and restaurants; mellow Calistoga, known for spas and hot springs, feels a bit like an Old West frontier town, and has a more casual attitude.

ESSENTIALS

Contacts **Napa Valley Destination Council** (☎ *707/226–7459* 🌐 *www.legendarynapavalley.com*).

NAPA

46 mi from San Francisco via I–80 east and north, Rte. 37 west, and Rte. 29 north.

The town of Napa is the valley's largest, and visitors who get a glimpse of the strip malls and big-box stores from Highway 29 often speed right past on the way to smaller and more seductive Yountville or St. Helena. But Napa doesn't entirely deserve its dowdy reputation. After many years as a blue-collar town that more or less turned its back on the Wine Country scene, Napa has spent the last few years attempting to increase its appeal to visitors, with somewhat mixed results. A walkway that follows the river through town, completed in 2008, makes the city more pedestrian-friendly, and in the last two years a surprising number of high-profile new restaurants have popped up, but you'll still find a handful of empty storefronts among the wine bars and tasting rooms.

Many visitors choose to stay in Napa after experiencing hotel sticker shock; prices in Napa are marginally more reasonable than elsewhere. If you set up your home base here, you'll undoubtedly want to spend some time getting out of town and into the beautiful countryside, but don't neglect taking a stroll to see what Napa's least pretentious town has to offer, or checking out the culinary landscape, which seems to be changing faster here than anywhere else in the valley.

GETTING HERE AND AROUND

To get to downtown Napa from Route 29, take the 1st Street exit and follow the signs for Central Napa less than a mile through town until you reach the corner of 2nd Street and Main Street. Most of the town's sights and many of its restaurants are clustered in an easily walkable area around this intersection.

EXPLORING

Artesa Vineyards & Winery. With its modern, minimalist look in the tasting room, which is dug into a Carneros hilltop, and contemporary sculptures and fountains on the property, Artesa Vineyards & Winery is a far cry from the many faux French châteaus and rustic Italian-style villas in the region. Although the Spanish owners once made only sparkling wines, now they produce primarily still wines, mostly Chardonnay and Pinot Noir, but also Cabernet Sauvignon and a smattering of other limited-release wines such as Syrah and Albariño. Call ahead to reserve a spot on one of the specialty tours, such as a wine-and-cheese pairing or the walk through the vineyard ($45). ✉ *1345 Henry Rd., north off Old Sonoma Rd. and Dealy La., Napa* ☎ *707/224–1668* 🌐 *www.artesawinery.com* 🎫 *Tasting $10–$15, tour $20* 🕒 *Daily 10–5; tour daily at 11 and 2.*

Clos du Val. Although this austere winery doesn't seduce you with dramatic architecture or lush grounds, it doesn't have to: the wines, crafted by winemaker John Clews, have a wide following, especially among those who are patient enough to cellar the wines for a number of years. Though Clews's team makes great Pinot Noir and Chardonnay (grown in the nearby Carneros region), the real claim to fame is the intense reserve Cabernet, made with fruit from the Stags Leap District. The few

Continued on page 314

WINE
TASTING *in*
NAPA *and*
SONOMA

The tantalizing pop of a cork. Roads unspooling through hypnotically even rows of vines. Sun glinting through a glass of sparkling wine or ruby colored cabernet. If these are your daydreams, you won't be disappointed when you get to Napa and Sonoma. The vineyard-blanketed hills, shady town squares, and ivy-draped wineries—not to mention the luxurious restaurants, hotels, and spas—really *are* that captivating.

(opposite page) Carneros vineyards in autumn, Napa Valley. (top) Pinot Gris grapes (bottom) Bottles from Far Niente winery.

VISITING WINERIES

Napa and Sonoma are outstanding destinations for both wine newcomers and serious wine buffs. Tasting rooms range from modest to swanky, offering everything from a casual conversation over a few sips of wine to in-depth tours of winemaking facilities and vineyards. And there's a tremendous variety of wines to taste. The one constant is a deep, shared pleasure in the experience of wine tasting.

Wineries in Napa and Sonoma range from faux châteaux with vast gift shops to rustic converted barns where you might have to step over the vintner's dog in the doorway. Many are regularly open to the public, usually daily from around 10 am to 5 pm. Others require advance reservations to visit, and still others are closed to the public entirely. When in doubt, call ahead.

There are many, many more wineries in Napa and Sonoma than we could possibly include here. Free maps pinpointing most of them are widely available, though; ask the staff at the tasting rooms you visit or look for the ubiquitous free tourist magazines.

Pick a designated driver before setting out for the day. Although wineries rarely advertise it, many will provide a free nonalcoholic drink for the designated driver; it never hurts to ask.

Fees. In the past few years, tasting fees have skyrocketed. Most Napa wineries charge \$10 to \$20 to taste four or so wines, though \$30 or even \$40 fees aren't unheard of. Sonoma wineries are often a bit cheaper, in the \$5 to \$15 range, and you'll still find the occasional freebie.

Some winery tours are free, in which case you're usually required to pay a separate fee if you want to taste the wine. If you've paid a fee for the tour—often \$15 to \$30—your wine tasting is usually included in that price.

MAKING THE MOST OF YOUR TIME

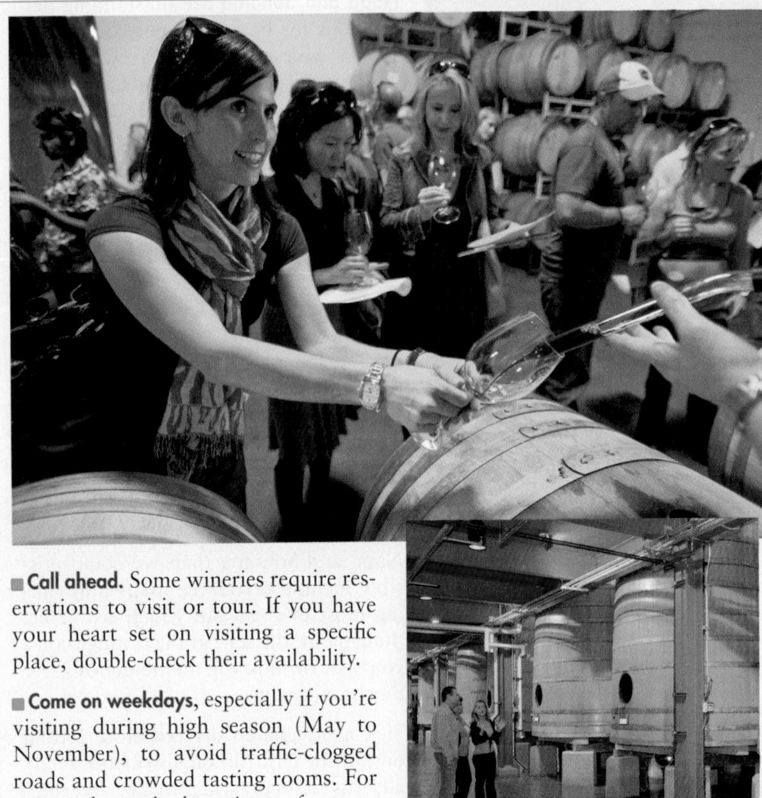

(top) Sipping and swirling in the De Loach tasting room. (bottom) Learning about barrel aging at Robert Mondavi Winery.

Call ahead. Some wineries require reservations to visit or tour. If you have your heart set on visiting a specific place, double-check their availability.

Come on weekdays, especially if you're visiting during high season (May to November), to avoid traffic-clogged roads and crowded tasting rooms. For more info on the best times of year to visit, see this chapter's Planner.

Get an early start. Tasting rooms are often deserted before 11 am or so, when most visitors are still lingering over a second cup of coffee. If you come early, you'll have the staff's undivided attention. You'll usually encounter the largest crowds between 3 and 5 pm.

Consider skipping Napa. If you've got less than two days to spend in the Wine Country, dip into the Carneros area or the Sonoma Valley rather than Napa Valley or northern Sonoma County. Though you might find fewer big-name wineries and critically acclaimed restaurants, these regions are only about an hour and half away from the city . . . if you don't hit traffic.

Divide your attention. If you're lucky enough to have three nights or more here, split your overnights between Napa and Sonoma to easily see the best that both counties have to offer.

A tasting at Heitz Cellar.

AT THE BAR

In most tasting rooms, you'll be handed a list of the wines available that day. The wines will be listed in a suggested tasting order, starting with the lightest-bodied whites, progressing to the most intense reds, and ending with dessert wines. If you can't decide which wines to choose, tell the server what types of wines you usually like and ask for a recommendation.

The server will pour you an ounce or so of each wine you select. As you taste it, feel free to take notes or ask questions. Don't be shy—the staff are there to educate you about their wine. If you don't like a wine, or you've simply tasted enough, feel free to pour the rest into one of the dump buckets on the bar.

TOURS

Tours tend to be the most exciting (and the most crowded) in September and October, when the harvest and crushing are underway. Tours typically last from 30 minutes to an hour and give you a brief overview of the winemaking process. At some of the older wineries, the tour guide might focus on the history of the property.

■ **TIP→ If you plan to take any tours, wear comfortable shoes, since you might be walking on wet floors or dirt or gravel pathways or stepping over hoses or other equipment.**

MONEY-SAVING TIPS

■ Many hotels and B&Bs distribute coupons for free or discounted tastings to their guests—don't forget to ask.

■ If you and your travel partner don't mind sharing a glass, servers are happy to let you split a tasting.

■ Some wineries will refund all or part of the tasting fee if you buy a bottle, making it so much easier to rationalize buying that $80 bottle of cabernet.

■ Almost all wineries will also waive the fee if you join their wine club program. However, this typically commits you to buying a certain number of bottles of their wine for a period of time, so be sure you really like their wines before signing up.

Preston Vineyards bottles only estate-grown grapes.

TOP 2-DAY ITINERARIES

First-Timer's Napa Tour

Start: Oxbow Public market, Napa. Get underway by browsing the shops selling wines, spices, locally grown produce, and other fine foods, for a taste of what the Wine Country has to offer.

Rubicon Estate, Rutherford. The tour here is a particularly fun way to learn about the history

of Napa winemaking—and you can see the old, atmospheric, ivy-covered château.

Frog's Leap, Rutherford. Friendly, unpretentious, and knowledgeable staff makes this place great for wine newbies. (Make sure you get that advance reservation lined up.)

Dinner and Overnight: St. Helena. Spluge at Meadowood Resort and you won't need to leave the property for an

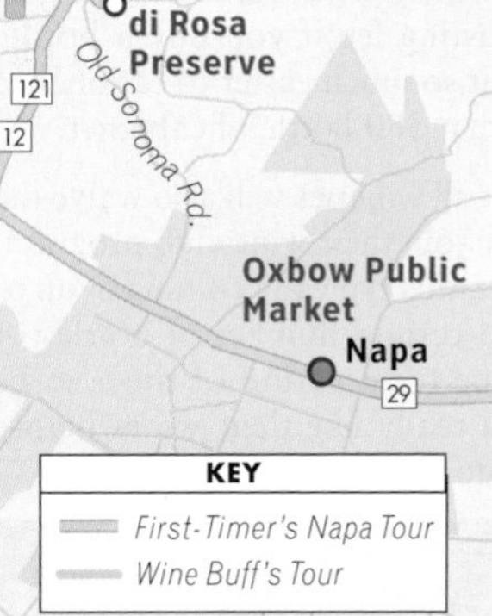

Wine Buff's Tour

Start: Stag's Leap Wine Cellars, Yountville. Famed for its cabernet sauvignon and Bordeaux blends.

Beaulieu Vineyard, Rutherford. Pony up the extra fee to visit the reserve tasting room to try their flagship cabernet sauvignon.

Caymus Vineyards, Rutherford. The low-key tasting room is a great place to learn more about Rutherford and Napa cabernet artistry. Reserve in advance.

Dinner and Overnight: Yountville. Have dinner at one of the Thomas Keller restaurants. Splurge at Bardessono; save at Maison Fleurie.

Next Day: Robert Mondavi, Oakville. Spring for the reserve room tasting so you can sip the top-of-the-line wines, especially the stellar cabernet. Head across Highway 29 to the Oakville Grocery to pick up a picnic lunch.

extravagant dinner at their restaurant. Save at El Bonita Motel with dinner at Taylor's.

Next Day: Poke around St. Helena's shops, then drive to Yountville for lunch.

di Rosa, Napa. Call ahead to book a one- or two-hour tour of the acres of gardens and galleries, which are chock-full of thousands of works of art.

Domaine Carneros, Napa. Toast your trip with a glass of outstanding bubbly.

Far Niente, Oakville. You have to reserve in advance and the fee for the tasting and tour is steep, but the payoff is an especially intimate winery experience. You'll taste excellent cabernet and chardonnay, then end your trip on a sweet note with a dessert wine.

Sonoma Backroads

Start: Iron Horse Vineyards, Russian River Valley. Soak up a view of vine-covered hills and Mount St. Helena while sipping a sparkling wine or pinot noir at this beautifully rustic spot.

Hartford Family Winery, Russian River Valley. A terrific source for pinot noir and chardonnay, the stars of this valley.

Dinner and Overnight: Forestville. Go all out with a stay at the Farmhouse Inn, whose award-winning restaurant is one of the best in all of Sonoma.

Next Day: Westside Road, Russian River Valley. This scenic route, which follows the river, is crowded with worthwhile wineries like Gary Farrell and Rochioli—but it's not crowded with visitors. Pinot fans will find a lot to love. Picnic at Rochioli and enjoy the lovely view.

Matanzas Creek Winery, near Santa Rosa. End on an especially relaxed note with a walk through their lavender fields (best in June).

WINE TASTING 101

TAKE A GOOD LOOK.

Hold your glass by the stem, raise it to the light, and take a close look at the wine. Check for clarity and color. (This is easiest to do if you can hold the glass in front of a white background.) Any tinge of brown usually means that the wine is over the hill or has gone bad.

BREATHE DEEP.

1. Sniff the wine once or twice to see if you can identify any smells.

2. Swirl the wine gently in the glass. Aerating the wine this way releases more of its aromas. (It's called "volatilizing the esters," if you're trying to impress someone.)

3. Take another long sniff. You might notice that experienced wine tasters spend more time sniffing the wine than drinking it. This is because this step is where the magic happens. The number of scents you might detect is almost endless, from berries, apricots, honey, and wildflowers to leather, cedar, or even tar. Does the wine smell good to you? Do you detect any "off" flavors, like wet dog or sulfur?

AT LAST! TAKE A SIP.

1. Swirl the wine around your mouth so that it makes contact with all your taste buds and releases more of its aromas. Think about the way the wine feels in your mouth. Is it watery or rich? Is it crisp or silky? Does it have a bold flavor, or is it subtle? The weight and intensity of a wine are called its body.

2. Hold the wine in your mouth for a few seconds and see if you can identify any developing flavors. More complex wines will reveal many different flavors as you drink them.

SPIT OR SWALLOW.

The pros typically spit, since they want to preserve their palate (and sobriety!) for the wines to come, but you'll find that swallowers far outnumber the spitters in the winery tasting rooms. Whether you spit or swallow, notice the flavor that remains after the wine is gone (the finish).

Swirl

Sniff

Sip

DODGE THE CROWDS

To avoid bumping elbows in the tasting rooms, look for wineries off the main drags of Highway 29 in Napa and Highway 12 in Sonoma. The back roads of the Russian River, Dry Creek, and Alexander valleys, all in Sonoma, are excellent places to explore. In Napa, try the northern end. Also look for wineries that are open by appointment only; they tend to schedule visitors carefully to avoid a big crush at any one time.

HOW WINE IS MADE

1. CRUSHING

Harvested grapes go into a stemmer-crusher, which separates stems from fruit and crushes the grapes to release "free-run" juice.

2. PRESSING

Remaining juice is gently extracted from grapes. Usually done by pressing grapes against the walls of a tank with an inflatable bladder.

3. FERMENTING

Extracted juice (and also grape skins and pulp, when making red wine) goes into stainless-steel tanks or oak barrels to ferment. During fermentation, sugars convert to alcohol.

4. AGING

Wine is stored in stainless-steel or oak casks or barrels to develop flavors.

5. RACKING

Wine is transferred to clean barrels; sediment is removed. Wine may be filtered and fined (clarified) to improve its clarity, color, and sometimes flavor.

6. BOTTLING

Wine is bottled either at the winery or at a special facility, then stored again for bottle-aging.

WHAT'S AN APPELLATION?

A specific region with a particular set of grape-growing conditions, such as soil type, climate, and elevation, is called an appellation. What makes things a little confusing is that appellations, which are defined by the Alcohol and Tobacco Tax and Trade Bureau, often overlap. California is an appellation, for example, but so is the Napa Valley. Napa and Sonoma counties are each county appellations, but they, too, are divided into even smaller regions, usually called subappellations or AVAs (American Viticultural Areas). You'll hear a lot about these AVAs from the staff in the tasting rooms; they might explain, for example, why the Russian River Valley AVA is such an excellent place to grow pinot noir grapes.

By law, if the label on a bottle of wine lists the name of an appellation, then at least 85% of the grapes in that wine must come from that appellation.

Wine and contemporary art find a home at di Rosa.

picnic tables fill up early on summer weekends, and anyone is welcome to try a hand at the bocce-style French game of pétanque. ✉ *5330 Silverado Trail, Napa* ☎ *707/259–2200* 🌐 *www.closduval.com* 🎫 *Tasting $15–$25* ⏲ *Daily 10–5; tour by appointment.*

Fodor's Choice ★ **di Rosa.** While you're driving along the Carneros Highway on your way to Napa from San Francisco, it would be easy to zip by one of the region's best-kept secrets: di Rosa. Metal sculptures of sheep grazing in the grass mark the entrance to this sprawling, art-stuffed property. Thousands of 20th-century artworks by hundreds of Northern California artists crop up everywhere—in galleries, in the former di Rosa residence, on every lawn, in every courtyard, and even on the lake. Some of the works were commissioned especially for the preserve, such as Paul Kos's meditative *Chartres Bleu,* a video installation in a chapel-like setting that replicates a stained-glass window of the cathedral in Chartres, France. If you stop by without a reservation, you'll only gain access to the Gatehouse Gallery, where there's a small collection of riotously colorful figurative and abstract sculpture and painting. **■ TIP→ To see the rest of the property and artwork, you'll have to sign up for one of the various tours of the grounds (from 1 to 2½ hours).** Reservations for the tours are recommended, but they can sometimes accommodate walk-ins. ✉ *5200 Sonoma Hwy./Carneros Hwy., Napa* ☎ *707/226–5991* 🌐 *www.dirosaart.org* 🎫 *Free, tour $10–$15* ⏲ *Wed.–Fri. 9:30–3; Sat. by reservation; call for tour times.*

★ **Domaine Carneros.** The majestic château here looks for all the world like it belongs in France, and in fact it does: it's modeled after the Château de la Marquetterie, an 18th-century mansion owned by the Taittinger family near Epernay, France. Carved into the hillside beneath the winery, Domaine Carneros's cellars produce delicate sparkling wines reminiscent of those made by Taittinger, using only grapes grown locally in the Carneros wine district. The winery sells full glasses, flights, and bottles of their wines, which also include still wines like a handful of Pinot Noirs and a Merlot, and serves them with cheese plates or caviar to those seated in the Louis XV–inspired salon or on the terrace overlooking the vineyards. Though this makes a visit here a tad more expensive than some stops on a winery tour, it's also one of the most opulent ways to enjoy the Carneros District, especially on fair days, when the views over the vineyards are spectacular. ⊠ *1240 Duhig Rd., Napa* ☎ *707/257–0101* 🌐 *www.domainecarneros.com* 🎟 *Tasting $6.75–$25, tour $25* ⏲ *Daily 10–6; tour daily at 11, 1, and 3.*

Fodor's Choice ★ **Hess Collection Winery.** Nine miles northwest of the city of Napa, up a winding road ascending Mt. Veeder, this winery is a delightful discovery. The simple limestone structure, rustic from the outside but modern and airy within, contains Swiss owner Donald Hess's personal art collection, including mostly large-scale works by such contemporary European and American artists as Robert Motherwell, Andy Goldsworthy, and Frank Stella. Cabernet Sauvignon is the real strength here, though Hess also produces some fine Chardonnays. Self-guided tours of the art collection and guided tours of the winery's production facilities are both free. On weekdays, ask to borrow an iPod for the free audio tour, which includes commentary by Donald Hess and some of the artists featured in the collection. ⊠ *4411 Redwood Rd., west of Rte. 29, Napa* ☎ *707/255–1144* 🌐 *www.hesscollection.com* 🎟 *Tasting $10–$30* ⏲ *Daily 10–5:30; guided tours daily, usually hourly 10:30–3:30.*

Luna Vineyards. Established in 1995 by veterans of the Napa wine industry, this spot on the southern end of the Silverado Trail originally focused on Italian varieties such as Sangiovese and Pinot Grigio. Though these days you're just as likely to taste a Merlot or a Cabernet blend, it's still well worth visiting its Tuscan-style tasting room with a coffered ceiling, especially for a nip of late-harvest Sauvignon Blanc and Semillon dessert wine called Mille Baci ("a thousand kisses" in Italian). ⊠ *2921 Silverado Trail, Napa* ☎ *707/255–5862* 🌐 *www.lunavineyards.com* 🎟 *Tasting $15–$25* ⏲ *Daily 10–5.*

Oxbow Public Market. Though it's not terribly large, this collection of about 25 small shops, wine bars, and artisanal food producers is a fun place to begin your introduction to the wealth of food and wine available in the Napa Valley. Swoon over the decadent charcuterie at the Fatted Calf, slurp down some oysters on the half shell at Hog Island Oyster Company, sample a large variety of local olive oils at The Olive Press, or get a whiff of the hard-to-find seasonings at the Whole Spice Company before sitting down to a glass of wine at one of the wine bars. A branch of the retro fast-food joint Gott's Roadside tempts those who prefer hamburgers to duck-liver mousse. ⊠ *610 and 644 1st St., Napa* ☎ *No phone* 🌐 *www.oxbowpublicmarket.com* 🎟 *Free* ⏲ *Generally weekdays 9–9, weekends 10–9; hrs of some merchants vary.*

6

Napa Valley
Mount St Helena
Robert Louis Stevenson State Park
THE PALISADES
Aetna Springs
POPE VALLEY
Pope Canyon Rd.
Pope Valley
Howell Mtn Rd.
Angwin
Angwin Airport
Lake Berryessa
Lake Berryessa Recreation Area
Knoxville Rd.
Calistoga
Tubbs Ln.
Dunaweal Ln.
Larkmead Ln.
Petrified Forest Rd.
Chiles Pope Valley Rd.
NAPA COUNTY
Diamond Mountain
Bothe-Napa State Park
Deer Park
Sanitarium Rd.
Bale Grist Mill State Historic Park
SONOMA COUNTY
Silverado Trail
Hennessy Lake
Sage Canyon Rd.
Saint Helena
NAPA VALLEY
Lake Hennessy City Recreation Area
Sugarloaf Ridge State Park
Hood Mountain Regional Park
Rutherford
Atlas Peak
FOSS VALLEY
Sonoma Hwy.
Adobe Canyon Rd.
Bald Mountain
Mt St. John
Oakville Cross Rd.
Oakville
Annadel State Park
Kenwood
SONOMA VALLEY
Oakville Grade Rd.
Yountville Hills
Yountville Cross Rd.
Napa River
Trinity Rd.
Yountville
Mt Veeder
Bennett Valley Rd.
Glen Ellen
Dry Creek Rd.
Oak Knoll
Big Ranch Rd.
Sonoma Mountain
VALLEY OF THE MOON
SONOMA MOUNTAINS
REDWOOD CANYON
Eldridge
Jack London State Park
CARNEROS VALLEY
Agua Caliente
Arnold Dr.
Boyes Hot Springs
Redwood Rd.
Trancas St.
Monticello
Pueblo
Lincoln
Browns Valley Rd.
1st
El Verano
Napa
Sonoma
Henry Rd.
Napa Rd.
Old Sonoma Rd.
Imola Ave.
Dealy La.
Washington
Adobe Rd.
Temelec
Petaluma
Lakeville Hwy.
Carneros Hwy.
Bonness Rd.
0 4 mi
0 4 km
Napa County Airport
Artesa Vineyards & Winery . 3
Beaulieu Vineyard 22
Beringer Vineyards 28
Cakebread Cellars 19
Castello di Amorosa 33
Caymus Vineyards 18
Charles Krug Winery 31
Clos du Val 8
Clos Pegase 34
Culinary Institute 29
di Rosa 2
Domaine Carneros 1
Domaine Chandon 9
Far Niente 14
Frog's Leap 24
Hess Collection Winery 5
Indian Springs 35
Joseph Phelps Vineyards .. 30
Luna Vineyards 6
Mumm Napa 25
Napa Valley Museum 7
Oakville Grocery 15
Opus One 17
Oxbow Public Market 4
PlumpJack 13
Robert Louis Stevenson State Park 36
Robert Mondavi 16
Robert Sinskey 11
Round Pond 23
Rubicon Estate 20
Rutherford Hill Winery 26
Schramsberg 32
Spring Mountain 27
St. Supéry 21
Stag's Leap Wine Cellars .. 10
Storybook Mountain 37
V Marketplace 12

Climbing ivy and lily pads decorate the Hess Collection's rustic exterior.

WHERE TO EAT

$$$ FRENCH **Angèle.** An 1890s boathouse with a vaulted wood-beam ceiling sets the scene for romance at this cozy French bistro. Though the style is casual—tables are close together, and the warm, crusty bread is plunked right down on the paper-top tables—the food is always well executed. Look for classic French dishes like duck breast accompanied with confit, guinea hen wrapped in house-cured pancetta, or a starter of *ris de veau* (veal sweetbreads) with a poached duck egg. In fair weather, ask for one of the charming outdoor tables. ✉ *540 Main St.* ☎ *707/252–8115* 🌐 *www.angelerestaurant.com.*

$ AMERICAN **BarBersQ.** Hardly a down-home ramshackle barbecue shack, this temple to meat in the middle of a shopping center has a clean, modern aesthetic, with black-and-white photos on the wall and brushed aluminum chairs. The menu of barbecue favorites includes a half or full rack of smoked baby back ribs and a Memphis-style pulled pork sandwich, all served with your choice of three different sauces. The supremely juicy fried chicken, made with free-range chicken and served with mashed potatoes and vinegary collard greens, is also popular. If you can save any room, the root-beer float or chocolate bourbon pecan pie is a fitting end to a homey meal. Outside seating (on a patio facing the parking lot) is available on fair days. ✉ *3900D Bel Aire Plaza* ☎ *707/224–6600* 🌐 *www.barbersq.com.*

$$ ITALIAN ★ **Bistro Don Giovanni.** Co-owner and host Giovanni Scala might be around to warmly welcome you to this lively bistro, where you can peek past the copper pots hanging in the open kitchen to see the 750-degree wood-burning oven. The Cal-Italian food is simultaneously inventive and comforting: an excellent fritto misto of onions, fennel, calamari,

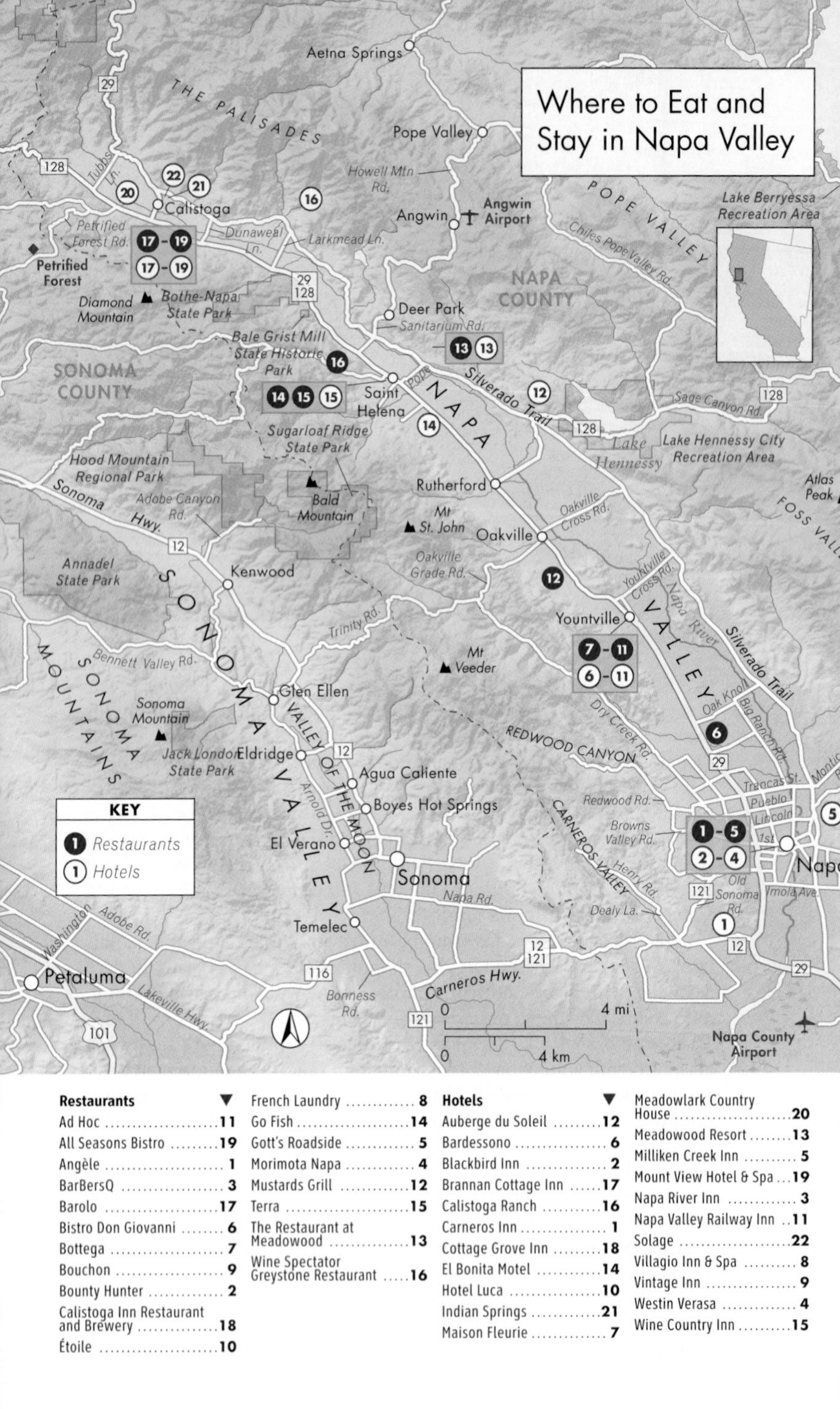

Restaurants

Ad Hoc ... 11
All Seasons Bistro ... 19
Angèle ... 1
BarBersQ ... 3
Barolo ... 17
Bistro Don Giovanni ... 6
Bottega ... 7
Bouchon ... 9
Bounty Hunter ... 2
Calistoga Inn Restaurant and Brewery ... 18
Étoile ... 10
French Laundry ... 8
Go Fish ... 14
Gott's Roadside ... 5
Morimota Napa ... 4
Mustards Grill ... 12
Terra ... 15
The Restaurant at Meadowood ... 13
Wine Spectator Greystone Restaurant ... 16

Hotels

Auberge du Soleil ... 12
Bardessono ... 6
Blackbird Inn ... 2
Brannan Cottage Inn ... 17
Calistoga Ranch ... 16
Carneros Inn ... 1
Cottage Grove Inn ... 18
El Bonita Motel ... 14
Hotel Luca ... 10
Indian Springs ... 21
Maison Fleurie ... 7
Meadowlark Country House ... 20
Meadowood Resort ... 13
Milliken Creek Inn ... 5
Mount View Hotel & Spa ... 19
Napa River Inn ... 3
Napa Valley Railway Inn ... 11
Solage ... 22
Villagio Inn & Spa ... 8
Vintage Inn ... 9
Westin Verasa ... 4
Wine Country Inn ... 15

and plump rock shrimp; pizza with caramelized onions and Gorgonzola; and whole roasted fish. Children are unusually welcome here, catered to with crayons and paper-topped tables and a menu with items like pizza topped with cheese, french fries, and "no green stuff." Fodors.com Forum users suggest snagging a table on the covered patio for a "more intimate and quiet" experience. ✉ *4110 Howard La. /Rte. 29* ☎ *707/224–3300* 🌐 *www.bistrodongiovanni.com.*

$$ AMERICAN ★ **Bounty Hunter.** A triple threat, Bounty Hunter is a wine store, wine bar, and restaurant in one. You can stop by for just a glass of wine from their impressive list—a frequently changing list with 40 available by the glass in both 2- and 5-ounce pours, and 400 by the bottle—but it's best to come with an appetite. A miniscule kitchen means the menu is also small, but every dish is a standout, including the pulled pork and beef brisket sandwiches served with three types of barbecue sauce, the signature beer-can chicken, and meltingly tender St. Louis–style ribs. The space is whimsically rustic, with stuffed game trophies mounted on the wall and leather saddles standing in for seats at a couple of tables. **TIP→ It's open until midnight on Friday and Saturday, making it a popular spot among locals for a late-night bite.** ✉ *975 1st St.* ☎ *707/226–3976* 🌐 *www.bountyhunterwinebar.com* *Reservations not accepted.*

$$$ JAPANESE **Morimoto Napa.** Masuharu Morimoto, known to many as the star of Iron Chef but also well regarded for his eponymous restaurants around the world, is the big name behind this hot restaurant that opened in downtown Napa in 2010. Organic materials like twisting grapevines above the bar and rough-hewn wooden tables seem simultaneously earthy and modern, which seems a fitting setting for the gorgeously plated Japanese fare, from super-fresh sashimi served with grated fresh wasabi to more elaborate concoctions like sea-urchin carbonara, made with udon noodles. For the full experience, consider the omakase menu ($110). If no tables are available, you can still order many dishes in the lounge, where a young and lively crowd drinks specialty cocktails along with appetizers like a tempura calamari salad and pork gyoza. ✉ *610 Main St., Napa* ☎ *707/252–1600* 🌐 *www.morimotonapa.com* *No lunch Mon. or Tues.*

WHERE TO STAY

For expanded hotel reviews, visit Fodors.com.

$$ **Blackbird Inn.** Arts and Crafts style infuses this 1905 building, from the lobby's enormous fieldstone fireplace to the lamps that cast a warm glow over the impressive wooden staircase to the attractive guest rooms, with sturdy turn-of-the-20th-century oak beds and matching night tables. **Pros:** gorgeous architecture and period furnishings; convenient to downtown Napa; free afternoon wine service. **Cons:** must be booked well in advance; some rooms are on the small side. ✉ *1755 1st St.* ☎ *707/226–2450 or 888/567–9811* 🌐 *www.blackbirdinnnapa.com* *8 rooms* *In-room: a/c, Wi-Fi. In-hotel: some pets allowed* *Breakfast.*

$$$$ Fodor's Choice ★ **Carneros Inn.** Freestanding board-and-batten cottages with rocking chairs on each porch are simultaneously rustic and chic at this luxurious property, where each cottage is flooded with natural light but still manages to maintain privacy, with windows and French doors leading to a private garden, some of which are equipped with fire pits and outdoor

6

soaking tubs. **Pros:** cottages have lots of privacy; beautiful views from the hilltop pool and hot tub; heaters on each private patio encourage lounging outside in the evening. **Cons:** a long drive from destinations up-valley; smallish rooms with limited seating options. ✉ *4048 Sonoma Hwy.* ☎ *707/299–4900* 🌐 *www.thecarnerosinn.com* *76 cottages, 10 suites* *In-room: a/c, Wi-Fi. In-hotel: restaurants, room service, bar, pool, gym, spa, some pets allowed.*

$$$$ **Milliken Creek Inn.** Wine and cheese at sunset set a romantic mood in the intimate lobby with its terrace overlooking the Napa River and a lush lawn, while chic rooms take a page from the stylebook of British-colonial Asia with a khaki-and-cream color scheme and gauzy canopies over the beds in some rooms alongside hydrotherapy spa tubs and some of the fluffiest beds in the Wine Country. **Pros:** soft-as-clouds beds; serene hotel-guests-only spa; breakfast delivered to your room (or wherever you'd like to eat on the grounds); gratuities are not accepted (except at the spa). **Cons:** expensive; road noise can be heard from the admittedly beautiful outdoor areas. ✉ *1815 Silverado Trail* ☎ *707/255–1197 or 800/835–6112* 🌐 *www.millikencreekinn.com* *12 rooms* *In-room: a/c, Wi-Fi. In-hotel: spa, some age restrictions apply* *Breakfast.*

MAKING TRACKS IN NAPA

Turn the driving over to someone else—a train conductor. The **Napa Valley Wine Train** (✉ *1275 McKinstry St.* ☎ *707/253–2111 or 800/427–4124* 🌐 *www.winetrain.com*) runs a scenic route between Napa and St. Helena with several restored 1915–17 Pullman railroad cars. The ride often includes a meal, such as brunch or dinner. While it's no bargain (starting at around $90 for lunch, $100 for dinner) and can feel a bit hokey, the train gives you a chance to enjoy the vineyard views without any driving worries.

$$$ **Napa River Inn.** Almost everything's close here: this waterfront inn is part of a complex of restaurants, shops, a gallery, and a spa, all within easy walking distance of downtown Napa. **Pros:** a pedestrian walkway connects the hotel to downtown Napa; unusual pet-friendly policy; wide range of room sizes and prices. **Cons:** river views could be more scenic; some rooms get noise from nearby restaurants. ✉ *500 Main St.* ☎ *707/251–8500 or 877/251–8500* 🌐 *www.napariverinn.com* *65 rooms, 1 suite* *In-room: a/c, Wi-Fi. In-hotel: restaurants, bar, gym, spa, business center, some pets allowed* *Breakfast.*

$$$$ **Westin Verasa.** Across the street from the Wine Train depot and just behind the Oxbow Public Market, this spacious hotel-condo complex, opened in 2008, is sophisticated and soothing, with pristine white bedding and furniture in warm earth tones. **Pros:** pool is heated year-round; most rooms have well-equipped kitchenettes; spacious double-headed showers. **Cons:** $20 "amenities fee" charged in addition to room rate. ✉ *1314 Mckinstry St.* ☎ *707/257–1800* 🌐 *www.westin.com/napa* *130 rooms, 50 suites* *In-room: a/c, kitchen (some), Wi-Fi. In-hotel: restaurants, room service, bar, pool, gym, some pets allowed.*

NIGHTLIFE AND THE ARTS

The interior of the 1879 Italianate Victorian **Napa Valley Opera House** isn't quite as majestic as the facade, but the intimate 500-seat venue is still an excellent place to see all sorts of performances, from Pat Metheny and Mandy Patinkin to the Napa Valley Film Festival and, yes, even the occasional opera. ✉ *1030 Main St.* ☎ *707/226–7372* 🌐 *www.napavalleyoperahouse.org.*

SPORTS AND THE OUTDOORS

BICYCLING

Thanks to the scenic country roads that wind through the region, bicycling is a practically perfect way to get around the Wine Country. And whether you're interested in an easy spin to a few wineries or a strenuous haul up a mountainside, there's a way to make it happen. ■ **TIP→ There are almost no designated bike lanes in the Wine Country, though, so be sure to pay attention to traffic.**

Napa Valley Bike Tours (✉ *6795 Washington St., Yountville* ☎ *707/944–2953*) will deliver the bikes, which go for $35 to $70 a day, to many hotels in the Napa Valley if you're renting at least two bikes for a full day. In addition to hourly rentals, a variety of guided and self-guided winery tours are available.

6

YOUNTVILLE

13 mi north of the town of Napa on Rte. 29.

These days Yountville is something like Disneyland for food-lovers. It all started with Thomas Keller's French Laundry, simply one of the best restaurants in the United States. Now Keller is also behind two more casual restaurants a few blocks from his mother ship—and that's only the tip of the iceberg. You could stay here for a week and not exhaust all the options in this tiny town with a big culinary reputation.

Yountville is full of small inns and high-end hotels that cater to those who prefer to walk (not drive) after an extravagant meal. It's also well located for excursions to many big-name Napa wineries, especially those in the Stags Leap District, where big, bold Cabernet Sauvignons helped put the Napa Valley on the wine-making map.

GETTING HERE AND AROUND

To get to Yountville from Highway 29 traveling north, take the Yountville exit and then take the first left, onto Washington Street. Almost all of Yountville's business and restaurants are clustered along Washington Street in the first half-mile. Yountville Cross Road connects tiny downtown Yountville to the Silverado Trail, along which many of the area's best wineries are located.

EXPLORING

Domaine Chandon. On a knoll west of downtown dotted with whimsical sculptures and shaded with ancient oak trees, this French-owned winery claims one of Yountville's prime pieces of real estate. Basic tours of the sleek, modern facilities are available for $12 (not including a tasting), but other tours ($30 each), which focus on various topics (food-and-wine pairing or Pinot production, for example), end with a seated tasting. The top-quality sparklers are made using the laborious

CLOSE UP

A Quick Wine Glossary

Like any activity, wine making and wine tasting have specialized vocabularies, and most of the terms are actually quite helpful, once you have them down. Here are some core terms to know:

American Viticultural Area (AVA). More commonly termed an "appellation," this is a region with unique soil, climate, and other grape-growing conditions. When a label lists an appellation—Napa Valley or Mt. Veeder, for example—at least 75% of the grapes used to make the wine must come from that region.

Aroma and bouquet. Aroma is the fruit-derived scent of young wine. It diminishes with fermentation and becomes a more complex **bouquet** as the wine ages.

Corked. Describes wine that is flawed by the musty, wet-cardboard flavor imparted by cork mold.

Estate bottled. A wine entirely made by one winery at a single facility. The grapes must come from the winery's own vineyards within the same appellation (which must be printed on the label).

Horizontal tasting. A tasting of several different wines of the same vintage.

Library wine. An older vintage that the winery has put aside to sell at a later date.

Méthode champenoise. The traditional, time-consuming method of making sparkling wines that are fermented in individual bottles.

Oaky. A vanilla-woody flavor that develops when wine is aged in oak barrels. Too much overpowers the other flavors.

Reserve wine. Fuzzy term applied by vintners to indicate that a wine is better in some way (through aging, source of the grapes, etc.) than others from their winery.

Table wine. Any wine that has at least 7% but not more than 14% alcohol by volume. The term doesn't necessarily imply anything about the wine's quality or price—both super-premium and jug wines can be labeled as table wine.

Tannins. These natural grape compounds produce a sensation of drying or astringency in the mouth and throat.

Terroir. French for "soil." Typically used to describe the soil and climate conditions that influence the quality and characteristics of grapes and wine.

Varietal. A wine that takes its name from the grape variety from which it is predominantly made. California wines that qualify are almost always labeled with the variety of the source grape.

Vertical tasting. A tasting of several wines of different vintages.

Vinification. Wine making, the process by which grapes are made into wine.

Vintage. The grape harvest of a given year, and the year in which the grapes are harvested. A vintage date on a bottle indicates the year in which the grapes were harvested rather than the year in which the wine was bottled.

Viticulture. The cultivation of grapes.

méthode champenoise. For the complete experience, you can order hors d'oeuvres to accompany the wines in the tasting room, which can be ordered either by tasting flights or by the glass. Although Chandon is best known for its bubblies, still wines like their Chardonnay, Pinot Noir, and Pinot Meunier are also worth a try. ✉ *1 California Dr., west of Rte. 29* ☎ *707/944–2280* 🌐 *www.chandon.com* 🎫 *Tasting $5.50–$25 by the glass, $16–$22 by the flight* ⏲ *Daily 10–6; tours daily at 1:30.*

Napa Valley Museum. Although it's not worth a long detour, if you need a break from wine tasting you can visit this small museum, next to Domaine Chandon on the grounds of the town's Veterans Home. Downstairs its permanent exhibit, The Land and People of Napa Valley, focuses on the geology and history of the area, from the Native Americans who once lived here through the pioneer period to the modern winemakers who made it famous. The rotating fine-arts shows upstairs feature the work of Napa Valley artists. ✉ *55 Presidents Circle* ☎ *707/944–0500* 🌐 *www.napavalleymuseum.org* 🎫 *$5* ⏲ *Wed.–Mon. 10–5.*

Robert Sinskey Vineyards. Although the winemaker here produces well-regarded Cabernet blends, as well as a variety of aromatic white wines, from their all-organic, certified biodynamic vineyards, Sinskey is best known for its intense, brambly Pinot Noirs, grown in the cooler Carneros District, where the grape thrives. The influence of Rob's wife, Maria Helm Sinskey—a chef and cookbook author and the winery's culinary director—is evident during the tastings, which come with a few bites of food paired with each wine (her books and other culinary items are also available in the gift shop, next to the open kitchen). But for the best sense of how Sinskey wines pair with food, reserve a spot on the culinary tour, which takes you through the winery's gardens and ends with a seated pairing of foods and wine. ✉ *6320 Silverado Trail, Napa* ☎ *707/944–9090* 🌐 *www.robertsinskey.com* 🎫 *Tasting $25, tour $60* ⏲ *Daily 10–4:30; tour by appointment.*

Stag's Leap Wine Cellars. It was the 1973 Cabernet Sauvignon produced by Stag's Leap Wine Cellars that put the winery—and the California wine industry—on the map by placing first in the famous Paris tasting of 1976. A visit to the winery is a no-frills affair; visitors in the tasting room are clearly serious about tasting wine, and aren't interested in distractions like a gift shop. It costs $30 to taste the top-of-the-line wines, including their limited-production estate-grown Cabernets, a few of which sell for well over $100. If you're interested in more modestly priced wines, try the $15 tasting, which usually includes a Sauvignon Blanc, Chardonnay, Merlot, and Cabernet. ✉ *5766 Silverado Trail, Napa* ☎ *707/265–2441* 🌐 *www.cask23.com* 🎫 *Tasting $15–$30, tour $40* ⏲ *Daily 10–4:30; tour by appointment.*

V Marketplace. In between bouts of eating and drinking, you might stop by V Marketplace. The vine-covered brick complex, which once housed a winery, livery stable, and a brandy distillery, contains a smattering of clothing boutiques, art galleries, and gift stores. NapaStyle, a large store, deli, and wine bar, sells cookbooks, luxury food items, and kitchenware, as well as an assortment of prepared foods perfect for picnics. The complex's signature restaurant, Bottega, features the food of celebrity chef Michael Chiarello. ✉ *6525 Washington St.* ☎ *707/944–2451.*

WHERE TO EAT

$$$$ AMERICAN Fodor's Choice ★ ✕ **Ad Hoc.** When superstar chef Thomas Keller opened this relatively casual spot in 2006, he meant to run it for only six months until he opened a burger joint in the same space—but locals were so charmed by the homey food that they clamored for the stopgap to stay. Now a single, seasonal fixed-price menu ($52) is served nightly, with a small menu of decadent brunch items served on Sunday. The selection might include a juicy pork loin and buttery polenta, served family style, or a delicate *panna cotta* with a citrus glaze. The dining room is warmly low-key, with zinc-top tables, wine served in tumblers, and rock and jazz on the stereo. If you just can't wait to know what's going be served before you visit, you can call a day in advance for the menu. ✉ *6476 Washington St.* ☎ *707/944–2487* 🌐 *www.adhocrestaurant.com* ⊙ *No lunch Mon.–Sat.; no dinner Tues. and Wed.*

$$$ ITALIAN Fodor's Choice ★ ✕ **Bottega.** At this lively trattoria the menu is simultaneously soulful and inventive, transforming local ingredients into regional Italian dishes with a twist. The antipasti in particular shine: you can order olives grown on chef Michael Chiarello's own property in St. Helena, house-made charcuterie, or an incredibly fresh fish crudo. Potato gnocchi might be served with duck and a chestnut ragu, and hearty main courses like braised short ribs could come on a bed of spinach prepared with preserved lemons. The vibe is more festival than formal, with exposed brick walls, an open kitchen, and paper-topped tables, but service is spot on, and the reasonably priced wine list offers lots of interesting choices from both Italy and California. This is one of the hottest spots on Yountville at the moment, so try to reserved well in advance, or visit at lunch, when it tends to be a little less crowded. ✉ *6525 Washington St.* ☎ *707/945–1050* 🌐 *www.botteganapavalley.com* ⊙ *No lunch Mon.*

$$$ FRENCH ✕ **Bouchon.** The team that brought French Laundry to its current pinnacle is also behind this place, where everything—the lively and crowded zinc bar, the elbow-to-elbow seating, the traditional French onion soup—could have come straight from a Parisian bistro. Roast chicken with mustard greens and fingerling potatoes and steamed mussels served with crispy, addictive *frites* (french fries) are among the hearty dishes served in the high-ceilinged room. ■ **TIP→ Late-night meals from a limited menu are served until 12:30 am—a rarity in the Wine Country, where it's often difficult to find a place to eat after 10.** ✉ *6534 Washington St.* ☎ *707/944–8037* 🌐 *www.bouchonbistro.com.*

$$$ AMERICAN ✕ **Étoile.** Housed at Domaine Chandon, this quietly elegant stunner seems built for romance, with delicate orchids on each table and views of the beautiful wooded winery grounds from the large windows. After a few years of being off the radar of many local critics, the restaurant has gotten more attention lately under the young chef Perry Hoffman, who turns out sophisticated California cuisine. Starters like lobster carpaccio with pickled carrots play with a variety of textures, and luxe ingredients like shavings of black truffle dress up pappardelle with maitake mushrooms. Four- and six-course tasting menus can be ordered with or without wine pairings. The wine list naturally features plenty of Domaine Chandon sparklers, but it's strong in wines from through-

out California as well. ✉ *1 California Dr.* ☎ *888/242–6366* 🌐 *www.chandon.com/etoile-restaurant* ⊗ *Closed Tues. and Wed. and Jan.*

$$$$ AMERICAN Fodor's Choice ★ ✕ **French Laundry.** An old stone building laced with ivy houses the most acclaimed restaurant in Napa Valley—and, indeed, one of the most highly regarded in the country. The restaurant's two nine-course prix-fixe menus (both $250), one of which is vegetarian, vary, but "oysters and pearls," a silky dish of pearl tapioca with oysters and white sturgeon caviar, is a signature starter. Some courses rely on luxe ingredients like foie gras, while others take humble foods like fava beans and elevate them to art. Reservations at French Laundry are hard-won, and not accepted more than two months in advance. **■ TIP→ Call two months ahead to the day at 10 am on the dot. Didn't get a reservation? Call on the day you'd like to dine here to be considered if there's a cancellation.** ✉ *6640 Washington St.* ☎ *707/944–2380* *Reservations essential* *Jacket required* 🌐 *www.frenchlaundry.com* ⊗ *Closed 1st 2 or 3 wks in Jan. No lunch Mon.–Thurs.*

$$ AMERICAN ✕ **Mustards Grill.** There's not an ounce of pretension at Cindy Pawlcyn's longtime Napa favorite, despite the fact that it's filled every day and night with fans of her hearty cuisine. The menu mixes updated renditions of traditional American dishes (what they like to call "deluxe truck stop classics"), such as barbecued baby back pork ribs and a lemon-lime tart piled high with browned meringue, with a handful of more innovative choices such as sweet corn tamales with tomatillo-avocado salsa and wild mushrooms. A black-and-white marble tile floor and upbeat artwork set a scene that one Fodors.com reader describes as "pure fun, if not fancy." ✉ *7399 St. Helena Hwy. /Rte. 29, 1 mi north of town* ☎ *707/944–2424* 🌐 *www.mustardsgrill.com* *Reservations essential.*

6

WHERE TO STAY

For expanded hotel reviews, visit Fodors.com.

$$$$ **Bardessono.** Although Bardessono bills itself as the "greenest luxury hotel in America," there's nothing spartan about its large, spare rooms, arranged around four landscaped courtyards, which have luxurious organic white bedding, gas fireplaces, and huge bathrooms with walnut floors. **Pros:** large rooftop lap pool; exciting restaurant on-site; polished service. **Cons:** expensive, the view from many rooms is uninspiring. ✉ *6526 Yount St.* ☎ *707/204–6000* 🌐 *www.bardessono.com* *50 rooms, 12 suites* *In-room: a/c, Internet, Wi-Fi. In-hotel: restaurant, room service, bar, pool, spa, some pets allowed.*

$$$$ **Hotel Luca.** Although this 20-room newcomer to Yountville just opened in December 2009, the property embodies a rustic Tuscan style through and through, with dark-wood furniture and soothing decor in brown and sage. **Pros:** extremely comfortable beds; attentive service; breakfast, included in rates, is served in the restaurant or delivered to your room. **Cons:** rooms are soundproofed, but outdoor areas get some traffic noise. ✉ *6774 Washington St.* ☎ *707/944–8080* 🌐 *www.hotellucanapa.com* *20 rooms* *In-room: a/c, Wi-Fi. In-hotel: restaurant, room service, bar, pool, gym, spa* *Breakfast.*

$$ ★ **Maison Fleurie.** If you'd like to be within easy walking distance of most of Yountville's best restaurants, and possibly score a great bargain, look into this casual, comfortable inn. **Pros:** smallest rooms are some of

the most affordable in town; free bike rental; refrigerator stocked with free soda. **Cons:** breakfast room can be crowded at peak times; bedding could be nicer. ✉ *6529 Yount St.* ☎ *707/944–2056, 800/788–0369* 🌐 *www.maisonfleurienapa.com* *13 rooms* *In-room: a/c, no TV (some), Wi-Fi. In-hotel: pool* *Breakfast.*

$ **Napa Valley Railway Inn.** Budget-minded travelers and those with kids appreciate these very basic accommodations—inside actual railcars—just steps away from most of Yountville's best restaurants. **Pros:** central Yountville location; guests have access to adjacent gym. **Cons:** minimal service, since the office is often unstaffed; rooms on the parking-lot side get some noise. ✉ *6523 Washington St.* ☎ *707/944–2000* 🌐 *www.napavalleyrailwayinn.com* *9 rooms* *In-room: a/c, no phone, Wi-Fi.*

$$$$ ★ **Villagio Inn & Spa.** The luxury here is quiet and refined, not flashy as is evident in a stroll along fountains and clusters of low buildings to the pool, where automated misters cool the sunbathers. **Pros:** amazing buffet breakfast; no extra charge for hotel guests to use the spa facilities; steps away from Yountville's best restaurants. **Cons:** can be bustling with large groups; you can hear the highway from many of the room's balconies or patios. ✉ *6481 Washington St.* ☎ *707/944–8877 or 800/351–1133* 🌐 *www.villagio.com* *86 rooms, 26 suites* *In-room: a/c, Internet, Wi-Fi. In-hotel: room service, tennis courts, bar, pool, spa.* *Breakfast.*

$$$$ **Vintage Inn.** Rooms in this lavish inn are housed in two-story villas scattered around a lush, landscaped 3½-acre property. **Pros:** spacious bathrooms with spa tubs; lavish breakfast buffet; luscious bedding. **Cons:** some exterior rooms get highway noise; pool area is smaller than the one at its sister property, the Villagio Inn & Spa. ✉ *6541 Washington St.* ☎ *707/944–1112 or 800/351–1133* 🌐 *www.vintageinn.com* *68 rooms, 12 suites* *In-room: a/c, Internet, Wi-Fi. In-hotel: room service, tennis courts, bar, pool, some pets allowed* *Breakfast.*

OAKVILLE

2 mi west of Yountville on Rte. 29.

There are three reasons to visit the town of Oakville: its gourmet grocery store; its scenic mountain road; and its magnificent, highly exclusive wineries.

GETTING HERE AND AROUND

Those driving along Route 29 will know they're reached Oakville when they see the Oakville Grocery Store on the east side of the road. Here the Oakville Cross Road provides access to the Silverado Trail, which runs parallel to Route 29. Oakville wineries are scattered along Route 29, Oakville Cross Road, and the Silverado Trail in roughly equal measure.

EXPLORING

Fodor's Choice ★ **Far Niente.** Though the fee for the combined tour and tasting is at the high end, Far Niente is especially worth visiting if you're tired of elbowing your way through crowded tasting rooms and are looking for a more personal experience. Here you're welcomed by name and treated to a glimpse of one of the most beautiful Napa properties. Small groups are shepherded through the historic 1885 stone winery, including some

Far Niente's wine cellars have a touch of ballroom elegance.

of the 40,000 square feet of caves, for a lesson on the labor-intensive method for making Far Niente's two wines, a Cabernet blend and a Chardonnay. (The latter is made without undergoing malolactic fermentation, so it doesn't have that buttery taste that's characteristic of many California Chards.) The next stop is the Carriage House, where you can see the founder's gleaming collection of classic cars. The tour ends with a seated tasting of wines and cheeses, capped by a sip of the spectacular Dolce, a late-harvest dessert wine made by Far Niente's sister winery. ✉ *1350 Acacia Dr.* ☎ *707/944–2861* 🌐 *www.farniente.com* 🎫 *$50* ⏲ *Tasting and tour by appointment.*

Oakville Grade. Along the mountain range that divides Napa and Sonoma, the Oakville Grade is a twisting half-hour route with breathtaking views of both valleys. Although the surface of the road is good, it can be difficult to negotiate at night, and the continual curves mean that it's not ideal for those who suffer from motion sickness. ✉ *West of Rte. 29*

Oakville Grocery. Built in 1881 as a general store, this popular spot carries a surprisingly wide range of unusual and chichi groceries and prepared foods. Unbearable crowds pack the narrow aisles on weekends, but it's still a fine place to sit on a bench out front and sip an espresso between winery visits. ✉ *7856 St. Helena Hwy. /Rte. 29* ☎ *707/944–8802*

Opus One. The combined venture of the late California winemaker Robert Mondavi and the late French baron Philippe de Rothschild, Opus One produces only one wine: a big, inky Bordeaux blend that was the first of Napa's ultra-premium wines, fetching unheard-of prices before it was overtaken by cult wines like Screaming Eagle. The winery's futuristic limestone-clad structure, built into the hillside, seems to be pushing itself out of the earth. Although the tour, which focuses on why it costs so much to produce this exceptional wine, can come off as "stuffy" (in the words of one Fodors.com reader), the facilities are undoubtedly impressive, with gilded mirrors, exotic orchids, and a large semicircular cellar modeled on the Château Mouton Rothschild winery in France. You can also taste the current vintage without the tour ($30), as long as you've called ahead for a reservation. **■ TIP→ Take your glass up to the rooftop terrace if you want to appreciate the views out over the vineyards.** ✉ *7900 St. Helena Hwy. /Rte. 29* ☎ *707/944–9442* 🌐 *www.opusonewinery.com* 🎫 *Tour $40* ⏲ *Daily 10–4; tasting and tour by appointment.*

PlumpJack. If Opus One is the Rolls-Royce of the Oakville District—expensive, refined, and a little snooty—then PlumpJack is the Mini Cooper: fun, casual, and sporty. With its metal chandelier and wall hangings, the tasting room looks like it could be the stage set for a modern Shakespeare production. (The name "PlumpJack" is a nod to Shakespeare's Falstaff.) The reserve Chardonnay has a good balance of baked fruit and fresh citrus flavors, while a Merlot is blended with a bit of Cabernet Sauvignon, giving the wine enough tannins to ensure it can be aged for another five years or more. If the tasting room is crowded, take a breather under the shady arbor on the back patio, where you can enjoy a close-up view of the vines. ✉ *620 Oakville Cross Rd.* ☎ *707/945–1220* 🌐 *www.plumpjack.com* 🎫 *Tasting $10* ⏲ *Daily 10–4.*

Robert Mondavi. The arch at the center of the sprawling Mission-style building at Robert Mondavi perfectly frames the lawn and the vineyard behind, inviting a stroll under the lovely arcades. If you've never been on a winery tour before, the comprehensive Signature Tour and Tasting ($25), which concludes with a seated tasting, is a good way to learn about enology, as well as the late Robert Mondavi's role in California wine making (shorter and longer tours are also available). And those new to tasting and mystified by all that swirling and sniffing should consider the 45-minute Wine Tasting Basics experience ($25). You can also head straight for one of the two tasting rooms. Serious wine lovers should definitely consider springing for the $30 reserve-room tasting, where you can enjoy four tastes of Mondavi's top-of-the-line wines, including both the current vintage and several previous vintages of the reserve Cabernet that cemented the winery's reputation. Concerts, mostly jazz and R&B, take place in summer on the lawn; call ahead for tickets. ✉ *7801 St. Helena Hwy. /Rte. 29* ☎ *888/766–6328* 🌐 *www.robertmondaviwinery.com* 🎫 *Tasting $20–$30, tour $15–$50* ⏲ *Daily 10–5; tour times vary.*

RUTHERFORD

2 mi northwest of Oakville on Rte. 29.

From a fast-moving car, Rutherford is a quick blur of vineyards and a rustic barn or two, but don't speed by this tiny hamlet. With its singular microclimate and soil, this is an important viticultural center, with more big-name wineries than you can shake a corkscrew at. Cabernet Sauvignon is king here. The well-drained, loamy soil is ideal for those vines, and since this part of the valley gets plenty of sun, the grapes develop exceptionally intense flavors. The late, great winemaker André Tchelistcheff claimed that "it takes Rutherford dust to grow great Cabernet."

GETTING HERE AND AROUND

Wineries around Rutherford are dotted along Route 29 and the parallel Silverado Trail just north and south of Rutherford Road/Conn Creek Road, which connect these two major thoroughfares.

EXPLORING

Beaulieu Vineyard. The Cabernet Sauvignon produced at the ivy-covered Beaulieu Vineyard is a benchmark of the Napa Valley. The legendary André Tchelistcheff, who helped define the California style of wine making, worked his magic here from 1938 until his death in 1973. This helps explain why Beaulieu's flagship, the Georges de Latour Private Reserve Cabernet Sauvignon, still garners high marks from major wine publications. The wines being poured in the main tasting room, which might include anything from a zesty Gewürztraminer to a lush Petite Syrah are notably good. Still, it's worth paying the extra money to taste that special Cabernet in the more luxe, less-crowded reserve tasting room. ✉ *1960 St. Helena Hwy. /Rte. 29* ☎ *707/967–5200* 🌐 *www.bvwines.com* 🎫 *Tasting $15–$35, tour $40* 🕐 *Daily 10–5.*

6

Cakebread Cellars. Jack and Dolores Cakebread snapped up the property at Cakebread Cellars in 1973, after Jack fell in love with the area while visiting on a photography assignment. Since then, they've been making luscious Chardonnays, as well as Merlot, a great Sauvignon Blanc, and a beautifully complex Cabernet Sauvignon. You must make an appointment for a tasting, for which there are several different options. The most basic usually involves a stroll through the winery's barrel room and crush pad and past Dolores's kitchen garden before ending in a taste of current releases. Other options focus on red, reserve, or library wines, and might take place in the winery's modern wing, where an elevator is crafted out of a stainless-steel fermentation tank and the ceiling is lined with thousands of corks. ✉ *8300 St. Helena Hwy.* ☎ *707/963–5221* 🌐 *www.cakebread.com* 🎫 *Tasting $15–$40, tour $25* 🕐 *Daily 10–4:30; tasting and tour by appointment.*

Caymus Vineyards. Wine master Chuck Wagner, who started making wine on the property in 1972, runs this well-regarded winery. His family, however, had been farming in the valley since 1906. Though they make a fine Zinfandel and Sauvignon Blanc, Cabernet is the winery's claim to fame, a ripe, powerful wine that's known for its consistently high quality. ■ **TIP→ There's no tour, and you have to reserve to taste, but it's still worth planning ahead to visit, because the low-key seated tasting (limited to 10 guests) is a great opportunity to learn about the valley's Cabernet artistry.** ✉ *8700 Conn Creek Rd.* ☎ *707/967–3010* 🌐 *www.caymus.com* 🎫 *Tasting $25* 🕐 *Sales daily 10–4; tasting by appointment.*

Fodor's Choice ★

Frog's Leap. The owner, John Williams, maintains a goofy sense of humor about wine that translates into an entertaining yet informative experience, making Frog's Leap the perfect places for wine novices to begin their education. You'll also find some fine Zinfandel, Cabernet Sauvignon, Merlot, Chardonnay, Sauvignon Blanc, Rosé, and also their

Frog's Leap's picturesque country charm extends all the way to the white picket fence.

take on the German dessert wine Trockenbeerenauslese. The winery includes a red barn built in 1884, 5 acres of organic gardens, an eco-friendly visitor center, and, naturally, a frog pond topped with lily pads. The fun tour is highly recommended, but you can also just do a seated tasting of their wines, which takes place on a porch overlooking the garden. ✉ *8815 Conn Creek Rd.* ☎ *707/963–4704* 🌐 *www.frogsleap.com* 🎫 *Tasting $20, tour $20.* 🕑 *Daily 10–4; tour by appointment.*

Mumm Napa. Although this is one of California's best-known sparkling-wine producers, enjoying the bubbly from the light-filled tasting room—available in either single flutes or by the flight—isn't the only reason to visit Mumm. There's also an excellent photography gallery with 30 Ansel Adams prints and rotating exhibits. You can even take that glass of wonderfully crisp Brut Rosé with you as you wander. For a leisurely tasting of a flight of their library wines while seated on their outdoor terrace ($30), reserve in advance. ✉ *8445 Silverado Trail* ☎ *707/967–7700* 🌐 *www.mummnapa.com* 🎫 *Tasting $6–$30, tour free–$20* 🕑 *Daily 10–5; tour daily at 10 (free; tasting not including), 11, 1, and 3 ($20, tasting including).*

★ **Round Pond.** It's not all grapevines here—you can switch your fruit focus to olives at Round Pond. This small farm grows five varieties of Italian olives and three types of Spanish olives. Within an hour of being hand-picked, the olives are crushed in the mill on the property to produce pungent, peppery oils that are later blended and sold. Call at least a day or two in advance to arrange a tour of the mill followed by an informative tasting, during which you can sample several types of oil, both alone and with Round Pond's own red-wine vinegars and other tasty foods. ■ **TIP→ If you can arrange to visit between mid-November and the end of December, you might be lucky enough to see the mill in action.** ✉ *886 Rutherford Rd.* ☎ *888/302–2575* 🌐 *www.roundpond.com* 🎫 *Tour $25* ⏲ *Tour by appointment.*

Word of Mouth

"If you're in Napa and want a truly exceptional meal (and don't mind paying for it), then the French Laundry is your ticket. In Sonoma, Cyrus in Healdsburg fills a similar need for high-end dining."
—Otis_B_Driftwood

Rubicon Estate. It's the house *The Godfather* built. Filmmaker Francis Ford Coppola began his wine-making career in 1975, when he bought part of the historic, renowned Inglenook estate. He eventually reunited the original Inglenook land and snagged the ivy-covered 19th-century château to boot. In 2006 he renamed the property Rubicon Estate, intending to focus on his premium wines, including the namesake Cabernet Sauvignon–based blend. (The less expensive wines are showcased at the Francis Ford Coppola Winery in Sonoma County's Geyserville.) A variety of tours and seminars cover topics that include the history of the estate, the Rutherford climate and geology, and the sensory evaluation of wine, but many just come to taste in the opulent, high-ceilinged tasting room. The wine bar, Mammarella, has seating in a picturesque courtyard. ✉ *1991 St. Helena Hwy./Rte. 29* ☎ *707/963–9099* 🌐 *www.rubiconestate.com* 🎫 *Tasting $15–$50, tours free (included in the $25 and $50 tastings)–$45.* ⏲ *Daily 10–5; call for tour times.*

Rutherford Hill Winery. A Merlot lover's paradise in a Cabernet Sauvignon world. When the winery's founders were deciding what grapes to plant, they discovered that the climate and soil conditions of their vineyards resembled those of Pomerol, a region of Bordeaux where Merlot is king. The wine caves here are some of the most extensive of any California winery—nearly a mile of tunnels and passageways. You can get a glimpse of the tunnels and the 5,000 barrels inside on the tours, then cap your visit with a picnic in their oak or olive groves. With views over the valley from a perch high on a hill, the picnic grounds are more charming than many others in Napa, which tend to be rather close to one of the busy thoroughfares. ✉ *200 Rutherford Hill Rd., east of Silverado Trail* ☎ *707/963–1871* 🌐 *www.rutherfordhill.com* 🎫 *Tasting $15–$30, tour $25* ⏲ *Daily 10–5; tour daily at 11:30, 1:30, and 3:30.*

St. Supéry. Your instinct may be to enter the beautifully restored 1882 Queen Anne Victorian at St. Supéry looking for the tasting room; actually the wines are being poured in the building behind it, a bland, unappealing, officelike structure. But you'll likely forgive the atmospheric lapse once you taste their fine Sauvignon Blancs, Merlots, and Chardonnays, as well as a couple of unusual wines that are made primarily of either Cabernet Franc or Petit Verdot, both of which are usually used for blending with Cabernet Sauvignon. An excellent, free self-guided tour also allows you a peek at the barrel and fermentation rooms, as well as a gallery of rotating art exhibits. At the "Smell-a-Vision" station you can test your ability to identify different smells that might be present in wine, and a small demonstration vineyard allows you to see the differences between different types of vines and even taste the grapes when they're in season. ✉ *8440 St. Helena Hwy. S /Rte. 29* ☎ *707/963–4507* 🌐 *www.stsupery.com* 🎫 *Tasting $10–$25* ⏲ *Daily 10–5.*

WHERE TO STAY

For expanded hotel reviews, visit Fodors.com.

$$$$ ★ **Auberge du Soleil.** Taking a cue from the olive-tree-studded landscape, this renowned hotel cultivates a luxurious Mediterranean look: earth-tone tile floors, heavy wood furniture, and terra-cotta colors. **Pros:** stunning views over the valley; spectacular pool and spa areas; the most expensive suites are fit for a superstar. **Cons:** stratospheric prices; the two least expensive rooms (in the main house) get some noise from the bar and restaurant. ✉ *180 Rutherford Hill Rd., off Silverado Trail north of Rte. 128* ☎ *707/963–1211 or 800/348–5406* 🌐 *www.aubergedusoleil.com* *31 rooms, 21 suites* *In-room: a/c, Internet, Wi-Fi. In-hotel: restaurants, room service, tennis court, bar, pool, gym, spa* *Breakfast.*

ST. HELENA

2 mi northwest of Oakville on Rte. 29.

Downtown St. Helena is a symbol of how well life can be lived in the Wine Country. Sycamore trees arch over Main Street (Route 29), a funnel of outstanding restaurants and tempting boutiques. At the north end of town looms the hulking stone building of the Culinary Institute of America. Weathered stone and brick buildings from the late 1800s give off that gratifying whiff of history.

By the time pioneer winemaker Charles Krug planted grapes in St. Helena around 1860, quite a few vineyards already existed in the area. Today the town is hemmed in by wineries, and you could easily spend days visiting vintners within a few miles.

GETTING HERE AND AROUND

Downtown St. Helena stretches along Route 29, which is called Main Street here. Many of the shops and restaurants are clustered on two pleasant pedestrian-friendly blocks of Main Street, between Pope Street and Adams Street. Wineries in the area are found both north and south of downtown along both Route 29 and the Silverado Trail, but some of the less touristed and more scenic spots are on the slopes of Spring Mountain, which rises southwest of town.

EXPLORING

Beringer Vineyards. Arguably the most beautiful winery in Napa Valley, the 1876 Beringer Vineyards is also the oldest continuously operating property. In 1884 Frederick and Jacob Beringer built the Rhine House Mansion to serve as Frederick's family home. Today it serves as the reserve tasting room, where you can sample wines surrounded by Belgian art-nouveau hand-carved oak and walnut furniture and stained-glass windows. The assortment includes a limited-release Chardonnay, a few big but very drinkable Cabernets, and a luscious white dessert wine named Nightingale. Another, less expensive tasting takes place in the less photogenic original stone winery. **■ TIP→ If you're looking for an undiscovered gem, pass this one by, but first-time visitors to the valley will**

learn a lot about the history of wine making in the region on the introductory tour. Longer tours, which might pass through a demonstration vineyard or end with a seated tasting in the Rhine House, are also offered a few times a day. ✉ *2000 Main St. /Rte. 29* ☎ *707/963–4812* 🌐 *www.beringer.com* 🎫 *Tasting $15–$25, tour $20–$30* ⏲ *May 29–Oct. 22, daily 10–6; Oct. 23–May 28, daily 10–5; call for tour times.*

Charles Krug Winery. The first winery founded in the Napa Valley, Charles Krug Winery, opened in 1861 when Count Haraszthy lent Krug a small cider press. Today the Peter Mondavi family runs it. Though the tasting room is fairly modest, the knowledgeable and friendly servers ensure a relaxed visit. The winery is best known for its lush red Bordeaux blends, but its Zinfandel is also good—or go for something unusual with the New Zealand–style Sauvignon Blanc. Its zingy flavor of citrus and tropical fruit is rare in wines from this area. The picnic area behind the tasting room has a view of the redwood cellar (not open to the public), where their wines are aged. ✉ *2800 N. Main St.* ☎ *707/963–5057* 🌐 *www.charleskrug.com* 🎫 *Tasting $10–$20* ⏲ *Daily 10:30–5.*

6

Culinary Institute of America. The West Coast headquarters of the Culinary Institute of America, the country's leading school for chefs, are in the **Greystone Winery,** an imposing building that was the largest stone winery in the world when it was built in 1889. On the ground floor you can check out the quirky corkscrew display and shop at a well-stocked culinary store that tempts aspiring chefs with gleaming gadgets and an impressive selection of cookbooks. Attached to the store, at the Flavor Bar, you can experience a guided tasting of certain types of ingredients (for example, chocolate or olive oil) to gain a greater understanding of them ($10 to $15). Upstairs, if there are no special events going on, you can browse their Vintners Hall of Fame, where winemakers past and present are commemorated on plaques fastened to 2,200-gallon redwood wine barrels. One-hour cooking demonstrations ($15) take place on Saturday on Sunday; call or visit the Web sites for time and reservations, or to get information on longer, hands-on cooking classes on a variety of subjects. ✉ *2555 Main St.* ☎ *707/967–1100* 🌐 *www.ciachef.edu* 🎫 *Free* ⏲ *Restaurant Sun.–Thurs. 11:30–9, Fri. and Sat. 11:30–10; store and museum daily 10–6.*

Fodor's Choice ★ **Joseph Phelps Vineyards.** Although an appointment is required to taste here, it's worth the trouble. In fair weather the casual, self-paced wine tastings are held on the terrace of a huge, modern barnlike building with stunning views down the slopes over oak trees and orderly vines. Though the Sauvignon Blanc and Viognier are good, the blockbuster wines are reds. The 2002 vintage of their flagship wine, a Bordeaux-style blend called Insignia, was selected as *Wine Spectator*'s wine of the year, immediately pushing up prices and demand. Luckily, you'll get a taste of the current vintage of Insignia (which goes for around $200 a bottle). A variety of 90-minute tasting seminars, available by appointment, are $40. The popular blending seminar, during which you get to try your hand at mixing the various varietals that go into their Insignia blend, is $60. ✉ *200 Taplin Rd.* ☎ *707/963–2745* 🌐 *www.jpvwines.com* 🎫 *Tasting $25* ⏲ *Weekdays 10–3:30, weekends 10–2:30; tasting by appointment.*

★ **Spring Mountain Vineyard.** Hidden off a winding road behind a security gate, Spring Mountain Vineyard has the feeling of a private estate in the countryside, even though it's only a few miles from downtown St. Helena. Though some Sauvignon Blanc, Pinot Noir, and Syrah is produced, the calling card here is Cabernet—big, chewy wines that demand some time in the bottle but promise great things. A tasting of their current releases ($25) gives you a good sense of the charms of their wines, but consider springing for the estate ($35) or reserve tasting ($50), both of which include a meander through the beautiful property, from the cellars to the beautifully preserved 1885 mansion. The latter two conclude in either the mansion's dining room or their wine cellar for a seated tasting. ✉ *2805 Spring Mountain Rd.* ☎ *707/967–4188* 🌐 *www.springmountainvineyard.com* 🎫 *Tour and tasting $25–$50* ⏲ *Tour and tasting by appointment.*

WHERE TO EAT

$$ SEAFOOD ★ ✕ **Go Fish.** Prolific restaurateur Cindy Pawlcyn is the big name behind this bustling bistro, one of the first restaurants in the Wine Country to specialize in seafood. You can either sit at the long marble bar and watch the chefs whip up inventive sushi rolls and raw-bar bites, or head into the dining room to study the mouthwatering menu, with listings that include a French-inflected sole almondine and Asian-inspired dishes like miso-marinated black cod. Hearty sandwiches like the bigeye tuna Reuben are popular at lunch. The large, lively space works a modern-chic look, with stainless-steel lamps and comfortable banquettes, and tables on the terrace are popular on fair evenings. ✉ *641 Main St.* ☎ *707/963–0700* 🌐 *www.gofishrestaurant.net.*

$ AMERICAN ★ ✕ **Gott's Roadside.** A slick 1950s-style outdoor hamburger stand goes upscale at this hugely popular spot, where locals are willing to brave long lines to order juicy burgers, root-beer floats, and garlic fries. There are also plenty of choices you wouldn't have found 50 years ago, such as the *ahi* tuna burger and chicken club with pesto mayo. Try to get here early or late for lunch, or all the shaded picnic tables on the lawn might be filled with happy throngs. Lines are usually shorter at the Gott's in downtown Napa's Oxbow Public Market. ✉ *933 Main St.* ☎ *707/963–3486* 🌐 *www.gottsroadside.com.*

$$$$ AMERICAN Fodor's Choice ★ ✕ **The Restaurant at Meadowood.** Chef Christopher Kostow has garnered rave reviews for transforming seasonal local products (some grown right on the property) into elaborate, elegant fare. The "composition of carrots," constructed of the tiniest carrots imaginable accompanied by delicate shavings of chocolate, foie gras, and candied tangerine (it sounds odd, but it works) is just one example of Kostow's inventiveness and playfulness. The slow-cooked black cod with chorizo and lamb demonstrates an earthier approach. The chef's menu ($175, $300 with wine pairings), composed of seven or so courses, is the best way to appreciate the experience, but the gracious and well-trained servers provide some of the best service in the valley even if you're ordering a less extravagant three-, four-, or five-course menu. The warm lighting and well-spaced tables in the dining room, which looks out onto a lovely stand of trees and the property's golf course, makes it a top choice for a romantic tête-à-tête. ✉ *900 Meadowood La.* ☎ *707/967–1205* 🌐 *www.meadowood.com* ⏲ *Closed Sun. No lunch.*

$$$ MEDITERRANEAN ★ ✕ **Terra.** St. Helena may have newer, flashier, and more dramatic restaurants, but for old-school romance and service, many diners return year after year to this quiet favorite in an 1884 fieldstone building. Since 1988, chef Hiro Sone has been giving unexpected twists to Italian and southern French cuisine in dishes such as the mussel soup with caramelized onions and garlic croutons, heavily perfumed with the scent of saffron. A few, like the signature sake-marinated black cod in a *shiso* broth, draw on Sone's Japanese background. Homey yet elegant desserts, courtesy of Sone's wife, Lissa Doumani, might include a chocolate caramel tart topped with fleur de sel. The gracious staff unobtrusively attends to every dropped fork or half-full water glass. ✉ *1345 Railroad Ave.* ☎ *707/963–8931* 🌐 *www.terrarestaurant.com* ⊗ *Closed Tues. and 1st 2 wks in Jan. No lunch.*

$$$ MEDITERRANEAN ✕ **Wine Spectator Greystone Restaurant.** The Culinary Institute of America runs this place in the handsome old Christian Brothers Winery. Century-old stone walls house a spacious restaurant that bustles at both lunch and dinner, with several cooking stations in full view. On busy nights you may find the hard-at-work chefs more entertaining than your dining companions. The tables on the terrace, shaded by red umbrellas, are away from the action, but on fair days they're even more appealing, providing a panoramic view down the hillside. The menu has a Mediterranean spirit and emphasizes locally grown produce. Typical main courses on the frequently changing menu include prosciutto-wrapped cod and house-made pasta with trumpet mushrooms and a sherry cream sauce. ✉ *2555 Main St.* ☎ *707/967–1010* 🌐 *www.ciachef.edu.*

6

WHERE TO STAY

For expanded hotel reviews, visit Fodors.com.

$$ **El Bonita Motel.** Only in St. Helena would a basic room in a roadside motel cost around $200 a night in high season, but for budget-minded travelers the tidy rooms here are pleasant enough, and the landscaped grounds and picnic tables elevate this property over similar places. **Pros:** cheerful rooms; hot tub; microwaves and mini refrigerators. **Cons:** road noise is a problem in some rooms. ✉ *195 Main St. / Rte. 29* ☎ *707/963–3216 or 800/541–3284* 🌐 *www.elbonita.com* *38 rooms, 4 suites* *In-room: a/c, Wi-Fi. In-hotel: pool, business center, some pets allowed* *Breakfast.*

$$$$ Fodor's Choice ★ **Meadowood Resort.** A rambling lodge and several gray clapboard bungalows are scattered across this sprawling property, giving it an exclusive New England feel, and every unit runs seamlessly—starting with the gatehouse staff who alert the front desk to arrivals. **Pros:** site of one of Napa's best restaurants; lovely hiking trail on the property; the most gracious service in all of Napa. **Cons:** very expensive; most bathrooms are not as extravagant as at other similarly priced resorts. ✉ *900 Meadowood La.* ☎ *707/963–3646 or 800/458–8080* 🌐 *www.meadowood.com* *40 rooms, 45 suites* *In-room: a/c, Internet, Wi-Fi. In-hotel: golf course, restaurants, room service, tennis courts, bar, pools, gym.*

$$$$ **Wine Country Inn & Gardens.** A pastoral landscape of vine-covered hills surrounds this retreat, which was styled after the traditional New England inns its owners liked to visit in the 1970s. **Pros:** free shuttle to some restaurants (reserve early); lovely grounds; swimming pool is heated

year-round. **Cons:** some rooms let in noise from neighbors; some areas could use updating. ✉ *1152 Lodi La., east of Rte. 29* ☎ *707/963–7077* 🌐 *www.winecountryinn.com* *24 rooms, 5 suites* *In-room: a/c, no TV, Wi-Fi. In-hotel: pool* *Breakfast.*

SHOPPING

Dean & Deluca (✉ *607 St. Helena Hwy. S /Rte. 29* ☎ *707/967–9980*), a branch of the famous Manhattan store, is crammed with everything you need in the kitchen—including terrific produce and deli items—as well as a large wine selection. The **Spice Islands Marketplace** (✉ *Culinary Institute of America, 2555 Main St.* ☎ *888/424–2433*) is the place to shop for cookbooks, kitchenwares, and everything else related to cooking and preparing food. Elaborate confections handmade on the premises are displayed like miniature works of art at **Woodhouse Chocolate** (✉ *1367 Main St.* ☎ *707/963–8413*), a lovely shop that resembles an 18th-century Parisian salon.

CALISTOGA

3 mi northwest of St. Helena on Rte. 29.

With false-fronted, Old West–style shops, 19th-century hotels, and unpretentious cafés lining Lincoln Avenue, the town's main drag, Calistoga has a slightly rough-and-tumble feel that's unique in the Napa Valley. It comes across as more down-to-earth than some of the polished towns to the south. And it's easier to find a bargain here, making it a handy home base for exploring the surrounding vineyards and back roads.

Ironically, Calistoga was developed as a swell, tourist-oriented getaway. In 1859 maverick entrepreneur Sam Brannan snapped up 2,000 acres of prime property and laid out a resort, intending to use the area's natural hot springs as the main attraction. Brannan's gamble didn't pay off as he'd hoped, but the hotels and bathhouses won a local following. Many of them are still going, and you can come for an old-school experience of a mud bath or a dip in a warm spring-fed pool.

GETTING HERE AND AROUND

To get to downtown Calistoga from anywhere farther south in the valley, take Route 29 north and then turn right on Lincoln Avenue. Most of the town's sights are found along a five-block stretch of Lincoln Avenue, or just off one of the side streets that intersect it. After about a mile, Lincoln Avenue (which changes names to Lake County Highway) intersects with the Silverado Trail.

EXPLORING

★ **Castello di Amorosa.** Possibly the most astounding sight in Napa Valley is your first glimpse of the Castello di Amorosa, which looks for all the world like a medieval castle, complete with drawbridge and moat, chapel, stables, and secret passageways. Some of the 107 rooms contain replicas of 13th-century frescoes, and the dungeon has an actual iron maiden from Nuremberg, Germany. You must pay for the tour to see the most of the extensive eight-level property, though paying for a tasting allows you access to a small portion of the astounding complex, as well as a taste of several of their excellent Italian-style wines, including

All it needs is a fair maiden: Castello di Amorosa's re-created castle.

a "super Tuscan," which is a blend of Sangiovese and Merlot with Cabernet Sauvignon, which gives it a bit more heft than your average Italian red. ✉ *4045 N. Saint Helena Hwy.* ☎ *707/967–6272* 🌐 *www.castellodiamorosa.com* 🎫 *Tasting $16–$26, tour $31–$41* 🕑 *Mar.–Oct., daily 9:30–6; Nov.–Feb., daily 9:30–5; tour by appointment.*

Clos Pegase. Designed by postmodern architect Michael Graves, the Clos Pegase winery is a one-of-a-kind "temple to wine and art" packed with unusual art objects from the collection of owner and publishing entrepreneur Jan Shrem. After tasting the wines, which include a bright Sauvignon Blanc, fruity Chardonnays, and mellow Pinot Noir, Merlot, and Cabernet (they're made in a soft, approachable style and meant to be drunk somewhat young), be sure to check out the surrealist paintings near the main tasting room, which include a Jean Dubuffet painting you may have seen on one of their labels. Better yet, bring a picnic and have lunch in the courtyard, where a curvaceous Henry Moore sculpture is one of about two dozen works of art. ✉ *1060 Dunaweal La.* ☎ *707/942–4981* 🌐 *www.clospegase.com* 🎫 *Tasting $7.50–$15, tour free* 🕑 *Daily 10:30–5; tour daily at 11:30 and 2.*

Indian Springs. Even before Sam Brannan constructed a spa and mud baths here in the 1860s, the Wapoo Indians were building sweat lodges over the thermal geysers at this, the oldest continually operating pool and spa in California. You can choose from the various spa treatments and volcanic-ash mud baths, after which you can relax in the small Zen-inspired garden out back. Best of all, clients of the spa and guests of the lodge rooms or bungalows ($–$$$) have access to the Olympic-size mineral-water pool, kept at 92°F in summer and a toasty 102°F in winter. ✉ *1712 Lincoln Ave. /Rte. 29* ☎ *707/942–4913* 🌐 *www.indianspringscalistoga.com* ⏲ *Daily 9–8.*

Petrified Forest. Here you'll find the remains of the volcanic eruptions of Mt. St. Helena 3.4 million years ago: petrified giant redwoods. Pick up a brochure before starting off on the leisurely 15-minute walk around the property, which takes you by the largest specimen, "The Queen of the Forest," a 65-by-8-foot petrified log. The property doesn't take long to visit unless you're a geology buff. For the best experience, consider taking a meadow hike for an additional $6, which leads through the woodland until you have a view of Mt. St. Helena. The 45-minute excursion, led by a naturalist, is offered on Saturday at 11 am, weather permitting. ✉ *4100 Petrified Forest Rd., 5 mi west of Calistoga* ☎ *707/942–6667* 🌐 *www.petrifiedforest.org* *$10* ⏲ *Mid-Mar.–early Nov., daily 9–6; early Nov.–mid-Mar., daily 9–5.*

Robert Louis Stevenson State Park. Encompassing the summit of Mt. St. Helena, this state park was where Stevenson and his bride, Fanny Osbourne, spent their honeymoon in an abandoned bunkhouse of the Silverado Mine. This stay in 1880 inspired the writer's travel memoir *The Silverado Squatters,* and Spyglass Hill in *Treasure Island* is thought to be a portrait of Mt. St. Helena. The park's approximately 3,600 acres are mostly undeveloped except for a trail leading to the site of the bunkhouse—which is marked with a marble memorial in the form of an open book on top of a pedestal—and a fire trail to the summit beyond. **TIP→ If you're planning on attempting the hike to the top, a 10-mi round-trip, bring plenty of water and dress appropriately: the trail is steep and lacks shade in spots, but the summit is often cool and breezy.** ✉ *Rte. 29, 7 mi north of Calistoga* ☎ *707/942–4575* 🌐 *www.parks.ca.gov* *Free* ⏲ *Daily sunrise–sunset.*

Fodor's Choice ★ **Schramsberg.** Founded in the 1860s, Schramsberg, one of Napa's oldest wineries, produces a variety of bubblies made using the traditional méthode champenoise (which means, among other things, that the wine undergoes a second fermentation in the bottle before being "riddled," or turned every few days over a period of weeks, to nudge the sediment into the neck of the bottle). If you want to taste, you must tour first, but what a tour: in addition to getting a glimpse of the winery's historic architecture, you get to tour the cellars dug in the late 19th century by Chinese laborers, where a mind-boggling 2 million bottles are stacked in gravity-defying configurations. The tour fee includes generous pours of several very different sparkling wines. ✉ *1400 Schramsberg Rd.* ☎ *707/942–4558* 🌐 *www.schramsberg.com* *Tasting and tour $40* ⏲ *Tasting and tour by appointment.*

Storybook Mountain Vineyards. Tucked into a rock face in the Mayacamas range, Storybook Mountain Vineyards is one of the more beautiful wineries in Napa, with vines rising steeply from the winery in dramatic tiers. Zinfandel is king here, and they even make a Zin Gris, an unusual dry Rosé of Zinfandel grapes. (In Burgundy, *Vin Gris*—pale Rosé—is made from Pinot Noir grapes.) Tastings are preceded by a low-key tour, during which you take a short walk up the hillside into the picture-perfect vineyard and then visit the atmospheric tunnels, parts of which have the same rough-hewn look as they did when Chinese laborers painstakingly dug them around 1888. ✉ *3835 Hwy. 128* ☎ *707/942–5310* 🌐 *www.storybookwines.com* 🎫 *Free* ⏲ *Tour and tasting by appointment Mon.–Sat.*

WHERE TO EAT

$$ AMERICAN ✕ **All Seasons Bistro.** Bistro cuisine takes a California spin in this cheerful sun-filled space, where tables topped with flowers stand on an old-fashioned black-and-white checkerboard floor. The seasonal menu might include risotto with shiitake mushroom and duck confit or fettuccine puttanesca. Homey desserts include crème brûlée and pear-and-golden-raisin bread pudding. You can order reasonably priced wines from their extensive list, or buy a bottle at the attached wineshop and have it poured at your table. Attentive service contributes to the welcoming atmosphere. ✉ *1400 Lincoln Ave.* ☎ *707/942–9111* 🌐 *www.allseasonsnapavalley.net* ⏲ *Closed Mon.*

$$ ITALIAN ✕ **Barolo.** With red-leather seats, artsy light fixtures, and a marble bar indoors and café seating out, this Italian-inflected wine bar is a stylish, modern spot for a glass of wine, with many from small producers you probably haven't heard of. Small plates that could have come straight from Tuscany—fried calamari, risotto croquettes, a selection of *salumi*—are great for sharing. A handful of well-executed large plates, like the *pappardelle* with shrimp and braised short ribs, round out the menu. ✉ *Mount View Hotel, 1457 Lincoln Ave.* ☎ *707/942–9900* 🌐 *www.barolocalistoga.com* ⏲ *No lunch.*

$$$ AMERICAN ✕ **Calistoga Inn Restaurant and Brewery.** On pleasant days this riverside restaurant and its sprawling, tree-shaded patio come into their own. At lunchtime, casual plates like a grilled-turkey-and-Brie sandwich or a vegetarian black-bean chili are light enough to leave some energy for an afternoon of wine tasting. And at night, when there's often live jazz played on the patio during the warm months, you'll find heartier dishes such as braised lamb shank or Sonoma duck breast with a fennel-and-Parmesan stuffing. Service can be a bit lackadaisical, so order one of the house-made brews and enjoy the atmosphere while you're waiting. ✉ *1250 Lincoln Ave.* ☎ *707/942–4101* 🌐 *www.calistogainn.com.*

WHERE TO STAY

For expanded hotel reviews, visit Fodors.com.

$$ **Brannan Cottage Inn.** Housed inside the only one of Sam Brannan's 1860 resort cottages still standing on its original site, this inn, a pristine Victorian house with lacy white fretwork, large windows, and a shady porch, is on the National Register of Historic Places. **Pros:** innkeepers go the extra mile; most rooms have fireplaces; a five-minute walk from most of Calistoga's restaurants. **Cons:** owners' dog may be a problem for those with allergies; beds may be too firm for some. ✉ *109 Wapoo Ave.* ☎ *707/942–4200* 🌐 *www.brannancottageinn.com* *6 rooms* *In-room: a/c, no phone, no TV (some), Wi-Fi. In-hotel: some pets allowed* *Breakfast.*

$$$$ ★ **Calistoga Ranch.** Spacious cedar-shingle bungalows throughout this posh, wooded property have outdoor living areas, and even the restaurant, spa, and reception space have outdoor seating areas and fireplaces. **Pros:** almost half the cottages have private hot tubs on the deck; lovely hiking trails on the property; guests have reciprocal privileges at Auberge

6

Floor-to-ceiling stacked bottles are no exaggeration in Schramsberg's cellars.

du Soleil. **Cons:** innovative indoor-outdoor organization works better in fair weather than in rain or cold; staff, though friendly, sometimes seems inexperienced compared to similarly priced places. ✉ *580 Lommel Rd.* ☎ *707/254–2800 or 800/942–4220* 🌐 *www.calistogaranch.com* *48 rooms* *In-room: a/c, Wi-Fi. In-hotel: restaurant, room service, bar, pool, gym, spa, some pets allowed.*

$$$$ **Cottage Grove Inn.** A long driveway lined with 16 freestanding cottages, each shaded by elm trees and with rocking chairs on the porch, looks a bit like Main Street, U.S.A., but inside the sky-lighted buildings are all the perks you could want for a romantic weekend away. **Pros:** bicycles available for loan; freestanding cottages offer lots of privacy; bathtubs so big you could swim in them. **Cons:** no pool; decor may seem a bit frumpy for some. ✉ *1711 Lincoln Ave.* ☎ *707/942–8400 or 800/799–2284* 🌐 *www.cottagegrove.com* *16 rooms* *In-room: a/c, Internet, Wi-Fi. In-hotel: business center* *Breakfast.*

$$ ★ **Indian Springs.** Since 1861, this old-time spa has welcomed clients to its mud baths, mineral pool, and steam room, all of them supplied with mineral water from its four geysers. **Pros:** lovely grounds with outdoor seating areas; stylish for the price; enormous mineral pool. **Cons:** lodge rooms are small; service could be more polished. ✉ *1712 Lincoln Ave.* ☎ *707/942–4913* 🌐 *www.indianspringscalistoga.com* *24 rooms, 17 suites* *In-room: no phone, kitchen (some), Wi-Fi. In-hotel: tennis court, pool, spa.*

$$ Fodor's Choice ★ **Meadowlark Country House.** Twenty hillside acres just north of downtown Calistoga surround this decidedly laid-back but sophisticated inn, and each of the rooms in the main house and guest wing has its own charms: one has a deep whirlpool tub looking onto a green hillside, and others have a deck with a view of the mountains. **Pros:** sauna next

CLOSE UP

Best Wine Country Spas

Spas in Napa and Sonoma have two special angles. First, there are the local mud baths and mineral-water sources, concentrated particularly around Calistoga. Admittedly, it can seem really strange to lower yourself into a vat of thick, muddy paste, but once you've had a few minutes to get used to the intense heat and peaty smell, you may never want to leave your cocoon. Second, there are all those grapes: their seeds, skins, and vines are credited with all sorts of antioxidant and other healthful properties by those who use them in scrubs, lotions, and other spa products.

Below are some of the best spas of the bunch.

■ **Dr. Wilkinson's.** The oldest spa in Calistoga. Although it's the least chic of the bunch, it's still well loved for its reasonable prices and its friendly, unpretentious vibe. Their mud baths are a mix of volcanic ash and peat moss. ✉ *1507 Lincoln Ave., Calistoga* ☎ *707/942–4102* 🌐 *www.drwilkinson.com.*

■ **Fairmont Sonoma Mission Inn & Spa.** The largest spa of its type in the Wine Country. The vast complex covers every amenity you could want in a spa, including several pools and Jacuzzis fed by local thermal mineral springs. ✉ *100 Boyes Blvd. /Rte. 12, Boyes Hot Springs* ☎ *707/938–9000* 🌐 *www.fairmont.com/sonoma.*

■ **Kenwood Inn & Spa.** The prettiest spa setting in the Wine Country, thanks to the vineyards across the road and the Mediterranean style of the inn. The "wine wrap" body treatment is finished off with a slathering of lotion made from various grape-seed oils and red-wine extract. ✉ *10400 Sonoma Hwy. /Rte. 12, Kenwood* ☎ *707/833–1293* 🌐 *www.kenwoodinn.com.*

■ **Spa at Villagio.** This 13,000-square-foot spa with fieldstone walls and a Mediterranean theme has all the latest gadgets, including men's and women's outdoor hot tubs and showers with an extravagant number of showerheads. Huge spa suites—complete with flat-panel TV screens and wet bars—are perfect for couples and groups. ✉ *6481 Washington St., Yountville* ☎ *707/948–5050.*

to the pool and hot tub; welcoming vibe attracts diverse guests; some of the most gracious innkeepers in Napa. **Cons:** clothing-optional pool policy isn't for everyone. ✉ *601 Petrified Forest Rd.* ☎ *707/942–5651 or 800/942–5651* 🌐 *www.meadowlarkinn.com* *5 rooms, 5 suites* *In-room: a/c, no phone, kitchen (some), Wi-Fi. In-hotel: pool, business center, some pets allowed* *Breakfast.*

$$$ **Mount View Hotel & Spa.** A National Historic Landmark built in 1917 in the Mission Revival style, the Mount View nevertheless feels up-to-date, after renovations in 2008 resulted in repainted rooms (some are a dramatic red and black), feather duvets, and high-tech touches like iPod alarm clocks. **Pros:** convenient location; excellent spa treatments. **Cons:** ground-floor rooms dark; mediocre continental breakfast; some bathrooms could use updating. ✉ *1457 Lincoln Ave.* ☎ *707/942–6877 or 800/816–6877* 🌐 *www.mountviewhotel.com* *18 rooms, 13 suites* *In-room: a/c, Wi-Fi. In-hotel: restaurant, bar, pool, spa* *Breakfast.*

$$$$ **Solage.** The cottages at this Calistogan, which spreads over 22 acres, don't look particularly luxurious from the outside, but inside they flaunt a Napa-Valley-barn-meets-San-Francisco-loft aesthetic, with high ceilings, polished concrete floors, recycled walnut furniture, and all-natural fabrics in soothing muted colors. **Pros:** great service; bike cruisers parked at every cottage for guests' use; separate pools for kids and adults. **Cons:** new landscaping needs some more time to fill out; some rooms don't have tubs. ✉ *755 Silverado Trail* ☎ *866/942–7442* 🌐 *www.solagecalistoga.com* *89 rooms* *In-room: a/c, Internet, Wi-Fi. In-hotel: restaurant, room service, bar, pools, gym, spa.*

SPORTS AND THE OUTDOORS

Calistoga Bikeshop (✉ *1318 Lincoln Ave. Calistoga* ☎ *707/942–9687*) offers a self-guided Calistoga Cool Wine Tour package ($79), which includes free tastings at a number of small wineries. Best of all, they'll pick up any wine you purchase along the way if you've bought more than will fit in the handy bottle carrier on your bike.

SHOPPING

Enoteca Wine Shop (✉ *1348B Lincoln Ave.* ☎ *707/942–1117*), on Calistoga's main drag, displays almost all their wines with extensive tasting notes. This makes it easier to choose from among this unusually fine collection, which includes both hard-to-find bottles from Napa and Sonoma and many rare French wines. The **Wine Garage** (✉ *1020 Foothill Blvd.* ☎ *707/942–5332*) is the stop for bargain hunters, since all their bottles go for $25 or less. It's a great way to discover the work of smaller wineries producing undervalued wines. The unusually helpful staffers are happy to share information on all the wines they stock.

THE SONOMA VALLEY

Although the Sonoma Valley may not have quite the cachet of the neighboring Napa Valley, wineries here entice with their unpretentious attitude and smaller crowds. The Napa-style glitzy tasting rooms with enormous gift shops and $25 tasting fees are the exception here. Sonoma's landscape seduces, too, its roads gently climbing and descending on their way to wineries hidden from the road by trees.

The scenic valley, bounded by the Mayacamas Mountains on the east and Sonoma Mountain on the west, extends north from San Pablo Bay nearly 20 mi to the eastern outskirts of Santa Rosa. The varied terrain, soils, and climate (cooler in the south because of the bay influence and hotter toward the north) allow grape growers to raise cool-weather varietals such as Chardonnay and Pinot Noir as well as Merlot, Cabernet Sauvignon, and other heat-seeking vines. The valley is home to dozens of wineries, many of them on or near Route 12, which runs the length of the valley.

ESSENTIALS

Contacts **Sonoma County Tourism Bureau** (✉ *3637 Westwind Blvd., Santa Rosa* ☎ *707/522–5800 or 800/576–6662* 🌐 *www.sonomacounty.com*).
Sonoma Valley Visitors Bureau (✉ *453 1st St. E, Sonoma* ☎ *707/996–1090 or 866/996–1090* 🌐 *www.sonomavalley.com*).

SONOMA

14 mi west of Napa on Rte. 12; 45 mi from San Francisco, north on U.S. 101, east on Rte. 37, and north on Rte. 121/12.

Founded in the early 1800s, Sonoma is the oldest town in the Wine Country, and one of the few where you can find some attractions not related to food and wine. The central Sonoma Plaza dates from the Mission era; surrounding it are 19th-century adobes, atmospheric hotels, and the swooping marquee of the 1930s Sebastiani Theatre. On summer days the plaza is a hive of activity, with children blowing off steam in the playground while their folks stock up on picnic supplies and browse the boutiques surrounding the square.

On your way into town from the south, you pass through the Carneros wine district, which straddles the southern sections of Sonoma and Napa counties.

GETTING HERE AND AROUND

To get to the town of Sonoma from San Francisco, cross the Golden Gate Bridge, then go north on U.S. 101, east on Route 37 toward Vallejo, and north on Route 121, aka the Carneros Highway. When you reach Route 12, take it north. It turns into Broadway, which dead-ends at Sonoma's Central Plaza. If you park here, a pleasant stroll around the plaza will take you by many of the town's restaurants and shops. Many of the town's most interesting wineries are a mile or less east of this downtown area. If you drive east from the plaza on East Spain Street or East Napa Street, signs will direct you to most of them.

6

EXPLORING

Fodor's Choice ★ **Bartholomew Park Winery.** Although this winery was founded only in 1994, grapes were grown in some of its vineyards as early as the 1830s. The emphasis here is on handcrafted, single-varietal wines—Cabernet, Merlot, Zinfandel, Syrah, and Sauvignon Blanc. The wines themselves, available only at the winery, make a stop worth it, but another reason to visit is its small museum, with vivid exhibits about the history of the winery and the Sonoma region. Another plus is the beautiful, slightly off-the-beaten-path location in a 375-acre private park about 2 mi from downtown Sonoma. Pack a lunch to enjoy on the woodsy grounds, one of the prettier picnic spots in Sonoma. ✉ *1000 Vineyard La.* ☎ *707/939–3026* 🌐 *www.bartpark.com* 🎫 *Tasting $10, tour $20* ⏲ *Daily 11–4:30, tour Fri.–Sat. at 11:30 by reservation.*

Buena Vista Carneros Winery. It was here in 1857, at California's oldest premium winery, that Count Agoston Haraszthy de Mokcsa laid the basis for modern California wine making, bucking the conventional wisdom that vines should be planted on well-watered ground by instead planting on well-drained hillsides. Chinese laborers dug tunnels 100 feet into the hillside, and the limestone they extracted was used to build the main house, which is now surrounded by redwood and eucalyptus trees and a picnic area. Their best wines are their Chardonnay, Pinot Noir, Syrah, and Merlot grown in the Ramal Vineyard in the Carneros District. ✉ *18000 Old Winery Rd., off Napa Rd.* ☎ *800/678–8504* 🌐 *buenavistacarneros.com* 🎫 *Tasting $10* ⏲ *Daily 10–5.*

Cloverdale
128
Cobb Mountain
175
Geyser Peak
Geysers Rd.
Black Mountain
ALEXANDER VALLEY
Lake Sonoma
Dutcher Creek Rd.
101
Geyserville
Russian River
128
27
22
Pine Flat Rd
Lake Sonoma Recreation Area
West Dry Creek Rd.
Dry Creek Rd.
Lytton Springs Rd.
23
Lytton
25
26
24
Dry Creek Rd.
Healdsburg Ave.
KNIGHTS VALLEY
128
IDA Calyton
Chalk Hill Rd.
Healdsburg
Mill Creek Rd.
Los Amigos Rd.
Franz Valley Rd.
Austin Creek State Recreation Area
Westside Rd.
RUSSIAN RIVER VALLEY
21
15
Eastside Rd.
Armstrong Redwoods State Reserve
Sweetwater Springs Rd.
Windsor
Mark West Springs
20
Rio Nido
River Rd.
19
101
Main St.
Guerneville
Russian River
Sonoma County Airport
Fulton
SONOMA COUNTY
116
River Rd.
18
Forestville
Piner Rd.
Fulton Rd.
Olivet Rd.
Monte Rio
Martinelli Rd.
17
116
16
Guerneville Rd.
Santa Rosa
Bohemian Hwy
Graton
Santa Rosa Creek
Hall Rd.
Occidental Rd.
13
14
Willow Creek Rd.
Graton Rd.
Bennett Va
Sebastopol Hwy.
Occidental
12
Sebastopol
Coleman Valley Rd.
Taylo Mtn
Bodega Hwy.
Petaluma Hill Rd.
Freestone
Stony Point Rd.
Bodega Hwy.
Rohnert Park
Cunningham
Salmon Creek
Rd.
116
Bloomfield
Bodega
1
Bodega Bay
Bay Hwy.
Valley Ford Cutoff
Valley Ford
Roblar Rd.
Cotati
Old Redwood Hwy.
Bloomfield
101
Petaluma Valley Ford Rd.
Bodega Bay
1
Fallon
Two Rock
Bodega Ave.
Dillon Beach
Tomales
MARIN COUNTY
0
4 mi
0
4 km
Laguna Lake
Point Reyes National Seashore
Tomales Bay

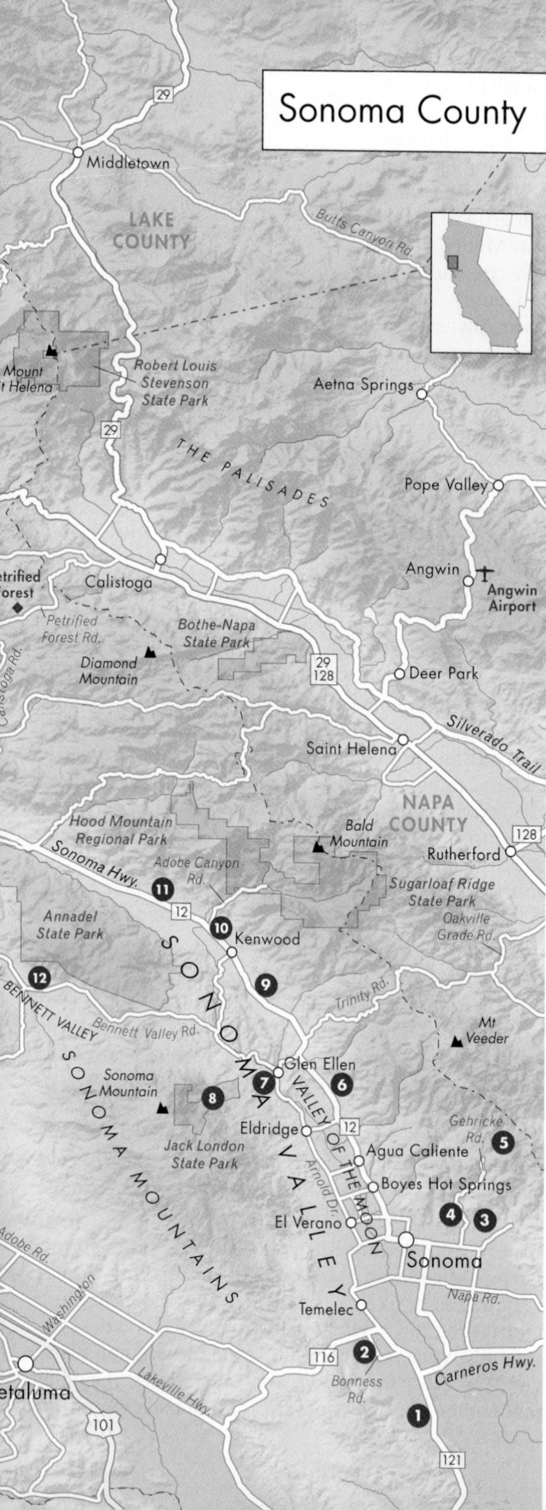

Arrowood Vineyards & Winery	6
Bartholomew Park Winery	5
Benziger Family Winery	7
Buena Vista Carneros Winery	3
Charles M. Schulz Museum	14
Cline Cellars	1
De Loach Vineyards	16
Dry Creek Vineyard	24
Family Wineries	10
Francis Ford Coppola Winery	23
Gary Farrell Winery	19
Hartford Family Winery	18
Iron Horse Vineyards	17
J Vineyards and Winery	21
Jack London State Historic Park	8
Kunde Estate Winery & Vineyards	9
Luther Burbank Home and Gardens	13
Matanzas Creek Winery	12
Michel-Schlumberger	26
Preston Vineyards	27
Quivira	25
Ravenswood	4
Robledo Family Winery	2
Rochioli Vineyards and Winery	20
Safari West	15
St. Francis Winery	11
Stryker Sonoma	22

Cline Cellars. Although many Carneros wineries specialize in Pinot Noir and Chardonnay, Cline Cellars goes its own way by focusing on Rhône varietals, such as Syrah, Roussanne, and Viognier, all grown here in Carneros, as well as Mourvèdre and Carignane, which are cultivated in Contra Costa County. They're also known for their Ancient Vines Zinfandel, produced from vines that are around 100 years old. The 1850s farmhouse that houses the tasting room has a pleasant wraparound porch for enjoying the weeping willows, ponds, fountains, and thousands of rosebushes on the property. Pack a picnic and plan to stay for a while. ✉ *24737 Hwy. 121/Arnold Dr.* ☎ *707/940–4030* 🌐 *www.clinecellars.com* 🎫 *Tasting free–$1 per reserve wine, tour free* 🕒 *Daily 10–6; tour daily at 11, 1, and 3.*

WORD OF MOUTH

"Take a look at the historic and lovely town of Sonoma, built around an 11-acre plaza during the Mexican occupation days of the early 1800s. It has some outstanding restaurants within walking distance of the plaza and several hotels as well, and cottages and bed-and-breakfasts."
—jtrandolph

★ **De Loach Vineyards.** Just far enough off the beaten track to feel like a real find, this winery produces a variety of old-vine Zinfandels, Chardonnays, and handful of other varietals, but it is best for known for its Pinot Noir, some of which is made using open-top wood fermentation vats that are uncommon in Sonoma but have been used in France for centuries. (Some think they intensify a wine's flavor.) Tours focus on the estate vineyards outside the tasting room door, where you can learn about the labor-intensive biodynamic and organic farming methods used, and take you through their culinary garden. Call a day or two in advance if you want to taste their wines paired with regional cheeses ($20) or purchase a picnic basket to enjoy in their attractive picnic area. ✉ *1791 Olivet Rd.* ☎ *707/526–9111* 🌐 *www.deloachvineyards.com* 🎫 *Tasting $10, tour free* 🕒 *Daily 10–5; tours by appointment.*

Ravenswood. Housed in a stone building covered in climbing vines, Ravenswood's tasting room lives up to the winery's punchy mission statement: "no wimpy wines." They generally succeed, especially with their signature big, bold Zinfandels, which are sometimes blended with Petit Syrah, Carignane, or other varietals that grow in the same field (this is called a "field blend"). Also be sure to taste the Bordeaux-style blends, early-harvest Gewürztraminer, and lightly sparkling Moscato, too. Tours that focus on their viticultural practices, held 10:30 daily, include a barrel tasting of wines in progress in the cellar. ✉ *18701 Gehricke Rd., off E. Spain St.* ☎ *707/938–1960* 🌐 *www.ravenswood-wine.com* 🎫 *Tasting $10–$15, tour $15* 🕒 *Daily 10–4:30.*

Robledo Family Winery. Founded by Reynaldo Robledo Sr., a former migrant worker from Michoacán, Mexico, Robledo Family Winery is truly a family affair. You're likely to encounter one of the charming Robledo sons in the tasting room, where he'll proudly tell you the story of the immigrant family while pouring tastes of their Sauvignon Blanc, Pinot Noir, Merlot, Cabernet Sauvignon, and other wines, including a Chardonnay that comes from the vineyard right outside the tasting room's door. All seven Robledo sons and two Robledo daughters, as well as matriarch Maria, are involved in the winery operations. If you don't run into them on your visit to the winery, you'll see their names and pictures on the bottles of wine, such as the Dos Hermanas late-harvest dessert wine, or one of the ports dedicated to Maria Robledo. ✉ *21901 Bonness Rd.* ☎ *707/939–6903* 🌐 *www.robledofamilywinery.com* *Tasting $5–$10* 🕓 *Mon.–Sat. 10–5, Sun. 11–4, by appointment.*

WHERE TO EAT

$$ AMERICAN ★ **Cafe La Haye.** In a postage-stamp-size open kitchen, skillful chefs turn out about half a dozen main courses that star on a small but worthwhile seasonal menu emphasizing local ingredients. Chicken, beef, pasta, and fish get deluxe treatment without fuss or fanfare. The daily roasted chicken and the risotto specials are always good. Butterscotch pudding is a homey signature dessert. The dining room is also compact, but the friendly owner, who is often there to greet diners, gives it a particularly welcoming vibe. ✉ *140 E. Napa St.* ☎ *707/935–5994* 🌐 *www.cafelahaye.com* 🕓 *Closed Sun. and Mon. No lunch.*

$ ITALIAN **Della Santina's.** This longtime favorite, with a charming heated brick patio out back, serves the most authentic Italian food in town. (The Della Santina family, which has been running the restaurant since 1990, hails from Lucca, Italy.) Daily fish and veal specials join classic northern Italian pastas such as linguine with pesto and lasagna Bolognese. Of special note are the roasted meat dishes and, when available, petrale sole and sand dabs. ✉ *133 E. Napa St.* ☎ *707/935–0576* 🌐 *www.dellasantinas.com.*

$$ FRENCH **The Girl & the Fig.** Chef Sondra Bernstein has turned the historic barroom of the Sonoma Hotel into a hot spot for inventive French cooking. You can always find something with the signature figs in it here, whether it's a fig-and-arugula salad or an aperitif of sparkling wine with a fig liqueur. Also look for duck confit with French lentils, a burger with matchstick fries, or wild boar braised in red wine. The wine list is notable for its emphasis on Rhône varietals, and a counter in the bar area sells artisanal cheese platters for eating here as well as cheese by the pound to go. Sunday brunch brings rib-sticking dishes such as steak and eggs and a Basque frittata with potatoes, onions, and tomatoes. ✉ *Sonoma Hotel, Sonoma Plaza, 110 W. Spain St.* ☎ *707/938–3634* 🌐 *www.thegirlandthefig.com.*

$$ AMERICAN ★ **Harvest Moon Cafe.** It's easy to feel like one of the family at this little restaurant with an odd, zigzagging layout. Diners seated at one of the two tiny bars chat with the servers like old friends, but the husband-and-wife team in the kitchen is serious about the food, much of which relies on local produce. The daily menu sticks to homey dishes like half a grilled chicken served with polenta and tapenade, rib-eye steak with a red wine sauce, and a marinated-beet-and-frisée salad. Everything is so perfectly executed and the vibe so genuinely warm that a visit here is deeply satisfying. In fair weather a spacious back patio, with seats arranged around a fountain, more than doubles the number of seats. ✉ *487 W. 1st St.* ☎ *707/933–8160* 🌐 *www.harvestmooncafesonoma.com* 🕓 *Closed Tues.; no lunch Mon.–Sat.*

CLOSE UP

A Grape Primer

Well more than 50 varieties of grapes are grown in the California Wine Country. Although you don't need to be on a first-name basis with them all, you'll see the following dozen again and again as you visit the wineries.

WHITES

■ **Chardonnay.** Now as firmly associated with California wine making as it is with Burgundy, where it's used extensively. California Chardonnays spent many years chasing big, buttery flavor, but the current trend is toward more restrained wines.

■ **Gewürztraminer.** Cooler California climes such as the Russian River Valley are great for growing this German-Alsatian grape, which is turned into a boldly perfumed, fruity wine.

■ **Riesling.** This cool-climate German grape has a sweet rep in America. When made in a dry style, as it more and more often is, it can be crisply refreshing, with lush aromas.

■ **Sauvignon Blanc.** Hails from Bordeaux and the Loire Valley. Wines made from this grape vary widely, from herbaceous to tropical-fruity.

■ **Viognier.** Once rarely planted outside France's Rhône Valley, it's one of the hottest white-wine varietals in California today. The best Viogniers have an intense fruity or floral bouquet; they're usually dry.

REDS

■ **Cabernet Franc.** Most often used in blends, often to add complexity to Cabernet Sauvignon, this French grape can produce aromatic, soft, and subtle wine.

■ **Cabernet Sauvignon.** The king of California reds, this Bordeaux grape grows best in austere, well-drained soils. At its best, the California version is dark, bold, and tannic, with black-currant notes. It's often blended with Cabernet Franc, Merlot, and other red varieties to soften the resulting wine and make it ready for earlier drinking.

■ **Merlot.** A blue-black Bordeaux variety that in California makes soft, full-bodied wine. Was well on its way to being the most popular red until anti-Merlot jokes in the movie *Sideways* damaged its rep, but it's staged for a comeback.

■ **Pinot Noir.** The darling of grape growers in cooler parts of Napa and Sonoma, such as the Carneros region and the Russian River Valley. At its best it has a subtle but addictive earthy quality.

■ **Sangiovese.** The main red grape of Italy's Chianti District and of much of central Italy. It can be made into vibrant, light- to medium-bodied wines, as well as into long-lived, very complex reds. Increasingly planted in California.

■ **Syrah.** A big red from France's Rhône Valley. With good tannins it can become a full-bodied beauty, but without them it can be flabby and forgettable. Also known as Shiraz, particularly when it's grown in Australia.

■ **Zinfandel.** A quintessential California grape. Rich, jammy, and often spicy, Zinfandel wines can be quite high in alcohol.

$$ PORTUGUESE ✕ **LaSalette.** Chef-owner Manuel Azevedo, born in the Azores and raised in Sonoma, serves dishes inspired by his native Portugal in this warmly decorated spot, where the best seats are on the patio, along a pedestrian alleyway off of Sonoma's plaza. Boldly flavored dishes such as *pork tenderloin recheado,* stuffed with olives and almonds and topped with a port sauce, or one of the daily seafood specials might be followed by a dish of rice pudding with Madeira-braised figs or a port from the varied list. ✉ *452 E. 1st St.* ☎ *707/938–1927* 🌐 *www.lasalette-restaurant.com.*

WORD OF MOUTH

"Just got back from a weekend in Sonoma and I really have to recommend Gary Farrell Winery. The winery is on a hillside on Westside Road south of Healdsburg and the view from the tasting room is stunning. But of course, the star is the wine, and they have some incredible Pinot Noirs that we tasted (and bought) along with Chardonnays and a Zinfandel. Not cheap, but excellent."

—hazel1

$$$$ AMERICAN Fodor's Choice ★ ✕ **Santé.** Under the leadership of chef Andrew Cain, this elegant dining room in the Sonoma Mission Inn has gained a reputation as a destination restaurant through its focus on seasonal and locally sourced ingredients. The room is understated, with drapes in rich earth tones and softly lighted chandeliers, but the food is anything but. Dishes on the frequently changing menu, such as a roasted Sonoma duck breast with braised Swiss chard and duck confit, are complex without being fussy, while some dishes, like the butter-poached Maine lobster with flageolet beans and lardons, are pure decadence. Brunch is also served in summer. ✉ *Fairmont Sonoma Mission Inn & Spa, 100 Boyes Blvd./Rte. 12, at Boyes Blvd., 2 mi north of Sonoma, Boyes Hot Springs* ☎ *707/939–2415* ⊙ *Closed 1st 2 wks in Jan. No lunch.*

6

$ AMERICAN ✕ **Sunflower Caffé.** Although you wouldn't realize it as you walk by, this casual café has one of Sonoma's prettiest patios. Equipped with both heating lamps and plenty of shade, it's comfortable in all but the most inclement weather. On dreary days, cheerful artworks brighten up the interior, where locals hunker over their computers and take advantage of the free Wi-Fi. The menu, composed mostly of salads and sandwiches (as well as omelets and waffles for breakfast), is simple but satisfying, and it relies largely on local ingredients. It's also a comfortable spot to take a quick break with an excellent coffee drink or something from the well-stocked outdoor wine bar. ✉ *421 W. 1st St.* ☎ *707/996–6645* 🌐 *www.sonomasunflower.com* ◬ *Reservations not accepted* ⊙ *No dinner fall and winter.*

WHERE TO STAY

For expanded hotel reviews, visit Fodors.com.

$ **El Dorado Hotel.** Rooms in this remodeled 1843 building strike a spare, modern pose, with rectilinear four-poster beds and pristine white bedding, but the Mexican-tile floors hint at Sonoma's mission-era past. **Pros:** stylish for the price; hip restaurant downstairs; central location. **Cons:** rooms are small; lighting could be better; noisy. ✉ *405*

1st St. W ☎ 707/996–3030 🌐 www.eldoradosonoma.com ⇨ 27 rooms ♁ In-room: a/c, Wi-Fi. In-hotel: restaurants, bar, pool.

$$$$ **The Fairmont Sonoma Mission Inn & Spa.** The real draw at this Mission-style resort is the extensive, swanky spa, easily the biggest in Sonoma, with a vast array of massages and treatments, some using locally sourced grape and lavender products. **Pros:** enormous spa; excellent, well-reviewed restaurant on-site; free shuttle to downtown. **Cons:** rooms on the smaller side; not as intimate as some similarly priced places. ✉ *100 Boyes Blvd. /Rte. 12, 2 mi north of Sonoma, Boyes Hot Springs* ☎ *707/938–9000* 🌐 *www.fairmont.com/sonoma* ⇨ *168 rooms, 60 suites* ♁ *In-room: a/c, Internet, Wi-Fi (some). In-hotel: golf course, restaurants, room service, bars, pools, gym, spa, some pets allowed.*

$ **Sonoma Creek Inn.** The small but cheerful rooms at this roadside inn with a sunny yellow exterior are individually decorated with painted wooden armoires, cozy quilts, and brightly colored contemporary artwork, elevating this bargain option well above your average motel. **Pros:** clean, well-lighted bathrooms; a lot of charm for the low price. **Cons:** office not staffed 24 hours a day; slightly out-of-the-way location (about a 10-minute drive from Sonoma's plaza). ✉ *239 Boyes Blvd.* ☎ *707/939–9463* 🌐 *www.sonomacreekinn.com* ⇨ *16 rooms* ♁ *In-room: a/c, Wi-Fi. In-hotel: restaurant, some pets allowed.*

NIGHTLIFE AND THE ARTS

The **Sebastiani Theatre** (✉ *476 1st St. E* ☎ *707/996–2020*), built on Sonoma's plaza in 1934 by Italian immigrant and entrepreneur Samuele Sebastiani, schedules first-run films, as well as the occasional musical or theatrical performance.

Hit the bar at the **Swiss Hotel** (✉ *18 W. Spain St.* ☎ *707/938–2884*) to sip a Glariffee, a cold and potent cousin to Irish coffee that's unique to this 19th-century spot.

SHOPPING

Sonoma's plaza is the town's main shopping magnet, with tempting boutiques and specialty food purveyors facing the square or just a block or two away. **Sign of the Bear** (✉ *Sonoma Plaza, 435 1st St. W* ☎ *707/996–3722*) sells the latest and greatest in kitchenware and cookware, as well as a few Wine Country–theme items, like lazy Susans made from wine barrels.

Although their Sonoma Jack cheese and tangy Sonoma Teleme are no longer made on the premises, the **Sonoma Cheese Factory** (✉ *Sonoma Plaza, 2 Spain St.* ☎ *707/996–1931*) does offer samples of many local cheeses. They also have everything you need for a picnic, from sandwiches to wine to about a dozen types of homemade fudge.

A block east of Sonoma Plaza, the **Vella Cheese Company** (✉ *315 2nd St. E* ☎ *707/938–3232*) has been making superb cheeses, such as raw-milk cheddars and several varieties of jack, since 1931.

GLEN ELLEN

7 mi north of Sonoma on Rte. 12.

Craggy Glen Ellen embodies the difference between the Napa and Sonoma valleys. In small Napa towns such as St. Helena well-groomed sidewalks are lined with upscale boutiques and restaurants, but in Glen Ellen the crooked streets are shaded with stands of old oak trees and occasionally bisected by the Sonoma and Calabasas creeks.

Jack London, who represents Glen Ellen's rugged spirit, lived in the area for many years; the town commemorates him with place names and nostalgic establishments.

GETTING HERE AND AROUND

To get to tiny Glen Ellen from Sonoma's Plaza, drive west on East Spain Street. After about a mile, turn right onto Route 12. Drive about 7 miles, then take the Arnold Drive exit and turn left. Many of Glen Ellen's few restaurants and inns are along a half-mile stretch of Arnold Drive. Though distances in town are short, the road is winding and lacks a sidewalk in most spots, so it might be safer to drive than to walk between spots.

6

EXPLORING

Arrowood Vineyards & Winery. Although it's neither as famous or as old as some of its neighbors, Arrowood still produces well-regarded wines, especially the Chardonnays, Syrahs, and age-worthy Cabernets. A wraparound porch with wicker chairs invites you to linger outside the tasting room, built to resemble a New England farmhouse. In fact, if you're more interested in lounging than learning about their wines, you can pay $5 for a glass to enjoy outside. Tours, offered daily at 10:30 by appointment, conclude with a seated tasting. ■ **TIP→ If you're doing a reserve tasting on a weekend, and you're interested in discovering what Arrowood wines taste like after several years in the bottle, ask whether they happen to have any library wines open they can pour.** ✉ *14347 Sonoma Hwy./Rte. 12* ☎ *707/935–2600* 🌐 *www.arrowoodvineyards.com* 🎫 *Tasting $5–$10, tour $25* ⏲ *Daily 10–4:30; tour by appointment.*

★ **Benziger Family Winery.** One of the best-known local wineries is Benziger Family Winery, on a sprawling estate in a bowl with 360-degree sun exposure. Benziger is noted for its Merlot, Pinot Noir, Cabernet Sauvignon, Chardonnay, and Sauvignon Blanc. The tram tours here are especially interesting (they're first come, first served). On a ride through the vineyards, guides explain the regional microclimates and geography and give you a glimpse of the extensive cave system. Tours depart several times a day, weather permitting. Reservations are needed for smaller tours that conclude with a seated tasting ($40). ■ **TIP→ Arrive before lunch for the best shot at joining a tour—and bring a picnic, since the grounds here are lovely.** ✉ *1883 London Ranch Rd.* ☎ *707/935–3000* 🌐 *www.benziger.com* 🎫 *Tasting $10–$20, tour $15–$40* ⏲ *Daily 10–5.*

Jack London Saloon. Built in 1905, the Jack London Saloon is decorated with photos of London and other London memorabilia. ✉ *13740 Arnold Dr.* ☎ *707/996–3100* 🌐 *www.jacklondonlodge.com*

Cloverdale
Cobb Mountain
Geyser Peak
Black Mountain
ALEXANDER VALLEY
Lake Sonoma
Dutcher Creek Rd.
Geysers Rd.
Geyserville
Russian River
Clos du Bois
Lake Sonoma Recreation Area
West Dry Creek Rd.
Dry Creek Rd.
Lytton Springs Rd.
Lytton
Pine Flat Rd
KNIGHTS VALLEY
Healdsburg Ave.
Chalk Hill Rd.
IDA Calyton
Healdsburg
Mill Creek Rd.
Los Amigos Rd.
Franz Valley Rd.
Austin Creek State Recreation Area
Westside Rd.
RUSSIAN RIVER VALLEY
Eastside Rd.
Armstrong Redwoods State Reserve
Sweetwater Springs Rd.
Windsor
Mark West Springs
Korbel Champagne Cellars
Rio Nido
Main St.
River Rd.
Guerneville
Sonoma County Airport
Fulton
SONOMA COUNTY
Russian River
Martinelli Rd.
Forestville
River Rd.
Olivet Rd.
Fulton Rd.
Piner Rd.
Monte Rio
Guerneville Rd.
Santa Rosa
Graton
Santa Rosa Creek
Bohemian Hwy
Hall Rd.
Occidental Rd.
Willow Creek Rd.
Graton Rd.
Sebastopol Hwy.
Bennett Va
Occidental
Sebastopol
Petaluma Hill Rd.
Coleman Valley Rd.
Bodega Hwy.
Freestone
Stony Point Rd.
Cunningham
Rohnert Park
Bodega Hwy.
Salmon Creek
Rd.
Bodega
Bodega Bay
Bloomfield Rd.
Roblar Rd.
Cotati
Bay Hwy.
Valley Ford Cutoff
Old Redwood Hwy.
Bloomfield
Bodega Bay
Petaluma Valley Ford Rd.
Fallon
Two Rock
Bodega Ave.
Tomales
MARIN COUNTY
Laguna Lake
0
4 mi
0
4 km
101
128
175
116
12
1
KEY
Restaurants
Hotels

Where to Eat and Stay in Sonoma County

Restaurants

Hotels

Jack London State Historic Park. In the hills above Glen Ellen—known as the Valley of the Moon—lies Jack London State Historic Park, where you could easily spend the afternoon hiking along the edge of vineyards and through stands of oak trees. Several of the author's manuscripts and a handful of personal effects are on view at the House of Happy Walls museum, once the home of London's widow. A short hike away from Happy Walls are the ruins of Wolf House. Designed by London, it mysteriously burned down just before he was to move in. Also open to the public are a few restored farm outbuildings, and on weekends you can visit the Cottage, a restored wood-framed building where he wrote many of his later works. London is buried on the property. ✉ *2400 London Ranch Rd.* ☎ *707/938–5216* 🎫 *Parking $8, admission to buildings free* ⏲ *Park and museum daily 10–5, cottage weekends 10–4..*

FARMERS MARKET

The **Sonoma Farmers' Market** overflows with locally farmed produce, artisanal cheeses, and baked goods. It's held year-round at Depot Park, just north of Sonoma Plaza, on Friday from 9 am to noon. From April through October it gets extra play on Tuesday evenings 5:30 pm–dusk at Sonoma Plaza.

WHERE TO EAT

$$ FRENCH Fodor's Choice ★

✕ **The Fig Cafe.** Pale sage walls, a high, sloping ceiling, and casual but very warm service set a sunny mood in this little bistro that's run by the same team behind Sonoma's The Girl & the Fig. The restaurant's eponymous fruit shows up in all sorts of places, from salads to the wintertime apple-and-fig bread pudding. The small menu focuses on California and French comfort food, like steamed mussels served with terrific crispy fries, and a roast quail served with faro and olives. Don't forget to look on the chalkboard for frequently changing desserts, such as butterscotch pots de crème. ■ **TIP→ The unusual no-corkage-fee policy makes it a great place to drink the wine you just discovered down the road.** ✉ *13690 Arnold Dr.* ☎ *707/938–2130* 🌐 *www.thegirlandthefig.com* *Reservations not accepted* ⏲ *No lunch weekdays.*

$$ ECLECTIC

✕ **Glen Ellen Inn Oyster Grill & Martini Bar.** Tucked inside a creek-side 1940s cottage, this cozy restaurant exudes romance, especially if you snag a seat in the shady garden or on the patio strung with tiny lights. After taking the edge off your hunger with some oysters on the half shell and an ice-cold martini, order from the eclectic, frequently changing menu that plucks elements from California, French, and occasionally Asian cuisines. For instance, you might try ginger tempura calamari with mango salsa or grilled rib-eye steak with Gorgonzola mashed potatoes. Desserts tend toward the indulgent; witness the warm pecan bread pudding with a chocolate center that sits in a puddle of brandy sauce. ✉ *13670 Arnold Dr.* ☎ *707/996–6409* 🌐 *www.glenelleninn.com* ⏲ *No lunch Wed. or Thurs.*

Horseback riding tours loop around Jack London State Historic Park.

WHERE TO STAY

For expanded hotel reviews, visit Fodors.com.

$$ ★ **Beltane Ranch.** On a slope of the Mayacamas range a few miles from Glen Ellen, this 1892 ranch house, shaded by magnificent oak trees, contains charmingly old-fashioned rooms, each individually decorated with antiques and thick old-fashioned bedcovers. **Pros:** casual, friendly atmosphere; reasonably priced; beautiful grounds with ancient oak trees. **Cons:** downstairs rooms get some noise from upstairs rooms; cooled with ceiling fans instead of air-conditioning. ✉ *11775 Sonoma Hwy. / Rte. 12* ☎ *707/996–6501* 🌐 *www.beltaneranch.com* *3 rooms, 3 suites* *In-room: no phone, no TV, Wi-Fi. In-hotel: tennis court* *Breakfast.*

$$$$ Fodor's Choice ★ **Gaige House.** Gorgeous Asian objets d'art and leather club chairs cozied up to the fireplace in the lobby are just a few of the graceful touches in this luxurious but understated B&B. **Pros:** beautiful lounge areas; cottages are very private; excellent service. **Cons:** sound carries in the main house; the least expensive rooms are on the small side. ✉ *13540 Arnold Dr.* ☎ *707/935–0237 or 800/935–0237* 🌐 *www.gaige.com* *10 rooms, 13 suites* *In-room: a/c, Wi-Fi. In-hotel: pool, spa* *Breakfast.*

$$ **Glenelly Inn and Cottages.** On a quiet side street a few blocks from the town center, this sunny little establishment has a long history as a getaway. **Pros:** children are welcome; quiet location; hot tub in a pretty garden. **Cons:** some may not appreciate the presence of children; a few of the rooms could be freshened up. ✉ *5131 Warm Springs Rd.* ☎ *707/996–6720* 🌐 *www.glenellyinn.com* *8 rooms, 2 suites* *In-room: a/c (some), no phone (some), Wi-Fi. In-hotel: laundry facilities, some pets allowed* *Breakfast.*

KENWOOD

3 mi north of Glen Ellen on Rte. 12.

Blink and you might miss tiny Kenwood, which consists of little more than a few restaurants and shops and a historic train depot, now used for private events. But hidden in this pretty landscape of meadows and woods at the north end of Sonoma Valley are several good wineries, most just off the Sonoma Highway.

GETTING HERE AND AROUND

To get to Kenwood from Glen Ellen, drive 3 miles north on Route 12. Most of the wineries in Kenwood are strung along Route 12, a short drive from one another.

EXPLORING

Family Wineries. Many wineries around the Kenwood area are small, so tiny that they don't have tasting rooms of their own. At Family Wineries you can sample the output of several such spots. Though the lineup of participating wineries occasionally changes, look for sweet flavored sparklers produced by SL Cellars and still wines from Sonoma producers such as David Noyes and Collier Falls. ✉ *9380 Sonoma Hwy.* ☎ *888/433–6555* 🌐 *www.familywines.com* 🎫 *Tasting $5* ⏲ *Daily 10:30–5.*

Kunde Estate Winery & Vineyards. On your way into Kunde Estate Winery & Vineyards you pass a terrace flanked with fountains, virtually coaxing you to stay for a picnic with views over the vineyard. The tour of the grounds includes its extensive caves, some of which stretch 175 feet below a Syrah vineyard. Kunde is perhaps best known for its toasty Chardonnays, although tastings might include Sauvignon Blanc, Cabernet Sauvignon, and Zinfandel as well. If you skip the tour, take a few minutes to wander around the demonstration vineyard outside the tasting room. Reserve in advance if you want to take advantage of the Mountain Top Tasting, a tour that ends with a sampling of their reserve wines at the highest point on their property, overlooking their vineyards ($25). ✉ *9825 Sonoma Hwy. /Rte. 12* ☎ *707/833–5501* 🌐 *www.kunde.com* 🎫 *Tasting $10–$20, tour free* ⏲ *Daily 10:30–5; tours Mon.–Thurs. at 11, Fri.–Sun on the hr 11–3; Mountain Top Tasting Mon.–Thurs. at 12:30 and 2:30, Fri.–Sun. hourly 11:30–2:30.*

★ **St. Francis Winery.** Named for St. Francis of Assisi, founder of the Franciscan order, which established missions and vineyards throughout California, St. Francis Winery has one of the most scenic locations in Sonoma, nestled at the foot of Mt. Hood. The visitor center beautifully replicates the California Mission style, with its red-tile roof and dramatic bell tower (a plaque explains that the bell was actually blessed in the Basilica di San Francesco in Assisi, Italy). Out back, a slate patio overlooks vineyards, lavender gardens, and hummingbirds flitting about the flower beds. The charm of the surroundings is matched by the wines, most of them red, including rich, earthy Zinfandels from both the Russian River and Sonoma valleys. In addition to the usual wine tastings, there are a variety of food and wine pairings available ($20 to $35); call or check their Web site for times and details. ✉ *100 Pythian Rd.* ☎ *800/543–7713* *www.stfranciswinery.com Tasting $10, tour $25, food and wine pairings $20–$35. Daily 10–5, tour weekdays at 11 and 2.*

WHERE TO EAT AND STAY

$ ITALIAN **Café Citti.** Classical music in the background and a friendly staff (as well as a roaring fire when the weather's cold) keep this no-frills roadside café from feeling too spartan. Order dishes such as roast chicken and slabs of tiramisu from the counter and they're delivered to your table, a few of which are on an outdoor patio. An ample array of prepared salads and sandwiches means they do a brisk business in takeout for picnic packers, but you can also choose pasta made to order, mixing and matching linguine, penne, and other pastas with sauces like pesto or marinara. *9049 Sonoma Hwy. /Rte. 12 707/833–2690 www.cafecitti.com.*

$$$$ ★ **Kenwood Inn and Spa.** Buildings resembling graceful old haciendas and mature fruit trees shading the courtyards make it seem like this inn has been here for more than a century (it was actually built in 1990). **Pros:** large rooms; lavish furnishings; extremely romantic. **Cons:** Wi-Fi can be spotty in some areas; expensive. *10400 Sonoma Hwy. 707/833–1293 www.kenwoodinn.com 25 rooms, 4 suites In-room: a/c, no TV, Internet, Wi-Fi. In-hotel: restaurant, bar, pool, spa, some age restrictions apply. Breakfast.*

6

ELSEWHERE IN SONOMA COUNTY

At nearly 1,598 square mi, there's much more to Sonoma County than the day-tripper favorites of Sonoma, Glen Ellen, and Kenwood. To the north is Healdsburg, a lovely small town with a rapidly rising buzz. The national media have latched onto it for its swank hotels and remarkable restaurants, and many Fodors.com readers recommend it as an ideal home base for wine tasting.

Within easy striking distance of Healdsburg are some of the Wine Country's most scenic vineyards, in the Alexander, Dry Creek, and Russian River valleys. And these lookers also happen to produce some of the country's best Pinot Noir, Cabernet Sauvignon, Zinfandel, and Sauvignon Blanc. Though these regions are hardly unknown names, their quiet, narrow roads feel a world away from Highway 29 in Napa.

The western stretches of Sonoma County, which reach all the way to the Pacific Ocean, are sparsely populated in comparison to the above destinations, with only the occasional vineyard popping up in between isolated ranches. Guerneville, a popular destination for weekending San Franciscans, who come to canoe down the Russian River, is a convenient place for picking up River Road, then Westside Road, which passes through Pinot Noir paradise on its way to Healdsburg.

SANTA ROSA

8 mi northwest of Kenwood on Rte. 12.

Santa Rosa, the Wine Country's largest city, isn't likely to charm you with its office buildings, department stores, and frequent snarls of traffic along U.S. 101. It is, however, home to a couple of interesting cultural

Hitching a ride on the Benziger Family Winery tram tour.

offerings. Its chain motels and hotels are also handy if you're finding that everything else is booked up, especially since Santa Rosa is roughly equidistant from Sonoma, Healdsburg, and the Russian River Valley, three of the most popular wine-tasting destinations.

GETTING HERE AND AROUND

To get to Santa Rosa from San Francisco, drive north over the Golden Gate Bridge and continue north on U.S. 101 to the downtown Santa Rosa exit. To get to Santa Rosa from Sonoma Valley, take Route 12 north. After passing through Santa Rosa's outskirts it will deposit you at U.S. 101. Santa Rosa's hotels, restaurants, and wineries are spread over a fairly wide area, and you should factor in a little extra time whenever driving around Santa Rosa, especially during morning and evening commute hours.

EXPLORING

Charles M. Schulz Museum. Fans of Snoopy and Charlie Brown should head to the Charles M. Schulz Museum, dedicated to the cartoonist who lived in Santa Rosa for the last 30 years of his life, until his death in 2000. Permanent installations such as a re-creation of the artist's studio share the space with temporary exhibits, which often focus on a particular theme in Schulz's work. Both children and adults can try their hand at creating cartoons in the Education Room or wander through the labyrinth in the form of Snoopy's head. Check the Web site or call for information about occasional kid-friendly workshops and events. ✉ *2301 Hardies La.* ☎ *707/579–4452* 🌐 *www.schulzmuseum.org* 🎟 *$10* 🕘 *Labor Day–Memorial Day, Wed.–Fri. and Mon. 11–5, weekends 10–5; Memorial Day–Labor Day, weekdays 11–5, weekends 10–5.*

Luther Burbank Home and Gardens. The Luther Burbank Home and Gardens commemorates the great botanist who lived and worked on these grounds and single-handedly developed the modern techniques of hybridization. The 1.6-acre garden and a greenhouse show the results of some of Burbank's experiments to develop spineless cactus, fruit trees, and flowers such as the Shasta daisy. Instructions for accessing the free self-guided garden tour using visitors' own cell phones is posted near the carriage house. In the music room of his house, a modified Greek Revival structure that was Burbank's home from 1884 to 1906, a dictionary lies open to a page on which the verb "burbank" is defined as "to modify and improve plant life." (To see the house, you'll need to join one of the docent-led tours, which leave from the gift shop every half hour.) ✉ *Santa Rosa and Sonoma Aves.* ☎ *707/524–5445* 🌐 *www.lutherburbank.org* 🎫 *Gardens free, tour $7* ⏲ *Gardens daily 8–dusk; museum and gift shop Apr.–Oct., Tues.–Sun. 10–4.*

Fodor's Choice ★ **Matanzas Creek Winery.** The visitor center at this beautiful winery sets itself apart with an understated Japanese aesthetic, extending to a tranquil fountain and a koi pond. Best of all, huge windows overlook a vast field of lavender plants. ■ **TIP→ The ideal time to visit is in May and June, when the lavender blooms and perfumes the air.** The winery specializes in Sauvignon Blanc, Merlot, and Chardonnay, although they also produce a popular dry Rosé as well as some Syrah, Pinot Noir, and Cabernet. Guided tours range from an hour-long intro to the Bennett Valley, the tiny AVA where the winery is located, to a more expensive one that concludes with a taste of limited-production and library wines paired with artisanal cheeses. If you'd like to go it on your own, ask for a printed vineyard tour guide, which will point you toward a stroll through their Merlot, Grenache, and Malbec vineyards. ✉ *6097 Bennett Valley Rd.* ☎ *707/528–6464 or 800/590–6464* 🌐 *www.matanzascreek.com* 🎫 *Tasting $5, tour $10–$35* ⏲ *Daily 10–4:30; tour by appointment.*

Safari West. An unexpected bit of wilderness in the Wine Country, this African wildlife preserve covers 400 acres on the outskirts of Santa Rosa. Reserve in advance and set aside an entire morning or afternoon for a visit, which begins with a stroll around various enclosures housing lemurs, cheetahs, giraffes, and many varieties of rare birds, like the brightly colored scarlet ibis. Next guests climb onto open-air vehicles that spend about two hours driving around the expansive property, where more than eighty species, such as African cape buffalo, gazelles, wildebeests, and zebras make their home on the hillsides. All the while you're accompanied by a staff member who informs you about the animals, their behavior, and the threats they face in the wild. If you'd like to extend your stay, lodging in well-equipped tent cabins ($–*$$) is also available.* ✉ *3115 Porter Creek Rd.* ☎ *707/579–2551* 🌐 *www.safariwest.com* 🎫 *$68, $30 children 3–12* ⏲ *By reservation only.*

WHERE TO EAT

$$$ ITALIAN Fodor's Choice ★ ✕ **Zazu.** A low wooden ceiling, rustic copper tables, and rock music on the stereo create a casual vibe at this roadhouse. It's a few miles from downtown Santa Rosa, but the hearty, soulful cooking of owners Duskie Estes and John Stewart brings passionate fans from all over the Wine Country. About 30 percent of the produce comes from their

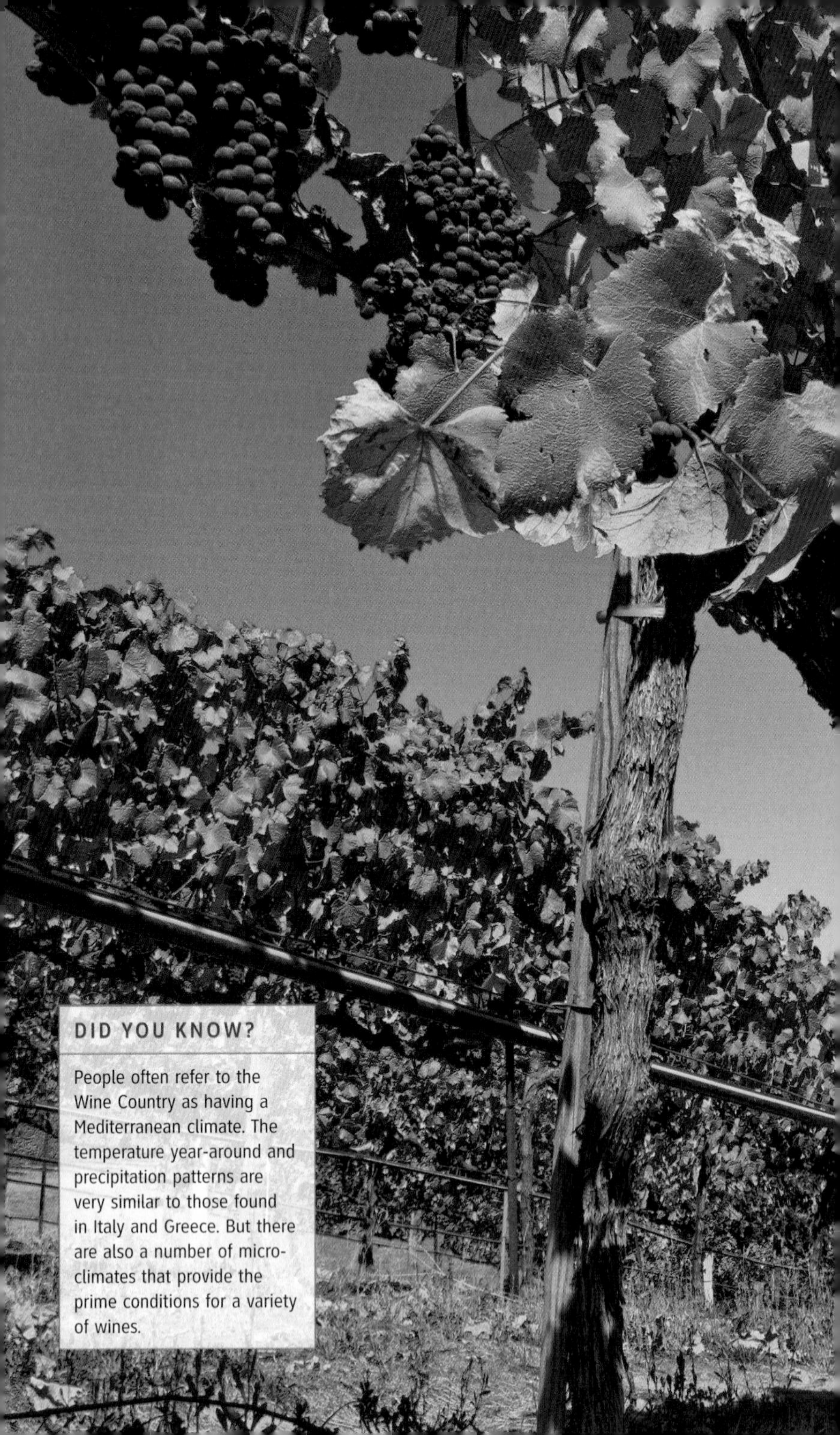

DID YOU KNOW?

People often refer to the Wine Country as having a Mediterranean climate. The temperature year-around and precipitation patterns are very similar to those found in Italy and Greece. But there are also a number of microclimates that provide the prime conditions for a variety of wines.

own garden, and the meats are house-cured, so the antipasto plate or a pizza with house-made pepperoni are both excellent choices. The small seasonal menu—a mix of Italian-influenced dishes and updated American classics—tends toward rich flavors, with choices like rabbit braised in red wine and served with a mushroom risotto. On Saturday and Sunday mornings hearty brunch dishes like cornmeal waffles and corned-beef hash lay the foundation for a busy day of wine tasting. ✉ *3535 Guerneville Rd.* ☎ *707/523–4814* 🌐 *www.zazurestaurant.com.*

RUSSIAN RIVER VALLEY

10 mi northwest of Santa Rosa.

The Russian River flows all the way from Mendocino to the Pacific Ocean, but in terms of wine making, the Russian River Valley is centered on a triangle with points at Healdsburg, Guerneville, and Sebastopol. Tall redwoods shade many of the two-lane roads that access this scenic area, where, thanks to the cooling marine influence, Pinot Noir and Chardonnay are the king and queen of grapes.

ESSENTIALS

Contacts Russian River Wine Road (✉ *Box 46, Healdsburg* ☎ *707/433–4335 or 800/723–6336* 🌐 *www.wineroad.com*).

GETTING HERE AND AROUND

Many people visit the Russian River Valley while based in nearby Healdsburg. To get to the wineries along Westside Road from Healdsburg's central plaza, head south on Center Street and turn right at Mill Street, which turns into Westside Road after it crosses U.S. 101. Keep heading west on River Road toward Guerneville if you want to explore the western reaches of the Russian River Valley. Or, for a shorter day trip, from Westside Road turn left on Wohler Road and left again on Eastside Road to loop back to U.S. 101 just south of Healdsburg. Wineries are somewhat more widely spaced in this rural area than in other parts of the Wine Country, and you should plan on spending some leisurely time driving along the winding roads. This is also a particularly scenic area for biking.

EXPLORING

Gary Farrell Winery. Pass through an impressive metal gate and wind your way up a steep hill to reach Gary Farrell, a spot with knockout views over the rolling hills and vineyards below. Although the winery has changed hands a few times since Farrell sold it in 2004, it's managed to continue producing well-regarded bottles under Susan Reed, who worked alongside him. Though their earthy, full-bodied Zinfandels and Carneros and Russian River Chardonnays are winners, the winery has built its reputation on its Pinot Noirs. ✉ *10701 Westside Rd., Healdsburg* ☎ *707/473–2900* 🌐 *www.garyfarrellwines.com* 🎫 *Tasting $10–$15, tour $25* ⏲ *Daily 10:30–4:30; tour by appointment.*

Hartford Family Winery. Fans of Pinot Noir will surely want to stop at this surprisingly opulent winery off a meandering country road in Forestville. Here grapes from the cooler areas of the Russian River Valley, Sonoma coast, and other regions are turned into crisp Chardonnays, old-vine

Zinfandels, and a wide variety of Pinots, many of which are single-vineyard wines. Call ahead if you're interested in scheduling a tour of the barrel room ($10, not including tasting) or a seated tasting of library wines ($25). ✉ *8075 Martinelli Rd., Forestville* ☎ *707/887–1756* 🌐 *www.hartfordwines.com* 🎫 *Tasting $5–$15* ⏲ *Daily 10–4:30.*

WORD OF MOUTH

"We opted for the car and driver and loved it! Not only did they suggest a route, the driver was very knowledgeable about the area. A big relief not to be concerned with the driving."
—patandhank

Fodor's Choice ★ **Iron Horse Vineyards.** Down a one-lane country road from Forestville, Iron Horse Vineyards makes a wide variety of sparkling wines, from the bright and austere to the rich and toasty, as well as estate Chardonnays and Pinot Noirs. Three hundred acres of rolling, vine-covered hills, barnlike winery buildings, and a beautifully rustic outdoor tasting area with a view of Mt. St. Helena set it apart from stuffier spots. (Instead of providing buckets for you to dump out the wine you don't want to finish, they ask you to toss it into the grass behind you.) Tours are available by appointment on weekdays at 10 am. ✉ *9786 Ross Station Rd., Sebastopol* ☎ *707/887–1507* 🌐 *www.ironhorsevineyards.com* 🎫 *Tasting $10, tour $20* ⏲ *Daily 10–4:30; tour weekdays at 10 by appointment.*

6

J Vineyards and Winery. Behind the bar in the tasting room is a dramatic steel sculpture studded with illuminated chunks of glass that suggests a bottle of bubbly. It's a big clue to what's most important here. The dry sparkling wines, made from Pinot Noir and Chardonnay grapes planted in Russian River vineyards, have wonderfully complex fruit and floral aromas and good acidity. Still best known for its sparklers, J also makes fine still wines, often from Pinot and Chardonnay grapes, as well as brandy-fortified dessert wine and a pear eau-de-vie. Although you can sample wines on their own at the tasting bar, for a truly indulgent experience make a reservation for the Bubble Room, where you should set aside a couple of hours for a selection of top-end still and sparkling wines served with different foods. Tours are offered twice daily by appointment. ✉ *11447 Old Redwood Hwy., Healdsburg* ☎ *707/431–3646* 🌐 *www.jwine.com* 🎫 *Tasting $20–$60* ⏲ *Daily 11–5; Bubble Room hrs vary.*

Rochioli Vineyards and Winery. Claiming one of the prettiest picnic sites in the area, with tables overlooking vineyards, this winery also has an airy little tasting room hung with modern artwork. Production is small—about 12,000 cases annually—and fans on the winery's mailing list snap up most of the bottles, but the wines are still worth a stop. Because of the cool growing conditions in the Russian River Valley, the flavors of their Chardonnay and Sauvignon Blanc are intense and complex. It's their Pinot, though, that is largely responsible for the winery's stellar reputation; it helped cement the Russian River's status as a Pinot powerhouse. ■ **TIP→ Though Rochioli typically pours only a couple of wines for visitors, it's one of the few wineries of its stature that doesn't charge for a tasting.** ✉ *6192 Westside Rd., Healdsburg* ☎ *707/433–2305* 🌐 *www.rochioliwinery.com* 🎫 *Tasting free* ⏲ *Thurs.–Mon. 11–4, Tues. and Wed. by appointment; closed mid-Dec.–early Jan.*

WHERE TO EAT

$$$$ FRENCH Fodor's Choice ★ **The Farmhouse Inn.** From the personable sommelier who arrives at the table to help you pick wines from the excellent list to the servers who lovingly describe the provenance of the black truffles shaved over your pasta stuffed with salt-roasted pears and Parmesan, the staff match the quality of the outstanding French-inspired cuisine. The signature dish "rabbit, rabbit, rabbit," a rich trio of confit of leg, rabbit loin wrapped in applewood-smoked bacon, and roasted rack of rabbit with a whole-grain mustard sauce, is typical of the dishes that are both rustic and refined and the starters often include a seared Sonoma foie gras served with an apple cider sauce. **TIP→ The inn's a favorite of local foodies in the wine industry, who also know that their head sommelier is one of only about a hundred Master Sommeliers working in the United States, so reserve well in advance.**

If you've forgotten to call ahead, a few tables in the small lounge area can often accommodate walk-ins. The small dining room, which has casual country yet elegant appeal, is warmed by a fireplace in winter. *7871 River Rd., Forestville 707/887–3300 or 800/464–6642 www.farmhouseinn.com Reservations essential Closed Tues. and Wed. No lunch.*

WHERE TO STAY

For expanded hotel reviews, visit Fodors.com.

$$$$ Fodor's Choice ★ **The Farmhouse Inn.** Inside a pale yellow 1873 farmhouse and its adjacent cottages, this hotel maintains individually decorated guest rooms with comfortable touches such as down comforters and whirlpool tubs, and most of the cottages have wood-burning fireplaces and even their own private saunas, which make this place especially inviting during the rainy months. **Pros:** one of Sonoma's best restaurants is on-site; free snacks, games, movies, and luxury bath products available; full-service spa uses many products made from local ingredients. **Cons:** rooms closest to the street get a bit of road noise. *7871 River Rd., Forestville 707/887–3300 or 800/464–6642 www.farmhouseinn.com 12 rooms, 6 suites In-room: a/c, Wi-Fi. In-hotel: restaurant, pool, spa Breakfast.*

$ **Sebastopol Inn.** Simple but cheerful rooms, freshly painted a sunny yellow and equipped with blue-and-white striped curtains, have a spare California country style at this reasonably priced inn. **Pros:** friendly staff; just steps from a café, wine bar, and spa. **Cons:** at least a 30-minute drive from most Russian River wineries; some will find the beds too firm. *6751 Sebastopol Ave., Sebastopol 707/829–2500 www.sebastopolinn.com 29 rooms, 2 suites In-room: a/c, Wi-Fi. In-hotel: restaurant, pool, laundry facilities.*

SPORTS AND THE OUTDOORS

At **Burke's Canoe Trips** (*River Rd. and Mirabel Rd., 1 mi north of Forestville 707/887–1222*) you can rent a canoe for a leisurely paddle 10 mi downstream to Guerneville. A shuttle bus will return you to your car at the end of the day. Late May through mid-October is the best time for boating.

Annual barrel tasting along Russian River's wine road.

HEALDSBURG

17 mi north of Santa Rosa on U.S. 101.

Just when it seems that the buzz about Healdsburg couldn't get any bigger, there's another article published in a glossy food or wine magazine about posh properties like the restaurant Cyrus and the ultra-luxe Hôtel Les Mars. But you don't have to be a tycoon to stay here and enjoy the town. For every ritzy restaurant there's a great bakery or relatively modest B&B. A whitewashed bandstand on Healdsburg's plaza hosts free summer concerts, where you might hear anything from bluegrass to Sousa marches. Add to that the fragrant magnolia trees shading the square and the bright flower beds, and the whole thing is as pretty as a Norman Rockwell painting.

The countryside around Healdsburg is the sort you dream about when you're planning a Wine Country vacation. Alongside the relatively untrafficked roads, country stores offer just-plucked fruits and vine-ripened tomatoes. The wineries here are barely visible, since they're tucked behind groves of eucalyptus or hidden high on fog-shrouded hills.

GETTING HERE AND AROUND

To get to Healdsburg from San Francisco, cross the Golden Gate Bridge and continue north on U.S. 101. About 65 miles from San Francisco, take the Central Healdsburg exit and follow Healdsburg Avenue a few blocks to the town's central plaza. Many of the town's hotels and restaurants ring the scenic town square and the few blocks radiating out from here.

WHERE TO EAT

$$$ AMERICAN ✕ **Barndiva.** This hip joint abandons the homey vibe of so many Wine Country spots for a younger, more urban feel. Electronic music plays quietly in the background while hipster servers ferry inventive seasonal cocktails. The food is as stylish as the well-dressed couples cozying up next to one another on the banquette seats. Make a light meal out of starters like goat-cheese croquettes or "The Artisan," a bountiful plate of cheeses and charcuterie, or settle in for the evening with dishes like pork tenderloin with tarragon risotto or rosemary roasted leg of lamb. During warm weather the patio is the place to be. ✉ *231 Center St.* ☎ *707/431–0100* 🌐 *www.barndiva.com* ⏲ *Closed Mon. and Tues.*

$ ITALIAN ✕ **Bovolo.** Husband-and-wife team John Stewart and Duskie Estes serve what they call "slow food . . . fast." Though you might pop into this casual café at the back of Copperfield's Books for half an hour, the staff will have spent hours curing the meats that star in the menu of salads, pizzas, pastas, and sandwiches. For instance, the Salumist's Salad mixes a variety of cured meats with greens, white beans, and a tangy vinaigrette; and a thin-crust pizza might come topped with house-made Italian pork sausage and roasted peppers. House-made gelato served with a dark chocolate sauce or *zeppole* (Italian donuts) are a simply perfect ending to a meal. Their closing hours sometimes vary according to the season and what's taking place on Healdsburg's plaza, so call ahead if you're planning an evening visit. ✉ *106 Matheson St.* ☎ *707/431–2962* 🌐 *www.bovolorestaurant.com* ✍ *Reservations not accepted* ⏲ *Often closed dinner Wed.–Tues.; closed dinner Sun.–Thurs. fall–spring.*

$$$$ AMERICAN Fodor's Choice ★ ✕ **Cyrus.** Hailed as the best thing to hit the Wine Country since French Laundry, Cyrus has collected lots of awards and many raves from guests. From the moment you're seated to the minute your dessert plates are whisked away, you'll be carefully tended by gracious servers and an expert sommelier. The formal dining room, with its vaulted Venetian-plaster ceiling, is a suitably plush setting for chef Douglas Keane's creative, subtle cuisine. Each night (and at some Saturday lunchtimes as well), diners have their choice of four set menus: five- and eight-course extravaganzas ($102 and $130), for both omnivores and vegetarians. Set aside three hours to work your way from savory starters like the terrine of foie gras with curried apple compote, through fragrant dishes like the truffled wine risotto with Parmesan broth, to desserts such as the hazelnut *dacquoise* (layers of hazelnut and buttercream). If you've failed to make reservations, you can order à la carte at the bar, which also has the best collection of cocktails and spirits in all of the Wine Country. ✉ *29 North St., Healdsburg* ☎ *707/433–3311* 🌐 *www.cyrusrestaurant.com* ✍ *Reservations essential* ⏲ *Closed Tues. and Wed. in winter. No lunch, except some Sat. Call to confirm.*

$ ITALIAN ✕ **Scopa.** At this tiny eatery chef Ari Rosen cooks up rustic Italian specialties such as house-made ravioli stuffed with ricotta cheese, braised chicken with greens and polenta, and *polpette Calabrese* (spicy meatballs served with smoked mozzarella in a tomato sauce). Simple thin-crust pizzas are worth ordering, too. Locals love the restaurant for its lack of pretension: wine is served in juice glasses, and the friendly hostess visits guests frequently to make sure all are satisfied. You'll be packed in elbow-to-elbow with your fellow diners, but for a convivial evening over a bottle of Nebbiolo, there's no better choice. Though they're often booked weeks in advance, patient diners can often get a seat at the bar by putting their name on the waiting list. ✉ *109A Plaza St.* ☎ *707/433–5282* 🌐 *www.scopahealdsburg.com* ⏲ *Closed Mon. No lunch.*

$$ MEDITERRANEAN ✕ **Spoonbar.** Cantina doors that open wide onto Healdsburg Avenue make this newcomer especially appealing in summer, when the warm breeze wafts into the stylish space. Concrete walls, mid-century modern chairs, and a long communal table fashioned from rough-hewn acacia wood make an urbane setting for the modern Mediterranean fare. "Small bites" like the marinated quail eggs, spicy lamb meatballs, and house-cured olives are standouts, and several of the dishes demonstrate a Moroccan flair (the Moorish-style chicken with grilled lemon and couscous is especially popular). Though the fare is simultaneously inventive and satisfying, the perpetually packed bar, where celebrity bartender Scott Beattie and his staff mix inventive seasonal cocktails, is the real draw for many locals. Show up early or late for your best shot at a seat at the bar. ✉ *219 Healdsburg Ave. Healdsburg* ☎ *707/433–7222* 🌐 *www.h2hotel.com/spoonbar* ⏲ *Closed lunch Mon.–Thurs.*

$$ AMERICAN ✕ **Zin Restaurant and Wine Bar.** Concrete walls and floors and large canvases on the walls make the restaurant casual, industrial, and slightly artsy. The American cuisine—such as grilled pork chop with homemade applesauce or the wine-braised lamb shank—is hearty and highly seasoned. Portions are large, so consider sharing if you hope to save room for desserts like the brownie sundae with house-made coffee ice cream. As you might have guessed, Zinfandel is the drink of choice here: the varietal makes up roughly half of the 100 or so bottles on the wine list. From Sunday through Thursday, blue-plate specials featuring their homiest fare (like pot roast and chicken and dumplings) make this place a particular bargain. ✉ *344 Center St.* ☎ *707/473–0946* ⏲ *No lunch weekends.*

6

WHERE TO STAY

For expanded hotel reviews, visit Fodors.com.

$$ **Camellia Inn.** In a well-preserved Victorian constructed in 1869, this colorful B&B is on a quiet residential street a block from the town's main square. **Pros:** reasonable rates for the neighborhood; a rare family-friendly inn; within easy walking distance of dozens of restaurants. **Cons:** a few rooms have a shower but no bath; the only TV on the property is in the common sunroom. ✉ *211 North St.* ☎ *707/433–8182 or 800/727–8182* 🌐 *www.camelliainn.com* *8 rooms, 1 suite* *In-room: a/c, no phone, no TV, Wi-Fi. In-hotel: pool, some pets allowed* *Breakfast.*

$$$ **h2hotel.** There are lots of eco-friendly touches at this LEED-certified newcomer to downtown Healdsburg, from the undulating plant-covered "green roof" to wooden decks made from salvaged lumber. **Pros:** stylish modern design; Healdsburg's most popular bar on the ground floor; king beds can be converted to two twins. **Cons:** least expensive rooms lack bathtubs; no fitness facilities on-site. ✉ *219 Healdsburg Ave.* ☎ *707/922–5251* 🌐 *www.h2hotel.com* *34 rooms, 2 suites* *In-room: a/c, Wi-Fi. In-hotel: restaurant, room service, bar, pool, business center, some pets allowed* *Breakfast.*

$$$$ ★ **The Honor Mansion.** An 1883 Italianate Victorian houses this photogenic hotel, and rooms in the main house preserve a sense of the building's heritage, while the larger suites are comparatively understated. **Pros:** spacious grounds with boccie and tennis courts, a putting green, and half-court for basketball; homemade sweets available at all hours; spa pavilions by pool available for massages in fair weather. **Cons:** almost a mile from Healdsburg's plaza; on a moderately busy street. ✉ *14891 Grove St.* ☎ *707/433–4277 or 800/554–4667* 🌐 *www.honormansion.com* *5 rooms, 8 suites* *In-room: a/c, Wi-Fi. In-hotel: tennis court, pool, business center* *Closed 2 wks around Christmas* *Breakfast.*

FARMERS' MARKETS

During two weekly **Healdsburg farmers' markets** you can buy locally made goat cheese, fragrant lavender, and olive oil in addition to the usual produce. On Saturday from May through November the market takes place one block west of the town plaza, at the corner of North and Vine streets, from 9 am to noon. The smaller Tuesday market, which runs from June through October, takes place two blocks northwest of the plaza, in a parking lot off North Street, from 4 pm to 7 pm.

$$$$ **Hotel Healdsburg.** Across the street from Healdsburg's tidy town plaza, this spare, sophisticated hotel caters to travelers with an urban sensibility. **Pros:** several rooms overlook the town plaza; comfortable lobby with a small attached bar; extremely comfortable beds. **Cons:** exterior rooms get some street noise, rooms could use better lighting. ✉ *25 Matheson St.* ☎ *707/431–2800 or 800/889–7188* 🌐 *www.hotelhealdsburg.com* *45 rooms, 10 suites* *In-room: a/c, Wi-Fi. In-hotel: restaurant, room service, bar, pool, gym, spa, some pets allowed* *Breakfast.*

$$$$ **Hôtel Les Mars.** In 2005 posh Healdsburg got even more chichi with the opening of this opulent Relais & Châteaux hotel, featuring guest rooms spacious and elegant enough for French nobility, with 18th- and 19th-century antiques and reproductions, canopied beds, and gas-burning fireplaces. **Pros:** large rooms; just off Healdsburg's plaza; Bulgari bath products. **Cons:** very expensive. ✉ *27 North St.* ☎ *707/433–4211* 🌐 *www.lesmarshotel.com* *16 rooms* *In-room: a/c, Internet, Wi-Fi. In-hotel: restaurant, bar, pool, gym* *Breakfast.*

$$$$ **Madrona Manor.** The oldest continuously operating inn in the area, this 1881 Victorian mansion is surrounded by 8 acres of wooded and landscaped grounds, and rooms in the three-story mansion, the carriage house, and the three separate cottages are splendidly ornate, with mirrors in gilt frames and paintings covering every wall. **Pros:** old-fashioned and romantic; pretty veranda perfect for a cocktail. **Cons:** pool heated May through October only; decor might be too fussy for some. ✉ *1001 Westside Rd., central Healdsburg exit off U.S. 101, then left on Mill St.* ☎ *707/433–4231 or 800/258–4003* 🌐 *www.madronamanor.com* *17 rooms, 5 suites* *In-room: a/c, no TV, Wi-Fi. In-hotel: restaurant, bar, pool* *Breakfast.*

SHOPPING

Oakville Grocery (✉ *124 Matheson St.* ☎ *707/433–3200*) has a bustling Healdsburg branch filled with wine, condiments, and deli items. A terrace with ample seating makes a good place for an impromptu picnic, but you might want to lunch early or late to avoid the worst crowds. You'll have to get in your car to head north on Healdsburg Avenue to **Tip Top Liquor Warehouse** (✉ *90 Dry Creek Rd., Healdsburg* ☎ *707/431–0841*), a nondescript spot that stocks an interesting selection of wines and spirits at fair prices. Though it's strongest in bottles from Sonoma, you'll also find a few Napa wines, including some rare cult Cabernets.

DRY CREEK AND ALEXANDER VALLEYS

On the west side of U.S. 101, Dry Creek Valley remains one of the least-developed appellations in Sonoma. Zinfandel grapes flourish on the benchlands, whereas the gravelly, well-drained soil of the valley floor is better known for Chardonnay and, in the north, Sauvignon Blanc. The wineries in this region tend to be smaller, which makes them a good bet on summer weekends, when larger spots and those along the main thoroughfares fill up with tourists.

The Alexander Valley, which lies northeast of Healdsburg, is similarly rustic, and you can see as many folks cycling along Highway 128 here as you can behind the wheel of a car. The largely family-owned wineries often produce Zinfandel and Chardonnay.

GETTING HERE AND AROUND

The Dry Creek Valley is to the west of downtown Healdsburg, across U.S. 101. To get here from the plaza, drive north on Healdsburg Avenue and turn left on Dry Creek Road. This takes you under the freeway and veers north. Many of the region's wineries are along Dry Creek Road or on West Dry Creek Road, which runs roughly parallel about a mile to the west, accessible by the cross streets Lambert Bridge Road and Yoakim Bridge Road.

The Alexander Valley is just northeast of Healdsburg. To get here from the plaza, drive north on Healdsburg Avenue and veer right on Alexander Valley Road. Although there are a few wineries on Alexander Valley Road itself, most of them on are on Highway 128, which intersects is after about 3.3 mi.

EXPLORING

Dry Creek Vineyard. Fumé Blanc is king here, where they have been making this refreshing white wine in the style of those made in Sancerre, France, since the beginning of the 1970s. But Dry Creek also makes well-regarded Zinfandels, a zesty dry Chenin Blanc, a Pinot Noir, and a handful of Cabernet Sauvignon blends. Since many of their quality wines go for less than $20 or $30 a bottle, it's a popular stop for those who want to stock their cellars for a reasonable price. After picking up a bottle you might want to picnic on the lawn, next to the flowering magnolia tree. Conveniently, a general store and deli with plenty of picnic fixings is just steps down the road. ✉ *3770 Lambert Bridge Rd., Healdsburg* ☎ *707/433–1000* 🌐 *www.drycreekvineyard.com* 🎫 *Tasting $5–$10* ⏲ *Daily 10:30–4:30.*

CLOSE UP

Best Wine Country Festivals

■ **February–March: Napa Valley Mustard Festival.** When Napa is at its least crowded, and wild mustard blooms in between the vines, locals celebrate wine, food, and art with exhibitions, auctions, dinners, and cooking and photography competitions. (*www.mustardfestival.org*)

■ **March: Wine Road Barrel Tasting Weekends.** For two weekends in March more than 100 wineries in the Russian River, Dry Creek, and Alexander valleys open their cellars to visitors who want to taste the wine in the barrels, getting a preview of what's to come. (*www.wineroad.com*)

■ **Late May: Sonoma Jazz + Festival.** Headlining jazz, rock, and world music performers play in a large tent in downtown Sonoma, while smaller music, food, and wine events take place around town. (*www.sonomajazz.org*)

■ **Early June: Auction Napa Valley.** The world's biggest charity wine auction is one of Napa's glitziest gatherings. Events hosted by various wineries culminate in a hotly contested auction followed by an opulent dinner and party. (*www.napavintners.com*)

■ **Early October: Sonoma County Harvest Fair.** This festival celebrates agriculture in Sonoma County, with wine tastings, cooking demos, livestock shows, crafts, carnival rides, and local entertainers filling the Sonoma County Fairgrounds in Santa Rosa. (*www.harvestfair.org*)

■ **Mid-November: Napa Valley Film Festival.** Film premieres, pre-movie wine tastings, and food- and wine-related events where you can meet some of the filmmakers whose works are being shown take place in downtown Napa and St. Helena. (*www.napavalleyfilmfest.org*)

Francis Ford Coppola Winery. In 2006 filmmaker-winemaker Francis Ford Coppola snapped up a majestic French-style château, formerly Château Souverain, to showcase his less-expensive wines. (His Napa winery, Rubicon Estate, focuses on the high-end vintages). After years of renovation the château has been turned into an impressive fantasyland where you could easily spend all day. In addition to tasting their wines or ordering a cocktail at the full bar, you can select from a variety of tours, from a vineyard walk to an opportunity to watch the bottling facility in action. Scattered throughout the gift shop are mementos of Coppola's film career, from his Oscars, to Don Corleone's desk in *The Godfather,* to a display on the filming of *Apocalypse Now.* Kids (and some adults), though, will be most excited by the large pool on the terrace, where you'll also see a band shell that is a replica of the one that appears in *Godfather II.* Guests rent cabines to shower and change into their swimsuits before spending the afternoon lounging under the striped umbrellas, perhaps even ordering food from the poolside café. The winery's restaurant, Rustic, serves a more elaborate menu from a spacious dining room and a terrace overlooking the vineyards. Prices, pool hours, and tour times are still being finalized, so check the winery's Web site or call ahead for the latest. ✉ *300 Via Archimedes (formerly Souverain Rd.), Geyserville* ☎ *707/857–1400* *www.franciscoppolawinery.com* *Tasting free–$10; tour $20; pool pass*

$15. See prices and family plans online. ⏲ Tasting room daily 11–6, restaurant daily 11–9; pool hours vary seasonally.

Fodor's Choice ★ **Michel-Schlumberger.** Down a narrow road at the westernmost edge of the Dry Creek Valley, Michel-Schlumberger is one of Sonoma's finest producers of Cabernet Sauvignon. A spin through their organically farmed vineyard is like taking a walk through France, and though they're best known for their Bordeaux varietals, you'll also find Burgundian grapes next to ones from Alsace and the Rhône. The tour is unusually casual and friendly. Weather permitting, you'll wander up a hill on a gravel pathway to the edge of their lovely terraced vineyards before swinging through the barrel room in the California Mission–style building that once served as the home of the winery's founder, Jean-Jacques Michel. To taste older vintages of their Cabernet and learn what their wines will taste like after 10 or so years in the bottle, reserve in advance for a vertical library tasting ($30). Wine and cheese pairings ($35) are also available by reservation. ✉ *4155 Wine Creek Rd., Healdsburg* ☎ *707/433–7427 or 800/447–3060* 🌐 *www.michelschlumberger.com* 🎫 *Tasting $10–$15, tour $20* ⏲ *Daily 11–5; tours at 11 and 2, by appointment.*

Fodor's Choice ★ **Preston Vineyards.** Once you wind your way down Preston Vineyards' long driveway, flanked by vineyards and punctuated by the occasional olive tree, you'll be welcomed by the sight of a few farmhouses encircling a shady yard prowled by several friendly cats. In summer a small selection of organic produce grown in their gardens is sold from an impromptu stand on the front porch, and house-made bread and olive oil are available year-round. Their down-home style is particularly in evidence on Sunday, the only day of the week that tasting-room staffers sell a 3-liter bottle of Guadagni Red, a primarily Zinfandel blend filled from the barrel right in front of you. Owners Lou and Susan Preston are committed to organic growing techniques, and use only estate-grown grapes in their wines, like Sauvignon Blanc, and Rhône varietals such as Syrah and Viognier. ✉ *9282 W. Dry Creek Rd., Healdsburg* ☎ *707/433–3372* 🌐 *www.prestonvineyards.com* 🎫 *$5 tasting* ⏲ *Daily 11–4:30.*

Quivira. An unassuming winery in a modern wooden barn topped by solar panels, Quivira produces some of the most interesting wines in Dry Creek Valley. It's known for its dangerously drinkable reds, including a Petite Syrah, and a few hearty Zinfandel blends. The excellent tour provides information about their biodynamic and organic farming practices and also offers a glimpse of their beautiful garden and the pigs, chickens, and beehives kept on the property. Redwood and olive trees shade the picnic area. ✉ *4900 W. Dry Creek Rd., Healdsburg* ☎ *707/431–8333* 🌐 *www.quivirawine.com* 🎫 *Tasting $5, tour $15* ⏲ *Daily 11–5; tour by appointment.*

★ **Stryker Sonoma.** Inside the tasting room at Stryker Sonoma, vaulted ceilings and seemingly endless walls of windows onto the vineyards suggest you've entered a cathedral to viniculture. The wines are almost as impressive as the architecture: most of their bottles are single varietals, such as Chardonnay, Merlot, Zinfandel, and Cabernet Sauvignon. An exception, however, are a few Bordeaux-style blends, including the powerful E1K, which, unfortunately, is not usually poured in the tasting room (though it never hurts to ask whether they have a bottle open). The picnic tables are a particularly lovely way to enjoy the quiet countryside of the Alexander Valley. Call ahead at least a day in advance to book a spot on a tour that concludes on the observation deck overlooking the vineyards. ✉ *5110 Hwy. 28, Geyserville* ☎ *707/433–1944* 🌐 *www.strykersonoma.com* 🎫 *Tasting $10, tour $15.* ⏲ *Daily 10:30–5.*

OFF THE BEATEN PATH

Though it's certainly possible to get a great drink in downtown Healdsburg at either Cyrus or Spoonbar *(see above)*, those who want to feel a million miles away from the bustle of downtown Healdsburg should drive the 6 miles to the **Alexander Valley Bar** (✉ *3487 Alexander Valley Rd.* ☎ *707/431–1904*), a dimly lit Victorian-style speakeasy where you'll find historic photos on the walls and a vintage photo booth to document the occasion. A mostly local crowd gathers to enjoy fine cocktails, some using produce grown in their own gardens. The place is poorly marked; to get there from Healdsburg's plaza, drive 3 mi north on Healdsburg Avenue and then turn right on Alexander Valley Road. The bar, which is attached to the Medlock Ames tasting room, is in another 3 mi, at the intersection of Alexander Valley Road and Sausal Lane.

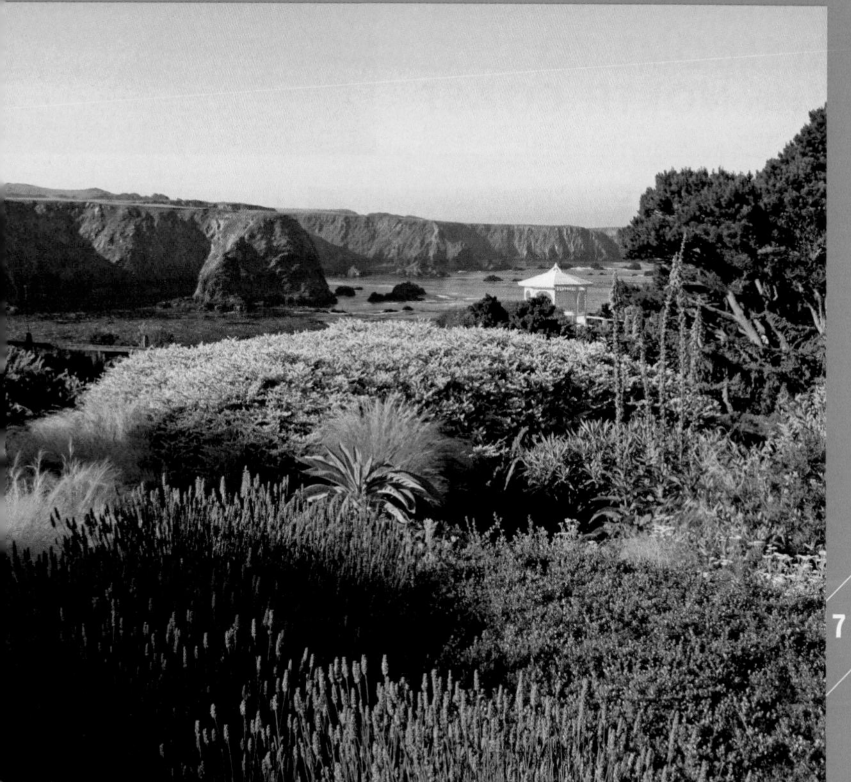

The North Coast

FROM THE SONOMA COAST TO REDWOOD NATIONAL PARK

WORD OF MOUTH

"Mendocino is a charming old town, and the Mendocino Headlands are beautiful. . . . Highway 1 from Mendocino to Bodega Bay is a very beautiful drive. It is a lot of work, but it is worth the effort."

—happytrailstoyou

WELCOME TO THE NORTH COAST

TOP REASONS TO GO

★ **Scenic coastal drives:** There's hardly a road here that *isn't* scenic.

★ **Wild beaches:** This stretch of California is one of nature's masterpieces. Revel in the unbridled, rugged coastline, without a building in sight.

★ **Dinnertime:** When you're done hiking the beach, refuel with delectable food; you'll find everything from burritos to bouillabaisse.

★ **Romance:** Here you can end almost every day with a perfect sunset.

★ **Wildlife:** Sea lions and otters and deer, oh my!

1 The Sonoma Coast. Heading up through northwestern Marin into Sonoma County, Highway 1 traverses gently rolling pastureland. North of Bodega Bay dramatic shoreline scenery takes over. The road snakes up, down, and around sheer cliffs and steep inclines—some without guardrails—where cows seem to cling precariously. Stunning vistas (or cottony fog) and hairpin turns make this one of the most exhilarating drives north of San Francisco.

2 The Mendocino Coast. The timber industry gave birth to most of the small towns strung along this stretch of the California coastline. Although tourism now drives the economy, the region has retained much of its old-fashioned charm. The beauty of the coastal landscape, of course, has not changed.

3 Redwood Country. There's a different state of mind in Humboldt County. Here, instead of spas, there are old-time hotels. Instead of wineries, there are breweries. The landscape is primarily thick redwood forest, which gets snow in winter and sizzles in summer while the coast sits covered in fog. Until as late as 1924, there was no road that went north of Willits; the coastal towns were reachable only by sea. That legacy is apparent in the communities here today: Eureka and Arcata, both former ports, are sizeable, but otherwise towns are tiny and nestled in the woods, and people have an independent spirit that recalls the original homesteaders. Coming from the south, Garberville is a good place to stop for picnic provisions and stretch your legs.

4 Redwood National Park. For a pristine encounter with giant redwoods, make the trek to this seldom-visited park where even casual visitors have easy access to the trees. *(See Chapter 8, Redwood National Park.)*

GETTING ORIENTED

It's all but impossible to explore the northern California coast without a car. Indeed, you wouldn't want to—driving here is half the fun. The main road is Highway 1, two lanes that twist and turn (sometimes 180 degrees) up cliffs and down through valleys. Towns appear every so often, but this is mostly a land of green pasture, dense forest, and natural, undeveloped coastline. Pace yourself: Most drivers stop frequently to appreciate the views (and you can't drive faster than 20–40 mph on many portions of the highway), so don't plan to drive too far in one day.

Updated by Sura Wood

The spectacular coastline between Marin County and the Oregon border defies expectations. The landscape is defined by the Pacific Ocean, but instead of boardwalks and bikinis there are ragged cliffs and pounding waves—and the sunbathers are mostly sea lions. Instead of strip malls and freeways, there are small towns that retire around sundown and a single-lane road that follows the fickle shoreline. And that's exactly why many Californians, especially those from the Bay Area, come here to escape the Sturm und Drang of daily life.

This stretch of Highway 1 is made up of numerous little worlds, each different from the next. From Point Reyes toward Bodega Bay, the land spreads out into green, rolling pastures and sandy beaches. The road climbs higher and higher as it heads north through Sonoma County, where cows graze on precipitous cliffs and the ocean views are breathtaking. In Mendocino the coastline follows the ins and outs of lush valleys where rivers pour down from the forests and into the ocean. At Humboldt County the highway heads inland to the redwoods, then returns to the shoreline at the tidal flats surrounding the ports of Eureka and Arcata. Heading north to the Oregon border, the coast is increasingly wild and lined with redwood trees.

Although the towns along the way vary from deluxe spa retreat to hippie hideaway, all are reliably sleepy. Most communities have fewer than 1,000 inhabitants, and most main streets are shuttered by 9 pm. Exceptions are Mendocino and Eureka, but even they are loved best by those who would rather cozy up in bed rather than paint the town.

PLANNING

WHEN TO GO

The North Coast is a year-round destination, though when you go determines what you will see. The migration of the Pacific gray whales is a wintertime phenomenon, which lasts roughly from mid-December to early April. Wildflowers follow the winter rain, as early as January in southern areas through June and July farther north. Summer is the high season for tourists, but spring, fall, and even winter are arguably better times to visit because everything is quieter.

The coastal climate is quite similar to San Francisco's, although with greater extremes: winter nights are colder than in the city, and in July and August thick fog can drop temperatures to the high 50s. If you do get caught in the summer fog, fear not! You need only drive inland to find temperatures that are often 20 degrees higher.

GETTING HERE AND AROUND

BY AIR

The only North Coast airport with commercial air service, Arcata/Eureka Airport (ACV) receives flights on United Express, Delta, and Horizon airlines. The airport is in McKinleyville, which is 16 mi from Eureka.

A taxi to Eureka costs about $50 and takes roughly 20 minutes. Door-to-door airport shuttles cost $19 to Arcata and Trinidad, $23 to Eureka, and $50 to Ferndale. All prices are for the first person, and go up only $5 total for each additional person.

7

Airport Contact Arcata/Eureka Airport ✉ *3561 Boeing Ave., McKinleyville* ☎ *707/839–5401.*

Shuttle Contact Door to Door Airport Shuttle ☎ *888/338–5497* 🌐 *www.doortodoorairporter.com.*

BY BUS

Greyhound buses travel along U.S. 101 from San Francisco to Seattle, with regular stops in Eureka and Arcata. Bus drivers will stop in other towns along the route if you specify your destination when you board. Humboldt Transit Authority connects Eureka, Arcata, and Trinidad.

Bus Contacts Greyhound ☎ *800/231–2222* 🌐 *www.greyhound.com.* **Humboldt Transit Authority** ☎ *707/443–0826* 🌐 *www.hta.org.*

BY CAR

Although there are excellent services along U.S. 101, long, lonesome stretches separate towns (with their resident gas stations and mechanics) along Highway 1, and services are even fewer and farther between on the smaller roads. ■ **TIP→ If you're running low on fuel and see a gas station, stop for a refill.** Driving directly to Mendocino from San Francisco is quicker if, instead of driving up the coast on Highway 1, you take U.S. 101 north to Highway 128 west (from Cloverdale) to Highway 1 north. The quickest way to the far North Coast from the Bay Area is a straight shot up U.S. 101, which runs inland all way until Eureka. Weather sometimes forces closure of parts of Highway 1, but it's rare. For information on the condition of roads in Northern California, call the Caltrans Highway Information Network's voice-activated system.

HIGHWAY 1: SAN FRANCISCO TO FORT BRAGG

Mendocino Coast Botanical Garden

THE PLAN

Distance: 177 mi

Time: 2-4 days

Good Overnight Options: San Francisco, Olema, Bodega Bay, Gualala, Mendocino, Fort Bragg

For more information on the sights and attractions along this portion of Highway 1, please see San Francisco, Bay Area, and North Coast chapters

SAN FRANCISCO

The official Highway 1 heads straight through **San Francisco** along 19th Avenue through **Golden Gate Park** and the **Presidio** toward the **Golden Gate Bridge.** For a more scenic tour, watch for signs announcing exits for 35 North/Skyline Boulevard, then Ocean Beach/The Great Highway (past Lake Merced). The Great Highway follows the coast along the western border of San Francisco; you'll cruise past entrances to the **San Francisco Zoo, Golden Gate Park,** and the **Cliff House.** Hike out to **Point Lobos** or **Land's End** for awesome vistas, then drive through **Lincoln Park** and the **Palace of the Legion of Honor** and follow El Camino del Mar/Lincoln Boulevard all the way to the Golden Gate Bridge.

Golden Gate Bridge

The best way to see San Francisco is on foot and public transportation. A **Union Square** stroll—complete with people-watching, window-shopping, and architecture-viewing—is a good first stop. In **Chinatown,** department stores give way to storefront temples, open-air markets, and delightful dim-sum shops. After lunch in one, catch a **Powell Street cable car** to the end of the line and get off to see the bay views and the antique arcade games at **Musée Mécanique** (the gem of otherwise mindless **Fisherman's Wharf**). For dinner and live music, try cosmopolitan **North Beach.**

SAN FRANCISCO TO OLEMA

(approx. 37 mi)

Leaving the city the next day, your drive across the Golden Gate Bridge and a stop at a **Marin Headlands** overlook will yield memorable views (if fog hasn't socked in the bay). So will a hike in **Point Reyes National Seashore,** farther up Highway 1 (now called Shoreline Highway). On this wild swath of coast you'll likely be able to claim an unspoiled beach for yourself. You should expect company, however, around the lighthouse at the tip of Point Reyes because year-round views—and seasonal elephant seal- and whale-watching—draw crowds. If you have time, poke around tiny **Olema,** which has some excellent restaurants, and **Inverness,** home to the historic Olema Inn & Restaurant.

Point Reyes National Seashore

OLEMA TO MENDOCINO

(approx. 131 mi)

Passing only a few minuscule towns, this next stretch of Highway 1 showcases the northern coast in all its rugged glory. The reconstructed compound of eerily foreign buildings at **Fort Ross State Historic Park** recalls the era of Russian fur trading in California. Pull into **Gualala** for an espresso, a sandwich, and a little human contact

Point Reyes National Seashore

TOP 5 PLACES TO LINGER

- San Francisco
- Marin Headlands
- Point Reyes National Seashore
- Fort Ross State Historic Park
- Mendocino

before rolling onward. After another 50 mi of tranquil state beaches and parks you'll return to civilization in **Mendocino.**

MENDOCINO TO FORT BRAGG

(approx. 9 mi)

Exploring Mendocino you may feel like you've fallen through a rabbit hole: the weather screams Northern California, but the 19th-century buildings—erected by homesick Yankee loggers—definitely say New England. Once you've browsed around the artsy shops, continue on to the **Mendocino Coast Botanical Gardens;** then travel back in time on the **Skunk Train,** which follows an old logging route from **Fort Bragg** deep into the redwood forest.

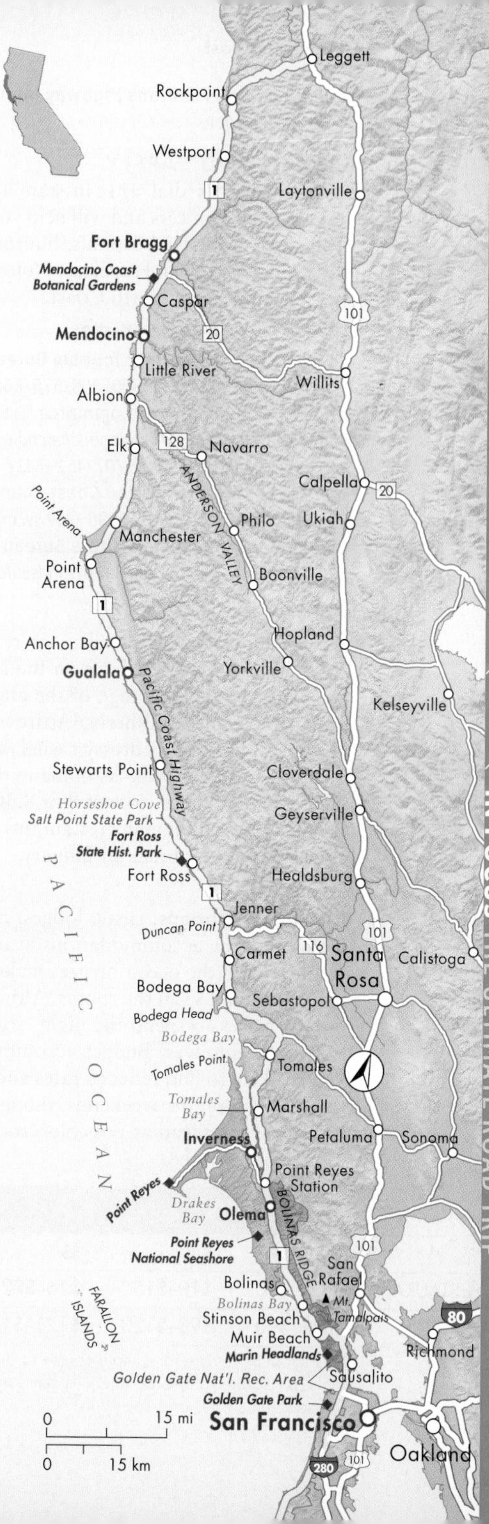

Road Conditions **Caltrans Highway Information Network** ☎ *800/427–7623* 🌐 *www.dot.ca.gov.*

HEALTH AND SAFETY

In an emergency dial 911. In state and national parks, park rangers serve as police officers and will help you in any emergency. Bigger towns along the coast have hospitals, but for major medical emergencies you will need to go to San Francisco. Note that cell phones don't work along large swaths of the North Coast.

VISITOR INFORMATION

Contacts **Sonoma County Tourism Bureau** ✉ *420 Aviation Blvd., Suite 106, Santa Rosa* ☎ *707/522–5800, 800/576–6662* 🌐 *www.sonomacounty.com.* **Redwood Coast Chamber of Commerce** ✉ *Box 199, Gualala* ☎ *707/884–1080, 800/778–5252* 🌐 *www.redwoodcoastchamber.com.* **Visit Mendocino County** ✉ *525 S. Main St., Ukiah* ☎ *707/462–7417, 866/466–3636* 🌐 *www.gomendo.com.* **Fort Bragg–Mendocino Coast Chamber of Commerce** ✉ *217 S. Main St., Fort Bragg* ☎ *707/961–6300* 🌐 *www.mendocinocoast.com.* **Humboldt County Convention and Visitors Bureau** ✉ *1034 2nd St., Eureka* ☎ *707/443–5097, 800/346–3482* 🌐 *www.redwoods.info.*

RESTAURANTS

A few restaurants with national reputations, plus several more of regional note, entice palates on the North Coast. Even the workaday local spots take advantage of the abundant fresh seafood and locally grown vegetables and herbs. Attire is usually informal, though at the pricier establishments dressy casual (somewhere between flip-flops and high heels) is the norm. As in many rural areas, plan to dine early: the majority of kitchens close at 8 or 8:30 and virtually no one serves past 9:30. Also note that many restaurants in the northern part of this region close for a winter break in January.

HOTELS

Restored Victorians, rustic lodges, country inns, and vintage motels are among the accommodations available here. Hardly any have air-conditioning (the ocean breezes make it unnecessary), and many have no phones or TVs in the rooms. Although several towns have only one or two places to spend the night, some of these lodgings are destinations in themselves. Budget accommodations are rare, but in winter you're likely to find reduced rates and nearly empty inns and B&Bs. In summer and on the weekends, though, make bed-and-breakfast reservations as far ahead as possible—rooms at the best inns often sell out months in advance.

WHAT IT COSTS

	¢	$	$$	$$$	$$$$
RESTAURANTS	under $10	$10–$15	$16–$22	$23–$30	over $30
HOTELS	under $90	$90–$120	$121–$175	$176–$250	over $250

Restaurant prices are for a main course at dinner, excluding sales tax of 9.00%. Hotel prices are for two people in a standard double room in high season, excluding service charges and 8%–11% tax.

THE SONOMA COAST

BODEGA BAY

21 mi north of Marshall on Hwy. 1.

From the busy harbor here, commercial boats pursue fish and Dungeness crab. There's nothing quaint about this working town without a center—it's just a string of businesses along several miles of Highway 1. But some tourists still come to see where Alfred Hitchcock shot *The Birds* in 1962. The buildings that appeared in the movie are long gone, but in nearby Bodega you can find Potter Schoolhouse and the Tides Wharf complex, which was an important, if no longer unrecognizable, location used for the movie.

GETTING HERE AND AROUND

Reach Bodega Bay from Highway 101 north or south to Santa Rosa, then Highway 12 west (Bodega Highway west of Sebastopol) 23 mi to the coast. From San Francisco you can also take Valley Ford Road (Highway 1) northwest about 27 mi from Petaluma. Mendocino Transit Authority (*www.4mta.org*) Route 95 buses connect Bodega Bay with coastal towns and Santa Rosa.

WHERE TO EAT AND STAY

$$ SEAFOOD **Sandpiper Restaurant.** A local favorite for breakfast, this friendly café on the marina does a good job for a fair price. Peruse the board for the day's fresh catch or order a menu regular such as crab stew or wasabi tuna; clam chowder is the house specialty. *1400 Hwy. 1* *707/875–2278* *www.sandpiperrestaurant.com.*

$$$ **Bodega Bay Lodge.** Looking out to the ocean across a wetland, a group of shingle-and-river-rock buildings houses Bodega Bay's finest accommodations. **Pros:** pampering; ocean views. **Cons:** on the highway. *103 Hwy. 1* *707/875–3525, 888/875–2250* *www.bodegabaylodge.com* *78 rooms, 5 suites* *In-room: no a/c, Wi-Fi. In-hotel: restaurant, pool, gym, business center.*

SPORTS AND THE OUTDOORS

Bodega Bay Sportfishing. Bodega Bay Sportfishing charters ocean-fishing boats and rents equipment. They also offer whale-watching trips mid-winter through spring. *1410 B Bay Flat Rd.* *707/875–3344* *www.bodegabaysportfishing.com.*

Sonoma Villa Horse Rental. Sonoma Villa Horse Rental, at the Sonoma Coast Villa & Spa, offers guided horseback trail rides, some along the beach. *16702 Hwy. 1* *707/876–3374* *www.scvilla.com.*

Links at Bodega Harbour. At the incredibly scenic oceanfront Links at Bodega Harbour you can play an 18-hole Robert Trent Jones–designed course. *21301 Heron Dr.* *707/875–3538, 800/503–8158* *www.bodegaharbourgolf.com.*

7

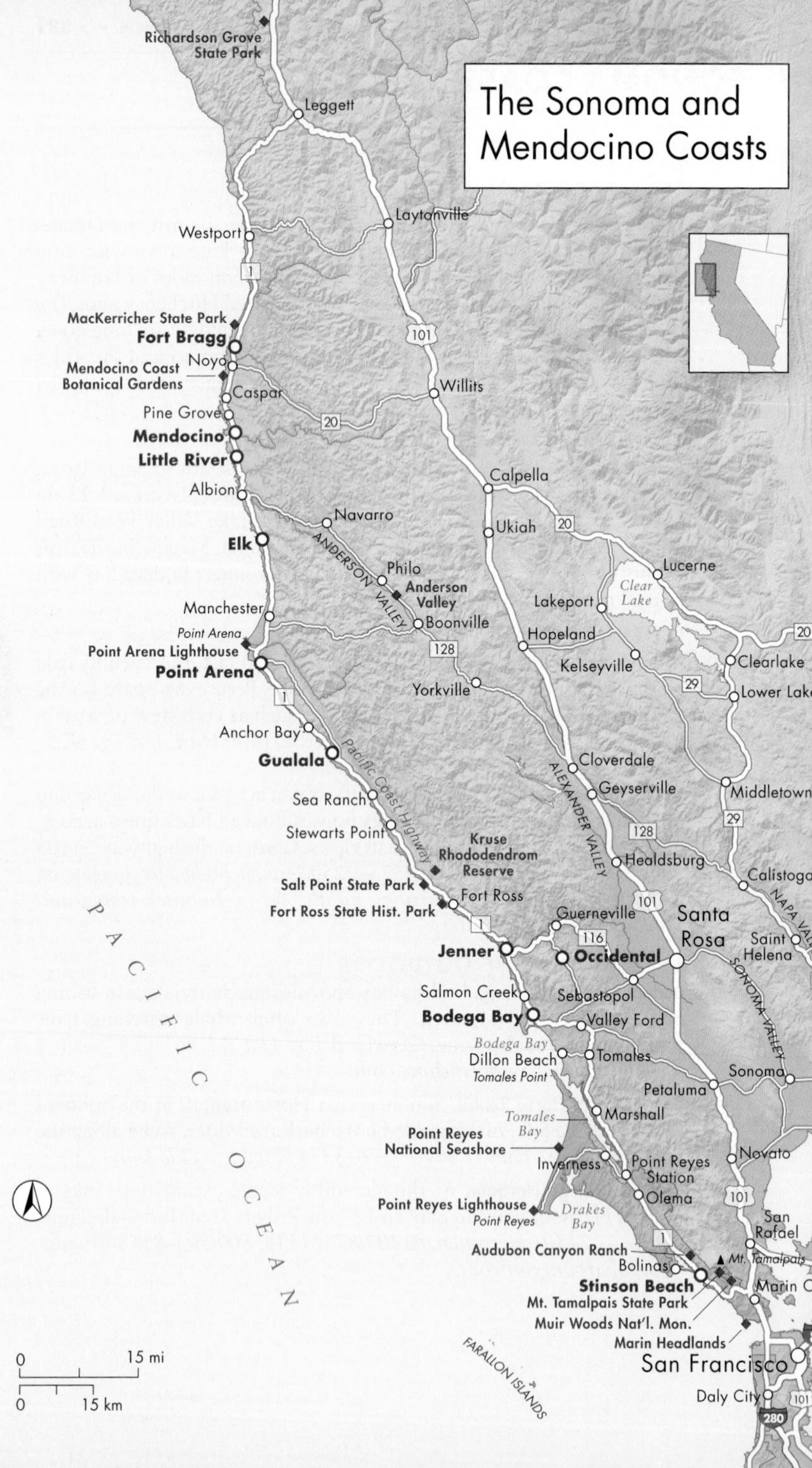

The Sonoma and Mendocino Coasts
Richardson Grove State Park
Leggett
Laytonville
Westport
1
MacKerricher State Park
Fort Bragg
101
Noyo
Mendocino Coast Botanical Gardens
Willits
Caspar
Pine Grove
20
Mendocino
Little River
Calpella
Albion
Navarro
Ukiah
20
Elk
ANDERSON VALLEY
Philo
Anderson Valley
Lucerne
Clear Lake
Lakeport
Manchester
Boonville
Point Arena
Point Arena Lighthouse
Point Arena
128
Hopeland
20
Kelseyville
Clearlake
29
Yorkville
Lower Lake
1
Anchor Bay
Gualala
Pacific Coast Highway
Cloverdale
ALEXANDER VALLEY
Geyserville
Middletown
Sea Ranch
29
Stewarts Point
128
Kruse Rhododendrom Reserve
Healdsburg
Calistoga
Salt Point State Park
Fort Ross
NAPA VALLEY
Fort Ross State Hist. Park
101
Guerneville
Santa Rosa
1
116
Saint Helena
Jenner
Occidental
SONOMA VALLEY
PACIFIC OCEAN
Salmon Creek
Sebastopol
Bodega Bay
Valley Ford
Bodega Bay
Dillon Beach
Tomales
Tomales Point
Sonoma
Petaluma
Tomales Bay
Marshall
Point Reyes National Seashore
Novato
Inverness
Point Reyes Station
Olema
101
Point Reyes Lighthouse
Point Reyes
Drakes Bay
San Rafael
1
Audubon Canyon Ranch
Mt. Tamalpais
Bolinas
Stinson Beach
Marin Ci
Mt. Tamalpais State Park
Muir Woods Nat'l. Mon.
Marin Headlands
San Francisco
FARALLON ISLANDS
0
15 mi
0
15 km
Daly City
101
280

OCCIDENTAL

14 mi northeast of Bodega Bay on Bohemian Hwy.

A village surrounded by redwood forests, orchards, and vineyards, Occidental is a former logging hub with a bohemian vibe. The 19th-century downtown offers a top-notch B&B, good food, and a handful of art galleries and boutiques. The neighboring town of Freestone offers much of the same, but on a smaller scale.

GETTING HERE AND AROUND

To reach Occidental, take Highway 12 (Bodega Highway) east 5 mi from Highway 1. Take a left onto Bohemian Highway, where you'll find Freestone; another 3½ mi and you'll be in Occidental. From Highway 101 north or south take Highway 12 west from Santa Rosa about 13 mi, then head north on Bohemian Highway about 3½ mi to the village.

EXPLORING

Osmosis–The Enzyme Bath Spa. A traditional Japanese detoxifying treatment awaits you at this spa, which claims to be the only such facility in America. Your bath is a deep redwood tub of damp cedar shavings and rice bran, naturally heated to 140°F by the action of enzymes. Serene attendants bury you up to the neck and during the 20-minute treatment bring you sips of water and place cool cloths on your forehead. After a shower, lie down and listen to brain-balancing music through headphones or have a massage, perhaps in one of the creek-side pagodas. A treatment and access to the gardens costs $85 per person (less for parties of two or more people); reservations are recommended. ✉ *209 Bohemian Hwy., Freestone* ☎ *707/823–8231* 🌐 *www.osmosis.com* ⏲ *Daily 9–8.*

7

Occidental Church chamber music. Once a month, usually on Friday or Saturday evening, chamber music concerts featuring notable musicians from California and around the country are held at the Occidental Community Church. ✉ *2nd and Church Sts.* ☎ *707/874–1124* 🌐 *www.redwoodarts.org.*

WHERE TO EAT AND STAY

¢ CAFÉ ✕ **Wild Flour Bread.** There are no appliances at this bakery, which occupies a renovated barn. Dough is kneaded by hand, and baked in a wood-fired oven. The result: delectable breads both savory and sweet. (Don't miss the sticky bun bread.) ✉ *140 Bohemian Hwy., Freestone* ☎ *707/874–2938* 🌐 *www.wildflourbread.com* ▬ *No credit cards* ⏲ *Closed Tues.–Thurs.*

$$$ ★ **The Inn at Occidental.** Quilts, folk art, and original paintings and photographs fill this colorful and friendly inn. **Pros:** colorful; luxurious; friendly. **Cons:** not for those with minimalist tastes; not for kids. ✉ *3657 Church St.* ✉ *Box 857* ☎ *707/874–1047, 800/522–6324* 🌐 *www.innatoccidental.com* *13 rooms, 3 suites, 1 cottage* *In-room: a/c, no TV, Wi-Fi. In-hotel: some age restrictions* 🍽 *Breakfast.*

JENNER

10 mi north of Bodega Bay on Hwy. 1.

The broad, lazy Russian River empties into the Pacific Ocean at Jenner, a wide spot in the road where houses dot a mountainside high above the sea. Facing south, the village looks across the river's mouth to **Goat Rock State Beach,** home to a colony of sea lions for most of the year; pupping season is March through June. The beach, accessed for free off Highway 1 a couple of miles south of town, is open daily from 8 am to sunset. Bring binoculars and walk north from the parking lot to view the sea lions.

GETTING HERE AND AROUND

From Highway 101 in Santa Rosa head west on Highway 12 (Bodega Highway west of Sebastopol) 23 mi to the coast, then travel 10 mi north on Highway 1 to Jenner. From Santa Rosa you can also use Highway 116 west through Guerneville (about 31 mi to Jenner). Mendocino Transit Authority (*www.4mta.org*) Route 95 buses stop in Jenner and connect with Bodega Bay, Santa Rosa, and other coastal towns.

WHERE TO EAT

$$$$ NEW AMERICAN

River's End. A magnificent ocean view makes lunch or an evening here memorable. Come for cocktails and Hog Island oysters on the half shell and hope for a splashy sunset. If you stay for dinner, choose from elaborate entrées such as grilled wild king salmon on cucumber noodles or elk with a red-wine-poached pear and Gorgonzola. The execution may not always justify the prices and the dining room is plain-Jane, but just look at that view. Open hours sometimes vary, so call to confirm. River's End also rents out a few ocean-view rooms and cabins ($$$–$$$$). *11048 Hwy. 1* *707/865–2484* *www.ilovesunsets.com* *Reservations essential* *Closed mid-week fall through spring.*

FORT ROSS STATE HISTORIC PARK

12 mi north of Jenner on Hwy. 1.

GETTING HERE AND AROUND

From Santa Rosa, head west on Highway 116 about 31 mi to Jenner, then north 12 mi on Highway 1 to the park entrance. Mendocino Transit Authority (*www.4mta.org*) Route 95 provides service between Fort Ross and other coastal towns and cities.

Fort Ross State Historic Park. Established in 1812, Fort Ross became Russia's major outpost in California, meant to produce crops and other supplies for northerly fur-trading operations. The Russians brought Aleut sea-otter hunters down from Alaska. By 1841 the area was depleted of seals and otters, and the Russians sold their post to John Sutter, later of gold-rush fame. After a local Anglo rebellion against the Mexicans, the land fell under U.S. domain, becoming part of California in 1850. The state park service has reconstructed Fort Ross, including its Russian Orthodox chapel, a redwood stockade, the officers' barracks, and a blockhouse. The excellent museum here documents the history of the fort and this part of the North Coast. *19005 Hwy. 1* *707/847–3286* *$8 per vehicle* *Fri.–Sun., sunrise–sunset; visitor center Fri.–Sun. 10–4:30* *No dogs allowed past parking lot and picnic area.*

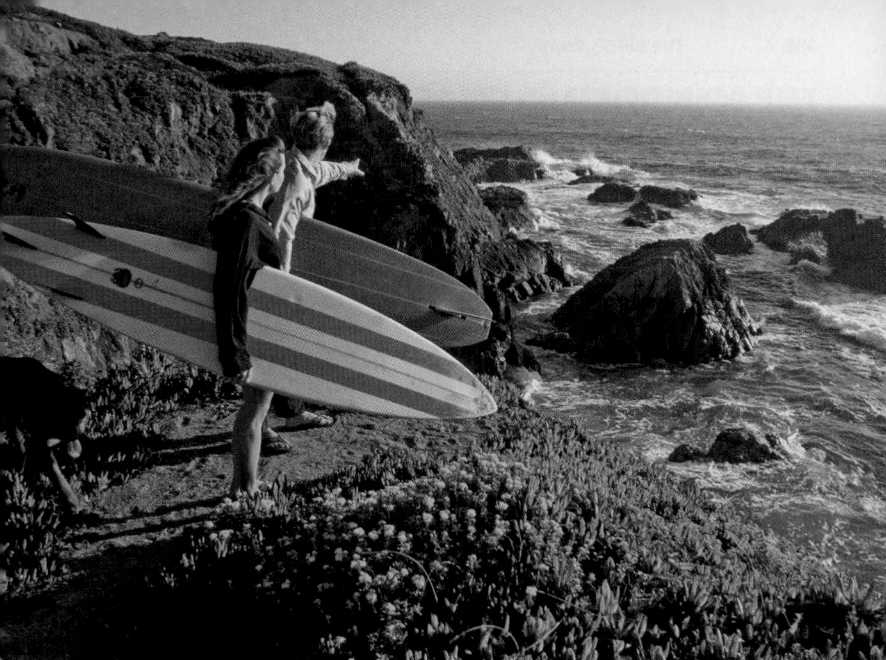

Surfers check out the waves near Bodega Bay on the Sonoma Coast.

SALT POINT STATE PARK

6 mi north of Fort Ross on Hwy. 1.

GETTING HERE AND AROUND

Exit U.S. 101 in Santa Rosa and travel west on Highway 116 about 31 mi to Jenner, then north 18 mi on Highway 1 to reach the park. Mendocino Transit Authority (🌐 *www.4mta.org*) Route 95 buses stop at Salt Point and connect with other North Coast towns.

Salt Point State Park. For 5 mi, Highway 1 winds through this park, 6,000 acres of forest, meadows, and rocky shoreline. Heading north, the first park entrance (on the right) leads to forest hiking trails and several campgrounds. The next entrance—the park's main road—winds through meadows and along the wave-splashed coastline (a great place to stop so the kids can let off steam). This is also the route to the visitor center (open April to October, weekends 10–3) and Gerstle Cove, a favorite spot for abalone divers and sunbathing seals. Next along the highway is Stump Beach Cove, with picnic tables, toilets, and a ¼-mi walk to the sandy beach. The park's final entrance is at Fisk Mill Cove, where centuries of wind and rain erosion have carved unusual honeycomb patterns in the sandstone called "tafonis." A five-minute walk uphill from the parking lot leads to a dramatic view of Sentinel Rock, an excellent spot for sunsets.

Kruse Rhododendron State Reserve. Just up the highway, narrow, unpaved Kruse Ranch Road leads to the Kruse Rhododendron State Reserve, where each May thousands of rhododendrons bloom within a quiet forest of redwoods and tan oaks. ✉ *20705 Hwy. 1* ☎ *707/847–3221* 🎟 *$8 per vehicle* 🕓 *Daily sunrise–sunset.*

THE MENDOCINO COAST

GUALALA

16 mi north of Salt Point State Park on Hwy. 1.

This former lumber port on the Gualala River has become a headquarters for exploring the coast. The busiest town between Bodega Bay and Mendocino, it has all the basic services plus a number of galleries and gift shops.

GETTING HERE AND AROUND

From San Francisco exit Highway 101 at Cloverdale and follow Highway 128 northwest 28 mi to Boonville. From Ukiah, take Highway 253 west about 17 mi to Boonville/Highway 128. From Boonville, turn west on Mountain View Road and travel 24 mi to Highway 1, then head south 18½ mi to Gualala. South Mendocino Coast Bus routes 75 and 95 (⊕ *www.4mta.org*) connect Gualala with coastal and inland towns.

EXPLORING

Gualala Point Regional Park. This park has a long, sandy beach, picnic areas ($6 day-use fee), and is an excellent whale-watching spot December through April. Along the river, shaded by redwoods, are two dozen campsites. ✉ *1 mi south of Gualala on Hwy. 1* ☎ *707/785–2377* ⊙ *Daily 8 am–sunset.*

WHERE TO EAT AND STAY

$$$$ AMERICAN ✕ **St. Orres.** Resembling a traditional Russian dacha with two onion-dome towers, this intriguing lodge stands on 42 acres of redwood forest and meadow. In one of the towers is a spectacular atrium dining room. Here, locally farmed and foraged ingredients appear as garlic flan with black chanterelles, venison medallions with yam waffles and wild huckleberries. The prix-fixe menu ($45) includes soup and salad but no appetizer or dessert (available à la carte). ✉ *36601 Hwy. 1, 3 mi north of Gualala* ☎ *707/884–3303* ⊕ *www.saintorres.com* ✍ *Reservations essential* ⊙ *Dec.–May, closed Tues. and Wed. No lunch weekdays.*

$$ **Mar Vista Cottages.** The thoughtfully appointed, sparkling clean 1930s cottages at Mar Vista are intentionally slim on modern gadgetry (no TV, phone, radio, or even a clock) and big on retro charm. **Pros:** charming, peaceful retreat. **Cons:** no other businesses in walking distance. ✉ *35101 S. Hwy 1, 5 mi north of Gualala* ☎ *707/884–3522, 877/855–3522* ⊕ *www.marvistamendocino.com* *8 1-bedroom cottages, 4 2-bedroom cottages* *In-room: no a/c, kitchen, no TV, Wi-Fi. In-hotel: some pets allowed.*

$$ **Seacliff on the Bluff.** Wedged behind a downtown shopping center, it's not much to look at—the interiors are motel standard—but you'll spend your time here staring at the Pacific panorama. Surprising extras ice the cake: take the binoculars out to your balcony or patio; stay in and watch the sunset from your jetted tub; snuggle into a robe and pop that complimentary sparkling cider in front of your gas fireplace. Upstairs rooms have cathedral ceilings; Wi-Fi is available throughout. **Pros:** budget choice; great views. **Cons:** less-than-scenic setting. ✉ *39140 Hwy. 1* ☎ *707/884–1213, 800/400–5053* ⊕ *www.seacliffmotel.com* *16 rooms* *In-room: no a/c, Wi-Fi.*

POINT ARENA

★ *14 mi north of Gualala on Hwy. 1.* Occupied by an eclectic mix of long-time locals and long-haired surfers, this former timber town is part New Age, part rowdy—and always laid back. The one road going west out of downtown will lead you to the harbor, where fishing boats unload urchins and salmon and there's almost always someone riding the waves.

SCENIC STOP

Sonoma Coast State Beach. The gorgeous sandy coves of Sonoma Coast State Beach stretch along the shoreline from Bodega Head to a point several miles north of Jenner. Rock Point, Duncan's Landing, and Wright's Beach, clustered at about the halfway mark, have picnic areas. Wright's Beach and Bodega Dunes have developed campsites. ☎ *707/875-3483* *$8 per vehicle.*

GETTING HERE AND AROUND

From the south, exit Highway 101 at Cloverdale and follow Highway 128 northwest 28 mi to Boonville. From Ukiah, take Highway 253 west about 17 mi to Boonville/Highway 128. From Boonville, Mountain View Road dead-ends after 25 mi at Highway 1; travel south 4 mi to reach Point Arena. South Mendocino Coast Bus Routes 75 and 95 (*www.4mta.org*) stop in Point Arena and travels to most towns in the region.

EXPLORING

Point Arena Lighthouse. For an outstanding view of the ocean and, in winter, migrating whales, take the marked road off Highway 1 north of town to the 115-foot Point Arena Lighthouse. The lighthouse is open for tours daily from 10 until 3:30; admission is $7.50. It's possible to stay out here, in one of four rental units ($$), all of which have full kitchens. (On weekends there's a two-night minimum.) ✉ *6300 S. Hwy. 1* ☎ *707/882–2777* *www.pointarenalighthouse.com.*

Manchester State Park. As you head north on Highway 1 from Point Arena toward Elk, you'll pass several beaches. Most notable is the one at Manchester State Park, 3 miles north of Point Arena, which has 5 miles of sandy, usually empty shoreline and lots of trails through the dunes.

WHERE TO EAT AND STAY

¢ CAFÉ **Arena Market.** The simple café at this all-organic grocery store offers hot soups, good sandwiches, and an ample salad bar. Picnickers can stock up on cheese, bread, and other good stuff in the market, which specializes in food from local farms. ✉ *185 Main St.* ✉ *185 Main St.* ☎ *707/882–3663.*

¢ CAFÉ **Franny's Cup and Saucer.** Aided by her mother, Barbara, a former pastry chef at Chez Panisse, Franny turns out baked goods that are sophisticated and inventive. Take the coffee crunch cake: vanilla chiffon cake layered with coffee whipped cream, topped with chocolate ganache and puffs of coffee caramel "seafoam." More familiar options include berry tarts and strawberry-apricot crisp. While normally closed on Sunday, once a month during spring and summer they open for a decadent brunch. ✉ *213 Main St.* ☎ *707/882–2500* 🌐 *www.frannyscupandsaucer.com* ▭ *No credit cards* ⏲ *Closed Sun.–Tues. No dinner.*

$$$$ ★ **Inn at Victorian Gardens.** Set amid 100 acres of meadows and trees, this exquisite Victorian house dates to 1904, but owner-architect Pauline Zamboni has updated and expanded it seamlessly over the past 17 years—skylights open up bathrooms with original hardwood floors, and peaked alcoves frame windows that look out onto lush gardens. **Pros:** total relaxation; total quiet; total elegance. **Cons:** 6 miles from the nearest town. ✉ *14409 S. Hwy. 1* ☎ *707/882–3606* 🌐 *www.innatvictoriangardens.com* *4 rooms* *In-room: no a/c, no TV. In-hotel: some age restrictions* *Breakfast.*

ELK

33 mi north of Gualala on Hwy. 1.

This quiet town is arranged on the cliff above Greenwood Cove, and just about every spot has a view of the rocky coastline and stunning Pacific sunsets. Beyond walking the beach there's little here for visitors, aside from a handful of restaurants and inns—and that's exactly why people come. Families don't tend to stay here, perhaps because it's such a romantic place.

GETTING HERE AND AROUND

From Ukiah, take Highway 253 west about 17 mi to Boonville/Highway 128, then follow Highway 128 northwest 29 mi until it ends at Highway 1; you'll find Elk about 6 mi south. From San Francisco, travel north on Highway 101 and exit at Cloverdale/Highway 128 West. Follow the road northwest about 56 mi to Highway 1, then head south 6 mi to Elk. South Mendocino Coast Bus Route 75 (🌐 *www.4mta.org*) stops in town.

WHERE TO EAT AND STAY

¢ AMERICAN ✕ **Queenie's Roadhouse Cafe.** The chrome and patent-leather diner-style chairs here are usually occupied by locals, as it's a good bet for big breakfasts (served all day) and casual lunches (the cheeseburgers are highly recommended). On sunny days, grab one of the two picnic tables out front. ✉ *6061 S. Hwy. 1* ☎ *707/877–3285* ⏲ *No dinner; closed Jan.; closed Tues. and Wed.*

$$ **Elk Cove Inn & Spa.** Perched on a bluff above pounding surf and a driftwood-strewn beach, this property has stunning views from most rooms. **Pros:** steps to the beach; gorgeous views; great breakfast. **Cons:** rooms in main house are smallish and within earshot of common TV. ✉ *6300 S. Hwy. 1* ☎ *707/877–3321, 800/275–2967* 🌐 *www.elkcoveinn.com* *7 rooms, 4 suites, 4 cottages* *In-room: no a/c, no TV, Wi-Fi. In-hotel: spa, beach* *Breakfast.*

$$$$ **Harbor House.** Constructed in 1916, this redwood Craftsman-style house is as elegant as its location is rugged. **Pros:** luxurious; romantic. **Cons:** not a place for kids. ✉ *5600 S. Hwy. 1* ☎ *707/877–3203, 800/720–7474* 🌐 *www.theharborhouseinn.com* *6 rooms, 4 cottages* *In-room: no a/c, no TV, Wi-Fi. In-hotel: restaurant, some pets allowed* *Some meals.*

ANDERSON VALLEY

6 mi north of Elk on Hwy. 101, then 22 mi southeast on Hwy. 128.

At the town of Albion, Highway 128 leads southeast into the Anderson Valley, whose hot summer weather might lure those weary of persistent coastal fog. Most of the first 13 mi wind through redwood forest along the Navarro River, then the road opens up to reveal farms and vineyards. While the community here is anchored in ranching, in the past few decades a progressive, gourmet-minded counterculture has taken root and that is what defines most visitors' experience. In the towns of Philo and Boonville you'll find B&Bs with classic Victorian style as well as small eateries.

Anderson Valley is best known to outsiders for its wineries. Tasting rooms here are more low-key than in Napa; most are in farmhouses and are more likely to play reggae than classical music. That said, Anderson Valley wineries produce world-class wines, particularly Pinot Noirs and Gewürztraminers, whose grapes thrive in the cool, coastal climate. All the wineries are along Highway 128, mostly in Philo with a few east of Boonville. The following are our favorites and are listed here from west to east.

GETTING HERE AND AROUND

Highway 128 West travels through the Anderson Valley; access it from Highway 101 from Cloverdale, or from Ukiah take Highway 253 west about 17 mi. The South Mendocino Coast Bus Route 75 offers limited service in the Anderson Valley between the coast and Ukiah.

7

EXPLORING

Husch Vineyards. The valley's oldest winery has a cozy tasting room next to sheep pastures and picnic tables under a grapevine-covered arbor. ✉ *4400 Hwy. 128* ☎ *800/554–8724* 🌐 *www.huschvineyards.com* ⏲ *Tasting room daily 10–5.*

Roederer Estate. To experience the more polished side of Anderson Valley wine production, stop in at Roederer to sample one of their delicious sparkling wines and take in the beautiful view from the patio. ✉ *4501 Hwy. 128* ☎ *707/895–2288* 🌐 *www.roedererestate.com* ⏲ *Tasting room daily 11–5.*

Greenwood Ridge Vineyards. White Riesling is the specialty here. Awards line the walls of the tasting room (built from a single redwood), and you can picnic at tables on an island in the middle of a pond. ✉ *5501 Hwy. 128* ☎ *707/895–2002* 🌐 *www.greenwoodridge.com* ⏲ *Tasting room daily 10–5.*

★ **Navarro Vineyards.** A visit to family-run Navarro is a classic Anderson Valley experience. Make time if you can for a vineyard tour (conducted daily by appointment at 10:30 and 3); guides draw from years of hands-on experience to explain every aspect of production, from organic farming techniques to the choices made in aging and blending. They're best known for their Alsatian varietals, but Navarro offers a wide range of other wines as well, with up to15 at a time open for tasting. The tasting room sells cheese and charcuterie for picnickers. ✉ *5601 Hwy. 128* ☎ *707/895–3686* 🌐 *www.navarrowine.com* ⏲ *Apr.–Oct. daily 9–6; Nov.–Mar. daily 9–5.*

Navarro River Redwoods State Park. This park just off Highway 128 is great for walks in the second-growth redwood forest and for swimming in the gentle Navarro River. There's also fishing and kayaking in the late winter and spring, when the river is higher. The two campgrounds (one on the river "beach") are quiet and clean. ✉ *Hwy. 128, Navarro* ☎ *707/937–5804*.

WHERE TO EAT AND STAY

¢ CAFÉ ✕ **The Boonville General Store.** The café menu here is nothing surprising, but the exacting attention paid to ingredients elevates each dish above the ordinary. Sandwiches are served on fresh-baked bread, the beet salad comes with roasted pecans and local blue cheese. Even the macaroni and cheese—freshly made—is noteworthy. For breakfast there are granola and pastries, made in-house. ✉ *14077A Hwy. 128, Boonville* ☎ *707/895–9477* ⊙ *No dinner.*

$$$$ ✕ **Table 128.** The restaurant at the Boonville Hotel takes small-town dining into the 21st century. Proprietor Johnny Schmitt and his kitchen prepare one prix fixe meal per night ($40 for three courses, $50 for four) and serve it up family-style, with platters of food brought to the table to be shared. Expect an expertly grilled or roasted meat (such as pork chops or flank steak), a sophisticated side (raddichio with polenta; heirloom bean ragout with salsa verde), and a soulful dessert (rhubarb galette; panna cotta with fresh berries). The lack of choices may feel limiting (menus are posted on the Web a few days in advance), but this is essentially home cooking done at a high level, and it's likely to satisfy most diners. ✉ *14050 Hwy. 128, Boonville* ☎ *707/895–2210* 🌐 *www.boonvillehotel.com* ⊙ *No lunch; closed Tues. and Wed.*

$$$ **Boonville Hotel.** From the street this looks like a fairly standard small-town hotel, but once you cross the threshold you start picking up on the laid-back sophistication that captures a lot of what's most appealing about Anderson Valley. **Pros:** stylish but homey; building is the town's main hub. **Cons:** service isn't overly attentive—don't expect to be pampered; two-night stay required most weekends. ✉ *14050 Hwy. 128, Boonville* ☎ *707/895–2210* 🌐 *www.boonvillehotel.com* *8 rooms, 4 suites* *In-room: no a/c, no TV, Wi-Fi. In-hotel: restaurant, bar, some pets allowed* *Breakfast.*

$$$ **The Philo Apple Farm.** Set in an orchard of organic, heirloom apples, the three cottages and one guest room here are tasteful, spare, and inspired by the surrounding landscape. **Pros:** pretty; quiet; country feel. **Cons:** hard to get a reservation on weekends; occasionally hot in summer. ✉ *18501 Greenwood Rd., Philo* ☎ *707/895–2333* 🌐 *www.philoapplefarm.com* *1 room, 3 cottages* *In-room: no a/c, no TV* *Breakfast.*

LITTLE RIVER

14 mi north of Elk on Hwy. 1.

The town of Little River is not much more than a post office and a convenience store; Albion, its neighbor to the south, is even smaller. Along the winding road, though, you'll find numerous inns and restaurants, all of them quiet and situated to take advantage of the breathtaking ocean.

You'll find excellent vintages and great places to taste wine in the Anderson Valley—but it's much more laid back than Napa.

GETTING HERE AND AROUND

To reach Little River from San Francisco, exit Highway 101 at Cloverdale and follow Highway 128 northwest about 56 mi until it merges with Highway 1, then head north 7 mi. From the north, exit Highway 101 in Ukiah at Highway 253 West and follow it 17 mi to Boonville/Highway 128. Then travel along Highway 128 northwest 29 mi and Highway 1 north 7 mi to town. South Mendocino Coast Bus Route 75 (🌐 *www.4mta.org*) provides public transit.

EXPLORING

Van Damme State Park. Van Damme State Park is best known for its beach and for being a prime abalone diving spot. Upland trails lead through lush riparian habitat and the bizarre **Pygmy Forest,** where acidic soil and poor drainage have produced mature cypress and pine trees that are no taller than a person. The visitor center has displays on ocean life and Native American history. ✉ *Hwy. 1* ☎ *707/937–5804 visitor center* 🌐 *www.parks.ca.gov.*

WHERE TO EAT AND STAY

$$$ FRENCH ★ ✕ **Ledford House.** The only thing separating this bluff-top wood-and-glass restaurant from the Pacific Ocean is a great view. Entrées evoke the flavors of southern France and include hearty bistro dishes—stews, cassoulets, and pastas—and large portions of grilled meats and freshly caught fish (though it also is vegetarian friendly). The long bar, with its unobstructed water view, is a scenic spot for a sunset aperitif. ✉ *3000 N. Hwy. 1* ☎ *707/937–0282* 🌐 *www.ledfordhouse.com* ⏲ *Closed Mon. and Tues. No lunch.*

$$$ **Albion River Inn.** Contemporary New England–style cottages at this inn overlook the dramatic bridge and seascape where the Albion River empties into the Pacific. **Pros:** great views; great bathtubs. **Cons:** newer buildings aren't as quaint as they could be. ⊠ *3790 N. Hwy. 1* ☎ *707/937–1919, 800/479–7944* 🌐 *www.albionriverinn.com* *18 rooms, 4 cottages* *In-room: no a/c, no TV, Wi-Fi. In-hotel: restaurant, bar* *Breakfast.*

$$$ ★ **Glendeven Inn.** If Mendocino is the New England village of the West Coast, then Glendeven is the local country manor. **Pros:** picture-book pretty; elegant; romantic. **Cons:** not within walking distance of town; on the main drag. ⊠ *8205 N. Hwy. 1* *P.O. Box 914* ☎ *707/937–0083, 800/822–4536* 🌐 *www.glendeven.com* *6 rooms, 4 suites* *In-room: no a/c, no TV, Wi-Fi. In-hotel: some age restrictions* *Breakfast.*

MENDOCINO

3 mi north of Little River on Hwy. 1; 153 mi from San Francisco, north on U.S. 101, west on Hwy. 128, and north on Hwy. 1.

Many of Mendocino's original settlers came from the Northeast and built houses in the New England style. Thanks to the logging boom, the town flourished for most of the second half of the 19th century. As the timber industry declined, many residents left, but the town's setting was too beautiful to be ignored. Artists and craftspeople began flocking here in the 1950s, and Elia Kazan chose Mendocino as the backdrop for his 1955 film adaptation of John Steinbeck's *East of Eden,* starring James Dean. As the arts community thrived, restaurants, cafés, and inns sprung up. Today, the small downtown area consists almost entirely of places to eat and shop.

GETTING HERE AND AROUND

From San Francisco, exit Highway 101 at Cloverdale and follow Highway 128 northwest about 56 mi and Highway 1 north 10 mi. You can also exit at Willits and head west on Highway 20 about 33 mi to Highway 1, then head south 8 mi to Mendocino. From Ukiah, use Highway 253 West 17 mi to Boonville, Highway 128 northwest 29 mi and Highway 1 north 7 mi. South Mendocino Coast Bus Route 75 (🌐 *www.4mta.org*) provides public transit.

EXPLORING

Ford House. The restored Ford House, built in 1854, serves as the visitor center for Mendocino Headlands State Park. The house has a scale model of Mendocino as it looked in 1890, when the town had 34 water towers and a 12-seat public outhouse. From the museum, you can head out on a 3-mi trail across the spectacular seaside cliffs that border the town. ⊠ *Main St., west of Lansing St.* ☎ *707/937–5397* *$2 suggested donation* ⏲ *Daily 11–4.*

Kelley House Museum. An 1861 structure holds this museum, whose artifacts include Victorian-era furniture and historical photographs of Mendocino's logging days. ⊠ *45007 Albion St.* ☎ *707/937–5791* 🌐 *www.kelleyhousemuseum.org* *$2* ⏲ *June–Sept., Thurs.–Tues. 11–3; Oct.–May, Fri.–Mon. 11–3.*

Mendocino Art Center. The art center has an extensive program of workshops, mounts rotating exhibits in its galleries, and is the home of the Mendocino Theatre Company. ✉ *45200 Little Lake St.* ☎ *707/937–5818, 800/653–3328* 🌐 *www.mendocinoartcenter.org.*

WHERE TO EAT AND STAY

$$$ AMERICAN ✕ **Cafe Beaujolais.** The Victorian cottage that houses this popular restaurant is surrounded by a garden of heirloom and exotic plantings. A commitment to the freshest possible organic, local, and hormone-free ingredients guides the chef here. The menu is eclectic and ever-evolving, but often includes free-range fowl, line-caught fish, and edible flowers. The bakery turns out several delicious varieties of bread from a wood-fired oven. ✉ *961 Ukiah St.* ☎ *707/937–5614* 🌐 *www.cafebeaujolais.com* ⊗ *No lunch Mon. and Tues.*

$$$$ ★ **Brewery Gulch Inn.** This tasteful inn gives a modern twist to the elegance of Mendocino. **Pros:** stylish; peaceful; intimate. **Cons:** must drive to town. ✉ *9401 Hwy. 1, 1 mi south of Mendocino* ☎ *707/937–4752, 800/578–4454* 🌐 *www.brewerygulchinn.com* *10 rooms* *In-room: no a/c, Wi-Fi. In-hotel: business center* *Breakfast.*

$$$ Fodor's Choice ★ **MacCallum House.** Set on two flower-filled acres in the middle of town, this inn is a perfect mix of Victorian charm and modern luxury. **Pros:** best B&B around; excellent breakfast; great in-town location. **Cons:** new luxury suites on a separate property are less charming. ✉ *45020 Albion St.* ☎ *707/937–0289, 800/609–0492* 🌐 *www.maccallumhouse.com* *11 rooms, 13 suites, 7 cottages* *In-room: no a/c, Internet, Wi-Fi. In-hotel: restaurant, bar, business center, some pets allowed* *Breakfast.*

7

NIGHTLIFE AND THE ARTS

Mendocino Theatre Company. The repertoire of this well-established company ranges all over the contemporary map, including works by David Mamet, Neil Simon, and local playwrights. Performances take place Thursday through Saturday evenings, with some weekend matinees. ✉ *Mendocino Art Center, 42500 Little Lake St.* ☎ *707/937–4477* 🌐 *mendocinotheatre.org.*

SPORTS AND THE OUTDOORS

Catch-A-Canoe and Bicycles Too. Rent kayaks and regular and outrigger canoes here, as well as mountain and suspension bicycles. ✉ *Stanford Inn by the Sea, Comptche-Ukiah Rd., off Hwy. 1* ☎ *707/937–0273.*

FORT BRAGG

10 mi north of Mendocino on Hwy. 1.

The commercial center of Mendocino County, Fort Bragg is a working-class town that many feel is the most authentic place around; it's certainly less expensive than its neighbors to the south. The declining timber industry has been steadily replaced by booming tourism, but the city maintains a local feel since most people who work at the area hotels and restaurants also live here, as do many local artists. A stroll down Franklin Street (one block east of Highway 1) takes you past numerous bookstores, antiques shops, and boutiques.

GETTING HERE AND AROUND

From Highway 101 at Willits follow Highway 20 west about 33 mi to Highway 1 and go north 2 mi. Route 75 MTA buses service the town and region.

EXPLORING

★ **Mendocino Coast Botanical Gardens.** The gardens have something for nature lovers in every season. Even in winter, heather and camellias bloom. Along 2 miles of trails with ocean views and observation points for whale-watching is a splendid profusion of flowers. The rhododendrons are at their peak from April through June, and the dahlias are spectacular in August. ✉ *18220 N. Hwy. 1, 1 mi south of Fort Bragg* ☎ *707/964–4352* 🌐 *www.gardenbythesea.org* 🎟 *$10* 🕑 *Mar.–Oct., daily 9–5; Nov.–Feb., daily 9–4.*

The Skunk Train. Back in the 1920s, a fume-spewing gas-powered train car shuttled passengers along a rail line dating from the logging days of the 1880s. Nicknamed the Skunk Train, it traversed redwood forests inaccessible to automobiles. The reproduction that you can ride today travels the same route, making a 3½-4 hour round-trip between Fort Bragg and the town of Northspur, 21 miles inland. The schedule varies depending on the season and in summer includes evening barbecue excursions and wine parties. ✉ *Foot of Laurel St., west of Main St.* ☎ *707/964–6371, 866/457–5865* 🌐 *www.skunktrain.com* 🎟 *$49–$70.*

MacKerricher State Park. This park has 9 miles of sandy beach and several square miles of dunes. The headland is a good place for whale-watching from December to mid-April. Fishing (at a freshwater lake stocked with trout), canoeing, hiking, jogging, bicycling, beachcombing, camping, and harbor seal watching at Laguna Point are among the popular activities, many of which are accessible to the mobility-impaired. Rangers lead nature hikes in summer. ✉ *Hwy. 1, 3 mi north of Fort Bragg* ☎ *707/964–9112* 🎟 *$8 per vehicle.*

Glass Beach. The ocean is not visible from most of Fort Bragg, but go three blocks west of Main Street and a flat, dirt path leads to wild coastline where you can walk for miles in either direction along the bluffs. The sandy coves in the area you first reach from the road are called Glass Beach because this used to be the dumping ground for the city. That history is still apparent—in a good way. Look closely at the sand and you'll find the top layer is comprised almost entirely of sea glass, likely more than you've ever seen in one place before. ✉ *Elm St. and Glass Beach Dr.*

Museum in the Triangle Tattoo Parlor. This museum is an unexpected nod to Fort Bragg's rough-and-tumble past. The two-room display shows a wonderful collection of tattoo memorabilia, including pictures of astonishing tattoos from around the world, early 20th-century Burmese tattooing instruments, and a small shrine to sword-swallowing sideshow king Captain Don Leslie. ✉ *356-B N. Main St.* ☎ *707/964–8814* 🎟 *Free* 🕑 *Daily noon–6.*

The North Coast is famous for its locally caught Dungeness crab; be sure to try some during your visit.

WHERE TO EAT AND STAY

$ ITALIAN **Piaci.** The seats are stools and your elbows might bang a neighbor's, but nobody seems to mind at this cozy little spot—this is hands down the most popular casual restaurant around. The food is simple, mostly pizza and calzones, but everything is given careful attention and comes out tasty. Alongside the selective list of wines is a distinctive beer list that has been given equal respect; noted are the origin, brewmaster, and alcohol content for each brew. Dogs and their owners are welcome at the tables outside. ✉ *120 W. Redwood Ave.* ☎ *707/961–1133* 🌐 *www.piacipizza.com* ⏲ *No lunch weekends.*

$$ **Weller House Inn.** It's hard to believe that when Ted and Eva Kidwell found this house in 1994, it was abandoned and slated for demolition; they've hammered and quilted it into the loveliest Victorian in Fort Bragg. **Pros:** handcrafted details; homey; friendly innkeepers. **Cons:** some may find it too old-fashioned. ✉ *524 Stewart St.* ☎ *707/964–4415, 877/893–5537* 🌐 *www.wellerhouse.com* *9 rooms* *In-room: no a/c, Wi-Fi* *Breakfast.*

SPORTS AND THE OUTDOORS

All Aboard Adventures. From December through mid-April they operate whale-watching trips, as well as fishing excursions all year. ✉ *32410 N. Harbor Dr.* ☎ *707/964–1881* 🌐 *www.allaboardadventures.com.*

Ricochet Ridge Ranch. Come here for private and group trail rides through redwood forest and on the beach. ✉ *24201 N. Hwy. 1* ☎ *707/964–7669, 888/873–5777* 🌐 *www.horse-vacation.com.*

REDWOOD COUNTRY

HUMBOLDT REDWOODS STATE PARK

20 mi north of Garberville on U.S. 101.

GETTING HERE AND AROUND

Access the park right off U.S. 101, about 43 mi south of Eureka and 20 mi north of Garberville. Contact Humboldt Transit Authority (*www.hta.org*) for public transportation details.

Avenue of the Giants. The Avenue of the Giants (Highway 254) traverses Humbolt Redwoods State Park south–north, branching off U.S. 101 about 7 mi north of Garberville and more or less paralleling that road for 33 mi north to Pepperwood. Some of the tallest trees on the planet tower over the stretch of two-lane blacktop that follows the south fork of the Eel River.

Humboldt Redwoods State Park Visitor Center. At the visitor center you can pick up information about the redwoods, waterways, and recreational activities in the 53,000-acre park. One brochure describes a self-guided auto tour of the park, with short and long hikes into redwood groves. *Ave. of the Giants, 2 mi south of Weott 707/946–2263 visitor center www.humboldtredwoods.org Free; $8 day-use fee for parking and facilities in Williams Grove Park daily; visitor center Apr–Oct., daily 9–5; Nov.–Mar., daily 10–4.*

Founders Grove. One of the most impressive trees here—the 362-foot-long Dyerville Giant—fell to the ground in 1991; its root base points skyward 35 feet. You reach the grove via a ½-mile trail off Avenue of the Giants. *Hwy. 254, 4 mi north of Humboldt Redwoods State Park Visitor Center.*

Rockefeller Forest. The largest remaining coastal redwood forest contains 40 of the 100 tallest trees in the world. *Mattole Rd., 6 mi north of Humboldt Redwoods State Park Visitor Center.*

FERNDALE

35 mi northwest of Weott; 57 mi northwest of Garberville via U.S. 101 north to Hwy. 211 west.

Though gift shops and ice-cream stores comprise a fair share of the businesses here, Ferndale remains a fully functioning small town. There's a butcher, a small grocery, and a local saloon (the westernmost in the contiguous United States), and descendants of the Portuguese and Scandinavian dairy farmers who settled this town continue to raise dairy cows in the surrounding pastures. Ferndale is best known for its colorful Victorian architecture, the queen of which is the Gingerbread Mansion, built in 1899. Many shops carry a self-guided tour map that highlights the town's most interesting historical buildings.

GETTING HERE AND AROUND

Ferndale is about 15 mi south of Eureka and 35 mi northwest of Weott. Exit U.S. 101 at Highway 211 and follow it southwest 5 mi.

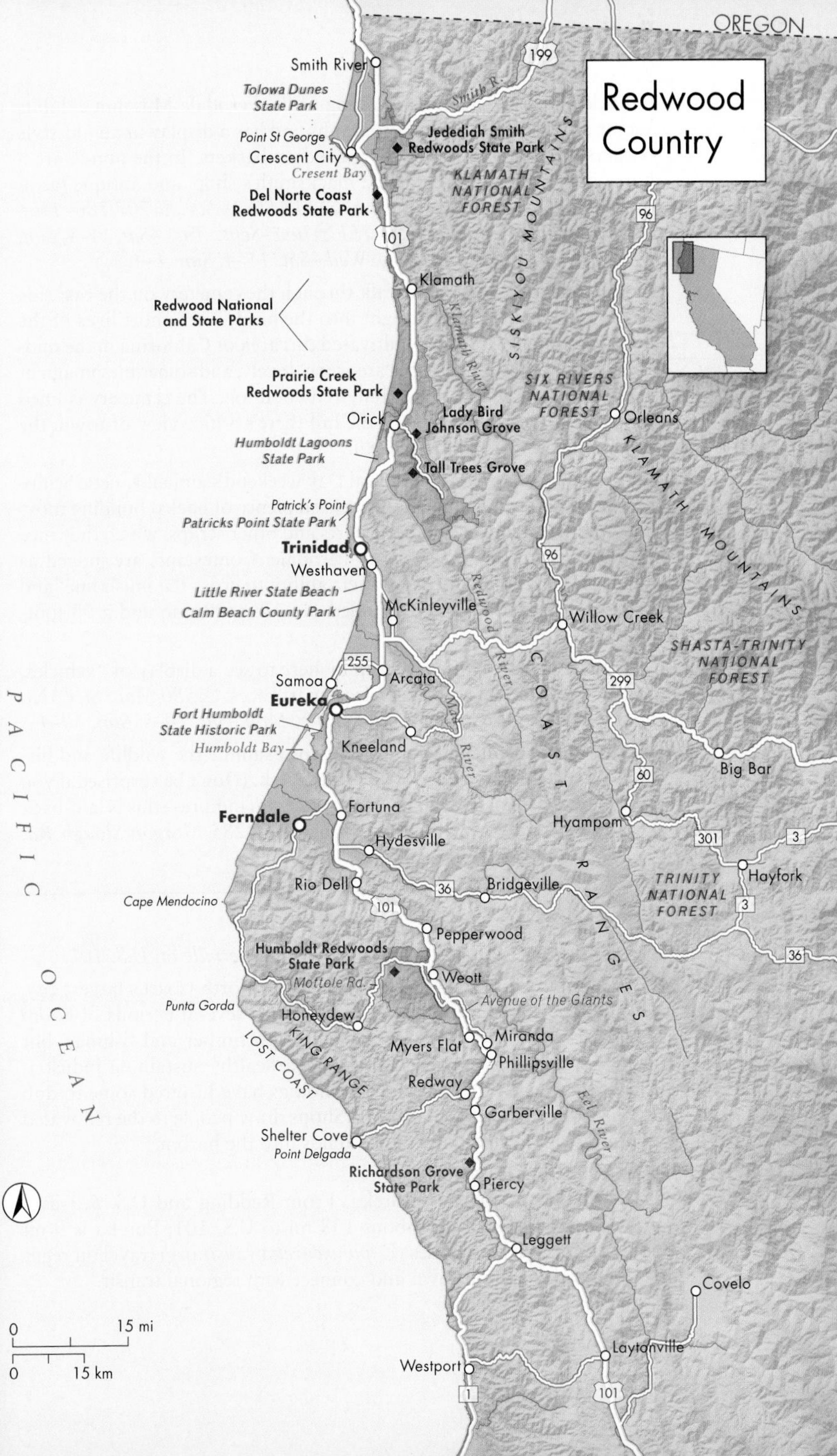

Redwood Country
OREGON
Smith River
Tolowa Dunes State Park
Smith R.
Jedediah Smith Redwoods State Park
Point St George
Crescent City
Cresent Bay
KLAMATH NATIONAL FOREST
Del Norte Coast Redwoods State Park
SISKIYOU MOUNTAINS
Klamath
Redwood National and State Parks
Klamath River
Prairie Creek Redwoods State Park
SIX RIVERS NATIONAL FOREST
Orick
Lady Bird Johnson Grove
Orleans
Humboldt Lagoons State Park
Tall Trees Grove
KLAMATH MOUNTAINS
Patrick's Point
Patricks Point State Park
Trinidad
Westhaven
Little River State Beach
Calm Beach County Park
McKinleyville
Redwood River
Willow Creek
SHASTA-TRINITY NATIONAL FOREST
Samoa
Arcata
Eureka
Fort Humboldt State Historic Park
Humboldt Bay
Kneeland
Mad River
COAST RANGES
Big Bar
PACIFIC OCEAN
Fortuna
Ferndale
Hyampom
Hydesville
Hayfork
Rio Dell
Bridgeville
TRINITY NATIONAL FOREST
Cape Mendocino
Pepperwood
Humboldt Redwoods State Park
Weott
Mattole Rd.
Avenue of the Giants
Punta Gorda
Honeydew
Miranda
Myers Flat
Phillipsville
LOST COAST
KING RANGE
Redway
Garberville
Eel River
Shelter Cove
Point Delgada
Richardson Grove State Park
Piercy
Leggett
Covelo
0
15 mi
0
15 km
Laytonville
Westport
199
96
101
255
299
60
301
3
36
1

EXPLORING

Ferndale Museum. The main building of the Ferndale Museum exhibits Victoriana and historical photographs and has a display of an old-style barbershop and another of Wiyot Indian baskets. In the annex are a horse-drawn buggy, a re-created blacksmith's shop, and antique farming, fishing, and dairy equipment. ✉ *515 Shaw Ave.* ☎ *707/786–4466* 🌐 *www.ferndale-museum.org* 🎫 *$1* ⏲ *June–Sept., Tues.–Sat. 11–4, Sun. 1–4; Oct.–Dec. and Feb.–May, Wed.–Sat. 11–4, Sun. 1–4.*

Ferndale Historic Cemetery. A walk through the cemetery on the east side of town gives interesting insight into the hard, often short lives of the European immigrants who cultivated this area of California in the mid-18th century. The gravestones are worn, lovely, and sometimes imaginative, one in the shape of a nubbly redwood log. The cemetery is lined by forest, and from the top of the hill there's a nice view of town, the surrounding farms, and the ocean.

The Kinetic Sculpture Race. Memorial Day weekend's annual Kinetic Sculpture Race has artists and engineers (and plenty of hacks) building moving sculptures from used bicycle parts and other scraps, which they race from Arcata to the finish line in Ferndale. Contestants are judged as much on their creativity as on their ability to cross the finish line, and as a result sculptures have included the Albino Rhino and a 93-foot-long fish.

Ferndale Kinetic Museum. Stop by here to see a display of "vehicles, costumes, awards, and bribes" from past races. ✉ *580 Main St.* ☎ *No phone* 🎫 *Free (donation encouraged)* ⏲ *Mon.–Sat. 10–5, Sun. 10–4*

Eel River Delta Tours. Two-hour boat trips examine the wildlife and history of the Eel River's estuary and salt marsh. (Don't be surprised if you get an informal answering machine when you inquire—this is laid-back Humboldt, and you will get a call back.) ✉ *285 Morgan Slough Rd.* ☎ *707/786–4902.*

EUREKA

18 mi north of Ferndale; 66 mi north of Garberville on U.S. 101.

With a population of 26,381, Eureka is the North Coast's largest city. Over the past century, it has cycled through several periods of boom and bust—first with mining and later with timber and fishing—but these days, tourism is developing into a healthy sustaining industry. The town's nearly 100 Victorian buildings have inspired some to dub it "the Williamsburg of the West." Shops draw people to the renovated downtown, and a walking pier extends into the harbor.

GETTING HERE AND AROUND

U.S. 101 travels through Eureka. From Redding and U.S. 5, travel west along Highway 299 about 138 mi to U.S. 101; Eureka is 9 mi south. Eureka Transit buses (🌐 *www.eurekatransit.org*) travel on regular routes throughout town and connect with regional transit.

EXPLORING

Eureka Chamber of Commerce. You can pick up maps here with self-guided driving tours of Eureka's Victorian architecture, and also learn about organized tours. ✉ *2112 Broadway* ☎ *707/442–3738, 800/356–6381* 🌐 *www.eurekachamber.com* ⏲ *June–Aug., Mon.–Thurs. 8:30–5, Fri. 8:30–4, Sat. 10–3; Sept.–May, Mon.–Thurs. 8:30–5, Fri. 8:30–4.*

Clarke Memorial Museum. The Native American Wing of the Clarke Memorial Museum contains a beautiful collection of northwestern California basketry. Artifacts from Eureka's Victorian, logging, and maritime eras fill the rest of the museum. ✉ *240 E St.* ☎ *707/443–1947* 🌐 *www.clarkemuseum.org* 🎫 *Donations accepted* ⏲ *Wed.–Sat. 11–4.*

Fort Humboldt State Historic Park. The structure that gives this park its name was built in response to conflicts between white settlers and Native Americans. It no longer stands, but on its grounds are some reconstructed buildings, fort and logging museums, and old logging locomotives. Demonstrators steam up the machines on the third Saturday of the month, April through September. At this writing the museums are closed due to earthquake damage, but the park, which is a good place for a picnic, remains open. ✉ *3431 Fort Ave.* ☎ *707/445–6547* 🌐 *www.parks.ca.gov* 🎫 *Free* ⏲ *Daily 8–5.*

Blue Ox Millworks. Blue Ox is one of only a handful of woodshops in the country that specialize in Victorian-era architecture, but what makes it truly unique is that it uses antique tools to do the work. The most modern tool here is a 1948 band saw. Lucky for curious craftspeople and history buffs, the shop doubles as a dusty historical park. Visitors can watch craftsmen use printing presses, lathes, and even a mill that pares down whole redwood logs into the ornate fixtures for Victorians like those around town. The museum is less interesting on Saturday, when the craftspeople mostly take the day off. ✉ *1 X St.* ☎ *707/444–3437, 800/248–4259* 🌐 *www.blueoxmill.com* 🎫 *$7.50* ⏲ *Weekdays 9–5, Sat. 9–4.*

7

WHERE TO EAT AND STAY

$$$ AMERICAN Fodor's Choice ★

✕ **Restaurant 301.** Eureka's most elegant restaurant, housed in the lovely Carter House, uses ingredients hand selected from the farmers' market, local cheese makers and ranchers, and the on-site gardens. Dishes are prepared with a delicate hand and a sensuous imagination—the ever-changing menu has featured sturgeon with house-made mushroom pasta, braised fennel, and white wine sauce. The extensive wine cellar has over 3,800 bottles. ✉ *301 L St.* ☎ *707/444–8062, 800/404–1390* 🌐 *www.carterhouse.com* ⏲ *No lunch.*

$ AMERICAN

✕ **Samoa Cookhouse.** Originally a cafeteria that fed 500 local mill workers, the cookhouse became a public restaurant in the 1950s—though not much but the clientele has changed. Take a seat at one of the long, communal tables, and waiters will bring bottomless, family-style bowls of whatever is being served at that meal. For breakfast that means eggs, sausage, biscuits and gravy, and the like. Lunch and dinner usually feature soup, potatoes, salad, and pie, plus daily changing entrées such as pot roast and pork loin. A back room contains a museum of logging culture, but really the whole place is a tribute to the rough-and-tumble life and hard work that tamed this wild land. Dieters and vegetarians should look elsewhere for sustenance. ✉ *Cookhouse Rd.; from U.S. 101 cross Samoa Bridge, turn left onto Samoa Rd., then left 1 block later onto Cookhouse Rd.* ☎ *707/442–1659* 🌐 *www.samoacookhouse.net.*

$ **Abigail's Elegant Victorian Mansion.** Innkeepers Doug and Lily Vieyra have devoted themselves to honoring this National Historic Landmark (once home to the town's millionaire real-estate sultan) by decorating it with authentic, Victorian-era opulence. **Pros:** unique; lots of character; fun innkeepers. **Cons:** downtown is not within walking distance; bedrooms are a bit worn. ✉ *1406 C St.* ☎ *707/444–3144* 🌐 *www.eureka-california.com* *4 rooms, 2 with shared bath* *In-room: a/c, Wi-Fi. In-hotel: tennis court, laundry facilities.*

A COLD ONE

Lost Coast Brewery & Cafe. This bustling microbrewery is the best place in town to relax with a pint of ale or porter. Soups, salads, and light meals are served for lunch and dinner. ✉ *617 4th St.* ☎ *707/445–4480* 🌐 *www.lostcoast.com.*

$$$ Fodor's Choice ★ **Carter House.** According to owner Mark Carter, his staff has been trained always to say yes; whether it's breakfast in bed or an in-room massage, someone here will make sure you get what you want. **Pros:** elegant; every detail in place; excellent dining at Restaurant 301. **Cons:** while kids are allowed, it's better suited for grown-ups. ✉ *301 L St.* ☎ *707/444–8062, 800/404–1390* 🌐 *www.carterhouse.com* *22 rooms, 8 suites, 2 cottages* *In-room: no a/c, kitchen, Wi-Fi. In-hotel: restaurant, bar, beach, business center, some pets allowed* *Breakfast.*

SPORTS AND THE OUTDOORS

Hum-Boats. Kayak rental and lessons are available here, along with a variety of group kayak tours, including popular whale-watching trips ($75, December–June) that get you close enough to get good photos of migrating gray whales and resident humpback whales. ✉ *A Dock, Woodley Island Marina* ☎ *707/443–5157* 🌐 *www.humboats.com.*

SHOPPING

Eureka has several art galleries and numerous antiques stores in the district running from C to I streets between 2nd and 3rd streets.

First Street Gallery. Run by Humboldt State University, this is the best for spot contemporary art by local artists. ✉ *422 1st St.* ☎ *707/443–6363.*

Eureka Books. This bibliophile's haven has an exceptional collection of used books on all topics. ✉ *426 2nd St.* ☎ *707/444–9593.*

TRINIDAD

21 mi north of Eureka on U.S. 101.

Trinidad got its name from the Spanish mariners who entered the bay on Trinity Sunday, June 9, 1775. The town became a principal trading post for the mining camps along the Klamath and Trinity rivers. Mining and whaling have faded from the scene, and now Trinidad is a quiet and genuinely charming community with ample sights and activities to entertain low-key visitors.

GETTING HERE AND AROUND

Access Trinidad via U.S. 101. If you're driving on Highway 5 south from Oregon, exit at Grants Pass and take U.S. 199 southwest to Crescent City (about 78 mi), then U.S. 101 south to Trinidad (another 66 mi). Redwood Transit System (*www.redwoodtransit.org*) provides bus service to Trinidad, Eureka, and nearby towns.

EXPLORING

Patrick's Point State Park. On a forested plateau almost 200 feet above the surf, Patrick's Point State Park has stunning views of the Pacific, great whale- and sea lion–watching in season, picnic areas, bike paths, and hiking trails through old-growth spruce forest. There are also tidal pools at Agate Beach, a re-created Yurok Indian village, and a small museum with natural-history exhibits. Because the park is far from major tourist hubs, there are few visitors (most are local surfers), which leaves the land sublimely quiet. In spruce and alder forest above the ocean, the park's three campgrounds have all amenities except RV hookups. In summer it's best to reserve in advance.

7

Campgrounds. In spruce and alder forest above the ocean, the park's three campgrounds have all amenities except RV hookups. In summer it's best to reserve in advance. *800/444–7275* *$35* *5 mi north of Trinidad on U.S. 101* *707/677–3570* *$8 per vehicle.*

Clam Beach County Park and Little River State Beach. Together these make a park that stretches from Trinidad to as far as one can see south. The sandy beach here is exceptionally wide, perfect for kids who need to get out of the car and burn off some energy. It's also the rare sort of beach where vehicles are allowed, so those with four-wheel-drive can drive to a perfect fishing spot or tailgate on the sand. *6½ mi south of Trinidad, on Hwy. 1* *707/445–7651* *5 am–midnight.*

WHERE TO EAT AND STAY

¢ SEAFOOD **Katy's Smokehouse.** Purchase delectable picnic fixings at this tiny shop that has been doing things the same way since the 1940s, curing day-boat, line-caught fish with its original smokers. Salmon cured with brown sugar, albacore jerky, and smoked scallops are popular. Buy bread and drinks in town and walk to the waterside for alfresco snacking. Katy's closes at 6 pm. *740 Edwards St.* *707/677–0151* *www.katyssmokehouse.com.*

$$$$ AMERICAN **Larrupin' Cafe.** Locals consider this restaurant one of the best places to eat on the North Coast. Set in a two-story house on a quiet country road north of town, it's often thronged with people enjoying fresh seafood, Cornish game hen, or mesquite-grilled ribs. While the garden setting

and candlelight stir thoughts of romance, service is sometimes rather rushed. ✉ *1658 Patrick's Point Dr.* ☎ *707/677–0230* 🌐 *www.larrupin.com* ✍ *Reservations essential* ⊙ *No lunch; closed Wed. in winter.*

$$$ **Trinidad Bay Bed and Breakfast Inn.** Staying at this small Cape Cod–style inn perched above Trinidad Bay is like spending the weekend at a friend's vacation house. **Pros:** great location above bay; lots of light. **Cons:** if all rooms are full, the main house can feel a bit crowded. ✉ *560 Edwards St., Box 849* ☎ *707/677–0840* 🌐 *www.trinidadbaybnb.com* *4 rooms* *In-room: no a/c, no TV, Wi-Fi* *Breakfast.*

$$$$ **Turtle Rocks Oceanfront Inn.** This comfortable inn has the best view in Trinidad, and the builders have made the most of it. **Pros:** great ocean views; comfy king beds. **Cons:** no businesses within walking distance; not as deluxe as you might expect for the price. ✉ *3392 Patrick's Point Dr., 4½ mi north of town* ☎ *707/677–3707* 🌐 *www.turtlerocksinn.com* *5 rooms, 1 suite* *In-room: no a/c, Wi-Fi* *Breakfast.*

8

Redwood National Park

WORD OF MOUTH

"I thought that Stout Grove and the drive through was fantastic in Jedediah Smith area of the Redwoods. It is easy to get confused about the Redwoods as certain groves are within certain state parks within the national park itself."

—spirobulldog

WELCOME TO REDWOOD NATIONAL PARK

TOP REASONS TO GO

★ **Giant trees:** These mature coastal redwoods are the tallest trees in the world.

★ **Hiking to the sea:** The park's trails wind between majestic redwood groves, and many connect to the Coastal Trail running along the western edge of the park.

★ **Rare wildlife:** Mighty Roosevelt elk favor the park's flat prairie and open lands; seldom-seen black bears roam the backcountry; trout and salmon leap through streams, and Pacific gray whales swim along the coast during their biannual migrations.

★ **Stepping back in time:** Hike Fern Canyon Trail, which weaves through a prehistoric scene of lush vegetation and giant ferns.

★ **Cheeps, not beeps:** Amid the majestic redwoods you're out of range for cell-phone service—and in range for the soothing sounds of warblers and burbling creeks.

1 Del Norte Coast Redwoods State Park. The rugged terrain of this far northwest corner of California combines stretches of treacherous surf, steep cliffs, and forested ridges. On a clear day it's postcard-perfect; with fog, it's simply mesmerizing.

2 Jedediah Smith Redwoods State Park. Gargantuan old growth redwoods dominate the scenery here. The Smith River cuts through canyons and splits across boulders, carrying salmon to the inland creeks where they spawn.

3 Prairie Creek Redwoods State Park. The forests here give way to spacious, grassy plains where abundant wildlife thrives. Roosevelt elk are a common sight in the meadows and down to Gold Bluffs Beach.

4 Orick Area. The highlight of the southern portion of Redwood National Park is the Tall Trees Grove. It's difficult to reach and requires a special pass, but it's worth the hassle—this section has the tallest coastal redwood trees, with a new record holder discovered in 2006.

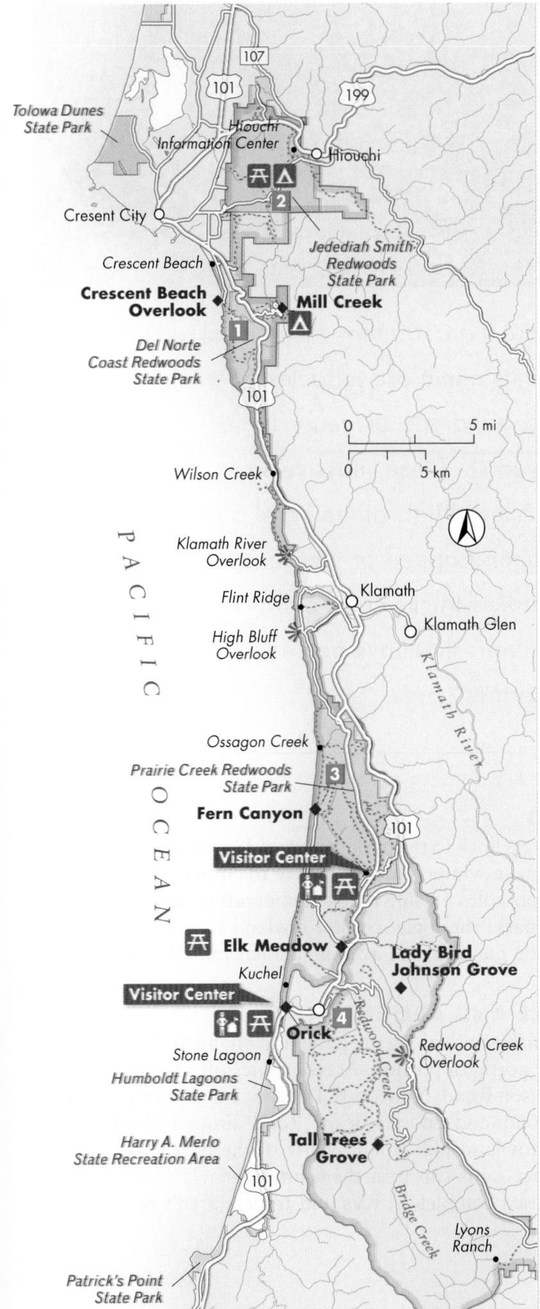

Tolowa Dunes State Park
Hiouchi Information Center
Hiouchi
Cresent City
Crescent Beach
Crescent Beach Overlook
Mill Creek
Jedediah Smith Redwoods State Park
Del Norte Coast Redwoods State Park
Wilson Creek
0 5 mi
0 5 km
Klamath River Overlook
Flint Ridge
Klamath
Klamath Glen
High Bluff Overlook
Klamath River
PACIFIC OCEAN
Ossagon Creek
Prairie Creek Redwoods State Park
Fern Canyon
Visitor Center
Elk Meadow
Lady Bird Johnson Grove
Kuchel
Visitor Center
Orick
Redwood Creek
Redwood Creek Overlook
Stone Lagoon
Humboldt Lagoons State Park
Tall Trees Grove
Harry A. Merlo State Recreation Area
Bridge Creek
Lyons Ranch
Patrick's Point State Park
101
107
199

GETTING ORIENTED

U.S. 101 weaves through the southern portion of the park, skirts around the center, and then slips back through redwoods in the north and on to Crescent City. Kuchel Visitor Center, Prairie Creek Redwoods State Park and Visitor Center, Tall Trees Grove, Fern Canyon, and Lady Bird Johnson Grove are all in the park's southern section. The graveled Coastal Drive curves along ocean vistas and dips down to the Klamath River in the park's central section.
To the north you'll find Mill Creek Trail, Enderts Beach, and Crescent Beach Overlook in Del Norte Coast Redwoods State Park as well as Jedediah Smith Redwoods State Park, Stout Grove, Little Bald Hills, and Simpson-Reed Grove.

Updated by Sura Wood and Christine Vovakes

Soaring to more than 300 feet, the coastal redwoods that give this park its name are miracles of efficiency—some have survived hundreds of years (a few live for more than 2,000 years). These massive trees glean nutrients from the rich alluvial flats at their feet and from the moisture and nitrogen trapped in their uneven canopy. Their huge, thick-barked trunks can hold thousands of gallons of water, reservoirs that have helped them withstand centuries of firestorms.

PLANNING

WHEN TO GO

Campers and hikers flock to the park from mid-June to early September. Crowds disappear in winter, but you'll have to contend with frequent rains and nasty potholes on side roads. Temperatures fluctuate widely throughout the park: the foggy coastal lowland is much cooler than the higher-altitude interior. The average annual rainfall here is 90 to 100 inches.

GETTING HERE AND AROUND

U.S. 101 runs north–south along the park, and Highway 199 cuts east–west through its northern portion. Access routes off 101 include Bald Hills Road, Davison Road, Newton B. Drury Scenic Parkway, Coastal Drive, Requa Road, and Enderts Beach Road. From 199 take South Fork Road to Howland Hill Road. Many of the park's roads aren't paved, and winter rains can turn them into obstacle courses; sometimes they're closed completely. RVs and trailers aren't permitted on some routes.

FLORA AND FAUNA

A healthy redwood forest is diverse and includes Douglas firs, western hemlocks, tan oaks, and madrone trees. In the park's backcountry, you might spot mountain lions, black bears, black-tailed deer, river otters, beavers, and minks. Roosevelt elk roam the flatlands, and the rivers and streams teem with salmon and trout. Gray whales, seals, and sea lions cavort near the coastline. And thanks to the area's location along the Pacific Flyway, an amazing 402 species of birds have been sighted here.

PARK ESSENTIALS

ADMISSION FEES AND PERMITS

Admission to Redwood National Park is free. There's an $8 day-use fee to enter one or all of Redwood's state parks; for camping at these state parks it's an additional $35. To visit Tall Trees Grove, you must get a free permit at the Kuchel Information Center in Orick. Permits also are needed to camp in Redwood Creek backcountry.

ADMISSION HOURS

The park is open year-round, 24 hours a day.

PARK CONTACT INFORMATION

Redwood National Park ✉ *1111 2nd St., Crescent City, CA* ☎ *707/465–7306* 🌐 *www.nps.gov/redw.*

SCENIC DRIVES

★ **Coastal Drive.** This 8-mi, partially paved road is closed to trailers and RVs and takes about one hour to drive one way. The slow pace alongside stands of redwoods offers close-up views of the Klamath River and expansive panoramas of the Pacific. From here you'll find access to the Flint Ridge section of the Coastal Trail.

8

EXPLORING

SCENIC STOPS

Crescent Beach Overlook. The scenery here includes ocean views and, in the distance, Crescent City and its working harbor; in balmy weather this is a great place for a picnic. From the overlook you can spot migrating gray whales November through December and March through April. ✉ *2 mi south of Crescent City off Enderts Beach Rd.*

★ **Fern Canyon.** Enter another world and be surrounded by 30-foot canyon walls covered with sword, maidenhair, and five-finger ferns. Allow an hour to explore the ¼-mi long vertical garden along a 0.7-mi loop. From the north end of Gold Bluffs Beach it's an easy walk, although you'll have to wade across a small stream several times (in addition to driving across streams on the way to the parking area). But the lush surroundings are otherworldly, and worth a visit when creeks aren't running too high. Be aware that RVs longer than 24 feet and all trailers are not allowed here. ✉ *10 mi northwest of Prairie Creek Visitor Center, via Davison Rd. off U.S. 101.*

CLOSE UP

Camping in Redwood National Park

ABOUT THE CAMPGROUNDS

Within a 30-minute drive of Redwood National and State parks there are nearly 60 public and private camping facilities. None of the four primitive areas in Redwood—DeMartin, Flint Ridge, Little Bald Hills, and Nickel Creek—is a drive-in site. Although you don't need a permit at these four hike-in sites, stop at a ranger station to inquire about availability. You will need to get a permit from a ranger station for camping along Redwood Creek in the backcountry. Bring your own water, since drinking water isn't available in any of these sites.

If you'd rather drive than hike in, Redwood has four developed campgrounds—Elk Prairie, Gold Bluffs Beach, Jedediah Smith, and Mill Creek—that are within the state park boundaries. None has RV hookups, and some length restrictions apply. Fees are $35 in state park campgrounds. For details and reservations, call ☎ *800/444-7275* or check 🌐 *www.reserveamerica.com*. Be sure to check the Web site for when park/campgrounds are open; some may adopt reduced schedules due to budget cuts.

⛺ **Gold Bluffs Beach Campground.** You can camp in tents or RVs right on the beach at this Prairie Creek Redwoods State Park campground near Fern Canyon. Keep your eyes open for Roosevelt elk. Note that RVs must be less than 24 feet long and 8 feet wide, and trailers aren't allowed on the access road. You pay the fee at the campground. ✉ *At end of Davison Rd., 5 mi north of Redwood Information Center off U.S. 101* ☎ *707/465-7354.*

⛺ **Jedediah Smith Campground.** This is one of the few places to camp—in tents or RVs—within groves of old-growth redwood forest. The length limit on RVs is 36 feet; for trailers it's 31 feet. ✉ *8 mi northeast of Crescent City on U.S. 199* ☎ *800/444-7275.*

⛺ **Mill Creek Campground.** Mill Creek is the largest of the state park campgrounds. ✉ *West of U.S. 101, 7 mi southeast of Crescent City* ☎ *800/444-7275.*

Lady Bird Johnson Grove. This section of the park was dedicated by, and named for, the former first lady. A 1-mi, wheelchair-accessible nature loop follows an old logging road through a mature redwood forest. Allow 45 minutes to complete the trail. ✉ *5 mi east of Kuchel Visitor Center, along U.S. 101 and Bald Hills Rd.*

★ **Tall Trees Grove.** From the Kuchel Visitor Center, you can get a free permit to make the drive up the steep 17-mi Tall Trees Access Road (the last 6 mi are gravel) to the grove's trailhead (trailers and RVs not allowed). Access to the popular grove is first-come, first-served, and a maximum of 50 permits are handed out each day. ✉ *Access road is 10 mi drive east of Kuchel Visitor Center, via U.S. 101 and Bald Hills Rd.*

VISITOR CENTERS

Crescent City Information Center. As the park's headquarters, this center is the main information stop if you're approaching the redwoods from the north. A gift shop and picnic area are here. ✉ *Off U.S. 101* *at 2nd and K Sts., Crescent City ☎ 707/465–7306 ⊕ www.nps.gov/redw ⏲ Mid-May–mid-Oct., daily 9–6; mid-Oct.–mid-May, daily 9–4.*

Hiouchi Information Center. Located in Jedediah Smith Redwoods State Park, 2 mi west of Hiouchi and 9 mi east of Crescent City off U.S. 199, this center has a bookstore, film, and exhibits about the flora and fauna in the park. It's also a starting point for seasonal ranger programs. ✉ *Hiouchi Information Center, Hwy. 199, Hiouchi* ☎ *707/458–3294* ⊕ *www.nps.gov/redw* ⏲ *Late May–mid-Sept., daily 9–6.*

Jedediah Smith Visitor Center. Located off U.S. 199, this center has information about ranger-led walks and evening campfire programs in the summer in Jedediah Smith Redwoods State Park. Also here are nature and history exhibits, a gift shop, a pay phone, and a picnic area. ✉ *Off U.S. 199, Hiouchi* ☎ *707/465–2144* ⊕ *www.parks.ca.gov* ⏲ *Late May–early Sept., daily 9–5; late Sept–late Feb. Hours are in flux, visitors should call to check hrs. of operation.*

★ **Prairie Creek Visitor Center.** This center, housed in a redwood lodge, has wildlife displays and a massive stone fireplace that was built in 1933. Several trailheads begin here. Stretch your legs with an easy stroll along Revelation Trail, a short loop behind the lodge. Pick up information about summer programs in Prairie Creek Redwoods State Park. There's a pay phone, nature museum, gift shop, picnic area, and exhibits on flora and fauna. ✉ *Off southern end of Newton B. Drury Scenic Pkwy., Orick* ☎ *707/465–7354* ⊕ *www.parks.ca.gov* ⏲ *Late May–early Sept., daily 9–6; early Sept.–late May, daily 9–5.*

★ **Thomas H. Kuchel Visitor Center.** Here you can get brochures, advice, and a free permit to drive up the access road to Tall Trees Grove. Whale-watchers will find the deck of the visitor center an excellent observation point, and bird-watchers will enjoy the nearby Freshwater Lagoon, a popular layover for migrating waterfowl. ✉ *Off U.S. 101, Orick* ☎ *707/465–7765* ⊕ *www.nps.gov/redw* ⏲ *Late May–early Sept., daily 9–6; early Sept.–late May, daily 9–4.*

OUTFITTERS

Coast True Value (✉ *900 Northcrest Dr., Crescent City* ☎ *707/464-4724*) is a good place to get fishing licenses (valid for both river and ocean fishing; $44.60 annual fee or $20.75 two-day fee for California residents; two-day and 10-day licenses for $20.75 and $41.20 can also be purchased by nonresidents).

You can rent hard-shell kayaks at **Adventure's Edge** (✉ *650 10th St., Arcata* ☎ *707/822-4673* ⏲ *Mon.-Sat. 9-6, Sun. 10-5*) for $40 a day. In business since 1970, this Arcata outfitter also rents camping equipment and tents.

8

SPORTS AND THE OUTDOORS

FISHING

Both deep-sea and freshwater fishing are popular here. Anglers often stake out sections of the Klamath and Smith rivers in their search for salmon and trout. (A single fishing license covers both ocean and river fishing.) Less serious anglers go crabbing and clamming on the coast, but check the tides carefully: rip currents and sneaker waves are deadly.

HIKING

★ **Coastal Trail.** Although this easy-to-difficult trail runs along most of the park's length, smaller sections—of varying degrees of difficulty—are accessible via frequent, well-marked trailheads. The moderate to difficult DeMartin section leads past 5 mi of old growth redwoods and through prairie. If you're up for a real workout, you'll be well rewarded with the brutally difficult but stunning Flint Ridge section, a 4.5-mi stretch of steep grades and numerous switchbacks that leads past redwoods and Marshall Pond. The moderate 4-mi-long Hidden Beach section connects the Lagoon Creek picnic area with Klamath Overlook and provides coastal views and whale-watching opportunities. ⊠ *Flint Ridge trailhead: Douglas Bridge parking area, north end of Coastal Dr.*

KAYAKING

With many miles of often-shallow rivers and streams in the area, kayaking is a popular pastime in the park.

WHALE-WATCHING

Good vantage points for whale-watching include Crescent Beach Overlook, the Kuchel Visitor Center in Orick, points along the Coastal Drive, and the Klamath River Overlook. Late November through January are the best months to see their southward migrations; February through April they return and generally pass closer to shore.

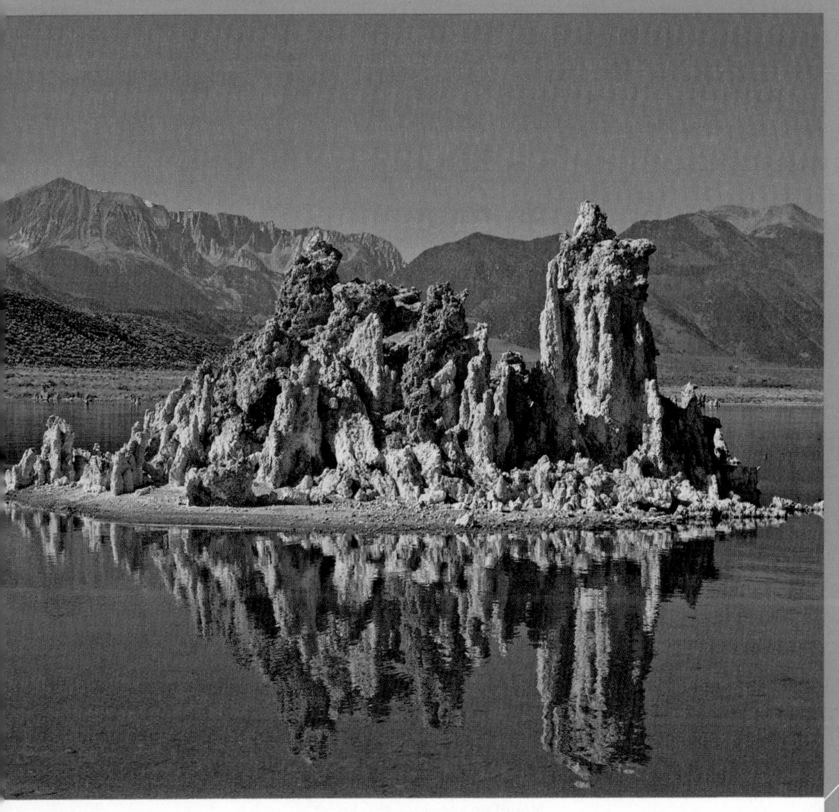

9

The Southern Sierra

AROUND SEQUOIA, KINGS CANYON, AND YOSEMITE NATIONAL PARKS

WORD OF MOUTH

"Sitting on the edge of [the] Sierra Nevada Mountains, Mono Lake is an ancient saline lake. It is home to trillions of brine shrimp and alkali flies. You can see many limestone formations known as Tufa Towers, such as this, rising from the water's surface. Mono Lake is visited by millions of migratory birds each year."

—photo by Randall Pugh, Fodors.com member

WELCOME TO THE SOUTHERN SIERRA

TOP REASONS TO GO

★ **Take a hike:** Whether you walk the paved loops in the national parks (⇨ *Chapter 10, Yosemite National Park, and Chapter 11, Sequoia and Kings Canyon National Parks)* or head off the beaten path into the backcountry, a hike through groves and meadows or alongside streams and waterfalls will allow you to see, smell, and feel nature up close.

★ **Hit the slopes:** Famous for its incredible snowpack—some of the deepest in the North American continent—the Sierra Nevada has something for every winter-sports fan.

★ **Mammoth fun:** Mammoth Lakes is eastern California's most exciting resort area.

★ **Old-world charm:** Tucked in the hills south of Oakhurst, the elegant Château du Sureau will make you feel as if you've stepped into a fairy tale.

★ **Go with the flow:** Three Rivers, the gateway to Sequoia National Park, is the launching pad for white-water trips down the Kaweah River.

1 South of Yosemite National Park. Several gateway towns to the south and west of Yosemite National Park (⇨ *Chapter 10)*, most within an hour's drive of Yosemite Valley, have food, lodging, and other services.

2 Mammoth Lakes. A jewel in the vast eastern Sierra Nevada, the Mammoth Lakes area lies just east of the Sierra crest, on the back side of Yosemite and the Ansel Adams Wilderness. It's a place of rugged beauty, where giant sawtooth mountains drop into the vast deserts of the Great Basin. In winter, 11,053-foot-high Mammoth Mountain provides the finest skiing and snowboarding in California—sometimes as late as June or even July. Once the snows melt, Mammoth transforms itself into a warm-weather playground, with fishing, mountain biking, golfing, hiking, and horseback riding. Nine deep-blue lakes are spread through the Mammoth Lakes Basin, and another 100 lakes dot the surrounding countryside.

3 East of Yosemite National Park. The area to the east of Yosemite National Park (⇨ *Chapter 10)* includes some ruggedly handsome, albeit desolate, terrain, most notably around Mono Lake. The area is best visited by car, as distances are great and public transportation is negligible. U.S. 395 is the main north–south road on the eastern side of the Sierra Nevada, at the western edge of the Great Basin. It's one of California's most beautiful highways; plan to snap pictures at roadside pullouts.

GETTING ORIENTED

The transition between the Central Valley and the rugged Southern Sierra may be the most dramatic in California sightseeing; as you head into the mountains, your temptation to stop the car and gawk will increase with every foot gained in elevation. Although you should spend most of your time here in the national parks ⇨ be sure to check out some of the mountain towns on the parks' fringes—in addition to being great places to stock up on supplies, they have a variety of worthy attractions, restaurants, and lodging options.

9

4 South of Sequoia and Kings Canyon: Three Rivers. Scenic Three Rivers is the main gateway for Sequoia and Kings Canyon National Parks (⇨ *Chapter 11*).

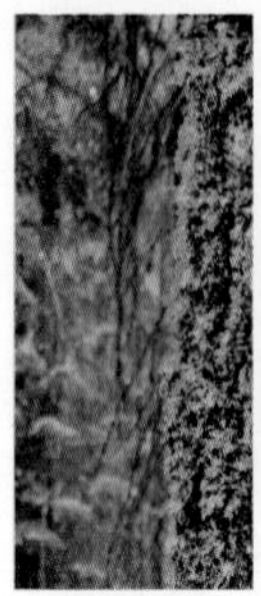

Updated by Reed Parsell

Vast granite peaks and giant sequoias are among the mind-boggling natural wonders of the Southern Sierra, many of which are protected in three national parks.

(⇨ *Chapter 10, Yosemite National Park, and Chapter 11, Sequoia and Kings Canyon National Parks).* Outside the parks, pristine lakes, superb skiing, rolling hills, and small towns complete the picture of the Southern Sierra. Heading up Highway 395, on the Sierra's eastern side, you'll be rewarded with outstanding vistas of dramatic mountain peaks, including Mt. Whitney, the highest point in the contiguous United States, and Mono Lake, a vast but slowly vanishing expanse of deep blue—one of the most-photographed natural attractions in California.

PLANNING

GETTING HERE AND AROUND

Fresno Yosemite International Airport (FYI) is the nearest airport to the national parks; Reno–Tahoe is the closest major airport to Mammoth Lakes.

Airports **Fresno Yosemite International Airport** (✉ *5175 E. Clinton Ave., Fresno* ☎ *559/621–4500 or 559/498–4095* 🌐 *www.flyfresno.org*). **Reno–Tahoe International Airport** (✉ *U.S. 395, Exit 65B, Reno, NV* ☎ *775/328–6400* 🌐 *www.renoairport.com*).

From San Francisco, interstates 80 and 580 are the most efficient connecting routes to Interstate 5 and Highway 99 on the western side of the Sierra Nevada range. To best reach the eastern side from the Bay Area, take Interstate 80 to Highway 395, then head south.

To get to Mammoth Lakes in summer and early fall (or whenever snows aren't blocking Tioga Road), you can travel via Highway 120 (to U.S. 395 south) through the Yosemite high country; the quickest route in winter is Interstate 80 to U.S. 50 to Highway 207 (Kingsbury Grade) to U.S. 395 south; either route takes about seven hours.

Contacts **California Road Conditions** (☎ *800/427–7623* 🌐 *www.dot.ca.gov/hq/roadinfo*).

RESTAURANTS

Most small towns in the Sierra Nevada have at least one restaurant; with few exceptions, dress is casual. You'll most likely be spending a lot of time in the car while you're exploring the area, so pick up snacks and drinks to keep with you. With picnic supplies on hand, you'll be able to enjoy an impromptu meal under giant trees.

HOTELS

If you're planning to stay on the Sierra's western side, book your hotel in advance—especially in summer. Otherwise, you may end up driving pretty far to find a place to sleep. Thanks to the surge in hotel development in Mammoth Lakes, making an advance reservation is not as critical on the Sierra's less-traveled eastern side. Wherever you visit, however, be prepared for sticker shock—rural and rustic does not mean inexpensive here.

BOOKING A ROOM

If you'd like assistance booking your lodgings, try the following agencies: **Mammoth Lakes Visitors Bureau Lodging Referral** (☎ *760/934–2712 or 888/466–2666* 🌐 *www.visitmammoth.com*). **Mammoth Reservations** (☎ *800/223–3032* 🌐 *www.mammothreservations.com*). **Three Rivers Reservation Center** (☎ *866/561–0410 or 559/561–0410* 🌐 *www.rescentre.com*).

WHAT IT COSTS

	¢	$	$$	$$$	$$$$
Restaurants	under $10	$10–$15	$16–$22	$23–$30	over $30
Hotels	under $90	$90–$120	$121–$175	$176–$250	over $250

Restaurant prices are for a main course at dinner, excluding sales tax of 7.25%–7.75% (depending on location). Hotel prices are for two people in a standard double room in high season, excluding service charges and 9%–10% tax.

9

SOUTH OF YOSEMITE NATIONAL PARK

People heading to Yosemite National Park, especially those interested in seeing the giant redwoods on the park's south side, pass through Oakhurst and Fish Camp on Highway 41.

OAKHURST

40 mi north of Fresno and 23 mi south of Yosemite National Park's south entrance on Hwy. 41.

Motels, restaurants, gas stations, and small businesses line both sides of Highway 41 as it cuts through Oakhurst. This is the last sizeable community before Yosemite (⇨ *Chapter 10*) and a good spot to find provisions. There are two major grocery stores near the intersection of highways 41 and 49. Three miles north of town, then 6 mi east, honky-tonky Bass Lake is a popular spot in summer with motorboaters, Jet Skiers, and families looking to cool off in the reservoir.

GETTING HERE AND AROUND

Sitting at the junction of highways 41 and 49, Oakhurst is not near any freeways and is a solid hour's drive north of Fresno. It's the southern gateway to Yosemite, so many people fly to Fresno and rent a car to get here and beyond. In town, there's no public transportation system of any consequence.

ESSENTIALS

Visitor Information **Yosemite Sierra Visitors Bureau** (*41969 Hwy. 41, Box 1998, Oakhurst 93644* *559/683–4636* *www.yosemitethisyear.com*).

DRIVING TIPS

Keep your tank full. Distances between gas stations can be long, and there's no fuel available in Yosemite Valley, Sequoia, or Kings Canyon ⇨ If you're traveling between October and May, rain on the coast can mean heavy snow in the mountains. Carry tire chains, know how to put them on (on Interstate 80 and U.S. 50 you can pay a chain installer $30 to do it for you, but on other routes you'll have to do it yourself), and always check road conditions before you leave. Traffic in national parks in summer can be heavy, and there are sometimes travel restrictions.

WHERE TO EAT

$$$ AMERICAN **Ducey's on the Lake.** For great views of Bass Lake and food that consistently impresses locals and tourists alike, make your way a few miles east of Oakhurst to this steakhouse-style restaurant, operated within The Pines Resort. Be sure to try the mashed potatoes. Alcoholic drinks are notably strong, so consider spending the night! *39255 Marina Dr.* *559/642–3131* *www.basslake.com* *Reservations recommended* *Brunch Sun.*

$$$$ CONTINENTAL Fodor's Choice ★ **Erna's Elderberry House.** Austrian-born Erna Kubin-Clanin, the grande dame of Château du Sureau, has created a culinary oasis, stunning for its elegance, gorgeous setting, and impeccable service. Crimson walls and dark beams accent the dining room's high ceilings, and arched windows reflect the glow of candles. The seasonal six-course prix-fixe dinner can be paired with superb wines, a must-do for oenophiles. When the waitstaff places all the plates on the table in perfect synchronicity, you know this will be a meal to remember. Premeal drinks are served in the former wine cellar. *48688 Victoria La.* *559/683–6800* *www.elderberryhouse.com* *Reservations essential* *No lunch Mon.–Sat.*

WHERE TO STAY

For expanded hotel reviews, visit Fodors.com.

$ **Best Western Yosemite Gateway Inn.** Oakhurst's best motel has carefully tended landscaping and rooms with attractive dark-wood American colonial–style furniture and slightly kitsch hand-painted wall murals of Yosemite. **Pros:** pretty close to Yosemite; clean; comfortable. **Cons:** chain property; some walls may seem thin. *40530 Hwy. 41* *559/683–2378 or 888/256–8042* *www.yosemitegatewayinn.com* *121 rooms, 16 suites* *In-room: a/c, Wi-Fi. In-hotel: restaurant, bar, pools, laundry facilities.*

$$$$ Fodor's Choice ★ **Château du Sureau.** This romantic inn, adjacent to Erna's Elderberry House, is straight out of one of Grimm's fairy tales: From the moment you drive through the wrought-iron gates and up to the enchanting

castle, you feel pampered. **Pros:** luxurious; stunning spa; spectacular property. **Cons:** you'll need to take out a second mortgage to stay here. ✉ *48688 Victoria La., Oakhurst* ☎ *559/683–6860* 🌐 *www.elderberryhouse.com* *10 rooms, 1 villa* *In-room: a/c, Wi-Fi. In-hotel: restaurant, bar, pool, spa, some age restrictions* 🍽 *Breakfast.*

$$ ★ **Homestead Cottages.** If you're looking for peace and quiet, Homestead is the place, because serenity is the order of the day at this secluded getaway in Ahwahnee, 6 mi west of Oakhurst. **Pros:** remote; quiet; friendly owners. **Cons:** remote; some urbanites might find it *too* quiet. ✉ *41110 Rd. 600, 2½ mi off Hwy. 49, Ahwahnee* ☎ *559/683–0495 or 800/483–0495* 🌐 *www.homesteadcottages.com* *5 cottages, 1 loft* *In-room: a/c, kitchen.*

FISH CAMP

57 mi north of Fresno and 4 mi south of Yosemite National Park's south entrance.

As you climb in elevation along Highway 41 northbound, you see nothing but trees until you get to the small settlement of Fish Camp, where there's a post office and general store, but no gasoline (for gas, head 10 mi north to Wawona, in the park, or 17 mi south to Oakhurst).

GETTING HERE AND AROUND

Arrive here by car via Highway 41, from Yosemite National Park a few miles to the north, or from Oakhurst (and, farther down the road, Fresno) to the south. Unless you're on foot or a bicycle, cars are your only option.

EXPLORING

Yosemite Mountain Sugar Pine Railroad. A narrow-gauge steam train chugs through the forest, following 4 mi of the route the Madera Sugar Pine Lumber Company cut through the forest in 1899 to harvest timber. The steam train, as well as Jenny railcars, runs year-round on fluctuating schedules; call for details. On Saturday (and Wednesday in summer), the Moonlight Special dinner excursion (reservations essential) includes a picnic with toe-tappin' music by the Sugar Pine Singers, followed by a sunset steam-train ride. ✉ *56001 Hwy. 41* ☎ *559/683–7273* 🌐 *www.ymsprr.com* *$18 steam train; Jenny railcar $14.50; Moonlight Special $48* ⏲ *Mar.–Oct., daily.*

9

WHERE TO STAY

For expanded hotel reviews, visit Fodors.com.

$$ ★ **Narrow Gauge Inn.** All of the rooms at this well-tended, family-owned property have balconies (some shared) and great views of the surrounding woods and mountains. **Pros:** close to Yosemite's south entrance; well appointed; wonderful balconies. **Cons:** rooms can feel a bit dark; dining options are limited (especially for vegetarians). ✉ *48571 Hwy. 41* ☎ *559/683–7720 or 888/644–9050* 🌐 *www.narrowgaugeinn.com* *26 rooms, 1 suite* *In-room: no a/c (some), Internet, Wi-Fi (some). In-hotel: restaurant, bar, pool, some pets allowed* 🍽 *Breakfast.*

$$$$ ★ **Tenaya Lodge.** One of the region's largest hotels, the Tenaya Lodge is ideal for people who enjoy wilderness treks by day but prefer creature comforts at night. **Pros:** rustic setting with modern comforts;

good off-season deals. **Cons:** so big it can seem impersonal; few dining options. ✉ *1122 Hwy. 41* 📭 *Box 159, 93623* ☎ *559/683–6555 or 888/514–2167* 🌐 *www.tenayalodge.com* *244 rooms, 6 suites* *In-room: a/c, Wi-Fi. In-hotel: restaurants, bar, pool, gym, children's programs.*

EL PORTAL

14 mi west of Yosemite Valley on Hwy. 140.

The market in town is a good place to pick up provisions before you get to Yosemite (⇨ *Chapter 20*). There's also a post office and a gas station, but not much else.

GETTING HERE AND AROUND

The drive here on Highway 140 from Mariposa and, farther west, Merced, is the prettiest and gentlest (in terms of steep uphill and downhill portions) route to Yosemite National Park. Much of the road follows the Merced River in a rugged canyon. The Yosemite Area Regional Transportation System (YARTS; 🌐 *www.yarts.com*) is a cheap and dependable way to go between Merced and Yosemite Valley; all its buses stop in El Portal, where many park employees reside.

WHERE TO STAY

For expanded hotel reviews, visit Fodors.com.

$$$ **Evergreen Lodge at Yosemite.** Near Hetch Hetchy on Yosemite National Park's northwest side, this recently renovated, 22-acre property is a dream come true for families. **Pros:** near the underrated Hetch Hetchy; family atmosphere; clean cabins. **Cons:** about an hour's drive from Yosemite Valley. ✉ *33160 Evergreen Road* ☎ *209/379–2606 or 888/935–6343* 🌐 *www.evergreenlodge.com* *90 cabins* *In-hotel: restaurant, bar, laundry facilities, some pets allowed.*

$$ **Yosemite View Lodge.** The motel-like design aesthetic is ameliorated by its location right on the banks of the boulder-strewn Merced River and its proximity to the park entrance 2 mi east. **Pros:** huge spa baths; great views; friendly service. **Cons:** air-conditioning inconsistent; restaurant can get crowded; can be pricey. ✉ *11136 Hwy. 140* ☎ *209/379–2681 or 888/742–4371* 🌐 *www.yosemiteresorts.us* *335 rooms* *In-room: a/c, kitchen (some). In-hotel: restaurant, bar, pools, laundry facilities, some pets allowed.*

MAMMOTH LAKES

30 mi south of eastern edge of Yosemite National Park on U.S. 395.

Much of the architecture in Mammoth Lakes (elevation 7,800 feet) is of the faux-alpine variety. You'll find increasingly sophisticated dining and lodging options here. International real-estate developers joined forces with Mammoth Mountain Ski Area and have worked hard to transform the once sleepy town into a chic ski destination. The Village at Mammoth (⇨ *below*) is the epicenter of all the recent development. Winter is high season at Mammoth; in summer room rates plummet. Highway 203 heads west from U.S. 395, becoming Main Street as it

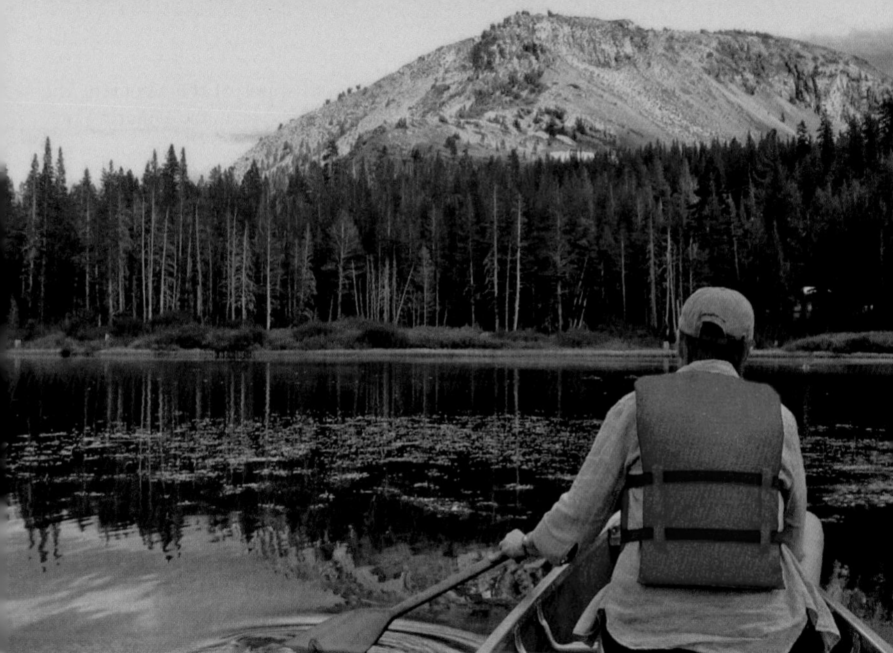

Twin Lakes, in the Mammoth Lakes region, is a great place to unwind.

passes through the town of Mammoth Lakes, and later Minaret Road (which makes a right turn) as it continues west to the Mammoth Mountain ski area and Devils Postpile National Monument.

GETTING HERE AND AROUND

The best way to get here, no surprise, is by private automobile. The town is a couple of miles west of Highway 395; take one of two exits to get here. The Yosemite Area Regional Transportation System (YARTS; 🌐 *www.yarts.com*) has once-a-day service between here and Yosemite Valley. The Eastern Sierra Transit Authority (☎ 800/922–1930 🌐 *www.easternsierratransitauthority.com*) operates shuttle buses among Mammoth Lakes, Bishop, and nearby tourist sites.

9

ESSENTIALS

Visitor Information **Mammoth Lakes Visitors Bureau** (✉ *Along Hwy. 203, Main St., near Sawmill Cutoff Rd., Box 48, Mammoth Lakes* ☎ *760/934–2712 or 888/466–2666* 🌐 *www.visitmammoth.com*).

EXPLORING

Mammoth Lakes Basin. The lakes, reached by Lake Mary Road off Highway 203 southwest of town, are popular for fishing and boating in summer. First comes Twin Lakes, at the far end of which is Twin Falls, where water cascades 300 feet over a shelf of volcanic rock. Also popular are Lake Mary, the largest lake in the basin; Lake Mamie; and Lake George. Horseshoe Lake is the only lake in which you can swim.

Minaret Vista. The glacier-carved sawtooth spires of the Minarets, the remains of an ancient lava flow, are best viewed from the Minaret Vista, off Highway 203 west of Mammoth Lakes.

Fodor's Choice ★ **Panorama Gondola.** Even if you don't ski, ride the gondola to see Mammoth Mountain, the aptly named dormant volcano that gives Mammoth Lakes its name. Gondolas serve skiers in winter and mountain bikers and sightseers in summer. The high-speed, eight-passenger gondolas whisk you from the chalet to the summit, where you can read about the area's volcanic history and take in top-of-the-world views. Standing high above the tree line atop this dormant volcano, you can look west 150 mi across the state to the Coastal Range; to the east are the highest peaks of Nevada and the Great Basin beyond. You won't find a better view of the Sierra High Country without climbing. Remember, though, that the air is thin at the 11,053-foot summit; carry water, and don't overexert yourself. The boarding area is at the Main Lodge. ✉ *Off Hwy. 203* ☎ *760/934–2571 Ext. 2400 information, Ext. 3850 gondola station* 🎫 *$21 in summer* ⏲ *July 4–Oct., daily 9–4:30; Nov.–July 3, daily 8:30–4.*

Village at Mammoth. The overwhelming popularity of Mammoth Mountain has generated a real-estate boom, and a huge new complex of shops, restaurants, and luxury accommodations, called the Village at Mammoth, has become the town's tourist center. Parking can be tricky. There's a lot across the street on Minaret Road; pay attention to time limits.

WHERE TO EAT

$$$ AMERICAN ✕ **Petra's Bistro & Wine Bar.** Other restaurateurs speak highly of Petra's as the most convivial restaurant in town. Its lovely ambience—quiet, dark, and warm—complements the carefully prepared meat main dishes and seasonal sides, and the more than two dozen California wines from behind the bar. The service is top-notch. Downstairs, the Clocktower Cellar bar provides a late-night, rowdy alternative—or chaser. ✉ *6080 Minaret Rd.* ☎ *760/934–3500* 🌐 *www.petrasbistro.com* ✍ *Reservations essential* ⏲ *No lunch.*

$$$$ AMERICAN ✕ **Restaurant at Convict Lake.** Tucked in a tiny valley ringed by mile-high peaks, Convict Lake is one of the most spectacular spots in the eastern Sierra. Thank heaven the food lives up to the view. The chef's specialties include beef Wellington, rack of lamb, and pan-seared local trout, all beautifully prepared. The woodsy room has a vaulted knotty-pine ceiling and a copper-chimney fireplace that roars on cold nights. Natural light abounds in the daytime, but if it's summer, opt for a table outdoors under the white-barked aspens. Service is exceptional, as is the wine list, with reasonably priced European and California varietals. ✉ *2 mi off U.S. 395, 4 mi south of Mammoth Lakes* ☎ *760/934–3803* ✍ *Reservations essential* ⏲ *No lunch early Sept.–July 4.*

$$$$ FRENCH ✕ **Restaurant LuLu.** The sunny, sensual, and assertive flavors of Provençale cooking—think olive tapenade, aioli, and lemony vinaigrettes—are showcased here. At this outpost of the famous San Francisco restaurant, the formula remains the same: small plates of southern French cooking

served family-style in a spare, modern, and sexy dining room. Standouts include rotisserie meats, succulent roasted mussels, homemade gnocchi, and a fantastic wine list, with 50 vintages available in 2-ounce pours. Outside, the sidewalk café includes a fire pit where kids will love do-it-themselves s'mores. LuLu's only drawback is price, but if you can swing it, it's worth every penny. The waiters wear jeans, so you can, too. ✉ *Village at Mammoth, 1111 Forest Trail, Unit 201* ☎ *760/924–8781* 🌐 *www.restaurantlulu.com* *Reservations essential.*

$ CAFÉ ✕ **Side Door Café.** Half wine bar, half café, this is a laid-back spot for an easy lunch or a long, lingering afternoon. The café serves grilled panini sandwiches, sweet and savory crepes, and espresso. At the wine bar, order cheese plates and charcuterie platters, designed to pair with the 25 wines (fewer in summertime) available by the glass. If you're lucky, a winemaker will show up and hold court at the bar. ✉ *Village at Mammoth, 1111 Forest Trail, Unit 229* ☎ *760/934–5200.*

$ AMERICAN ✕ **The Stove.** A longtime family favorite for down-to-earth, folksy cooking, this is the kind of place you take the family to fill up before a long car ride. The omelets, pancakes, huevos rancheros, and meat loaf won't win any awards, but they're tasty. The room is cute, with gingham curtains and pinewood booths, and service is friendly. Breakfast and lunch are the best bets here. ✉ *644 Old Mammoth Rd.* ☎ *760/934–2821* *Reservations not accepted.*

WHERE TO STAY

For expanded hotel reviews, visit Fodors.com.

$ **Alpenhof Lodge.** The owners lucked out when developers built the fancy-schmancy Village at Mammoth right across the street from their mom-and-pop motel. **Pros:** convenient for skiers; good price. **Cons:** could use an update; rooms above the pub can be noisy. ✉ *6080 Minaret Rd., Box 1157* ☎ *760/934–6330 or 800/828–0371* 🌐 *www.alpenhof-lodge.com* *54 rooms, 3 cabins* *In-room: no a/c, kitchen (some), Wi-Fi. In-hotel: restaurant, bar, pool, laundry facilities.*

$ **Cinnamon Bear Inn Bed and Breakfast.** In a business district off Main Street, this bed-and-breakfast feels more like a small motel, with nicely decorated rooms, many with four-poster beds. **Pros:** quiet; affordable; friendly. **Cons:** a bit tricky to find; limited parking. ✉ *113 Center St.* *Box 3338, 93546* ☎ *760/934–2873 or 800/845–2873* 🌐 *www.cinnamonbearinn.com* *22 rooms* *In-room: no a/c, kitchen (some), Wi-Fi. In-hotel: bar* *Breakfast.*

$$$ **Double Eagle Resort and Spa.** You won't find a better spa retreat in the eastern Sierra than the Double Eagle, which is in a spectacularly beautiful spot under towering peaks and along a creek, near June Lake, 20 minutes north of Mammoth Lakes. **Pros:** pretty setting; generous breakfast; good for families. **Cons:** expensive, remote. ✉ *5587 Hwy. 158, Box 736, June Lake* ☎ *760/648–7004 or 877/648–7004* 🌐 *www.doubleeagleresort.com* *16 2-bedroom cabins, 16 cabin suites, 1 3-bedroom cabin* *In-room: no a/c, kitchen (some), Internet. In-hotel: restaurant, bar, pool, gym, spa, some pets allowed.*

9

$$$ **Juniper Springs Lodge.** Tops for slope-side comfort, these condominium-style units have full kitchens and ski-in ski-out access to the mountain. **Pros:** bargain during summer; direct access to the slopes; good views. **Cons:** no nightlife within walking distance; no a/c; some complaints about service. *4000 Meridian Blvd. Box 2129, 93546 760/924–1102 or 800/626–6684 www.mammothmountain.com 10 studios, 99 1-bedrooms, 92 2-bedrooms, 3 3-bedrooms In-room: no a/c, kitchen, Internet. In-hotel: restaurant, bar, golf course, pool, laundry facilities.*

$$$ **Mammoth Mountain Inn.** If you want to be within walking distance of the Mammoth Mountain Main Lodge, this is the place. **Pros:** great location; big rooms; a traditional place to stay. **Cons:** can be crowded in ski season; won't be around for many more years. *Minaret Rd., 4 mi west of Mammoth Lakes Box 353, 93546 760/934–2581 or 800/626–6684 www.mammothmountain.com 124 rooms, 91 condos In-room: no a/c, kitchen (some), Internet. In-hotel: 2 restaurants, bar, pool, laundry facilities.*

$$ Fodor's Choice ★ **Tamarack Lodge Resort & Lakefront Restaurant.** Tucked away on the edge of the John Muir Wilderness Area, where cross-country ski trails loop through the woods, this original 1924 lodge looks like something out of a snow globe, and the lake it borders is serenely beautiful. **Pros:** rustic but not run-down; plenty of eco-sensitivity; tons of nearby outdoor activities. **Cons:** thin walls; some main lodge rooms have shared bathrooms. *Lake Mary Rd., off Hwy. 203 Box 69, 93546 760/934–2442 or 800/626–6684 www.tamaracklodge.com 11 rooms, 35 cabins In-room: no a/c, kitchen (some), no TV. In-hotel: restaurant, bar.*

$$$ **Village at Mammoth.** At the epicenter of Mammoth's dining and nightlife scene, this cluster of four-story timber-and-stone condo buildings nods to Alpine style, with exposed timbers and peaked roofs. **Pros:** central location; clean; big rooms; lots of good restaurants nearby. **Cons:** pricey; can be noisy outside. *100 Canyon Blvd. Box 3459, 93546 760/934–1982 or 800/626–6684 www.mammothmountain.com 277 units In-room: no a/c, kitchen (some), Internet. In-hotel: pool, gym, laundry facilities, parking.*

The Village at Mammoth hosts events and has several rockin' bars and clubs.

SPORTS AND THE OUTDOORS

For information on winter conditions around Mammoth, call the **Snow Report** (*760/934–7669 or 888/766–9778*). The **U.S. Forest Service ranger station** (*760/924–5500*) can provide general information year-round.

BICYCLING

Mammoth Mountain Bike Park (*Mammoth Mountain Ski Area 760/934–3706 www.mammothmountain.com*) opens when the snow melts, usually by July, with 70-plus mi of single-track trails—from mellow to super-challenging. Chairlifts and shuttles provide trail access, and rentals are available. Various shops around town also rent bikes and provide trail maps, if you don't want to ascend the mountain.

FISHING

Crowley Lake is the top trout-fishing spot in the area; Convict Lake, June Lake, and the lakes of the Mammoth Basin are other prime spots. One of the best trout rivers is the San Joaquin, near Devils Postpile. Hot Creek, a designated Wild Trout Stream, is renowned for fly-fishing (catch-and-release only). The fishing season runs from the last Saturday in April until the end of October.

Kittredge Sports (✉ *3218 Main St., at Forest Trail* ☎ *760/934–7566* 🌐 *www.kittredgesports.com*) rents rods and reels and also conducts guided trips.

To maximize your time on the water, get tips from local anglers, or better yet, book a guided fishing trip with **Sierra Drifters Guide Service** (☎ *760/935–4250* 🌐 *www.sierradrifters.com*).

HIKING

Hiking in Mammoth is stellar, especially along the trails that wind through the pristine alpine scenery around the Lakes Basin. Carry lots of water; and remember, you're above 8,000-foot elevation, and the air is thin. Stop at the **U.S. Forest Service ranger station** (✉ *Hwy. 203* ☎ *760/924–5500* 🌐 *www.fs.fed.us/r5/inyo*), on your right just before the town of Mammoth Lakes, for a Mammoth area trail map and permits for backpacking in wilderness areas.

HORSEBACK RIDING

Stables around Mammoth are typically open from June through September. **Mammoth Lakes Pack Outfit** (✉ *Lake Mary Rd., between Twin Lakes and Lake Mary* ☎ *760/934–2434 or 888/475–8747* 🌐 *www.mammothpack.com*) runs day and overnight horseback trips, or will shuttle you to the high country. **McGee Creek Pack Station** (☎ *760/935–4324 or 800/854–7407* 🌐 *www.mcgeecreekpackstation.com*) customizes pack trips or will shuttle you to camp alone. Operated by the folks at McGee Creek, **Sierra Meadows Ranch** (✉ *Sherwin Creek Rd., off Old Mammoth Rd.* ☎ *760/934–6161*) conducts horseback and wagon rides that range from one-hour to all-day excursions.

9

SKIING

June Mountain Ski Area. In their rush to Mammoth Mountain, most people overlook June Mountain, a compact, low-key resort 20 mi north of Mammoth. Snowboarders especially dig it. Two freestyle terrain areas are for both skiers and boarders, including a huge 16-foot-wall super pipe. Best of all, there's rarely a line for the lifts—if you want to avoid the crowds but must ski on a weekend, this is the place. And in a storm, June is better protected from wind and blowing snow than Mammoth Mountain. (If it starts to storm, you can use your Mammoth ticket at June.) Expect all the usual services, including a rental-and-repair shop, ski school, and sports shop, but the food quality is better at Mammoth. Lift tickets run $69, with discounts for multiple days. ✉ *3819 Hwy. 158, off June Lake Loop, June Lake* ☎ *760/648–7733 or 888/586–3686* 🌐 *www.junemountain.com* ☞ *35 trails on 500 acres, rated 35% beginner, 45% intermediate, 20% advanced. Longest run 2½ mi, base 7,510 feet, summit 10,174 feet. Lifts: 7.*

Fodor's Choice ★ **Mammoth Mountain Ski Area.** If you ski only one mountain in California, make it Mammoth Mountain Ski Area. One of the West's largest and best ski areas, Mammoth has more than 3,500 acres of skiable terrain and a 3,100-foot vertical drop. The views from the 11,053-foot summit are some of the most stunning in the Sierra. Below, you'll find a 6½-mi-wide swath of groomed boulevards and canyons, as well as pockets of tree-skiing and a dozen vast bowls. Snowboarders are everywhere on the slopes; there are three outstanding freestyle terrain parks of varying technical difficulty, with jumps, rails, tabletops, and giant super pipes (this is the location of several international snowboarding competitions). Mammoth's season begins in November and often lingers into May. Lift tickets cost $65. Lessons and equipment are available, and there's a children's ski and snowboard school. Mammoth runs free shuttle-bus routes around town and to the ski area, and the Village Gondola runs from the Village complex to Canyon Lodge. However, only overnight guests are allowed to park at the Village for more than a few hours. Warning: The main lodge is dark and dated, unsuited in most every way for the crush of ski season. Within a decade, it's likely to be replaced. ✉ *Minaret Rd., west of Mammoth Lakes* ☎ *760/934–2571; 800/626–6684; 760/934–0687 shuttle* ☞ *150 trails on 3,500 acres, rated 30% beginner, 40% intermediate, 30% advanced. Longest run 3 mi, base 7,953 feet, summit 11,053 feet. Lifts: 27, including 9 high-speed and 2 gondolas.*

Trails at **Tamarack Cross Country Ski Center** (✉ *Lake Mary Rd., off Hwy. 203* ☎ *760/934–5293 or 760/934–2442* 🌐 *www.tamaracklodge.com*), adjacent to Tamarack Lodge, meander around several lakes. Rentals are available.

SKI RENTALS

★ When the U.S. Ski Team visits Mammoth and needs their boots adjusted, they head to **Footloose** (✉ *3043 Main St.* ☎ *760/934–2400* 🌐 *www.footloosesports.com*), the best place in town—and possibly all California—for ski-boot rentals and sales, as well as custom insoles (ask for Kevin or Corty).

Advanced skiers should rent from **Kittredge Sports** (✉ *3218 Main St.* ☎ *760/934–7566* 🌐 *www.kittredgesports.com*). **Mammoth Sporting Goods** (✉ *1 Sierra Center Mall, Old Mammoth Rd.* ☎ *760/934–3239* 🌐 *www.mammothsportinggoods.com*) rents good skis for intermediates, and sells equipment, clothing, and accessories.

EAST OF YOSEMITE NATIONAL PARK

Most people enter Yosemite National Park from the west, having driven out from the Bay Area or Los Angeles. The eastern entrance on Tioga Pass Road (Highway 120), however, provides stunning, sweeping views of the High Sierra. Gray rocks shine in the bright sun, with scattered, small vegetation sprinkled about the mountainside. To drive from Lee Vining to Tuolumne Meadows is an unforgettable experience, but keep in mind the road tends to be closed for at least seven months of the year.

LEE VINING

20 mi east of Tuolumne Meadows via Hwy. 120 to U.S. 395; 30 mi north of Mammoth Lakes on U.S. 395.

Tiny Lee Vining is known primarily as the eastern gateway to Yosemite National Park (summer only; ⇨ *Chapter 10*) and the location of vast and desolate Mono Lake. Pick up supplies at the general store year-round, or stop here for lunch or dinner before or after a drive through the high country. In winter the town is all but deserted, except for the ice climbers who come to scale frozen waterfalls. You can meet these hearty souls at Nicely's restaurant, where the climbers congregate for breakfast around 8 on winter mornings.

GETTING HERE AND AROUND

Lee Vining is on Highway 395, just north of the intersection with Highway 120 and on the south side of massive Mono Lake. Greyhound can get you here from Reno and the Yosemite Area Regional Transportation System (YARTS; *www.yarts.com*) from Yosemite Valley, but you're much better off with a car.

ESSENTIALS

Visitor Information **Lee Vining Chamber of Commerce** (*Box 130, Lee Vining 93541* *760/647–6629* *www.leevining.com*). **Mono Lake** (*Box 49, Lee Vining 93541* *760/647–3044* *www.monolake.org*).

To try your hand at ice climbing, contact **Sierra Mountain Guides** (*760/648–1122 or 877/423–2546* *www.themountainguide.com*).

EXPLORING

★ **Mono Lake.** Eerie tufa towers—calcium carbonate formations that often resemble castle turrets—rise from impressive Mono Lake. Since the 1940s, the city of Los Angeles has diverted water from streams that feed the lake, lowering its water level and exposing the tufa. Court victories by environmentalists in the 1990s forced a reduction of the diversions, and the lake has since risen about 9 feet. From April through August, millions of migratory birds nest in and around Mono Lake. The best place to view the tufa is at the south end of the lake along the mile-long **South Tufa Trail.** To reach it, drive 5 mi south from Lee Vining on U.S. 395, then 5 mi east on Highway 120. There's a $3 fee. You can swim (or float) in the salty water at Navy Beach near the South Tufa Trail or take a kayak or canoe trip for close-up views of the tufa (check with rangers for boating restrictions during bird-nesting season). You can rent kayaks in Mammoth Lakes. The sensational **Scenic Area Visitor Center** (*U.S. 395* *760/647–3044*) is open daily from June through September (Sunday–Thursday 8–5, Friday and Saturday 8–7), and the rest of the year Thursday–Monday 9–4. Its hilltop and sweeping views of Mono Lake, along with its interactive exhibits inside, make this one of California's best visitor centers. Rangers and naturalists lead walking tours of the tufa daily in summer and on weekends (sometimes on cross-country skis) in winter. In town, the **Mono Lake Committee Information Center & Bookstore** (*U.S. 395 and 3rd St.* *760/647–6595* *www.monolake.org*) has more information about this beautiful area.

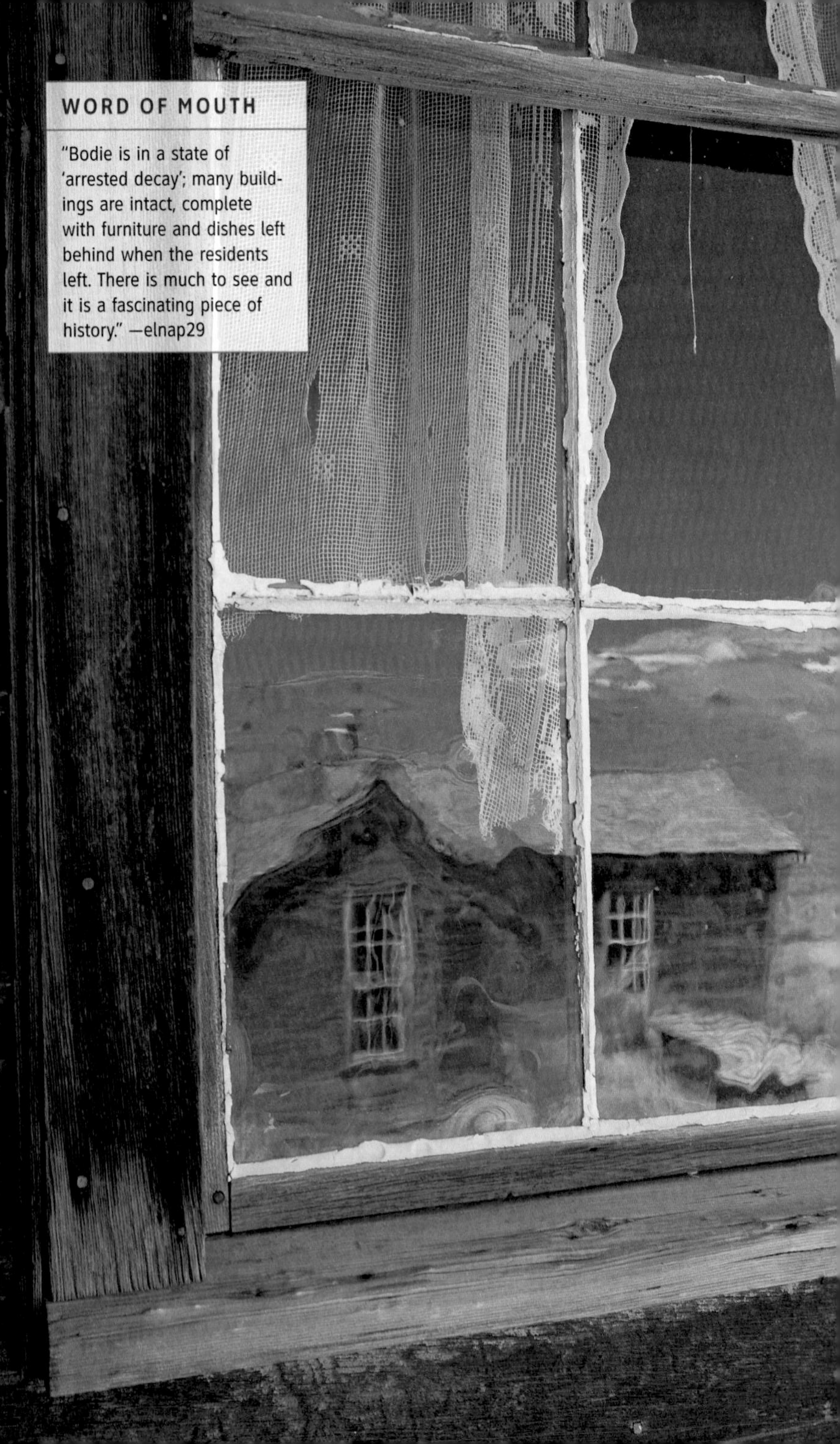

WORD OF MOUTH

"Bodie is in a state of 'arrested decay'; many buildings are intact, complete with furniture and dishes left behind when the residents left. There is much to see and it is a fascinating piece of history." —elnap29

EN ROUTE

Heading south from Lee Vining, U.S. 395 intersects the **June Lake Loop** (✉ *Hwy. 158 W*). This gorgeous 17-mi drive follows an old glacial canyon past Grant, June, Gull, and other lakes before reconnecting with U.S. 395 on its way to Mammoth Lakes. The loop is especially colorful in fall.

WHERE TO EAT AND STAY

$ DELI **Tioga Gas Mart & Whoa Nelli Deli.** Near the eastern entrance to Yosemite, Whoa Nelli serves some of Mono County's best food, including lobster taquitos, pizzas, and enormous slices of multilayered cakes. But what makes it special is that it's in a gas station—possibly the only one in America where you can order cocktails (a pitcher of mango margaritas, anyone?)—and outside there's a full-size trapeze where you can take lessons (by reservation). This wacky spot is well off the noisy road, and has plenty of shaded outdoor tables with views of Mono Lake; bands play here on summer evenings, and locals love it, too. ✉ *Hwy. 120 and U.S. 395* ☎ *760/647–1088* ⊗ *Closed mid-Nov.–mid-Apr.*

$$ **Lake View Lodge.** Lovely landscaping, which includes several inviting and shaded places to sit, is what sets this clean motel apart from its handful of competitors in town. **Pros:** attractive; clean; friendly staff. **Cons:** could use updating. ✉ *51285 U.S. 395* ☎ *760/647–6543 or 800/990–6614* 🌐 *www.lakeviewlodgeyosemite.com* *76 rooms, 12 cottages* *In-room: no a/c, kitchen (some).*

BODIE STATE HISTORIC PARK

23 mi northeast of Lee Vining via U.S. 395 to Hwy. 270 (last 3 mi are unpaved).

GETTING HERE AND AROUND

You need to get here by private car. About 15 mi north of Lee Vining (7 mi south of Bridgeport), look for signs pointing you east toward the ghost town, another 13 mi via Highway 270. The last 3 mi are unpaved, and possibly treacherous depending on erosion and the weather.

EXPLORING

Fodor's Choice ★ **Bodie Ghost Town.** Old shacks and shops, abandoned mine shafts, a Methodist church, the mining village of Rattlesnake Gulch, and the remains of a small Chinatown are among the sights at fascinating Bodie Ghost Town. The town, at an elevation of 8,200 feet, boomed from about 1878 to 1881, as gold prospectors, having worked the best of the western Sierra mines, headed to the high desert on the eastern slopes. Bodie was a mean place—the booze flowed freely, shootings were commonplace, and licentiousness reigned. Evidence of the town's wild past survives today at an excellent museum, and you can tour an old stamp mill and a ridge that contains many mine sites. Bodie, unlike Calico in Southern California near Barstow, is a genuine ghost town, its status proudly stated as "arrested decay." No food, drink, or lodging is available in Bodie. Though the park stays open in winter, snow may close Highway 270. Still, it's a fantastic time to visit: rent cross-country skis in Mammoth Lakes, drive north, ski in, and have the park to yourself. ✉ *Museum: Main and Green Sts.* ☎ *760/647–6445* 🌐 *www.bodie.net* *Park $3, museum free* ⊗ *Park: late May–early Sept., daily 8–7; early Sept.–late May, daily 8–4. Museum: late May–early Sept., daily 9–6; early Sept.–late May, hrs vary.*

9

SOUTH OF SEQUOIA AND KINGS CANYON: THREE RIVERS

200 mi north of Los Angeles via I–5 to Hwy. 99 to Hwy. 198; 8 mi south of Ash Mountain/Foothills entrance to Sequoia National Park on Hwy. 198.

In the foothills of the Sierra along the Kaweah River, this sparsely populated, serpentine hamlet serves as the main gateway town to Sequoia and Kings Canyon national parks (⇨ *Chapter 11, Sequoia and Kings Canyon National Parks*). Its livelihood depends largely on tourism from the parks, courtesy of two markets, a few service stations, banks, a post office, and several lodgings, which are good spots to find a room when park accommodations are full.

GETTING HERE AND AROUND

From Memorial Day through Labor Day, you can ride the city of Visalia's Sequoia Shuttle (☎ 877/404–6473 🌐 *www.ci.visalia.ca.us*) to and from Three Rivers, up to and down from Sequoia National Park. You probably should count on driving here yourself, however, via Highway 198. The town is slender and long, and to walk from your hotel to a restaurant might take longer than you think.

WHERE TO EAT AND STAY

¢ ECLECTIC ✕ **We Three Bakery.** This friendly, popular-with-the-locals spot packs lunches for trips into the nearby national parks; they're also open for breakfast. ✉ *43688 Sierra Dr.* ☎ *559/561–4761.*

$$ **Buckeye Tree Lodge.** Every room at this two-story motel has a patio facing a sun-dappled lawn, right on the banks of the Kaweah River. **Pros:** scenic setting; clean. **Cons:** could use an update. ✉ *46000 Sierra Dr., Hwy. 198* ☎ *559/561–5900* 🌐 *www.buckeyetree.com* *11 rooms, 1 cottage* *In-room: a/c. In-hotel: pool, some pets allowed* *Breakfast.*

RAFTING

Kaweah White Water Adventures (☎ *559/561–1000 or 800/229–8658* 🌐 *www.kaweah-whitewater.com*) guides two-hour and full-day rafting trips in spring and early summer, with some Class III rapids; longer trips may include some Class IV.

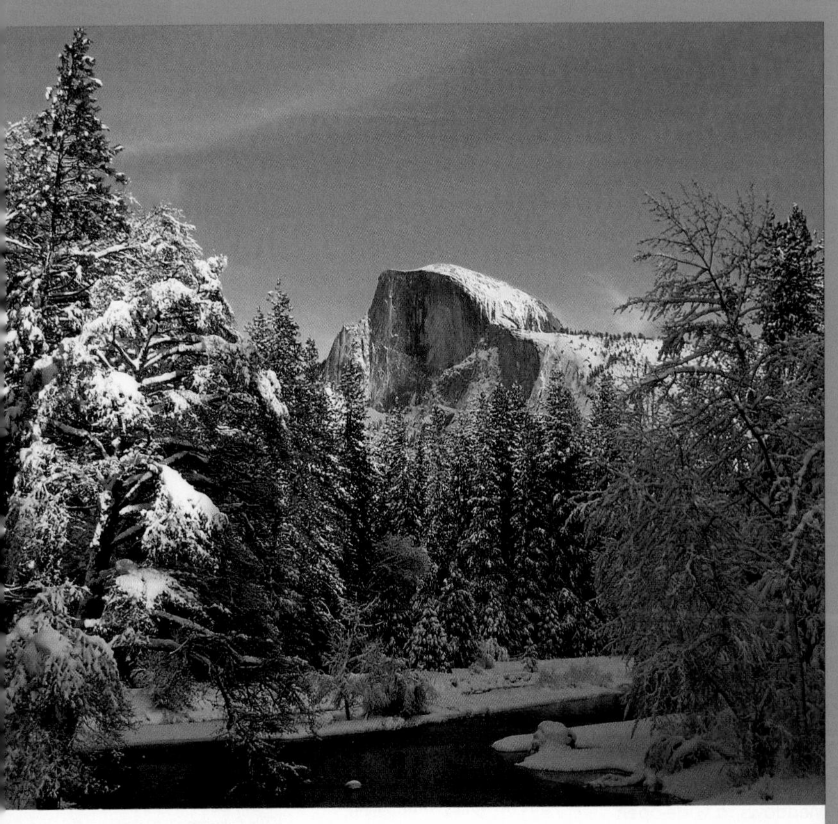

Yosemite National Park

10

WORD OF MOUTH

"I don't really have a favorite park, but we all agreed that Yosemite definitely gets the prize for waterfalls. I thought that Columbia River Gorge couldn't be beat, but it doesn't come close to Yosemite for waterfalls."

—spirobulldog

WELCOME TO YOSEMITE NATIONAL PARK

TOP REASONS TO GO

★ **Feel the earth move:** An easy stroll brings you to the base of Yosemite Falls, America's highest, where thundering springtime waters shake the ground.

★ **Tunnel to heaven:** Winding down into Yosemite Valley, Wawona Road passes through a mountainside and emerges before one of the park's most heart-stopping vistas.

★ **Touch the sky:** Watch clouds scudding across the bright blue dome that arches above the High Sierra's Tuolumne Meadows, a wide-open alpine valley ringed by 10,000-foot granite peaks.

★ **Walk away from it all:** Early or late in the day, leave the crowds behind and take a forest hike on a few of Yosemite's 800 mi of trails.

★ **Powder your nose:** Winter's hush floats into Yosemite on snowflakes. Wade into a fluffy drift, lift your face to the sky, and listen to the trees.

1 Yosemite Valley. At an elevation of 4,000 feet, in roughly the center of the park, beats Yosemite's heart. This is where you'll find the park's most famous sights and biggest crowds.

2 Wawona and Mariposa Grove. The park's southeastern tip holds Wawona, with its grand old hotel and pioneer history center, and the Mariposa Grove of Big Trees, filled with giant sequoias. These are closest to the South Entrance, 35 mi (a one-hour drive) south of Yosemite Village.

3 Tuolumne Meadows. The highlight of east-central Yosemite is this wildflower-strewn valley with hiking trails, nestled among sharp, rocky peaks. It's a two-hour drive northeast of Yosemite Valley along Tioga Road (closed mid-October–late May).

4 Hetch Hetchy. The most remote, least-visited part of Yosemite accessible by automobile, this glacial valley is dominated by a reservoir and veined with wilderness trails. It's near the park's western boundary, about a half-hour drive north of Big Oak Flat Entrance.

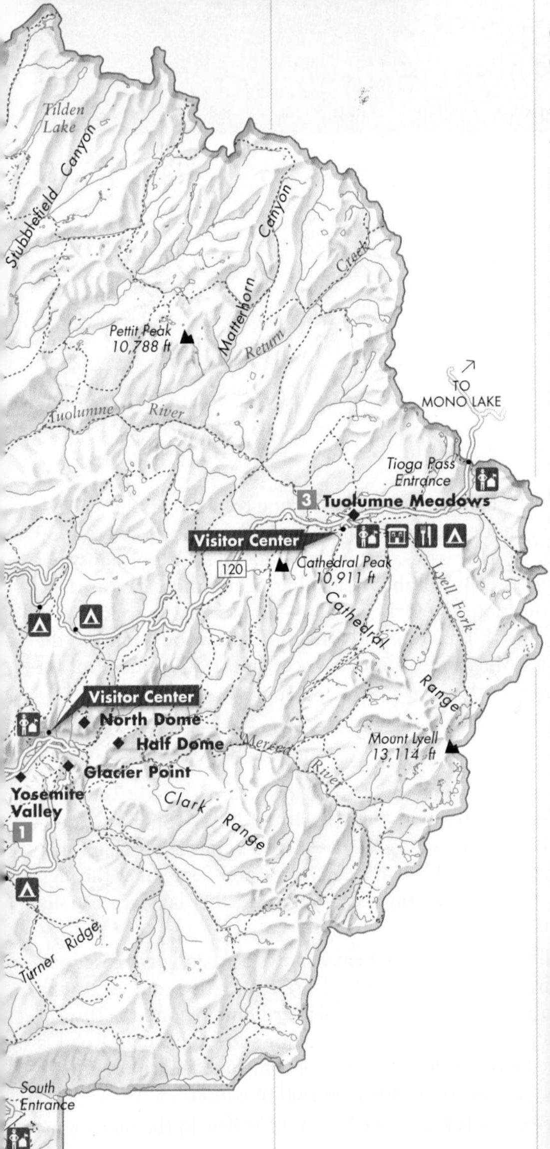

Tilden Lake
Stubblefield Canyon
Matterhorn Canyon
Return Creek
Pettit Peak 10,788 ft
Tuolumne River
TO MONO LAKE
Tioga Pass Entrance
3 Tuolumne Meadows
Visitor Center
120
Cathedral Peak 10,911 ft
Lyell Fork
Cathedral Range
Visitor Center
North Dome
Half Dome
Merced River
Mount Lyell 13,114 ft
Glacier Point
Yosemite Valley
1
Clark Range
Turner Ridge
South Entrance

GETTING ORIENTED

Yosemite is so large that you can think of it as five parks. Yosemite Valley, famous for waterfalls and cliffs, and Wawona, where the giant sequoias stand, are open all year. Hetch Hetchy, home of less-used backcountry trails, closes after the first big snow and reopens in May or June. The subalpine high country, Tuolumne Meadows, is open for summer hiking and camping; in winter it's accessible only via cross-country skis or snowshoes. Badger Pass Ski Area is open in winter only. Most visitors spend their time along the park's south-western border, between Wawona and Big Oak Flat Entrance; a bit farther east in Yosemite Valley and Badger Pass Ski Area; and along the east–west corridor of Tioga Road, which spans the park north of Yosemite Valley and bisects Tuolumne Meadows.

By Sura Wood and Reed Parsell

By merely standing in Yosemite Valley and turning in a circle, you can see more natural wonders in a minute than you could in a full day pretty much anywhere else. Half Dome, Yosemite Falls, El Capitan, Bridalveil Fall, the meadows, Sentinel Dome, the Merced River, white-flowering dogwood trees, maybe even bears ripping into the bark of fallen trees or sticking their snouts into beehives—it's all in the Valley.

In the mid-1800s, when tourists were arriving to the area, the Valley's special geologic qualities, and the giant sequoias of Mariposa Grove 30 mi to the south, so impressed a group of influential Californians that they persuaded President Abraham Lincoln to grant those two areas to the state for protection. On Oct. 1, 1890—thanks largely to lobbying efforts by naturalist John Muir and Robert Underwood Johnson, the editor of *Century Magazine*—Congress set aside 1,500 square mi for Yosemite National Park.

PLANNING

WHEN TO GO

During extremely busy periods—like the 4th of July—you may experience delays at the entrance gates. ■ **TIP→ For less crowds, visit midweek.** Or come mid-April through Memorial Day or mid-September through October, when the park is only a bit busy and the days are usually sunny and clear.

Summer rainfall is rare. In winter, heavy snows occasionally cause road closures, and tire chains or four-wheel drive may be required on the roads that remain open. The road to Glacier Point beyond the turnoff for Badger Pass is closed after the first major snowfall; Tioga Road is closed from late October through May or mid-June. Mariposa Grove Road is typically closed for a shorter period in winter.

The temperature chart below is for Yosemite Valley. In the high country, it's cooler.

GETTING HERE AND AROUND

Roughly 200 mi from San Francisco, 300 mi from Los Angeles, and 500 mi from Las Vegas, Yosemite takes a while to reach—and its sites and attractions merit much more time than what rangers say is the average visit: four hours. Most people arrive via car or tour bus, but public transportation (courtesy of Amtrak and the regional YARTS bus system) also can get you here.

Of the park's four entrances, Arch Rock is the closest to Yosemite Valley. The road that goes through it, Route 140 from Merced and Mariposa, is a scenic western approach that snakes alongside the boulder-packed Merced River. Route 41, through Wawona, is the way to come from Los Angeles. Route 120, through Crane Flat, is the most direct route from San Francisco. The only way in from the east is Tioga Road, which may be the best route in terms of scenery—though due to snow accumulation it's open for a frustratingly short amount of time each year (typically early June through mid-October).

However you get to the Valley, once you're there you can take advantage of the free shuttle buses, which make 21 stops, and run every 10 minutes or so from 9 am to 6 pm year-round; a separate (and also free) summer-only shuttle runs out to El Capitan. Also during the summer, from Yosemite Valley you can pay to take the morning "hikers' bus" to Tuolumne or the bus up to Glacier Point. Bus service from Wawona is geared for people who are staying there and want to spend the day in Yosemite Valley. Free and frequent shuttles transport people between the Wawona Hotel and Mariposa Grove. During the snow season, buses run regularly between Yosemite Valley and Badger Pass Ski Area. For more information, visit *www.nps.gov/yose/planyourvisit/bus.htm* or call *209/372–1240*.

There are few gas stations within Yosemite (Crane Flat, Tuolumne Meadows, and Wawona; none in the Valley), so fuel up before you reach the park. From late fall until early spring, the weather is unpredictable, and driving can be treacherous. You should carry chains. For road condition updates, call *800/427–7623 or 209/372–0200* from within California or go to *www.dot.ca.gov*.

10

WHAT IT COSTS

	¢	$	$$	$$$	$$$$
RESTAURANTS	under $10	$10–$15	$16–$22	$23–$30	over $30
HOTELS	under $90	$90–$120	$121–$175	$176–$250	over $250

Restaurant prices are for a main course at dinner, excluding sales tax. Hotel prices are for two people in a standard double room in high season, excluding service charges and tax.

FLORA AND FAUNA

Dense stands of incense cedar and Douglas fir—as well as ponderosa, Jeffrey, lodgepole, and sugar pines—cover much of the park, but the stellar standout, quite literally, is the *Sequoia sempervirens,* the giant sequoia. Sequoias grow only along the west slope of the Sierra Nevada

GOOD READS ON YOSEMITE

- *The Photographer's Guide to Yosemite*, by Michael Frye, is an insider's guide to the park, with maps for shutterbugs looking to capture perfect images.
- John Muir penned his observations of the park he long advocated for in *The Yosemite*.
- *Yosemite and the High Sierra*, edited by Andrea G. Stillman and John Szarkowski, features beautiful reproductions of landmark photographs by Ansel Adams, accompanied by excerpts from the photographer's journals written when Adams traveled in Yosemite National Park in the early 20th century.
- An insightful collection of essays accompany the museum-quality artworks in *Yosemite: Art of an American Icon*, by Amy Scott.
- Perfect for beginning wildlife watchers, *Sierra Nevada Wildflowers*, by Karen Wiese, indentifies more than 230 kinds of flora growing in the Sierra Nevada region.

between 4,500 and 7,000 feet in elevation. Starting from a seed the size of a rolled-oat flake, each of these ancient monuments assumes remarkable proportions in adulthood; you can see them in the Mariposa Grove of Big Trees. In late May the Valley's dogwood trees bloom with white, starlike flowers. Wildflowers, such as black-eyed Susan, bull thistle, cow parsnip, lupine, and meadow goldenrod, peak in June in the Valley and in July at higher elevations.

The most visible animals in the park—aside from the omnipresent western gray squirrel—are the mule deer. Though sightings of bighorn sheep are infrequent in the park itself, you can sometimes see them on the eastern side of the Sierra Crest, just off Route 120 in Lee Vining Canyon. You may also see the American black bear, which often has a brown, cinnamon, or blond coat. The Sierra Nevada is home to thousands of bears, and you should take all necessary precautions to keep yourself—and the bears—safe. For one, do not feed the bears. Bears that acquire a taste for human food can become very aggressive and destructive and sometimes must be put down by rangers.

Watch for the blue Steller's jay along trails, near public buildings, and in campgrounds, and look for Golden eagles soaring over Tioga Road.

PARK ESSENTIALS

ADMISSION FEES AND PERMITS

The admission fee, valid for seven days, is $20 per vehicle or $10 per individual.

If you plan to camp in the backcountry, you must have a wilderness permit. Availability of permits, which are free, depends upon trailhead quotas. It's best to make a reservation, especially if you will be visiting May through September. You can reserve two days to 24 weeks in advance by phone, mail, or fax (✉ *P.O. Box 545, Yosemite, CA 95389* ☎ *209/372–0740* 🖷 *209/372–0739*); a $5 per person processing fee is charged if and when your reservations are confirmed. Requests must include your name, address, daytime phone, the number of people in your party, trip date, alternative dates, starting and ending trailheads, and a brief itinerary. Without a reservation, you may still get a free permit on a first-come, first-served basis at wilderness permit offices at Big Oak Flat, Hetch Hetchy, Tuolumne, Wawona, the Wilderness Center (in Yosemite Village), and Yosemite Valley in summer; fall through spring, visit the Valley Visitor Center.

ADMISSION HOURS

The park is open 24/7 year-round. All entrances are open at all hours, except for Hetch Hetchy Entrance, which is open roughly dawn to dusk. Yosemite is in the Pacific time zone.

PARK CONTACT INFORMATION

Yosemite National Park *Information Office, P.O. Box 577, Yosemite National Park, CA 95389 ☎ 209/372–0200 www.nps.gov/yose.*

SAFETY

In an emergency, call 911. You can also call the Yosemite Medical Clinic in Yosemite Village at 209/372–4637. The clinic provides 24-hour emergency care.

EXPLORING YOSEMITE NATIONAL PARK

HISTORIC SITES

★ **Ahwahnee Hotel.** Gilbert Stanley Underwood, the architect for Grand Canyon Lodge on the North Rim in Arizona, also designed the Ahwahnee. Opened in 1927, it is generally considered to be his best work. The Great Lounge, 77 feet long with magnificent 24-foot-high ceilings and all manner of Indian artwork on display, is the most special interior space in Yosemite. You can stay here (for $459 or more a night), or simply explore the first-floor shops and perhaps have breakfast or lunch in the lovely Dining Room. ✉ *Ahwahnee Rd., about ¾ mi east of Yosemite Valley Visitor Center, Yosemite Village* ☎ *209/372–1489.*

Ahwahneechee Village. This solemn smattering of re-created structures, accessed by a short loop trail, is an imagination of what Indian life might have resembled here in the 1870s. One interpretive sign points out that Miwok referred to the 19th century newcomers as "Yohemite" or "Yohometuk," which have been translated as "some of them are killers." ✉ *Northside Dr., Yosemite Village* *Free* *Daily sunrise–sunset.*

Pioneer Yosemite History Center. Some of Yosemite's first structures—those not occupied by American Indians, that is—were relocated from various parts of the park and placed here in the 1950s and 1960s. You can spend a pleasurable and informative half-hour walking about them and reading the signs, perhaps springing for a self-guided-tour pamphlet (50¢) to further enhance the history lesson. Wednesdays through Sundays in the summer, costumed docents conduct free blacksmithing and "wet-plate" photography demonstrations, and for a small fee you can take a stagecoach ride. ✉ *Rte. 41, Wawona* ☎ *209/375–9531 or 209/379–2646* *Free* *Building interiors are open mid-June–Labor Day, Daily 9–5.*

10

★ **Wawona Hotel.** One can imagine an older Mark Twain relaxing in a rocking chair on one of the broad verandas of Yosemite's first lodge, a whitewashed series of two-story buildings from the Victorian era. Across the road is a somewhat odd sight: Yosemite's only golf course, one of the few links in the world that does not employ fertilizers or other chemicals. The Wawona is an excellent place to stay or to stop for lunch, but be aware that the hotel is closed in January. ✉ *Rte. 41, Wawona* ☎ *209/375–1425.*

SCENIC STOPS

★ **El Capitan.** Rising 3,593 feet—more than 350 stories—above the Valley, El Capitan is the largest exposed-granite monolith in the world. Since 1958, people have been climbing its entire face, including the famous "nose." You can spot adventurers with your binoculars by scanning the smooth and nearly vertical cliff for specks of color. ✉ *Off Northside Dr., about 4 mi west of the Valley Visitor Center.*

Fodor's Choice ★ **Glacier Point.** If you lack the time, desire, or stamina to hike more than 3,200 feet up to Glacier Point from the Yosemite Valley floor, you can drive here—or take a bus from the Valley—for a bird's-eye view. You are likely to encounter a lot of day-trippers on the short, paved trail that leads from the parking lot to the main overlook. Take a moment to veer off a few yards to the Geology Hut, which succinctly explains and illustrates how the Valley looked like 10 million, 3 million, and 20,000 years ago. For details about the summer-only buses, call ☎ *209/372–1240.* ✉ *Glacier Point Rd., 16 mi northeast of Rte. 41.*

★ **Half Dome.** Visitors' eyes are continually drawn to this remarkable granite formation that tops out at more than 4,700 feet above the Valley floor. Despite its name, the dome is actually about three-quarters "intact." You can hike to the top of Half Dome on an 8.5-mi (one-way) trail whose last 400 feet must be ascended while holding onto a steel cable. Park officials now require a permit to climb above the sub-dome mid-May to mid-October ($1.50). Permits must be scheduled in advance. Call the main line for reservations (☎ *209/372–0200*). To see Half Dome reflected in the Merced River, view it from Sentinel Bridge just before sundown. But stay for sunset, when the setting sun casts a brilliant orange light onto Half Dome, a stunning sight.

Hetch Hetchy Reservoir. When Congress green-lighted the O'Shaughnessy Dam in 1913, pragmatism triumphed over aestheticism. Some 2.4 million residents of the San Francisco Bay Area continue to get their water from this 117-billion-gallon reservoir, although spirited efforts are being made to restore the Hetch Hetchy Valley to its former, pristine glory. Eight miles long, the reservoir is Yosemite's largest body of water, and one that can be seen up close from several trails. ✉ *Hetch Hetchy Rd., about 15 mi north of the Big Oak Flat entrance station.*

★ **Mariposa Grove of Big Trees.** Of Yosemite National Parks' three sequoia groves—the others being Merced and Tuolumne, both near Crane Flat well to the north—Mariposa is by far the largest and easiest to walk around. Grizzly Giant, whose base measures 96 feet around, has been estimated to be the world's 25th largest tree by volume. Perhaps more astoundingly, it's about 2,700 years old. On up the hill, you'll find

Yosemite's Valley Floor
KEY
Ranger Station
Campground
Picnic Area
Restaurant
Lodge
Trailhead
Restrooms
Scenic Viewpoint
Walking/Hiking Trails
John Muir Trail
Bicycle Path
Valley Floor
Half Dome 8,836 ft
Yosemite Falls
YOSEMITE VILLAGE
Yosemite Museum
Ansel Adams Gallery
P.O.
Medical Clinic
Village Store
Auto Repair
The Ahwahnee Hotel
Valley Visitor Center
Yosemite Lodge
Road open only to bicycles and Shuttlebuses
Merced River
bicycle path
Chapel
LeConte Memorial Lodge
Royal Arch Cascade
Royal Arches
Washington Column
Mirror Lake
North Pines
Lower Pines
Upper Pines
Clarks Bridge
Curry Village Store
CURRY VILLAGE
Happy Isles Bridge
Nature Center at Happy Isles
Union Point
Moran Point
Staircase Falls
Four Mile Trail
Glacier Point 7,214 ft
Sentinel Rock
Sentinel Fall
Glacier Point Road
Pohono Trail
Panorama Trail
Illilouette Gorge
Grizzly Peak
Sierra Point
John Muir Trail
Vernal Falls
Emerald Pools
Mist Trail
Footbridge
Clark Point
Liberty Cap
Nevada Falls
Panorama Cliff
0
1/2 mi
1/2 km

"This is us taking a break before conquering the top of Lembert Dome, while enjoying the beautiful view over Yosemite's high country." —photo by Rebalyn, Fodors.com member

many more sequoias, a small museum, and fewer people. Summer weekends are especially crowded here. Consider taking the free shuttle from Wawona. ✉ *Rte. 41, 2 mi north of the South Entrance station.*

★ **Tuolumne Meadows.** The largest subalpine meadow in the Sierra (at 8,600 feet) is a popular way station for backpack trips along the Pacific Crest and John Muir trails. The setting is not as dramatic as Yosemite Valley, 56 mi away, but the almost perfectly flat basin, about 2½ mi long, is intriguing, and in July it's resplendent with wildflowers. The most popular day hike is up Lembert Dome, atop which you'll have breathtaking views of the basin below. Keep in mind that Tioga Road rarely opens sooner than June and usually closes by mid-October. ✉ *Tioga Rd. (Rte. 120), about 8 mi west of the Tioga Pass entrance station.*

WATERFALLS

Yosemite's waterfalls are at their most spectacular in May and June. When the snow starts to melt (usually peaking in May), almost every rocky lip or narrow gorge becomes a spillway for streaming snowmelt churning down to meet the Merced River. By summer's end, some falls, including the mighty Yosemite Falls, dry up. They begin flowing again in late fall, and in winter they may be hung dramatically with ice. Even in drier months, the waterfalls can be breathtaking. If you choose to hike any of the trails to or up the falls, be sure to wear shoes with good, no-slip soles; the rocks can be extremely slick. Stay on trails at all times.

■ TIP→ Visit the park during a full moon, and you can stroll in the evening without a flashlight and still make out the ribbons of falling water, as well as silhouettes of the giant granite monoliths.

Bridalveil Fall. The filmy waterfall of 620 feet is often diverted as much as 20 feet one way or the other by the breeze. It is the first marvelous view of Yosemite Valley you will see if you come in via Route 41. ✉ *Yosemite Valley, access from parking area off Wawona Rd.*

Nevada Fall. Climb Mist Trail from Happy Isles for an up-close view of this 594-foot cascading beauty, the first major fall as the Merced River plunges out of the high country toward the eastern end of Yosemite Valley. If you don't want to hike, you can see it—distantly—from Glacier Point. ✉ *Yosemite Valley, access via Mist Trail from Nature Center at Happy Isles.*

Ribbon Fall. At 1,612 feet, this is the highest single fall in North America. It's also the first valley waterfall to dry up in summer; the rainwater and melted snow that create the slender fall evaporate quickly at this height. Look just west of El Capitan from the Valley floor for the best view of the fall from the base of Bridalveil Fall. ✉ *Yosemite Valley, west of El Capitan Meadow.*

Vernal Fall. Fern-covered black rocks frame this 317-foot fall, and rainbows play in the spray at its base. You can get a distance view from Glacier Point, or hike to see it close up. ✉ *Yosemite Valley, access via Mist Trail from Nature Center at Happy Isles.*

Fodor's Choice ★ **Yosemite Falls.** Actually three falls, they together constitute the highest waterfall in North America and the fifth-highest in the world. The water from the top descends a total of 2,425 feet, and when the falls run hard, you can hear them thunder all across the Valley. When they dry up—usually in late summer—the Valley seems naked without the wavering tower of spray. ■ **TIP→ If you hike the partially paved, mile-long loop trail to the base of the Lower Falls during the peak water flow in May, expect to get soaked.** You can get a view of the falls from the lawn of Yosemite Chapel, off Southside Drive. ✉ *Yosemite Valley, access from Yosemite Lodge or trail parking area.*

VISITOR CENTERS

Le Conte Memorial Lodge. This small but striking National Historic Landmark, with its granite walls and steeply pitched shingle roof, is Yosemite's first permanent public information center. Step inside to see the cathedral-like interior, which contains a library and environmental exhibits. To find out about evening programs, check the kiosk out front, look in the park's newspaper, or visit 🌐 *www.sierraclub.org.* ✉ *Southside Dr., about ½ mi west of Curry Village* ⏲ *Memorial Day–Labor Day, Wed.–Sun. 10–4.*

Valley Visitor Center. At this center—which was overhauled in 2007—you can learn how Yosemite Valley was formed and about its vegetation, animals, and human inhabitants. Don't leave without watching the superb *Spirit of Yosemite*, a 23-minute introductory film that runs every half-hour in the theater behind the visitor center. ✉ *Yosemite Village* ☎ *209/372–0200* 🌐 *www.nps.gov/yose* ⏲ *Late May–early Sept., daily 9–7; early Sept.–late May, daily 9–5.*

SPORTS AND THE OUTDOORS

BICYCLING

There may be no more enjoyable way to see Yosemite Valley than to ride a bike beneath its lofty granite monoliths. The eastern valley has 12 mi of paved, flat bicycle paths across meadows and through woods, with bike racks at convenient stopping points. For a greater challenge, you can ride on 196 mi of paved park roads—but bicycles are not allowed on hiking trails or in the backcountry. Kids under 18 must wear a helmet.

You can get **Yosemite bike rentals** (✉ *Yosemite Lodge or Curry Village* ☎ *209/372–1208* 🌐 *www.yosemitepark.com* 🎟 *$9.50/hour, $25.50/day* ⏲ *Apr.–Oct.*) from either Yosemite Lodge or Curry Village bike stands. Bikes with child trailers, baby-jogger strollers, and wheelchairs are available.

BIRD-WATCHING

Nearly 250 bird species have been spotted in the park, including the sage sparrow, pygmy owl, blue grouse, and mountain bluebird. Park rangers lead free bird-watching walks in Yosemite Valley one day each week in summer; check at a visitor center or information station for times and locations. Binoculars are sometimes available for loan.

The Yosemite Association sponsors one- to four-day **birding seminars** (☎ *209/379–2321* 🌐 *www.yosemite.org* 🎟 *$82–$254* ⏲ *Apr.–Aug.*) for beginner and intermediate birders.

HIKING

The staff at the **Wilderness Center** (☎ *209/372–0655*), in Yosemite Village, provides free wilderness permits, which are required for overnight camping (advance reservations are available for $5 and are highly recommended for popular trailheads from May through September and on weekends). The staff here also provide maps and advice to hikers heading into the backcountry. From April through November, **Yosemite Mountaineering School and Guide Service** (✉ *Yosemite Mountain Shop, Curry Village* ☎ *209/372–8344*) leads two-hour to full-day treks.

EASY

★ **Yosemite Falls Trail.** This is the highest waterfall in North America. The upper fall (1,430 feet), the middle cascades (675 feet), and the lower fall (320 feet) combine for a total of 2,425 feet and, when viewed from the valley, appear as a single waterfall. The ¼-mi trail leads from the parking lot to the base of the falls. Upper Yosemite Fall Trail, a strenuous 3½-mi climb rising 2,700 feet, takes you above the top of the falls. ✉ *Trailhead off Camp 4, north of Northside Dr.*

MODERATE

★ **Mist Trail.** More visitors take this trail (or portions of it) than any other in the park other than Lower Yosemite Falls. The trek up to and back from Vernal Fall is 3 mi. Add another 4 mi total by continuing up to 594-foot Nevada Fall; the trail becomes quite steep and slippery in its final stages. The elevation gain to Vernal Fall is 1,000 feet, and to Nevada Fall an additional 1,000 feet. Merced River tumbles down both falls on its way to a tranquil flow through the Valley. ✉ *Trailhead at Happy Isles.*

DID YOU KNOW?

Waterfalls in Yosemite Valley are especially famous for their heart-stopping drops over sheer granite cliffs. At peak times, hydrologists estimate that almost 135,000 gallons of water tumble down Yosemite Falls' triple cascade every minute.

★ **Panorama Trail.** Few hikes come with the visual punch that this 8½-mi trail provides. The star attraction is Half Dome, visible from many intriguing angles, but you also see three waterfalls up close and walk through a manzanita grove. Before you begin, look down on Yosemite Valley from Glacier Point, a special experience in itself. ✉ *Trailhead at Glacier Point.*

DIFFICULT

Fodor's Choice ★ **John Muir Trail to Half Dome.** Ardent and courageous trekkers can continue on from the top of Nevada Fall, off Mist Trail, to the top of Half Dome. Some hikers attempt this entire 10- to 12-hour, 16¾-mi round-trip trek from Happy Isles in one day; if you're planning to do this, remember that the 4,800-foot elevation gain and the 8,842-foot altitude will cause shortness of breath. Another option is to hike to a campground in Little Yosemite Valley near the top of Nevada Fall the first day, then climb to the top of Half Dome and hike out the next day; it's highly recommended that you get your wilderness permit reservations at least a month in advance. Be sure to wear hiking boots and bring gloves. The last pitch up the back of Half Dome is very steep—the only way to climb this sheer rock face is to pull yourself up using the steel cable handrails, which are in place only from late spring to early fall. Those who brave the ascent will be rewarded with an unbeatable view of Yosemite Valley below and the high country beyond. ✉ *Trailhead at Happy Isles.*

HORSEBACK RIDING

Reservations for guided trail rides must be made in advance at the hotel tour desks or by phone. For overnight saddle trips, which use mules, go online to 🌐 *www.yosemitepark.com* and fill out a lottery application for the following year. Scenic trail rides range from two hours to a full day; six-day High Sierra saddle trips are also available.

Tuolumne Meadows Stables (✉ *Off Tioga Rd., 2 mi east of Tuolumne Meadows Visitor Center* ☎ *209/372–8427* 🌐 *www.yosemitepark.com*) runs two-, four-, and eight-hour trips—which cost $53, $69, and $96, respectively—and High Sierra four- to six-day camping treks on mules, beginning at $625. Reservations are essential. **Wawona Stables** (✉ *Rte. 41, Wawona* ☎ *209/375–6502*) has two- and five-hour rides, starting at $53. Reservations are essential. You can tour the valley and the start of the high country on two-hour and four-hour rides at **Yosemite Valley Stables** (✉ *At entrance to North Pines Campground, 100 yards northeast of Curry Village* ☎ *209/372–8348* 🌐 *www.yosemitepark.com*). Reservations are required for the $60 and $80 trips.

RAFTING

Rafting is permitted only on designated areas of the Middle and South Forks of the Merced River. Check with the Valley Visitor Center for closures and other restrictions.

The per-person rental fee at **Curry Village raft stand** (✉ *South side of Southside Dr., Curry Village* ☎ *209/372–8319* 🌐 *www.yosemitepark.com* 🎫 *$20.50* ⏲ *Late May–July*) covers the four- to six-person raft, two paddles, and life jackets, plus a shuttle to the launch point on Sentinel Beach.

DID YOU KNOW?

Yosemite's granite formations provide sturdy ground for climbers of all skill levels. The sheer granite monolith El Capitan—simply "El Cap" to climbers—is the most famous, climbed by even Captain Kirk (if you believe the opening scene of *Star Trek V: The Final Frontier*), but climbers tackle rocks up in the mountains, too.

ROCK CLIMBING

Fodor's Choice ★ The one-day basic lesson at **Yosemite Mountaineering School and Guide Service** (✉ *Yosemite Mountain Shop, Curry Village* ☎ *209/372–8344* 🌐 *www.yosemitepark.com* 🎟 *$117–$300* ⏲ *Apr.–Nov.*) includes some bouldering and rappelling, and three or four 60-foot climbs. Climbers must be at least 10 (kids under 12 must be accompanied by a parent or guardian) and in reasonably good physical condition. Intermediate and advanced classes include instruction in belays, self-rescue, summer snow climbing, and free climbing.

ICE-SKATING

Curry Village ice-skating rink. Winter visitors have skated at this outdoor rink for decades, and there's no mystery why: it's a kick to glide across the ice while soaking up views of Half Dome and Glacier Point. ✉ *South side of Southside Dr., Curry Village* ☎ *209/372–8319* 🎟 *$8 per 2 hrs, $3 skate rental* ⏲ *Mid-Nov.–mid-Mar. afternoons and evenings daily, morning sessions weekends; 12–2:30 pm on weekends as well (hrs vary).*

SKIING AND SNOWSHOEING

Badger Pass Ski Area. California's first ski resort has five lifts and 10 downhill runs, as well as 90 mi of groomed cross-country trails. Free shuttle buses from Yosemite Valley operate during ski season (December through early April, weather permitting). Lift tickets are $42, downhill equipment rents for $31, and snowboard rental with boots is $35. The gentle slopes of Badger Pass make

Yosemite Ski School (☎ *209/372–8430*) an ideal spot for children and beginners to learn downhill skiing or snowboarding for as little as $35 for a group lesson. The highlight of Yosemite's cross-country skiing center is a 21-mi loop from Badger Pass to Glacier Point. You can rent cross-country skis for $23.00 per day at the

Cross-Country Ski School (☎ *209/372–8444*), which also rents snowshoes ($22.00 per day), telemarking equipment ($29), and skate-skis ($24).

Yosemite Mountaineering School (✉ *Badger Pass Ski Area* ☎ *209/372–8344* 🌐 *www.yosemitemountaineering.com*) conducts snowshoeing, cross-country skiing, telemarking, and skate-skiing classes starting at $30. ✉ *Badger Pass Rd., off Glacier Point Rd., 18 mi from Yosemite Valley* ☎ *209/372–8434.*

EDUCATIONAL PROGRAMS

CLASSES AND SEMINARS

Art Classes. Professional artists conduct workshops in watercolor, etching, drawing, and other mediums. Bring your own materials or purchase the basics at the Art Activity Center, next to the Village Store. Call to verify scheduling. ✉ *Art Activity Center, Yosemite Village* ☎ *209/372–1442* 🌐 *www.yosemitepark.com* 🎟 *Free* ⏲ *April.–early Oct., Tues.–Sat., 10 am–2 pm.*

Yosemite Outdoor Adventures. Naturalists, scientists, and park rangers lead multi-hour to multiday educational outings on topics from woodpeckers to fire management to pastel painting. Most sessions take place spring through fall, but a few focus on winter phenomena. ✉ *Various locations* ☎ *209/379–2321* 🌐 *www.yosemite.org* 🎫 *$82–$465.*

RANGER PROGRAMS

Junior Ranger Program. Children ages 3 to 13 can participate in the informal, self-guided Little Cub and Junior Ranger programs. A park activity handbook ($8) is available at the Valley Visitor Center or the Nature Center at Happy Isles; once your child has completed the book, a ranger will present him or her with a certificate and a badge. ✉ *Valley Visitor Center or the Nature Center at Happy Isles* ☎ *209/372–0299.*

Ranger-Led Programs. Rangers lead walks and hikes and give informative and entertaining talks on a range of topics at different locations several times a day from spring through fall. The schedule is reduced in winter, but most days you can usually find a ranger program somewhere in the park. In the evenings at Yosemite Lodge and Curry Village, lectures by rangers, slide shows, and documentary films present unique perspectives on Yosemite. On summer weekends, Camp Curry and Tuolumne Meadows Campground host sing-along campfire programs. There's usually at least one ranger-led activity each night in the Valley; schedules and locations are posted on bulletin boards throughout the park and published in the *Yosemite Guide* you receive when you enter the park.

TOURS

★ **Ansel Adams Photo Walks.** Photography enthusiasts shouldn't miss these two-hour guided camera walks that are offered four mornings each week—Monday; Tuesday, Thursday, and Saturday—by professional photographers. Some walks are hosted by the Ansel Adams Gallery, others by Delaware North; meeting points vary. All are free, but participation is limited to 15 people. Reservations are essential. To reserve a spot, call up to 3 days in advance or visit the gallery. ☎ *209/372–4413 or 800/568–7398* 🌐 *www.anseladams.com* 🎫 *Free.*

DNC Parks and Resorts. The main concessionaire at Yosemite National Park, this organization operates several guided tours and programs throughout the park, including the **Big Trees Tram Tour** of the Mariposa Grove of Big Trees, the **Glacier Point Tour,** the **Grand Tour** (both Mariposa Grove and Glacier Point), the **Moonlight Tour** of Yosemite Valley, the **Tuolumne Meadows Tour,** and the **Valley Floor Tour.** ☎ *209/372–1240* 🌐 *www.yosemitepark.com* 🎫 *shuttle buses, free; tours $26–$83, check Web site exact prices.*

10

WHERE TO EAT

RESTAURANTS

$$$$ CONTINENTAL ✕ **Ahwahnee Hotel Dining Room.** Rave reviews about the dining room's appearance are fully justified—it features floor-to-ceiling windows, a 34-foot-high ceiling with interlaced sugar-pine beams, and massive chandeliers. Although many continue to applaud the food, others have reported that they sense a recent dip in the quality both in the service and what is being served. Diners must spend a lot of money here, so perhaps that inflates the expectations and amplifies the disappointments. In

CLOSE UP

Camping in Yosemite

The 464 campsites within Yosemite Valley are the park's most tightly spaced and, along with the 304-site campground at Tuolumne Meadows, the most difficult to secure on anything approaching short notice.

The park's backcountry and the surrounding wilderness have some unforgettable campsites that can be reached only via long and often difficult hikes or horseback rides. Delaware North operates five High Sierra Camps with comfortable, furnished tent cabins in the remote reaches of Yosemite; rates include breakfast and dinner service. The park concessionaire books the extremely popular backcountry camps by lottery; applications are due by late November for the following summer season. Phone ☎ *801/559–4909* for more information, or check for current availability by navigating from ⊕ *www.yosemitepark.com* to the High Sierra Camps pages.

To camp in a High Sierra campground you must obtain a wilderness permit. Make reservations up to 24 weeks in advance first by visiting the park's Web site (⊕ *www.nps.gov/yose/planyourvisit/backpacking.htm*) and checking availability. For a $5 nonrefundable fee, you can make reservations by phone (☎ *209/372–0740*) or by mail (✉ *P.O. Box 545, Yosemite, CA 95389*); make checks payable to "Yosemite Association."

Reservations are required at most of Yosemite's campgrounds, especially in summer. You can reserve a site up to five months in advance; bookings made more than 21 days in advance require prepayment. Unless otherwise noted, book your site through the central **National Park Service Reservations Office** (✉ *P.O. Box 1600, Cumberland, MD 21502* ☎ *800/436–7275* ⊕ *www.recreation.gov* ⏲ *Daily 7–7.*

Delaware North Companies Parks and Resorts (✉ *6771 N. Palm Ave., Fresno, CA 93704* ☎ *801/559–5000* ⊕ *www.yosemitepark.com*), which handles most in-park reservations, takes reservations beginning one year plus one day in advance of your proposed stay. Or, you can roll the dice by showing up at the front desk and asking if there have been any cancellations.

any event, the Sunday brunch ($49) is consistently praised. Reservations are always advised, and for dinner, the attire is "resort casual." ✉ *Ahwahnee Hotel, Ahwahnee Rd., about ¾ mi east of Yosemite Valley Visitor Center, Yosemite Village* ☎ *209/372–1489* ✍ *Reservations essential.*

$$$ AMERICAN ★ ✕ **Mountain Room.** Though good, the food becomes secondary when you see Yosemite Falls through this dining room's wall of windows—almost every table has a view. The chef makes a point of using locally sourced, organic ingredients, so you can be assured of fresh greens and veggies here. The Mountain Room Lounge, a few steps away in the Yosemite Lodge complex, has a broad bar with about 10 beers on tap. ✉ *Yosemite Lodge, Northside Dr. about ¾ mi west of the visitor center, Yosemite Village* ☎ *209/372–1281* ⏲ *No lunch.*

$$ AMERICAN ✕ **Tuolumne Meadows Lodge.** At the back of a small building that contains the lodge's front desk and small gift shop, this restaurant serves hearty American fare at breakfast and dinner. Let the front desk know

in advance if you have any dietary restrictions, and the cooks will not let you down. ✉ *Tioga Rd. (Rte. 120)* ☎ *209/372–8413* ✍ *Reservations essential* ⊙ *Closed late Sept.–Memorial Day. No lunch.*

$$$$ AMERICAN ★ ✕ **Wawona Hotel Dining Room.** Watch deer graze on the meadow while you dine in the romantic, candlelit dining room of the whitewashed Wawona Hotel, which dates from the late 1800s. The American-style cuisine favors fresh California ingredients and flavors; trout is a menu staple. ✉ *Wawona Hotel, Rte. 41, Wawona* ☎ *209/375–1425* ✍ *Reservations essential* ⊙ *Closed Jan.–mid-March.*

PICNIC AREAS

Considering how large the park is and how many visitors come here—some 3.5 million people every year, most of them just for the day—it is somewhat surprising that Yosemite has so few formal picnic areas, though in many places you can find a smooth rock to sit on and enjoy breathtaking views along with your lunch. The convenience stores all sell picnic supplies, and prepackaged sandwiches and salads are widely available. Those options can come in especially handy during the middle of day, when you might not want to spend precious daylight hours in such a spectacular setting sitting in a restaurant for a formal meal. None of these spots have drinking water available; most have some type of toilet. Good spots to hit include Cathedral Beach, Church Bowl, Swinging Bridge, and Yellow Pine.

WHERE TO STAY

■ **TIP→ Reserve your room or cabin in Yosemite as far in advance as possible.** You can make a reservation up to a year before your arrival (within minutes after the reservation office makes a date available, the Ahwahnee, Yosemite Lodge, and Wawona Hotel often sell out their weekends, holiday periods, and all days between May and September).

For expanded hotel reviews, visit Fodors.com.

$$$$ Fodor's Choice ★ **The Ahwahnee.** A National Historic Landmark, this hotel is constructed primarily of concrete and sugar-pine logs. **Pros:** best lodge in Yosemite (if not all of California); concierge. **Cons:** expensive; some reports that service has slipped in recent years. ✉ *1 Ahwahnee Rd., about ¾ mi east of Yosemite Valley Visitor Center, Yosemite Village* ☎ *209/372–1407 or 801/559–5000* ⊕ *www.yosemitepark.com* *99 lodge rooms, 4 suites, 24 cottage rooms* *In-room: a/c, Wi-Fi. In-hotel: restaurant, room service, bar, pool.*

10

$$ **Curry Village.** Opened in 1899 as a place where travelers could enjoy the beauty of Yosemite for a modest price, Curry Village has plain accommodations: standard motel rooms, cabins, and tent cabins, which have rough wood frames, canvas walls, and roofs. **Pros:** comparatively economical; family-friendly atmosphere. **Cons:** can be crowded; sometimes a bit noisy. ✉ *South side of Southside Dr., Yosemite Valley* ☎ *801/559–5000* ⊕ *www.yosemitepark.com* *18 rooms, 527 cabins* *In-room: no a/c, no phone, no TV. In-hotel: restaurants, bar, pool.*

$$$ **Wawona Hotel.** This 1879 National Historic Landmark sits at Yosemite's southern end, a 15-minute drive (or free shuttle bus ride) from the Mariposa Grove of Big Trees. **Pros:** lovely; peaceful atmosphere; close

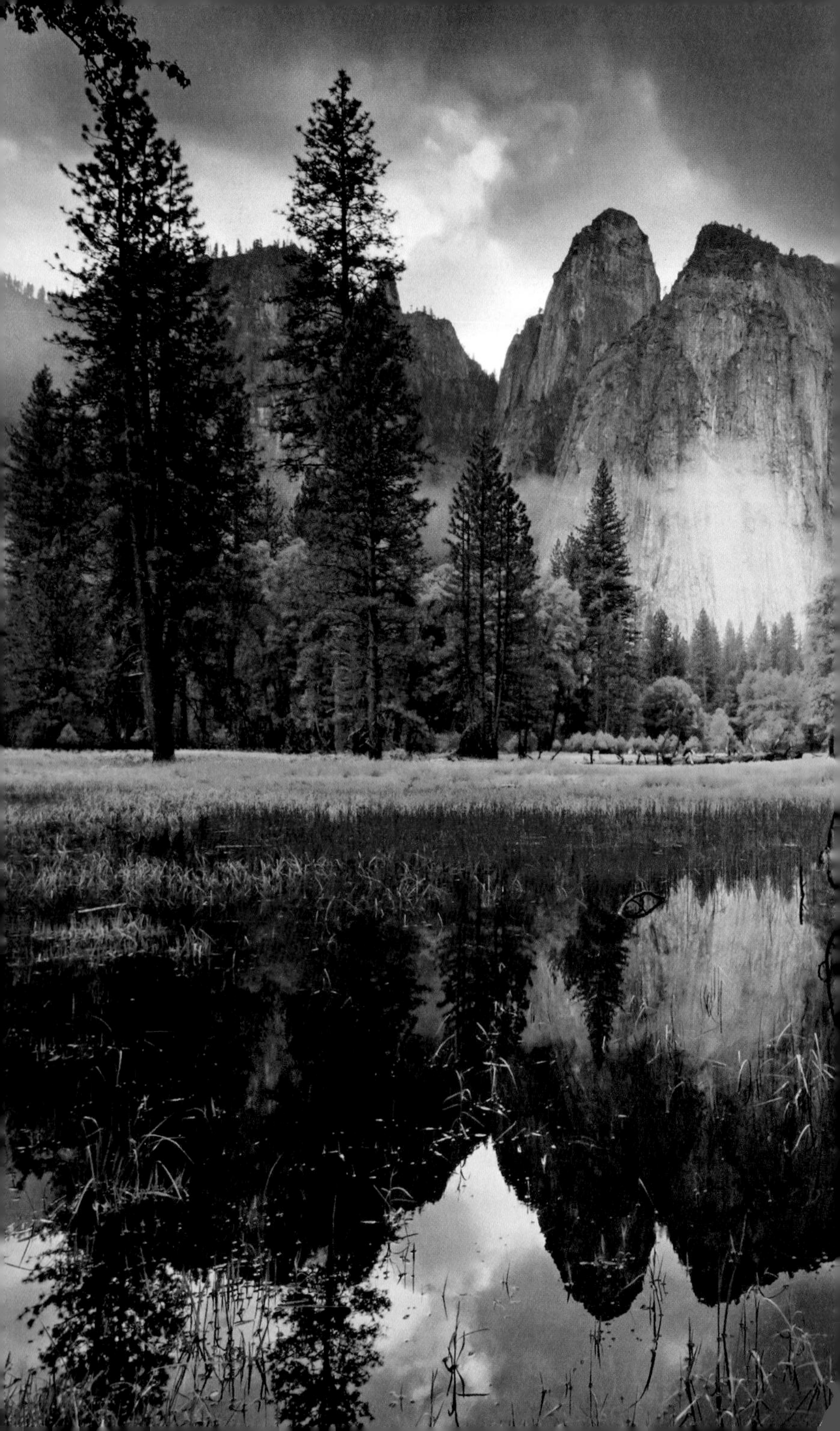

DID YOU KNOW?

In the Sierra's mixed-conifer forests, telling the many types of pines apart can be difficult if you don't know the trick: sizing up the cones and examining the branches to count how many needles are in discrete clusters. If the needles are paired, you're likely looking at a lodgepole pine. If the needles are long and come in threes, chances are you've come upon a ponderosa pine.

to Mariposa Grove. **Cons:** few modern in-room amenities; half of the rooms have no baths. ✉ *Hwy. 41, Wawona* ☎ *801/559–5000* 🌐 *www.yosemitepark.com* *104 rooms, 50 with bath* *In-room: no a/c, no phone, no TV. In-hotel: restaurant, bar, golf course, tennis court, pool* ⏲ *Closed Jan. 2–Apr. 6; Nov 27–Dec. 14; call ahead to check for seasonal closures.*

$ **White Wolf Lodge.** Set in a subalpine meadow, White Wolf offers rustic accommodations in tent cabins. **Pros:** quiet; convenient for hikers; good restaurant. **Cons:** far from the Valley; not much to do here other than hiking. ✉ *Off Tioga Rd. (Rte. 120), 25 mi west of Tuolumne Meadows and 15 mi east of Crane Flat 95389* ☎ *801/559–5000* *24 tent cabins, 4 cabins* *In-room: no a/c, no phone, no TV. In-hotel: restaurant* ⏲ *Closed mid-Sept.–early June.*

$$$ **Yosemite Lodge at the Falls.** This lodge near Yosemite Falls, which dates from 1915, looks like a 1960s motel-resort complex, with numerous brown, two-story buildings tucked beneath the trees, surrounded by large parking lots. **Pros:** centrally located; dependably clean rooms; lots of tours leave from out front. **Cons:** can feel impersonal; appearance is little dated. ✉ *Northside Dr. about ¾ mi west of the visitor center, Yosemite Village95389* ☎ *DNC reservations line: 801/559–5000; direct line: 209/372–1274* 🌐 *www.yosemitepark.com* *245 rooms* *In-room: no a/c, Wi-Fi. In-hotel: restaurant, bar, pool.*

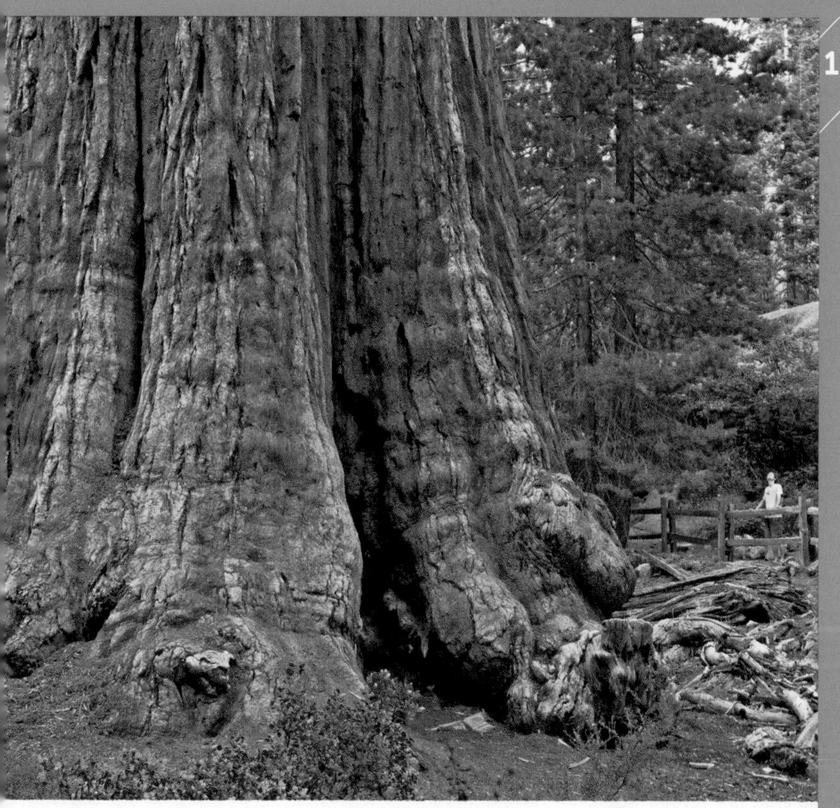

Sequoia and Kings Canyon National Parks

WORD OF MOUTH

"At the south end of Sequoia, Giant Forest is the best area for viewing the Big trees. . . . At the edge of Giant Forest, there are amazing views down into the valley . . . The best view is from the top of Moro Rock."

—Sequoia370

WELCOME TO SEQUOIA AND KINGS CANYON NATIONAL PARKS

TOP REASONS TO GO

★ **Gentle giants:** You'll feel small—in a good way—walking among some of the world's largest living things in Sequoia's Giant Forest and Kings Canyon's Grant Grove.

★ **Because it's there:** You can't even glimpse it from the main part of Sequoia, but the sight of majestic Mount Whitney is worth the trek to the eastern face of the High Sierra.

★ **Underground exploration:** Far older even than the giant sequoias, the gleaming limestone formations in Crystal Cave will draw you along dark, marble passages.

★ **A grander-than–Grand Canyon:** Drive the twisting Kings Canyon Scenic Byway down into the jagged, granite Kings River Canyon, deeper in parts than the Grand Canyon.

★ **Regal solitude:** To spend a day or two hiking in a subalpine world of your own, pick one of the 11 trailheads at Mineral King.

1 Giant Forest–Lodgepole Village. The most heavily visited area of Sequoia lies at the base of the "thumb" portion of Kings Canyon National Park and contains major sights such as Giant Forest, General Sherman Tree, Crystal Cave, and Moro Rock.

2 Grant Grove Village–Redwood Canyon. The "thumb" of Kings Canyon National Park is its busiest section, where Grant Grove, General Grant Tree, Panoramic Point, and Big Stump are the main attractions.

3 Cedar Grove. Most visitors to the huge, high-country portion of Kings Canyon National Park don't go farther than Roads End, a few miles east of Cedar Grove on the canyon floor. Here, the river runs through Zumwalt Meadow, surrounded by magnificent granite formations.

4 Mineral King. In the southeast section of Sequoia, the highest road-accessible part of the park is a good place to hike, camp, and soak up the unspoiled grandeur of the Sierra Nevada.

5 Mount Whitney. The highest peak in the Lower 48 stands on the eastern edge of Sequoia; to get there from Giant Forest you must either backpack eight days through the mountains or drive nearly 400 mi around the park to its other side.

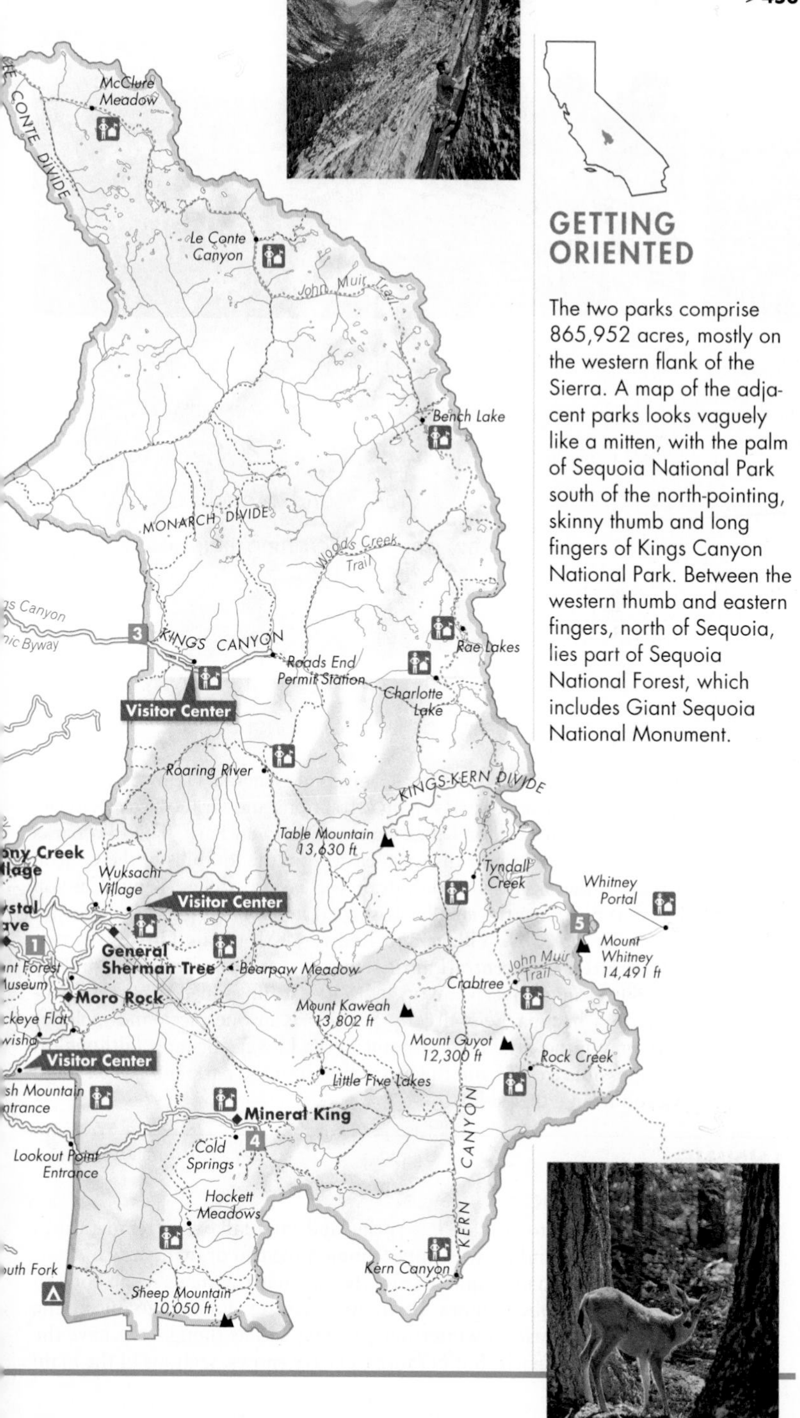

GETTING ORIENTED

The two parks comprise 865,952 acres, mostly on the western flank of the Sierra. A map of the adjacent parks looks vaguely like a mitten, with the palm of Sequoia National Park south of the north-pointing, skinny thumb and long fingers of Kings Canyon National Park. Between the western thumb and eastern fingers, north of Sequoia, lies part of Sequoia National Forest, which includes Giant Sequoia National Monument.

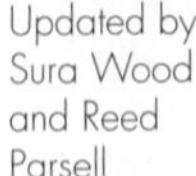

Updated by Sura Wood and Reed Parsell

Although *Sequoiadendron giganteum* is the formal name for the redwoods that grow here, everyone outside the classroom calls them sequoias, big trees, or Sierra redwoods. Their monstrously thick trunks and branches, remarkably shallow root systems, and neck-craning heights are almost impossible to believe, as is the fact they can live for more than 2,500 years. Many of these towering marvels are in the Giant Forest stretch of Generals Highway, which connects Sequoia and Kings Canyon national parks.

Next to or a few miles off the 43-mi road Generals Highway are most of Sequoia National Park's main attractions and Grant Grove Village, the orientation hub for Kings Canyon National Park. The two parks share a boundary that runs west–east, from the foothills of the Central Valley to the Sierra Nevada's dramatic eastern ridges. Kings Canyon has two portions: the smaller is shaped like a bent finger and encompasses Grant Grove Village and Redwood Mountain Grove (the two parks' largest concentration of sequoias), and the larger is home to stunning Kings River Canyon, whose vast, unspoiled peaks and valleys are a backpacker's dream. Sequoia is in one piece and includes Mount Whitney, the highest point in the Lower 48 states (although it is impossible to see from the western part of the park and is a chore to ascend from either side).

PLANNING

WHEN TO GO

The best times to visit are late spring and early fall, when temperatures are moderate and crowds thin. Summertime can draw hoards of tourists to see the giant sequoias, and the few, narrow roads mean congestion at peak holiday times. If you must visit in summer, go during the week. By contrast, in wintertime you may feel as though you have the parks all to yourself. But because of heavy snows, sections of the main park roads can be closed without warning, and low-hanging clouds can move in and obscure mountains and valleys for days. Check road and weather conditions before venturing out mid-November to late April.

Temperatures in the chart below are for the mid-level elevations, generally between 4,000 and 7,000 feet.

GETTING HERE AND AROUND

Sequoia is 36 mi east of Visalia on Route 198; Kings Canyon is 53 mi east of Fresno on Route 180. There is no automobile entrance on the eastern side of the Sierra. Routes 180 and 198 are connected by Generals Highway, a paved two-lane road that sometimes sees delays at peak times due to ongoing improvements. The road is extremely narrow and steep from Route 198 to Giant Forest, so keep an eye on your engine temperature gauge, as the incline and congestion can cause vehicles to overheat; to avoid overheated brakes, use low gears on downgrades.

If you are traveling in an RV or with a trailer, study the restrictions on these vehicles. Do not travel beyond Potwisha Campground with an RV longer than 22 feet on Route 198; take straighter, easier Route 180 instead. Maximum vehicle length on Generals Highway is 40 feet, or 50 feet combined length for vehicles with trailers.

Generals Highway between Lodgepole and Grant Grove is sometimes closed by snow. The Mineral King Road from Route 198 into southern Sequoia National Park is closed 2 mi below Atwell Mill either on November 1 or after the first heavy snow. The Buckeye Flat–Middle Fork Trailhead Road is closed mid-October–mid-April when the Buckeye Flat Campground closes. The lower Crystal Cave Road is closed when the cave closes in November. Its upper 2 mi, as well as the Panoramic Point and Moro Rock–Crescent Meadow roads, are closed with the first heavy snow. Because of the danger of rockfall, the portion of Kings Canyon Scenic Byway east of Grant Grove closes in winter. For current conditions, call ☎ *559/565–3341 Ext. 4*.

WHAT IT COSTS

	¢	$	$$	$$$	$$$$
Restaurants	under $10	$10–$15	$16–$22	$23–$30	over $30
Hotels	under $90	$90–$120	$121–$175	$176–$250	over $250

Restaurant prices are per person for a main course at dinner. Hotel prices are per night for two people in a standard double room in high season, excluding taxes and service charges.

PARK ESSENTIALS

ADMISSION FEES AND PERMITS

The admission fee is $20 per vehicle and $10 for those who enter by bus, on foot, bicycle, motorcycle, or horse; it is valid for seven days in both parks. U.S. residents over the age of 62 pay $10 for a lifetime pass, and permanently disabled U.S. residents are admitted free.

If you plan to camp in the backcountry, you need a permit, which costs $15. One permit covers the group. Availability of permits depends upon trailhead quotas. Advance reservations are accepted by mail or fax beginning March 1, and must be made at least two weeks in advance (✉ *Sequoia and Kings Canyon National Park, Wilderness Permit Reservations, 47050 Generals Hwy. #60, Three Rivers, CA 9327* ☎ *559/565–3766* ℻ *559/565–4239*). Without a reservation, you may still get a permit on a first-come, first-served basis starting at 1 pm the day before you plan to hike. For more information on backcountry camping or travel with pack animals (horses, mules, burros, or llamas), contact the Wilderness Permit Office (☎ *559/565–3761*).

ADMISSION HOURS

The parks are open 24/7 year-round.

EMERGENCIES

Call 911 from any telephone within the park in an emergency. Rangers at the Cedar Grove, Foothills, Grant Grove, and Lodgepole visitor centers and the Mineral King ranger station are trained in first aid. National Park rangers have legal jurisdiction within park boundaries: contact the closest ranger station or visitor center for police matters. For nonemergencies, call the parks' main number (☎ *559/565–3341*).

PARK CONTACT INFORMATION

Delaware North Park Services (✉ *P.O. Box 89, Sequoia National Park, CA 93262* ☎ *559/565–4070 or 888/252–5757* 🌐 *www.visitsequoia.com*). This concessionaire operates the lodgings and visitor services in Sequoia, and some in Kings Canyon. **Kings Canyon Park Services** (✉ *P.O. Box 909, Kings Canyon National Park, CA 93633* ☎ *559/335–5500 or 866/522–6966* 🌐 *www.sequoia-kingscanyon.com*). Some park services, including lodging, are operated by this company. **Sequoia and Kings Canyon National Parks** (✉ *47050 Generals Hwy. [Rte. 198], Three Rivers, CA 93271–9651* ☎ *559/565–3341* 🌐 *www.nps.gov/seki*). **Sequoia Natural History Association** (✉ *HCR 89 P.O. Box 10, Three Rivers, CA 93271* ☎ *559/565–3759* 🌐 *www.sequoiahistory.org*). The SNHA operates Crystal Cave and the Pear Lake Ski Hut, and provides educational materials and programs. **U.S. Forest Service, Sequoia National Forest** (✉ *900 W. Grand Ave., Porterville, CA 93527* ☎ *559/338–2251* 🌐 *www.fs.fed.us/r5/sequoia*).

SEQUOIA NATIONAL PARK

EXPLORING

SCENIC STOPS

Crescent Meadow. John Muir called this the "gem of the Sierra." Take an hour or two to walk around, and see if you agree. Wildflowers bloom here throughout the summer. ✉ *End of Moro Rock–Crescent Meadow Rd., 2.6 mi east off Generals Hwy.*

★ **Crystal Cave.** One of more than 200 caves in Sequoia and Kings Canyon national parks, Crystal Cave is unusual in that it's composed largely of marble, the result of limestone being hardened under heat and pressure. It contains several impressive formations, even more visible now that an environmentally sensitive relighting project has completed. Unfortunately, some of the cave's formations have been damaged or destroyed by early 20th-century dynamite blasting. The standard tour will give you 45 minutes inside the cave. ✉ *Crystal Cave Rd., 6 mi west off Generals Hwy.* ☎ *559/565–3759* 🌐 *www.sequoiahistory.org* 🎟 *$11* ⏲ *Mid-May–mid-Oct., daily 10–4.*

★ **General Sherman Tree.** Neither the world's tallest nor oldest sequoia, General Sherman is nevertheless tops in volume—and it is still putting on weight, adding the equivalent of a 60-foot-tall tree every year to its 2.7 million-pound mass. ✉ *Generals Hwy. (Rte. 198), 2 mi south of Lodgepole Visitor Center.*

Mineral King. This subalpine valley sits at 7,800 feet at the end of a steep, winding road. The trip from the park's entrance can take up to two hours. This is the highest point to which you can drive in the park. ✉ *End of Mineral King Rd., 25 mi east of Generals Hwy. (Rte. 198), east of Three Rivers.*

★ **Moro Rock.** Sequoia National Park's best non-tree attraction offers panoramic views to those fit and determined enough to mount its 350-ish steps. In a case where the journey rivals the destination, Moro's stone stairway is so impressive in its twisty inventiveness that it's on the National Register of Historic Places. The rock's 6,725-foot summit overlooks the Middle Fork Canyon, sculpted by the Kaweah River and approaching the depth of Arizona's Grand Canyon. ✉ *Moro Rock–Crescent Meadow Rd., 2 mi east off Generals Hwy. (Rte. 198) to parking area.*

Tunnel Log. This 275-foot tree fell in 1937, and soon a 17-foot-wide, 8-foot-high hole was cut through it for vehicular passage that continues today. Large vehicles take the nearby bypass. ✉ *Moro Rock–Crescent Meadow Rd., 2 mi east of Generals Hwy. (Rte. 198).*

VISITOR CENTERS

Foothills Visitor Center. Exhibits focusing on the foothills and resource issues facing the parks are on display here. You can also pick up books, maps, and a list of ranger-led walks, and get wilderness permits. ✉ *Generals Hwy. (Rte. 198), 1 mi north of the Ash Mountain entrance* ☎ *559/565–4212* ⏲ *Oct.–mid-May, daily 8–4:30; mid-May–Sept., daily 8–5.*

Lodgepole Visitor Center. Along with exhibits on the area's geologic history, wildlife, and longtime American Indian inhabitants, the center screens an outstanding 22-minute film about bears. You can also buy books and maps here. ✉ *Generals Hwy. (Rte. 198), 21 mi north of Ash Mountain entrance* ☎ *559/565–4436* ⏲ *June–Oct., daily 7–6; Closed from Nov.–May.*

Mineral King Ranger Station. The small visitor center here houses a few exhibits on the history of the area; wilderness permits and some books and maps are available. ✉ *End of Mineral King Rd., 25 mi east of East Fork entrance* ☎ *559/565–3768* ⏲ *Late May–mid-Sept., daily 8–4:30.*

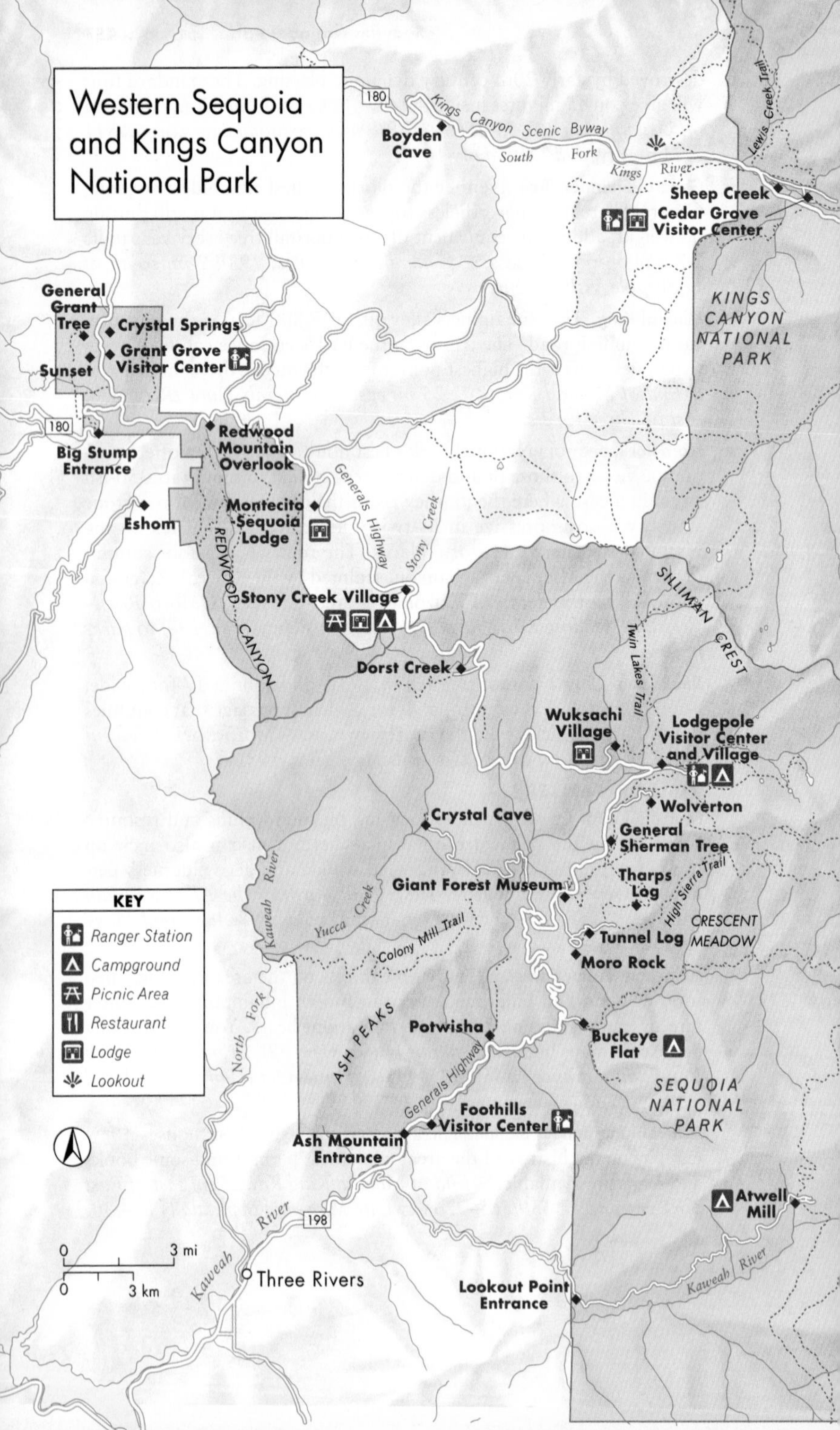

Western Sequoia and Kings Canyon National Park
180
Kings Canyon Scenic Byway
Boyden Cave
South Fork Kings River
Lewis Creek Trail
Sheep Creek
Cedar Grove Visitor Center
KINGS CANYON NATIONAL PARK
General Grant Tree
Crystal Springs
Grant Grove Visitor Center
Sunset
180
Big Stump Entrance
Redwood Mountain Overlook
Generals Highway
Stony Creek
Montecito-Sequoia Lodge
Eshom
REDWOOD CANYON
Stony Creek Village
SILLIMAN CREST
Twin Lakes Trail
Dorst Creek
Wuksachi Village
Lodgepole Visitor Center and Village
Wolverton
Crystal Cave
General Sherman Tree
Tharps Log
High Sierra Trail
Giant Forest Museum
Kaweah River
Yucca Creek
Colony Mill Trail
CRESCENT MEADOW
Tunnel Log
Moro Rock
KEY
Ranger Station
Campground
Picnic Area
Restaurant
Lodge
Lookout
North Fork
ASH PEAKS
Potwisha
Buckeye Flat
Generals Highway
SEQUOIA NATIONAL PARK
Foothills Visitor Center
Ash Mountain Entrance
Atwell Mill
198
River
0 3 mi
0 3 km
Kaweah
Three Rivers
Kaweah River
Lookout Point Entrance

CLOSE UP

Flora and Fauna

The parks can be divided into three distinct zones. In the west (1,500–4,500 feet) are the rolling, lower elevation foothills, covered with shrubby chaparral vegetation or golden grasslands dotted with oaks. Chamise, red-barked manzanita, and the occasional yucca plant grow here. Fields of white popcorn flower cover the hillsides in spring, and the yellow fiddleneck flourishes. In summer, intense heat and absence of rain cause the hills to turn golden brown. Wildlife includes the California ground squirrel, noisy blue-and-gray scrub jay, black bears, coyotes, skunks, and gray fox.

At middle elevation (5,000–9,000 feet), where the giant sequoia belt resides, rock formations mix with meadows and huge stands of evergreens—red and white fir, incense cedar, and ponderosa pines, to name a few. Wildflowers like yellow blazing star and red Indian paintbrush, bloom in spring and summer. Mule deer, golden-mantled ground squirrels, Steller's jays, mule deer, and black bears (most active in fall) inhabit the area, as does the chickaree.

The high alpine section of the parks is extremely rugged, with a string of rocky peaks reaching above 13,000 feet to Mt. Whitney's 14,494 feet. Fierce weather and scarcity of soil make vegetation and wildlife sparse. Foxtail and whitebark pines have gnarled and twisted trunks, the result of high wind, heavy snowfall, and freezing temperatures. In summer you can see yellow-bellied marmots, pikas, weasels, mountain chickadees, and Clark's nutcrackers.

SPORTS AND THE OUTDOORS

The best way to see Sequoia is to take a hike. Unless you do so, you'll miss out on the up-close grandeur of mist wafting between deeply scored, red-orange tree trunks bigger than you've ever seen. If it's winter, put on some snowshoes or cross-country skis and plunge into the outscale woodland swaddled in snow. There are not too many other outdoor options: no off-road driving is allowed in the parks, and no special provisions have been made for bicycles. Boating, rafting, and snowmobiling are also prohibited.

BIRD-WATCHING

More than 200 species of birds inhabit Sequoia and Kings Canyon national parks. Not seen in most parts of the United States, the white-headed woodpecker and the pileated woodpecker are common in most mid-elevation areas here. There are also many hawks and owls, including the renowned spotted owl. Species are diverse in both parks due to the changes in elevation, and range from warblers, kingbirds, thrushes, and sparrows in the foothills to goshawk, blue grouse, red-breasted nuthatch, and brown creeper at the highest elevations. Ranger-led bird-watching tours are held on a sporadic basis. Call the park's main information number to find out more about these tours.

Contact the **Sequoia Natural History Association** (✉ *HCR 89, P.O. Box 10, Three Rivers, CA 93271* ☎ *559/565–3759* 🌐 *www.sequoiahistory.org*) for information on bird-watching in the southern Sierra.

CROSS-COUNTRY SKIING

Pear Lake Ski Hut. Primitive lodging is available at this backcountry hut, reached by a steep and extremely difficult 7-mi trail from Wolverton. Only expert skiers should attempt this trek. Space is limited; make reservations well in advance. ✉ *Trailhead at end of Wolverton Rd., 1½ mi northeast off Generals Hwy. (Rte. 198)* ☎ *559/565–3759* 🎟 *$38* ⏲ *Mid-Dec.–mid-Apr.*

Wuksachi Lodge. Rent skis here. Depending on snowfall amounts, instruction may also be available. Reservations are recommended. Marked trails cut through Giant Forest, just 5 mi south of the lodge. ✉ *Off Generals Hwy. (Rte. 198), 2 mi north of Lodgepole* ☎ *559/565–4070* 🎟 *$15–$20 ski rental* ⏲ *Nov.–May (unless no snow), daily 9–4.*

HIKING

The best way to see the park is to hike it. The grandeur and majesty of the Sierra is best seen up close. Carry a hiking map—available at any visitor center—and plenty of water. Check with rangers for current trail conditions, and be aware of rapidly changing weather. As a rule of thumb, plan on trekking 1 mph.

EASY

★ **Congress Trail.** This easy 2-mi trail is a paved loop that begins near General Sherman Tree and winds through the heart of the Sequoia forest. You'll get close-up views of more big trees here than on any other Sequoia hike. Watch for the clusters known as the House and Senate. ✉ *Trail begins off Generals Hwy. (Rte. 198), 2 mi north of Giant Forest.*

★ **Crescent Meadow Trails.** John Muir reportedly called Crescent Meadow the "gem of the Sierra." Brilliant wildflowers bloom here by midsummer, and a 1.8-mi trail loops around the meadow. A 1.6-mi trail begins at Crescent Meadow and leads to Tharp's Log, a cabin built from a fire-hollowed sequoia. ✉ *Trail begins end of Moro Rock–Crescent Meadow Rd., 2.6 mi east off Generals Hwy. (Rte. 198).*

MODERATE

Tokopah Falls Trail. This moderate trail follows the Marble Fork of the Kaweah River for 1.75 mi one way and dead-ends below the impressive granite cliffs and cascading waterfall of Tokopah Canyon. It takes 2½ to 4 hours to make the 3.5-mi round-trip journey. The trail passes through a mixed-conifer forest. ✉ *Trail begins off Generals Hwy. (Rte. 198), ¼ mi north of Lodgepole Campground.*

DIFFICULT

Mineral King Trails. Many trails to the high country begin at Mineral King. The two most popular day hikes are Eagle Lake and Timber Gap, both of which are somewhat strenuous. At 7,800 feet, this is the highest point to which one can drive in either of the parks. Get a map and provisions, and check with rangers about conditions. ✉ *Trailhead at end of Mineral King Rd., 25 mi east of Generals Hwy. (Rte. 198).*

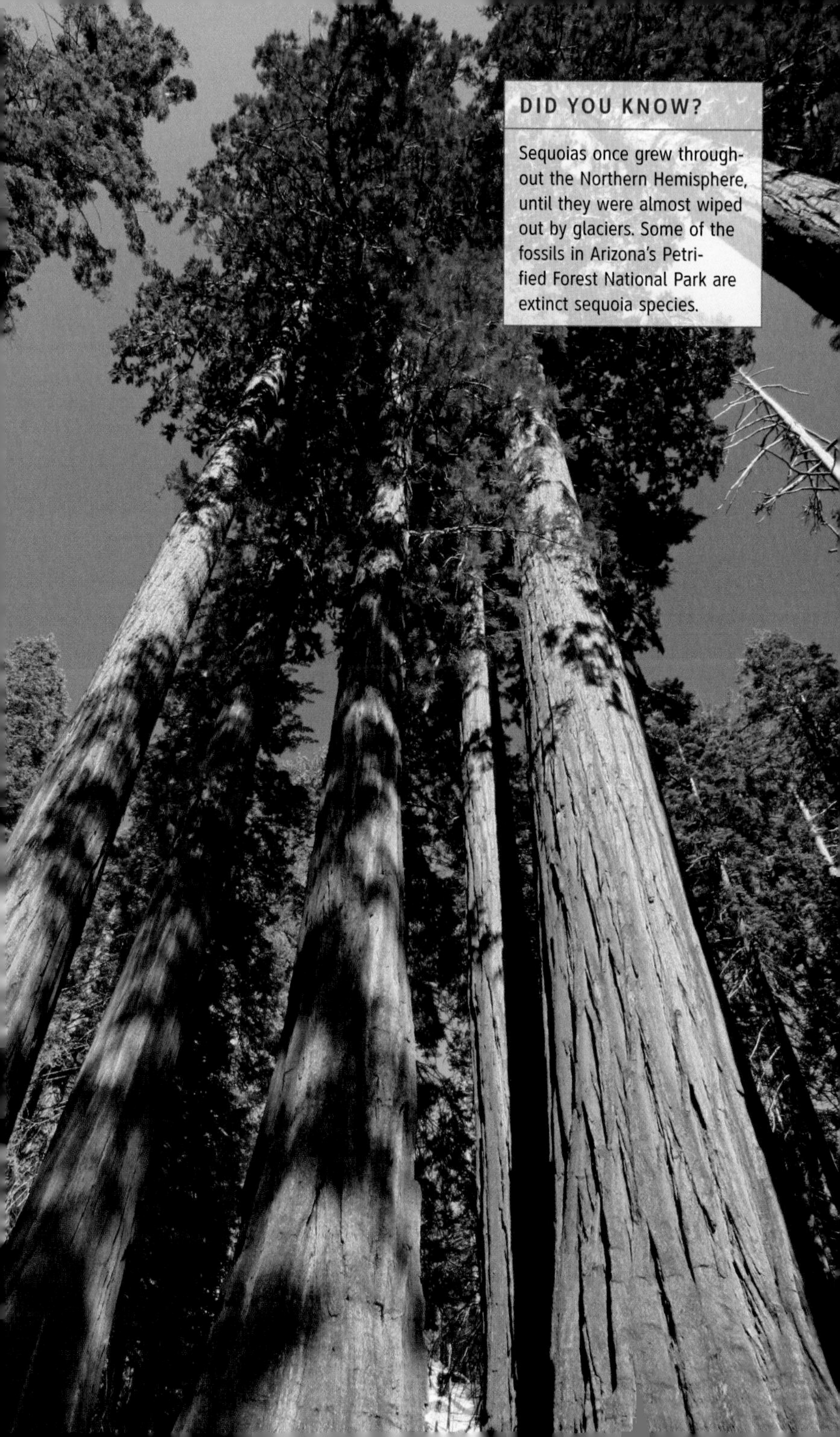

DID YOU KNOW?

Sequoias once grew throughout the Northern Hemisphere, until they were almost wiped out by glaciers. Some of the fossils in Arizona's Petrified Forest National Park are extinct sequoia species.

HORSEBACK RIDING

Trips take you through redwood forests, flowering meadows, across the Sierra, or even up to Mt. Whitney. Costs per person range from $25 for a one-hour guided ride to around $200 per day for fully guided trips for which the packers do all the cooking and camp chores.

Grant Grove Stables is the stable to choose if you want a short ride. ✉ *Rte. 180, ½ Mi north of Grant Grove Visitor Center, near Grant Grove Village, Gran Grove* ☎ *559/337–2314 mid-June–Sept., 559/337–2314 Oct.–mid-June*

Horse Corral Pack Station. Hourly, half-day, full-day, or overnight trips through Sequoia are available for beginning and advanced riders. ✉ *Off Big Meadows Rd., 12 mi east of Generals Hwy. (Rte. 198) between Sequoia and Kings Canyon national parks* ☎ *559/565–3404 in summer, 559/564–6429 in winter* 🌐 *www.horsecorralpackers.com* 🎫 *$35–$145 day trips* ⏲ *May–Sept.*

Mineral King Pack Station. Day and overnight tours in the high-mountain area around Mineral King are available here. ✉ *End of Mineral King Rd., 25 mi east of East Fork entrance* ☎ *559/561–3039 in summer, 520/855–5885 in winter* 🌐 *mineralking.tripod.com* 🎫 *$25–$75 day trips* ⏲ *July to late Sept. or early Oct.*

SLEDDING AND SNOWSHOEING

The Wolverton area, on Route 198 near Giant Forest, is a popular sledding spot, where sleds, inner tubes, and platters are allowed. You can buy sleds and saucers, starting at $8, at the **Wuksachi Lodge** (☎ *559/565–4070*), 2 mi north of Lodgepole. You can also rent snowshoes for $15–$20. Naturalists lead snowshoe walks around Giant Forest and Wuksachi Lodge, conditions permitting, on Saturdays and holidays. Snowshoes are provided for a $1 donation. Make reservations and check schedules at **Giant Forest Museum** (☎ *559/565–4480*) or **Wuksachi Lodge.**

EDUCATIONAL OFFERINGS

CLASSES AND SEMINARS

Evening Programs. In summer, the park shows documentary films and slide shows, and has evening lectures. Locations and times vary; pick up a schedule at any visitor center or check bulletin boards near ranger stations. ☎ *559/565–3341.*

★ **Seminars.** Expert naturalists lead seminars on a range of topics, including birds, wildflowers, geology, botany, photography, park history, backpacking, and pathfinding. Some courses offer transferable credits. Reserve in advance. For information and prices, pick up a course catalogue at any visitor center or contact the **Sequoia Natural History Association** (☎ *559/565–3759* 🌐 *www.sequoiahistory.org*).

Sequoia Sightseeing Tours. The only licensed tour operator in either park offers daily interpretive sightseeing tours in a 10-passenger van with a friendly, knowledgeable guide. Reservations are essential. They also offer private tours of Kings Canyon. ☎ *559/561–4189* 🌐 *www.sequoiatours.com.*

RANGER PROGRAMS

Free Nature Programs. Almost any summer day, half-hour to 1½-hour ranger talks and walks explore subjects such as the life of the sequoia, the geology of the park, and the habits of bears. Giant Forest, Lodgepole Visitor Center, Wuksachi Village, and Dorst Creek Campground are frequent starting points. Check bulletin boards throughout the park for the week's offerings.

Junior Ranger Program. This self-guided program is offered year-round for children over five. Pick up a Junior Ranger booklet at any of the visitor centers. When your child finishes an activity, a ranger signs the booklet. Kids earn a patch upon completion, which is given at an awards ceremony. It isn't necessary to complete all activities to be awarded a patch. ☎ *559/565–3341.*

KINGS CANYON NATIONAL PARK

SCENIC DRIVES

★ **Kings Canyon Scenic Byway.** About 10 mi east of Grant Grove Village is Jackson View, where you'll first see Kings River Canyon. Near Yucca Point, it's thousands of feet deeper than the much more famous Grand Canyon. Continuing through Sequoia National Forest past Boyden Cavern, you'll enter the larger portion of Kings Canyon National Park and, eventually, Cedar Grove Village. Past there, the U-shaped canyon becomes broader. Be sure to allow an hour to walk through Zumwalt Meadow. Also, be sure to park and take the less-than-five-minute walks to the base of Grizzly Falls and Roaring River Falls. The drive dead-ends at a big parking lot, the launch point for many backpackers. Driving the byway takes about one hour each way (without stops).

EXPLORING

Kings Canyon National Park consists of two sections that adjoin the northern boundary of Sequoia National Park. The western portion, covered with sequoia and pine forest, contains the park's most visited sights, such as Grant Grove. The vast eastern portion is remote high country, slashed across half its southern breadth by the deep, rugged Kings River Canyon. Separating the two is Sequoia National Forest, which encompasses Giant Sequoia National Monument. The Kings Canyon Scenic Byway (Route 180) links the major sights within and between the park's two sections.

HISTORIC SITES

★ **Fallen Monarch.** This Sequoia's hollow base was used in the second half of the 19th century as a home for settlers, a saloon, and even to stable U.S. Cavalry horses. As you walk through it (assuming entry is permitted, which has not always been the case in recent years), check out how little the wood has decayed, and imagine yourself tucked safely inside, sheltered from a storm or protected from the searing heat. ✉ *Trailhead 1 mi north of Grant Grove Visitor Center.*

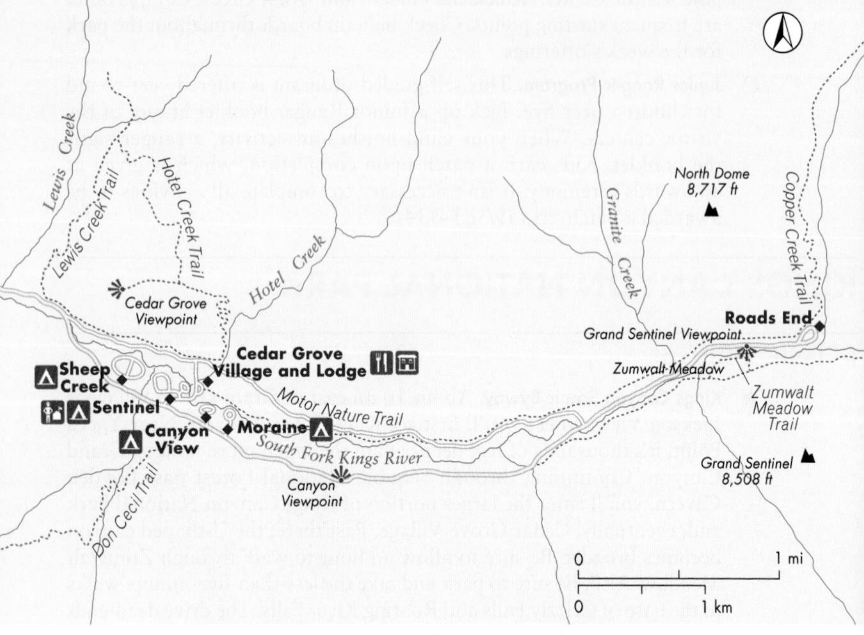

SCENIC STOPS

Canyon View. There are many places along the scenic byway to pull over for sightseeing, but this special spot showcases evidence of the canyon's glacial history. Here, maybe more than anywhere else, you'll understand why John Muir compared Kings Canyon vistas with those in Yosemite. ✉ *Kings Canyon Scenic Byway (Rte. 180), 1 mi east of the Cedar Grove turnoff.*

★ **Redwood Mountain Grove.** If you are serious about sequoias, you should consider visiting this, the world's largest big-tree grove. Within its 2,078 acres are 2,172 sequoias whose diameters exceed 10 feet. Your options range from the distant (pulling off the Generals Highway onto an overlook) to the intimate (taking a 6- to 10-mi hike down into its richest regions, which include two of the world's 25 heaviest trees). ✉ *Drive 5 mi south of Grant Grove on Generals Hwy. (Rte. 198), then turn right at Quail Flat; follow it 1½ mi to the Redwood Canyon trailhead.*

VISITOR CENTERS

Cedar Grove Visitor Center. Off the main road and behind the Sentinel Campground, this small ranger station has books and maps, plus information about hikes and other things to do in the area. ✉ *Kings Canyon Scenic Byway, 30 mi east of park entrance* ☎ *559/565–3793* ⏲ *mid-May–late September, daily 9–5.*

Grant Grove Visitor Center. Acquaint yourself with the varied charms of this two-section national park by watching a 15-minute film and perusing the center's exhibits on the canyon, sequoias, and human history. Books, maps, and free wilderness permits are available, as are updates on the parks' weather and air-quality conditions. ✉ *Generals Hwy. (Rte. 198), 3 mi northeast of Rte. 180, Big Stump entrance* ☎ *559/565–4307* ⏲ *Summer, daily 8–6; mid-May–late Sept., daily 9–4:30; winter, daily 9–4:30.*

SPORTS AND THE OUTDOORS

CROSS-COUNTRY SKIING

Roads to Grant Grove are easily accessible during heavy snowfall, making the trails here a good choice over Sequoia's Giant Forest when harsh weather hits.

HIKING

You can enjoy many of Kings Canyon's sights from your car, but the giant gorge of the Kings River Canyon and the sweeping vistas of some of the highest mountains in the United States are best seen on foot. Carry a hiking map—available at any visitor center—and plenty of water. Check with rangers for current trail conditions, and be aware of rapidly changing weather.

If you're planning to hike the backcountry, you can pick up a permit and information on the backcountry at **Road's End Permit Station** (✉ *5 mi east of Cedar Grove Visitor Center, at the end of Kings Canyon Scenic Byway* ☎ *No phone* ⏲ *Late May–late Sept., daily 7–3:30*). You can also rent or buy bear canisters, a must for campers. When the station is closed, you can still complete a self-service permit form.

EASY

Fodor's Choice ★ **Zumwalt Meadow Trail.** Rangers say this is the best (and most popular) day hike in the Cedar Grove area. Just 1.5 mi long, it offers three visual treats: the South Fork of the Kings River, the lush meadow, and the high granite walls above, including those of Grand Sentinel and North Dome. ✉ *Trailhead 4½ mi east of Cedar Grove Village turnoff from Kings Canyon Scenic Byway.*

MODERATE

★ **Big Baldy.** This hike climbs 600 feet and 2 mi up to the 8,209-feet summit of Big Baldy. Your reward is the view of Redwood Canyon. The round-trip hike is 4 mi. ✉ *Trailhead 8 mi south of Grant Grove on Generals Hwy. (Rte. 198).*

★ **Redwood Canyon Trail.** Avoid the hubbub of Giant Forest and its General Sherman Tree by hiking down to Redwood Canyon, the world's largest grove of sequoias. Opt for the trail toward Hart Tree, and you'll soon lose track of how many humongous trees you pass along the 6-mi loop. Count on spending four to six peaceful hours here—although some backpackers linger overnight (wilderness permit required). ✉ *Trail begins off Quail Flat* ✣ *Drive 5 mi south of Grant Grove on Generals Hwy. (Rte. 198), then turn right at Quail Flat; follow it 1½ mi to the Redwood Canyon trailhead.*

DIFFICULT

★ **Hotel Creek Trail.** For gorgeous canyon views, take this trail from the canyon floor at Cedar Grove up a series of switchbacks until it splits. Follow the route left through chaparral to the forested ridge and rocky outcrop known as Cedar Grove Overlook, where you can see the Kings River Canyon stretching below. This strenuous 5-mi round-trip hike gains 1,200 feet and takes three to four hours to complete. For a longer hike, return via Lewis Creek Trail for an 8-mi loop. ✉ *Trailhead at Cedar Grove pack station, 1 mi east of Cedar Grove Village.*

MOUNT WHITNEY

At 14,494 feet, Mt. Whitney is the highest point in the contiguous United States and the crown jewel of Sequoia National Park's wild eastern side. Despite the mountain's scale, you can't see it from the more traveled west side of the park, because it is hidden behind the Great Western Divide. The only way to access Mt. Whitney from the main part of the park is to circumnavigate the Sierra Nevada via a 10-hour, nearly 400-mi drive outside the park. No road ascends the peak; the best vantage point from which to catch a glimpse of the mountain is at the end of Whitney Portal Road. (Whitney Portal Road is closed in winter.)

HORSEBACK RIDING

One-day destinations by horseback out of Cedar Grove include Mist Falls and Upper Bubb's Creek. In the backcountry, many equestrians head for Volcanic Lakes or Granite Basin, ascending trails that reach elevations of 10,000 feet. Costs per person range from $25 for a one-hour guided ride to around $200 per day for fully guided trips for which the packers do all the cooking and camp chores.

Take a day or overnight trip along the Kings River Canyon with **Cedar Grove Pack Station** (✉ *Kings Canyon Scenic Byway, 1 mi east of Cedar Grove Village* ☎ *559/565–3464 in summer, 559/337–2314 off-season* 🎫 *Call for prices* ⏲ *May–Oct.*). Popular routes include the Rae Lakes Loop and Monarch Divide. A one- or two-hour trip through Grant Grove leaving from **Grant Grove Stables** (✉ *Rte. 180, ½ mi north of Grant Grove Visitor Center* ☎ *559/335–9292 mid-June–Sept., 559/337–2314 Oct.–mid-June* 🎫 *$40–$60* ⏲ *June–Labor Day, daily 8–6*) is a good way to get a taste of horseback riding in Kings Canyon.

SLEDDING AND SNOWSHOEING

In winter, Kings Canyon has a few great places to play in the snow. Sleds, inner tubes, and platters are allowed at both the Azalea Campground area on Grant Tree Road, ¼ mi north of Grant Grove Visitor Center, and at the Big Stump picnic area, 2 mi north of the lower Route 180 entrance to the park.

Snowshoeing is good around Grant Grove, where you can take naturalist-guided snowshoe walks on Saturdays and holidays mid-December through mid-March as conditions permit.

Hiking in the Sierra mountains is a thrilling experience, putting you amid some of the world's highest trees.

WHERE TO EAT

$$ AMERICAN **Cedar Grove Restaurant.** For a small operation, the menu here is surprisingly extensive, with dinner entrées such as pasta, pork chops, and steak. For breakfast, try the biscuits and gravy, French toast, pancakes, or cold cereal. Burgers (including vegetarian patties) and hot dogs dominate the lunch choices. Outside, a patio dining area overlooks the Kings River. ✉ *Cedar Grove Village* ☎ *559/565–0100* ⏲ *Closed Oct.–May.*

$$$ AMERICAN **Grant Grove Restaurant.** In a no-frills, open room, you can order basic American fare such as pancakes for breakfast or hot sandwiches and chicken for later meals. Vegetarians and vegans will have to content themselves with a simple salad. Take-out service is available. ✉ *Grant Grove Village* ☎ *559/335–5500.*

¢ CAFÉ **Lodgepole Market and Snack Bar.** The choices here run the gamut from simple to very simple, with the three counters only a few strides apart in a central eating complex. For hot food, venture into the snack bar. The deli sells prepackaged sandwiches along with ice cream scooped from tubs. You'll find other prepackaged foods in the market. ✉ *Next to Lodgepole Visitor Center* ☎ *559/565–3301* ⏲ *Closed early Sept.–mid-Apr.*

$$$ BARBECUE **Wolverton Barbecue.** Weather permitting, diners congregate on a wooden porch that looks directly out onto a small but strikingly verdant meadow. In addition to the predictable meats such as ribs and chicken, the all-you-can-eat buffet has sides that include baked beans, corn on the cob, and potato salad. Following the meal, listen to a ranger talk and clear your throat for a campfire sing-along. Purchase tickets at Lodgepole Market, Wuksachi Lodge, or Wolverton

Recreation Area's office. ✉ *Wolverton Rd., 1½ mi northeast off Generals Hwy. (Rte. 198)* ☎ *559/565–4070 or 559/565–3301* ⌚ *Open in summer only, seven days a week.*

$$$ AMERICAN ★ ✕ **Wuksachi Village Dining Room.** Huge windows run the length of the high-ceilinged dining room, and a large fireplace on the far wall warms both the body and the soul. The diverse dinner menu—by far the best in the two parks—includes filet mignon, rainbow trout, and vegetarian pasta dishes, in addition to the ever-present burgers. The children's menu is economically priced. Breakfast and lunch also are served. ✉ *Wuksachi Village* ☎ *559/565–4070* ✍ *Reservations essential.*

WHERE TO STAY

For expanded hotel reviews, visit Fodors.com.

$$$ **John Muir Lodge.** This modern, timber-sided lodge is nestled in a wooded area in the hills above Grant Grove Village and offers year-round accommodations. **Pros:** common room stays warm; it's far enough from the main road to be quiet. **Cons:** check-in is down in the village. ✉ *Kings Canyon Scenic Byway, ¼ mi north of Grant Grove Village* 📫 *Sequoia Kings Canyon Park Services Co., P.O. Box 907, Suite 101, Kings Canyon National Park CA 93633* ☎ *559/335–5500 or 866/522–6966* 🌐 *www.sequoia-kingscanyon.com* 36 rooms *In-room: no a/c, no TV.*

$$$ Fodor's Choice ★ **Wuksachi Lodge.** The striking cedar-and-stone main building here is a fine example of how a man-made structure can blend effectively with lovely mountain scenery. **Pros:** best place to stay in the parks; lots of wildlife. **Cons:** rooms can be small; main lodge is a few minutes' walk from guest rooms. ✉ *Wuksachi Village* ☎ *559/565–4070 front desk, 888/252–5757 reservations* 🌐 *www.visitsequoia.com* 102 rooms *In-room: a/c (some), Internet, Wi-Fi. In-hotel: restaurant, bar.*

Sacramento and the Gold Country

WORD OF MOUTH

"Highway 49 travels through the California Gold Country steeped with history and small towns. . . . Much, much more interesting than taking Highway 99."

—BarbAnn

WELCOME TO SACRAMENTO AND THE GOLD COUNTRY

TOP REASONS TO GO

★ **Golden opportunities:** Marshall Gold Discovery State Park and Hangtown's Gold Bug & Mine conjure up California's mid-19th century boom.

★ **Capital connections:** Sacramento may no longer be home to Arnold Schwarzenegger—actually it never was; he commuted from L.A.—but it's a vibrant if not glitzy city with much to offer visitors.

★ **That festive feeling:** Sacramento is home to the California state fair in July and many ethnic food festivals. Nevada City and environs are known for summer mountain music festivals and Victorian and Cornish winter holiday celebrations.

★ **The next Napa:** With bucolic scenery and friendly tasting rooms, the Shenandoah Valley is like Napa, without the traffic.

★ **Back to nature:** Moaning Cavern's main chamber is big enough to hold the Statue of Liberty, and Calaveras Big Trees State Park is filled with giant sequoias.

1 Sacramento and Vicinity. The gateway to the Gold Country, the seat of state government, and an agricultural hub, Sacramento plays many important contemporary roles. About 2 million people live in the metropolitan area, which offers up opportunity, sunshine, and lower housing costs than in coastal California.

2 The Gold Country—South. South of its junction with U.S. 50, Highway 49 traces in asphalt the famed Mother Lode. The sleepy former gold-rush towns strung along the road have for the most part been restored and made presentable to visitors with an interest in one of the most frenzied episodes of American history.

3 The Gold Country—North. Highway 49 north of Placerville links the towns of Coloma, Auburn, Grass Valley, and Nevada City. Most are gentrified versions of once-rowdy mining camps, vestiges of which remain in roadside museums, old mining structures, and restored homes now serving as inns.

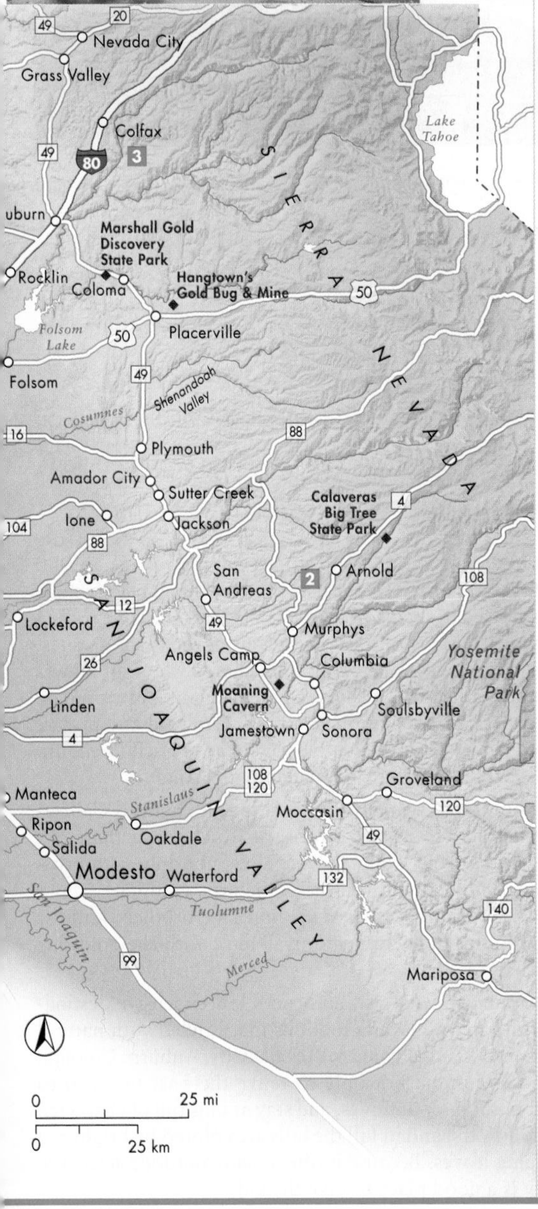

GETTING ORIENTED

The Gold Country is a largely laid-back and lower-tech destination for those seeking to escape Southern California and the Bay Area. Sacramento, Davis, and Woodland are in an enormous valley bordered to the east by the Sierra Nevada mountain range. Foothill communities Nevada City, Placerville, and Sutter Creek were products of the gold rush.

Updated by Reed Parsell

A new era dawned for California when James Marshall turned up a gold nugget in the tailrace of a sawmill he was constructing along the American River. Before January 24, 1848, Mexico and the United States were still wrestling for ownership of what would become the Golden State. With Marshall's discovery, the United States tightened its grip on the region, and prospectors from all over the world came to seek their fortunes in the Mother Lode.

As gold fever seized the nation, California's population of 15,000 swelled to 265,000 within three years. The mostly young, mostly male adventurers who arrived in search of gold—the '49ers—became part of a culture that discarded many of the conventions of the eastern states. It was also a violent time. Yankee prospectors chased Mexican miners off their claims, and California's leaders initiated a plan to exterminate the local Native American population. Bounties were paid and private militias were hired to wipe out the Native Americans or sell them into slavery. California was now to be dominated by the Anglo.

The gold rush boom lasted scarcely 20 years, but it changed California forever. It produced 546 mining towns, of which fewer than 250 remain. The hills of the Gold Country were alive, not only with prospecting and mining but also with business, the arts, gambling, and a fair share of crime. Opera houses went up alongside brothels, and the California State Capitol, in Sacramento, was built with the gold dug out of the hills.

Today the Gold Country is one of California's less expensive destinations, a region of the Sierra Nevada foothills that is filled with natural and cultural pleasures. Visitors come to Nevada City, Auburn, Coloma, Sutter Creek, and Columbia not only to relive the past but also to explore art galleries, shop for antiques, and stay at inns full of character. Spring brings wildflowers, and in fall the hills are colored by bright red berries and changing leaves. Because it offers many outdoor activities, the Gold Country is a good place to take the kids.

Visiting Old Sacramento's museums is a good way to immerse yourself in history, but the Gold Country's heart lies along Highway 49, which winds the 325-mi north–south length of the historic mining area. The highway, often a twisting, hilly, two-lane road, begs for a convertible with the top down.

PLANNING

WHEN TO GO

The Gold Country is most pleasant in spring, when the wildflowers are in bloom, and in fall. Summers can be hot: temperatures of 100°F are fairly common. Sacramento winters tend to be cool with occasionally foggy and/or rainy days; many Sacramentans drive to the foothills (or to the coast) to get some winter sunshine. Throughout the year Gold Country towns stage community and ethnic celebrations. In December many towns are decked out for Christmas.

GETTING HERE AND AROUND

Traveling by car or motorcycle is the only practical way to explore the Gold Country (bicyclists flirt with disaster on the often-narrow, twisty roads). From Sacramento, three highways fan out toward the east, all intersecting with Highway 49: I–80 heads 34 mi northeast to Auburn; U.S. 50 goes east 40 mi to Placerville; and Highway 16 angles southeast 45 mi to Plymouth. Highway 49 is an excellent two-lane road that winds and climbs through the foothills and valleys, linking the principal Gold Country towns.

AIR TRAVEL

Sacramento International Airport is served by Alaska, American, Continental, Delta, Frontier, Hawaiian, Horizon Air, JetBlue, Mexicana, Southwest, United, and US Airways. A private taxi from the airport to downtown Sacramento is about $35. The cost of the Super Shuttle from the airport to downtown Sacramento is $25. Call in advance to arrange transportation from your hotel to the airport.

Contacts Sacramento International Airport (✉ *6900 Airport Blvd., 12 mi northwest of downtown off I–5, Sacramento* ☎ *916/874–0700* 🌐 *www.sacairports.org*). **Super Shuttle** (☎ *800/258–3826*).

BUS TRAVEL

Getting to and from SIA can be accomplished via taxi, the Super Shuttle (⇨ *By Air*), or by Yolo County Public Bus 42, which operates a circular service around SIA, downtown Sacramento, West Sacramento, Davis, and Woodland. Other Gold Country destinations are best reached by private car.

Greyhound serves Sacramento, Davis, Auburn, and Placerville. It's a two-hour trip from San Francisco's Transbay Terminal, at First and Mission streets, to the Sacramento station, at Seventh and L streets.

Sacramento Regional Transit buses and light-rail vehicles transport passengers in Sacramento. Most buses run from 6 am to 10 pm, most trains from 5 am to midnight. A transit-system-operated DASH (Downtown Area Shuttle) bus and the No. 30 city bus link Old Sacramento, midtown, and Sutter's Fort.

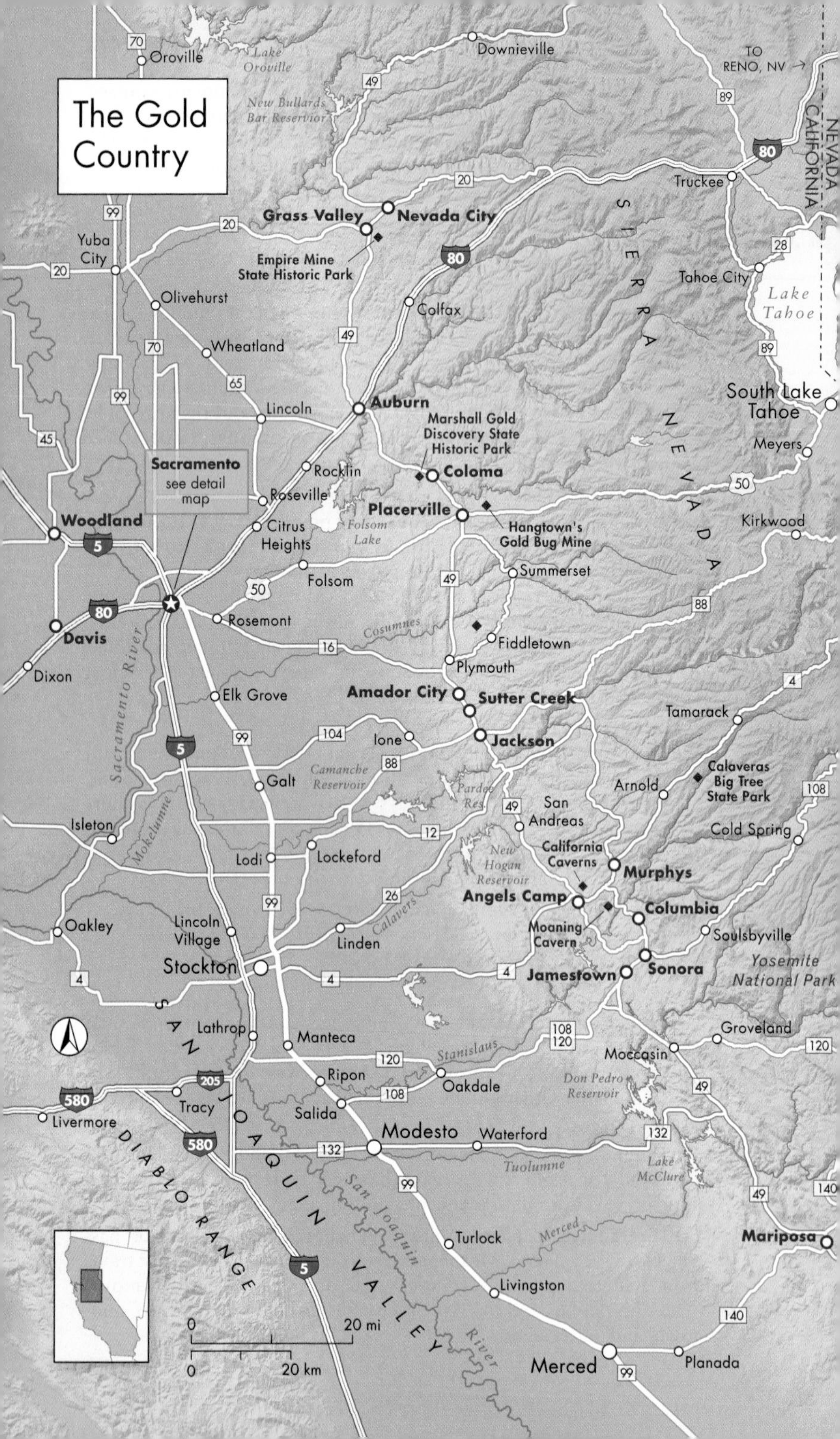
The Gold Country
Oroville
Lake Oroville
Downieville
TO RENO, NV
New Bullards Bar Reservior
NEVADA
CALIFORNIA
Truckee
Grass Valley
Nevada City
Empire Mine State Historic Park
SIERRA NEVADA
Yuba City
Olivehurst
Tahoe City
Lake Tahoe
Colfax
Wheatland
South Lake Tahoe
Auburn
Lincoln
Marshall Gold Discovery State Historic Park
Meyers
Sacramento see detail map
Rocklin
Coloma
Roseville
Placerville
Woodland
Citrus Heights
Folsom Lake
Hangtown's Gold Bug Mine
Kirkwood
Folsom
Summerset
Davis
Rosemont
Cosumnes
Fiddletown
Dixon
Plymouth
Amador City
Sutter Creek
Elk Grove
Tamarack
Sacramento River
Ione
Jackson
Camanche Reservoir
Calaveras Big Tree State Park
Galt
Pardee Res.
Arnold
San Andreas
Isleton
Cold Spring
Mokelumne
New Hogan Reservoir
California Caverns
Lodi
Lockeford
Murphys
Angels Camp
Columbia
Calaveras
Moaning Cavern
Oakley
Lincoln Village
Soulsbyville
Linden
Yosemite National Park
Stockton
Jamestown
Sonora
SAN JOAQUIN VALLEY
Lathrop
Manteca
Groveland
Stanislaus
Moccasin
Ripon
Oakdale
Don Pedro Reservoir
Tracy
Livermore
Salida
DIABLO RANGE
Modesto
Waterford
Tuolumne
Lake McClure
San Joaquin
Turlock
Merced
Mariposa
Livingston
River
0
20 mi
0
20 km
Merced
Planada

Contacts Greyhound (☎ *800/231–2222* 🌐 *www.greyhound.com*). **Sacramento Regional Transit** (☎ *916/321–2877* 🌐 *www.sacrt.com*). **Yolo County Bus** (☎ *530/666–2837* 🌐 *www.yolobus.com*).

TRAIN TRAVEL

Several Capitol Corridor trains operated by Amtrak stop in Sacramento and Davis. Trains making the 2½-hour trip from Jack London Square, in Oakland, stop in Emeryville (across the bay from San Francisco), Richmond, Martinez, and Davis before reaching Sacramento; some stop in Berkeley and Suisun-Fairfield as well; a few venture as far south as San Jose and as far north as Auburn. Amtrak also runs trains and buses down through the Central Valley.

Contacts **Amtrak** (☎ *800/872–7245* 🌐 *www.amtrakcalifornia.com*).

Capitol Corridor (☎ *877/974–3322* 🌐 *www.capitolcorridor.org*).

HEALTH AND SAFETY

In an emergency dial 911. Each of the following medical facilities has an emergency room open 24 hours a day.

Hospitals Mercy Hospital of Sacramento (✉ *4001 J St., Sacramento* ☎ *916/453–4424*). **Sutter General Hospital** (✉ *2801 L St., Sacramento* ☎ *916/733–8900*). **Sutter Memorial Hospital** (✉ *52nd and F Sts., Sacramento* ☎ *916/733–1000*).

TOUR OPTIONS

Gold Prospecting Adventures, LLC (☎ *209/984–4653 or 800/596–0009* 🌐 *www.goldprospecting.com*), based in Jamestown, arranges gold-panning trips.

VISITOR INFORMATION

Contacts Amador County Chamber of Commerce & Visitors Bureau (✉ *571 S. Hwy. 49, Jackson* ☎ *209/223–0350* 🌐 *www.amadorcountychamber.com*). **El Dorado County Chamber of Commerce** (✉ *542 Main St., Placerville* ☎ *530/621–5885 or 800/457–6279* 🌐 *www.eldoradocounty.org*). **Grass Valley/Nevada County Chamber of Commerce** (✉ *248 Mill St., Grass Valley* ☎ *530/273–4667 or 800/655–4667* 🌐 *www.grassvalleychamber.com*). **Mariposa County Visitors Bureau** (✉ *5158 Hwy. 140, Mariposa* ☎ *209/966–7081 or 866/425–3366* 🌐 *www.homeofyosemite.com*). **Tuolumne County Visitors Bureau** (✉ *542 W. Stockton Rd., Sonora* ☎ *209/533–4420 or 800/446–1333* 🌐 *www.thegreatunfenced.com*).

RESTAURANTS

American, Italian, and Mexican are common Gold Country fare, but chefs also prepare ambitious Continental, French, and California cuisine. Grass Valley's meat- and vegetable-stuffed *pasties,* introduced by 19th-century gold miners from Cornwall, are one of the region's more unusual treats.

HOTELS

Full-service hotels, budget motels, and small inns can be found in Sacramento. Larger towns along Highway 49—among them Placerville, Nevada City, Auburn, and Mariposa—have chain motels and inns.

Many Gold Country bed-and-breakfasts occupy former mansions, miners' cabins, and other historic buildings.

A number of organizations can supply information about Gold Country B&Bs and other accommodations.

Contacts Amador County Innkeepers Association (☎ *209/267-1710 or 800/726-4667*). **Gold Country Inns of Tuolumne County** (☎ *209/533-1845*). **Historic Bed & Breakfast Inns of Grass Valley & Nevada City** (☎ *530/477-6634 or 800/250-5808*).

WHAT IT COSTS

	¢	$	$$	$$$	$$$$
Restaurants	under $10	$10–$15	$16–$22	$23–$30	over $30
Hotels	under $90	$90–$120	$121–$175	$176–$250	over $250

Restaurant prices are for a main course at dinner, excluding sales tax of 7%–8% (depending on location). Hotel prices are for two people in a standard double room in high season, excluding service charges and 7%–8% tax.

SACRAMENTO AND VICINITY

California's capital is one of the country's most ethnically diverse cities, with sizable Hmong and Ukrainian populations, among many others.

SACRAMENTO

Driving 87 mi northeast of San Francisco (I–80 to Highway 99 or I–5) brings you to the Golden State's seat of government and to echoes of the gold-rush days. Wooden sidewalks and horse-drawn carriages on cobblestone streets lend a 19th-century feel to Old Sacramento, a 28-acre district along the Sacramento River waterfront. The museums at the north end hold artifacts of state and national significance, and historic buildings house shops and restaurants. River cruises and train rides are fun family diversions for an hour or two.

The midtown area, just east of downtown between 15th Street and the Capital City Freeway, contains many of the city's best restaurants and trendy boutiques. Midtown is a vibrant mix of genteel Victorian edifices, ultramodern lofts, and—slowed when the recession hit—a rapidly growing number of innovative restaurants and cozy wine bars. It really springs to life the second Saturday evening of every month, when art galleries hold open houses and the sidewalks are packed, though lately the scene's been more rowdy than arty. A couple of intersections are lively most evenings when the weather's good; they include the corner of 20th and L streets in what's known as Lavender Heights, the center of the city's gay and lesbian community. Overall, midtown is a safe and interesting place to explore, and is the city's most interesting neighborhood.

Downtown, pedestrian-only K Street Mall has for years struggled to gain momentum but cannot shrug off a persistent homeless problem

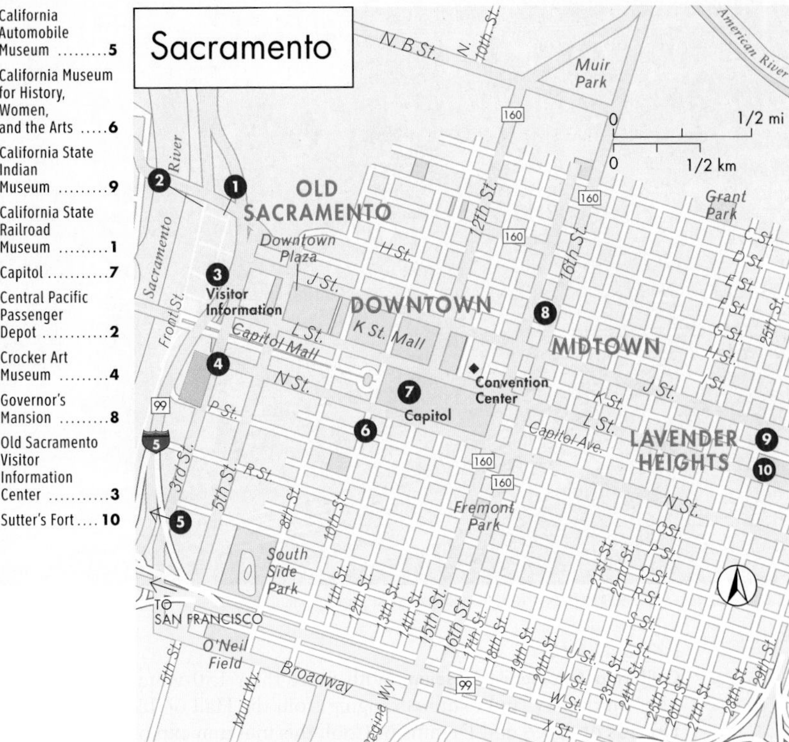

and a scattering of boarded-up storefronts. Sacramento's mayor, former Phoenix Suns guard Kevin Johnson, was viewed as development-friendly when elected in November 2008. Progress since then has been undetectable, and in late 2011, K Street was reopened to vehicular traffic.

Call the **Old Sacramento Events Hotline** (☎ *916/558–3912*) for information about living-history re-creations and merchant hours.

GETTING HERE AND AROUND

Assuming traffic is not a factor, though often it is, Sacramento is a 90-minute drive from San Francisco (and a seven-hour drive from Los Angeles). In town, most people get around by car but Sacramento Regional Transit (🌐 *www.sacrt.com*) operates light-rail and bus lines, the latter reduced significantly in recent years by budget cuts. Taxis are a minor presence. Bike lanes abound, but often they come to sudden ends and leave riders in dicey circumstances.

ESSENTIALS

Visitor Information Sacramento Convention and Visitors Bureau (✉ *1608 I St., Suite 600, Sacramento* ☎ *916/808–7777* 🌐 *www.sacramentocvb.org*).

The California State Railroad Museum is North America's most popular railroad museum.

EXPLORING

California Automobile Museum. With more than 150 vintage automobiles on display, and exhibits ranging from the Hall of Technology to Dreams of Speed and Dreams of Cool, this museum explores automotive history and car culture. A 1920s roadside café and garage exhibit re-creates the early days of motoring. Friendly docents are ready to explain everything. The gift shop sells vintage-car magazines, model kits, and other car-related items. The museum is near downtown and Old Sacramento, with ample free parking. ✉ *2200 Front St., 1 block off Broadway* ☎ *916/442–6802* 🌐 *www.calautomuseum.org* 🎫 *$8* ⏲ *Daily 10–6, Third Thurs. of the month, 10–9.*

California Museum for History, Women, and the Arts. When Arnold Schwarzenegger was governor, Maria Shriver took an active role in having this museum stress women's issues. Though many exhibits use modern technology, there are also scores of archival drawers that you can pull out to see the real artifacts of history and culture—from the California State Constitution to surfing magazines. Board a 1949 cross-country bus to view a video on immigration, visit a Chinese herb shop maintained by a holographic proprietor, or find familiar names inducted into the annually expanded California Hall of Fame. There's also a café that's open weekdays until 2:30 pm. ✉ *1020 O St.* ☎ *916/653–7524* 🌐 *www.californiamuseum.org* 🎫 *$8.50* ⏲ *Mon.–Sat. 10–5, Sun. noon–5.*

California State Indian Museum. Among the interesting displays at this well-organized museum a few strides from Sutter's Fort is one devoted to Ishi, the last Yahi Indian to emerge from the mountains, in 1911. Ishi provided scientists with insight into the traditions and culture of this group of Native Americans. Arts-and-crafts exhibits, a demonstration village, and an evocative 10-minute video bring to life the multifaceted past and present of California's native peoples. ✉ *2618 K St.* ☎ *916/324–0971* 🌐 *www.parks.ca.gov* 🎫 *$3* ⏲ *Daily 10–5.*

12

Fodor's Choice ★ **California State Railroad Museum.** Near what was once the terminus of the transcontinental and Sacramento Valley railroads (the actual terminus was at Front and K streets), this 100,000-square-foot museum—the best of its kind in the region, if not the country—has 21 locomotives and railroad cars on display along with dozens of other exhibits. You can walk through a post-office car and peer into cubbyholes and canvas mailbags, enter a sleeping car that simulates the swaying on the roadbed and the flashing lights of a passing town at night, or glimpse the inside of the first-class dining car. One thousand vintage toy trains constitute a much-heralded permanent exhibit, and the "Last Spike" room is compelling. Kids have lots of fun here, especially in the big play area upstairs. ✉ *125 I St.* ☎ *916/445–6645* 🌐 *www.csrmf.org* 🎫 *$9* ⏲ *Daily 10–5.*

★ **Capitol.** The lacy plasterwork of the Capitol's 120-foot-high rotunda has the complexity and colors of a Fabergé egg. Underneath the gilded dome are marble floors, glittering chandeliers, monumental staircases, reproductions of 19th-century state offices, and legislative chambers decorated in the style of the 1890s (the Capitol was built in 1869). Guides conduct tours of the building and the 40-acre Capitol Park, which contains a rose garden, an impressive display of camellias (Sacramento's city flower), and the California Vietnam Veterans Memorial. ✉ *Capitol Mall and 10th St.* ☎ *916/324–0333* 🌐 *www.statecapitolmuseum.com* 🎫 *Free* ⏲ *Daily 9–5; tours hourly 10–4.*

Central Pacific Passenger Depot, At this reconstructed 1876 station there's rolling stock to admire, a typical waiting room, and a small restaurant. A steam-powered train ($8) departs hourly on weekends April through September, and for special occasions October through December from the freight depot, south of the passenger depot, making a 40-minute out-and-back trip along the Sacramento riverfront. ✉ *930 Front St.* ☎ *916/445–6645* 🎫 *$4, free with same-day ticket from California State Railroad Museum* ⏲ *Daily 10–4.*

Crocker Art Museum. The oldest art museum in the American West has a collection of art from Europe, Asia, and California, including *Sunday Morning in the Mines* (1872), a large canvas by Charles Christian Nahl depicting aspects of the original mining industry, and the magnificent *Great Canyon of the Sierra, Yosemite* (1871), by Thomas Hill. An expansion completed in 2010 tripled the Crocker's size; it now rivals San Francisco's best art museums in scope if not quite in permanent collections. ✉ *216 O St.* ☎ *916/264–5423* 🌐 *www.crockerartmuseum.org* 🎫 *$10, free Sun. 10–1* ⏲ *Tues.–Wed. 10–7, Thurs. 10–9, Fri.–Sat. 10–5.*

★ **Governor's Mansion.** This 15-room house was built in 1877 and used by the state's chief executives from the early 1900s until 1967, when Ronald Reagan vacated it in favor of an upscale private residence. Many of the Italianate mansion's interior decorations were ordered from the Huntington, Hopkins & Co. hardware store, one of whose partners,

Albert Gallatin, was the original occupant. Each of the seven marble fireplaces has a petticoat mirror that ladies strolled past to see if their slips were showing. ✉ *1526 H St.* ☎ *916/323–3047* 🎟 *$5* 🕐 *Daily 10–5; tours hourly, last tour at 4.*

QUICK BITES

The River City Brewing Co. (✉ *Downtown Plaza* ☎ *916/447–2739*) is the best of several breweries in the capital city. The brewery is at the west end of the K Street Mall, between the Capitol and Old Sacramento.

Old Sacramento Visitor Information Center. Find brochures about nearby attractions, check local restaurant menus, and get advice from the helpful staff here. ✉ *1004 Second St., at K St.* ☎ *916/442–7644* 🌐 *www.oldsacramento.com* 🕐 *Daily 10–5.*

★ **Sutter's Fort.** German-born Swiss immigrant John Augustus Sutter founded Sacramento's earliest Euro-American settlement in 1839. Audio speakers give information at each stop along a self-guided tour that includes a blacksmith's shop, bakery, prison, living quarters, and livestock areas. Costumed docents sometimes reenact fort life, demonstrating crafts, food preparation, and firearms maintenance. ✉ *2701 L St.* ☎ *916/445–4422* 🌐 *www.parks.ca.gov* 🎟 *$5* 🕐 *Tues.–Sun. 10–5.*

WHERE TO EAT

$$$ ITALIAN Fodor's Choice ★ ✕ **Biba.** Owner Biba Caggiano is a nationally recognized authority on Italian cuisine. The Capitol crowd flocks here for homemade ravioli, osso buco, grilled pork loin, and veal and rabbit specials. A pianist adds to the upscale ambience nightly. ✉ *2801 Capitol Ave.* ☎ *916/455–2422* 🌐 *www.biba-restaurant.com* ✍ *Reservations essential* 🕐 *Closed Sun. No lunch Sat.*

$ MEXICAN ✕ **Ernesto's Mexican Food.** Customers wait up to an hour for a table on Friday and Saturday evenings at this popular midtown restaurant. Fresh ingredients are stressed in the wide selection of entrées, and the margaritas are especially refreshing. Sister restaurant **Zocalo** (✉ *1801 Capitol Ave.* ☎ *916/441–0303*) has a striking indoor-outdoor atmosphere and is a popular launching spot for nights out on the town. Its menu differs slightly from Ernesto's. ✉ *16th and S Sts.* ☎ *916/441–5850* 🌐 *www.ernestosmexicanfood.com.*

$$$$ CONTINENTAL Fodor's Choice ★ ✕ **The Firehouse.** Consistently ranked by local publications as one of the city's top 10 restaurants, this formal and historic restaurant has a full bar, courtyard seating (its signature attraction), and creative American cooking, such as char-grilled spring rack of lamb served with roasted French fingerling potatoes and baby artichoke and fava bean succotash. Visitors who can afford to treat themselves to a fine and leisurely meal can do no better in Old Sacramento—although they might also opt for the equally upscale Ten 22, located a block away and under the same ownership as the Firehouse. ✉ *1112 2nd St.* ☎ *916/442–4772* 🌐 *www.firehouseoldsac.com* 🕐 *No lunch Sat.*

$$ ECLECTIC ✕ **The Park Downtown.** Atmosphere is what it's all about at this complex of cutting-edge eateries across from Capitol Park. Ma Jong's Asian Diner has inexpensive fare, some suitable for vegetarians; the indoor-outdoor Park Lounge is a supermodern bar and dance club; and the Park To Go

puts a classy spin on breakfasts and lunches for people to take away. ✉ *1116 15th St.* ☎ *916/492–1960* 🌐 *www.theparkdowntown.com.*

WHERE TO STAY

For expanded hotel reviews, visit Fodors.com.

12

$$$ ★ **Amber House Bed & Breakfast Inn.** This B&B about a mile from the Capitol encompasses two homes: the original house is a Craftsman-style home with five bedrooms, and the second is an 1897 Dutch colonial–revival home. **Pros:** midtown location; attentive service. **Cons:** no nearby freeway access. ✉ *1315 22nd St.* ☎ *916/444–8085 or 800/755–6526* 🌐 *www.amberhouse.com* *10 rooms* *In-room: a/c, Internet, Wi-Fi* *Breakfast.*

$$$ **Citizen Hotel.** Billed as Sacramento's first luxury boutique hotel, the Citizen makes its home downtown, in the 1926 Cal Western Life building. *926 J St.* ☎ *916/447–2700* 🌐 *www.jdvhotels.com* *175 rooms, 23 suites* *In-room: a/c. In-hotel: restaurant, bar, gym* *Breakfast.*

$$$ ★ **Hyatt Regency Sacramento.** With a marble-and-glass lobby and luxurious rooms, this hotel across from the Capitol and adjacent to the convention center is arguably Sacramento's finest. **Pros:** beautiful Capitol Park is across the street. **Cons:** downtown streets can be dodgy at night; somewhat impersonal. ✉ *1209 L St.* ☎ *916/443–1234 or 800/633–7313* 🌐 *www.hyatt.com* *500 rooms, 24 suites* *In-room: a/c, Internet. In-hotel: restaurants, bar, pool, gym, parking.*

SHOPPING

The Galleria at Roseville (✉ *1 mi west of I–80 in northern suburb*) is a sprawling, heavily trafficked collection of chain stores and restaurants.

WOODLAND

20 mi northwest of Sacramento on I–5.

Woodland's downtown lies frozen in a quaint and genteel past. In its heyday it was one of the wealthiest cities in California, established in 1861 by gold seekers and entrepreneurs. Once the boom was over, attention turned to the rich surrounding land, and the area became an agricultural gold mine. The legacy of the old land barons lives on in the Victorian homes that line Woodland's wide streets. Many of the houses have been restored and are surrounded by lavish gardens.

GETTING HERE AND AROUND

Yolobus (🌐 *www.yolobus.com*) serves Woodland and Davis, with one route venturing to Sacramento International Airport and downtown Sacramento. As a visitor, you're far better off having access to a private automobile here (or anywhere else in the region, for that matter.

ESSENTIALS

Visitor Information Woodland Chamber of Commerce (✉ *307 1st St., Woodland* ☎ *530/662–7327 or 888/843–2636* 🌐 *www.woodlandchamber.org*).

EXPLORING

Woodland Opera House. More than 300 touring companies, including John Philip Sousa's marching band, and Frank Kirk, the Acrobatic Tramp, appeared at the opera house, built in 1885 (and rebuilt after it burned in 1892). Now restored, the building is the site of concerts and, September through July, a season of musical theater. Free, guided tours reveal old-fashioned stage technology. ✉ *Main and 2nd Sts.* ☎ *530/666–9617* 🌐 *www.wohtheatre.org* ⏲ *Weekdays 10–5, weekends noon–5, tours Tues. 1–4.*

Yolo County Historical Museum. This 10-room classical-revival home of settler William Byas Gibson was purchased by volunteers and restored to what you see today. You can see collections of furnishings and artifacts from the 1850s to 1930s. Old trees and an impressive lawn cover the 2½-acre site off Highway 113. ✉ *512 Gibson Rd.* ☎ *530/666–1045* 🌐 *www.gibsonhouse.org* 🎟 *Free* ⏲ *Mon. and Tues. 10–4, Sat. noon–4.*

Heidrick Ag History Center. Old trucks and farm machinery seem to rumble to life within this shedlike center, where you can see the world's largest collection of antique agricultural equipment. Also here are multimedia exhibits and a gift shop. ✉ *1962 Hays La.* ☎ *530/666–9700* 🌐 *www.aghistory.org* 🎟 *$8* ⏲ *Weekdays 10–5, Sat. 10–6, Sun. 10–4.*

DAVIS

10 mi west of Sacramento on I–80.

Though it began as—and still is—a rich agricultural area, Davis doesn't feel like a cow town. It's home to the University of California at Davis, whose students hang at the cafés and bookstores in the central business district, making the city feel a little more cosmopolitan. Downtown is compact and walkable; bicyclists are everywhere (and are treated with respect by drivers) throughout town. The city has long enjoyed a progressive, liberal reputation (it's been called "the People's Republic of Davis"), but a rash of 1990s-built yuppie-stocked subdivisions reflect how Davis is becoming more of a mainstream commuter community, whether residents admit it or not.

GETTING HERE AND AROUND

If you can, bring your bicycle and "go native." Otherwise, use your feet to get around downtown, your car to get about town, and Yolobus (🌐 *www.yolobus.com*) if you're among the tiny percentage of visitors who don't have an automobile handy.

ESSENTIALS

Visitor Information **Davis Chamber of Commerce** (✉ *130 G St., Davis* ☎ *530/756–5160* 🌐 *www.davischamber.com*).

EXPLORING

Davis Campus of the University of California. The center of action in town, UC Davis often ranks among the top 25 research universities in the United States. You can take tours of the campus, which depart from Buehler Alumni and Visitors Center. The **Mondavi Center for the Performing Arts,** a strikingly modern glass structure off I–80, offers a busy and varied schedule of performances by top-tier musical, dance and other artists. ✉ *1 Shields Ave.* ☎ *530/752–8111* 🌐 *www.ucdavis.edu* ⏲ *Tours weekends at 11:30, weekdays by appointment.*

THE GOLD COUNTRY—SOUTH

This hilly region has an old-timey vibe. It's rich with antiques shops, quaint coffee shops, and delightfully appointed Victorian B&Bs.

PLACERVILLE

10 mi south of Coloma on Hwy. 49; 44 mi east of Sacramento on U.S. 50.

It's hard to imagine now, but in 1849 about 4,000 miners staked out every gully and hillside in Placerville, turning the town into a rip-roaring camp of log cabins, tents, and clapboard houses. The area was then known as Hangtown, a graphic allusion to the nature of frontier justice. It took on the name Placerville in 1854 and became an important supply center for the miners. Mark Hopkins, Philip Armour, and John Studebaker were among the industrialists who got their starts here.

GETTING HERE AND AROUND

Placerville is a 45-minute drive east of downtown Sacramento via Highway 50. Although many Placerville residents work in the capital, there is no public bus link worth mentioning. You'll need a car to get here and around.

EXPLORING

★ **Hangtown's Gold Bug Park & Mine,** owned by the City of Placerville, centers on a fully lighted mine shaft open for self-guided touring. ■ **TIP→** An audio tour is included with admission and greatly enriches the experience. A shaded stream runs through the park, and there are picnic facilities. ✉ *North on Bedford Ave., 1 mi off U.S. 50* ☎ *530/642–5207* 🌐 *www.goldbugpark.org* *$5* ⏲ *Tours mid-Apr.–Oct., daily 10–4; Nov.–Apr., weekends noon–4. Gift shop Apr.–Oct., daily 10–4.*

WHERE TO EAT AND STAY

¢ VEGETARIAN ✕ **The Cozmic Cafe.** Crowds convene here at any time of day for healthful wraps, burritos, sandwiches, salads, and the like, plus breakfasts (served anytime), smoothies, and coffee drinks; vegetarians are well served here. The portions are big, prices are low, and the ambience is among the most distinctive in Placerville. The eatery is in the 1859 Pearson's Soda Works Building, and extends back into the side of a mountain, into what used to be a mineshaft. Live music here is among the best in the foothills, and an upstairs pub beckons with local wines and microbrews; unwind with yoga classes there before the evening's libations. ✉ *594 Main St.* ☎ *530/642–8481* 🌐 *www.ourcoz.com.*

APPLE HILL

The **Apple Hill** roadside stand sells fresh produce from more than 50 family farms in this area. During the fall harvest season (from September through December), members of the Apple Hill Growers Association open their orchards and vineyards for apple and berry picking, picnicking, and wine and cider tasting. Many sell baked items and picnic food. ✉ *About 5 mi east of Hwy. 49; take Camino exit from U.S. 50* ☎ *530/644–7692.*

$ **Seasons Bed & Breakfast.** A 10-minute walk from downtown, one of Placerville's oldest homes has been transformed into a lovely and relaxing oasis. **Pros:** quiet setting; attentive hosts; great breakfasts. **Cons:** B&B environment not for everyone. *2934 Bedford Ave.* *530/626–4420* *www.theseasons.net* *1 room, 2 suites* *In-room: a/c, Wi-Fi* *Breakfast.*

SHENANDOAH VALLEY

20 mi south of Placerville on Shenandoah Rd., east of Hwy. 49.

The most concentrated Gold Country wine-touring area lies in the hills of the Shenandoah Valley, east of Plymouth. **TIP→ This region is gaining steam as a less-congested alternative to overrun Napa Valley.** Robust zinfandel is the primary grape grown here, but vineyards also produce other varietals. Most wineries are open on weekend afternoons; several have shaded picnic areas, gift shops, and galleries or museums; all have tasting rooms.

GETTING HERE AND AROUND

Reach the Shenandoah Valley by turning east on Fiddletown Road in Plymouth, between Placerville and Sutter Creek. You will need a car to explore the valley and its vineyards.

EXPLORING

Charles Spinetta Winery. Here, you can see a wildlife art gallery in addition to tasting the wine. The winery's Zinfandel and Syrah are quite popular. *12557 Steiner Rd., Plymouth* *209/245–3384* *www.charlesspinettawinery.com* *Mon., Thurs., and Fri. 8–4, weekends 9–5.*

Shenandoah Vineyards. The gallery at this Sobon-affiliated winery (one of the valley's original four) displays contemporary art, and sells pottery, framed photographs, and souvenirs. *12300 Steiner Rd., Plymouth* *209/245–4455* *www.sobonwine.com* *Daily 10–5.*

Sobon Estate. Its Shenandoah Valley Museum illustrates pioneer life and wine-making in the valley. The family-owned business is listed as a California State Historic Landmark. *14430 Shenandoah Rd., Plymouth* *209/245–6554* *www.sobonwine.com* *Daily 9:30–5.*

AMADOR CITY

6 mi south of Plymouth on Hwy. 49.

The history of tiny Amador City mirrors the boom-bust-boom cycle of many Gold Country towns. With an output of $42 million in gold, its Keystone Mine was one of the most productive in the Mother Lode. After all the gold was extracted, the miners cleared out, and the area suffered. Amador City now derives its wealth from tourists, who come to browse through its antiques and specialty shops, most of them on or just off Highway 49.

Continued on page 490

EUREKA! CALIFORNIA'S GOLD RUSH

When James W. Marshall burst into John Sutter's Mill on January 24, 1848, carrying flecks of gold in his hat, the millwright unleashed the glittering California gold rush with these immortal words:

 **"Boys, I believe I've found a gold mine!"** 

Before it was over, drowsy San Francisco had become the boomtown of the Golden West, Columbia's mines alone yielded $87,000,000, and California's Mother Lode—a vein of gold-bearing quartz that stretched 150 miles across the Sierra Nevada foothills—had been nearly tapped dry. Even though the gold rush soon became the gold bust, today you can still strike it rich by visiting the historic sites where it all happened.

Journey down the Gold Country Highway—a serpentine, nearly 300-mi-long two-lane route appropriately numbered 49—to find pure vacation treasure: fascinating mother lode towns, rip-roaring mining camps, and historic strike sites. In fact, in Placerville—as the former Hangtown, this spot saw so much new money and crime that outlaws were hanged in pairs—you can still pan the streams. And after you've seen the sights, the prospects remain just as golden: the entire region is a trove of gorgeous wineries, fun eateries, and Victorian-era hotels.

by: Reed Parsell and Robert I.C. Fisher

ALL THAT GLITTERED: '49ER FEVER

From imagination springs adventure, and perhaps no event in the 19th century provoked more wild adventures than the California gold rush of 1848 to 1855.

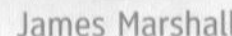

James Marshall

1856 U.S. quarter

John Sutter

GOLD IN THEM THAR HILLS California's golden lava was discovered purely by accident. Upon finding his cattle ranch had gone to ruin while he was away fighting in the Mexican-American War, New Jersey native James W. Marshall decided to build a sawmill, with John Sutter, outside the town of Coloma, 40 miles upstream of Sutter's Fort on the American River. To better power the mill, he had a wider siphon created to divert the river water and, one morning, spotted golden flakes in the trench. Rich fur magnate Sutter tried to keep the mother strike quiet, but his own staff soon decamped to pan the streams and the secret was out. The gold rush's impact was so profound that, practically overnight, it catapulted San Francisco into one of the nation's—and the world's—wealthiest cities.

BROTHER, CAN YOU SPARE AN INGOT? After Marshall, 37 at the time, saw his fledgling mill abandoned by workers who went to pan the streams, he left Coloma for almost a decade. During the 1860s he made some money as a vintner there—a dicey profession for a reported alcoholic. Eventually Marshall's wine business dried up, and he returned to prospecting in the 1870s. But without success. For six years starting in 1872, the state Legislature gave him a small pension as an acknowledgment of his gold rush importance, but for the last years of his life he was practically penniless. He died on Aug. 10, 1885, at age 74.

THE GOLD CRUSH Before the gold rush ended, in 1855, it is estimated that it drew 300,000 people—Americans, Europeans, and Chinese—to the Sierra Nevada foothills to seek their fortune. Sadly, accidents, disease, and skirmishes with Native Americans took their toll on both the prospectors and the environment. In addition, the gold lust of '49er fever left more than a thousand murders in its wake (not counting the infamous "suspended" sentences meted out at Hangtown).

BOOM TO BUST

Jan. 24, 1848: James W. Marshall spies specks of bright rock in the streambed at his sawmill's site; Sutter certifies they are gold.
May, 1848: California's coastal communities empty out as prospectors flock to the hills to join the "forty-eighters."
Aug. 19, 1848: The *New York Herald* is the first East Coast newspaper to report a gold rush in California.
Oct. 13, 1849: California's state constitution is approved in Monterey. The state's new motto becomes "Eureka!"
1855: The California gold rush effectively ends, as digging for the precious mineral becomes increasingly difficult, and large corporations monopolize mining operations.

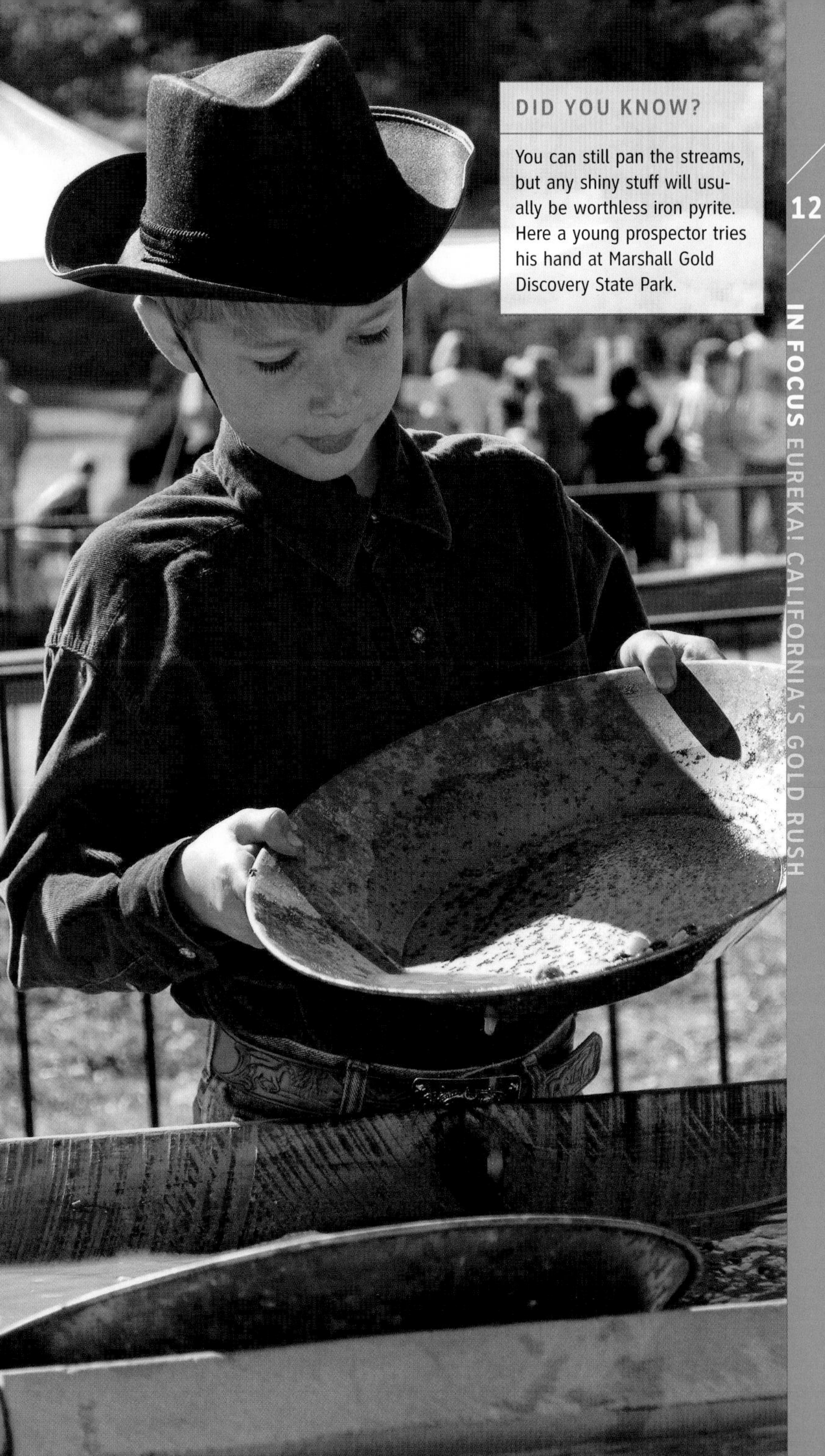

DID YOU KNOW?

You can still pan the streams, but any shiny stuff will usually be worthless iron pyrite. Here a young prospector tries his hand at Marshall Gold Discovery State Park.

GOING FOR THE GOLD

Marshall Gold Discovery State Park

If you want to go prospecting for the best sightseeing treasures in Gold Country, just follow this map.

Coloma

Empire Mine State Historic Park, Grass Valley: During the century that it was operating, Empire Mine produced some 5.6 million ounces of gold. More than 350 miles of tunnels were dug, most under water. Operations ceased in 1956, but today visitors to the 800-acre park can go on 50-minute guided tours of the mines and enjoy great hiking trails and picnic spots.

Marshall Gold Discovery State Historic Park, Coloma: Here's where it all began—a can't-miss gold rush site. See the stone cairn that marks the spot of James Marshall's discovery, the huge statue of him that rests on his grave site, and visit—together with crowds of schoolchildren—the updated museum, and more.

Hangtown's Gold Bug Park & Mine, Placerville: Put on a hardhat and step into the 19th century at Gold Bug, located a few miles south of Marshall's jackpot site. Take a self-guided audio tour of a mine that opened in 1888, or a special tour of a mine opened in the 1850s, and do some "placering" (panning for gold) yourself, outside the gift shop. "Fool's gold" (used for billiard tables and chalkboards) was mostly found here before digging stopped in 1942.

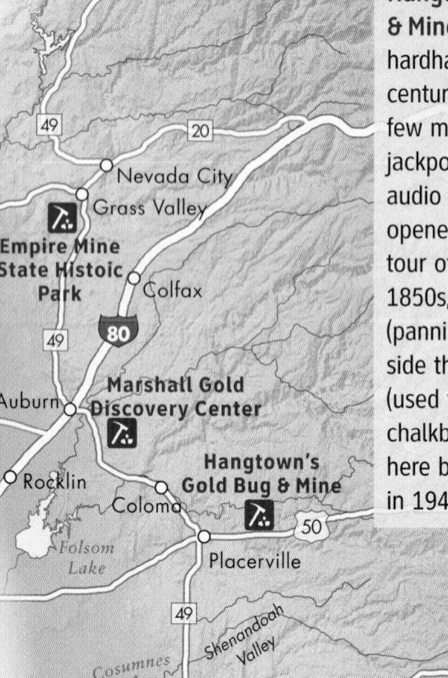

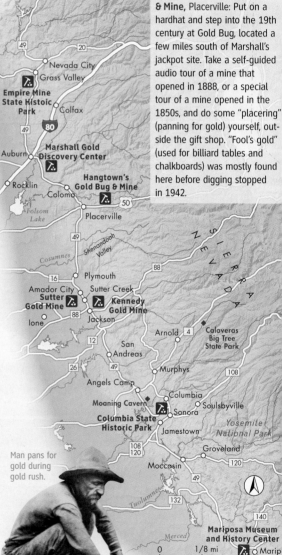

Man pans for gold during gold rush.

Empire Mine State Historic Park　　Gold sifting pan　　Columbia State Historic Park

Sutter Gold Mine: Between Amador City and Sutter Creek off Highway 49, this is the place to see how the so-called "Forty-Niner" individual prospectors were succeeded by large, deep-pocket mining companies. One-hour tours, offered daily April through most of October, take visitors deep into a hard-rock mine, where they can see ore veins that contain gold and learn the basics of hydraulic extraction.

Kennedy Gold Mine, Jackson: At 5,912 feet below ground, this is one of the world's deepest mines. Its head frame is one of the most dominant man-made sights along Highway 49's 295 miles. In operation from 1880 until World War II, the mine produced tens of millions of dollars of gold. One-hour tours, offered weekends and holidays from March through October, include a look inside the stately Mine Office.

Columbia State Historic Park

Columbia State Historic Park. Just north of Sonora, this is the best extant example of a gold rush-era town as it appeared in the mid-19th century. During its "golden" years, Columbia yielded more than $85 million in gold. Since World War II, the town has been restored. Fandango halls, Wells Fargo stage coaches, and a costumed staff bring a working 1850's mining town to life again.

Gold dollars

Mariposa Museum and History Center, Mariposa: Find all sorts of mining equipment, including a five-stamp ore mill, at this modest museum in the gold rush region's southernmost area. Also here is the fascinating California State Mining and Mineral Museum, home to a famous 13-pound golden nugget.

A PROSPECTING PRIMER

Grab any non-Teflon-coated pan with sloping sides and head up to "them thar hills." Find a stream—preferably one containing black sand—you can stoop beside, and then:

- Scoop out sediment to fill your pan.
- Add water, then gently shake the pan sideways, back and forth. This allows any gold to settle at the bottom.
- Pick out and toss away any larger rocks.
- Keep adding water, keep shaking the pan, and slowly pour the loosened waste gravel over the rim of the pan, making sure not to upend the pan while doing so.
- If you're left with gold, yell "Eureka!" then put it in a glass container. Your findings may not make you rich, but will entitle you to bragging rights for as long as you keep the gold handy to show friends.

TIP→ If you'd rather not pan on your own, plenty of attractions and museums in the Gold Country will let you try your hand at prospecting. See listings in this chapter for more details on these historic sites.

GETTING HERE AND AROUND

Park where you can along Old Highway 49 (in 2008 a bypass diverted Highway 49 traffic around Sutter Creek and Amador City) and walk from place to place. It won't take you but a few minutes in this blink-and-you'll-miss-it town.

WHERE TO STAY

For expanded hotel reviews, visit Fodors.com.

$$ ★ **Imperial Hotel.** The whimsically decorated mock-Victorian rooms at this 1879 hotel give a modern twist to the excesses of the era. **Pros:** comfortable; good restaurant and bar; tiny-town charm. **Cons:** the town's got no nightlife. ✉ 14202 Old *Hwy. 49* ☎ *209/267–9172* 🌐 *www.imperialamador.com* *6 rooms, 3 suites* *In-room: a/c, no TV, Wi-Fi. In-hotel: restaurant, bar* *Breakfast.*

SUTTER CREEK

★ *2 mi south of Amador City on Hwy. 49.*

Sutter Creek is a charming conglomeration of balconied buildings, Victorian homes, and neo–New England structures. The stores on Main Street (formerly part of busy Highway 49, which thankfully has been rerouted around town) are worth visiting for works by the many local artists and craftspeople.

GETTING HERE AND AROUND

There are no public transportation options here or anywhere else in the Gold Country. But Sutter Creek, like the Gold Country's other towns, is very walkable once you've found that parking spot.

EXPLORING

Monteverde Store Museum. This store, opened 1896, is a relic from the past. In the 1970s the owner walked out without telling a soul and never returned. What you see on the shelves today is what he left behind, including typical turn-of-the-20th-century goods, an elaborate antique scale, and a chair-encircled potbellied stove in the corner. The store is open Thursday–Monday provided there are volunteers available. ✉ *3 Randolph St.*

Sutter Creek Visitor Center. The visitor center organizes walking tours and has a helpful Web site. ✉ *71A Main St.* ☎ *209/267–1344 or 800/400–0305* 🌐 *www.suttercreek.org.*

WHERE TO EAT AND STAY

$$ AMERICAN **Susan's Place.** Fresh produce, prompt and attentive service, and a lovely patio (especially lovely on warm summer evenings) distinguish this local favorite a half-block off the main drag. The serving of wine is a big deal here; there's even a "mystery wine" option that leaves the bottle (or glass) choice up to the owner. Try the eggplant and Portobello mushrooms on grilled panini bread. ✉ *15 Eureka St.* ☎ *209/267–0945* 🌐 *www.susansplace.com* *Closed Mon.–Wed.*

$$ ★ **Eureka Street Inn.** Original redwood paneling, wainscoting, beams, and cabinets as well as lead- and stained-glass windows lend the Eureka Street Inn a certain coziness. **Pros:** quiet location; lovely porch; engaging owners. **Cons:** only four rooms. ✉ *55 Eureka St.,* ☎ *209/267–5500*

or 800/399–2389 ⊕ www.eurekastreetinn.com ⇆ 4 rooms ♁ In-room: a/c, no TV, Wi-Fi 🍽 Breakfast.

$$$ ★ **The Foxes Inn of Sutter Creek.** The rooms in this 1857 white-clapboard house are handsome, with high ceilings, antique beds, and armoires; five have gas fireplaces. **Pros:** lovely inside and out; friendly owners. **Cons:** pricey. ✉ *77 Main St.* ☎ *209/267–5882 or 800/987–3344* ⊕ *www.foxesinn.com* ⇆ *5 rooms, 2 suites* ♁ *In-room: a/c, Wi-Fi* 🍽 *Breakfast.*

$$ **Grey Gables Inn.** Charming yet modern, this inn brings a touch of the English countryside to the Gold Country. **Pros:** distinctively English feel; tasteful interiors. **Cons:** hovers over the main road; not much to do in town after dark. ✉ *161 Hanford St.* ☎ *209/267–1039 or 800/473–9422* ⊕ *www.greygables.com* ⇆ *8 rooms* 🍽 *Breakfast.*

JACKSON

8 mi south of Sutter Creek on Hwy. 49.

Jackson wasn't the Gold Country's rowdiest town, but the party lasted longer here than most anywhere else: "girls' dormitories" (aka brothels) and nickel slot machines flourished until the mid-1950s. Jackson also had the world's deepest and richest gold mines, the Kennedy and the Argonaut, which together produced $70 million in gold. These were deep-rock mines with tunnels extending as much as a mile underground. Most of the miners who worked the lode were of Serbian or Italian origin, and they gave the town a European character that persists to this day. Jackson has pioneer cemeteries whose headstones tell the stories of local Serbian and Italian families.

GETTING HERE AND AROUND

Arrive here via automobile via Highway 49. You'll need a car to see Jackson and the nearby sites; there's no public transportation worth noting.

EXPLORING

St. Sava Serbian Orthodox Church. The terraced cemetery on the grounds of the handsome church is the town's most impressive burial grounds. ✉ *724 N. Main St.*

WHERE TO EAT

$ AMERICAN **Mel and Faye's Diner.** For more than a half-century this roadside (looming over Highway 49 on a small hill) diner has been a local hangout, with its signature "Moo Burger" (so big it still makes cow sounds, presumably). Mel and Faye's son now runs the business and has supplemented the menu with slightly more sophisticated fare for breakfast, lunch, and dinner. ✉ *31 Main St.* ☎ *209/223–0853* ⊙ *Closed Tues. No dinner.*

ANGELS CAMP

20 mi south of Jackson on Hwy. 49.

Angels Camp is famed chiefly for its May jumping-frog contest, based on Mark Twain's short story "The Celebrated Jumping Frog of Calaveras County." The writer reputedly heard the story of the jumping frog from Ross Coon, proprietor of Angels Hotel, which has been in operation since 1856.

GETTING HERE AND AROUND

Angels Camp is at the intersection of Highway 49 and Highway 4, which from here heads northeast past Murphys up into the Sierra Nevada range past the popular Bear Valley Ski Resort and, during warm months only, connects with Highway 395 along the eastern Sierra. You'll need to get here and around in a car.

EXPLORING

Angels Camp Museum. Here you'll find gold-rush relics, including photos, rocks, petrified wood, old blacksmith and mining equipment, and a horse-drawn hearse. The carriage house out back holds 31 carriages and an impressive display of mineral specimens. ✉ *753 S. Main St.* ☎ *209/736–2963* 🎫 *$2* ⏲ *Jan. and Feb., weekends 10–3; Mar.–Dec., daily 10–3.*

California Cavern. A ½-mi subterranean trail winds through large chambers and past underground streams and lakes. There aren't many steps to climb, but it's a strenuous walk with some narrow passageways and steep spots. The caverns, at a constant 53°F, contain crystalline formations not found elsewhere, and the 80-minute guided tour explains local history and geology. Call ahead to check on hours of operation, which are subject to change. ✉ *9 mi east of San Andreas on Mountain Ranch Rd., then about 3 mi on Cave City Rd., follow signs* ☎ *209/736–2708* 🌐 *www.caverntours.com* 🎫 *$14.75* ⏲ *Mar.–Apr., daily 10–4; May–Oct., daily 10–5; Nov.–Feb. weekends 10–4.*

Fodor's Choice ★ **Moaning Cavern.** A 235-step spiral staircase leads into this vast cavern. More adventurous sorts can rappel into the chamber—ropes and instruction are provided. Otherwise, the only way inside is via the 45-minute tour, during which you'll see giant (and still growing) stalactites and stalagmites and an archaeological site that holds some of the oldest human remains yet found in America (an unlucky person has fallen into the cavern about once every 130 years for the last 13,000 years). Outside there are three zip lines, starting at $39 per person. ✉ *5350 Moaning Cave Rd., off Parrots Ferry Rd., about 2 mi south of Vallecito* ☎ *209/736–2708* 🌐 *www.caverntours.com* 🎫 *$14.75* ⏲ *May–Oct., daily 9–6; Nov.–Apr., weekdays 10–5, weekends 9–5.*

MURPHYS

10 mi northeast of Angels Camp on Hwy. 4.

Murphys is a well-preserved town of white-picket fences, Victorian houses, and interesting shops that exhibits an upscale vibe, with its nearby wineries and free-spending Bay Area visitors. Horatio Alger and Ulysses S. Grant came through here, staying at Murphys Historic Hotel & Lodge when they, along with many other 19th-century tourists, came to see the giant sequoia groves in nearby Calaveras Big Trees State Park.

DID YOU KNOW?

A stately giant sequoia rises above it all at Calaveras Big Trees State Park, which protects the northernmost grove of giant sequoias known to exist.

GETTING HERE AND AROUND

Although Murphys is 10 mi off Highway 49, the diversion on Highway 4 is worth it, as Murphys presents the Gold Country's most compact, orderly town, with enough shops and restaurants to keep most families busy for at least a half-day. You'll need to drive here, and parking can be a challenge on busy summer weekends.

CALAVERAS BIG TREE STATE PARK

The **Calaveras Big Tree State Park** protects hundreds of the largest and rarest living things on the planet—magnificent giant sequoia redwood trees. Some are 3,000 years old, 90 feet around at the base, and 250 feet tall. There are campgrounds and picnic areas; swimming, wading, fishing, and sunbathing on the Stanislaus River are popular in summer. ✉ *Off Hwy. 4, 15 mi northeast of Murphys, 4 mi northeast of Arnold* ☎ *209/795–2334* 🎫 *$6 per vehicle, day use; campsites $20* ⏲ *Park daily sunrise–sunset, day use; visitor center May–Oct., daily 11–3; Nov.–Apr., weekends 11–3.*

EXPLORING

Ironstone Vineyards. Tours take you through the spectacular gardens and into underground tunnels cooled by a waterfall from a natural spring, and include a performance on a massive automated pipe organ. ■ **TIP→ It's worth a visit even if you don't drink wine.** The winery schedules concerts during summer in its huge outdoor amphitheater, plus art shows and other events on weekends. On display is a 44-pound specimen of crystalline gold. Visit the deli for lunch. ✉ *1894 6 Mile Rd.* ☎ *209/728–1251* 🌐 *www.ironstonevineyards.com* ⏲ *Daily 10–5; open until 6 in summer.*

WHERE TO EAT AND STAY

$$$ AMERICAN ✕ **Grounds.** Light entrées, grilled vegetables, chicken, seafood, and steak are the specialties at this bustling bistro and coffee shop. Sandwiches, salads, and homemade soups are served for lunch. The crowd is friendly and the service attentive. ✉ *402 Main St.* ☎ *209/728–8663.*

$ **Murphys Historic Hotel & Lodge.** This 1855 stone hotel, whose register has seen the signatures of Mark Twain and the bandit Black Bart, figured in Bret Harte's short story "A Night at Wingdam." **Pros:** loads of historical ambience; great bar; smack in the middle of downtown. **Cons:** dated; creaky. ✉ *457 Main St.* ☎ *209/728–3444 or 800/532–7684* 🌐 *www.murphyshotel.com* *29 rooms, 20 with bath* *In-room: a/c, Wi-Fi. In-hotel: restaurant, bar.*

COLUMBIA

14 mi south of Angels Camp via Hwy. 49 to Parrots Ferry Rd.

Columbia is the gateway for Columbia State Historic Park, which is one of the Gold Country's most visited sites.

GETTING HERE AND AROUND

The only way to get here is by private automobile. Consider bringing picnic supplies, as there are several inviting spots within and around the town. The parking lot is huge.

12

EXPLORING

Fodor's Choice ★ **Columbia State Historic Park.** Although it definitely is showing wear from state budget cuts, Columbia comes as close to a gold-rush town in its heyday as any site in the Gold Country. Usually, you can ride a stagecoach, pan for gold, and watch a blacksmith working at an anvil. Street musicians perform in summer. Restored or reconstructed buildings include a Wells Fargo Express office, a Masonic temple, stores, saloons, two hotels, a firehouse, churches, a school, and a newspaper office. At times, all are staffed to simulate a working 1850s town. The park also includes the **Historic Fallon House Theater,** where entertainment is presented much of the year. Note: The town's two 19th-century historic lodgings, the Fallon Hotel (¢–$) and City Hotel ($–$$), which shuttered in 2008, reopened under new ownership in late 2010; find out more at *www.cityhotel.com*. ✉ *11175 Washington St.* ☎ *209/532–0150* *www.parks.ca.gov* *Free* *Daily 9–5.*

SONORA

4 mi south of Columbia via Parrots Ferry Rd. to Hwy. 49.

Miners from Mexico founded Sonora and made it the biggest town in the Mother Lode. Following a period of racial and ethnic strife, the Mexican settlers moved on, and Yankees built the commercial city that is visible today. Sonora's historic downtown section sits atop the Big Bonanza Mine, one of the richest in the state. Another mine, on the site of nearby Sonora High School, yielded 990 pounds of gold in a single week in 1879. Reminders of the gold rush are everywhere in Sonora, in prim Victorian houses, typical Sierra-stone storefronts, and awning-shaded sidewalks. Reality intrudes beyond the town's historic heart, with strip malls, shopping centers, and modern motels.

GETTING HERE AND AROUND

You'll more likely than not being arriving by private car. Sonora represents a bit of a parking challenge, what with its busy main drag (Washington St., which is Highway 49) and its narrow, often very steep side roads.

EXPLORING

Tuolumne County Museum and History Center. The small but chockablock museum occupies a gold rush–era building that served as a jail until 1960. Listed on the National Register of Historic Places, it houses a museum with vintage firearms and paraphernalia, a case with gold specimens, a MiWuk basket display, and the historical society's and genealogical society's libraries. ✉ *158 W. Bradford St.* ☎ *209/532–1317* *www.tchistory.org* *Free* *Daily 10–4.*

WHERE TO EAT AND STAY

$ AMERICAN ✕ **Diamondback Grill.** Burgers are what this place is about, although the bright decor and refined atmosphere suggest more ambitious fare. Locals regard this place as the best restaurant in town, and seem to back that up by crowding the tables, especially after 6 pm. Aside from the ground-meat patties, the beer-battered onion rings, Veggie Burger, and wine collection draw raves. ✉ *93 S. Washington St.* ☎ *209/532–6661* ⏲ *Closed Sun.*

$$ **Barretta Gardens Bed and Breakfast Inn.** This inn is perfect for a romantic getaway, with elegant Victorian rooms varying in size, all furnished with period pieces. **Pros:** lovely grounds; yummy breakfasts; romantic. **Cons:** only seven rooms. ✉ *700 S. Barretta St.* ☎ *209/532–6039 or 800/206–3333* ⊕ *www.barrettagardens.com* *7 rooms* *In-room: Wi-Fi* *Breakfast.*

A LIVING BACKDROP

If the countryside surrounding Sonora seems familiar, that's because it has been the backdrop for many movies over the years. Scenes from *High Noon, For Whom the Bell Tolls, The Virginian, Back to the Future III,* and *Unforgiven* were filmed here.

JAMESTOWN

4 mi south of Sonora on Hwy. 49.

Compact Jamestown supplies a lightly touristy view of gold rush–era life. Shops in brightly colored buildings along Main Street sell antiques and gift items.

GETTING HERE AND AROUND

Highway 49, which is joined by Highway 108 as the latter passes through on its way to cross (warm months only) the Sierra Nevada mountain range, is a car town. There is a railroad museum, all right, but there is no rail service.

EXPLORING

Railtown 1897. This low-key but extensive (mostly) outdoor museum preserves what were the headquarters and general shops of the Sierra Railway from 1897 to 1955. The railroad has appeared in more than 200 movies and television productions, including *Petticoat Junction, The Virginian, High Noon,* and *Unforgiven.* You can view the roundhouse, an air-operated 60-foot turntable, shop rooms, and old locomotives and coaches. Six-mile, 40-minute steam train rides through the countryside operate weekends in warm months and on some holiday weekends. ✉ *5th Ave. and Reservoir Rd., off Hwy. 49* ☎ *209/984–3953* ⊕ *www.railtown1897.org* *Roundhouse tour $5; train ride $13* ⏲ *Apr.–Oct., daily 9:30–4:30; Nov.–Mar., daily 10–3. Train rides Apr.–Oct., weekends 11–3.*

WHERE TO STAY

For expanded hotel reviews, visit Fodors.com.

$$ **National Hotel.** The National has been in business since 1859, and the furnishings—brass beds, regal comforters, and lace curtains—are authentic but not overly embellished. **Pros:** wonderful historic feel; great brunches—especially the crepes. **Cons:** only nine rooms. ✉ *18183 Main St.* ☎ *209/984–3446; 800/894–3446 in CA* ⊕ *www.national-hotel.com* *9 rooms* *In-room: a/c, Internet. In-hotel: restaurant, bar* *Breakfast.*

12

MARIPOSA

50 mi south of Jamestown on Hwy. 49.

Mariposa marks the southern end of the Mother Lode. Much of the land in this area was part of a 44,000-acre land grant Colonel John C. Fremont acquired from Mexico before gold was discovered and California became a state.

GETTING HERE AND AROUND

Many people stop here on their way to Yosemite National Park, about an hour's drive east on Highway 140. The Yosemite Area Regional Transportation System (YARTS *www.yarts.com*) is a cheap and dependable way to travel among Merced (off the Central Valley's busy Highway 99), Mariposa, and Yosemite Valley. YARTS partners with Amtrak so that riders on the Central Valley's San Joaquin line can detrain in Merced and catch a bus right at the train station. Otherwise, you'll need a car to get here.

EXPLORING

California State Mining and Mineral Museum. A glittering 13-pound chunk of crystallized gold makes it clear what the rush was about. Displays include a reproduction of a typical tunnel dug by hard-rock miners, a miniature stamp mill, and a panning and sluicing exhibit. ✉ *Mariposa County Fairgrounds, Hwy. 49* ☎ *209/742–7625* *$3* ⏲ *May–Sept., daily 10–6; Oct.–Apr., Wed.–Mon. 10–4.*

WHERE TO EAT AND STAY

$ AMERICAN ✕ **Butterfly Cafe.** The quiet and shady outdoor patio behind the front shop is where you'll want to sit—weather permitting, of course. This friendly place shines brightest for breakfast and lunch, and has several options for vegans and vegetarians. The beer and wine selections are solid, and the cheesecake is superb. ✉ *Hwy. 140* ☎ *209/742–4114* *www.thebutterflycafe.com*

$$$ AMERICAN ✕ **Charles Street Dinner House.** Ever since Ed Uebner moved here from Chicago to become the owner-chef in 1980, Charles Street has been firmly established as the classiest dinner joint in town—plus, it's centrally located. The extensive menu includes beef, chicken, pork, lamb, duck, and lobster; recently a few vegetarian options were added. ✉ *Hwy. 140, at 7th St.* ☎ *209/966–2366* *www.charlesstreetdinnerhouse.com* ⏲ *No lunch.*

$ **Little Valley Inn.** Historical photos and old mining tools recall Mariposa's heritage at this modern B&B set on extensive grounds that include a creek where you can pan for gold. **Pros:** quiet; comfortable; about halfway between Yosemite's western entrances. **Cons:** still about 40 minutes outside the park. ✉ *3483 Brooks Rd., off Hwy. 49* ☎ *209/742–6204 or 800/889–5444* *www.littlevalley.com* *4 rooms, 1 suite, 1 cabin* *In-room: a/c, Wi-Fi.* *Breakfast.*

THE GOLD COUNTRY—NORTH

Gold has had a significant presence along this northern stretch of Highway 49, which encompasses the lovely Empire State Historic Park and also Coloma, where the rush began in 1848.

COLOMA

8 mi northwest of Placerville on Hwy. 49.

The California gold rush started in Coloma. "My eye was caught with the glimpse of something shining in the bottom of the ditch," James Marshall recalled. Marshall himself never found any more "color," as gold came to be called.

GETTING HERE AND AROUND

The only practical way to get here is by car. Once you've parked, it's easy enough to walk about town and see all the worthwhile sites.

EXPLORING

★ **Marshall Gold Discovery State Historic Park.** Most of Coloma lies within the historic park. Though crowded with tourists in summer, Coloma hardly resembles the mob scene it was in 1849, when 2,000 prospectors staked out claims along the streambed. The town's population grew to 4,000, supporting seven hotels, three banks, and many stores and businesses. But when reserves of the precious metal dwindled, prospectors left as quickly as they had come. A working reproduction of an 1840s mill lies near the spot where James Marshall first saw gold. A trail leads to a sign marking his discovery. **TIP→ The museum is not as interesting as the outdoor exhibits.** *Hwy. 49 530/622–3470 www.parks.ca.gov $5 per vehicle, day use Park daily 8–sunset. Museum daily 10–3.*

WHERE TO STAY

For expanded hotel reviews, visit Fodors.com.

$$ **Coloma Country Inn.** Four of the rooms at this B&B on 2½ acres in the state historic park are inside an 1850s farmhouse, and two suites with kitchenettes occupy the carriage house. *345 High St. 530/622–6919 www.colomacountryinn.com 4 rooms, 2 suites In-room: a/c, kitchen, Wi-Fi Breakfast.*

AUBURN

18 mi northwest of Coloma on Hwy. 49; 34 mi northeast of Sacramento on I–80.

Auburn is the Gold Country town most accessible to travelers on I–80. An important transportation center during the gold rush, Auburn has a small Old Town district with narrow climbing streets, cobblestone lanes, wooden sidewalks, and many original buildings. **TIP→ Fresh produce, flowers, baked goods, and gifts are for sale at the farmers' market, held Saturday morning year-round.**

GETTING HERE AND AROUND

You can reach here via Amtrak or Greyhound. Otherwise, count on driving here and needing the car to see all other Gold Country attractions.

Almost 6 million ounces of gold were extracted from the Empire Mine.

EXPLORING

Bernhard Museum Complex. The Bernhard Museum Complex, whose centerpiece is the former Traveler's Rest Hotel, was built in 1851. A residence and adjacent winery buildings reflect family life in the late Victorian era. The carriage house contains period conveyances. ✉ *291 Auburn–Folsom Rd.* ☎ *530/889–6500* 🎫 *Free* ⏲ *Tues.–Sun. 11–4.*

Gold Country Museum. This museum surveys life in the mines. Exhibits include a walk-through mine tunnel, a gold-panning stream, and a reproduction saloon. ✉ *1273 High St., off Auburn–Folsom Rd.* ☎ *530/889–6500* 🎫 *Free* ⏲ *Tues.–Sun. 11–4.*

Placer County Courthouse. Auburn's standout structure is the Placer County Courthouse. The classic gold-dome building houses the Placer County Museum, which documents the area's history—Native American, railroad, agricultural, and mining—from the early 1700s to 1900. ✉ *101 Maple St.* ☎ *530/889–6500* 🎫 *Free* ⏲ *Daily 10–4.*

WHERE TO EAT

$$ ECLECTIC ✕ **Latitudes.** Delicious multicultural cuisine is served in an 1870 Victorian. The menu (with monthly specials from diverse geographical regions) includes meat entrées prepared with the appropriate Mexican spices, curries, cheeses, or teriyaki sauce. Vegetarians and vegans have several inventive choices, too, including several tofu and tempeh dishes. Sunday brunch is deservedly popular. ✉ *130 Maple St.* ☎ *530/885–9535* 🌐 *www.latitudesrestaurant.com* ⏲ *Closed Mon. and Tues.*

GRASS VALLEY

24 mi north of Auburn on Hwy. 49.

More than half of California's total gold production was extracted from mines around Grass Valley, including the Empire Mine, which, along with the North Star Mining Museum, is among the Gold Country's most fascinating attractions. Unlike neighboring Nevada City, urban sprawl surrounds Grass Valley's historic downtown.

GETTING HERE AND AROUND

Highway 20 arrives here from Interstate 5 to the west and Interstate 80 to the east; otherwise, you'll likely get here via Highway 49 from Placerville. Buy a one-day pass from Gold Country Stage (☎ *530/447–0103*), and its buses and trolleys can deliver you about various attractions here and in nearby Nevada City. Amtrak also serves the area with bus service.

EXPLORING

★ **Empire Mine State Historic Park.** The hard-rock gold mine at Empire Mine State Historic Park was one of California's richest. An estimated 5.8 million ounces were extracted from its 367 mi of underground passages between 1850 and 1956. On the 50-minute tours you can walk into a mine shaft, peer into the mine's deeper recesses, and view the owner's "cottage," which has exquisite woodwork. With its shaded picnic areas and gentle hiking trails, this is a pleasant place for families. ✉ *10791 E. Empire St., south of Empire St. exit of Hwy. 49* ☎ *530/273–8522* 🌐 *www.parks.ca.gov* 🎫 *$5* 🕒 *May–Aug., daily 9–6; Sept.–Apr., daily 10–5. Tours May–Aug., daily on hr 11–4; Sept.–Apr., weekends at 1 (cottage only) and 2 (mine yard only), weather permitting.*

Holbrooke Hotel. The landmark Holbrooke Hotel, built in 1851, was host to Lola Montez and Mark Twain as well as a stream of U.S. presidents including Ulysses S. Grant. Its restaurant-saloon is one of the oldest operating west of the Mississippi. ✉ *212 W. Main St.* ☎ *530/273–1353 or 800/933–7077* 🌐 *www.holbrooke.com.*

Lola Montez House. In the center of town, on the site of the original, stands a reproduction of the home of Lola Montez, the notorious dancer, singer, and courtesan. Montez, who arrived in Grass Valley in the early 1850s, was no great talent—her popularity among miners derived from her suggestive "spider dance"—but her loves, who reportedly included composer Franz Liszt, were legendary. According to one account, she arrived in California after having been "permanently retired from her job as Bavarian king Ludwig's mistress," literary muse, and political adviser. She apparently pushed too hard for democracy, which contributed to his overthrow and her banishment as a witch—or so the story goes. The Grass Valley/Nevada County Chamber of Commerce is headquartered here. ✉ *248 Mill St.* ☎ *530/273–4667; 800/655–4667 in CA.*

North Star Mining Museum. Housed in the former North Star powerhouse, the museum displays the 32-foot-high enclosed Pelton Water Wheel, said to be the largest ever built. It was used to power mining operations and was a forerunner of the modern turbines that generate hydroelectricity. Hands-on displays are geared to children. There's a picnic area nearby. ✉ *Empire and McCourtney Sts., north of Empire St. exit of Hwy. 49* ☎ *530/273–4255* *Donation requested* ⏱ *May–mid-Oct., daily 10–5.*

WHERE TO EAT AND STAY

¢ BRITISH ✕ **Cousin Jack Pasties.** Meat- and vegetable-stuffed pasties are a taste of the region's history, having come across the Atlantic with Cornish miners and their families in the mid-19th century. The flaky crusts practically melt in your mouth. A simple food stand, which sometimes closes early on dreary winter days, Jack's is nonetheless a local landmark and dear to its loyal clientele. ✉ *Auburn and Main Sts.* ☎ *530/272–9230* *No credit cards.*

¢ **Holiday Lodge.** This modest hotel is close to many of the town's main attractions, and its staff can help arrange historical tours of Nevada City, Grass Valley, and the small town of Washington. **Pros:** good price; friendly staff. **Cons:** feels a bit dated. ✉ *1221 E. Main St.* ☎ *530/273–4406 or 800/742–7125* 🌐 *www.holidaylodge.biz* *35 rooms* *In-room: a/c, Wi-Fi. In-hotel: pool* *Breakfast.*

NEVADA CITY

4 mi north of Grass Valley on Hwy. 49.

Nevada City, once known as the Queen City of the Northern Mines, is the most appealing of the northern Mother Lode towns. The iron-shutter brick buildings that line the narrow downtown streets contain antiques shops, galleries, bookstores, boutiques, B&Bs, restaurants, and a winery. Horse-drawn carriage tours add to the romance, as do gas street lamps. At one point in the 1850s, Nevada City had a population of nearly 10,000—enough to support much cultural activity. Today, about 3,000 people reside in Nevada City.

GETTING HERE AND AROUND

As is the case with nearby Grass Valley, Highway 20 arrives here from Interstate 5 to the west and Interstate 80 to the east; otherwise, you'll likely get here via Highway 49 from Placerville. Buy a one-day pass from Gold Country Stage (☎ *530/447–0103*) and its buses and trolleys can deliver you about various attractions in the two towns.

ESSENTIALS

Visitor Information Nevada City Chamber of Commerce (✉ *132 Main St., Nevada City* ☎ *530/265–2692* 🌐 *www.nevadacitychamber.com*).

EXPLORING

Firehouse No. 1. With its gingerbread-trim bell tower, Firehouse No. 1 is one of the Gold Country's most distinctive buildings. A museum, it houses gold-rush artifacts and a Chinese joss house (temple). ✉ *214 Main St.* ☎ *530/265–5468* *Donation requested* ⏱ *Apr.–Nov., daily 11–4; Dec.–Mar., Thurs.–Sun. 11:30–4.*

Miners Foundry. The Miners Foundry, erected in 1856, produced machines for gold mining and logging. The Pelton Water Wheel, a source of power for the mines (the wheel also jump-started the hydroelectric power industry), was invented here. A cavernous building, the foundry is the site of plays, concerts, weddings, receptions, and other events; call for a schedule. ✉ *325 Spring St.* ☎ *530/265–5040* 🌐 *www.minersfoundry.org.*

Nevada City Winery. You can watch wine being created while you sip at the Nevada City Winery, where the tasting room overlooks the production area. ✉ *Miners Foundry Garage, 321 Spring St.* ☎ *530/265–9463 or 800/203–9463* 🌐 *www.ncwinery.com* *Free* ⏲ *Tastings Mon.–Sat. 11–5, Sun. noon–5.*

Nevada Theatre. This redbrick edifice, constructed in 1865, is California's oldest theater building. Mark Twain, Emma Nevada, and many other notable people appeared on its stage. Several local theatrical troupes perform here, and old films are screened as well. ✉ *401 Broad St.* ☎ *530/265–6161; 530/274–3456 for film showtimes* 🌐 *www.nevadatheatre.com.*

WHERE TO EAT AND STAY

$$$$ ECLECTIC ✕ **Friar Tuck's.** This popular restaurant specializes in aromatic, interactive fondues and also has an extensive seafood menu. The sparkling interior has a late-19th century ambience—it's one of Nevada City's best indoor spaces. ✉ *111 N. Pine St.* ☎ *530/265–9093* 🌐 *www.friartucks.com* ⏲ *No lunch.*

$$ AMERICAN ✕ **South Pine Cafe.** Locals flock here, especially for brunch. Although lobster and beef are on the menu, the real attention-grabbers are vegetarian entrées and side dishes, such as breakfast potatoes and apple-ginger muffins. This place is a regional hit; it has branches in Grass Valley and Auburn, too. ✉ *110 S. Pine St.* ☎ *530/265–0260* 🌐 *www.southpinecafe.com* ⏲ *Daily 8–3.*

$$ Fodor's Choice ★ **Red Castle Historic Lodgings.** A state landmark, this 1857 Gothic-revival mansion stands on a forested hillside overlooking Nevada City, and is a special place for those who appreciate the finer points of Victorian interior design. **Pros:** friendly owners; spectacular food; fascinating architecture. **Cons:** you'll get a workout walking up the hill from downtown. ✉ *109 Prospect St.* ☎ *530/265–5135 or 800/761–4766* 🌐 *www.redcastleinn.com* *4 rooms, 3 suites* *In-room: a/c, Wi-Fi.* *Breakfast.*

Lake Tahoe

WITH RENO, NEVADA

WORD OF MOUTH

"The views from the top of Heavenly are, well, heavenly—really really jaw-dropping spectacular."

–sf7307

WELCOME TO LAKE TAHOE

TOP REASONS TO GO

★ **The lake:** Blue, deep, and alpine pure, Lake Tahoe is far and away the main reason to visit this high Sierra paradise.

★ **Snow, snow, snow:** Daring black-diamond runs or baby-bunny bumps—whether you're an expert, a beginner, or somewhere in between, there are many slopes to suit your skills at the numerous Tahoe area ski parks.

★ **The great outdoors:** A ring of national forests, recreation areas, and miles of trails make Tahoe a nature lover's paradise.

★ **Dinner with a view:** You can picnic lakeside at state parks or dine in restaurants perched along the shore.

★ **A date with lady luck:** Whether you want to roll dice, play the slots, or hope the blackjack dealer goes bust before you do, you'll find round-the-clock gambling at the casinos in Reno and on the Nevada side of the lake.

1 California Side. With the exception of Stateline, Nevada—which, aside from its casino-hotel towers, seems almost indistinguishable from South Lake Tahoe, California—the California side is more developed than the Nevada side. Here you can find both commercial enterprises—restaurants, motels, lodges, resorts, residential subdivisions—and public-access facilities, such as historic sites, parks, campgrounds, marinas, and beaches.

2 Nevada Side. You don't need a highway sign to know when you've crossed from California into Nevada: the flashing lights and elaborate marquees of casinos announce legal gambling in garish hues. But you'll find more here than tables and slot machines. Reno, the Biggest Little City in the World, has a vibrant art scene and a serene downtown RiverWalk. And when you really need to get away from the chip-toting crowds, you can hike through pristine wilderness at Lake Tahoe–Nevada State Park, or hit the slopes near Incline Village.

GETTING ORIENTED

In the northern section of the Sierra Nevada mountain range, the Lake Tahoe area covers portions of five national forests, several state parks, and rugged wilderness areas with names like Desolation and Granite Chief. Lake Tahoe, the star attraction, straddles California and Nevada and is one of the world's largest, clearest, and deepest alpine lakes. The region's proximity to the Bay Area and Sacramento to the west and Reno to the east draws hordes of thrill-seekers during ski season and summer, when water sports, camping, and hiking are the dominant activities.

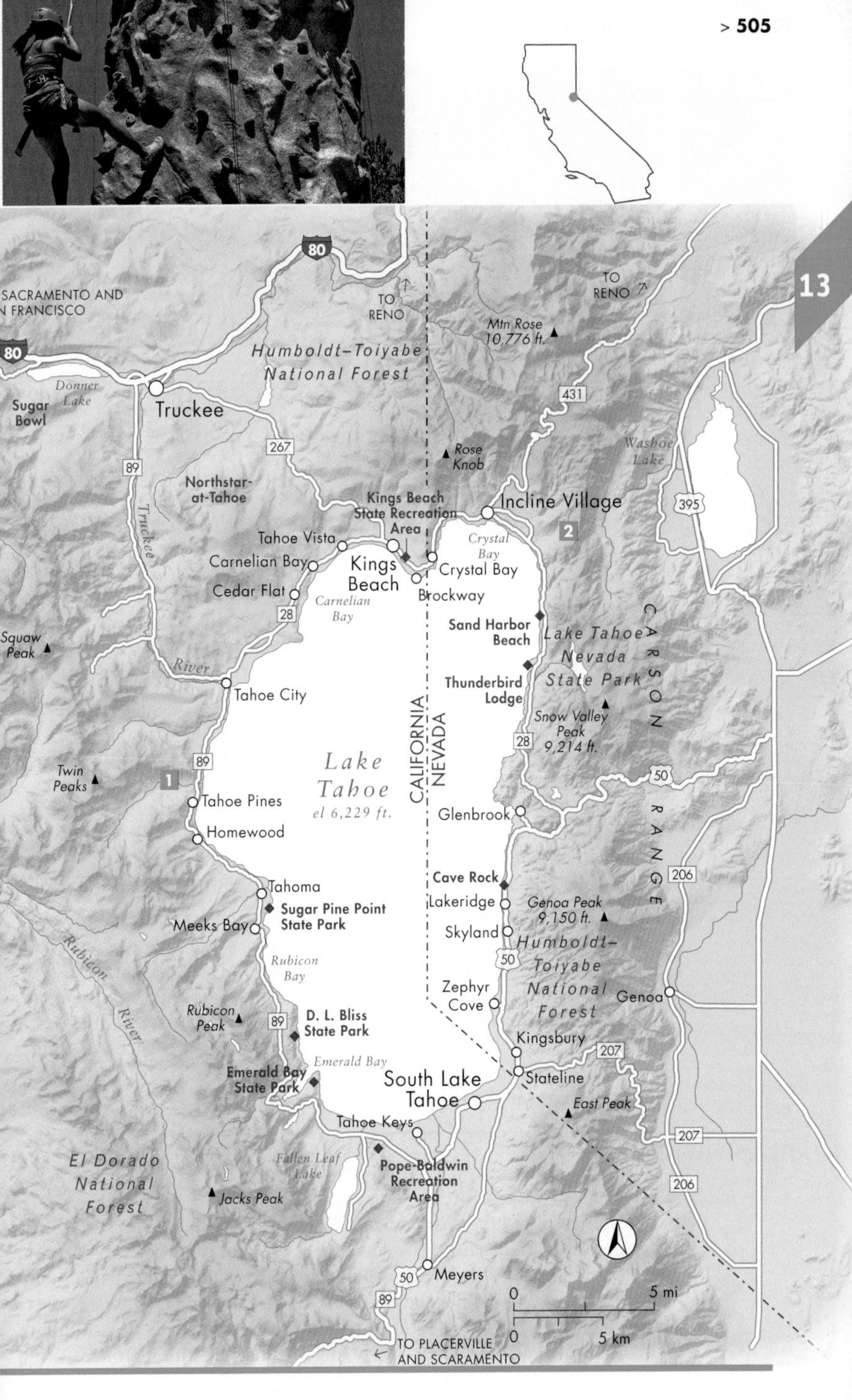
13
80
TO RENO
TO RENO
SACRAMENTO AND
N FRANCISCO
Mtn Rose
10,776 ft.
Humboldt–Toiyabe
National Forest
Donner
Lake
Sugar
Bowl
Truckee
431
267
89
Rose
Knob
Washoe
Lake
Northstar-
at-Tahoe
Truckee
Kings Beach
State Recreation
Area
Incline Village
395
Tahoe Vista
Crystal
Bay
2
Carnelian Bay
Kings
Beach
Crystal Bay
Cedar Flat
Brockway
Carnelian
Bay
28
Sand Harbor
Beach
Lake Tahoe
Nevada
State Park
CARSON
RANGE
Squaw
Peak
River
Thunderbird
Lodge
Tahoe City
CALIFORNIA
NEVADA
Snow Valley
Peak
9,214 ft.
Lake
Tahoe
el 6,229 ft.
Twin
Peaks
1
Tahoe Pines
Glenbrook
Homewood
Cave Rock
206
Tahoma
Lakeridge
Genoa Peak
9,150 ft.
Sugar Pine Point
State Park
Meeks Bay
Skyland
Humboldt-
Toiyabe
National
Forest
Rubicon
Bay
Rubicon
River
Zephyr
Cove
Genoa
Rubicon
Peak
D. L. Bliss
State Park
Kingsbury
207
Emerald Bay
Emerald Bay
State Park
Stateline
South Lake
Tahoe
East Peak
Tahoe Keys
207
El Dorado
National
Forest
Fallen Leaf
Lake
Pope-Baldwin
Recreation
Area
206
Jacks Peak
Meyers
50
89
0
5 mi
0
5 km
TO PLACERVILLE
AND SCARAMENTO

Updated by Christine Vovakes

Stunning cobalt-blue Lake Tahoe is the largest alpine lake in North America, famous for its clarity, deep blue water, and surrounding snowcapped peaks. Straddling the state line between California and Nevada, it lies 6,225 feet above sea level in the Sierra Nevada.

The border gives this popular resort region a split personality. About half its visitors are intent on low-key sightseeing, hiking, fishing, camping, and boating. The rest head directly for the Nevada side, where bargain dining, big-name entertainment, and the lure of a jackpot draw them into the glittering casinos.

The typical way to explore the Lake Tahoe area is to drive the 72-mi road that follows the shore through wooded flatlands and past beaches, climbing to vistas on the rugged southwest side of the lake and passing through busy commercial developments and casinos on its northeastern and southeastern edges. Another option is to actually go out *on* the 22-mi-long, 12-mi-wide lake on a sightseeing cruise or kayaking trip.

The lake, the communities around it, the state parks, national forests, and protected tracts of wilderness are the region's main draws, but other nearby destinations are gaining in popularity. Truckee, with an Old West feel and hot new restaurants, lures visitors looking for a relaxed pace and easy access to Tahoe's north shore and Olympic Valley ski parks. And today Reno, once known only for its casinos, attracts tourists with its buzzing arts scene, revitalized downtown riverfront, and campus events at the University of Nevada.

PLANNING

WHEN TO GO

A sapphire blue lake shimmering deep in the center of an ice-white wonderland—that's Tahoe in winter. But those blankets of snow mean lots of storms that often close roads and force chain requirements on the interstate. In summer the roads are open, but the lake and lodgings are clogged with visitors seeking respite from valley heat. If you don't ski, the best times to visit are early fall—September and October—and late spring. The crowds thin, prices dip, and you can count on Tahoe being beautiful year-round.

Most Lake Tahoe accommodations, restaurants, and even a handful of parks are open year-round, but many visitor centers, mansions, state parks, and beaches are closed from November through May. During those months, multitudes of winter-sports enthusiasts are attracted to Tahoe's downhill resorts and cross-country centers, North America's largest concentration of skiing facilities. In summer it's cooler here than in the scorched Sierra Nevada foothills, the clean mountain air is bracingly crisp, and the surface temperature of Lake Tahoe is an invigorating 65°F to 70°F (compared with 40°F to 50°F in winter). This is also the time, however, when it may seem as if every tourist at the lake—100,000 on peak weekends—is in a car on the main road circling the 72-mi shoreline (especially on Highway 89, just south of Tahoe City; on Highway 28, east of Tahoe City; and on U.S. 50 in South Lake). Christmas week and July 4th are the busiest times, and prices go through the roof; plan accordingly.

GETTING HERE AND AROUND

AIR TRAVEL

The nearest airport to Lake Tahoe is Reno–Tahoe International Airport, in Reno, 50 mi northeast of the closest point on the lake. It's served by nearly a dozen airlines—including Alaska, American, Continental, Delta, Horizon, Southwest, United, and US Airways—and all the major car-rental agencies. If you're also visiting the Bay Area or California's northern towns, fly into San Francisco, Oakland, or Sacramento airport.

Airport Contact **Reno–Tahoe International Airport** (✉ *U.S. 395, Exit 65B, 2001 E. Plumb La., Reno, NV* ☎ *775/328–6400* 🌐 *www.renoairport.com*).

BUS TRAVEL

Greyhound stops in Sacramento, Truckee, and Reno, Nevada. Blue Go runs along U.S. 50 and through the neighborhoods of South Lake Tahoe daily from morning to evening (times vary, check schedules; $2 per ride, exact change only); it also operates a 24-hour door-to-door van service to most addresses in South Lake Tahoe and Stateline for $6 per person (reservations essential). Tahoe Area Regional Transit (TART) operates buses along Lake Tahoe's northern and western shores between Tahoma and Incline Village daily, plus five shuttles daily to Truckee ($1.75 per ride, exact change only). In summer TART buses have bike racks; in winter they have ski racks. Shuttle buses run among the casinos, major ski resorts, and motels of South Lake Tahoe. South Tahoe Express runs 10 daily buses between Reno–Tahoe Airport and resort hotels in the South Lake Tahoe area in winter (eight daily the rest of the year). Reserve online or by telephone. A nonrefundable adult ticket is $27 one-way, $48 round-trip. RTC RIDE is the public transportation bus service in the greater Reno area ($2 per ride, exact change only).

Bus Contacts **Greyhound** (☎ *800/231–2222* 🌐 *www.greyhound.com*). **Blue Go** (☎ *530/541–7149* 🌐 *www.bluego.org*). **RTC RIDE** (☎ *775/348–7433* 🌐 *www.rtcwashoe.com*). **Tahoe Area Regional Transit (TART)** (☎ *530/550–1212 or 800/736–6365* 🌐 *www.laketahoetransit.com*). **South Tahoe Express** (☎ *775/325–8944 or 866/898–2463* 🌐 *www.southtahoeexpress.com*).

CAR TRAVEL

Lake Tahoe is 198 mi northeast of San Francisco, a drive of less than four hours in good weather and light traffic—if possible avoid heavy weekend traffic, particularly leaving the San Francisco area for Tahoe on Friday afternoon and returning on Sunday afternoon. The major route is I–80, which cuts through the Sierra Nevada about 14 mi north of the lake. From there Highway 89 and Highway 267 reach the west and north shores, respectively. U.S. 50 is the more direct route to the south shore, a two-hour drive from Sacramento. From Reno you can get to the north shore by heading south on U.S. 395 for 10 mi, then west on Highway 431 for 25 mi. For the south shore, head south on U.S. 395 through Carson City, and then turn west on U.S. 50 (50 mi total).

The scenic 72-mi highway around the lake is marked Highway 89 on the southwest and west shores, Highway 28 on the north and northeast shores, and U.S. 50 on the east and southeast. Sections of Highway 89 sometimes close during snowy periods, usually at Emerald Bay because of avalanche danger, which makes it impossible to complete the circular drive around the lake. Interstate 80, U.S. 50, and U.S. 395 are all-weather highways, but there may be delays as snow is cleared during major storms. (Note that I–80 is a four-lane freeway; a large part of U.S. 50 is only two lanes with no center divider.) Carry tire chains from October through May, or rent a four-wheel-drive vehicle. (Most rental agencies do not allow tire chains to be used on their vehicles; ask when you book.)

Contacts California Highway Patrol (☎ *530/577–1001 South Lake Tahoe* ⊕ *www.chp.ca.gov*). **Cal-Trans Highway Information Line** (☎ *800/427–7623* ⊕ *www.dot.ca.gov/hq/roadinfo*). **Nevada Department of Transportation Road Information** (☎ *877/687–6237* ⊕ *www.nevadadot.com/traveler/roads*). **Nevada Highway Patrol** (☎ *775/687–5300* ⊕ *www.nhp.nv.gov*).

TRAIN TRAVEL

Amtrak's cross-country rail service makes stops in Truckee and Reno. The *California Zephyr* stops in both towns once daily eastbound (Salt Lake, Denver, and Chicago) and once daily westbound (Sacramento and Oakland). Amtrak also operates several buses daily between Reno and Sacramento to connect with the *Coast Starlight*, which runs south to Southern California and north to Oregon and Washington.

Train Contact Amtrak (☎ *775/329–8638 or 800/872–7245* ⊕ *www.amtrakcalifornia.com*).

HEALTH AND SAFETY

In an emergency dial 911.

Hospital Contacts Barton Memorial Hospital (✉ *2170 South Ave., South Lake Tahoe* ☎ *530/541–3420*). **St. Mary's Regional Medical Center** (✉ *235 W. 6th St., Reno, NV* ☎ *775/770–3000 general information, 775/770–3188 emergency room*). **Tahoe Forest Hospital** (✉ *10121 Pine Ave., Truckee* ☎ *530/587–6011*).

TOUR OPTIONS

The 350-passenger *Tahoe Queen*, a glass-bottom paddle wheeler, departs from South Lake Tahoe daily for 2½-hour sightseeing cruises year-round by reservation and three-hour dinner-dance cruises daily from late spring to early fall (weekly the rest of the year). Fares range from $46 to $75. A few times in winter the boat becomes the only waterborne ski shuttle in the world: $127 covers hotel transfers, a bus transfer from South Lake Tahoe or Stateline to Squaw Valley, lift ticket, and boat transportation back across the lake to South Lake. There's a full bar on board, live music, and an optional dinner.

The *Sierra Cloud,* a large 50-passenger catamaran owned by the Hyatt Hotel, cruises the north shore area morning and afternoon, May through September. The fare is $50. The 570-passenger MS *Dixie II,* a stern-wheeler, sails year-round from Zephyr Cove to Emerald Bay on sightseeing, lunch, and dinner cruises. Fares range from $39 to $65.

Also in Zephyr Cove, Woodwind Cruises operates the *Woodwind II,* a 50-passenger catamaran that sails on regular and champagne cruises April through October. Fares range from $34 to $49. Woodwind Cruises also offers half-day round-the-lake cruises aboard the *Safari Rose,* an 80-foot-long wooden motor yacht; $95 includes lunch.

Lake Tahoe Balloons conducts excursions over the lake May through October; the hour-long flights cost $250 (the entire experience takes four hours total). Soar Minden offers glider rides and instruction over the lake and the Great Basin. Flights cost $155 to $295 and depart from Minden–Tahoe Airport, a municipal facility in Minden, Nevada.

Tour Contacts **Lake Tahoe Balloons** (☎ *530/544–1221 or 800/872–9294* 🌐 *www.laketahoeballoons.com*). **MS *Dixie II*** (✉ *Zephyr Cove Marina, 760 U.S. Hwy. 50, Zephyr Cove* ☎ *775/589–4906 or 888/896–3830* 🌐 *www.zephyrcove.com*). **Sierra Cloud** (✉ *Hyatt Regency Lake Tahoe, 111 Country Club Dr., Incline Village* ☎ *775/832–1234*). **Soar Minden** (☎ *775/782–7627 or 800/345–7627* 🌐 *www.soarminden.com*). ***Tahoe Queen*** (✉ *Ski Run Marina, off U.S. 50, 900 Ski Run Blvd., South Lake Tahoe* ☎ *775/589–4906 or 888/896–3830* 🌐 *www.zephyrcove.com*). **Woodwind Cruises** (✉ *Zephyr Cove Resort, 760 U.S. Hwy. 50, Zephyr Cove* ☎ *775/588–1881 or 888/867–6394* 🌐 *www.sailwoodwind.com*).

RESTAURANTS

On weekends and in high season, expect a long wait in the more popular restaurants. And expect to pay resort prices almost everywhere. Remember, restaurants see business only 6 out of 12 months. During the "shoulder seasons" (April to May and September to November), some places may close temporarily or limit their hours, so call ahead. Also, check local papers for deals and discounts during this time, especially two-for-one coupons. Many casinos use their restaurants to attract gamblers. Marquees often tout "$8.99 prime rib dinners" or "$1.99 breakfast specials." Some of these meals are downright lousy and they are usually available only in the coffee shops and buffets, but at those prices, it's hard to complain. The finer restaurants in casinos deliver pricier food, as well as reasonable service and a bit of atmosphere. Unless otherwise noted, even the most expensive area restaurants welcome customers in casual clothes.

HOTELS

Quiet inns on the water, suburban-style strip motels, casino hotels, slope-side ski lodges, and house and condo rentals throughout the area constitute the lodging choices at Tahoe. The crowds come in summer and during ski season; reserve as far in advance as possible, especially for holiday periods, when prices skyrocket. Spring and fall give you a little more leeway and lower—sometimes significantly lower—rates. Check hotel Web sites for the best deals.

Head to South Lake Tahoe for the most activities and the widest range of lodging options.

Tahoe City, on the west shore, has a small-town atmosphere and is accessible to several nearby ski resorts.

Looking for a taste of old Tahoe? The north shore with its woodsy backdrop is your best bet, with Carnelian Bay and Tahoe Vista on the California side.

WHAT IT COSTS

	¢	$	$$	$$$	$$$$
Restaurants	under $10	$10–$15	$16–$22	$23–$30	over $30
Hotels	under $90	$90–$120	$121–$175	$176–$250	over $250

Restaurant prices are based on the median main course price at dinner. Hotel prices are for two people in a standard double room in high season.

SKIING AND SNOWBOARDING

The mountains around Lake Tahoe are bombarded by blizzards throughout most winters and sometimes in fall and spring; 10- to 12-foot bases are common. Indeed, the Sierra often has the deepest snowpack on the continent, but because of the relatively mild temperatures over the Pacific, falling snow can be very heavy and wet—it's nicknamed Sierra Cement for a reason. The upside is that you can sometimes ski and board as late as July (snowboarding is permitted at all Tahoe ski areas). Note that the major resorts get extremely crowded on weekends. If you're going to ski on a Saturday, arrive early and quit early. Avoid moving with the masses: eat at 11 am or 1:30 pm, not noon. Also consider visiting the ski areas with few high-speed lifts or limited lodging and real estate at their bases: Alpine Meadows, Sugar Bowl, Homewood, Mt. Rose, Sierra-at-Tahoe, Diamond Peak, and Kirkwood. And to find out the true ski conditions, talk to waiters and bartenders—most of whom are ski bums.

The Lake Tahoe area is also a great destination for Nordic skiers. "Skinny" (i.e., cross-country) skiing at the resorts can be costly, but you get the benefits of machine grooming and trail preparation. If it's bargain Nordic you're after, take advantage of thousands of acres of public forest and parkland trails.

VISITOR INFORMATION

Contacts Lake Tahoe Visitors Authority (✉ *169 U.S. Hwy. 50, Stateline* ☎ *775/588–5900 or 800/288–2463* 🌐 *www.tahoesouth.com*). **U.S. Forest Service** (☎ *530/587–2158 backcountry recording* 🌐 *www.fs.fed.us/r5*).

THE CALIFORNIA SIDE

The most hotels, restaurants, ski resorts, and state parks are on the California side of the lake, but you'll also encounter the most congestion and developed areas.

SOUTH LAKE TAHOE

13

50 mi south of Reno on U.S. 395 and U.S. 50; 198 mi northeast of San Francisco on I–80 and U.S. 50.

The city of South Lake Tahoe's raison d'être is tourism: the casinos of adjacent Stateline, Nevada; the ski slopes at Heavenly Mountain; the beaches, docks, bike trails, and campgrounds all around the south shore; and the backcountry of Eldorado National Forest and Desolation Wilderness. The town itself, however, is disappointingly unattractive, with its mix of cheap motels, strip malls, and low-rise prefab-looking buildings that line both sides of U.S. 50. Though there are lots and lots of places to stay, we haven't recommended many because they're not cream-of-the-crop choices. The small city's saving grace is its convenient location and bevy of services, as well as its gorgeous lake views.

GETTING HERE AND AROUND

U.S. 50, the main route into South Lake Tahoe, changes its name to Lake Tahoe Boulevard and is the major road through the city. Arrive by car or, if coming from Reno Airport, take the South Tahoe Express. Blue Go operates daily bus service in the south shore area year-round, plus a ski shuttle from the large hotels to Heavenly Ski Resort in the winter.

ESSENTIALS

Visitor Information **Lake Tahoe Visitors Authority** (✉ *169 U.S. Hwy. 50, Stateline* ☎ *775/588–5900 or 800/288–2463* 🌐 *www.tahoesouth.com*).

EXPLORING

Fodor's Choice ★ **Heavenly Gondola.** Whether you ski or not, you'll appreciate the impressive view of Lake Tahoe from the Heavenly Gondola. Its 138 eight-passenger cars travel from the middle of town 2½ mi up the mountain in 15 minutes. When the weather's fine, you can take one of three hikes around the mountaintop and then have lunch at Adventure Peak Grill. Heavenly also offers day care for children. ✉ *Downtown* ☎ *775/586–7000 or 800/432–8365* 🌐 *www.skiheavenly.com* *$32* *Hrs vary; summer, daily 10–5; winter, daily 9–4.*

Heavenly Village. At the base of the gondola the Heavenly Village is the centerpiece of South Lake Tahoe's efforts to reinvent itself and provide a focal point for tourism. Essentially a pedestrian mall, it includes some good shopping, a cinema, an arcade for kids, and the Heavenly Village Outdoor Ice Rink.

WHERE TO EAT

$ ECLECTIC ✕ **Blue Angel Café.** A favorite of locals, who fill the dozen or so wooden tables, the Blue Angel serves everything from basic sandwiches and salads to internationally inspired dishes like sweet potato tamales and a curry-of-the-day. Prices are extremely reasonable. This cozy café has Wi-Fi and is open daily from 9 am to 9 pm. ✉ *1132 Ski Run Blvd.* ☎ *530/544–6544.*

$ MEXICAN **The Cantina.** One of Tahoe's most popular casual restaurants, the Cantina serves generous portions of traditional Mexican dishes, such as burritos, enchiladas, and rellenos, as well as more stylized Southwestern cooking, including smoked chicken polenta with grilled vegetables, and crab cakes in jalapeño cream sauce. The bar makes great margaritas and serves 30 different kinds of beer. *765 Emerald Bay Rd. 530/544–1233 Reservations not accepted.*

$$$ ECLECTIC **Evan's.** The top choice for high-end dining in South Lake, Evan's creative American cuisine includes such specialties as roasted rack of lamb with citrus couscous, along with daily seafood specials. Although some might find the tables a tad close to each other, the 40-seat dining room in the converted Tahoe cabin is intimate. The excellent service, world-class food, and superb wine list merit a special trip. *536 Emerald Bay Rd. 530/542–1990 No lunch.*

$$$$ ASIAN **Kalani's.** Fresh-off-the-plane seafood gets flown directly from the Honolulu fish market to Heavenly Village's sexiest (and priciest) restaurant. The sleek, white-tablecloth dining room is decked out with carved bamboo, a burnt-orange color palette, and a modern-glass sculpture, all of which complement contemporary Pacific Rim specialties such as melt-from-the-bone baby back pork ribs with sesame-garlic soy sauce. Sushi selections with inventive rolls and sashimi combos, plus less expensive vegetarian dishes, add depth to the menu. *1001 Heavenly Village Way, #26 530/544–6100.*

¢ AMERICAN **Red Hut Café.** A vintage-1959 Tahoe diner, all chrome and red plastic, the Red Hut is a tiny place with a wildly popular breakfast menu: huge omelets; banana, pecan, and coconut waffles; and other tasty vittles. A sparkling new branch opened in South Lake Tahoe in 2009, and there's a third location in Stateline. The menu and prices are the same at each location. *2749 U.S. 50 530/541–9024 Reservations not accepted No credit cards No dinner 3660 Lake Tahoe Blvd. 530/544–1595 227 Kingsbury Grade, Stateline, NV 775/588–7488.*

$$ ITALIAN **Scusa!** The kitchen here turns out big plates of linguine with clam sauce, veal scallopine, and chicken piccata. There's nothing fancy about the menu, just straightforward Italian-American food—and lots of it. *1142 Ski Run Blvd. 530/542–0100 No lunch.*

WHERE TO STAY

For expanded reviews, visit Fodors.com.

$$$ Fodor's Choice ★ **Black Bear Inn Bed and Breakfast.** South Lake Tahoe's most luxurious inn feels like one of the grand old lodges of the Adirondacks. **Pros:** intimate; within walking distance of several good restaurants; massive stone fireplace in great room. **Cons:** not appropriate for children under 16; pricey. *1202 Ski Run Blvd. 530/544–4451 or 877/232–7466 www.tahoeblackbear.com 5 rooms, 3 cabins In-room: a/c, kitchen (some), Wi-Fi. In-hotel: some age restrictions Breakfast.*

$$ **Camp Richardson.** An old-fashioned family resort, Camp Richardson is built around a 1920s lodge, with a few dozen cabins and a small inn, all tucked beneath giant pine trees on 80 acres of lakefront land on the southwest shore of Lake Tahoe. **Pros:** wide choice of accommodations; beautiful lakeside location. **Cons:** no phones or TVs in some rooms. *1900 Jameson Beach Rd. 530/541–1801 or 800/544–1801 www.*

Continued on page 520

TAHOE A LAKE FOR ALL SEASONS

by Christine Vovakes

Best known for its excellent skiing, Lake Tahoe is a year-round resort and outdoor sports destination. All kinds of activities are available, from snowboarding some of the best runs in North America and gliding silently along the lakeshore on cross-country skis in winter, to mountain biking through lush forests and puttering around the alpine lake in a classic yacht in summer. Whatever you do—and whenever you visit—the sapphire lake is at the center of it all, pulling you out of your posh resort or rustic cabin rental like a giant blue magnet. There are many ways to enjoy and experience Lake Tahoe, but here are some of our favorites.

(top) Heavenly Mountain Resort, (bottom) Sand Harbor Beach.

WINTER WONDERLAND

Home to a host of world-famous Sierra resorts, Tahoe is a premier ski destination. Add sledding, ice skating, cross-country skiing, and jingly sleigh rides under the stars to the mix, and you begin to get a glimpse of Tahoe's cold-weather potential.

DOWNHILL SKIING AND SNOWBOARDING

Even if you've never made it off the bunny hill before, you should definitely hit the slopes here at least once. The Lake Tahoe region has the deepest snowpack in North America, and you can ski from Thanksgiving until it melts—which is sometimes July.

One of the top-rated resorts in the country, Olympic Valley's **Squaw Valley USA** hosted the 1960 Winter Olympics that put Tahoe on the map. A great classic resort is **Sugar Bowl,** where you can revel in a bit of Disney nostalgia while you swoop down the slopes. Walt helped start the resort, which opened in 1939 and had Tahoe's first chair lift.

Even if you're not hitting the slopes at South Lake Tahoe's **Heavenly Mountain,** be sure to take a ride on their **Heavenly Gondola** so you can take in awe-inspiring views of the frozen circle of white ice that rings the brilliant lake.

(top) Skiing in Lake Tahoe,. (above left) Cross-country skiing, (above right) Snow boarding at Heavenly Mountain.

SKI RESORT	LOCATION	TRAILS	ACRES	BEGIN.	INTER.	ADV./ EXP.
CALIFORNIA						
Alpine Meadows	Tahoe City	100	2,400	25%	40%	35%
Heavenly Mountain	South Lake Tahoe	94	4,800	20%	45%	35%
Homewood Mountain	Homewood	60	1,260	15%	50%	35%
Kirkwood	Kirkwood	65	2,300	15%	50%	35%
Northstar-at-Tahoe	Truckee	93	3,000	13%	60%	27%
Sierra-at-Tahoe	South Lake Tahoe	46	2,000	25%	50%	25%
Squaw Valley USA	Olympic Valley	170	4,000	25%	45%	30%
Sugar Bowl	Truckee	95	1,500	17%	45%	38%
NEVADA						
Diamond Peak	Incline Village	30	655	18%	46%	36%
Mt. Rose Ski Tahoe	Incline Village	61	1,200	20%	30%	50%

CROSS-COUNTRY SKIING

Downhill skiing may get all the glory here, but Lake Tahoe is also a premier cross-country (or Nordic) skiing destination. "Skinny" skiers basically have two options: pony up the cash to ski the groomed trails at a resort, or hit the more rugged (but cheaper—or free) public forest and parkland trails.

Beautiful **Royal Gorge** is the country's largest cross-country ski resort. Other resorts with good skinny skiing include **Kirkwood, Squaw Valley USA, Tahoe Donner,** and **Northstar-at-Tahoe.** Private operators **Spooner Lake Cross Country** and **Hope Valley Cross Country** will also have you shushing through pristine powder in no time.

For bargain Nordic on public trails, head to **Sugar Pine Point State Park.** Other good low-cost cross-country skiing locations include **Donner Memorial State Park, Lake Tahoe—Nevada State Park,** and **Tahoe Meadows** near Incline Village.

CAUTION⚠ Cross-country skiing is relaxing and provides a great cardiovascular workout—but it's also quite strenuous. If it's your first time out or you're not in great shape, start out slow.

SLEDDING AND TUBING

Kirkwood, Squaw Valley USA, Boreal, Soda Springs, and many other Tahoe resorts have areas where you can barrel down hills in sleds and inflatable tubes. Some good non-resort sledding spots are **Tahoe National Forest** and **Tahoe Meadows,** near Incline Village.

ICE SKATING

Want to work on your triple lutz? You can skate seasonally at **Heavenly Village Outdoor Ice Rink,** or year-round at the **South Tahoe Ice Arena.** Other great gliding spots include **Squaw Valley USA's Olympic Ice Pavilion.**

WARMING UP

To defrost your ski-stiff limbs, take a dip in a resort's heated pool, de-stress in a hotel spa... or enjoy a brandy by the fire at a cozy restaurant. Our favorite places to warm up and imbibe include Graham's of Squaw Valley and Soule Domain, near Crystal Bay.

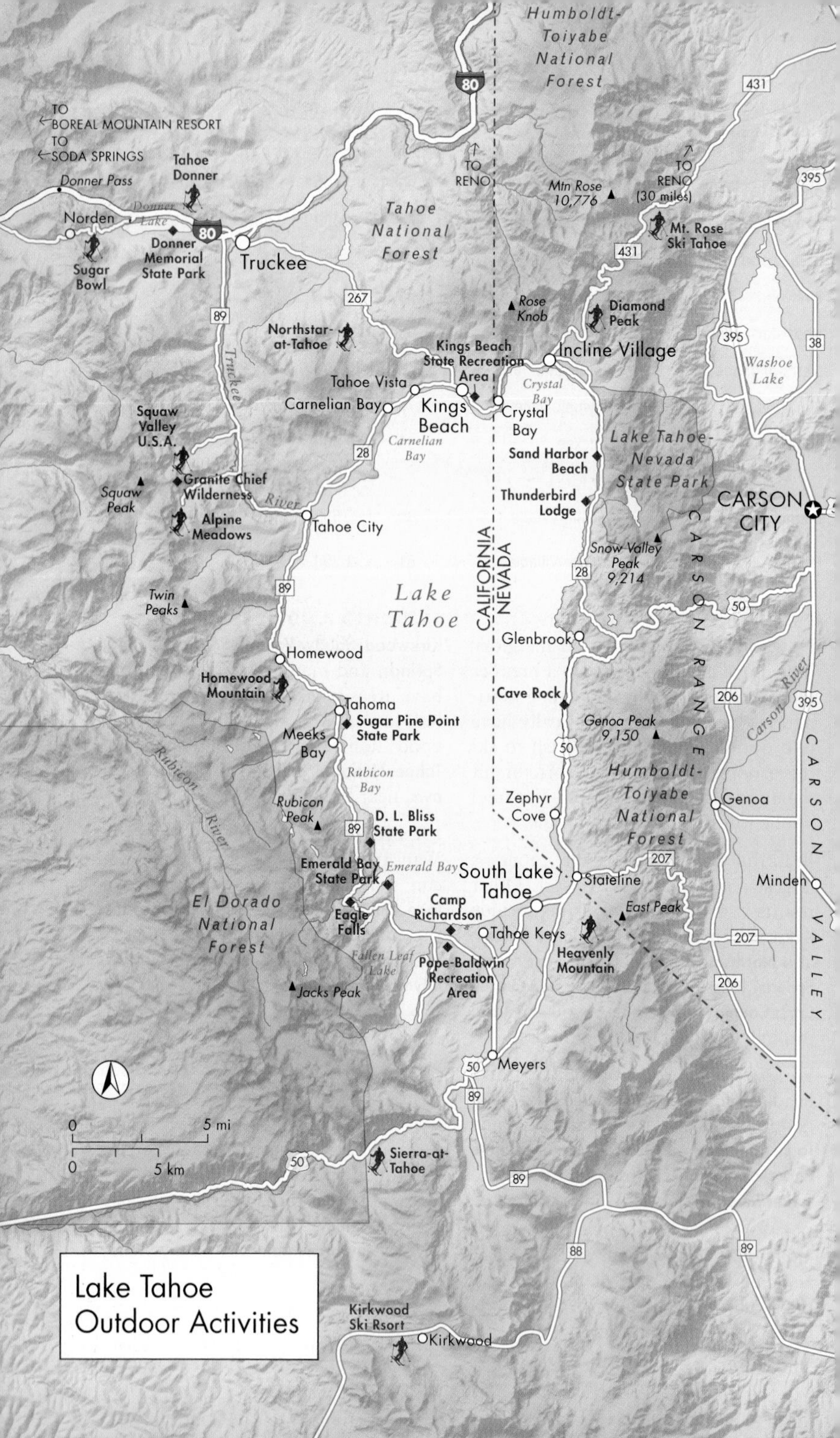

Lake Tahoe
Outdoor Activities
Humboldt-Toiyabe National Forest
TO BOREAL MOUNTAIN RESORT
TO SODA SPRINGS
Donner Pass
Tahoe Donner
Donner Lake
Norden
Sugar Bowl
Donner Memorial State Park
Truckee
TO RENO
TO RENO (30 miles)
Tahoe National Forest
Mtn Rose 10,776
Mt. Rose Ski Tahoe
Rose Knob
Diamond Peak
Northstar-at-Tahoe
Kings Beach State Recreation Area
Incline Village
Tahoe Vista
Carnelian Bay
Kings Beach
Crystal Bay
Washoe Lake
Squaw Valley U.S.A.
Squaw Peak
Granite Chief Wilderness
Truckee River
Alpine Meadows
Tahoe City
Sand Harbor Beach
Thunderbird Lodge
Lake Tahoe-Nevada State Park
CARSON CITY
CARSON RANGE
Snow Valley Peak 9,214
Lake Tahoe
CALIFORNIA
NEVADA
Twin Peaks
Glenbrook
Homewood
Homewood Mountain
Tahoma
Sugar Pine Point State Park
Meeks Bay
Cave Rock
Genoa Peak 9,150
Carson River
Rubicon River
Rubicon Bay
Rubicon Peak
Zephyr Cove
Humboldt-Toiyabe National Forest
Genoa
D. L. Bliss State Park
Emerald Bay State Park
Emerald Bay
South Lake Tahoe
Stateline
Minden
CARSON VALLEY
El Dorado National Forest
Eagle Falls
Camp Richardson
Tahoe Keys
East Peak
Heavenly Mountain
Fallen Leaf Lake
Pope-Baldwin Recreation Area
Jacks Peak
Meyers
0
5 mi
0
5 km
Sierra-at-Tahoe
Kirkwood Ski Rsort
Kirkwood
80
431
395
267
89
38
28
50
206
207
88

FROSTY CATCH

Too cold to fish? Nonsense. South Lake's Tahoe Sport Fishing runs charters year-round with crews that will clean and package your catch.

IN THE WARM CALIFORNIA SUN

Summer in Tahoe means diving into pure alpine waters, hiking a mountain trail with stunning lake views, or kayaking on glorious Emerald Bay. From tennis to golf to fishing, you can fill every waking moment with outdoor activity—or just stretch out on a sunny lakeside beach with a good book and a cool drink.

HIKING

The lake is surrounded by protected parkland, offering countless opportunities to take jaunts through the woods or rambles along lakeside trails.

One of the most unique hiking experiences in Tahoe is at Heavenly Mountain Resorts, where the **Heavenly Gondola** runs up to three nice trails. When you're done enjoying sky-high views of the lake, grab lunch at the nearby Adventure Peak Grill.

Another out-of-the-ordinary option is a romantic moonlit trek. **Camp Richardson** has lots of trails and a long curve of lake to catch the moonlight.

In **Eldorado National Forest and Desolation Wilderness,** you can hike a small portion of the famous Pacific Crest Trail and branch off to discover beautiful backcountry lakes. Nearby **Eagle Falls** has stunning views of Emerald Bay.

One of Tahoe's best hikes is a 4½-mi trail at **D.L. Bliss State Park;** it has lovely views of the lake and leads to bizarre **Vikingsholm** (*see box on next page*).

Other great places to hike in Lake Tahoe include **Sugar Pines Point State Park, Olympic Valley's Granite Chief Wilderness, Squaw Valley USA's High Camp, Donner Memorial State Park**, and **Lake Tahoe—Nevada State Park.**

You can pick up hiking maps at the U.S. Forest Service office at the Lake Tahoe Visitor Center.

HIT THE BEACH

Lake Tahoe has some gorgeous lakeside sunbathing terrain; get to perennial favorite **Kings Beach State Recreation Area** early to snag a choice spot. Or, if you never want to be far from the water, reserve one of the prime beachside spots at **D.L. Bliss State Park Campground.**

(left) Fannette Island in Emerald Bay. (right) A young man leaps off a cliff into Lake Tahoe.

MOUNTAIN BIKING AND CYCLING

You don't need to be preparing for the Tour de France to join the biking fun. While there are myriad rugged mountain biking trails to choose from, the region is also blessed with many flat trails.

Truly intrepid cyclists take the lift up **Northstar-at-Tahoe** and hit the resort's 100 mi of trails. Another good option is **Sugar Pine Point State Park,** where you can hop on a 10-mi trail to Tahoe City.

Tahoe Sports in South Lake Tahoe is a good place for bike rentals and tips for planning your trip. **Cyclepath Mountain Bikes Adventures** in Tahoe City leads guided mountain biking tours, and **Flume Trail Bikes** in Incline Village rents bikes and operates a bike shuttle to popular trails.

LAKE TOURS AND KAYAKING

One of the best ways to experience the lake is by getting out on the water.

The ***Tahoe Queen*** is a huge glass-bottomed paddle-wheel boat that offers sightseeing cruises and dinner-dance cruises; in winter, it's the only water-borne ski shuttle in the world. The ***Sierra Cloud, MS Dixie II,*** and ***Woodwind I and II*** also ply the lake, offering a variety of enjoyable cruises. *(See Tour Options in the Planning section at the beginning of this chapter for contact info.)*

Another enjoyable option is taking a throwback wooden cruiser from Tahoe Keys Marina in South Lake Tahoe to tour **Thunderbird Lodge,** the meticulously crafted stone mansion built in 1936 by socialite George Whittell.

For a more personal experience, rent a kayak and glide across **Emerald Bay. Kayak Tahoe** in South Lake Tahoe will have you paddling in no time.

VIKINGS?

As you kayak around Tahoe, you'll see many natural wonders...and a few manmade ones as well. One of the most impressive and strangest is **Vikingsholm**, a grand 1929 estate that looks like an ancient Viking castle. You can see it from **Emerald Bay** (which, appropriately, resembles a fjord), or hike to it via a steep one-mile trail.

(left top) Biking along the shore. (left bottom) Kayaking. (right) Steamboat cruise.

camprichardson.com ⇨ *27 lodge rooms, 40 cabins, 7 inn rooms, 200 campsites; 100 RV sites* ☝ *In-room: no phone (some), no a/c, kitchen (some), no TV (some). In-hotel: restaurant, beach.*

WORD OF MOUTH

"Bike trails are wonderful from Camp Richardson (near South Shore). It's like hiking in the middle of the woods, but on a bicycle. You can bike from beach to beach. Take a picnic lunch."

—elnap29

$$ ★ **Inn by the Lake.** Of all the mid-range lodgings in South Lake, this one is probably the best. **Pros:** great value; stellar service; next to a bowling alley and just a short drive from Heavenly Mountain. **Cons:** sits on Lake Tahoe Boulevard, the busy main route into town. ✉ *3300 Lake Tahoe Blvd.* ☎ *530/542–0330 or 800/877–1466* 🌐 *www.innbythelake.com* ⇨ *90 rooms, 10 suites* ☝ *In-room: a/c, kitchen (some), Wi-Fi. In-hotel: pool, gym, laundry facilities.*

$$$ ★ **Marriott's Grand Residence and Timber Lodge.** You can't beat the location of these two gigantic, modern condominium complexes right at the base of Heavenly Gondola, smack in the center of town. **Pros:** central location; great for families; within walking distance of excellent restaurants. **Cons:** can be jam-packed on weekends. ✉ *1001 Heavenly Village Way* ☎ *530/542–8400 or 800/627–7468* 🌐 *www.marriott.com* ⇨ *431 condos* ☝ *In-room: a/c, kitchen (some), Wi-Fi. In-hotel: pool, gym, laundry facilities, parking.*

$$$ **Sorensen's Resort.** Escape civilization by staying in a log cabin at this woodsy 165-acre resort within the Eldorado National Forest, 20 minutes south of town. **Pros:** gorgeous, rustic setting. **Cons:** nearest nightlife is 20 mi away in South Lake Tahoe. ✉ *14255 Hwy. 88, Hope Valley* ☎ *530/694–2203 or 800/423–9949* 🌐 *www.sorensensresort.com* ⇨ *2 rooms with shared bath, 35 cabins, 5 houses* ☝ *In-room: no phone, no a/c, kitchen (some), no TV, Wi-Fi (some). In-hotel: restaurant, children's programs, some pets allowed.*

$$$ **Tahoe Seasons Resort.** It's a 150-yard walk to California Lodge of Heavenly Mountain Resort from this all-suites time-share hotel, where every room has a two-person sunken hot tub. **Pros:** steps away from ski resort; a less touristy location. **Cons:** no restaurants or casinos within walking distance. ✉ *3901 Saddle Rd.* ☎ *530/541–6700 front desk, 800/540–4874 reservations* 🌐 *www.tahoeseasons.com* ⇨ *160 suites* ☝ *In-room: a/c, Internet. In-hotel: restaurant, bar, tennis courts, pool.*

NIGHTLIFE

Most of the area's nightlife is concentrated in the casinos over the border in Stateline. If you want to avoid slot machines and blinking lights, you can stay in California and hear live bands every night at **Mc P's Irish Pub & Grill** (✉ *4093 Lake Tahoe Blvd.* ☎ *530/542–4435*), across the street from the Heavenly Gondola.

SPORTS AND THE OUTDOORS

FISHING **Tahoe Sport Fishing** (✉ *900 Ski Run Blvd.* ☎ *530/541–5448, 800/696–7797 in CA* 🌐 *www.tahoesportfishing.com*) is one of the largest and oldest fishing-charter services on the lake. Morning trips cost $95, afternoon trips $85. Year-round outings include all necessary gear and bait, and the crew cleans and packages your catch.

GOLF The 18-hole, par-71 **Lake Tahoe Golf Course** (✉ *2500 Emerald Bay Rd* ☎ *530/577–0788* 🌐 *www.laketahoegc.com*) has a driving range. Greens fees start at $64 and go as high as $84; a cart (mandatory Friday to Sunday) costs $25. Twilight rates drop as low as $39.

HIKING The south shore is a great jumping-off point for day treks into nearby Eldorado National Forest and Desolation Wilderness. Hike a couple of miles on the **Pacific Crest Trail** (✉ *Echo Summit, about 12 mi southwest of South Lake Tahoe off U.S. 50 916/285–1846 or 888/728–7245* 🌐 *www.pcta.org*). The Pacific Crest Trail leads into **Desolation Wilderness** (✉ *El Dorado National Forest Information Center* ☎ *530/644–6048* 🌐 *www.fs.fed.us/r5/eldorado*), where you can pick up trails to gorgeous backcountry lakes and mountain peaks (bring a proper topographic map and compass, and carry water and food). Late May through early September, the easiest way to access Desolation Wilderness is via boat taxi ($10 one way) across Echo Lake from **Echo Chalet** (✉ *Echo Lakes Rd. off U.S. 50 near Echo Summit* ☎ *530/659–7207* 🌐 *www.echochalet.com*).

ICE-SKATING If you're here in winter, practice your jumps and turns at the **Heavenly Village Outdoor Ice Rink.** It's between the gondola and the cinema. ☎ *530/542–4230* *$20, includes skate rentals* ⏲ *Nov.–Mar., daily 10–8, weather permitting.*

For year-round fun, head to the city-operated **South Tahoe Ice Arena.** You can rent equipment and sign up for lessons at this NHL regulation size indoor rink. In the evening the lights are turned low and a disco ball lights up the ice. Call ahead to check on the irregular hours. ✉ *1176 Rufus Allen Blvd.* ☎ *530/542–6262* 🌐 *www.recreationintahoe.com/ice_arena* *$9, plus $3 skate rental* ⏲ *Daily.*

KAYAKING **Kayak Tahoe** (✉ *Timber Cove Marina; 3411 Lake Tahoe Blvd., behind Best Western Timber Cove Lodge* ☎ *530/544–2011* 🌐 *www.kayaktahoe.com*) has long been teaching people to kayak on Lake Tahoe and the Truckee River. Lessons and excursions (to the south shore, Emerald Bay, and Sand Harbor) are offered May through September. You can also rent a kayak and paddle solo.

MOUNTAIN BIKING With so much national forest land surrounding Lake Tahoe, you may want to try mountain biking. You can rent both road and mountain bikes and get tips on where to ride from the friendly staff at **Tahoe Sports Ltd.** (✉ *4000 Lake Tahoe Blvd.* ☎ *530/542–4000* 🌐 *www.tahoesportsltd.com*).

SKIING Fodor's Choice ★ Straddling two states, vast **Heavenly Mountain Resort**—composed of nine peaks, two valleys, and four base-lodge areas, along with the largest snowmaking system in the western United States—has terrain for every skier. Beginners can choose wide, well-groomed trails, accessed from the California Lodge or the gondola from downtown South Lake Tahoe; kids have short and gentle runs in the Enchanted Forest area all to themselves. The Sky Express high-speed quad chair whisks intermediate and advanced skiers to the summit for wide cruisers or steep tree-skiing. Mott and Killebrew canyons draw experts to the Nevada side for steep chutes and thick-timber slopes. For snowboarders and tricksters, there are four different terrain parks.

The ski school is big and offers everything from learn-to-ski packages to canyon-adventure tours. Call about ski and boarding camps. Skiing lessons are available for children ages four and up; there's day care for infants older than six weeks. ✉ *Ski Run Blvd., off U.S. 50, South Lake Tahoe, CA* ☎ *775/586–7000 or 800/432–8365* 🌐 *www.skiheavenly.com* ☞ *94 trails on 4,800 acres, rated 20% beginner, 45% intermediate, 35% expert. Longest run 5½ mi, base 6,540 feet, summit 10,067 feet. Lifts: 30, including 1 aerial tram, 1 gondola, 2 high-speed 6-passenger lifts, and 8 high-speed quads.*

★ Thirty-six miles south of Lake Tahoe, **Kirkwood Ski Resort** is the hard-core skiers' and boarders' favorite south-shore mountain, known for its craggy gulp-and-go chutes, sweeping cornices, steep-aspect glade skiing, and high base elevation. But there's also fantastic terrain for newbies and intermediates down wide-open bowls, through wooded gullies, and along rolling tree-lined trails. Tricksters can show off in the Stomping Grounds terrain park on jumps, wall rides, rails, and a half-pipe, all visible from the base area. The mountain gets hammered with more than 500 inches of snow annually, and often has the most in all of North America. If you're into out-of-bounds skiing, check out Expedition Kirkwood, a backcountry-skills program that teaches basic safety awareness. Kirkwood is also the only Tahoe resort to offer Cat-skiing. If you're into cross-country, the resort has 80 km (50 mi) of superb groomed-track skiing, with skating lanes, instruction, and rentals. Non-skiers can snowshoe, snow-skate, and go dogsledding or snow-tubing. The children's ski school has programs for ages 4 to 12, and there's day care for children two to six years old. ✉ *1501 Kirkwood Meadows Dr., off Hwy. 88, 14 mi west of Hwy. 89, Kirkwood* ☎ *209/258–6000 downhill, 209/258–7248 cross-country, 209/258–7293 lodging information, 877/547–5966 snow phone* 🌐 *www.kirkwood.com* ☞ *65 trails on 2,300 acres, rated 15% beginner, 50% intermediate, 20% advanced, 15% expert. Longest run 2½ mi, base 7,800 feet, summit 9,800 feet. Lifts: 14, including 2 high-speed quads.*

Often overlooked by skiers and boarders rushing to Heavenly or Kirkwood, **Sierra-at-Tahoe** has meticulously groomed intermediate slopes, some of the best tree-skiing in California, and gated backcountry access. Extremely popular with local snowboarders, Sierra also has six terrain parks, including a super-pipe with 17-foot walls. For nonskiers there's a snow-tubing hill. Sierra has a low-key atmosphere that's great for families. Kids and beginners take the slow routes in the Mellow Yellow Zone. ✉ *1111 Sierra-at-Tahoe Rd., 12 mi from South Lake Tahoe off U.S. 50, near Echo Summit, Twin Bridges* ☎ *530/659–7453* 🌐 *www.sierraattahoe.com* ☞ *46 trails on 2,000 acres, rated 25% beginner, 50% intermediate, 25% advanced. Longest run 2½ mi, base 6,640 feet, summit 8,852 feet. Lifts: 14, including 3 high-speed quads.*

Operating from a yurt at Pickett's Junction, **Hope Valley Cross Country** (✉ *Hwy. 88, at Hwy. 89, Hope Valley* ☎ *530/694–2266* 🌐 *www.hopevalleyoutdoors.com*) provides lessons and equipment rentals to prepare you for cross-country skiing and snowshoeing. The outfit has 60 mi of trails through Humboldt–Toiyabe National Forest, 10 of which are groomed.

If you don't want to pay the high cost of rental equipment at the resorts, you'll find reasonable prices and expert advice at **Tahoe Sports Ltd.** (✉ *4000 Lake Tahoe Blvd.* ☎ *530/542–4000* 🌐 *www.tahoesportsltd.com*).

POPE-BALDWIN RECREATION AREA

5 mi west of South Lake Tahoe on Hwy. 89.

To the west of downtown South Lake Tahoe, U.S. 50 and Highway 89 come together, forming an intersection nicknamed "the Y." If you head northwest on Highway 89, also called Emerald Bay Road, and follow the lakefront, commercial development gives way to national forests and state parks. One of these is Pope-Baldwin Recreation Area.

GETTING HERE AND AROUND

The entrance to the Pope-Baldwin Recreation Area is on the east side of Highway 89, also called Emerald Bay Road. Public transportation from South Lake Tahoe is available only in the summer months via Blue Go's seasonal Nifty 50 Trolley. From the northern and western communities, take the **Tahoe Area Regional Transit (TART)** bus to Tahoma and transfer to the trolley. The area is closed to vehicles in the winter but you can cross-country ski here.

EXPLORING

Tallac Historic Site. Stroll or picnic lakeside, then explore **Pope House,** the magnificently restored 1894 mansion of George S. Pope, who made his money in shipping and lumber and played host to the business and cultural elite of 1920s America. There are two other estates here. One belonged to entrepreneur "Lucky" Baldwin; today it houses the **Baldwin Museum,** a collection of family memorabilia and Washoe Indian artifacts. The **Valhalla** (🌐 *www.valhallatahoe.com*), with a spectacular floor-to-ceiling stone fireplace, belonged to Walter Heller. Its Grand Hall and a lakeside boathouse, refurbished as a theater, host summertime concerts, plays, and cultural activities. Docents conduct tours of the Pope House in summer; call for tour times. In winter you can cross-country ski around the site. ✉ *Hwy. 89* ☎ *530/541–5227* 🌐 *www.tahoeheritage.org* 🎫 *Free; Pope House tour $5* ⏲ *Grounds daily sunrise–sunset. Pope House and Baldwin Museum late May–mid-June, weekends 11–3; mid-June–early Sept., daily 11–4.*

Taylor Creek Visitor Center. At this center operated by the U.S. Forest Service you can visit the site of a Washoe Indian settlement; walk self-guided trails through meadow, marsh, and forest; and inspect the Stream Profile Chamber, an underground display with windows right into Taylor Creek (in fall you may see spawning kokanee salmon digging their nests). In summer U.S. Forest Service naturalists organize discovery walks and evening programs (call ahead). ✉ *Hwy. 89, 3 mi north of junction with U.S. 50* ☎ *530/543–2674 June–Oct., 530/543–2600 year-round* 🌐 *www.fs.fed.us/r5/ltbmu/recreation/summer-index.shtml* 🎫 *Free* ⏲ *Memorial Day–late Sept., daily 8–5; Oct., daily 8–4.*

EMERALD BAY STATE PARK

4 mi west of Pope-Baldwin Recreation Area on Hwy. 89.

GETTING HERE AND AROUND

The entrance to Emerald Bay State Park is on the east side of a narrow, twisty section of Highway 89. Caution is the keyword for both drivers and pedestrians. Public transportation from South Lake Tahoe is available only in the summer months via Blue Go's seasonal Nifty 50 Trolley. From the northern and western communities, take the **Tahoe Area Regional Transit** (TART) bus to Tahoma and transfer to the trolley. The park is closed to vehicles in the winter.

EXPLORING

Fodor's Choice ★ **Emerald Bay.** A 3-mi-long and 1-mi-wide fjordlike inlet on Lake Tahoe's shore, Emerald Bay was carved by a massive glacier millions of years ago. Famed for its jewel-like shape and colors, it surrounds Fannette, Tahoe's only island. Highway 89 curves high above the lake through Emerald Bay State Park; from the Emerald Bay lookout, the centerpiece of the park, you can survey the whole scene. This is one of the don't-miss views of Lake Tahoe. Come before the sun drops below the mountains to the west; the light is best in mid- to late morning, when the bay's colors really pop.

Vikingsholm. A steep 1-mi-long trail from the lookout leads down to Vikingsholm, a 38-room estate completed in 1929. The original owner, Lora Knight, had this precise copy of a 1,200-year-old Viking castle built out of materials native to the area. She furnished it with Scandinavian antiques and hired artisans to build period reproductions. The sod roof sprouts wildflowers each spring. There are picnic tables nearby and a gray-sand beach for strolling. The hike back up is hard (especially if you're not yet acclimated to the elevation), but there are benches and stone culverts to rest on. At the 150-foot peak of Fannette Island are the ruins of a stone structure known as the Tea House, built in 1928 so that Knight's guests could have a place to enjoy afternoon refreshments after a motorboat ride. The island is off-limits from February through June to protect nesting Canada geese. The rest of the year it's open for day use. ✉ *Hwy. 89* ☎ *530/541–6498 summer, 530/525–3345 year-round* 🌐 *www.vikingsholm.com* 🎫 *Day-use parking fee $7, mansion tour $5* ⏲ *Late May–Sept., daily 10–4.*

SPORTS AND THE OUTDOORS

HIKING Leave your car in the parking lot for Eagle Falls picnic area (near Vikingsholm; arrive early for a good spot), and head to **Eagle Falls,** a short but fairly steep walk-up canyon. You'll have a brilliant panorama of Emerald Bay from this spot, near the boundary of Desolation Wilderness. If you want a full-day's hike and you're in good shape, continue 5 mi, past Eagle Lake, to Upper and Middle Velma Lakes. You can pick up trail maps from the U.S. Forest Service at their Lake Tahoe Visitor Center in summer, or at park headquarters in South Lake Tahoe year-round.

Fjordlike Emerald Bay is quite possibly the prettiest part of Lake Tahoe.

D.L. BLISS STATE PARK

3 mi north of Emerald Bay State Park on Hwy. 89.

GETTING HERE AND AROUND

The entrance to D.L. Bliss State Park is on the east side of Highway 89 just north of Emerald Bay. Public transportation from South Lake Tahoe is available only in the summer months via Blue Go's seasonal Nifty 50 Trolley. From the northern and western communities, take the **Tahoe Area Regional Transit** (**TART**) bus to Tahoma and transfer to the trolley. From the north point of the park you can hoof scenic Rubicon Trail, a moderate 4.5-mi hike that winds through the forest, dips steeply toward the lake, and ends in Emerald Bay State Park.

EXPLORING

D.L. Bliss State Park. This park takes its name from Duane LeRoy Bliss, a 19th-century lumber magnate. At one time Bliss owned nearly 75% of Tahoe's lakefront, along with local steamboats, railroads, and banks. The park shares 6 mi of shoreline with Emerald Bay State Park; combined the two parks cover 1,830 acres, 744 of which were donated to the state by the Bliss family in 1929. At the north end of Bliss is Rubicon Point, which overlooks one of the lake's deepest spots. Short trails lead to an old lighthouse and Balancing Rock, which weighs 250,000 pounds and balances on a fist of granite. A 4.25-mi trail—one of Tahoe's premier hikes—leads to Vikingsholm and provides stunning lake views. Two white-sand beaches front some of Tahoe's warmest water. ✉ *Hwy. 89* ☎ *530/525–3345 or 800/777–0369* 🎫 *$8 per vehicle, day use* 🕒 *Late May–Sept., daily sunrise–sunset.*

SUGAR PINE POINT STATE PARK

8 mi north of D.L. Bliss State Park on Hwy. 89.

GETTING HERE AND AROUND

The entrance to Sugar Pine Point is on the east side of Hwy. 89, about a mile south of Tahoma. Public transportation from South Lake Tahoe is available only in the summer months via Blue Go's seasonal Nifty 50 Trolley. From north shore communities, take the Tahoe Area Regional Transit (TART) bus to Tahoma and transfer to the trolley for the short ride to the entrance. There's also a bike trail that links Tahoe City to the park.

EXPLORING

Sugar Pine Point State Park. The largest of the state parks at Lake Tahoe, Sugar Pine Point has 2,000 acres of dense forests and nearly 2 mi of shore frontage. A popular spot during snow season, this park provides cross-country trails and a minimal amount of winter camping on a first-come, first-served basis. Rangers lead three full-moon snowshoe tours during January–March.

★ **Ehrman Mansion.** The main attraction at Sugar Pine Point State Park is Ehrman Mansion, a 1903 stone-and-shingle summer home furnished in period style. In its day it was the height of modernity, with a refrigerator, an elevator, and an electric stove (tours leave hourly). Also in the park are a trapper's log cabin from the mid-19th century, a nature preserve with wildlife exhibits, a lighthouse, the start of the 10-mi-long biking trail to Tahoe City, and an extensive system of hiking and cross-country skiing trails. If you're feeling less ambitious, you can relax on the sun-dappled lawn behind the mansion and gaze out at the lake. ✉ *Hwy. 89* ☎ *530/525–7982 mansion in season, 530/525–7232 year-round* 🎫 *$8 per vehicle, day use; mansion tour $5* ⏲ *Mansion Memorial Day–Labor Day, daily 11–4.*

TAHOMA

1 mi north of Sugar Pine Point State Park on Hwy. 89; 23 mi south of Truckee on Hwy. 89.

Tahoma exemplifies life on the lake in its early days, with rustic water-front vacation cottages that are far from the blinking lights of South Shore's casinos. In 1960 Tahoma was host of the Olympic Nordic-skiing competitions. Today there's little to do here except stroll by the lake and listen to the wind in the trees, making it a favorite home base for mellow families and nature buffs.

GETTING HERE AND AROUND

Approach Tahoma by car on Highway 89, called West Lake Blvd. in this section. Public transportation from north shore communities is available year-round via the **Tahoe Area Regional Transit (TART).** There's also a bike trail that links Tahoe City to Tahoma.

WHERE TO STAY

For expanded reviews, visit Fodors.com

$$$ ★ **Tahoma Meadows B&B Cottages.** It's hard to beat Tahoma Meadows for atmosphere and woodsy charm; it's a great retreat for families and couples. **Pros:** lovely setting; good choice for families. **Cons:** far from the casinos. *6821 W. Lake Blvd. 530/525–1553 or 866/525–1553 www.tahomameadows.com 16 cabins In-room: no phone, no a/c, kitchen (some), Wi-Fi. In-hotel: some pets allowed Breakfast.*

13

SPORTS AND THE OUTDOORS

SKIING You'll feel as though you're going to ski into the lake when you schuss down the face of **Homewood Mountain Resort**—and you could if you really wanted to, because the mountain rises right off the shoreline. This is the favorite area of locals on a fresh-snow day, because you can find lots of untracked powder. It's also the most protected and least windy Tahoe ski area during a storm; when every other resort's lifts are on wind hold, you can almost always count on Homewood's to be open. There's only one high-speed chairlift, but there are rarely any lines, and the ticket prices are some of the cheapest around—kids 5 to 12 ski for $12 while those four and under are free. It may look small as you drive by, but most of the resort is not visible from the road. *5145 West Lake Blvd., (Hwy. 89), 6 mi south of Tahoe City, Homewood 530/525–2992 www.skihomewood.com 60 trails on 1,260 acres, rated 15% beginner, 50% intermediate, and 35% advanced. Longest run 2 mi, base 6,230 feet, summit 7,880 feet. Lifts: 4 chairlifts, 4 surface lifts.*

TAHOE CITY

★ *10 mi north of Sugar Pine Point State Park on Hwy. 89; 14 mi south of Truckee on Hwy. 89.*

Tahoe City is the only lakeside town with a compact downtown area good for strolling and window-shopping. Of the larger towns ringing the lake, it has the most bona-fide charm. Stores and restaurants are all within walking distance of the Outlet Gates, enormous Lake Tahoe's only outlet, where water is spilled into the Truckee River to control the surface level of the lake. You can spot giant trout in the river from Fanny Bridge, so-called for the views of the backsides of sightseers leaning over the railing.

GETTING HERE AND AROUND

Tahoe City is at the junction of Hwy. 28, also called North Lake Blvd., and Hwy. 89 where it turns northwest toward Squaw Valley and Truckee. **Tahoe Area Regional Transit (TART)** serves the communities along the north and west shores, and connects them to Truckee, with year-round public transportation. Or you could arrive in Truckee via Greyhound bus or Amtrak, rent a car there and drive to Tahoe City. The truly adventurous take the West Shore Bike Trail from Truckee to Tahoe City and further south to Sugar Pine Point State Park.

ESSENTIALS

Visitor Information North Lake Tahoe Resort Association (*Box 1757, Tahoe City 96145 530/583–3494 or 888/434–1262 www.gotahoenorth.com*).

EXPLORING

★ **Gatekeeper's Cabin Museum.** The Gatekeeper's Cabin Museum preserves a little-known part of the region's history. Between 1910 and 1968 the gatekeeper who lived on this site was responsible for monitoring the level of the lake, using a hand-turned winch system to keep the water at the correct level. That winch system is still used today. The site is also home to a fantastic Native American basket museum that displays 800 baskets from 85 tribes and is reason enough to visit. ✉ *130 W. Lake Blvd.* ☎ *530/583–1762* 🌐 *www.northtahoemuseums.org* 🎫 *$5* 🕐 *May–Sept., Wed.–Mon. 10–5; Oct.–Apr., weekends 11–3.*

Watson Cabin Living Museum. In the middle of town, the Watson Cabin Living Museum, a 1909 log cabin built by Robert M. Watson and his son, is filled with some century-old furnishings and many reproductions. Docents are available to answer questions and will lead tours with advance arrangements. ✉ *560 N. Lake Blvd.* ☎ *530/583–8717 or 530/583–1762* 🌐 *www.northtahoemuseums.org* 🎫 *$2 donation suggested* 🕐 *Late May–early Sept., Thurs.–Mon. 10–5.*

WHERE TO EAT

$$$ AMERICAN ✕ **Christy Hill.** Huge windows give diners here some of the best lake views in Tahoe. The menu features solid Euro–Cal preparations of fresh seafood, filet mignon, or vegetarian selections. An extensive wine list and exceptionally good desserts earn accolades, as do the gracious service and casual vibe. If the weather is balmy, have dinner on the deck. In any season, this is the romantic choice for lake gazing and wine sipping. Reservations are recommended. ✉ *Lakehouse Mall, 115 Grove St.* ☎ *530/583–8551* 🕐 *Open daily. No lunch.*

¢ AMERICAN ✕ **Fire Sign Café.** Watch the road carefully or you'll miss this great little diner 2 mi south of Tahoe City on Highway 89. There's often a wait at the west shore's best spot for breakfast and lunch, but it's worth it. The pastries are made from scratch, the salmon is smoked in-house, the salsa is hand cut, and there's real maple syrup for the many flavors of pancakes and waffles. The eggs Benedict are delicious. ✉ *1785 W. Lake Blvd.* ☎ *530/583–0871* ✍ *Reservations not accepted* 🕐 *No dinner.*

$$$$ ECLECTIC ✕ **Wolfdale's.** Going strong since 1978, Wolfdale's consistent, inspired cuisine makes it one of the top restaurants on the lake. Seafood is the specialty on the changing menu; the imaginative entrées merge Asian and European cooking (drawing on the chef-owner's training in Japan) and trend toward light and healthful, rather than heavy and overdone. And everything from teriyaki glaze to smoked fish is made in-house. Request a window table, and book early enough to see the lake view from the elegantly sparse dining room. ✉ *640 N. Lake Blvd.* ☎ *530/583–5700* ✍ *Reservations essential* 🕐 *Closed Tues. No lunch.*

WHERE TO STAY

For expanded reviews, visit Fodors.com

$$ 🏨 **Cottage Inn.** Avoid the crowds by staying just south of town in one of these charming circa-1938 log cottages under the towering pines on the lake's west shore. **Pros:** romantic, woodsy setting; each room has a fireplace; full breakfast. **Cons:** no kids under 12. ✉ *1690 W. Lake Blvd., Box 66* ☎ *530/581–4073 or 800/581–4073* 🌐 *www.thecottageinn.com*

22 rooms In-room: no phone, no a/c, kitchen (some). In-hotel: beach, some age restrictions.

$$ **River Ranch Lodge**. Tucked into a bend of the Truckee River, this intimate lodge is a short distance from major ski resorts and the town center. **Pros:** beautiful site on the Truckee River; great lounge with a gorgeous curved wall of windows. **Cons:** rooms fill quickly. *Hwy. 89, at Alpine Meadows Rd., Tahoe City 530/583–4264 or 866/991–9912 www.riverranchlodge.com 19 rooms In-room: no a/c, Wi-Fi. In-hotel: restaurant, bar Breakfast.*

13

$$$ ★ **Sunnyside Steakhouse and Lodge**. The views are superb at this pretty little lodge right on the lake, 3 mi south of Tahoe City. **Pros:** complimentary Continental breakfast and afternoon tea; most rooms have balconies overlooking the lake. **Cons:** can be pricey for families. *1850 W. Lake Blvd., Box 5969 530/583–7200 or 800/822–2754 www.sunnysideresort.com 18 rooms, 5 suites In-room: no a/c, Wi-Fi. In-hotel: restaurant, room service, bar, beach Breakfast.*

SPORTS AND THE OUTDOORS

GOLF Golfers use pull carts or caddies at the 9-hole **Tahoe City Golf Course** (*251 N. Lake Blvd. 530/583–1516*), which opened in 1917. **TIP→ All greens break toward the lake.** Though rates vary by season, the maximum greens fees are $40 for 9 holes, $75 for 18; a power cart costs $15 to $25.

MOUNTAIN BIKING **Cyclepaths Mountain Bike Adventures** (*1785 W. Lake Blvd. 530/581–1171 www.cyclepaths.com*) is a combination full-service bike shop and bike-adventure outfitter. It offers instruction in mountain biking, guided tours (from half-day to weeklong excursions), tips for self-guided bike touring, bike repairs, and books and maps on the area.

RIVER RAFTING In summer you can take a self-guided raft trip down a gentle 5-mi stretch of the Truckee River through **Truckee River Rafting** (*530/583–7238 or 888/584–7238 www.truckeeriverrafting.com*). They will shuttle you back to Tahoe City at the end of your two- to four-hour trip. On a warm day, this makes a great family outing.

SKIING ★ The locals' favorite place to ski on the north shore, **Alpine Meadows Ski Area**, is also the unofficial telemarking hub of the Sierra. With 495 inches of snow annually, Alpine has some of Tahoe's most reliable conditions. It's usually one of the first areas to open in November and one of the last to close in May or June. Alpine isn't the place for arrogant show-offs; instead, you'll find down-to-earth alpine fetishists. The two peaks here are well suited to intermediate skiers, with a number of runs for experts only. Snowboarders and hot-dog skiers will find a terrain park with a half-pipe, super-pipe, rails, and tabletops, as well as a boarder-cross course. Alpine is a great place to learn to ski and has a ski school that teaches and coaches those with physical and mental disabilities. There's also an area for overnight RV parking. On Saturday, because of the limited parking, there's more acreage per person than at other resorts. *2600 Alpine Meadows Rd., off Hwy. 89, 6 mi northwest of Tahoe City and 13 mi south of I–80 530/583–4232 or 800/441–4423, 530/581–8374 snow phone www.skialpine.com 100 trails on 2,400 acres, rated 25% beginner, 40% intermediate,*

TAHOE SPORTS TIPS

If you're planning to spend any time outdoors around Lake Tahoe, whether hiking, climbing, or camping, be aware that weather conditions can change quickly in the Sierra. To avoid a life-threatening case of hypothermia, always bring a pocket-size, fold-up rain poncho (available in all sporting-goods stores) to keep you dry. Wear long pants and a hat. Carry plenty of water. Because you'll likely be walking on granite, wear sturdy, closed-toe hiking boots, with soles that grip rock. If you're going into the backcountry, bring a signaling device (such as a mirror), emergency whistle, compass, map, energy bars, and water purifier. When heading out alone, tell someone where you're going and when you're coming back.

If you plan to ski, be aware of resort elevations. In the event of a winter storm, determine the snow level before you choose the resort you'll ski. Often the level can be as high as 7,000 feet, which means rain at some resorts' base areas but snow at others. For storm information, check the **National Weather Service's Web page** (🌐 *www.wrh.noaa.gov/rev*). If you plan to do any backcountry skiing, check with the **U.S. Forest Service** (☎ *530/587–2158 backcountry recording*) for conditions. A shop called the **Backcountry** (☎ *530/581–5861 Tahoe City, 530/582–0909 Truckee* 🌐 *www.thebackcountry.net*), with branches in Tahoe City and Truckee, operates an excellent Web site with current information about how and where to (and where not to) ski, mountain bike, and hike in the backcountry around Tahoe.

If you plan to camp in the backcountry, you'll need to purchase a wilderness permit, which you can pick up at the **U.S. Forest Service Office** (✉ *35 College Dr., South Lake Tahoe* ☎ *530/543–2600* 🌐 *www.fs.fed.us/r5/ltbmu*) or at a ranger station at the entrance to any of the national forests. For reservations at campgrounds in California state parks, contact **Reserve America** (☎ *800/444–7275* 🌐 *www.reserveamerica.com*).

35% advanced. Longest run 2½ mi, base 6,835 feet, summit 8,637 feet. Lifts: 14, including 1 high-speed 6-passenger lift and 2 high-speed quads.

You can rent skis, boards, and snowshoes at **Tahoe Dave's Skis and Boards** (✉ *590 N. Lake Blvd.* ☎ *530/583–0400*), which has the area's best selection of downhill rental equipment. If you plan to ski or board the backcountry, you'll find everything from crampons to transceivers at the **BackCountry** (✉ *690 N. Lake Blvd.* ☎ *530/581–5861 or 888/625–8444* 🌐 *www.thebackcountry.net*).

OLYMPIC VALLEY

7 mi north of Tahoe City via Hwy. 89 to Squaw Valley Rd.; 8½ mi south of Truckee via Hwy. 89 to Squaw Valley Rd.

Olympic Valley got its name in 1960, when Squaw Valley USA, the ski resort here, hosted the Winter Olympics. Snow sports remain the primary activity, but once summer comes, you can hike into the adjacent Granite Chief Wilderness, explore wildflower-studded alpine meadows, or lie by a swimming pool in one of the Sierra's prettiest valleys.

13

GETTING HERE AND AROUND

Squaw Valley Rd., the only way into Olympic Valley, branches west off Hwy. 89 about 8 mi south of Truckee. **Tahoe Area Regional Transit (TART)** connects the Squaw Valley ski area with the communities along the north and west shores, and Truckee, with year-round public transportation. Squaw Valley Ski Resort provides a free shuttle to many stops in those same areas.

EXPLORING

Village at Squaw Valley. The centerpiece of Olympic Valley is the Village at Squaw Valley, a pedestrian mall at the base of several four-story ersatz Bavarian stone-and-timber buildings, where you'll find restaurants, high-end condo rentals, boutiques, and cafés. The village often holds events and festivals. ✉ *1750 Village East Rd.* ☎ *530/584–1000 or 530/584–6205, 888/805–5022 condo reservations* 🌐 *www.thevillageatsquaw.com.*

High Camp. You can ride the Squaw Valley cable car to High Camp, which at 8,200 feet commands superb views of Lake Tahoe and the surrounding mountains. In summer, go for a hike, sit by the pool at the High Camp Bath and Tennis Club, or have a cocktail and watch the sunset. In winter, you can ski, ice-skate, or snow-tube. There's also a restaurant, lounge, and small Olympic museum. ✉ *Cable Car Bldg., Squaw Valley* ☎ *530/581–7278 High Camp, 530/583–6985 cable car* 🌐 *www.squaw.com* 🎫 *Cable car $24; special packages include swimming or skating* ⏲ *Daily; call for hrs.*

WHERE TO EAT

$$$ ECLECTIC ✕ **Graham's of Squaw Valley.** Sit by a floor-to-ceiling river-rock hearth under a knotty-pine peaked ceiling in the intimate dining room in the Christy Inn Lodge. The southern European–inspired menu changes often, but expect hearty entrées such as fillet of beef with wild mushroom sauce, along with lighter-fare small plates like salmon with orange saffron glaze. You can also stop in at the fireside bar for appetizers and wine from Graham's huge and highly regarded wine list. Reservations are recommended. ✉ *1650 Squaw Valley Rd.* ☎ *530/581–0454* ⏲ *Closed Mon. No lunch.*

$$ JAPANESE ✕ **Mamasake.** The hip and happening spot for sushi at Squaw serves stylized presentations in an industrial-warehouse-like room. In the evening, sit at the bar and watch extreme ski movies, many of which were filmed right outside the window. Or drop in from 3 to 5 to enjoy the incredibly inexpensive afternoon special: a spicy-tuna or salmon hand roll and a can of Bud for five bucks. ✉ *The Village at Squaw Valley* ☎ *530/584–0110.*

Squaw Valley USA has runs for skiers of all ability levels—from beginner trails to cliff drops for experts.

$$$ AMERICAN Fodor's Choice ★ **PlumpJack Café**. The best restaurant at Olympic Valley is also the finest in the entire Tahoe Basin, the epitome of discreet chic and a must-visit for all serious foodies. The menu changes seasonally, but look for roasted quail in a huckleberry compote, crispy sweetbreads, and seared diver scallops. Rather than complicated, heavy sauces, the chef uses simple reductions to complement a dish. The result: clean, dynamic, bright flavors. The wine list is exceptional for its variety and surprisingly low prices. If not for the view of the craggy mountains through the windows lining the cushy, 60-seat dining room, you might swear you were in San Francisco. A less expensive but equally adventurous menu is served at the bar. ✉ *1920 Squaw Valley Rd., Olympic Valley* ☎ *530/583–1578 or 800/323–7666* *Reservations essential.*

WHERE TO STAY

For expanded reviews, visit Fodors.com

$$$ Fodor's Choice ★ **PlumpJack Squaw Valley Inn.** If style and luxury are a must, make PlumpJack your first choice. **Pros:** small; intimate; lots of attention to details. **Cons:** not the best choice for families with small children. ✉ *1920 Squaw Valley Rd., Olympic Valley* ☎ *530/583–1576 or 800/323–7666* 🌐 *www.plumpjacksquawvalleyinn.com* *56 rooms, 8 suites* *In-room: a/c (some), Wi-Fi. In-hotel: restaurant, room service, bar, pool, gym, parking* *Breakfast.*

$$$ **The Village at Squaw Valley USA.** Right at the base of the slopes at the center point of Olympic Valley, the Village's studios and one-, two-, and three-bedroom condominiums were built in 2000 and still look fresh. **Pros:** family-friendly; near Village restaurants and shops. **Cons:** claustrophobia-inducing crowds. ✉ *1750 Village East Rd.* ☎ *530/584–1000 or*

866/818–6963 ⊕ www.thevillageatsquaw.com 198 suites In-room: no a/c, kitchen (some), Internet. In-hotel: laundry facilities, parking.

SPORTS AND THE OUTDOORS

GOLF The **Resort at Squaw Creek Golf Course** (✉ *400 Squaw Creek Rd.* ☎ *530/583–6300* ⊕ *www.squawcreek.com*), an 18-hole championship course, was designed by Robert Trent Jones Jr. Greens fees range from $60 for afternoon play to $95 for prime time, and include the use of a cart.

HIKING The Granite Chief Wilderness and the high peaks surrounding Olympic Valley are accessible by foot, but save yourself a 2,000-foot elevation gain by riding the Squaw Valley cable car to **High Camp** (☎ *530/583–6985* ⊕ *www.squaw.com*), the starting point for a variety of hikes. Pick up trail maps at the cable car building. In late summer, High Camp offers full-moon and sunset hikes.

ICE-SKATING Ice-skate from November to late September at the **Olympic Ice Pavilion** (✉ *1960 Squaw Valley Rd., High Camp, Squaw Valley* ☎ *530/452–4000 or 530/581–7246* ⊕ *www.squaw.com*). A ride up the mountain and a skating pass cost $29, including skate rental; pay $7 extra to end your outing in the hot tub.

MINIATURE GOLF ★ Next to the Olympic Village Lodge, on the far side of the creek, the **Squaw Valley Adventure Center** (☎ *530/583–7673* ⊕ *www.squawadventure.com*) has an 18-hole miniature golf course, a ropes course, and sometimes a bungee-trampoline, a blast for kids.

ROCK CLIMBING Before you rappel down a granite monolith, hone your skills at the **Headwall Climbing Wall** (✉ *1960 Squaw Valley Rd., near Village at Squaw Valley* ☎ *530/583–7673* ⊕ *www.squawadventure.com*), at the base of the cable car.

SKIING Fodor's Choice ★ Known for some of the toughest skiing in the Tahoe area, **Squaw Valley USA** was the centerpiece of the 1960 Winter Olympics. Today it's the definitive North Tahoe ski resort and among the top-three megaresorts in California (the other two are Heavenly and Mammoth). Although Squaw has changed significantly since the Olympics, the skiing is still world-class and extends across vast bowls stretched between six peaks. Experts often head directly to the untamed terrain of the infamous KT-22 face, which has bumps, cliffs, and gulp-and-go chutes, or to the nearly vertical Palisades, where many famous Warren Miller extreme-skiing films have been shot. Fret not, beginners and intermediates: you have plenty of wide-open, groomed trails at High Camp (which sits at the *top* of the mountain) and around the more challenging Snow King Peak. Snowboarders and show-off skiers can tear up the three fantastic terrain parks, which include a giant super-pipe. Lift prices include night skiing until 9 pm. Tickets for skiers 12 and under cost only $12. ✉ *1960 Squaw Valley Rd., off Hwy. 89, Olympic Valley, 7 mi northwest of Tahoe City* ☎ *530/583–6985, 800/545–4350 lodging reservations, 530/583–6955 snow phone* ⊕ *www.squaw.com* ☞ *170 trails on 4,000 acres, rated 25% beginner, 45% intermediate, 30% advanced. Longest run 3.2 mi, base 6,200 feet, summit 9,050 feet. Lifts: 33, including a gondola-style funitel, a cable car, 7 high-speed chairs, and 18 fixed-grip chairs.*

13

If you don't want to pay resort prices, you can rent and tune downhill skis and snowboards at **Tahoe Dave's Skis and Boards** (✉ *3039 Hwy. 89, at Squaw Valley Rd.* ☎ *530/583–5665* 🌐 *www.tahoedaves.com*).

Cross-country skiers will enjoy looping through the valley's giant alpine meadow. The **Resort at Squaw Creek** (✉ *400 Squaw Creek Rd.* ☎ *530/583–6300* 🌐 *www.squawcreek.com*) rents cross-country equipment and provides trail maps.

TRUCKEE

13 mi northwest of Kings Beach on Hwy. 267; 14 mi north of Tahoe City on Hwy. 89.

Formerly a decrepit railroad town in the mountains, Truckee is now the trendy first stop for many Tahoe visitors. Around 1863 the town was officially established; by 1868 it had gone from a stagecoach station to a major stopover for trains bound for the Pacific via the new transcontinental railroad. Freight trains and Amtrak's California Zephyr still stop every day at the depot right in the middle of town. Across from the station, where Old West facades line the main drag, you'll find galleries, gift shops, boutiques, old-fashioned diners, and several remarkably good restaurants. Look for outlet stores, strip malls, and discount skiwear shops along Donner Pass Road, north of the freeway. Because of its location on I–80, Truckee is a favorite stopover for people traveling from the San Francisco Bay Area to the north shore of Lake Tahoe, Reno, and points east.

GETTING HERE AND AROUND

Truckee is just off I–80 between Hwys. 89 and 267. Greyhound and Amtrak stop there. Enterprise and Hertz provide car rentals, and **Tahoe Area Regional Transit** can bus you to north shore communities.

ESSENTIALS

Visitor Information Truckee Donner Chamber of Commerce and the California Welcome Center (✉ *10065 Donner Pass Rd., Truckee, CA* ☎ *530/587–8808* 🌐 *www.truckee.com*) are inside the downtown Amtrak depot. Stop by for a walking-tour map of historic Truckee and for brochures about the towns, activities, and ski resorts in the Tahoe area.

EXPLORING

Donner Memorial State Park and Emigrant Trail Museum. A must-stop for history buffs, Donner Memorial State Park and Emigrant Trail Museum commemorates the Donner Party, a group of 89 westward-bound pioneers who were trapped in the Sierra in the winter of 1846–47 in snow 22 feet deep. Only 49 pioneers survived that fierce winter, some by resorting to cannibalism, though none consumed his own kin. (For the full story, pick up a copy of *Ordeal by Hunger,* by George R. Stewart.) The museum's hourly slide show details the Donner Party's plight. Other displays and dioramas relate the history of railroad development through the Sierra. In the park, you can picnic, hike, camp, and go boating, fishing, and waterskiing in summer; winter brings cross-country skiing and snowshoeing on groomed trails. The day-use parking fee includes admission to the museum. ✉ *12593 Donner Pass Rd., off I–80, 2 mi west of*

Truckee ☎ 530/582–7892 museum, 800/444–7275 camping reservations 🌐 www.parks.ca.gov 💳 $8 parking, day use ⏲ Museum daily 9–4.

OFF THE BEATEN PATH

Tahoe National Forest. Draped along the Sierra Nevada Crest above Lake Tahoe, the national forest offers abundant outdoor recreation: picnicking and camping in summer, and in winter, snowshoeing, skiing, and sledding over some of the deepest snowpack in the West. The **Big Bend Visitor Center** occupies a state historic landmark within the forest, 10 mi west of Donner Summit. This area has been on major cross-country routes for centuries, ever since Native Americans passed through trading acorns and salt for pelts, obsidian, and other materials. Between 1844 and 1860, more than 200,000 emigrants traveled to California along the Emigrant Trail, which passed nearby; you can see rut marks left by wagon wheels scraping the famously hard granite. Later the nation's first transcontinental railroad ran through here (and still does), as do U.S. 40 (the old National Road) and its successor, I–80. Exhibits in the visitor center explore the area's transportation history. Take the Rainbow–Big Bend exit off I–80. ✉ *49685 Hampshire Rocks Rd. (old U.S. Hwy. 40), Soda Springs ☎ 530/426–3609 or 530/265–4531 🌐 www.fs.fed.us/r5/tahoe/recreation 💳 Free ⏲ Hrs vary; open only during summer months; call ahead.*

WHERE TO EAT

$$$ ECLECTIC ✕ **Cottonwood**. Perched above town on the site of North America's first chairlift, the Cottonwood restaurant is a veritable institution. The bar is decked out with old wooden skis, sleds, skates, and photos of Truckee's early days. The dining area serves an ambitious menu—everything from grilled New York strip steak to baby back short ribs with Cajun spices to butternut squash enchiladas, plus fresh-baked breads and desserts—but people come here mainly for the atmosphere and hilltop views. There's live music on weekends. ✉ *10142 Rue Hilltop, off Brockway Rd., ¼ mi south of downtown ☎ 530/587–5711 ⏲ No lunch.*

$$ ASIAN ✕ **Dragonfly**. Flavors are bold and zingy at this old-town, Cal-Asian spot, where every dish is artfully prepared and stylishly presented—and most important, well executed. The bright tones of Southeast Asian cooking inspire most dishes on the changing menu, which you can savor in the bright, contemporary dining rooms—one for sushi—or an outdoor terrace overlooking Main Street and the train depot. Lunch is a bargain, and there are lots of choices for vegetarians. Look for the staircase: the restaurant is on the second floor, not street level. ✉ *10118 Donner Pass Rd. ☎ 530/587–0557.*

$$ AMERICAN ✕ **FiftyFifty Brewing Company**. In this Truckee brewpub, warm red tones and comfy booths, plus a pint of their Donner Party Porter, will take the nip out of a cold day on the slopes. The lunch menu includes salads, burgers, and the house specialty, a pulled pork sandwich. After 5 pm, you can tuck into barbecued ribs and crab cakes. Order one of their inventive pizzas anytime. There's a full bar along with the brews, and lots of après-ski action. ✉ *11197 Brockway Rd. ☎ 530/587–2337.*

$$$ ECLECTIC ✕ **Moody's**. Head here for contemporary-Cal cuisine in a sexy dining room with pumpkin-color walls, burgundy velvet banquettes, and art-deco fixtures. The chef-owner's earthy, sure-handed cooking features organically grown ingredients: look for ahi tuna "four ways,"

13

house-made charcuterie samplings, pan-roasted wild game, fresh seafood, and organic grass-fed steak. Lunch fare is lighter. In summer dine alfresco surrounded by flowers. Thursday through Saturday there's music in the borderline-raucous bar that gets packed with Truckee's bon vivants. ✉ *10007 Bridge St.* ☎ *530/587–8688.*

WHERE TO STAY

For expanded reviews, visit Fodors.com

$$$ **Cedar House Sport Hotel.** Built in 2006, Cedar House ups the ante for lodging at Tahoe. **Pros:** an environmentally friendly facility that's also comfortable and hip. **Cons:** some bathrooms are on the small side. ✉ *10918 Brockway Rd.* ☎ *530/582–5655 or 866/582–5655* 🌐 *www.cedarhousesporthotel.com* *41 rooms* *In-room: no a/c, Wi-Fi. In-hotel: restaurant, bar, parking* *Breakfast.*

$$$$ **Northstar-at-Tahoe Resort.** The area's most complete destination resort is perfect for families, thanks to its many sports activities—from golf and tennis to skiing and snowshoeing—and its concentration of restaurants, shops, recreation facilities, and accommodations. **Pros:** vast array of lodging types; on-site shuttle, several dining options in Northstar Village. **Cons:** family accommodations are very pricey. ✉ *Hwy. 267, 6 mi southeast of Truckee, Box 129* ☎ *530/562–1010 or 800/466–6784* 🌐 *www.northstarattahoe.com* *250 units* *In-room: a/c (some), kitchen (some), Internet (some). In-hotel: golf course, tennis courts, pool, gym, children's programs, laundry facilities.*

$$$$ **Ritz-Carlton Highlands Court, Lake Tahoe.** The first luxury hotel built in the Tahoe area in decades, the Ritz-Carlton opened in December 2009. **Pros:** superb service; gorgeous setting. **Cons:** prices as breathtaking as the views; must go off-site for golf and tennis. ✉ *13031 Ritz-Carlton Highlands Court* ☎ *530/562–3000 or 800/241–3333* 🌐 *www.ritzcarlton.com/laketahoe* *153 rooms, 17 suites* *In-room: a/c, Internet, Wi-Fi. In-hotel: restaurants, room service, bars, pools, gym, spa, children's programs, business center, parking, some pets allowed.*

$$ **River Street Inn.** On the banks of the Truckee River, this 1885 wood-and-stone inn was at times a boardinghouse and a brothel. **Pros:** nice rooms; good value. **Cons:** parking is a half-block from inn. ✉ *10009 E. River St.* ☎ *530/550–9290* 🌐 *www.riverstreetinntruckee.com* *11 rooms* *In-room: no phone, no a/c, Wi-Fi* *Breakfast.*

SPORTS AND THE OUTDOORS

GOLF The **Coyote Moon Golf Course** (✉ *10685 Northwoods Blvd.* ☎ *530/587–0886* 🌐 *www.coyotemoongolf.com*) is both challenging and beautiful, with no houses to spoil the view. Fees range from $95 to $145, including cart. **Northstar** (✉ *Hwy. 267* ☎ *530/562–3290*) has open links–style play and tight, tree-lined fairways, including water hazards. Fees range from $40 to $80, including cart. At **Old Greenwood** (✉ *12915 Fairway Dr., off Overland Trail exit, Exit 190, from I–80; call for specific directions* ☎ *530/550–7010* 🌐 *www.oldgreenwood.com*), north Lake Tahoe's only Jack Nicklaus signature course, the water hazards are trout streams where you can actually fish. The $100–$185 fee includes a cart.

MOUNTAIN BIKING In summer you can rent a bike and ride the lifts up the mountain at **Northstar-at-Tahoe** (✉ *Hwy. 267, at Northstar Dr.* ☎ *530/562–2268* *www.northstarattahoe.com*) for 100 mi of challenging terrain. A ride to the mountain-biking park on the lift is $42 for ages 13 and above; $27 for ages 9–12. The season extends from July through September with varying hours; call for times.

SKIING Several smaller resorts around Truckee give you access to the Sierra's slopes for less than half the price of the big resorts. Though you'll sacrifice vertical rise, acreage, and high-speed lifts, you can ski or ride and still have money left over for room and board. These are great places for first-timers and families with kids learning to ski.

13

Boreal (✉ *Boreal/Castle Peak exit off I–80, 19659 Boreal Ridge Rd., Truckee* ☎ *530/426–3666* 🌐 *www.rideboreal.com*) has 480 acres and 500 vertical feet of terrain visible from the freeway; there's also lift-served snow-tubing and night skiing until 9. **Donner Ski Ranch** (✉ *19320 Donner Pass Rd., Norden* ☎ *530/426–3635* 🌐 *www.donnerskiranch.com*) has 505 acres and 750 vertical feet and sits across from the more challenging Sugar Bowl (⇨ *below*). **Soda Springs** (✉ *Soda Springs exit off I–80, 10244 Soda Springs Rd., Soda Springs* ☎ *530/426–3901* 🌐 *www.skisodasprings.com*) has 200 acres and 652 vertical feet and lift-served snow-tubing. **Tahoe Donner** (✉ *11509 Northwoods Blvd., Truckee* ☎ *530/587–9444* 🌐 *www.tahoedonner.com*) is just north of Truckee and covers 120 acres and 560 vertical feet; the cross-country center includes 51 trails on 114 km (71 mi) of groomed tracks on 4,800 acres, with night skiing on Wednesdays January and February.

Northstar-at-Tahoe may be the best all-around family ski resort at Tahoe. With two tree-lined, northeast-facing, wind-protected bowls, it's the ideal place to ski in a storm. Hotshot experts unfairly call the mountain "Flatstar," but the meticulous grooming and long cruisers make it an intermediate skier's paradise. Boarders are especially welcome, with awesome terrain parks, including a 420-foot-long super-pipe, a half-pipe, rails and boxes, and lots of kickers. Experts can ski the steeps and bumps off Lookout Mountain, where there's rarely a line for the high-speed quad. Northstar-at-Tahoe's cross-country center has 40 km (25 mi) of groomed trails, including double-set tracks and skating lanes. The school has programs for skiers ages four and up, and day care is available for tots two and older. The mountain gets packed on busy weekends but when there's room on the slopes, Northstar is loads of fun. (⇨ *See "When to Go" at the beginning of this chapter for alternatives on busy days.*) ✉ *100 Northstar Dr., off Hwy. 267, 6 mi southeast of Truckee* ☎ *530/562–1010 or 800/466–6784, 530/562–1330 snow phone* 🌐 *www.northstarattahoe.com* ☞ *93 trails on 3,000 acres, rated 13% beginner, 60% intermediate, 27% advanced. Longest run 1.4 mi, base 6,330 feet, summit 8,610 feet. Lifts: 19, including a gondola and 6 high-speed quads.*

Opened in 1939 by Walt Disney, **Sugar Bowl** is the oldest—and one of the best—resorts at Tahoe. Atop Donner Summit, it receives an incredible 500 inches of snowfall annually. Four peaks are connected by 1,500 acres of skiable terrain, with everything from gentle groomed corduroy to wide-open bowls to vertical rocky chutes and outstanding tree skiing. Snowboarders can hit two terrain parks and a 20-foot-high by

450-foot-long super-pipe. Because it's more compact than some of the area's megaresorts, there's a certain gentility here that distinguishes Sugar Bowl from its competitors, making this a great place for families and a low-pressure, low-key place to learn to ski. It's not huge, but there's some very challenging terrain (experts: head to the Palisades). There's limited lodging at the base area. This is the closest resort to San Francisco (three hours via I–80). ✉ *Donner Pass Rd., 3 mi east of Soda Springs/Norden exit off I–80, 10 mi west of Truckee, Norden* ☎ *530/426–9000 information and lodging reservations, 530/426–1111 snow phone, 866/843–2695 lodging referral* 🌐 *www.sugarbowl.com* ☞ *95 trails on 1,500 acres, rated 17% beginner, 45% intermediate, 38% advanced. Longest run 3 mi, base 6,883 feet, summit 8,383 feet. Lifts: 13, including 5 high-speed quads.*

★ For the ultimate in groomed conditions, head to the nation's largest cross-country ski resort, **Royal Gorge** (✉ *9411 Hillside Dr., Soda Springs/Norden exit off I–80, Soda Springs* ☎ *530/426–3871* 🌐 *www.royalgorge.com*). It has 195 km (121 mi) of 18-foot-wide track for all abilities, 65 trails on a whopping 9,172 acres, a ski school, and eight warming huts. Two trailside cafés and two lodges round out the facilities. Since it's right on the Sierra Crest, the views are drop-dead gorgeous, and the resort feels like it goes on forever. If you love to cross-country, don't miss Royal Gorge.

You can save money by renting skis and boards at **Tahoe Dave's** (✉ *10200 Donner Pass Rd.* ☎ *530/582–0900*), which has the area's best selection and also repairs and tunes equipment.

CARNELIAN BAY TO KINGS BEACH

5–10 mi northeast of Tahoe City on Hwy. 28.

The small lakeside commercial districts of Carnelian Bay and Tahoe Vista service the thousand or so locals who live in the area year-round and the thousands more who have summer residences or launch their boats here. Kings Beach, the last town heading east on Highway 28 before the Nevada border, is to Crystal Bay what South Lake Tahoe is to Stateline: a bustling California town full of basic motels and rental condos, restaurants, and shops, used by the hordes of hopefuls who pass through on their way to the casinos.

GETTING HERE AND AROUND

From the California side, reach Kings Beach and Carnelian Bay via Hwy. 89 to Hwy. 28. If you're coming from Reno, take I–580 south to U.S. 395 toward Carson City. Take the exit to Mt. Rose Hwy. 431. Turn right on Tahoe Blvd. and follow it to Hwy. 28. **Tahoe Area Regional Transit (TART)** connects the serves the communities along the north and west shores.

EXPLORING

Kings Beach State Recreation Area. The 28-acre Kings Beach State Recreation Area, one of the largest such areas on the lake, is open year-round. The 700-foot-long sandy beach gets very crowded with people swimming, sunbathing, Jet Skiing, riding in paddleboats, spiking volleyballs, and tossing Frisbees. If you're going to spend the day, come early enough to snag a table in the picnic area; there's also a good playground. ✉ *N. Lake Blvd., Kings Beach* ☎ *530/546–7248* *$8 parking fee* ⏲ *Daily.*

WHERE TO EAT AND STAY

$$$ ECLECTIC ✕ **Gar Woods Grill and Pier.** The view's the thing at this lakeside stalwart, where you can watch the sun shimmer on the water through the dining room's plate-glass windows or from the heated outdoor deck. Grilled steak and fish are menu mainstays, but be sure to try specialties like crab chilis rellenos and margarita Hawaiian swordfish. At all hours in season, the bar gets packed with boaters who pull up to the restaurant's private pier. ✉ *5000 N. Lake Blvd., Carnelian Bay* ☎ *530/546–3366.*

13

$$ AMERICAN ✕ **Spindleshanks.** This handsome roadhouse, decorated with floor-to-ceiling knotty pine, serves mostly classic American cooking—ribs, steaks, and seafood updated with adventurous sauces—as well as house-made ravioli. On cold nights request seating near the crackling fireplace and enjoy a drink from the full bar or the extensive wine list. Reservations are recommended. ✉ *6873 N. Lake Blvd, Tahoe Vista* ☎ *530/546–2191* ⏲ *No lunch.*

$$ **Ferrari's Crown Resort.** One of the few remaining family-owned and -operated motels in Kings Beach, Ferrari's has straightforward motel rooms in a resort setting, great for families with kids. **Pros:** family-friendly; lakeside location. **Cons:** older facility. ✉ *8200 N. Lake Blvd., Kings Beach* ☎ *530/546–3388 or 800/645–2260* 🌐 *www.tahoecrown.com* *71 rooms* *In-room: a/c (some), kitchen (some), Internet, Wi-Fi. In-hotel: pools, beach* *Breakfast.*

$$$ ★ **Shore House.** Every room has a gas fireplace, down comforter, and featherbed at this lakefront B&B in Tahoe Vista. **Pros:** waterfront honeymoon cottage; massage appointments available. **Cons:** pricey (even off-season). ✉ *7170 N. Lake Blvd., Tahoe Vista* ☎ *530/546–7270 or 800/207–5160* 🌐 *www.shorehouselaketahoe.com* *8 rooms, 1 cottage* *In-room: no phone, no a/c, Wi-Fi. In-hotel: beach* *Breakfast.*

THE NEVADA SIDE

The difference on the Nevada side of the lake is, of course, gambling, with all its repercussions.

CRYSTAL BAY

1 mi east of Kings Beach on Hwy. 28; 30 mi north of South Lake Tahoe via U.S. 50 to Hwy. 28.

Right at the Nevada border, Crystal Bay has a cluster of casinos that look essentially the same, but have a few minor differences. These casinos tend toward the tacky, and most of the lodging is pretty lackluster.

GETTING HERE AND AROUND

From the California side, reach Crystal Bay via Hwy. 89 or 267 to Hwy. 28. If you're coming from Reno, take I–580 south to U.S. 395 toward Carson City. Take exit to Mt. Rose Hwy. 431. Turn right on Tahoe Blvd. and follow it to Hwy. 28. **Tahoe Area Regional Transit (TART)** connects the serves the communities along the north and west shores.

EXPLORING

Cal-Neva Lodge. Bisected by the state line, the Cal-Neva Lodge opened in 1927 and has weathered many scandals. The largest involved former owner Frank Sinatra (he lost his gaming license in the 1960s for alleged mob connections). The secret tunnel that Frank built so that he could steal away unnoticed to Marilyn Monroe's cabin is definitely worth a look; call for tour times. ✉ *2 Stateline Rd.* ☎ *800/225–6382* 🌐 *www.calnevaresort.com.*

Tahoe Biltmore. A daily happy hour keeps the Tahoe Biltmore hopping. ✉ *5 Hwy. 28, at Stateline Rd.* ☎ *800/245–8667* 🌐 *www.tahoebiltmore.com.*

Jim Kelley's Tahoe Nugget. Nearly 100 kinds of beer highlight the bar scene at Jim Kelley's Tahoe Nugget. ✉ *20 Hwy. 28, near Stateline Rd.* ☎ *775/831–0455.*

Crystal Bay Club. Known for its classic steak and lobster dinner, the restaurant at the Crystal Bay Club has a distinctive open-truss ceiling. ✉ *14 Hwy. 28, near Stateline Rd.* ☎ *775/833–6333* 🌐 *www.crystalbaycasino.com.*

WHERE TO EAT

$$$ ECLECTIC ✕ **Soule Domain.** Rough-hewn wood beams and a vaulted wood ceiling lend high romance to this cozy 1927 pine-log cabin, tucked beneath tall trees, next to the Tahoe Biltmore. On the eclectic menu, chef-owner Charles Soule's specialties include curried cashew chicken, lamb ravioli, fresh sea scallops poached in champagne with kiwi and mango cream sauce, and a vegan sauté with ginger, jalapeños, and tofu, but you'll find the chef's current passion in the always-great roster of nightly specials. Some find it a little pricey, but if you're looking for someplace with a solid menu where you can hold hands by candlelight, this is it. In winter request a table near the crackling fireplace. Reservations are recommended. ✉ *9983 Cove Ave., ½ block up Stateline Rd. from Hwy. 28, Kings Beach* ☎ *530/546–7529* ⏲ *No lunch.*

INCLINE VILLAGE

3 mi east of Crystal Bay on Hwy. 28.

Incline Village, Nevada's only privately owned town, dates to the early 1960s, when an Oklahoma developer bought 10,000 acres north of Lake Tahoe. His idea was to sketch out a plan for a town without a central commercial district, hoping to prevent congestion and to preserve the area's natural beauty. One-acre lakeshore lots originally fetched $12,000 to $15,000; today you couldn't buy the same land for less than several million.

GETTING HERE AND AROUND

From the California side, reach Incline Village via Hwy. 89 or 267 to Hwy. 28. If you're coming from Reno, take I–580 south to U.S. 395 toward Carson City. Take the exit to Mt. Rose Hwy. 431. Turn left on Tahoe Blvd. to Incline Village. From South Lake Tahoe, take U.S. 50 southeast around the lake and turn left onto Hwy. 28 just north of Glenbrook (U.S. 50 continues to Carson City at that point.) **Tahoe Area Regional Transit** (**TART**) serves the communities along the north and west shores from Incline Village to Tahoma.

13

ESSENTIALS

Visitor Information **Lake Tahoe Incline Village/Crystal Bay Visitors Bureau** (*969 Tahoe Blvd., Incline Village 775/832–1606 or 800/468–2463 www.gotahoenorth.com*).

EXPLORING

Lakeshore Drive. Check out Lakeshore Drive, along which you'll see some of the most expensive real estate in Nevada. The drive is discreetly marked: to find it, start at the Hyatt Hotel and drive westward along the lake.

Fodor's Choice ★ **Thunderbird Lodge.** George Whittell, a San Francisco socialite who once owned 40,000 acres of property along the lake, built the Thunderbird Lodge in 1936. You can tour the mansion and the grounds by reservation only, and though it's pricey, it provides a rare glimpse back to a time when only the very wealthy had homes at Tahoe. The lodge is accessible via a bus from the Incline Village Visitors Bureau, a catamaran from the Hyatt in Incline Village, or a 1950 wooden cruiser from Tahoe Keys Marina in South Lake Tahoe (which includes lunch). *2435 Venice Dr. E 775/832–8750 lodge, 800/468–2463 reservations, 775/588–1881, 888/867–6394 Tahoe Keys boat, 775/832–1234, 800/553–3288 Hyatt Incline Village boat www.thunderbirdlodge.org $39 bus tour, $110 boat tour May–Oct., call for tour times.*

OFF THE BEATEN PATH

Lake Tahoe–Nevada State Park. Protecting much of the lake's eastern shore from development, Lake Tahoe–Nevada State Park comprises several sections that stretch from Incline Village to Zephyr Cove. Beaches and trails provide access to a wilder side of the lake, whether you're into cross-country skiing, hiking, or just relaxing at a picnic. The east shore gets less snow and more sun than the west shore, making it a good early- or late-season outdoor destination. One of the most likable areas is **Sand Harbor Beach** (*Hwy. 28, 3 mi south of Incline Village 775/831–0494 parks.nv.gov/lt.htm*). It's so popular that it sometimes fills to capacity by 11 am on summer weekends. Stroll the boardwalk and read the information signs for a good lesson in the local ecology. Pets are not allowed.

WHERE TO EAT AND STAY

$$$ ECLECTIC **Frederick's.** Copper-top tables lend a chic look to the small dining room at this intimate bistro. The menu consists of a mélange of European and Asian cooking, mostly prepared using organic produce and free-range meats. Try the braised short ribs, roasted duck with caramel pecan glaze, or the deliciously fresh sushi rolls. Ask for a table by the fire. Reservations are recommended. *907 Tahoe Blvd. 775/832–3007 Closed Sun. and Mon. No lunch.*

$$$ FRENCH **Le Bistro.** Incline Village's hidden gem, Le Bistro serves expertly prepared French-country cuisine in a relaxed, cozy, romantic dining room. The chef-owner makes everything himself, using organically grown ingredients, and changes the menu almost daily. Expect such dishes as pâté de campagne, baked tomato bisque en croute, escargot, and herb-crusted roast lamb loin. Try the five-course prix-fixe menu ($49), which can be paired with their award-winning wine selections. Service is gracious and attentive. Be sure to ask directions when you book since the restaurant is hard to find. *120 Country Club Dr., #29 775/831–0800 Closed Sun. and Mon. No lunch.*

¢ SOUTHERN **T's Rotisserie.** There's nothing fancy about T's (it looks like a small snack bar), but the mesquite-grilled chicken and tri-tip steaks are delicious and inexpensive—a rare combination in pricey Incline Village. It's mainly a take-out spot; seating is limited. *901 Tahoe Blvd. 775/831–2832 No credit cards.*

$$$ **Hyatt Regency Lake Tahoe.** Once a dowdy casino hotel, the Hyatt underwent a $60 million renovation between 2001 and 2003 and is now a smart-looking, upmarket, full-service destination resort. **Pros:** incredible views; first-class spa. **Cons:** pricey (especially for families). *111 Country Club Dr., at Lakeshore Dr. 775/832–1234 or 888/899–5019 www.laketahoe.hyatt.com 422 rooms, 28 suites In-room: a/c, kitchen (some), Internet, Wi-Fi. In-hotel: restaurants, room service, bars, pool, gym, spa, beach, children's programs, business center, parking.*

SPORTS AND THE OUTDOORS

GOLF **Incline Championship** (*955 Fairway Blvd. 866/925–4653 www.inclinegolf.com*) is an 18-hole, par-72 Robert Trent Jones Sr. course with a driving range, both completely renovated between 2002 and 2004. The $179 greens fee includes an optional cart. **Incline Mountain** (*690 Wilson Way 866/925–4653 www.inclinegolf.com*) is an executive (shorter) 18-hole course; par is 58. Greens fees start at $65, including optional cart.

MOUNTAIN BIKING You can rent bikes and get helpful tips from **Flume Trail Bikes** (*Spooner Summit, Hwy. 28, ¾ mi north of U.S. 50, Glenbrook 775/749–5349 www.theflumetrail.com*), which also operates a bike shuttle to popular trailheads. Ask about the secluded backcountry rental cabins for overnight rides.

SKIING A fun family mood prevails at **Diamond Peak,** which has many special programs and affordable rates. Snowmaking covers 75% of the mountain, and runs are groomed nightly. The ride up the 1-mi Crystal chair rewards you with some of the best views of the lake from any ski area. Diamond Peak is less crowded than the larger areas and provides free shuttles to nearby lodging. It's a great place for beginners and intermediates, and it's appropriately priced for families. However, though there are some steep-aspect black-diamond runs, advanced skiers may find the acreage too limited. For snowboarders there's a half-pipe and super-pipe. *1210 Ski Way, Incline Village 775/832–1177 www.diamondpeak.com 30 trails on 655 acres, rated 18% beginner, 46% intermediate, 36% advanced. Longest run 2½ mi, base 6,700 feet, summit 8,540 feet. Lifts: 6, including 2 high-speed quads.*

Ski some of the highest slopes at Tahoe, and take in bird's-eye views of Reno and the Carson Valley at **Mt. Rose Ski Tahoe.** Though more compact than the bigger Tahoe resorts, Mt. Rose has the area's highest base elevation and consequently the driest snow. The mountain has a wide variety of terrain. The most challenging is the Chutes, 200 acres of gulp-and-go advanced-to-expert vertical. Intermediates can choose steep groomers or mellow, wide-open boulevards. Beginners have their own corner of the mountain, with gentle, nonthreatening, wide slopes. Boarders and tricksters have three terrain parks to choose from, on

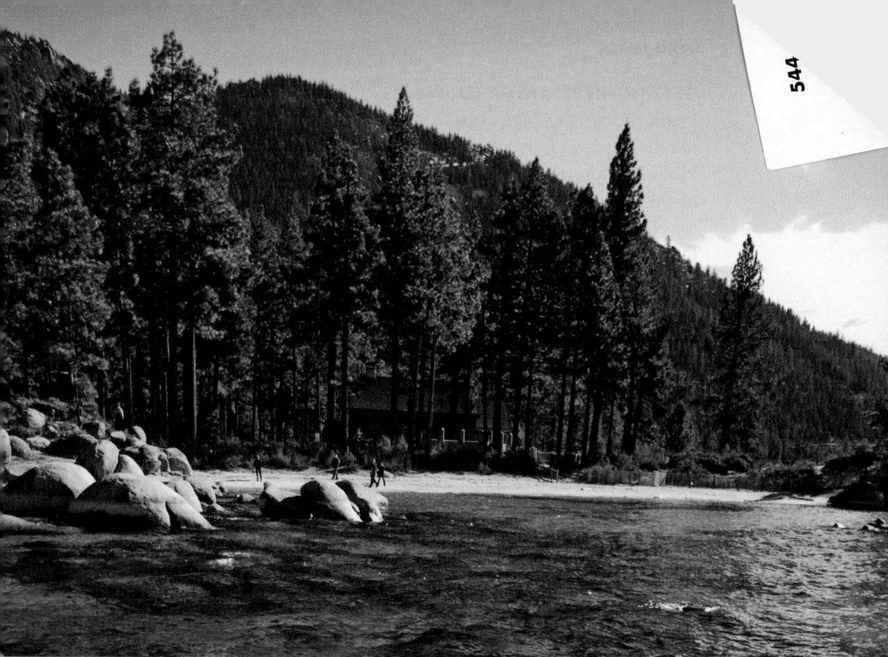

Get to Sand Harbor Beach in Lake Tahoe–Nevada State Park early; the park sometimes fills to capacity before lunchtime in summer.

opposite sides of the mountain, allowing them to follow the sun as it tracks across the resort. Because of its elevation, the mountain gets hit hard in storms; check conditions before heading up during inclement weather or on a windy day. ✉ *22222 Mt. Rose Hwy. (Hwy. 431), 11 mi north of Incline Village, Reno* ☎ *775/849–0704 or 800/754–7673* 🌐 *www.skirose.com* ☞ *61 trails on 1,200 acres, rated 20% beginner, 30% intermediate, 40% advanced, 10% expert. Longest run 2½ mi, base 8,260 feet, summit 9,700 feet. Lifts: 8, including 2 high-speed 6-passenger lifts.*

On the way to Mt. Rose from Incline Village, **Tahoe Meadows** (✉ *Hwy. 431*) is the most popular area near the north shore for noncommercial cross-country skiing, sledding, tubing, snowshoeing, and snowmobiling.

You'll find superbly groomed tracks and fabulous views of Lake Tahoe at **Spooner Lake Cross-Country** (✉ *Spooner Summit, Hwy. 28, ½ mi north of U.S. 50, Glenbrook* ☎ *775/749–5349* 🌐 *www.spoonerlake.com*). It has more than 50 mi of trails on more than 9,000 acres, and two rustic, secluded cabins are available for rent for overnight treks.

ZEPHYR COVE

22 mi south of Incline Village via Hwy. 28 to U.S. 50.

The largest settlement between Incline Village and the Stateline area is Zephyr Cove, a tiny resort. It has a beach, marina, campground, picnic area, coffee shop in a log lodge, rustic cabins, and nearby riding stables.

GETTING HERE AND AROUND

From the north shore communities, reach Zephyr Cove by following Hwy. 28 along the scenic eastern side of the lake. From South Lake Tahoe, take U.S. 50 southeast around the lake. If you're coming from Reno, head south out of the city on U.S. 395, then west on U.S. 50 until it curves south to the Nevada side of the lake. Public transportation isn't available in Zephyr Cove.

> **TAHOE TESSIE**
>
> Local lore claims this huge sea monster slithers around Lake Tahoe. Skeptics laugh, but true believers keep their eyes peeled for surprise sightings.

EXPLORING

★ **Cave Rock.** Near Zephyr Cove, Cave Rock, 75 feet of solid stone at the southern end of Lake Tahoe–Nevada State Park, is the throat of an extinct volcano. Tahoe Tessie, the lake's version of the Loch Ness monster, is reputed to live in a cavern below the impressive outcropping. Cave Rock towers over a parking lot, a lakefront picnic ground, and a boat launch. The views are some of the best on the lake; this is a good spot to stop and take a picture. However, this area is a sacred burial site for the Washoe Indians, and climbing up to the cave, or through it, is prohibited. ✉ *U.S. 50, 4 mi north of Zephyr Cove* ☎ *775/831–0494.*

WHERE TO STAY

For expanded reviews, visit Fodors.com

$$$ **Zephyr Cove Resort.** Tucked beneath towering pines at the lake's edge stand 28 cozy, modern vacation cabins with peaked knotty-pine ceilings. **Pros:** family-friendly. **Cons:** lodge rooms are very basic; can be noisy. ✉ *760 U.S. 50, 4 mi north of Stateline* ☎ *775/589–4907 or 888/896–3830* 🌐 *www.zephyrcove.com* *28 cabins* *In-room: no a/c, kitchen (some). In-hotel: restaurant, beach, laundry facilities, some pets allowed.*

STATELINE

5 mi south of Zephyr Cove on U.S. 50.

Stateline is the archetypal Nevada border town. Its four high-rise casinos are as vertical and contained as the commercial district of South Lake Tahoe, on the California side, is horizontal and sprawling. And Stateline is as relentlessly indoors oriented as the rest of the lake is focused on the outdoors. This strip is where you'll find the most concentrated action at Lake Tahoe: restaurants (including typical casino buffets), showrooms with famous headliners and razzle-dazzle revues, tower-hotel rooms and suites, and 24-hour casinos.

GETTING HERE AND AROUND

In South Lake Tahoe take U.S. 50, also called Lake Tahoe Blvd., south across the Nevada border to reach Stateline and its casinos. Arrive by car or, if coming from Reno Airport, take the South Tahoe Express. Blue Go operates daily bus service in the south shore area year-round, plus a ski shuttle from the large hotels to Heavenly ski resort in the winter.

WHERE TO EAT AND STAY

$$$ FRENCH ✕ **Mirabelle.** Don't be put off by this restaurant's nondescript exterior. Inside there's a lovely, airy dining room with creamy yellow walls and white tablecloths—and some of the most delectable dishes you'll find in the Tahoe area. Enticing scents drift from the kitchen where the French Alsatian–born chef-owner personally prepares everything from puff pastry to meringues to homemade bread. Specialties include sautéed veal sweetbreads and mushrooms in a cognac veal cream sauce, garlicky escargot, and rack of lamb with fresh thyme. There's always a fresh fish entrée, and on some evenings a fixed-price menu is available for $33.50 per person. ✉ *290 Kingsbury Grade* ☎ *775/586–1007* ⏲ *Closed Mon. No lunch.*

13

$$$ **Harrah's Tahoe Hotel/Casino.** Harrah's major selling point is that every room has two full bathrooms, each with a television and telephone, a boon if you're traveling with family. **Pros:** central location; great midweek values. **Cons:** can get noisy. ✉ *15 U.S. 50 at Stateline Ave.* ☎ *775/588–6611 or 800/427–7247* 🌐 *www.harrahstahoe.com* *470 rooms, 62 suites* *In-room: a/c, Internet, Wi-Fi. In-hotel: restaurants, room service, bars, pool, gym, spa, parking.*

$$$ **Harveys Resort Hotel/Casino.** Harveys began as a cabin in 1944, and now it's Tahoe's largest casino-hotel. **Pros:** hip entertainment; just a few blocks south of the Heavenly Gondola. **Cons:** can get loud at night. ✉ *18 U.S. 50, at Stateline Ave.* ☎ *775/588–2411 or 800/648–3361* 🌐 *www.harrahs.com* *705 rooms, 38 suites* *In-room: a/c, Internet, Wi-Fi. In-hotel: restaurants, room service, bars, pool, gym, spa, parking.*

$$ **MontBleu.** Formerly Caesar's Tahoe, MontBleu opened in summer 2006, and the tired Roman theme is gone. **Pros:** indoor pool; first-class spa; plush bedding. **Cons:** can get noisy. ✉ *55 U.S. 50, Box 5800* ☎ *775/588–3515 or 800/648–3353* 🌐 *www.montbleuresort.com* *328 rooms, 109 suites* *In-room: a/c, Internet, Wi-Fi. In-hotel: restaurants, room service, bars, pool, gym, spa parking.*

NIGHTLIFE

Each of the major casinos has its own showroom, including Harrah's **South Shore Room** (☎ *775/588–6611*). They feature everything from comedy to magic acts to sexy floor shows to Broadway musicals. If you want to dance to DJ grooves and live bands, check out the scene at MontBleu's **Blu** (✉ *55 U.S. 50* ☎ *775/588–3515*). At Harrah's, you can dance at **Vex** (✉ *U.S. 50, at state line* ☎ *775/588–6611*). **Harveys Outdoor Summer Concert Series** (☎ *800/427–7247* 🌐 *www.harrahs.com*) presents outdoor concerts on weekends in summer with headliners such as Elton John, Bob Dylan, Tim McGraw, and the Rascal Flats.

SPORTS AND THE OUTDOORS

One of the south shore's best, **Nevada Beach** (✉ *Elk Point Rd., 3 mi north of Stateline via U.S. 50* ☎ *530/543–2600*) has a superwide sandy beach that's great for swimming (most Tahoe beaches are rocky). There are also picnic tables, restrooms, barbecue grills, and a campground beneath towering pines. This is the best place to watch the July 4th or Labor Day fireworks. The beach is open Memorial Day weekend through October.

On the lake, **Edgewood Tahoe** (✉ *U.S. 50 and Lake Pkwy., 100 Lake Pwy., behind Horizon Casino* ☎ *775/588–3566 or 888/881–8659* 🌐 *www.edgewood-tahoe.com*) is an 18-hole, par-72 course with a driving range. Fees range $140–$240, depending on the month, and include a cart (though you can walk if you wish). You can have breakfast or lunch in the bar, but the best meal at Edgewood is at the lake-view restaurant inside the clubhouse ($$$–$$$$; dinner only).

RENO

32 mi east of Truckee on I–80; 38 mi northeast of Incline Village via Hwy. 431 and U.S. 395.

Established in 1859 as a trading station at a bridge over the Truckee River, Reno grew along with the silver mines of nearby Virginia City and the transcontinental railroad that chugged through town. Train officials named it in 1868, but gambling—legalized in 1931—put Reno on the map.

Today a sign over the upper end of Virginia Street proclaims Reno "The Biggest Little City in the World." This is still a gambling town, with most of the casinos crowded into five square blocks downtown. The city has lost significant business to California's Indian casinos over the past few years, which has resulted in cheaper rooms, but mediocre upkeep; there just isn't the money coming into town that there once was.

Though parts of downtown are sketchy, things are changing. Several defunct casinos are being converted into condominiums, and downtown is undergoing an urban renewal, sparked by the development of the riverfront, with new shops, boutiques, and nongaming, family-friendly activities like kayaking on the Truckee River. Excellent restaurants have shown up outside the hotels. Temperatures year-round in this high-mountain-desert climate are warmer than at Tahoe, though it rarely gets as hot here as in Sacramento and the Central Valley, making strolling around town a pleasure.

GETTING HERE AND AROUND

By car, Reno is just off I–80. Greyhound and Amtrak also make stops, plus several airlines fly into Reno-Tahoe International Airport. **RTC RIDE** provides bus service in the greater Reno area.

ESSENTIALS

Visitor Information Reno-Sparks Convention and Visitors Authority (✉ *4001 S. Virginia St., Reno, NV* ☎ *775/827–7600 or 800/367–7366* 🌐 *www.visitrenotahoe.com*).

EXPLORING

Circus Circus. Families with kids in tow head for Circus Circus. A midway above the casino floor has clowns, games, fun-house mirrors, and circus acts. ✉ *500 N. Sierra St.* ☎ *775/329–0711 or 800/648–5010* 🌐 *www.circusreno.com*

★ **Peppermill.** A few miles from downtown, the Peppermill is known for its excellent restaurants and neon-bright gambling areas. For cocktails, the Fireside Lounge is a blast. ✉ *2707 S. Virginia St.* ☎ *775/826–2121 or 800/648–6992* 🌐 *www.peppermillreno.com.*

Eldorado. Action packed, with tons of slots and popular bar-top video poker, the Eldorado also has good coffee-shop and food-court fare. ✉ *345 N. Virginia St.* ☎ *775/786–5700 or 800/648–5966* 🌐 *www.eldoradoreno.com.*

Harrah's. Occupying two city blocks, Harrah's has a sprawling casino and an outdoor promenade. ✉ *219 N. Center St.* ☎ *775/786–3232 or 800/648–3773* 🌐 *www.harrahs.com.*

RENO'S RIVERWALK

Stroll along the Truckee River and check out the art galleries, cinema, specialty shops, theater, and restaurants that line this lively refurbished section of town near Reno's casino district.

13

Silver Legacy. An antique 120-foot-tall mining rig and video poker games draw gamblers to the Silver Legacy. ✉ *407 N. Virginia St.* ☎ *775/329–4777 or 800/687–8733* 🌐 *www.silverlegacy.com.*

Downtown RiverWalk. Once dilapidated, Reno's waterfront district got a gentrified makeover when the Downtown RiverWalk brought in street performers, art exhibits, shops, and a lovely park. The 2,600-foot-long Truckee River white-water kayaking course runs right through downtown and has become a major attraction for water-sports enthusiasts. On the third Saturday of each month, from 2 to 5, local merchants host a **Wine Walk.** The cost is $20; stop inside the RiverWalk's participating shops, galleries, and boutiques, and they'll refill your wine glass. In July look for stellar outdoor art, opera, dance, and kids' performances as part of the monthlong **Artown festival** (🌐 *www.renoisartown.com*), presented mostly in Wingfield Park, along the river. ✉ *S. Virginia St. and the Truckee River* 🌐 *www.renoriver.org.*

Fleischmann Planetarium. On the University of Nevada campus, the sleekly designed Fleischmann Planetarium has films and astronomy shows, providing a great alternative to glittering casino lights. ✉ *1650 N. Virginia St.* ☎ *775/784–4811* 🌐 *www.planetarium.unr.nevada.edu* *Exhibits free, films and star shows $6* ⏲ *Fri.–Sat. 10–9, Sun. 10–5, Mon.–Tues. noon–5.*

★ **Nevada Museum of Art.** With its changing exhibits in a dramatic modern building this museum is a must-see for art aficionados. ✉ *160 W. Liberty St.* ☎ *775/329–3333* 🌐 *www.nevadaart.org* *$10* ⏲ *Wed. and Fri.–Sun. 10–5, Thurs. 10–8.*

National Automobile Museum. More than 220 antique and classic automobiles, including an Elvis Presley Cadillac and a 1949 Mercury coupe driven by James Dean in the movie *Rebel Without a Cause,* are on display at the National Automobile Museum. ✉ *10 S. Lake St., at Mill St.* ☎ *775/333–9300* 🌐 *www.automuseum.org* *$10* ⏲ *Mon.–Sat. 9:30–5:30, Sun. 10–4.*

WHERE TO EAT

$ THAI ✕ **Bangkok Cuisine.** If you want to eat well in a pretty dining room but don't want to break the bank, come to this cute little Thai restaurant where delicious soups, salads, stir-fries, and curries are prepared by a Thai national. ✉ *55 Mt. Rose St.* ☎ *775/322–0299* ⏲ *No lunch Sun.*

$$$ FRENCH ✕ **Beaujolais Bistro.** Consistently spot-on Beaujolais serves earthy, country-style French food with zero pretension. The understated chef-

owner is known for classics like beef bourguignon, roast duck, escargots, and steak frites, all lovingly prepared and seasoned just right. Less expensive small plate offerings are also on the menu. The comfortable, airy dining room has exposed brick walls, a parquet floor, and an inviting, casual vibe, making it a good choice for an unfussy meal a short walk from the casinos. ✉ *130 West St.* ☎ *775/323–2227* ⏲ *Closed Mon. No lunch weekends.*

$ CAFÉ ✕ **Chocolate Bar**. If you love chocolate, don't miss this place. Part café, part cocktail bar, this hip little joint a mile from downtown makes killer truffles, chocolate fondue, fabulous fruity cocktails, gourmet appetizers, and small-plate selections—and, of course, stellar hot chocolate, served at a small bar or at a dozen or so tables. It's open 4 pm to midnight and gets crowded on weekend evenings with twenty- and thirtysomethings. ✉ *475 S. Arlington Ave.* ☎ *775/337–1122* ⏲ *Closed Sun.–Mon.*

WHERE TO STAY

For expanded reviews, visit Fodors.com

$ **Harrah's**. Of the big-name casino hotels in downtown Reno, double-towered Harrah's does a good job, with no surprises. **Pros:** Harrah's sets the standard for downtown Reno; great midweek rates. **Cons:** huge property. ✉ *219 N. Center St.* ☎ *775/786–3232 or 800/648–3773* 🌐 *www.harrahs.com* *876 rooms, 52 suites* *In-room: a/c, Internet (some), Wi-Fi (some). In-hotel: restaurants, room service, bars, pool, gym, spa, parking.*

$ ★ **Peppermill**. A few miles removed from downtown Reno's flashy main drag, the Peppermill generates its own glitz with a neon-filled casino that's as dazzling as any. **Pros:** casino decor is worth a special trip; good (and inexpensive) coffee shop. **Cons:** some may find the amount of neon a bit over the top. ✉ *2707 S. Virginia St.* ☎ *775/826–2121 or 800/648–6992* 🌐 *www.peppermillreno.com* *915 rooms, 720 suites* *In-room: a/c, Wi-Fi. In-hotel: restaurants, room service, bars, pool, gym, spa, business center, parking.*

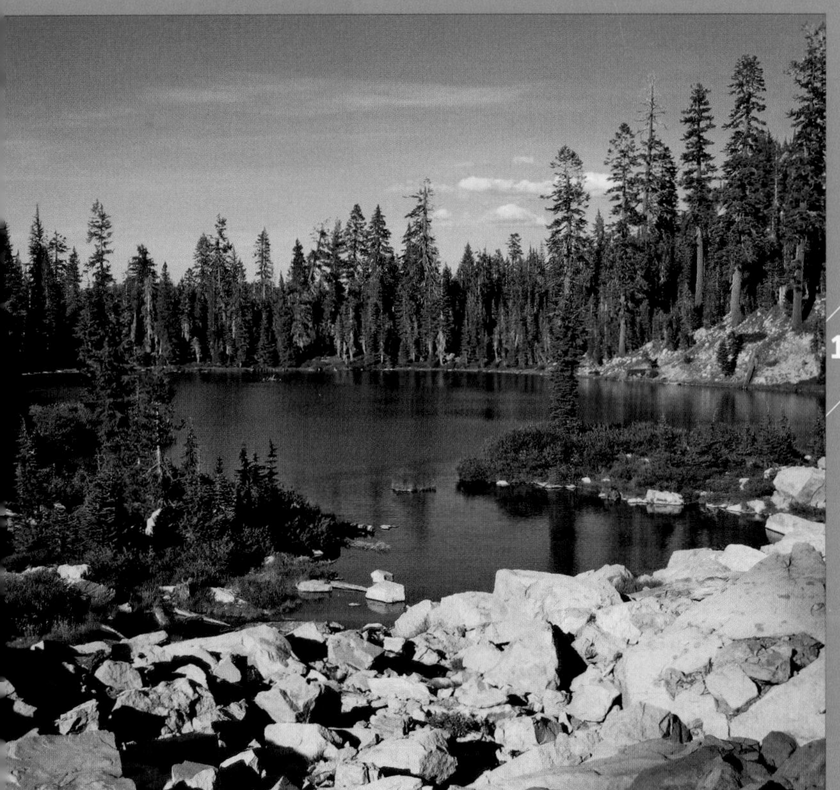

14

The Far North

WITH LAKE SHASTA, MT. SHASTA, AND LASSEN VOLCANIC NATIONAL PARK

WORD OF MOUTH

"Bumpass Hell is a very interesting hike, the thermal features are unusual and there is a boardwalk so you can get close to the steaming holes and pools. North of the park is the gorgeous Burney Falls, real easy walk, definitely worth a visit."

—Shanghainese

WELCOME TO THE FAR NORTH

TOP REASONS TO GO

★ **Mother Nature's wonders:** California's Far North has more rivers, streams, lakes, forests, and mountains than you'll ever have time to explore.

★ **Rock and roll:** With two volcanoes to entice you—Lassen and Shasta—you can learn firsthand what happens when a mountain blows its top.

★ **Fantastic fishing:** Whether you like casting from a riverbank or letting your line bob beside a boat, you'll find fabulous fishing in all the northern counties.

★ **Cool hops:** On a hot day there's nothing quite as inviting as a visit to Chico's world-famous Sierra Nevada Brewery. Take the tour and then savor a chilled glass on tap at the adjacent brewpub.

★ **Shasta:** Wonderful in all its forms: lake, dam, river, mountain, forest, and town.

1 From Chico to Mt. Shasta. The Far North is bisected, south to north, by I-5, which passes through several historic towns and state parks, as well as miles of mountainous terrain. Halfway to the Oregon border is Lake Shasta, a favorite recreation destination, and farther north stands the spectacular snowy peak of Mt. Shasta.

2 The Backcountry. East of I-5, the Far North's main corridor, dozens of scenic two-lane roads crisscross the wilderness, leading to dramatic mountain peaks and fascinating natural wonders. Small towns settled in the second half of the 19th century seem frozen in time, except that they are well equipped with tourist amenities.

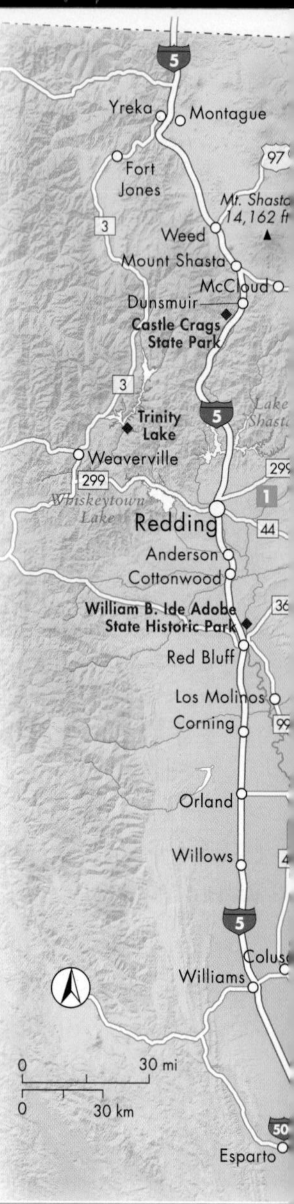

OREGON
Dorris
Tulelake
Lava Beds National Monument
Clear Lake
Goose Lake
139
395
Canby
Alturas
299
89
Adin
Burney
2
139
44
395
Old Station
Shingletown
Lassen Volcanic National Park
Mt. Lassen
Susanville
NEVADA
Chester
36
Westwood
Honey Lake (Dry)
Greenville
SIERRA NEVADA
395
32
70
Quincy
70
Portola
Chico
Loyalton
Reno
Oroville
99
Gridley
Nevada City
80
Truckee
Live Oak
70
20
Grass Valley
Yuba City
Olivehurst
49
Colfax
Lake Tahoe
70
Wheatland
65
Auburn
Rocklin
Woodland
Citrus Heights
Sacramento
50

GETTING ORIENTED

14

The Far North is a vast area that stretches from the upper reaches of the Sacramento Valley north to the Oregon border and east to Nevada. The region includes all or part of seven counties with sparsely populated rural farming and mountain communities, as well as thriving small cities in the valley. Much of the landscape was shaped by two volcanoes—Mt. Shasta and Mt. Lassen—that draw amateur geologists, weekend hikers, and avid mountain climbers to their rugged terrain. An intricate network of high mountain watersheds feeds lakes large and small, plus streams and rivers that course through several forests.

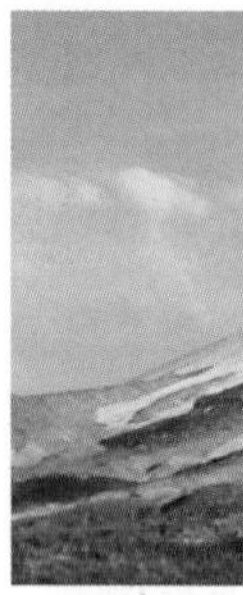

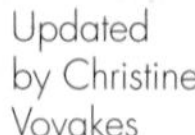

Updated by Christine Vovakes

The Wondrous Landscape of California's northeastern corner, relatively unmarred by development, congestion, and traffic, is the product of volcanic activity. At the southern end of the Cascade Range, Lassen Volcanic National Park is the best place to witness the Far North's fascinating geology. Beyond the sulfur vents and bubbling mud pots, the park owes much of its beauty to 10,457-foot Mt. Lassen and 50 wilderness lakes.

The most enduring image of the region, though, is Mt. Shasta, whose 14,162-foot snowcapped peak beckons outdoor adventurers of all kinds. There are many versions of Shasta to enjoy—the mountain, the lake, the river, the town, the dam, and the forest—all named after the Native Americans known as the Shatasla, or Sastise, who once inhabited the region. Its soaring mountain peaks, wild rivers teeming with trout, and almost unlimited recreational possibilities make the Far North the perfect destination for sports lovers. You won't find many hot nightspots or cultural enclaves, but you'll find some of the best hiking and fishing in the state.

PLANNING

WHEN TO GO

Heat scorches the valley in summer. Temperatures above 110°F are common, but the mountains provide cool respite. Fall throughout the Far North is beautiful, rivaled only by the spring months when wildflowers bloom and snowmelt sends mountain creeks splashing through forests. Winter is usually temperate in the valley, but cold and snowy in high country. A few favorite tourist attractions are closed in winter.

GETTING HERE AND AROUND

AIR TRAVEL

Both Chico—served by United Express—and Redding—served by United Express and Horizon Air—have small regional airports, but for the cheapest fares fly into Sacramento airport and rent a car for your northern explorations.

There's no shuttle service from either airport, but taxis can be ordered. The approximate cost from the airport to downtown Redding is $28 to $30, and it's $20 from the Chico airport to downtown.

Air Contacts **Chico Municipal Airport** (*150 Airpark Blvd., off Cohasset Rd., Chico* *530/896–7200*). **Redding Municipal Airport** (*Airport Rd., Redding* *530/224–4320*). **Taxi Service, Chico** (*530/893–4444 or 530/342–2929*). **Taxi Service, Redding** (*530/246–0577 or 530/222–1234*).

BUS TRAVEL

Greyhound buses travel I–5 and interior highways, serving Burney, Chico, Red Bluff, Redding, and Susanville. Butte County Transit serves Chico, Oroville, and elsewhere. Chico Area Transit System provides bus service within Chico. The vehicles of the Redding Area Bus Authority operate daily except Sunday within Redding, Anderson, and Shasta Lake. STAGE buses serve Siskiyou County, on weekdays only, from Yreka to Dunsmuir, stopping in Mt. Shasta and other towns, and provide service in Scott Valley, Happy Camp, Hornbrook, Lake Shastina, and the Klamath River area. Lassen Rural Bus serves the Susanville, northeast Lake Almanor, and south and east Lassen County areas, running weekdays except holidays. Lassen Rural Bus connects with Plumas County Transit, which serves the Quincy area, and with Modoc County Sage Stage, which serves the Alturas area.

Bus Contacts **Butte County Transit/Chico Area Transit System** (*530/342–0221 or 800/822–8145* *www.blinetransit.com*). **Greyhound** (*800/229–9424* *www.greyhound.com*). **Lassen Rural Bus** (*530/252–7433* *www.lassentransportation.org*). **Modoc County Sage Stage** (*530/233–3883 or 233–6410* *www.sagestage.com*). **Plumas County Transit** (*530/283–2538* *www.plumastransit.com*). **Redding Area Bus Authority** (*530/241–2877* *www.rabaride.com*). **STAGE** (*530/842–8295* *www.co.siskiyou.ca.us*).

CAR TRAVEL

Interstate 5 runs up the center of California through Red Bluff and Redding; the other main roads here are good two-lane highways that are, with few exceptions, open year-round. Check weather reports and carry detailed maps, warm clothing, and tire chains whenever you head into mountainous terrain in winter.

Chico is east of I–5 on Hwy. 32. Lassen Volcanic National Park can be reached by Hwy. 36 from Red Bluff or (except in winter) Hwy. 44 from Redding. Hwy. 299 connects Redding and Alturas. Hwy. 139 leads from Susanville to Lava Beds National Monument. Hwy. 89 will take you from Mt. Shasta to Quincy. Hwy. 36 links Chester and Susanville.

Road Conditions **Caltrans Highway Information Network** (*800/427–7623*).

TRAIN TRAVEL

Amtrak has stations in Chico, Redding, and Dunsmuir and operates buses that connect to Greyhound service through Redding, Red Bluff, and Chico.

Train Contacts Amtrak (✉ *W. 5th and Orange Sts., Chico* ✉ *1620 Yuba St. (for Amtrak's Coach Starlight) or 1530 Yuba St. (Amtrak motor coach connections to Sacramento), Redding* ✉ *5750 Sacramento Ave., Dunsmuir* ☎ *800/872–7245* 🌐 *www.amtrakcalifornia.com*).

RESTAURANTS

Redding, the urban center of the Far North, and college-town Chico have the greatest selection of restaurants. Cafés and simple eateries are the rule in the smaller towns, though trendy, innovative restaurants have been popping up. Dress is always informal.

HOTELS

The Far North—especially the mountainous backcountry—is gaining popularity as a tourist destination. For summer holiday weekends in towns at higher elevations that escape the valley heat, such as Mt. Shasta, Dunsmuir, and Chester, and at camping sites within state or national parks, make lodging reservations well in advance.

Rooms in Redding, Chico, and Red Bluff usually are booked solid only during popular local events. Aside from the large chain hotels and motels in Redding and Chico, most accommodations in the Far North blend rusticity, simplicity, and coziness. Wilderness resorts close in fall and reopen after the snow season ends in May.

The Web site of the **California Association of Bed & Breakfast Inns** (🌐 *www.cabbi.com*) lists numerous bed-and-breakfasts in the Far North region.

WHAT IT COSTS

	¢	$	$$	$$$	$$$$
Retaurants	under $10	$10–$15	$16–$22	$23–$30	over $30
Hotels	under $90	$90–$120	$121–$175	$176–$250	over $250

Restaurant prices are for a main course at dinner, excluding sales tax of 7.75%. Hotel prices are for two people in a standard double room in high season, excluding service charges and 7.25%–10% tax.

VISITOR INFORMATION

Contacts **Lassen County Chamber of Commerce** (✉ *75 N. Weatherlow, Susanville* ☎ *530/257–4323* 🌐 *www.lassencountychamber.com*). **Shasta Cascade Wonderland Association** (✉ *1699 Hwy. 273, Anderson* ☎ *530/365–7500 or 800/474–2782* 🌐 *www.shastacascade.com*). **Mt. Shasta Chamber of Commerce Visitors Bureau** (✉ *300 Pine St., Mt. Shasta* ☎ *530/926–3696 or 800/926–4865* 🌐 *www.visitsiskiyou.org*).

FROM CHICO TO MT. SHASTA

From the blooming almond orchards of the fertile Sacramento River Valley, through the forested mountains and to the dominating peak of a dormant volcano, this section of the Far North entices tourists in all seasons.

CHICO

180 mi from San Francisco, east on I–80, north on I–505 to I–5, and east on Hwy. 32; 86 mi north of Sacramento on Hwy. 99.

Chico (which is Spanish for "small") sits just west of Paradise in the Sacramento Valley and offers a welcome break from the monotony of Interstate 5. The Chico campus of California State University, the scores of local artisans, and the area's agriculture (primarily almond orchards) all influence the culture here. Chico's true claim to fame, however, is the popular Sierra Nevada Brewery, which keeps locals and beer drinkers across the country happy with its distinctive microbrews.

GETTING HERE AND AROUND

Both Hwy. 99, coming north from Sacramento or south off I–5 at Red Bluff, and Hwy. 32, going east off I–5 at Orland, intersect Chico. Amtrak and Greyhound stop here, and United Express flies into the Chico airport. Butte County Transit takes riders to nearby communities, while Chico Area Transit System provides service in the city. Anchored by a robust university scene, the downtown neighborhoods are great for walking.

ESSENTIALS

Visitor Information Chico Chamber of Commerce (✉ *300 Salem St., Chico* ☎ *530/891–5556 or 800/852–8570* 🌐 *www.chicochamber.com*).

EXPLORING

★ **Bidwell Park.** The sprawling 3,670-acre Bidwell Park is a community green space straddling Big Chico Creek, where scenes from *Gone With the Wind* and the 1938 version of *Robin Hood* (starring Errol Flynn) were filmed. The region's recreational hub, it includes a golf course, swimming areas, and paved biking, hiking, and in-line skating trails. One of the largest city-run parks in the country, Bidwell starts as a slender strip downtown and expands eastward 11 mi toward the Sierra foothills. ✉ *300 S. Park Dr.* ☎ *530/896–7800.*

★ **Sierra Nevada Brewing Company.** This pioneer of the microbrewery movement still has a hands-on approach to beer making. Tour the brew house and see how the beer is produced—from the sorting of hops through fermentation and bottling. You can also visit the gift shop and enjoy a hearty lunch or dinner in the brewpub where tastings are available (for a fee). ✉ *1075 E. 20th St.* ☎ *530/345–2739* 🌐 *www.sierranevada.com* 🎫 *Free* ⏲ *Tours daily, call for times.*

★ **Bidwell Mansion State Historic Park.** Built between 1865 and 1868 by General John Bidwell, the founder of Chico, this mansion was designed by Henry W. Cleaveland, a San Francisco architect. Bidwell and his wife welcomed many distinguished guests to their distinctive pink Italianate home, including President Rutherford B. Hayes, naturalist John Muir, suffragist Susan B. Anthony, and General William T. Sherman. A one-hour tour takes you through most of the mansion's 26 rooms. ✉ *525 The Esplanade* ☎ *530/895–6144* *$6* ⏲ *Tues.–Wed. noon–5, weekends 11–5; last tour at 4.*

WHERE TO EAT AND STAY

$$$ STEAKHOUSE ✕ **5th Street Steakhouse.** Hand-cut steak is the star in this refurbished early 1900s building, the place to come when you're craving red meat and a huge baked potato. Exposed redbrick walls warm the small dining area. A long mahogany bar catches the overflow crowds that jam the place on weekends. No reservations are accepted on Fridays and Saturdays, but it's worth the wait. ✉ *345 W. 5th St.* ☎ *530/891–6328* ⏲ *No lunch Sat.–Thurs.*

$$$ ★ **Hotel Diamond.** Crystal chandeliers and gleaming wood floors and banisters elegantly welcome guests into the foyer of this restored gem in downtown Chico near the university. **Pros:** refined; great location; excellent breakfast buffet included in room rate. **Cons:** pricey; not a good choice for families. ✉ *220 W. 4th St.* ☎ *530/893–3100 or 866/993–3100* ⊕ *www.hoteldiamondchico.com* *39 rooms, 4 suites* *In-room: a/c, Internet, Wi-Fi. In-hotel: restaurant, room service, bar* *Breakfast.*

$ **Johnson's Country Inn.** Nestled in an almond orchard five minutes from downtown, this Victorian-style farmhouse with a wraparound veranda is a welcome change from motel row. **Pros:** rural setting; beautifully maintained; serene walks. **Cons:** a car is essential. ✉ *3935 Morehead Ave.* ☎ *530/345–7829* ⊕ *www.chico.com/johnsonsinn* *4 rooms* *In-room: a/c, no TV, Wi-Fi* *Breakfast.*

RED BLUFF

41 mi north of Chico on Hwy 99.

Historic Red Bluff is a gateway to Lassen Volcanic National Park. Established in the mid-19th century as a shipping center and named for the color of its soil, the town is filled with dozens of restored Victorians. It's a great home base for outdoor adventures in the area.

GETTING HERE AND AROUND

Access Red Bluff via exits off I–5, or by driving north on Hwy. 99. Hwy. 36 is a long, twisty ride that begins near the Pacific Coast and goes to Red Bluff, then east to the towns near Lassen Volcanic National Park. TRAX (Tehama Rural Area Express) has a few routes in Red Bluff and links to neighboring small towns. Greyhound stops here and also provides connecting service to Amtrak.

ESSENTIALS

Visitor Information Red Bluff–Tehama County Chamber of Commerce (✉ *100 Main St., Red Bluff* ☎ *530/527–6220* ⊕ *www.redbluffchamber.com*).

EXPLORING

★ **William B. Ide Adobe State Historic Park.** Named for the first and only president of the short-lived California Republic of 1846, William B. Ide Adobe State Historic Park is on an oak-lined bank of the Sacramento River. The Bear Flag Party proclaimed California a sovereign nation, separate from Mexican rule, and the republic existed for 22 days before it was taken over by the United States. The republic's flag has survived, with only minor refinements, as California's state flag. The park's main attraction is an adobe home built in the 1850s and outfitted with period furnishings; tours are available on request. There's also a carriage shed, a blacksmith shop, and a small visitor center. ✉ *21659 Adobe Rd.* ☎ *530/529–8599* 🌐 *www.parks.ca.gov* *$6 per vehicle* ⏲ *Park and picnic facilities daily sunrise–sunset; adobe home and historic sites open Thurs.–Sun., varying hrs.*

RED BLUFF ROUND-UP

Check out old-time rodeo at its best during the Red Bluff Round-Up. Held the third weekend of April, this annual event attracts some of the best cowboys in the country. For more information, visit 🌐 *www.redbluffroundup.com.*

WHERE TO EAT AND STAY

$$ STEAKHOUSE ✕ **Green Barn Steakhouse.** You're likely to find cowboys sporting Stetsons and spurs, feasting on sizzling porterhouse, baby back ribs, and filet mignon at Red Bluff's premier steak house. For lighter fare, there's garlicky scampi or fettuccine primavera, along with fresh fish specials. As a sweet indulgence, don't miss the bread pudding with rum sauce. The lounge is usually hopping, especially when there's an event at the nearby rodeo grounds. ✉ *5 Chestnut Ave.* ☎ *530/527–3161* ⏲ *Closed Sun.*

$ **The Jeter Victorian Inn.** On sunny days, breakfast is served in the garden pavilion outside this 1881 Victorian home. **Pros:** quiet residential area; within walking distance of restaurants. **Cons:** no Internet access. ✉ *1107 Jefferson St.* ☎ *530/527–7574* 🌐 *www.jetervictorianinn.com* *4 rooms, 3 with bath; 1 cottage* *In-room: no phone, a/c,* *Breakfast.*

REDDING

32 mi north of Red Bluff on I–5.

As the largest city in the Far North, Redding is an ideal headquarters for exploring the surrounding countryside.

GETTING HERE AND AROUND

Reach Redding from exits off I–5 or via Hwy. 299, which originates near coastal Eureka and crosses Weaverville and Redding before heading northeast to Burney and Alturas. Hwy. 44 stretches from Susanville past Lassen Park's north entrance before ending in Redding. United Express and Horizon Air serve the Redding airport. Amtrak and Greyhound make stops here. Redding Area Bus Authority serves Redding and some of the surrounding communities.

ESSENTIALS

Visitor Information **Redding Convention and Visitors Bureau** (✉ *2334 Washington Ave., Ste. B, Redding* ☎ *530/225–4100* 🌐 *www.visitredding.com*).

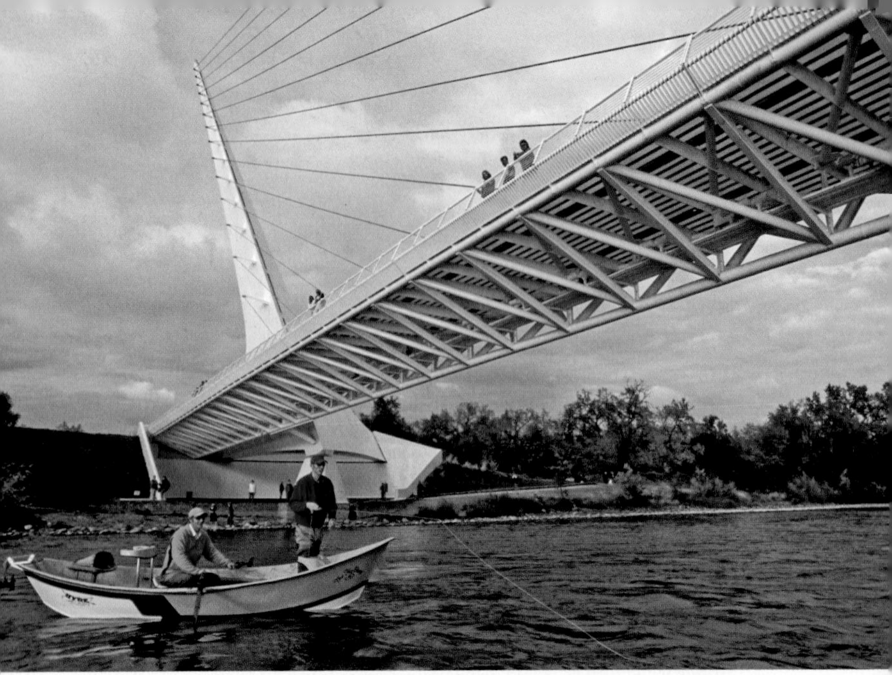

Fisherman under Santiago Calatrava's striking Sundial Bridge in Turtle Bay Exploration Park.

EXPLORING

Fodor's Choice ★ **Turtle Bay Exploration Park.** Curving along the Sacramento River, Turtle Bay Exploration Park has a museum, an arboretum with walking trails, and lots of interactive exhibits for children, including a miniature dam, a gold-panning area, and a seasonal Butterfly House where monarchs emerge from their cocoons. The main draw at the park, however, is the stunning **Sundial Bridge,** a modernist pedestrian footbridge designed by world-renowned Spanish architect Santiago Calatrava. The bridge's architecture consists of a translucent, illuminated span that stretches across the river, and—most strikingly—a soaring white 217-foot needle that casts a slender moving shadow, like a sundial's, over the water and surrounding trees. Watching the sun set over the river from this bridge is a magical experience. The bridge links to the Sacramento River Trail and the park's arboretum and botanical gardens. Access to the bridge and arboretum is free; a fee admits you to both the museum and the botanical gardens. ✉ *840 Sundial Bridge Dr.* ☎ *530/243–8850 or 800/887–8532* 🌐 *www.turtlebay.org* 🎫 *$14* 🕒 *Mid-Mar.–Sept., daily 9–5; Oct.–mid-Mar., Wed.–Sat. 9–4, Sun. 10–4.*

WHERE TO EAT AND STAY

$ SEAFOOD ✕ **Buz's Crab.** This casual restaurant in central Redding shares space with a bustling seafood market where locals snap up ocean-fresh Dungeness crab in season. The fish-and-chips is a favorite; seafood combos, including Cajun-style selections are also noteworthy. Try the wild salmon or trout charbroiled over mesquite wood. ✉ *2159 East St.* ☎ *530/243–2120.*

$$$ STEAKHOUSE **Jack's Grill.** Famous for its 16-ounce steaks, this popular bar and steak house also serves shrimp and chicken. A town favorite, the place is usually jam-packed and noisy. *1743 California St. 530/241–9705 Closed Sun. No lunch.*

$$ ★ **The Red Lion.** Adjacent to I–5, and close to Redding's convention center and regional recreation sites, this hotel is a top choice for both business and vacation travelers. **Pros:** family-friendly; close to a major shopping area. **Cons:** busy area. *1830 Hilltop Dr., Hwy. 44/299 exit off I–5 530/221–8700 or 800/733–5466 www.redlion.com 192 rooms, 2 suites In-room: a/c, Wi-Fi. In-hotel: restaurant, bar, pool, gym.*

SPORTS AND THE OUTDOORS

The **Fly Shop** (*4140 Churn Creek Rd. 530/222–3555*) sells fishing licenses and has information about guides, conditions, and fishing packages.

14

WEAVERVILLE

46 mi west of Redding on Hwy. 299, called Main St. in town.

A man known only as Weaver struck gold here in 1849, and the fledgling community at the base of the Trinity Alps was named after him. With its impressive downtown historic district, today Weaverville is a popular headquarters for family vacations and biking, hiking, fishing, and gold-panning excursions.

GETTING HERE AND AROUND

Highway 299 becomes Main St. down the center of Weaverville, a mountain community in the Trinity Alps. Take the highway either east from the Pacific Coast or west from Redding. Highway 36 from Red Bluff to Hwy. 3 heading north leads to Weaverville. Trinity Transit provides minimal local bus service plus a line that links Weaverville to I–5 at Redding and to Willow Creek near coastal U.S. 101.

EXPLORING

Fodor's Choice ★ **Weaverville Joss House.** Weaverville's main attraction is the Joss House, a Taoist temple built in 1874 and called Won Lim Miao ("the temple of the forest beneath the clouds") by Chinese miners. The oldest continuously used Chinese temple in California, it attracts worshippers from around the world. With its golden altar, antique weaponry, and carved wooden canopies, the Joss House is a piece of California history that can best be appreciated on a guided 30-minute tour. The original temple building and many of its furnishings—some of which came from China—were lost to fire in 1873, but members of the local Chinese community soon rebuilt it. *630 Main St. 530/623–5284 Museum free; guided tour $4 Thurs.–Sun. 10–5; last tour at 4.*

Trinity County Courthouse. Trinity County Courthouse, built in 1856 as a store, office building, and hotel, was converted to county use in 1865. The Apollo Saloon, in the basement, became the county jail. It's the oldest courthouse still in use in California. *Court and Main Sts.*

★ **Trinity County Historical Park.** For a vivid sense of Weaverville's past visit the Trinity County Historical Park. It houses the **Jake Jackson Memorial**

Museum, which has a blacksmith shop, a stamp mill (where ore is crushed) from the 1890s that is still in use, and the original jail cells of the Trinity County Courthouse. ✉ *508 Main St.* ☎ *530/623–5211* ⏲ *Late Apr.–Oct., daily 10–5; Nov. and Dec., Wed–Sat. 11-4; Jan.–late Apr., Tues. and Sat. noon–4.*

WHERE TO EAT

$$ AMERICAN ✕ **La Grange Café.** In two brick buildings dating from the 1850s (they're among the oldest edifices in town), this eatery serves buffalo and other game meats, pasta, fresh fish, and farmers' market vegetables when they're available. There's a full premium bar, and the wine list is extensive. ✉ *520 Main St.* ☎ *530/623–5325* ⏲ *Daily; hours sometimes sporadic in winter.*

SPORTS AND THE OUTDOORS

Below the Lewiston Dam, east of Weaverville on Highway 299, is the **Fly Stretch** of the Trinity River, an excellent fly-fishing area. The **Pine Cove Boat Ramp**, on Lewiston Lake, provides fishing access for those with disabilities—decks here are built over prime trout-fishing waters. Contact the **Weaverville Ranger Station** (✉ *360 Main St.* ☎ *530/623–2121*) for maps and information about hiking trails in the Trinity Alps Wilderness.

LAKE SHASTA AREA

★ *12 mi north of Redding on I–5.*

When you think of the Lake Shasta Area picture water, wilderness, dazzling stalagmites—and a fabulous man-made project in the midst of it all.

GETTING HERE AND AROUND

Interstate 5 north of Redding is the main link to the entire Lake Shasta area. Numerous exits spool off toward the lake, campgrounds, and the caverns, which also require bus and catamaran rides to reach. Get to the dam by going through tiny City of Shasta Lake.

ESSENTIALS

Visitor Information **Shasta Cascade Wonderland Association** (✉ *1699 Hwy. 273, Anderson* ☎ *530/365–7500 or 800/474–2782* 🌐 *www.shastacascade.com*).

EXPLORING

Lake Shasta. Twenty-one types of fish inhabit the lake, including rainbow trout and salmon. The lake region also has the largest nesting population of bald eagles in California. You can rent fishing boats, ski boats, sailboats, canoes, paddleboats, Jet Skis, and windsurfing boards at one of the many marinas and resorts along the 370-mi shoreline.

Lake Shasta Caverns. Stalagmites, stalactites, flowstone deposits, and crystals entice people of all ages to the Lake Shasta Caverns. To see this impressive spectacle, you must take the two-hour tour, which includes a catamaran ride across the McCloud arm of Lake Shasta and a bus ride up Grey Rock Mountain to the cavern entrance. The caverns are 58°F year-round, making them a cool retreat on a hot summer day. The most awe-inspiring of the limestone rock formations is the glistening Cathedral Room, which appears to be gilded. During peak summer months

(June through August), tours depart every half hour; in April, May, and September it's every hour. A gift shop is open from 8 to 4:30. ✉ *20359 Shasta Caverns Rd. exit off I–5, Lakehead* ☎ *530/238–2341 or 800/795–2283* 🌐 *www.lakeshastacaverns.com* 🎟 *$22* ⏲ *June–Aug., daily 9–4 with departures every ½ hr; Apr., May, and Sept., daily 9–3 with departures every hr; Oct.–Mar., daily 10–2 with departures every 2 hrs.*

★ **Shasta Dam.** Shasta Dam is the second-largest concrete dam in the United States (only Grand Coulee in Washington is bigger). The visitor center has computerized photographic tours of the dam construction, video presentations, fact sheets, and historical displays. Hour-long guided tours take visitors inside the dam and its powerhouse. Check in at the visitor center to take the free tour. ✉ *16349 Shasta Dam Blvd.* ☎ *530/275–4463* 🌐 *www.usbr.gov/mp/ncao* ⏲ *Visitor center daily 8–5; call for tour times.*

14

SPORTS AND THE OUTDOORS

FISHING **The Fishin' Hole** (✉ *3844 Shasta Dam Blvd., Shasta Lake City* ☎ *530/275–4123*) is a bait-and-tackle shop a couple of miles from the lake. It sells fishing licenses and provides information about conditions.

HOUSEBOATING Houseboats here come in all sizes except small. As a rule, rentals are outfitted with cooking utensils, dishes, and most of the equipment you'll need—all you supply are the food and the linens. When you rent a houseboat, you receive a short course in how to maneuver your launch before you set out. You can fish, swim, sunbathe on the flat roof, or sit on the deck and watch the world go by. The shoreline of Lake Shasta is beautifully ragged, with countless inlets; it's not hard to find privacy. Expect to spend a minimum of $350 a day for a craft that sleeps six. A three-day, two-night minimum is customary. Prices are often lower during the off-season (September through May). The **Shasta Cascade Wonderland Association** (✉ *1699 Hwy. 273, Anderson* ☎ *530/365–7500 or 800/474–2782* 🌐 *www.shastacascade.com*) provides names of rental companies and prices for Lake Shasta houseboating. **Bridge Bay Resort** (✉ *10300 Bridge Bay Rd., Redding* ☎ *800/752–9669*) rents houseboats, fishing boats, and patio boats.

DUNSMUIR

10 mi south of Mt. Shasta on I–5.

Castle Crags State Park surrounds the town of Dunsmuir, which was named for a 19th-century Scottish coal baron who offered to build a fountain if the town was renamed in his honor. The town's other major attraction is the Railroad Park Resort, where you can spend the night in restored railcars.

GETTING HERE AND AROUND

Reach tiny Dunsmuir via exits off I–5 at the north and south ends of town. When snow hasn't closed the route, you can take Hwy. 89 from the Lassen Park area toward Burney then northeast to I–5 at Mt. Shasta. From there it's a 10-mi drive south to Dunsmuir. Amtrak stops here; Greyhound stops in Weed, 20 mi north. There's no local bus transportation system, but during weekdays STAGE travels from Yreka to Dunsmuir, Mt. Shasta, and several other Siskiyou County communities.

FINE FISHING

The upper Sacramento River near Dunsmuir is consistently rated one of the best fishing spots in the country. Check with the chamber of commerce for local fishing guides.

EXPLORING

★ **Castle Crags State Park.** Named for its 6,000-foot glacier-polished crags, which tower over the Sacramento River, this park offers fishing in Castle Creek, hiking in the backcountry, and a view of Mt. Shasta. The crags draw climbers and hikers from around the world. The 4,350-acre park has 28 mi of hiking trails, including a 2.75-mi access trail to **Castle Crags Wilderness,** part of the **Shasta-Trinity National Forest.** There are excellent trails at lower altitudes, along with picnic areas, restrooms, showers, and campsites. ✉ *6 mi south of Dunsmuir, Castella/Castle Crags exit off I–5; follow for ¼ mi* ☎ *530/235–2684* *$8 per vehicle, day use.*

WHERE TO EAT AND STAY

$$ MEDITERRANEAN **Café Maddalena.** Café Maddalena serves an adventurous Mediterranean menu with a French influence that draws in diners from nearby mountain communities, and as far away as Redding. Selections change seasonally but always feature a vegetarian offering along with fresh fish and meat entrées such as Dungeness crab soufflé and chicken tagine in yellow curry with couscous. Wines from Spain, Italy, and France complement the meals. ✉ *5801 Sacramento Ave.* ☎ *530/235–2725* ⏲ *Closed Mon.–Wed. and Jan. No lunch.*

$ **Railroad Park Resort.** The antique cabooses here were collected over more than three decades and have been converted into cozy motel rooms in honor of Dunsmuir's railroad legacy. **Pros:** gorgeous setting; kitschy fun. **Cons:** cabooses can feel cramped; restaurant open mid-April through September. ✉ *100 Railroad Park Rd.* ☎ *530/235–4440* 🌐 *www.rrpark.com* *23 cabooses, 4 cabins* *In-room: a/c, kitchen (some). In-hotel: restaurant, pool, some pets allowed.*

MT. SHASTA

34 mi north of Lake Shasta on I–5.

GETTING HERE AND AROUND

Three exits off I–5 lead to the town of Mt. Shasta. When snow hasn't closed the route, you can take Hwy. 89 from the Lassen Park area toward Burney then northeast to Mt. Shasta. The ski park is off Hwy. 89. Greyhound stops at Weed, 10 mi north; Amtrak stops at Dunsmuir, 10 mi south. There's no local bus transportation system but during weekdays STAGE travels from Yreka to Mt. Shasta, Dunsmuir, and several other Siskiyou County communities.

ESSENTIALS

Visitor Information Mt. Shasta Chamber of Commerce Visitors Bureau (✉ *300 Pine St., Mt. Shasta* ☎ *530/926–3696 or 800/926–4865* 🌐 *www.visitsiskiyou.org*).

EXPLORING

Mt. Shasta. The crown jewel of the 2.5-million-acre Shasta-Trinity National Forest, Mt. Shasta, a 14,162-foot-high dormant volcano, is a mecca for day hikers. It's especially enticing in spring, when fragrant Shasta lilies and other flowers adorn the rocky slopes. The paved road reaches only as far as the timberline; the final 6,000 feet are a tough climb of rubble, ice, and snow (the summit is perpetually ice packed). Only a hardy few are qualified to make the trek to the top.

The town of Mt. Shasta has real character and some fine restaurants. Lovers of the outdoors and backcountry skiers abound, and they are more than willing to offer advice on the most beautiful spots in the region, which include out-of-the-way swimming holes, dozens of high mountain lakes, and a challenging 18-hole golf course with 360 degrees of spectacular views.

14

WHERE TO EAT AND STAY

$$ ECLECTIC **Lilys.** This restaurant in a white-clapboard home, framed by a picket fence and arched trellis, serves everything from steaks and pastas to Mexican and vegetarian dishes. Daily specials include prime rib and a fresh fish entrée. For innovative vegetarian fare try a roasted eggplant hoagie with three cheeses, or a *dal* burger, which is made with walnuts, fresh veggies, garbanzo beans, and rice. *1013 S. Mt. Shasta Blvd. 530/926–3372.*

¢ CAFÉ **Seven Suns Coffee and Cafe.** A favorite gathering spot for locals, this small coffee shop serves specialty wraps for breakfast and lunch, plus soup and salad selections. Pastries, made daily, include muffins and scones, and blackberry fruit bars in season. If the weather's nice, grab a seat on the patio. *1011 S. Mt. Shasta Blvd. 530/926–9701.*

$$$ ★ **Mount Shasta Resort.** Private chalets are nestled among tall pine trees along the shore of Lake Siskiyou, all with gas-log fireplaces and full kitchens. **Pros:** incredible views; romantic woodsy setting. **Cons:** kids may get bored. *1000 Siskiyou Lake Blvd. 530/926–3030 or 800/958–3363 www.mountshastaresort.com 65 units In-room: a/c, kitchen (some), Wi-Fi. In-hotel: restaurant, bar, golf course, spa.*

SPORTS AND THE OUTDOORS

HIKING The **Mt. Shasta Forest Service Ranger Station** (*530/926–4511 or 530/926–9613*) keeps tabs on trail conditions and gives avalanche reports.

MOUNTAIN CLIMBING **Fifth Season Mountaineering Shop** (*300 N. Mt. Shasta Blvd. 530/926–3606 or 530/926–5555*) rents skiing and climbing equipment and operates a recorded 24-hour climber-skier report. **Shasta Mountain Guides** (*530/926–3117 www.shastaguides.com*) leads hiking, climbing, and ski-touring groups to the summit of Mt. Shasta.

SKIING On the southeast flank of Mt. Shasta, **Mt. Shasta Board & Ski Park** has three triple-chair lifts and one surface lift on 425 skiable acres. It's a great place for novices because three-quarters of the trails are for beginning or intermediate skiers. The area's vertical drop is 1,390 feet, with a top elevation of 6,600 feet. The longest of the 32 trails is 1.75 mi. A package for beginners, available through the ski school, includes a lift ticket, ski rental, and a lesson. The school also runs ski and snowboard programs for children. There's night skiing for those who want to see the moon rise as they schuss. The base lodge has a simple café, a ski shop, and a ski-snowboard rental shop. The **Mt. Shasta Nordic Center,** with 25 km (15 mi) of groomed cross-country trails, is on the same road. ✉ *Hwy. 89 exit east from I–5, south of Mt. Shasta* ☎ *530/926–8610 or 800/754–7427, 530/926–2142 Mt. Shasta Nordic Center* 🌐 *www.skipark.com; www.mtshastanordic.org* ⏲ *Winter ski season schedule: Sun.–Wed. 9–4, Thurs.–Sat. 9–9.*

THE BACKCOUNTRY

Primitive, rugged, and mostly undeveloped, the Far North's backcountry is arguably full of more natural wonders than any other region in California.

MCARTHUR–BURNEY FALLS MEMORIAL STATE PARK

Hwy. 89, 52 mi southeast of Mt. Shasta and 41 mi north of Lassen Volcanic National Park.

GETTING HERE AND AROUND

From Mt. Shasta, take the I–5 exit to Hwy. 89 and follow it for about 51 mi to the park. From Redding, take the Lake Blvd./299E exit off I–5, heading east for about 55 mi; turn left onto Hwy. 89 and drive 6 mi to the park. From Alturas, head west on Hwy. 299E for about 86 mi and turn right onto Hwy. 89; drive 6 mi to the park.

EXPLORING

Fodor's Choice ★ **McArthur–Burney Falls Memorial State Park.** Just inside the park's southern boundary, Burney Creek wells up from the ground and divides into two falls that cascade over a 129-foot cliff into a pool below. Countless ribbonlike streams pour from hidden moss-covered crevices; resident bald eagles are frequently seen soaring overhead. You can walk a self-guided nature trail that descends to the foot of the falls, which Theodore Roosevelt—according to legend—called "the eighth wonder of the world." You can also swim at Lake Britton; lounge on the beach; rent motorboats, paddleboats, and canoes; or relax at one of the campsites or picnic areas. The camp store is open from early May to the end of October. ✉ *24898 Hwy. 89, Burney* ☎ *530/335–2777* 🎟 *$8 per vehicle, day use.*

ALTURAS

86 mi northeast of McArthur–Burney Falls Memorial State Park on Hwy. 299.

Alturas is the county seat and largest town in northeastern California's Modoc County. The Dorris family arrived in the area in 1874, built Dorris Bridge over the Pit River, and later opened a small wayside stop for travelers. Today the Alturas area is a land of few people but much rugged natural beauty. Travelers come to see eagles and other wildlife, the Modoc National Forest, and active geothermal areas.

GETTING HERE AND AROUND

To get to Alturas from Susanville take Main St./Hwy. 36 south for about 4 mi out of town; turn left at U.S. 395 and stay on that highway for 99 mi. From Redding, take the Lake Blvd./299E exit off I–5, head east and stay on Hwy. 299E for 140 mi. Sage Stage runs intermittent buses between Alturas and Redding, and Alturas and Susanville.

ESSENTIALS

Visitor Information **Alturas Chamber of Commerce** (✉ *600 S. Main St., Alturas* ☎ *530/233–4434* 🌐 *www.alturaschamber.org*).

EXPLORING

Modoc National Forest. Encompassing 1.6 million acres, Modoc National Forest protects 300 species of wildlife, including Rocky Mountain elk, wild horses, mule deer, and pronghorn antelope. In spring and fall, watch for migratory waterfowl as they make their way along the Pacific Flyway above the forest. Hiking trails lead to Petroglyph Point, one of the largest panels of rock art in the United States. ✉ *800 W. 12th St.* ☎ *530/233–5811.*

14

Modoc National Wildlife Refuge. The 7,021-acre Modoc National Wildlife Refuge was established in 1961 to protect migratory waterfowl. You might see Canada geese, sandhill cranes, mallards, teal, wigeon, pintail, white pelicans, cormorants, and snowy egrets. The refuge is open for hiking, bird-watching, and photography, but one area is set aside for hunters. Regulations vary according to season. ✉ *1½ mi south of Alturas on Hwy. 395* ☎ *530/233–3572* 🎫 *Free* ⏲ *Daily dawn–dusk.*

WHERE TO EAT

$$ SPANISH ✕ **Brass Rail.** This authentic Basque restaurant offers hearty dinners at fixed prices that include wine, homemade bread, soup, salad, side dishes, coffee, and ice cream. Steak, lamb chops, fried chicken, shrimp, and scallops are among the best entrée selections. A full bar and lounge adjoin the dining area. ✉ *395 Lakeview Hwy.* ☎ *530/233–2906* ⏲ *Closed Mon.*

SUSANVILLE

104 mi south of Alturas via Rte. 395; 65 mi east of Lassen Volcanic National Park via Hwy. 36.

Susanville tells the tale of its rich history through murals painted on buildings in the historic uptown area. Established as a trading post in 1854, it's the second-oldest town in the western Great Basin. You can take a self-guided tour around the original buildings and stop for a bite at one of the restaurants now housed within them; or, if you'd rather work up a sweat, you can hit the Bizz Johnson Trail and Eagle Lake recreation areas just outside of town.

GETTING HERE AND AROUND

U.S. 395 connects Susanville and Alturas, about a 100-mi trip. From Red Bluff, take Hwy. 36E/Fairgrounds I–5 exit east for about 3 mi; turn left at 36E and continue on that highway through the mountains for 103 mi, traveling past Chester and Lake Almanor to reach Susanville. Lassen Rural Bus serves Susanville and surrounding areas weekdays.

ESSENTIALS

Visitor Information Lassen County Chamber of Commerce (✉ *75 N. Weatherlow, Susanville* ☎ *530/257–4323* 🌐 *www.lassencountychamber.com*).

EXPLORING

Bizz Johnson Trail. Bizz Johnson Trail follows a defunct line of the Southern Pacific Railroad for 25 mi. Known to locals as the Bizz, the trail is open for hikers, walkers, mountain bikers, horseback riders, and cross-country skiers. It skirts the Susan River through a scenic landscape of canyons, bridges, and forests abundant with wildlife. ✉ *Trailhead: 601 Richmond Rd.* ☎ *530/257–0456* 🌐 *www.blm.gov/ca/eaglelake/bizztrail.html* 🎫 *Free.*

Eagle Lake. Anglers travel great distances to fish the waters of Eagle Lake, the second largest freshwater lake wholly in California. The Eagle Lake rainbow trout is prized for its size and fighting ability. Surrounded by high desert to the north and alpine forests to the south, the lake is also popular for picnicking, hiking, boating, waterskiing and windsurfing, and bird-watching—ospreys, pelicans, western grebes, and many other waterfowl visit the lake. On land you might see mule deer, small mammals, and even pronghorn antelope—and be sure to watch for bald eagle nesting sites. ✉ *16 mi north of Susanville on Eagle Lake Rd.* ☎ *530/257–0456 for Eagle Lake Recreation Area, 530/825–3454 for Eagle Lake Marina* 🌐 *www.blm.gov/ca/eaglelake.*

WHERE TO EAT AND STAY

$ MEXICAN ✕ **Mazatlan Grill.** The sauces and tortillas are prepared on-site in this friendly, family-run restaurant and lounge, which serves lunch and dinner daily. The dining room is simple and tidy, with comfortable upholstered booths. The extensive menu offers authentic, inexpensive Mexican fare ranging from fajitas and enchiladas to a vegetarian burrito. ✉ *1535 Main St.* ☎ *530/257–1800.*

¢ 🏨 **High Country Inn.** Rooms are spacious in this two-story, colonial-style motel on the east edge of town. **Pros:** great mountain views; neat and clean; a well-kept property. **Cons:** must drive to town's historic center. ✉ *3015 Riverside Dr.* ☎ *530/257–3450 or 866/454–4566* 🌐 *www.high-country-inn.com* *66 rooms* *In-room: a/c, Internet (some), Wi-Fi. In-hotel: pool, gym* 🍽 *Breakfast.*

LASSEN VOLCANIC NATIONAL PARK

45 mi east of Redding on Hwy. 44; 48 mi east of Red Bluff on Hwy. 36.

GETTING HERE AND AROUND

Whether coming from the west or the east, reach the southern entrance to the park via Hwy. 36E, and turn onto Hwy. 89 for a short drive to the park. The northwest entrance is reached via Hwy. 44 from Redding and Susanville. No buses serve the area.

EXPLORING

Fodor's Choice ★ **Lassen Volcanic National Park.** A dormant plug dome, Lassen Peak is the focus of Lassen Volcanic National Park's 165.6 square mi of distinctive landscape. The peak began erupting in May 1914, sending pumice, rock, and snow thundering down the mountain and gas and hot

DID YOU KNOW?

President Theodore Roosevelt supposedly called McArthur–Burney Falls "the eighth wonder of the world."

ash billowing into the atmosphere. Lassen's most spectacular outburst occurred in 1915 when it blew a cloud of ash some 7 mi into the stratosphere. The resulting mudflow destroyed vegetation for miles in some directions; the evidence is still visible today, especially in Devastated Area. The volcano finally came to rest in 1921. Now fumaroles, mud pots, lakes, and bubbling hot springs create a fascinating but dangerous landscape that can be viewed throughout the park, especially via a hiked descent into Bumpass Hell. Because of its significance as a volcanic landscape, Lassen became a national park in 1916. Several volcanoes—the largest of which is now Lassen Peak—have been active in the area for roughly 600,000 years. The four types of volcanoes found in the world are represented in the park, including shield (Prospect Peak), plug dome (Lassen Peak), cinder cone (Cinder Cone), and composite (Brokeoff Volcano). Lassen Park Road (the continuation of Highway 89 within the park) and 150 mi of hiking trails provide access to many of these volcanic wonders. Caution is key here: signs warn visitors to stay on the trails and railed boardwalks to avoid falling into boiling water or through dangerous thin-crusted areas of the park. Although the park is closed to cars in winter, it's usually open to intrepid cross-country skiers and snowshoers. The Kohm Yah-mah-nee Visitor Center, at the southwest entrance to the park, is open year-round. There is a $10 entrance fee per vehicle; those on foot, bicycle or motorcycle pay $5 per person. 🌐 *www.nps.gov/lavo.*

Sulphur Works Thermal Area. Proof of Lassen Peak's volatility becomes evident shortly after you enter the park at the southwest entrance. Sidewalks skirt bubbling mud, boiling springs, and sulfur-emitting steam vents. This site is usually the last to close because of snow. ✉ *Lassen Park Rd., 1 mi from Kohm Yah-mah-nee Visitor Center.*

Lassen Peak Hike. This trail winds 2½ mi to the mountaintop. It's a tough climb—2,000 feet uphill on a steady, steep grade—but the reward is a spectacular view. At the peak you can see into the rim and view the entire park (and much of the Far North). Bring sunscreen, water, and a jacket because it's often windy and much cooler at the summit. ✉ *Lassen Park Rd., 7 mi north of southwest entrance station.*

Lassen Scenic Byway. Beginning in Chester, this 185-mi scenic drive loops through the forests, volcanic peaks, geothermal springs, and lava fields of Lassen National Forest and Lassen National Park. It's an all-day excursion into dramatic wilderness; the road goes through the park and Lassen National Forest, veers southeast toward Susanville, then cuts west to make a loop around Lake Almanor before ending in Chester. The road is partially inaccessible in winter; call the Almanor Ranger District headquarters or Caltrans for current road conditions. From Chester, take Route 36 west to Route 89 north through the park (subject to closures due to snow), then Route 44 east to Route 36 west. Optionally, at Route 147, cut south to loop around Lake Almanor, and return to Route 89 north; at Route 36, turn east to return to Chester. ☎ *530/258–2141 Almanor Ranger District* ☎ *800/427–7623 Caltrans.*

Bumpass Hell Trail. Boiling springs, steam vents, and mud pots are featured on this 3.5-mi round-trip hike. There's an overall descent of 700

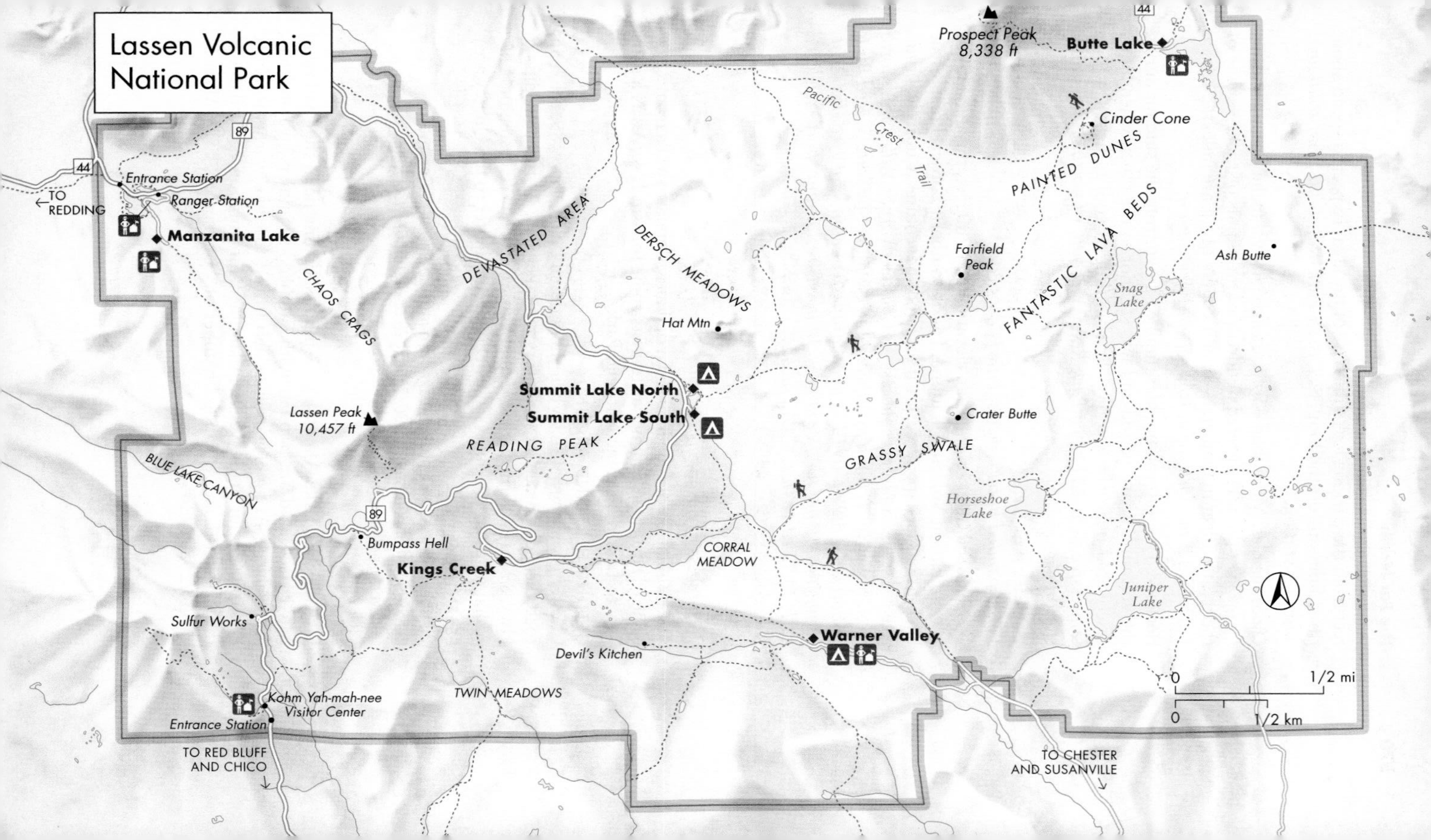

Lassen Volcanic National Park
Prospect Peak 8,338 ft
Butte Lake
44
Pacific Crest Trail
Cinder Cone
PAINTED DUNES
FANTASTIC LAVA BEDS
Ash Butte
Snag Lake
Fairfield Peak
Crater Butte
GRASSY SWALE
Horseshoe Lake
Juniper Lake
89
Entrance Station
Ranger Station
TO REDDING
Manzanita Lake
CHAOS CRAGS
DEVASTATED AREA
DERSCH MEADOWS
Hat Mtn
Summit Lake North
Summit Lake South
Lassen Peak 10,457 ft
READING PEAK
BLUE LAKE CANYON
Bumpass Hell
Kings Creek
CORRAL MEADOW
Sulfur Works
Devil's Kitchen
Warner Valley
TWIN MEADOWS
Kohm Yah-mah-nee Visitor Center
Entrance Station
TO RED BLUFF AND CHICO
TO CHESTER AND SUSANVILLE
0
1/2 mi
0
1/2 km

feet from the parking lot to the base of the area. Expect to spend about three hours to do the loop. ✉ *Lassen Park Rd., 6 mi from southwest entrance station.*

Chaos Jumbles. More than 350 years ago, an avalanche from the Chaos Crags lava domes scattered hundreds of thousands of rocks—many of them 2 to 3 feet in diameter—over a couple of square miles. ✉ *Lassen Park Rd., 2 mi north of northwest entrance station.*

Hot Rock. This 400-ton boulder tumbled down from the summit during the volcano's active period and was still hot to the touch when locals discovered it nearly two days later. Although cool now, it's still an impressive sight. ✉ *Lassen Park Rd., 7 mi south of northwest entrance station.*

WHERE TO STAY

For expanded hotel reviews, visit Fodors.com.

$$$$ **Drakesbad Guest Ranch**. At an elevation of 5,700 feet, this guest ranch is near Lassen Volcanic National Park's southern border. **Pros:** a true back-to-nature experience; great for family adventures. **Cons:** too primitive for some; no Internet access. ✉ *Chester–Warner Valley Rd., north from Hwy. 36* *Booking office: 2150 N. Main St., Suite 5, Red Bluff 96080* ☎ *866/999–0914* 🌐 *www.drakesbad.com* *19 rooms* *In-room: no phone, no a/c, no TV. In-hotel: restaurant, pool* *Closed early Oct.–early June* *All meals.*

CHESTER

36 mi west of Susanville on Hwy 36.

The population of this small town on Lake Almanor swells from 2,500 to nearly 5,000 in summer as tourists come to visit. It serves as a gateway to Lassen Volcanic National Park.

GETTING HERE AND AROUND

Chester is on Hwy. 36E. When snow doesn't close Hwy. 89, the main road through Lassen Park, visitors can take Hwy. 44 from Redding to Hwy. 89 through the park and to Hwy. 36E and onto Chester and Lake Almanor. Plumas County Transit connects Chester to the Quincy area.

ESSENTIALS

Visitor Information Chester–Lake Almanor Chamber of Commerce (✉ *529 Main St., Chester* ☎ *530/258–2426 or 800/350–4838* 🌐 *www.lakealmanorarea.com*).

EXPLORING

Lake Almanor. Lake Almanor's 52 mi of shoreline lie in the shadow of Mt. Lassen, and are popular with campers, swimmers, water-skiers, and anglers. At an elevation of 4,500 feet, the lake warms to above 70°F for about eight weeks in summer. Information is available at the Chester–Lake Almanor Chamber of Commerce. ✉ *529 Main St.* ☎ *530/258–2426*

WHERE TO EAT AND STAY

$ AMERICAN **Kopper Kettle Cafe.** Locals return again and again to this coffee shop–style restaurant that serves savory home-cooked lunch and dinner, and breakfast whenever you've got a hankering for eggs with biscuits and gravy or other morning fare. A junior-senior menu, and beer and wine are available. The patio is open in summer. *243 Main St. 530/258–2698.*

$ MEXICAN **Maria and Walker's Mexican Restaurant.** A festive atmosphere prevails in this family-friendly restaurant and lounge, where traditional south-of-the-border fare is served. Lunch specials and children's plates are available. It's one of the few restaurants in the area with a full bar, a great place to enjoy a margarita at the end of a long day spent hiking. *159 Main St. 530/258–2262 Closed Sun.*

$ **Best Western Rose Quartz Inn.** Down the road from Lake Almanor and close to Lassen Volcanic National Park, this small-town inn with its modern, wired rooms lets you venture into the wilderness and stay in touch with cyberspace. **Pros:** near Lake Almanor and Lassen Park; modern conveniences in a rural setting. **Cons:** on the pricey side. *306 Main St., Chester 530/258–2002 or 888/571–4885 www.bestwesterncalifornia.com 50 rooms In-room: a/c, Internet, Wi-Fi. In-hotel: gym, business center Breakfast.*

$ ★ **Bidwell House.** This 1901 ranch house sits on 2 acres of cottonwood-studded lawns and gardens, and has views of Lake Almanor and Mt. Lassen. **Pros:** unique decor in each room; standout breakfast. **Cons:** not ideal for kids. *1 Main St. 530/258–3338 www.bidwellhouse.com 14 rooms, 2 with shared bath In-room: no phone, no a/c, no TV (some), Wi-Fi Breakfast.*

14

QUINCY

67 mi southwest of Susanville via Hwys. 36 and 89.

A center for mining and logging in the 1850s, Quincy is nestled against the western slope of the Sierra Nevada. The county seat and largest community in Plumas County, the town is rich in historic buildings that have been the focus of preservation and restoration efforts. The four-story courthouse on Main Street, one of several stops on a self-guided tour, was built in 1921 with marble posts and staircases. The arts are thriving in Quincy, too: catch one of the plays or bluegrass performances at the Town Hall Theatre.

GETTING HERE AND AROUND

Quincy is on Hwy. 70 and is accessible from all directions via mountain roads. Hwy. 70 goes through the Feather River Canyon to Hwy. 149, then Hwy. 99 to Chico and Red Bluff, a 198-mi trip. From Quincy, Hwy. 70 connects to Hwy. 89 and then to Hwy. 36E toward Susanville in the east, or westward toward Chester and Lassen Park. Plumas County Transit goes from Quincy to Chester and also connects in Quincy with Lassen Rural Bus for rides to Susanville.

Lassen Volcanic National Park's King Creek Falls Hike, which takes you through forests and meadows dotted with wildflowers, is a good hike for nature photographers.

ESSENTIALS

Visitor Information **Plumas County Visitors Bureau** (✉ *550 Crescent St., Quincy* ☎ *530/283–6345 or 800/326–2247* 🌐 *www.plumascounty.org*). **Quincy Chamber of Commerce** (✉ *464 Main St., Quincy* ☎ *530/283–0188* 🌐 *www.quincychamber.com*).

EXPLORING

Bucks Lake Recreation Area. The main recreational attraction in central Plumas County is 17 mi southwest of Quincy at 5,200 feet. During warm months the lake's 17-mi shoreline, two marinas, and eight campgrounds attract anglers and water-sports enthusiasts. Trails through the tall pines beckon hikers and horseback riders. In winter much of the area remains open for snowmobiling and cross-country skiing. ✉ *Bucks Lake Rd.* ☎ *800/326–2247* 🌐 *www.plumascounty.org.*

Plumas National Forest. Plumas County is known for its wide-open spaces, and the 1.2-million-acre Plumas National Forest, with its high alpine lakes and crystal clear woodland streams, is a beautiful example. Hundreds of campsites are maintained in the forest, and picnic areas and hiking trails abound. You can enter the forest from numerous sites along highways 70 and 89. ✉ *159 Lawrence St.* ☎ *530/283–2050* 🕒 *U.S. Forest Service office weekdays 8–4:30.*

Plumas County Museum. The cultural, home arts, and industrial history displays at the Plumas County Museum contain artifacts dating to the 1850s. Highlights include collections of Maidu Indian basketry, pioneer weapons, and rooms depicting life in the early days of Plumas County. There are a blacksmith shop and gold-mining cabin, equipment from the early days of logging, a restored buggy, and railroad and mining exhibits. ✉ *500 Jackson St.* ☎ *530/283–6320* $2 ⏲ *Tues.–Sat. 9–4:30.*

WHERE TO EAT AND STAY

$$ AMERICAN **Sweet Lorraine's.** Hearty fare served in this casual, bustling restaurant in Quincy's historic downtown area includes meaty dishes like St. Louis ribs as well as vegetarian selections and lighter items; there's also a good selection of wines. If the weather is mild, dine alfresco on the patio. ✉ *384 Main St.* ☎ *530/283–5300* ⏲ *Closed Sun.–Mon.*

$ ★ **Ada's Place.** This place is actually four cottages, secluded on a quiet street one block from the county courthouse and downtown Quincy. **Pros:** on-site owners' meticulous upkeep. **Cons:** a bit pricey. ✉ *562 Jackson St.* ☎ *530/283–1954 or 877/234–2327* 🌐 *www.adasplace.com* *4 cottages* *In-room: a/c (some), kitchen, Wi-Fi. In-hotel: laundry facilities.*

Travel Smart Northern California

WORD OF MOUTH

"Yes, the distances here in California are huge. As you'll be spending many hours in the car, make sure that you get one that's not going to be too cramped. You ought to carry bottled water with you all the time, but especially when you're driving through the desert."

—Barbara

www.fodors.com/community

GETTING HERE AND AROUND

Wherever you plan to go in Northern California, getting there will likely involve driving (even if you fly). Major airports are usually far from main attractions. (In San Francisco, it's a 30-minute-plus trip between any Bay Area airport and downtown.) California's major airport hubs are LAX in Los Angeles and SFO in San Francisco, but satellite airports can be found around most major cities. When booking flights, it pays to check these locations, as you may find cheaper flights, more convenient times, and a better location in relation to your hotel. Most small cities have their own commercial airports, with connecting flights to larger cities—but service may be extremely limited, and it may be cheaper to rent a car and drive from San Francisco.

There are two basic north–south routes in California: I–5, an interstate highway, runs inland most of the way from the Oregon border to the Mexican border; and Highway 101 hugs the coast for part of the route from Oregon to Mexico. (A slower but much more scenic option is to take California State Route 1, also referred to as Highway 1 and the Pacific Coast Highway, which winds along much of the California coast and provides an occasionally hair-raising, but breathtaking, ride.) From north to south, the state's east–west interstates are I–80, I–15, I–10, and I–8. Much of California is mountainous, and you may encounter winding roads, frequently cliff-side, and steep mountain grades. In winter, roads crossing the Sierra east to west may close at any time due to weather, and chains may be required on these roads when they are open. Also in winter, I–5 north of Los Angeles closes during snowstorms. The flying and driving times in the following charts are best-case scenario estimates, but know that the infamous California traffic jam can occur at any time.

FROM SAN FRANCISCO TO	BY AIR	BY CAR
San Jose		1 hour 20 minutes
Monterey	40 minutes	2 hours 30 minutes
Los Angeles	1 hour 25 minutes	6 hours 30 minutes
Portland, OR	1 hour 45 minutes	10 hours 30 minutes
Mendocino		3 hours
Yosemite NP/ Fresno	55 minutes	4 hours
Lake Tahoe/Reno	55 minutes	4 hours

AIR TRAVEL

Flying time to California is about six hours from New York and four hours from Chicago. Travel from London to San Francisco is 11 hours and from Sydney approximately 14. Flying between San Francisco and Los Angeles takes about 90 minutes.

AIRPORTS

California's gateways are Los Angeles International Airport (LAX), San Francisco International Airport (SFO), San Diego International Airport (SAN), Sacramento International Airport (SMF), and San Jose International Airport (SJC). Oakland International Airport (OAK) is another option in the Bay Area, and other Los Angeles airports include Long Beach (LGB), Bob Hope Airport (BUR), LA/Ontario (ONT), and John Wayne Airport (SNA).

Airport Information Bob Hope Airport (☎ *818/840–8840* 🌐 *www.burbankairport.com*). **John Wayne Airport** (☎ *949/252–5200* 🌐 *www.ocair.com*). **LA/Ontario International Airport** (☎ *909/937–2700* 🌐 *www.flyontario.com*). **Los Angeles International Airport** (☎ *310/646–5252* 🌐 *www.lawa.org/lax*). **Long Beach Airport** (☎ *562/570–2619* 🌐 *www.lgb.org*). **Oakland International Airport** (☎ *510/563–3300* 🌐 *www.flyoakland.com*). **Sacramento International Airport**

(☎ *916/929–5411* 🌐 *www.sacairports.org/int*). **San Diego International Airport** (☎ *619/400–2404* 🌐 *www.san.org*). **San Francisco International Airport** (☎ *650/761–0800* 🌐 *www.flysfo.com*). **San Jose International Airport** (☎ *408/277–4759* 🌐 *www.sjc.org*).

FLIGHTS

United, with hubs in San Francisco and Los Angeles, has the greatest number of flights into and within California. But most national and many international airlines fly here. Southwest Airlines connects smaller cities within California, often from satellite airports near major cities.

Airline Contacts **Air Canada** (☎ *888/247–2262* 🌐 *www.aircanada.com*). **Alaska Airlines/Horizon Air** (☎ *800/252–7522* 🌐 *www.alaskaair.com*). **American Airlines** (☎ *800/433–7300* 🌐 *www.aa.com*). **British Airways** (☎ *800/247–9297* 🌐 *www.britishairways.com*). **Cathay Pacific** (☎ *800/233–2742* 🌐 *www.cathaypacific.com*). **Continental Airlines** (☎ *800/523–3273 for U.S. and Mexico reservations, 800/231–0856 for international reservations* 🌐 *www.continental.com*). **Delta Airlines** (☎ *800/221–1212 for U.S. reservations, 800/241–4141 for international reservations* 🌐 *www.delta.com*). **Frontier Airlines** (☎ *800/452–2022* 🌐 *www.frontierairlines.com*). **Japan Air Lines** (☎ *800/525–3663* 🌐 *www.jal.com*). **JetBlue** (☎ *800/538–2583* 🌐 *www.jetblue.com*). **Qantas** (☎ *800/227–4500* 🌐 *www.qantas.com.au*). **Southwest Airlines** (☎ *800/435–9792* 🌐 *www.southwest.com*). **Spirit Airlines** (☎ *800/772–7117* 🌐 *www.spirit.com*). **United Airlines** (☎ *800/864–8331 for U.S. reservations, 800/538–2929 for international reservations* 🌐 *www.united.com*). **US Airways** (☎ *800/428–4322 for U.S. and Canada reservations, 800/622–1015 for international reservations* 🌐 *www.usairways.com*).

BOAT TRAVEL

CRUISES

A number of major cruise lines offer trips that begin or end in California. Most voyages sail north along the Pacific Coast to Alaska or south to Mexico. California cruise ports include Los Angeles, San Diego, and San Francisco.

Cruise Lines **Carnival Cruise Line** (☎ *305/599–2600 or 800/227–6482* 🌐 *www.carnival.com*). **Celebrity Cruises** (☎ *800/647–2251 or 800/437–3111* 🌐 *www.celebritycruises.com*). **Crystal Cruises** (☎ *310/785–9300 or 800/446–6620* 🌐 *www.crystalcruises.com*). **Holland America Line** (☎ *206/281–3535 or 877/932–4259* 🌐 *www.hollandamerica.com*). **Norwegian Cruise Line** (☎ *305/436–4000 or 800/327–7030* 🌐 *www.ncl.com*). **Princess Cruises** (☎ *661/753–0000 or 800/774–6237* 🌐 *www.princess.com*). **Regent Seven Seas Cruises** (☎ *954/776–6123 or 800/477–7500* 🌐 *www.rssc.com*). **Royal Caribbean International** (☎ *305/539–6000 or 800/327–6700* 🌐 *www.royalcaribbean.com*). **Silversea Cruises** (☎ *954/522–4477 or 800/722–9955* 🌐 *www.silversea.com*).

BUS TRAVEL

Greyhound is the major bus carrier in California. Regional bus service is available in metropolitan areas.

Bus Information **Greyhound** (☎ *800/231–2222* 🌐 *www.greyhound.com*).

CAR TRAVEL

Three major highways—I–5, U.S. 101, and Highway 1—run north–south through California. The main east–west route is I–80 in northern California.

GASOLINE

Gasoline prices in California vary widely, depending on location, oil company, and whether you buy it at a full-serve or self-serve pump. It's less expensive to buy fuel in the southern part of the state than in the north. If you're planning to travel near Nevada, you can save a bit by purchasing gas over the border. Gas stations are plentiful throughout the state. Most stay open late (24 hours along major highways and in big cities), except in rural areas, where Sunday hours are limited and where you may drive long stretches without a chance to refuel.

ROAD CONDITIONS

Rainy weather can make driving along the coast or in the mountains treacherous. Some of the smaller routes over mountain ranges and in the deserts are prone to flash flooding. When the rains are severe, coastal Highway 1 can quickly become a slippery nightmare, buffeted by strong winds and obstructed by falling debris from the cliffs above. When the weather is particularly bad, Highway 1 may be closed due to mud and rock slides.

FROM SAN FRANCISCO TO	ROUTE	DISTANCE
San Jose	Hwy. 101	50 mi
Monterey	Hwy. 101 to Hwy. 156 to Hwy. 1	120 mi
Los Angeles	Hwy. 101 to Hwy. 156 to I–5	403 mi
Portland, OR	I–80 to I–505 to I–5	635 mi
Mendocino	Hwy. 1	174 mi
Yosemite NP	I–80 to I–580 to I–205 to Hwy. 120 east	184 mi
Lake Tahoe/ Reno	I–80	250 mi

Many smaller roads over the Sierra Nevada are closed in winter, and if it's snowing, tire chains may be required on routes that are open, most notably those to Yosemite and Lake Tahoe. From October through April, if it's raining along the coast, it's usually snowing at higher elevations. Consider renting a four-wheel-drive vehicle, or purchase chains before you get to the mountains. (Chains or cables generally cost $30 to $70, depending on tire size; cables are easier to apply than chains, but chains are more durable.) If you delay and purchase them in the vicinity of the chain-control area, the cost may double. Be aware that most rental-car companies prohibit chain installation on their vehicles. If you choose to risk it and do not tighten them properly, they may snap—your insurance likely will not cover any resulting damage. Uniformed chain installers on I–80 and U.S. 50 will apply them at the checkpoint for $30 or take them off for less than that. (Chain installers are independent business people, not highway employees, and set their own fees. They are not allowed to sell or rent chains.) On smaller roads, you're on your own. Always carry extra clothing, blankets, water, and food when driving to the mountains in the winter, and keep your gas tank full to prevent the fuel line from freezing.

Road Conditions Statewide Hotline (☎ *800/ GAS–ROAD [800/427–7623]* 🌐 *www.dot.ca.gov/hq/roadinfo*).

Weather Conditions National Weather Service (☎ *707/443–6484 northernmost California, 831/656–1725 San Francisco Bay area and central California, 775/673–8100 Reno, Lake Tahoe, and northern Sierra, 805/988–6610 Los Angeles area, 858/675–8700 San Diego area* 🌐 *www.weather.gov*).

ROADSIDE EMERGENCIES

Dial 911 to report accidents on the road and to reach the police, the California Highway Patrol (CHP), or the fire department. On some rural highways and on most interstates, look for emergency phones on the side of the road.

RULES OF THE ROAD

Children under age 6 or weighing less than 60 pounds must be secured in a federally approved child passenger restraint system and ride in the back seat. Seat belts are required at all times and children must wear them regardless of where they're seated (studies show that children are safest in the rear seats). Unless otherwise indicated, right turns are allowed at red lights after you've come to a full stop. Left turns between two one-way streets are allowed at red lights after you've come to a full stop. Drivers with a blood-alcohol level higher than 0.08 who are stopped by police are subject to arrest, and police officers can detain those with a level of 0.05 if they appear impaired. California's drunk-driving laws are extremely tough—violators may have their licenses immediately suspended, pay hefty fines, and spend the night in jail. The speed limit on many interstate highways is 70 mph; unlimited-access roads are usually 55 mph. In cities, freeway speed limits are between 55 mph and 65 mph. Many city routes have commuter lanes during rush hour.

Those 18 and older must use a hands-free device for their mobile phones while driving, while teenagers under 18 are not allowed to use mobile phones or wireless devices while driving. "Texting" on a wireless device is illegal for persons of all ages while driving in California. Smoking in a vehicle where a minor is present is an infraction. For more information refer to the Department of Motor Vehicles driver's handbook at 🌐 *www.dmv.ca.gov/dmv.htm*.

CAR RENTAL

When you reserve a car, ask about cancellation penalties, taxes, drop-off charges (if you're planning to pick up the car in one city and leave it in another), and surcharges (for being under or over a certain age, for additional drivers, or for driving across state or country borders or beyond a specific distance from your point of rental). All these things can add substantially to your costs. Request car seats and extras such as GPS when you book.

Rates are sometimes—but not always—better if you book in advance or reserve through a rental agency's Web site. There are other reasons to book ahead, though: for popular destinations, during busy times of the year, or to ensure that you get certain types of cars (vans, SUVs, exotic sports cars).

■ TIP→ Make sure that a confirmed reservation guarantees you a car. Agencies sometimes overbook, particularly for busy weekends and holiday periods.

A car is essential in most parts of California, but in compact San Francisco it's better to use public transportation to avoid parking headaches.

Rates statewide for the least expensive vehicle begin at around $52 a day and $209 a week (though they increase rapidly from here). This does not include additional fees or tax on car rentals, which is 9.25% in San Francisco. Be sure to shop around—you can get a decent deal by carefully shopping the major car rental companies' Web sites. Ask about "drop charges" if you plan to return the car in a city other than the one where you rented the vehicle. If you pick up at an airport, there may also be a facility charge of as much as $12 per rental; ask when you book. When you're returning your rental, be aware that gas stations can be few and far between near airports.

In California, you must have a valid driver's license and be 21 to rent a car; rates may be higher if you're under 25. Some agencies will not rent to those under 25; check when you book. Non-U.S. residents must have a license with text that is in the Roman alphabet that is valid for the entire rental period. Though it need not be entirely written in English, it must have English letters that clearly identify it as a driver's license. In addition, most companies also require an international license; check in advance.

Specialty Car Agencies In San Francisco **Specialty Rentals** (☎ *800/400–8412* 🌐 *www.specialtyrentals.com*);

Major Rental Agencies Alamo (☎ *800/462–5266* 🌐 *www.alamo.com*). **Avis** (☎ *800/331–1212* 🌐 *www.avis.com*). **Budget** (☎ *800/527–0700* 🌐 *www.budget.com*). **Hertz** (☎ *800/654–3131* 🌐 *www.hertz.com*). **National Car Rental** (☎ *800/227–7368* 🌐 *www.nationalcar.com*).

TRAIN TRAVEL

One of the most beautiful train trips in the country is along the Pacific Coast from Los Angeles to Oakland via Amtrak's *Coast Starlight,* which hugs the waterfront before it turns inland at San Luis Obispo for the rest of its journey to Seattle. (Be aware that this train is frequently late arriving at and departing from Central Coast stations.) The *California Zephyr* travels from Chicago to Oakland via Denver.

Information Amtrak (☎ *800/872–7245* 🌐 *www.amtrak.com*).

ESSENTIALS

ACCOMMODATIONS

The lodgings we list are the cream of the crop in each price category. We always list the facilities that are available, but we don't specify whether they cost extra; when pricing accommodations, ask what's included and what costs extra. ⇨ *For price information, see the planner in each chapter.*

Most hotels require you to give your credit-card details before they will confirm your reservation. If you don't feel comfortable e-mailing this information, ask if you can fax it (some places even prefer faxes). However you book, get confirmation in writing and have a copy of it handy when you check in.

BED-AND-BREAKFASTS

California has more than 1,000 bed-and-breakfasts. You'll find everything from simple homestays to lavish luxury lodgings, many in historic hotels and homes. The California Association of Bed and Breakfast Inns has about 300 member properties that you can locate and book through their Web site.

Reservation Services Bed & Breakfast.com (☎ *512/322–2710 or 800/462–2632* 🌐 *www.bedandbreakfast.com*). **Bed & Breakfast Inns Online** (☎ *310/280–4363 or 800/215–7365* 🌐 *www.bbonline.com*). **BnB Finder.com** (☎ *646/205–8016 or 888/547–8226* 🌐 *www.bnbfinder.com*). **California Association of Bed and Breakfast Inns** (☎ *800/373–9251* 🌐 *www.cabbi.com*).

COMMUNICATIONS

INTERNET

Internet access is widely available in California's urban areas, but it's usually more difficult to get online in the state's rural areas. Most hotels offer some kind of connection—dial-up, broadband, or Wi-Fi (which is becoming much more common). Most hotels charge a daily fee (about $10) for Internet access. Cybercafés are also located throughout California.

Contacts Cybercafés (🌐 *www.cybercafes.com*).

EATING OUT

Northern California has led the pack in bringing natural and organic foods to the forefront of American cooking. Though rooted in European cuisine, California cooking sometimes has strong Asian and Latin influences. Wherever you go, you're likely to find that dishes are made with fresh produce and other local ingredients.

The restaurants we list are the cream of the crop in each price category. ⇨ *For price information, see the planner in each chapter.*

CUTTING COSTS

TIP→ If you're on a budget, take advantage of the "small plates" craze sweeping California by ordering several appetizer-size portions and having a glass of wine at the bar, rather than having a full meal. Also, better grocery and specialty-food stores have grab-and-go sections, with prepared foods on par with restaurant cooking, perfect for picnicking. At resort areas in the off-season (such as Lake Tahoe in October and May), you can often find two-for-one dinner specials at upper-end restaurants; check local papers or with visitor bureaus.

RESERVATIONS AND DRESS

Regardless of where you are, it's a good idea to make a reservation if you can. We only mention them specifically when reservations are essential (there's no other way you'll ever get a table) or when they are not accepted. For popular restaurants, book as far ahead as you can (often 30 days), and reconfirm as soon as you arrive. (Large parties should always call ahead to check the reservations policy.) We mention dress only when men are required to wear a jacket or a jacket and tie.

Online reservation services make it easy to book a table before you even leave home. OpenTable covers most states, including 20 major cities, and has limited listings in Canada, Mexico, the United Kingdom, France and elsewhere. DinnerBroker has restaurants throughout the United States.

Contacts OpenTable (*www.opentable.com*). **DinnerBroker** (*www.dinnerbroker.com*).

WINES, BEER, AND SPIRITS

If you like wine, your trip to California won't be complete unless you sample a few of the local vintages. Throughout the state, most famously in the Napa and Sonoma valleys, you can visit wineries, many of which have tasting rooms and offer tours. Microbreweries are an emerging trend in the state's cities and in some rural areas in Northern California. The legal drinking age is 21.

HEALTH

Do not fly within 24 hours of scuba diving.

Smoking is illegal in all California bars and restaurants, including on outdoor dining patios in some cities. Hotels and motels are also decreasing their inventory of smoking rooms; inquire at the time you book your reservation if any are available. In addition, a tax is added to cigarettes sold in California, and prices can be as high as $6 per pack. You might want to bring a carton from home.

HOURS OF OPERATION

Banks in California are typically open weekdays from 9 to 6 and Saturday morning; most are closed on Sunday and most holidays. Smaller shops usually operate from 10 to 6, with larger stores remaining open until 8 or later. Hours vary for museums and historical sites, and many are closed one or more days a week, or for extended periods during off-season months. It's a good idea to check before you visit a tourist site.

MONEY

San Francisco tends to be expensive cities to visit, and rates at coastal and desert resorts are almost as high. Hotel rates average $150 to $250 a night (though you can find cheaper places), and dinners at even moderately priced restaurants often cost $20 to $40 per person. Costs in the Gold Country and the Far North regions are considerably less—some motels in the Far North charge $70 to $90.

CREDIT CARDS

Record all your credit-card numbers—as well as the phone numbers to call if your cards are lost or stolen—in a safe place, so you're prepared should something go wrong. Both MasterCard and Visa have general numbers you can call (collect if you're abroad) if your card is lost, but you're better off calling the number of your issuing bank, since MasterCard and Visa normally just transfer you to your bank; your bank's number is usually printed on your card.

Reporting Lost Cards American Express (*800/992–3404 in U.S., 336/393–1111 collect from abroad www.americanexpress.com*). **Discover** (*800/347–2683 in U.S., 801/902–3100 collect from abroad www.discovercard.com*). **Diners Club** (*800/234–6377 in U.S., 303/799–1504 collect from abroad www.dinersclubinternational.com*). **MasterCard** (*800/622–7747 in U.S., 636/722–7111 collect from abroad www.mastercard.com*). **Visa** (*800/847–2911 in U.S., 410/581–9994 collect from abroad www.visa.com*).

SAFETY

Northern California is a safe place to visit, as long as you take the usual precautions. In large cities ask the concierge or desk clerk to point out areas on your map that you should avoid. Lock valuables in a hotel safe when you're not using them. (Some hotels have in-room safes large enough to hold a laptop computer.) Keep an eye on your handbag when you're out in public. Security is high (but mostly invisible) at theme parks and resorts.

TAXES

Sales tax in California varies from about 8.25% to 9.75% and applies to all purchases except for food purchased in a grocery store; food consumed in a restaurant is taxed but take-out food purchases are not. Hotel taxes vary widely by region, from 10% to 15%.

TIME

California is in the Pacific time zone. Pacific daylight time (PDT) is in effect from mid-March through early November; the rest of the year the clock is set to Pacific standard time (PST).

TIPPING

Most service workers in California are fairly well paid compared to those in the rest of the country, and extravagant tipping is not the rule here. Exceptions include wealthy enclaves such as San Francisco as well as the more expensive resort areas.

TIPPING GUIDELINES FOR CALIFORNIA	
Bartender	$1 per drink, or 10%–15% of tab per round of drinks
Bellhop	$1–$5 per bag, depending on the level of the hotel
Hotel Concierge	$5 or more, if he/she performs a service for you
Hotel Doorman	$1–$2 if he/she helps you get a cab
Valet Parking Attendant	$2 when you get your car
Hotel Maid	$1–$2 per person, per day; more in high-end hotels
Waiter	15%–20% (20% is standard in upscale restaurants); nothing additional if a service charge is added to the bill
Skycap at Airport	$1–$3 per bag
Hotel Room-Service Waiter	$1–$2 per delivery, even if a service charge has been added
Taxi Driver	15%–20%, but round up the fare to the next dollar amount
Tour Guide	10% of the cost of the tour

TOURS

Guided tours are a good option when you don't want to do it all yourself. You travel along with a group (sometimes large, sometimes small), stay in prebooked hotels, eat with your fellow travelers (the cost of meals is sometimes included in the price of your tour, sometimes not), and follow a schedule.

But not all guided tours are an if-it's-Tuesday-this-must-be-Belgium experience. A knowledgeable guide can take you places that you might never discover on your own, and you may be pushed to see more than you would have otherwise. Tours aren't for everyone, but they can be just the thing for trips to places where making travel arrangements is difficult or time-consuming.

Whenever you book a guided tour, find out what's included and what isn't. A "land-only" tour includes all your travel (by bus, in most cases) in the destination, but not necessarily your flights to and from or even within it. Also, in most cases prices in tour brochures don't include fees and taxes. And remember that you'll be expected to tip your guide (in cash) at the end of the tour.

SPECIAL-INTEREST TOURS

BIKING

Bicycling is a popular way to see the California countryside, and commercial tours are available throughout the state. Most three- to five-day trips are all-inclusive—you'll stay in delightful country inns, dine at good regional restaurants, and follow experienced guides. The Northern California wine country, with its flat valley roads, is one of the most popular destinations. When booking, ask about level of difficulty, as nearly every trip will involve some hill work. Tours fill up early, so book well in advance.

■ TIP→ Most airlines accommodate bikes as luggage, provided they're dismantled and boxed.

Contacts Napa and Sonoma Valley Bike Tours (✉ *6795 Washington St., Bldg. B, Yountville* ☎ *800/707–2453* 🌐 *www.napavalleybiketours.com*). **Bicycle Adventures** (✉ *29700 S.E. High Point Way, Issaquah, WA* ☎ *800/443–6060* 🌐 *www.bicycleadventures.com*).

INDEX

A

B

N

T

PHOTO CREDITS

1, Yuen Kwan, Fodors.com member. 2-3, Bryan Brazil/Shutterstock. 5, Heavenly Mountain Resort. Chapter 1: Experience California: 8-9, Jay Anderson, Fodors.com member. 11, Helio San Miguel. 12 (top), Clinton Steeds/Flickr. 12 (bottom), Jose Vigano, Fodors.com member. 13, comfortablynirm, Fodors.com member. 14, Helio San Miguel. 15, vathomp, Fodors.com member. 16, Robert Holmes. 17 (left), sd_foodies, Fodors.com member. 17 (right), Lisa M. Hamilton. 18, Warren H. White. 19, Thomas Kranzel/Venture Media. 20 (left), Christophe Testi/iStockphoto. 20 (top right), Corbis. 20 (bottom right), Warren H. White. 21 (top left), Alan A. Tobey/iStockphoto. 21 (bottom left), Janet Fullwood. 21 (right), Aaron Kohr/iStockphoto. 23, Andrew Zarivny/iStockphoto. 24, Robert Holmes. 26, yummy-porky/Flickr. 27 (top and bottom), Lisa M. Hamilton. 28, John Elk III/Alamy. 29 (top), Janine Bolliger/iStockphoto. 29 (bottom), Lise Gagne/iStockphoto. 30, iStockphoto. Chapter 2: The Central Coast: 31, TweetieV, Fodors.com member. 32, Stephen Walls/iStockphoto. 33 (top), Bart Everett/iStockphoto. 33 (bottom), Robert Holmes. 34 (top), Evan Meyer/ iStockphoto. 34 (center), Kyle Maass iStockphoto. 34 (bottom left), iStockphoto. 34 (bottom right), iStockphoto. 35, Tom Baker/Shutterstock. 36, David M. Schrader/Shutterstock. 48, S. Greg Panosian/iStockphoto. 49, Ruben G. Mendoza. 50 (top), Richard Wong/www.rwongphoto.com/Alamy. 50 (bottom), Ruben G. Mendoza, 51 (top left), Witold Skrypczak/Alamy. 51 (top right), S. Greg Panosian/iStockphoto. 51 (bottom), Janet Fullwood. 52 (top left), GIPhotoStock Z/Alamy. 52 (top right), Craig Lovell/Eagle Visions Photography/Alamy. 52 (bottom) and 53 (top), S. Greg Panosian/iStockphoto. 53 (bottom), Eugene Zelenko/wikipedia.org. 56, David M. Schrader/Shutterstock. 67, Doreen Miller, Fodors.com member. 77, Robert Holmes. 92-93, Valhalla | Design & Conquer, Fodors.com member. Chapter 3: The Monterey Bay Area: 99, mellifluous, Fodors.com member. 100, Janet Fullwood. 101 (top), vittorio sciosia/age fotostock. 101 (bottom), Jeff Greenberg/age fotostock. 102 (left), SuperStock/age fotostock.102 (top right), CURAphotography/Shutterstock. 102 (bottom right), Michael Almond/iStockphoto. 103 (top), iStockphoto. 103 (bottom), Lise Gagne/iStockphoto. 104, Brent Reeves/Shutterstock. 111, Robert Holmes. 117, Holger Mette/iStockphoto. 125, laurel stewart/iStockphoto. Chapter 4: San Francisco: 145-148, Brett Shoaf/Artistic Visuals Photography. 157, Brett Shoaf/Artistic Visuals Photography. 158 (top), Arnold Genthe. 158 (bottom), Library of Congress Prints and Photographs Division. 159 (left), Sandor Balatoni/SFCVB. 159 (right), Detroit Publishing Company Collection, Photography Collection, Miriam and Ira D. Wallach Division of Art, Prints and Photographs, The New York Public Library, Astor, Lenox and Tilden Foundation. 160, Brett Shoaf/Artistic Visuals Photography. 161 (top), Gary Soup/Flickr. 161 (bottom), Albert Cheng/Shutterstock. 162 (top), Sheryl Schindler/SFCVB. 162 (center), Ronen/Shutterstock. 162 (bottom), Robert Holmes. 167, Walter Bibikow/age fotostock. 173, travelstock44/Alamy. 175, Brett Shoaf/Artistic Visuals Photography. 176, San Francisco Municipal Railway Historical Archives. 183, Lewis Sommer/SFCVB. 191, Robert Holmes. 200, aprillilacs, Fodors.com member. 205, Rafael Ramirez Lee/iStockphoto. 224, Queen Anne Hotel. 228 (top), George Apostolidis/Mandarin Oriental Hotel Group. 228 (center left), David Phelps/Argonaut Hotel. 228 (center right), Joie de Vivre Hospitality. 228 (bottom left), Starwood Hotels & Resorts. 228 (bottom right), Cris Ford/Union Street Inn. 229 (top), Rien van Rijthoven/InterContinental Hotels & Resorts. 229 (center left), Orchard Hotel. 229 (center right), Hotel Nikko San Francisco. 229 (bottom), The Ritz-Carlton, San Francisco. 234, Rough Guides/Alamy. 237, Robert Holmes. Chapter 5: The Bay Area: 239 and 240, Robert Holmes. 241, Jyeshern Cheng/iStockphoto. 242, Brett Shoaf/Artistic Visuals Photography. 248, Robert Holmes. 261, Mark Rasmussen/iStockphoto. 263, Robert Holmes. 269, S. Greg Panosian/iStockphoto. 275 and 287, Robert Holmes. Chapter 6: The Wine Country: 297, Robert Holmes. 298, iStockphoto. 299, Robert Holmes. 300, Warren H. White. 306, Robert Holmes. 307 (top), kevin miller/iStockphoto. 307 (bottom), Far Niente+Dolce+Nickel & Nickel. 308 (top and bottom) and 309 (top), Robert Holmes. 309 (bottom), star5112/Flickr. 310 (top left), Rubicon Estate. 310 (top right and bottom) and 311 (top and bottom), Robert Holmes. 312 (top), Philippe Roy/Alamy. 312 (center), Agence Images/Alamy. 312 (bottom), Cephas Picture Library/Alamy. 313 (top), Napa Valley Conference Bureau. 313 (second and third from top), Wild Horse Winery (Forrest L. Doud). 313 (fourth from top), Napa Valley Conference Bureau. 313 (fifth from top), Panther Creek Cellars (Ron Kaplan). 313 (sixth from top), Clos du Val (Marvin Collins). 313 (seventh from top), Panther Creek Cellars (Ron Kaplan). 313 (bottom), Warren H. White. 314 and 317, Robert Holmes. 327, Far Niente+Dolce+Nickel & Nickel. 330, Terry Joanis/Frog's Leap. 337, Castello di Amorosa. 340, Chuck Honek/Schramsberg Vineyard. 355, 358, 360-361, and 365, Robert Holmes. Chapter 7: The North Coast: 373, Thomas Barrat/Shutterstock. 374 (all), Robert Holmes. 375 (top), Russ Bishop/age fotostock. 375 (bottom), Robert Holmes. 376, Janet Fullwood. 378 (top), Ross Stapleton-Gray/iStockphoto. 378 (center), Jay Spooner/iStockphoto. 378 (bottom), TebNad/Shutterstock. 379 (top), Jay Spooner/iStockphoto. 379 (bottom), Lise Gagne/iStockphoto. 385, 391, and 395,

Robert Holmes. Chapter 8: Redwood National Park: 403, iStockphoto. 404 (top), Michael Schweppe/wikipedia.org. 404 (center), Agnieszka Szymczak/iStockphoto. 404 (bottom), Natalia Bratslavsky/Shutterstock. 406, WellyWelly/Shutterstock. Chapter 9: The Southern Sierra: 411, Randall Pugh, Fodors.com member. 412, Craig Cozart/iStockphoto. 413 (top), David T Gomez/iStockphoto. 413 (bottom left and bottom right), Robert Holmes. 414, christinea78, Fodors.com member. 419, moonjazz/Flickr. 426, Douglas Atmore/iStockphoto. Chapter 10: Yosemite National Park: 429, Sarah P. Corley, Fodors.com member. 430, Yosemite Concession Services. 431 (top), Andy Z./Shutterstock. 431 (bottom), Greg Epperson/age fotostock. 432, Doug Lemke/Shutterstock. 438, Rebalyn, Fodors.com member. 441, Nathan Jaskowiak/Shutterstock. 443, Greg Epperson/age fotostock. 448-49, Katrina Leigh/Shutterstock. Chapter 11: Sequoia and Kings Canyon National Parks: 451 and 452, Robert Holmes. 453 (top), Greg Epperson/age fotostock. 453 (bottom) and 454, Robert Holmes. 461, urosr/Shutterstock. 467, Robert Holmes. Chapter 12: Sacramento and the Gold Country: 469 and 471 (top and bottom), Robert Holmes. 472, Andy Z./Shutterstock. 478, Marcin Wichary/Flickr. 485, Image Asset Management/age fotostock. 486 (left) and 486 (right), wikipedia.org. 486 (center), Charles Danek. 487, Ambient Images Inc./Alamy. 488 (top), Trailmix.Net/Flickr. 488 (center), oger jones/Flickr. 488 (bottom), L. C. McClure/wikipedia.org. 489 (top left), Russ Bishop/age fotostock. 489 (top center), vera bogaerts/iStockphoto. 489 (top right and bottom left), Walter Bibikow/age fotostock. 489 (bottom right), Charles Danek. 493, Janet Fullwood. 499, RickC/Flickr. Chapter 13: Lake Tahoe: 503, Tom Zikas/North Lake Tahoe. 504 (top), Rafael Ramirez Lee/iStockphoto. 504 (bottom) and 505, Janet Fullwood. 506, Jay Spooner/iStockphoto. 513 (top), Heavenly Mountain Resort. 513 (bottom), Jake Foster/iStockphoto. 514 (top), Lake Tahoe Visitors Authority. 514 (bottom left), iStockphoto. 514 (bottom right), Heavenly Mountain Resort. 517 and 518 (left), Andrew Zarivny/iStockphoto. 518 (right), Harry Thomas/iStockphoto. 519 (top left), Joy Strotz/Shutterstock. 519 (bottom left), iStockphoto. 519 (right), Jennifer Stone/Shutterstock. 525, Jay Spooner/iStockphoto. 532, Tom O'Neill. 543, Christopher Russell/iStockphoto. Chapter 14: The Far North: 549, NPS. 550 (top and bottom), Robert Holmes. 551 (top), Andy Z./Shutterstock. 551 (bottom), NPS. 552, ThreadedThoughts/Flickr. 558, Robert Holmes. 567, kathycsus/Flickr. 572, NPS.

NOTES

NOTES

NOTES

NOTES

ABOUT OUR WRITERS

Native Californian **Cheryl Crabtree**—who updated the Bay Area, the Central Coast, and Monterey Bay Area chapters—has worked as a freelance writer since 1987. She has contributed to *Fodor's California* since 2003 and has also written for *Fodor's Complete Guide to the National Parks of the West.* Cheryl is editor of *Montecito Magazine.* She currently lives in Santa Barbara with her husband, two sons, and Jack Russell terrier.

A Northern California resident for 17 years, **Reed Parsell** has traveled extensively throughout the region and written hundreds of newspaper travel stories based on his experiences. A part-time copy editor and travel writer for the *Sacramento Bee,* Parsell also writes a "going green" column for *Sacramento* magazine and was the primary writer for *Fodor's InFocus Yosemite, Sequoia and Kings Canyon National Parks.* He updated our Central Valley, Southern Sierra, Sacramento and the Gold Country coverage.

Freelance writer **Christine Vovakes**—who updated the Far North, Lake Tahoe, and Travel Smart chapters—has also contributed to *Fodor's National Parks of the West* and *Essential USA.* Her travel articles and photographs have also appeared in many other publications, including *The Washington Post, The Christian Science Monitor, The Sacramento Bee,* and the *San Francisco Chronicle.*

Sura Wood is a San Francisco-based writer who has covered the Bay Area arts and lifestyle scene in particular and the film industry in general. Her profiles, reviews, and features have appeared in *The Hollywood Reporter,* the *San Jose Mercury News, San Francisco Arts Monthly* and many other publications. For this edition, she fact-checked our National Parks chapters, including Yosemite, Sequoia and Kings Canyon, and Redwood National Park.

Bobbi Zane—who updated the Experience Northern California chapter for this edition—grew up in Southern California, watching the region grow from its mostly rural roots into one of the most exciting places in the world. Her articles on Palm Springs have appeared in the *Orange County Register* and *Westways* magazine. She has contributed to *Fodor's Complete Guide to the National Parks of the West, Fodor's San Diego,* and *Escape to Nature Without Roughing It.* A lifelong Californian, Bobbi has visited every corner of the state on behalf of Fodor's.